Field Trials of Health Interventions: A Toolbox

Field Trials of Health Interventions: A Toolbox

3RD EDITION

Edited by

Peter G. Smith
Professor of Tropical Epidemiology
Medical Research Council Tropical Epidemiology Group
London School of Hygiene & Tropical Medicine
London, UK

Richard H. Morrow
Professor of International Health
Department of International Health
The Johns Hopkins Bloomberg School of Public Health
Baltimore, USA

David A. Ross
Professor of Epidemiology and International Public Health
Medical Research Council Tropical Epidemiology Group
London School of Hygiene & Tropical Medicine
London, UK

IEA International Epidemiological Association   **wellcome**trust

OXFORD
UNIVERSITY PRESS

OXFORD
UNIVERSITY PRESS

Great Clarendon Street, Oxford, OX2 6DP,
United Kingdom

Oxford University Press is a department of the University of Oxford.
It furthers the University's objective of excellence in research, scholarship,
and education by publishing worldwide. Oxford is a registered trade mark of
Oxford University Press in the UK and in certain other countries

© London School of Hygiene and Tropical Medicine 2015

The moral rights of the author have been asserted

First edition published 1991
Second edition published 1996 by Macmillan Press on behalf of the UNDP/World Bank/WHO
Special Programme for Research and Training in Tropical Disease
Third edition published 2015
Impression: 1

Some rights reserved. No part of this publication may be reproduced, stored in a retrieval system, or transmitted, in any form or by any means, electronic, mechanical or photocopying, recording, or otherwise, for commercial purposes, without the prior permission in writing of Oxford University Press.

This is an open access publication that is free to read at Oxford Medicine Online. Except where otherwise noted, this work is distributed under the terms of the Creative Commons Attribution NonCommercial 4.0 International licence (CC BY-NC), a copy of which is available at http://creativecommons.org/licenses/by-nc/4.0/. Enquiries concerning use outside the scope of the licence terms should be sent to the Rights Department, Oxford University Press, at the address above.

Published in the United States of America by Oxford University Press
198 Madison Avenue, New York, NY 10016, United States of America

British Library Cataloguing in Publication Data

Data available

Library of Congress Control Number: 2015936869

ISBN 978-0-19-873286-0

Printed and bound by
CPI Group (UK) Ltd

Oxford University Press makes no representation, express or implied, that the drug dosages in this book are correct. Readers must therefore always check the product information and clinical procedures with the most up-to-date published product information and data sheets provided by the manufacturers and the most recent codes of conduct and safety regulations. The authors and the publishers do not accept responsibility or legal liability for any errors in the text or for the misuse or misapplication of material in this work. Except where otherwise stated, drug dosages and recommendations are for the non-pregnant adult who is not breast-feeding

Links to third party websites are provided by Oxford in good faith and for information only. Oxford disclaims any responsibility for the materials contained in any third party website referenced in this work.

Published by Oxford University Press with financial support from the UNDP/World Bank/WHO Special Programme for Research and Training in Tropical Diseases and the Wellcome Trust and with sponsorship by the International Epidemiological Association.

The views expressed in this publication are those of the authors and do not necessarily reflect those of WHO, the Wellcome Trust, or the International Epidemiological Association. Furthermore, these organizations do not warrant that the information contained in this publication is correct and shall not be liable whatsoever for any damages incurred as a result of its use.

Dedication

Richard H. Morrow (1932–2013)

We dedicate this book to the memory of Dick Morrow who died after a short illness in the final stages of editing the book (Figure D.1). Dick Morrow had a profound influence on the careers and development of the very many students and colleagues he mentored, including my own. It was an enormous privilege to have worked with him in various locations over a period in excess of 40 years. We first met in 1970 when he was teaching epidemiology at Makerere University in Uganda, and I was a newly arrived lecturer. It was my great good fortune to be allocated an office next to Dick at the top of Mulago Hill. He guided me through writing my first grant application to the Wellcome Trust, for a trial to assess whether BCG vaccination protected against Buruli ulcer and, with his ever present optimism, persuaded me to start the study with my own funds, anticipating a positive outcome from the Trust! The short time we overlapped in Kampala cemented what was to become a lifelong friendship.

We both worked in Uganda on the ambitious cohort study designed to evaluate whether prior infection with the Epstein–Barr virus was the trigger for causing the African childhood cancer Burkitt's lymphoma. This study involved many players and was executed by the World Health Organization (WHO) International Agency for Research on Cancer, but what has been lost in the history of that research is the key role that Dick had in the genesis of the study and the enormous intellectual contribution he made to its design. However, one of the most endearing features of the man was his indifference to personal credit, believing that what was important was that the right things were done and what was key were the scientific insights, rather than who had them.

In the 1970s, Dick returned to Ghana to work in the newly formed Health Planning Unit, and, in extended visits, I worked with him and Ghanaian colleagues to pursue his idea of a new way of measuring the burden of different diseases in Ghana through the concept of 'years of healthy life lost', a combination measure of years lost due to premature mortality and time spent in different states of morbidity, each of which was accorded a weight according to severity. We published the method and data for Ghana, and Dick's insights were later taken up by others in developing the Global Burden of Disease exercise. The origination of this methodology from Dick has never been properly acknowledged, but this never really bothered Dick whose pleasure came from seeing the idea being taken forward and built upon.

In 1979, Dick became the epidemiologist for the then recently formed Tropical Disease Research (TDR) Programme at WHO in Geneva, first working under the directorship of Ade Lucas and then Tore Godal. Dick's emphasis of the fundamental importance of epidemiology and rigorous design in field research on tropical diseases did much to

Figure D.1 Richard H. Morrow (1932–2013).
Photograph Claudio Vazquez. Reproduced with the permission of Richard H Morrow's family, and the photographer, Claudio Vazquez. This image is distributed under the terms of the Creative Commons Attribution Non Commercial 4.0 International licence (CC-BY-NC), a copy of which is available at http://creativecommons.org/licenses/by-nc/4.0/.

lay the foundations of the TDR programme. The joy that Dick always had in helping and seeing others develop and succeed suited him ideally for work in a programme in which capacity development was a major part. I had the pleasure of accompanying him on a large number of field trips, promoting epidemiology and epidemiological methods in many low- and middle-income countries. In 1987, I was able to work with Dick for a year in Geneva with TDR, and it was then we devised the idea of producing a book on the aspects of field research methods that are rarely detailed in published papers. This was very much a labour of love on both our parts, and we were able to persuade numerous colleagues, with a wealth of field research experience, to contribute to the venture. The first edition of what came to be known as '*The toolbox*' was published in 1990, and we revised it in 1996. Sections of the book have become dated, and, a couple of years ago, we decided that a complete revision was required, taking on David Ross as a co-editor. We worked on this on a regular basis, again enlisting the help of numerous colleagues, during meetings and conference calls, every few weeks, between the three of us. We were revising the manuscript right up to the time of Dick's untimely short final illness, and he was able to complete his review and revisions of all of the chapters.

Dick's passing has left an enormous hole in my life and in that of all those who enjoyed his friendship and mentorship in a life devoted to improving the health and well-being of those in the most deprived communities. His legendary rock-like calmness, intellectual curiosity, and warm kindness were an inspiration. Appreciation of Dick's many qualities was shared by many friends and colleagues, including contributors to *The toolbox*—his intellect, integrity, sense of humour, creativity, willingness to give others credit for what he started, and making himself available and giving of himself to his colleagues and students, often to the detriment of his own work. He believed in the goodness of mankind, always saw the best in people, never spoke badly of anyone, and truly treated all equally, with respect and kindness, whether this was a first-year student or the Director General of WHO.

Peter G. Smith
2015

Foreword to the third edition

The organizations that we represent have a long-standing commitment to the development of capacity to conduct high-quality field research to evaluate the impact of interventions against diseases prevalent in low- and middle-income countries (LMICs). The idea of producing a book detailing the methods used to conduct intervention trials of health interventions in LMICs was conceived in the 1980s when one of us (T. G.) was the TDR Director. Since it was first published, the '*Toolbox*' has been very widely used, both by those undertaking intervention trials and epidemiological research in LMICs and in teaching courses. Since the 1980s, significant progress has been made in developing interventions that have reduced the burden of many diseases in impoverished communities, and much of this progress has been through the rigorous evaluation of interventions in randomized controlled trials before their adoption into public health use. Notable examples have been the evaluation and deployment of insecticide-impregnated bed-nets for malaria control and the development, testing, and introduction into public health programmes of vaccines against diseases which are major killers of infants and children, such as diarrhoeal diseases and respiratory infections.

The standards to which field trials of health interventions have been conducted have undoubtedly improved markedly over the last three decades, and dissemination and use of the *Toolbox* has contributed to this. In parallel, over this period, there has been a substantial increase in oversight and regulatory requirements related to clinical and field trials, and it was timely therefore for the authors of the *Toolbox* to produce a revised version, taking account not only of these regulatory changes, but also of the revolution in data collecting, processing, and computing methods.

Although the *Toolbox* is aimed at those conducting health intervention trials in LMICs, it is likely to be valuable for anyone undertaking field research or surveys in those countries, as many of the issues that arise in trials also arise in other kinds of investigation. We are confident that the *Toolbox* will continue to make an important contribution to building up epidemiological capacity in LMICs.

We congratulate the authors on their labours. We believe that this new edition of the *Toolbox* is likely to enhance the quality and quantity of field research that is being conducted on the health conditions afflicting those in LMICs, and this can only speed the control of these diseases that cause so much suffering to so much of mankind.

Tore Godal, Director (1986–98) of TDR, the Special Programme for Research and Training in Tropical Diseases

John Reeder, Present Director of TDR, the Special Programme for Research and Training in Tropical Diseases

Cesar Victora, President of the International Epidemiological Association

Jimmy Whitworth, Head of Department of Population Health, the Wellcome Trust

Preface to the third edition

Field trials of interventions against disease in LMICs may be complex and expensive undertakings, requiring the follow-up of hundreds, or thousands, of individuals for long periods. The conduct of such trials requires careful planning, in order to assure their timely and successful completion. Over the last several decades, an increasing number of large field trials have been conducted successfully in LMICs and have provided information critical to the assessment of the likely health impact of potential interventions. With a few exceptions, descriptions of the detailed procedures and methods that were essential for the conduct of successful trials are not published. A consequence of this is that those planning field trials have few practical guidelines available to them, and investigators have to design a study, often with little access to the knowledge and experience that has been accumulated previously. Personal experience is a good teacher, but, all too often, investigators have learned by repeating the mistakes of previous field researchers, at considerable cost and inconvenience.

Problems arise in the design, conduct, or analysis of many trials that may be unique to the particular study, but most potential problems have been faced by many investigators previously, some of whom devised good solutions and some not so good ones. Few publications exist which document this wealth of experience, and it is very difficult for potential field investigators to learn the practical issues in trial design and conduct.

The intention of this manual is to go some way towards filling this gap in the literature. It builds on the first two editions and has been comprehensively revised to take account of the evolution of methods that has taken place since the first edition in 1990. It has been compiled by contributors with extensive direct experience in the design, conduct, and analysis of field trials, and it attempts to document their accumulated experience for the guidance of those who might undertake field trials of health interventions in LMICs. It can be read in its entirety as an introduction to the field and/or can serve as a reference volume during each of the different stages of planning, conducting, and analysing a field trial.

The first edition had the title *Methods for field trials of interventions against tropical diseases: a toolbox*. We changed the title for the second edition to *Field trials of health interventions in developing countries: a toolbox*, recognizing that many issues discussed in the manual will be relevant to the conduct of field epidemiological studies on diseases that would not necessarily be classed as 'tropical'. For the third edition, we have changed the title again to *Field trials of health interventions: a toolbox*, as the 'developing country' terminology has been generally replaced by 'LMICs', but this would have made for a rather tortuous title! The focus of the book nonetheless is on field research in LMICs. Though some sections have wider relevance, we have preserved trials in the title because they are the main orientation of the book.

For the third edition, we have comprehensively reviewed the content of all the chapters that were included in the second edition. In addition, we have added chapters on topics or issues that were incompletely covered previously. Specifically, there are new chapters on conducting systematic literature reviews, trial governance, preliminary studies and pilot testing, budgeting and accounting, intervention costing and economic analysis, and Phase IV studies. Most of the other chapters have been rewritten, taking into account the substantial developments in trial methodology that have taken place since the second edition was published in 1996.

The *Toolbox* will always be a work in progress, and our intention is to continue to refine and improve it, as experience is gained with its practical use. We encourage those who use the manual to write to the editors if there are aspects of the manual that they think are in need of improvement.

Responsibility for producing initial drafts of the different chapters of the manual was assigned among the participants listed at the front of the book. The editors reviewed each of the contributions, and input was also sought from contributors other than those who had drafted the specific chapter. In this way, many different persons contributed to each chapter, and it seemed inappropriate therefore to attribute responsibility for any one chapter to individuals, as each chapter owes its final form to the collective contributions of those listed.

The text was discussed extensively and edited by the three of us to try to maintain a uniform style. The manual was also circulated to other field research scientists for their suggestions for any changes. We gratefully acknowledge valuable contributions from: Salim Abdulla, Martin Adjuik, Chris Grundy, Claudia Hanson, Adnan Hyder, Maria Merritt, Honorati Masanja, Luke Mullany, Hassan Mshinda, Annabelle South, and Susanne Wedner.

We are also very grateful to those who authored the first and second editions of the book, upon whose contributions the third edition is built. These are: Jackie Cattani, John Cleland, Nick Day, Joel Gittelsohn, Andy Hall, Birthe Høgh, Betty Kirkwood, Lindlwe Makubalo, Tom Marshall, Louis Molineaux, Jorg Pönnighaus, S. Radhakrishna, Ian Riley, Bob Snow, Harrison Spencer, Marcel Tanner, Carol Vlassoff, and Fred Wurapa. In addition, we are grateful to the following field research scientists who commented on chapters in the first two editions: Astier Almedon, Steve Bennett, Boachie Boatin, Loretta Brabin, David Brandling-Bennett, Gilbert Burnham, Peter Byass, Andreas de Francisco, Tony Degrement, Aime de Muynck, Isabelle de Zoysa, Anne Dick, Nicola Dollimore, Herbert Gillies, Brian Greenwood, Hazel Inskip, Japhet Killewo, Sarah Macfarlane, Bruce Macleod, Gilly Maude, Daan Mulder, Andrzej Radalowicz, Brian Southgate, Malcolm Pike, Roger Webber, Jimmy Whitworth, and Andrew Wilkins.

From the above, it is apparent that the *Toolbox* benefited from the wisdom of a large number of field research scientists. We apologize to those whose suggestions we have incorporated, but whose contribution we have inadvertently omitted to acknowledge!

We have been very keen to ensure that the *Toolbox* is made available as widely as possible, especially to those in LMICs. We are delighted therefore that, in addition to a paperback version, it has been possible to make the book available online and in open access through generous financial support from the UNDP/World Bank/WHO Special Programme for Research and Training in Tropical Diseases and from the Wellcome Trust.

London and Baltimore	P. G. S.
2015	R. H. M.
	D. A. R.

Contents

Contributors *xxix*
Acronyms *xxxii*

1 Introduction to field trials of health interventions *1*
2 Types of intervention and their development *5*
3 Reviewing the literature *19*
4 Trial design *37*
5 Trial size *71*
6 Ethical considerations *98*
7 Trial governance *120*
8 Preparing grant applications *132*
9 Community engagement *145*
10 Censuses and mapping *159*
11 Randomization, blinding, and coding *183*
12 Outcome measures and case definition *198*
13 Preliminary studies and pilot testing *216*
14 Questionnaires *223*
15 Social and behavioural research *249*
16 Field organization and ensuring data of high quality *268*
17 Field laboratory methods *285*
18 Budgeting and accounting *300*
19 Intervention costing and economic analysis *323*
20 Data management *338*
21 Methods of analysis *365*
22 Phase IV studies *394*
23 Reporting and using trial results *406*

Index *433*

Detailed contents

Contributors *xxix*

Acronyms *xxxii*

1 Introduction to field trials of health interventions *1*
   1 Scope of the book *1*
   2 Outline of contents *2*

2 Types of intervention and their development *5*
   1 Introduction to types of intervention and their development *5*
   2 Types of intervention *6*
      2.1 Preventive interventions *6*
          2.1.1 Vaccines *6*
          2.1.2 Nutritional interventions *7*
          2.1.3 Maternal and neonatal interventions *7*
          2.1.4 Education and behaviour change *8*
          2.1.5 Environmental alterations *9*
          2.1.6 Vector and intermediate host control *9*
          2.1.7 Drugs for the prevention of disease *10*
          2.1.8 Injury prevention *11*
      2.2 Therapeutic interventions *11*
          2.2.1 Treatment of infectious diseases *11*
          2.2.2 Surgical and radiation treatment *11*
          2.2.3 Diagnostics to guide therapy *12*
          2.2.4 Control of chronic diseases *12*
      2.3 Other forms of intervention *12*
          2.3.1 Legislation, legal action, taxation, and subsidies *12*
          2.3.2 Health systems interventions *13*
          2.3.3 Implementation research *13*
          2.3.4 Complex interventions *13*
   3 Evolution of new intervention products and sequence of study phases *16*
      3.1 Clinical studies: Phases I to IV *16*
      3.2 Registration of new interventions *17*

3.3 'Proof of principle' trials *17*

3.4 Trials of intervention delivery strategies *18*

3 Reviewing the literature *19*

1 Introduction to reviewing the literature *19*

2 Systematic reviews *20*

2.1 Defining the question *21*

2.2 Identifying relevant literature *22*

2.2.1 Electronic searching *22*

2.2.2 Reviewing abstracts *25*

2.2.3 Reviewing full articles *26*

2.2.4 Hand searching *26*

2.2.5 Flow chart of search strategy *26*

2.3 Descriptive synthesis of studies *26*

2.4 Assessing risk of bias in the studies *29*

2.5 Quantitative synthesis of results *30*

2.5.1 Forest plots *30*

2.5.2 Examining heterogeneity *31*

3 Software available for systematic reviews and meta-analyses *32*

4 Reporting findings from systematic reviews *32*

4 Trial design *37*

1 Introduction to trial design *38*

1.1 Planning a trial *38*

1.2 Ethical considerations in designing a trial *39*

1.3 Trial governance *40*

2 Definition of trial objectives *40*

2.1 The idea for a trial *40*

2.2 Trial purpose *41*

2.3 Specific objectives of the trial *42*

2.4 Subsidiary objectives of the trial *42*

3 Selection of interventions *43*

3.1 Intervention characteristics required *43*

3.2 Number of interventions compared *44*

3.3 Combined interventions *45*

3.4 Choice of comparison intervention *46*

3.5 Complex interventions *47*

    4   Allocation of interventions within the trial 47
        4.1   Randomization and 'blindness' 47
        4.2   Unit of application of the interventions 48
        4.3   'Stepped wedge' design 51
        4.4   Other approaches to allocation of the interventions 52
    5   Choice of outcome measures and trial duration 54
    6   Trial population 56
        6.1   Criteria for selection of trial population 56
        6.2   Inclusion and exclusion criteria 57
        6.3   The size of the trial population 57
        6.4   Compliance 58
    7   Implementation 59
        7.1   Community acceptance 59
        7.2   Feasibility studies and pilot testing 59
        7.3   Staff recruitment, training, and retention 59
        7.4   Field organization 60
    8   Data handling 60
        8.1   Data collection 60
        8.2   Data processing 60
    9   Quality control 60
        9.1   The intervention 61
        9.2   Follow-up 61
        9.3   Assessment of trial outcomes 62
        9.4   Other field and laboratory procedures 62
    10 Analysis, monitoring, and reporting 62
        10.1 Planning the main analyses 62
        10.2 Analyses during the trial 62
        10.3 Data and Safety Monitoring Committee 63
        10.4 Analysis methods 64
        10.5 Reporting results 64
        10.6 Further studies 64
    11 The 'SPIRIT' checklist for standard protocol items for clinical trials 65

5 Trial size 71

    1   Introduction to trial size 71
    2   Criteria for determining trial size 72

- 2.1 Precision of effect measures *72*
- 2.2 Power of the trial *73*
- 2.3 Choice of criterion *73*
- 2.4 Trials with multiple outcomes *74*
- 2.5 Practical constraints *75*
3 Size to give adequate precision *76*
- 3.1 Comparison of proportions *76*
- 3.2 Comparison of incidence rates *77*
- 3.3 Comparison of means *78*
4 Size to give adequate power *79*
- 4.1 Comparison of proportions *80*
- 4.2 Comparison of incidence rates *83*
- 4.3 Comparison of means *85*
5 More complex designs *86*
- 5.1 Two groups of unequal size *86*
- 5.2 Comparison of more than two groups *87*
- 5.3 Factorial designs *88*
- 5.4 Equivalence and non-inferiority trials *88*
6 Interventions allocated to groups *89*
- 6.1 Cluster randomized trials *90*
- 6.2 Stepped wedge trials *92*
7 Other factors influencing choice of trial size *93*
- 7.1 Allowance for interim analyses *93*
- 7.2 Allowance for losses *94*
8 The consequences of trials that are too small *94*
9 Computer software for sample size calculations *95*

6 Ethical considerations *98*

1 Introduction to ethical considerations *99*
2 Widely accepted ethical principles concerning research on human subjects *100*
- 2.1 Scientific merit *101*
- 2.2 Equitable selection of subjects *101*
- 2.3 Voluntariness *102*
- 2.4 Informed consent *102*
- 2.5 Confidentiality *105*
- 2.6 Coercion *105*

- 2.7 Review and approval by ethics committees *106*
- 2.8 Useful guidance documents *108*
  - 2.8.1 Operational guidelines for ethics committees that review biomedical research *108*
  - 2.8.2 International conference on harmonisation/WHO good clinical practice standards *108*
  - 2.8.3 The Declaration of Helsinki—ethical principles for medical research involving human subjects *108*
  - 2.8.4 International Ethical Guidelines for Epidemiological Studies *109*
  - 2.8.5 The ethics of research related to health care in developing countries *109*
  - 2.8.6 Consolidated Standards of Reporting Trials (CONSORT) *109*
  - 2.8.7 Extending the CONSORT statement to randomized trials of non-pharmacologic treatments *109*
  - 2.8.8 Other useful background documents *109*
- 3 Special issues in field trials in low- and middle-income countries *110*
  - 3.1 Obtaining communal and individual consent *110*
  - 3.2 Potential benefit and the risk of harm *111*
  - 3.3 Incentives *112*
  - 3.4 Standard of care *112*
  - 3.5 Choice of 'control' interventions *113*
  - 3.6 Choosing the primary endpoint *114*
  - 3.7 Duration and size of a trial *114*
  - 3.8 Monitoring safety during a trial *116*
  - 3.9 Special ethical issues in cluster randomized trials *117*
  - 3.10 Reporting and feedback of results *117*
  - 3.11 What happens after the trial? *118*
  - 3.12 Special ethical issues in Phase IV (post-licensure) studies *118*

7 Trial governance *120*

- 1 Introduction to trial governance *120*
- 2 The trial sponsor *121*
- 3 Steering committee *122*
- 4 Data and Safety Monitoring Board *122*

- 4.1 The functions of a Data and Safety Monitoring Board *124*
  - 4.1.1 Monitoring the conduct of the trial *124*
  - 4.1.2 Monitoring the safety of trial participants *124*
  - 4.1.3 Conducting interim analyses *125*
  - 4.1.4 Modification of trial procedures and other advice *126*
  - 4.1.5 Reporting to the sponsor *126*
- 4.2 Composition and appointment of the Data and Safety Monitoring Board *127*
- 4.3 The Data and Safety Monitoring Board charter *128*
5. Trial registration *129*

8 Preparing grant applications *132*

1. Introduction to preparing grant applications *132*
2. Grant awarding agencies *133*
   - 2.1 Understand the remit *133*
   - 2.2 Early contact *133*
3. Grant types *134*
   - 3.1 Project and programme grants *134*
   - 3.2 Personal fellowships *134*
   - 3.3 Special initiatives *134*
4. Grant awarding process *135*
   - 4.1 Peer review *135*
   - 4.2 Funding committees *135*
   - 4.3 Competitive process *136*
5. Developing the proposal *136*
   - 5.1 What is the problem, and why should it be studied? *136*
   - 5.2 What information is already available? *138*
   - 5.3 What are the objectives of the research? *138*
   - 5.4 How will relevant information be collected and analysed? *138*
   - 5.5 Community engagement plan *139*
   - 5.6 Who will do what and when? *139*
   - 5.7 What are the risks? *139*
   - 5.8 What resources are needed? *140*
   - 5.9 How will the project be supervised and administered? *140*
   - 5.10 How will results be disseminated? *140*

5.11　How will the application be presented to funding agencies?　*141*
　6　Responding to referees　*141*
　7　Funding decision　*142*
　8　Common problems in grant applications　*143*
　9　Roles and responsibilities　*143*
　10　Further advice　*144*

9 Community engagement　*145*
　1　Introduction to community engagement　*145*
　2　Planning and initiating community engagement　*146*
　　2.1　Defining communities and aims of engaging communities　*146*
　　2.2　Preliminary investigations in study communities　*147*
　　2.3　Setting up Community Advisory Groups or Boards　*149*
　3　Engaging community stakeholders　*151*
　　3.1　Engaging national and regional administrations　*151*
　　3.2　Engaging district health teams and health providers　*151*
　　3.3　Engaging community leaders　*152*
　　3.4　Working with the wider community　*153*
　　3.5　Roles of front-line research staff in community engagement　*153*
　4　Strategy and content of information for communication　*155*
　5　Sustaining community engagement　*156*

10 Censuses and mapping　*159*
　1　Introduction to conducting censuses and mapping　*159*
　2　Uses of maps and censuses in intervention trials　*160*
　3　Preparations for a census　*160*
　　3.1　Planning　*160*
　　3.2　Pre-testing　*162*
　　3.3　Recruitment and training of field staff　*162*
　　3.4　Mapping　*162*
　4　Enumeration　*166*
　　4.1　Organization of enumeration of households　*166*
　　4.2　Definition of dwelling units　*167*
　　4.3　*De facto* and *de jure* populations　*167*

4.4　Ensuring completeness of the census *168*
　　4.5　Numbering and identifying individuals *169*
　　4.6　Household or individual forms within a census? *170*
　　4.7　Coding relationships *171*
　　4.8　Names and addresses *173*
　　4.9　Ages *174*
　　4.10　Other identifying information *179*
　5　Processing of census data *180*
　6　Post-enumeration checks and quality control *180*
　7　Keeping the census up to date: demographic surveillance *180*

11 Randomization, blinding, and coding *183*
　1　Introduction to randomization, blinding, and coding *183*
　2　Randomization schemes for individual participants *185*
　　2.1　Unrestricted randomization *185*
　　2.2　Restricted randomization *186*
　　　2.2.1　Small block sizes *187*
　　　2.2.2　Larger block sizes *187*
　　2.3　Stratified randomization *188*
　3　Randomization schemes for community or group-based interventions *189*
　　3.1　Matched-pairs design *189*
　　3.2　Stratified design *189*
　　3.3　Constrained randomization design *190*
　4　Blinding *193*
　5　Coding systems *194*
　　5.1　Individual allocations *194*
　　5.2　Group allocations *195*

12 Outcome measures and case definition *198*
　1　Introduction to outcome measures and case definition *199*
　2　Types of outcome measures *200*
　　2.1　Primary, secondary, tertiary *200*
　　　2.1.1　Primary outcomes *200*
　　　2.1.2　Secondary and tertiary outcomes *201*
　　　2.1.3　Other variables which are not study outcomes *201*
　　2.2　Clinical case definitions *201*

- 2.2.1 Physician-based case definitions *201*
- 2.2.2 Laboratory-based case definitions, including any diagnostic procedure *202*
- 2.2.3 Lay worker-based case definitions *203*
- 2.2.4 Case definitions using secondary data sources *203*
- 2.2.5 Standardization *203*
- 2.2.6 Inclusion and exclusion criteria *204*
- 2.3 Death and verbal autopsies *204*
- 2.4 Non-clinical case definitions *205*
- 2.5 Proxy measurements as study outcomes *206*
  - 2.5.1 Behavioural changes *206*
  - 2.5.2 Transmission reduction *206*
- 2.6 Adverse events *207*
- 3 Factors influencing choice of outcome measures *208*
  - 3.1 Relevance *209*
  - 3.2 Feasibility *209*
  - 3.3 Acceptability *209*
  - 3.4 Opportunity for add-on studies *210*
- 4 Variability and quality control of outcome measures *210*
  - 4.1 Reproducibility *210*
  - 4.2 Sensitivity and specificity *211*
  - 4.3 Bias *213*
  - 4.4 The Hawthorne effect *214*
  - 4.5 Quality control issues *214*

13 Preliminary studies and pilot testing *216*
1 Introduction to preliminary studies and pilot testing *216*
2 Preliminary studies *216*
- 2.1 Purposes *216*
- 2.2 Design of preliminary studies *218*
3 Pilot testing *220*
- 3.1 Purpose *220*
- 3.2 Design of the pilot test *220*

14 Questionnaires *223*
1 Introduction to questionnaires *224*
2 The questions *225*

- 2.1 Relation to study objectives, content, and duration *225*
- 2.2 Development of questions *226*
- 2.3 Types of question *229*
    - 2.3.1 Historical recall *229*
    - 2.3.2 Open and closed questions *230*
- 2.4 Validation *230*
- 2.5 Translation *231*
- 3 The questionnaire *231*
    - 3.1 Length *231*
    - 3.2 Order of questions *232*
    - 3.3 Layout *233*
    - 3.4 Coding *233*
- 4 The interviewers *234*
    - 4.1 Selection *234*
    - 4.2 Training *235*
    - 4.3 Standardization *235*
    - 4.4 Interviewers' manual *236*
- 5 Data capture *237*
    - 5.1 Pen and paper *237*
    - 5.2 Electronic *237*
- 6 The interview *238*
    - 6.1 Who, where, and when *238*
    - 6.2 Non-response *239*
- Appendix 14.1 Options for recording responses on a questionnaire *240*
- Appendix 14.2 Pre-coded responses which are mutually exclusive *241*
- Appendix 14.3 Pre-coded responses which are not mutually exclusive *242*
- Appendix 14.4 Questions with a 'skip' instruction *242*
- Appendix 14.5 Recording of multiple items of information for direct computer entry *243*
- Appendix 14.6 'Open' questions *244*
- Appendix 14.7 Questions for self-completion by the respondent *245*
- Appendix 14.8 Questionnaires on a mobile phone *246*

Appendix 14.9   Collecting geolocation data on a mobile phone *247*

Appendix 14.10   Recording a laboratory test result on a mobile phone *248*

15 Social and behavioural research *249*

1   Purposes of social and behavioural research in intervention trials *249*

   1.1   Formative research to define the intervention package *250*

      1.1.1   Fieldwork *251*

      1.1.2   Literature review *252*

      1.1.3   Developing and pilot testing intervention delivery *254*

   1.2   Formative research to adapt the study protocol *255*

      1.2.1   Study design and procedures *255*

      1.2.2   Consent procedures and measurement tools *257*

2   Social and behavioural research in evaluation *257*

   2.1   Process evaluation to understand implementation *257*

   2.2   Evaluation of pathways of change *259*

      2.2.1   Hypothesis testing research *259*

      2.2.2   Hypothesis-generating research *259*

3   Commonly used methods in social research *260*

   3.1   Direct observation *261*

      3.1.1   Unstructured observation *262*

      3.1.2   Structured observation *262*

   3.2   In-depth interviews *263*

   3.3   Focus group discussions *264*

   3.4   Participatory research *265*

16 Field organization and ensuring data of high quality *268*

1   Introduction to field organization and ensuring data of high quality *268*

2   Manual of field operations and study diary *273*

3   Personnel issues *273*

4   Physical location and facilities *276*

5   Equipment and supplies *277*

6   Timetable for field activities *279*

7   Ensuring data of high quality *279*

DETAILED CONTENTS | xxiii

    7.1 Regulatory requirements and good clinical practice *280*

    7.2 Supervision and data checks *281*

17 Field laboratory methods *285*

  1 Introduction to field laboratory methods *285*

  2 Sample collection *286*

    2.1 Types of specimen *286*

    2.2 Handling specimens *287*

    2.3 Blood *288*

    2.4 Cerebrospinal fluid *289*

    2.5 Stool and urine *289*

    2.6 Sputum *290*

  3 Labelling and storage *290*

    3.1 Labelling *290*

    3.2 Storage *291*

    3.3 Aliquoting *292*

    3.4 Storage system *292*

  4 Documentation of laboratory procedures *292*

    4.1 Supplies *293*

    4.2 Equipment maintenance *293*

    4.3 Procedures and staff duties *293*

    4.4 Unusual or adverse events *294*

  5 Quality control and quality assurance *295*

    5.1 Reproducibility of test results *295*

    5.2 Internal quality control *296*

    5.3 External quality assurance *296*

  6 Accreditation and links between laboratories *297*

  7 Coding and linkage of results *297*

  8 Laboratory health and safety *298*

18 Budgeting and accounting *300*

  1 Introduction to budgeting and accounting *300*

  2 Budgeting *303*

    2.1 Capital costs *304*

    2.2 Recurrent costs *305*

        2.2.1 Personnel *305*

        2.2.2 Consultant or technical advisor costs *305*

        2.2.3 Supplies *305*

        2.2.4   Travel and per diems *306*

        2.2.5   Patient care and participant costs *306*

        2.2.6   Other expenses *306*

        2.2.7   Indirect costs (institutional overheads) *306*

    3   Accounting *307*

        3.1   Supporting documents *307*

        3.2   Books of account *308*

        3.3   Reconciliations *309*

            3.3.1   Bank reconciliation *310*

            3.3.2   Petty cash reconciliation *310*

            3.3.3   Trial balance *310*

        3.4   Cost codes *310*

    4   Budget monitoring *310*

        4.1   Analysis of expenditure *311*

        4.2   Balance sheet *311*

        4.3   Cash flow forecast *311*

    5   Accounts summaries and auditing *311*

    6   Prevention of fraud and other losses *313*

        6.1   Purchasing *314*

        6.2   Debtors *315*

        6.3   Cash payments *315*

    7   Glossary of financial terms *317*

19 Intervention costing and economic analysis *323*

    1   Introduction to intervention costing and economic analysis *323*

    2   Types of economic analyses *324*

        2.1   Cost-effectiveness analysis *325*

        2.2   Cost-utility analysis *325*

            2.2.1   Disability-adjusted life-years and quality-adjusted life-years *326*

        2.3   Cost–benefit analysis *326*

    3   Framing the analysis *327*

        3.1   Perspective *327*

        3.2   Range of inputs and outcomes *328*

        3.3   Time frame *328*

    4   Health intervention costs *329*

        4.1   Types of costs *329*

- 4.1.1 Provider costs *329*
- 4.1.2 User costs *329*
- 4.2 Approaches to costing *331*
  - 4.2.1 Valuing resource use *331*
- 5 Presentation of results *332*
- 6 Generalizability *333*
  - 6.1 Uncertainty *333*
    - 6.1.1 Sampling uncertainty *333*
    - 6.1.2 Parameter uncertainty *334*
  - 6.2 Policy inferences *334*
  - 6.3 External validity *334*
- 7 Modelling *334*
- 8 Publication of findings *335*

20 Data management *338*

- 1 Introduction to data management *339*
- 2 Before starting to collect data *340*
  - 2.1 Hardware *340*
  - 2.2 Software *342*
  - 2.3 Personnel *343*
  - 2.4 Data oversight *344*
  - 2.5 Summary *346*
- 3 Planning the data flow *346*
  - 3.1 Database design *346*
  - 3.2 Data cleaning and integrity *348*
  - 3.3 Programming issues *349*
  - 3.4 Standard operating procedures *349*
  - 3.5 Version control *349*
  - 3.6 Confidentiality *350*
  - 3.7 Training *350*
  - 3.8 Pilot testing and database testing *350*
- 4 Data collection systems *351*
  - 4.1 Questionnaires *351*
  - 4.2 Electronic data capture *351*
  - 4.3 Laboratory data *351*
  - 4.4 Clinic data *352*
  - 4.5 Longitudinal data collection *352*

    4.6 Quality control *353*
    4.7 Future trends *353*
5 Managing data *354*
    5.1 Data entry *354*
    5.2 Data checks *355*
    5.3 Data cleaning *357*
    5.4 Variable naming and coding *358*
    5.5 Data lock *359*
6 Archiving *359*
    6.1 Interim backups *359*
    6.2 Metadata *360*
    6.3 Data sharing policy *360*
    6.4 Archiving hard copies *361*
7 Preparing data for analysis *362*
    7.1 Data dictionary *362*
    7.2 Creating new variables *362*
    7.3 Coding and re-coding *362*
    7.4 Merging and linking data *363*

21 Methods of analysis *365*

1 Introduction to methods of analysis *366*
2 Basics of statistical inference *367*
    2.1 Types of outcome measure *367*
    2.2 Confidence intervals *367*
    2.3 Statistical tests *368*
3 Statistical analysis plan *369*
4 Analysis of proportions *371*
    4.1 Confidence interval for a single proportion *371*
    4.2 Difference between two proportions *371*
    4.3 Ratio of two proportions *372*
    4.4 Trend test for proportions *373*
5 Analysis of rates *374*
    5.1 Risks, rates, and person-time-at-risk *374*
    5.2 Confidence interval for a rate *375*
    5.3 Difference between two rates *376*
    5.4 Ratio of two rates *377*
    5.5 Trend test for rates *377*

6   Analysis of mean values *378*
  6.1   Confidence interval for a mean *378*
  6.2   Difference between two means *378*
  6.3   Analysis of more than two groups *379*
7   Controlling for confounding variables *380*
  7.1   The nature of confounding variables *380*
  7.2   Adjusting for confounding variables *381*
  7.3   Adjusting risks *381*
    7.3.1   Overall test of significance *381*
    7.3.2   Pooled estimate of risk difference *383*
    7.3.3   Pooled estimate of risk ratio *383*
    7.3.4   Confidence intervals *384*
  7.4   Adjusting rates *384*
    7.4.1   Overall test of significance *384*
    7.4.2   Pooled estimate of rate difference *385*
    7.4.3   Pooled estimate of rate ratio *385*
    7.4.4   Confidence intervals *385*
  7.5   Adjusting means *387*
8   Analyses when communities have been randomized *388*
  8.1   Calculation of standardized responses *389*
  8.2   Non-parametric rank sum test *390*
  8.3   Tests on paired data *391*
9   Prevented fraction of disease *392*

22 Phase IV studies *394*

1   Introduction to Phase IV studies *394*
  1.1   Efficacy and effectiveness *396*
  1.2   Stakeholders *397*
2   Types of Phase IV study *397*
  2.1   Safety/pharmacovigilance *397*
  2.2   Intervention effectiveness *398*
3   The conduct of Phase IV studies *400*
  3.1   Design issues *400*
  3.2   Study sites *400*
  3.3   Ethics and governance *401*
  3.4   Stakeholder involvement *401*

- 3.5 Data collection, processing, and analysis *401*
- 3.6 Contextual and confounding factors *402*
- 3.7 Reporting and dissemination *402*
- 3.8 Funding *402*
- 4 Examples of real-world effectiveness studies *403*
  - 4.1 The INDEPTH Effectiveness and Safety Studies (INESS) platform *403*
  - 4.2 Effectiveness of intermittent preventive treatment for malaria *404*

23 Reporting and using trial results *406*

- 1 Planning communications *406*
- 2 Communication before and during the trial *407*
- 3 Reporting the final results *408*
  - 3.1 Planning the sequence of communications *408*
  - 3.2 Report to the sponsor *408*
  - 3.3 Trial participants and the study communities *409*
  - 3.4 Local and government officials *409*
  - 3.5 Reporting in the scientific literature *409*
  - 3.6 Media coverage *410*
  - 3.7 The funding agency *411*
- 4 From research findings to public health action *412*
  - 4.1 Sharing and synthesizing findings *412*
  - 4.2 Researchers and policy *412*
  - 4.3 Introducing an intervention into public health programmes *415*
- Appendix 23.1 Guidance on how to write a scientific paper reporting the results of a trial *417*
- Appendix 23.2 Checklist of information to include when reporting a randomized trial *422*
- Appendix 23.3 A communication action plan for a trial (Annabelle South, Aoife Doyle, David Ross, personal communication) *424*

Index *433*

Contributors

The following persons had a major role in the production of this book, in contributing drafts of chapters and in subsequent revisions.

Richard Adegbola
Global Director, Scientific Affairs and Public Health, GlaxoSmithKline Vaccines, Wavre, Belgium

Kenneth Babigumira
Senior Analyst Programmer, Medical Research Council (MRC) Clinical Trials Unit at University College London, UK

Kathy Baisley
Lecturer in Epidemiology and Medical Statistics, MRC Tropical Epidemiology Group, London School of Hygiene & Tropical Medicine, London, UK

David Beckles
Data Processing Consultant, Upton, Oxfordshire, UK

Fred Binka
Vice-Chancellor, University of Health and Allied Sciences, Ho, Ghana

Clare Chandler
Lecturer in Social Science, Department of Global Health and Development, London School of Hygiene & Tropical Medicine, London, UK

Michael Chew
Science Portfolio Advisor, Wellcome Trust, London, UK

Aoife Doyle
Lecturer in Epidemiology, MRC Tropical Epidemiology Group, London School of Hygiene & Tropical Medicine, London, UK

Chris Drakeley
Professor of Infection and Immunity, Department of Immunology and Infection, London School of Hygiene & Tropical Medicine, London, UK

Anbrasi Edward
Associate Scientist, Department of International Health, Johns Hopkins Bloomberg School of Public Health, Baltimore, USA

Greg Fegan
Head of Statistics, Kenya Medical Research Institute (KEMRI)–Wellcome Trust, Centre for Geographic Medicine Research (Coast), Kilifi, Kenya and Centre for Tropical Medicine, University of Oxford, UK

Susan Foster
Professor of International Health, Department of International Health, Boston University School of Public Health, Boston, USA

Richard J. Hayes
Professor of Epidemiology and International Health, MRC Tropical Epidemiology Group, London School of Hygiene & Tropical Medicine, London, UK

Hilary Hunter
Planning and Governance Manager, London School of Hygiene & Tropical Medicine, London, UK

Anatoli Kamali
Deputy Director, MRC/Uganda Virus Research Institute Uganda Research Unit on AIDS, Entebbe, Uganda

Dorcas M. Kamuya
Researcher in Ethics and Community Engagement, The Ethox Centre, University of Oxford, UK; and KEMRI–Wellcome Trust, Centre for Geographic Medicine Research (Coast), Kilifi, Kenya

Saidi Kapiga
Reader in Epidemiology and International Health, Department of Infectious Disease Epidemiology, London School of Hygiene & Tropical Medicine, London, UK

Juntra Karbwang Laothavorn
Professor and Head, Department of Clinical Product Development, Institute of Tropical Medicine, Nagasaki University, Japan

Jane Kengeya-Kayondo
Coordinator, Strategic Alliances, Special Programme for Research and Training in Tropical Diseases, World Health Organization, Geneva, Switzerland

Irene Kuepfer
Scientist, Health Systems Research, Swiss Tropical and Public Health Institute, Basel, Switzerland

Claudio F. Lanata
Senior Researcher, Instituto de Investigacion Nutricional, Lima, Peru; and US Naval Medical Research Unit No. 6, Peru

Trudie Lang
Head of the Global Health Network, Centre for Tropical Medicine, University of Oxford, UK

Vicki Marsh
Senior Researcher, Health Systems and Social Science Group, KEMRI-Wellcome Trust, Centre for Geographic Medicine Research (Coast), Kilifi, Kenya; and Research Lecturer, Centre for Tropical Medicine and Research Associate, Ethox Centre, University of Oxford, UK

Sassy Molyneux
Lecturer and Group Head, Centre for Tropical Medicine and Ethox Centre, University of Oxford, UK; and KEMRI-Wellcome Trust, Centre for Geographic Medicine Research (Coast), Kilifi, Kenya

Richard H. Morrow
Professor of International Health, Department of International Health, Johns Hopkins Bloomberg School of Public Health, Baltimore, USA

Lawrence H. Moulton
Professor of Biostatistics, Department of International Health, Johns Hopkins Bloomberg School of Public Health, Baltimore, USA

Seth Owusu-Agyei
Director, Kintampo Health Research Centre, Kintampo, Ghana

David A. Ross
Professor of Epidemiology and International Public Health, MRC Tropical Epidemiology Group, London School of Hygiene & Tropical Medicine, London, UK

Donald de Savigny
Professor of Epidemiology and Public Health, Swiss Tropical and Public Health Institute, Basel, Switzerland

Joanna Schellenberg
Professor of Epidemiology and International Health and Head of Department of Disease Control, London

School of Hygiene & Tropical Medicine,
London, UK

Peter G. Smith
Professor of Tropical Epidemiology,
MRC Tropical Epidemiology Group,
London School of Hygiene & Tropical
Medicine, London, UK

Jim Todd
Reader in Applied Biostatistics,
Department of Population Health,
London School of Hygiene & Tropical
Medicine, London, UK

Cesar Victora
Emeritus Professor of Epidemiology,
Departmento de Medicina Social,
Faculdade de Medicina, Universidade
Federal de Pelotas, Brazil

Jimmy Volmink
Dean, Faculty of Medicine and Health
Sciences, Stellenbosch University; and
Director, South African (SA) Cochrane
Centre, SA Medical Research Council,
Tygerberg, South Africa

Damian G. Walker
Senior Program Officer, Integrated
Delivery, Bill and Melinda Gates
Foundation, Seattle, USA

Helen Weiss
Professor of Epidemiology and
Head of the MRC Tropical
Epidemiology Group,
London School of Hygiene
& Tropical Medicine, London, UK

Peter Winch
Director, Social and Behavioural
Interventions Program,
Department of International Health,
Johns Hopkins Bloomberg School
of Public Health, Baltimore,
USA

Fabio Zicker
Senior Visiting Professor,
Center for Technological Development
in Health, Oswaldo Cruz Foundation,
Fiocruz, Rio de Janeiro,
Brazil

Acronyms

#	number	ELISA	enzyme-linked immunosorbent assay
ABC	activity-based costing	EPI	Expanded Programme on Immunisation
ACT	artimisinen combination treatment	ERC	ethics review committee
AE	adverse event	ESR	erythrocyte sedimentation rate
ASRH	adolescent sexual and reproductive health	ESRC	Economic and Social Research Council
BCG	bacille Calmette–Guérin	GCP	Good Clinical Practice
BMI	body mass index	GCLP	Good Clinical Laboratory Practice
CAB	Community Advisory Board	GDP	gross domestic product
CAG	Community Advisory Group	GIS	geographical information system
CBA	cost–benefit analysis	GPS	global positioning system
CEA	cost-effectiveness analysis	GRADE	Grading of Recommendations Assessment, Development, and Evaluation
CI	confidence interval		
CIOMS	Council for International Organizations of Medical Sciences	HBV	hepatitis B virus
		HDSS	health and demographic surveillance system
CONSORT	Consolidated Standards of Reporting Trials	HIC	high-income country
CRO	clinical research organization	HIV	human immunodeficiency virus
CSF	cerebrospinal fluid	HLA	human leucocyte antigen
CT	*Chlamydia trachomatis*	HSV 2	herpes simplex virus type 2
CUA	cost-utility analysis	IATA	International Air Transport Association
CVD	cardiovascular disease		
DALY	disability-adjusted life-year	ICER	incremental cost-effectiveness ratio
DDI	Data Documentation Initiative		
DDT	dichlorodiphenyltrichloroethane	ICH	International Conference on Harmonisation
df	degree of freedom		
DFID	Department for International Development	ICMJE	International Committee of Medical Journal Editors
DHMT	district health management team	IDMC	Independent Data Monitoring Committee
DHS	Demographic and Health Surveys		
DMB	Data Monitoring Board	IEC	information, education, and communication
DMC	Data Monitoring Committee		
DNA	deoxyribonucleic acid	IMCI	Integrated Management Of Childhood Illness
DSMB	Data and Safety Monitoring Board		
		INDEPTH	International Network for the Demographic Evaluation of Populations and Their Health
DSMC	Data and Safety Monitoring Committee		

INESS	INDEPTH Effectiveness And Safety Studies
INSERM	Institut National de la Santé et de la Recherche Médicale
IPT	intermittent preventive therapy for malaria
IPTc	intermittent preventive treatment for malaria in children
IPTi	intermittent preventive treatment for malaria in infants
IPTi-SP	intermittent preventive treatment for malaria in infants using sulfadoxine–pyrimethamine
IPTp	intermittent preventive treatment for malaria in pregnancy
IRB	Institutional Review Board
ITN	insecticide-treated bed-net
IU	international unit
kg	kilogram
LAN	local area network
LDMS	Laboratory Data Management System
LIMS	Laboratory Information Management System
LMIC	low- and middle-income country
Mango	Management Accounting for Non-governmental Organisations
MeSH	medical subject heading
MkV	MEMA kwa Vijana
MOH	Ministry of Health
MTA	Material Transfer Agreement
NGO	non-governmental organization
ODK	Open Data Kit
OHRP	Office for Human Research Protections
OR	odds ratio
PCV	packed cell volume
PDA	personal digital assistant
PI	principal investigator
PICOS	Population; Interventions (or Exposure); Comparison; Outcomes; Study design
PLA	participatory learning and action
POC	point of care
PRA	participatory rural appraisal

PRISMA	Preferred Reporting Items for Systematic Reviews and Meta-Analyses
QA	quality assurance
QALY	quality-adjusted life-year
QC	quality control
RCT	randomized controlled trial
RDT	rapid diagnostic test
RR	relative risk *or* risk ratio *or* rate ratio
SAE	serious adverse event
SAP	statistical analysis plan
SMC	seasonal malaria chemoprevention
SOP	standard operating procedure
SP	sulfadoxine–pyrimethamine
SPIRIT	Standard Protocol Items: Recommendations for Intervention Trials
SRH	sexual and reproductive health
STD	sexually transmitted disease
STI	sexually transmitted infection
TB	tuberculosis
UK	United Kingdom
UMPC	ultra-mobile personal computer
UN	United Nations
UNAIDS	Joint United Nations Programme on HIV/AIDS
UNESCO	United Nations Educational, Scientific, and Cultural Organization
UNFPA	United Nations Population Fund
UNICEF	United Nations Children's Fund
USA	United States of America
USAID	United States Agency for International Development
vs	versus
WHO	World Health Organization
WHO ERC	World Health Organization Research Ethics Review Committee
XML	extensible markup language
YLD	years of life lived with disability
YLL	years of life lost

Chapter 1

Introduction to field trials of health interventions

1 Scope of the book 1
2 Outline of contents 2

1 Scope of the book

In this book, we aim to provide a practical and comprehensive guide to the design and conduct of field trials of health interventions directed against disease problems in low- and middle-income countries (LMICs). Our main emphasis is on randomized controlled trials (RCTs), but many of the issues discussed are of relevance to other kinds of field research in LMICs. Published papers reporting the results of intervention trials rarely include details of the practical aspects of preparation for a trial and its conduct, yet these are crucial to the execution of a successful trial. Those conducting trials for the first time often do not have access to references detailing the many practical issues that have to be addressed in the organization and conduct of a trial. New investigators generally have to learn by experience and, as a consequence, often repeat mistakes that others have learned not to make. While 'learning by doing' can be a valuable educational method, it is usually inefficient and wasteful. We have tried to synthesize the experience of investigators with substantial experience of conducting field trials in LMICs and describe procedures and practices found to work well in LMIC settings. Thereby, we hope that new investigators will build on and extend the experience of others, rather than repeat the same mistakes.

Trials of health interventions involve the implementation of a specific health intervention and comparison of the effects of that intervention with the effects of the currently available 'best' intervention or, if there is none, comparison with what happens with no intervention (or with a placebo). In order to avoid bias in the allocation of participants to the intervention or comparison group, assignment of individuals or groups to a particular intervention should be done by randomization. The 'trial' approach is in contrast to observational studies such as cross-sectional surveys, cohort studies, and case-control studies. But many of the methods and techniques described in this book may also be usefully deployed in observational studies.

We use the term 'field trial' for trials conducted outside clinical settings, in contrast to 'clinical trial' that is used for studies carried out in health facilities. Thus, field trials generally involve participants who are living at home in their normal environment, rather than being 'captive' in hospitals or outpatient clinics. Most trials of preventive measures, such as immunizations or health education, are 'field' trials. Important differences in field and clinical trials include inclusion and exclusion criteria that may be less stringent in field trials than criteria often imposed in clinical trials, in which it may be important to have a clearly defined disease condition for treatment. To the extent that there are less stringent inclusion and exclusion criteria, there may be fewer problems with the external validity of trial conclusions than there often are for clinical trials that limit the generalizability of conclusions. Another difference is that randomization of intervention by groups (clusters), rather than by individuals, is more often necessary or useful in field trials than in clinical trials (see Chapter 4, Section 4).

Clinical trials of drugs and vaccines are commonly carried out in successive phases, as described in Chapter 2, Section 3. Phase I trials are early studies conducted in a few human volunteers to test the safety of a promising new drug or vaccine. Thereafter, Phase II trials are carried out on larger numbers of volunteers, often to gauge immunogenicity (of a vaccine) and the effect of different doses or number of doses and to monitor for any adverse reactions. When these phases are successfully completed, Phase III trials are conducted on much larger numbers of volunteers who are randomized to receive either the new product or the comparison product, in order to establish the efficacy of the new intervention. The main focus of the book will be large-scale randomized field trials. For pharmaceuticals and vaccines, these will usually be Phase III trials, though this designation by phase does not fit so well with some other important types of interventions such as behaviour change interventions or environmental modification.

We do not envisage that many readers will sit down and read the book from beginning to end! We have called it a 'toolbox', because we think this reflects how it might be used, i.e. to consult different chapters and sections to guide different stages in the planning and execution of a trial.

2 Outline of contents

The chapters of this book can be considered in three main groupings. Chapters 2 through to 13 review issues to consider and steps to be taken before starting a trial. Chapters 14 through to 20 detail the tasks to be carried out during the conduct of a trial, with a focus on data collection. Chapters 21 and 23 discuss the analysis, interpretation, and reporting of trial results. We have also included a short chapter on Phase IV studies (Chapter 22), that are usually conducted after a product has been licensed and is in, or is about to go into, public health use. Phase IV studies are usually not randomized designs, because of the ethical issues in withholding a licensed intervention from participants, and such studies are not a main focus of this book. However, we have included this chapter because many of the design, conduct, and analysis issues discussed in other chapters have relevance for Phase IV studies and also because it will often be desirable for Phase III trials, which usually measure the efficacy of an intervention delivered in a highly controlled manner, to be followed by Phase IV evaluations in 'real-life' programmes.

Before embarking on a trial, the first steps are to define the goals, objectives, and key questions for the study. As background to this, the broad array of potential types of interventions is catalogued in Chapter 2. The importance of critically reviewing essential background information relevant to a trial, including trials of similar interventions, through a systematic review of literature is emphasized in Chapter 3. The heart of the book is concerned with the design of the trial, as outlined in Chapter 4, and making it of appropriate size (Chapter 5). Many of the design details are guided by ethical concerns (Chapter 6), regulatory requirements, and governance issues (Chapter 7). A major issue in planning a trial is generating the resources to carry it out, and guidance is given in Chapter 8 on the preparation of grant applications for trials to funding agencies.

Field trials are generally based in communities, and their successful conduct is highly dependent on investigators engaging appropriately with community members at all stages in the planning and execution of a trial (Chapter 9). Before a trial starts, the target population has to be defined and registered (Chapter 10), and then the interventions under test must be allocated to individuals or communities, in an unbiased way, by randomization, with the intervention allocations being kept 'blind', if possible, to investigators and participants. Ways of achieving this are discussed in Chapter 11. Evaluation of the impact of an intervention depends upon appropriate definition of the outcomes that the intervention is expected to affect. Choice of appropriate outcome measures and unambiguous definition of these is considered in Chapter 12.

Undertaking a trial is often a major activity, involving a large trial team for several years. It is rarely possible to start a trial immediately the protocol has been written and the funding obtained. Almost always, it is necessary to have collected preliminary data to facilitate the planning of the trial and to conduct studies to test out the procedures that are proposed for use in the trial, and modifying them appropriately if they are not found to be fit for purpose. Such preliminary studies and pilot testing of procedures are covered in Chapter 13. Information about trial participants is commonly collected through the administration of questionnaires. The various forms that these might take and different methods of administering them are summarized in Chapter 14.

Most intervention trials involve some element of behaviour change, both on the parts of those administering the intervention (for example, workers in the health service) and of those taking it up—the trial participants. The extent of behaviour change required will vary, according to the intervention under test. Evaluating a new vaccine which is administered at the same time as routine vaccinations in the childhood immunization programme may require relatively little behaviour change, but implementing an intervention to reduce high-risk sexual behaviour to lower the risk of human immunodeficiency virus (HIV) infection, or promoting hand-washing to reduce the risk of diarrhoeal diseases, will involve substantial behaviour changes. Undertaking social and behavioural research to facilitate the design and implementation of interventions is reviewed in Chapter 15.

Quality control of all aspects of conducting a trial is crucial if the findings from the trial are to be used to make important public health decisions about the use, or otherwise, of an intervention, based on the trial results. These issues are discussed in Chapter 16, while Chapter 17 specifically focuses on methods and quality control in field laboratories, which are an important component of most trials.

Nothing can be done without financial support for the trial. The essentials for the preparation of budgets for grant applications are given in Chapter 8. The efficient planning and management of finances during a trial are also key to success, and a requirement of funding agencies. The necessary budgeting and accounting methods are outlined in Chapter 18. Chapter 19 affords an overview of the main methods used to assess the costs of health interventions and summarizes the types of economic analyses that can be conducted to assist decisions concerning resource allocation to health interventions.

In all but the smallest trials, substantial amounts of data are collected and have to be efficiently processed, both during the conduct of the trial and for the analysis of the results during, and at the end of, the trial. Methods of data management are summarized in Chapter 20, and an outline of methods of statistical analysis of trials is given in Chapter 21. In most trials it will be necessary to employ a statistician to oversee the analysis of the data from the trial, but the relatively simple methods summarized in this chapter should be sufficient to elucidate the main results from most trials.

Finally, Chapter 23 stresses the importance of communication at all stages of the trial, how best to communicate to the many different audiences who should be informed about the trial, and the necessary steps to translate research findings into policy and public health action.

We have deliberately not included large numbers of references, as the book is intended to stand largely on its own, without readers needing access to a well-stocked library. Referencing has been reserved for where a particular study has been described, or as a guide for readers who may require a more detailed explanation of a concept than can be included in this text. Whenever possible, we have favoured open access or relatively low-cost resources.

Chapter 2

Types of intervention and their development

1 Introduction to types of intervention and their development 5
2 Types of intervention 6
   2.1 Preventive interventions 6
      2.1.1 Vaccines 6
      2.1.2 Nutritional interventions 7
      2.1.3 Maternal and neonatal interventions 7
      2.1.4 Education and behaviour change 8
      2.1.5 Environmental alterations 9
      2.1.6 Vector and intermediate host control 9
      2.1.7 Drugs for the prevention of disease 10
      2.1.8 Injury prevention 11
   2.2 Therapeutic interventions 11
      2.2.1 Treatment of infectious diseases 11
      2.2.2 Surgical and radiation treatment 11
      2.2.3 Diagnostics to guide therapy 12
      2.2.4 Control of chronic diseases 12
   2.3 Other forms of intervention 12
      2.3.1 Legislation, legal action, taxation, and subsidies 12
      2.3.2 Health systems interventions 13
      2.3.3 Implementation research 13
      2.3.4 Complex interventions 13
3 Evolution of new intervention products and sequence of study phases 16
   3.1 Clinical studies: Phases I to IV 16
   3.2 Registration of new interventions 17
   3.3 'Proof of principle' trials 17
   3.4 Trials of intervention delivery strategies 18

1 Introduction to types of intervention and their development

This book is about the evaluation of the effectiveness of health-related interventions. We use the term 'intervention' to apply to any activity undertaken with the objective of improving human health by preventing disease, by curing or reducing the severity or duration of an existing disease, or by restoring function lost through disease or injury. There are a wide variety of new interventions, and new strategies for the use of interventions, that are being developed against the major diseases common in LMICs. These include both public health and clinical care measures, and include drugs for acute and chronic conditions, vaccines, vector control, health education, behaviour change strategies, injury prevention, and better health planning and management methods that improve a spectrum of health-related activities. Research involving a wide range of disciplines is needed to develop, deploy, and assess these interventions, ranging from molecular biology and immunology to social sciences, epidemiology, and statistics. The focus of this book is on the evaluation of interventions through field trials. Field trials are required to assess how interventions, both old and new, may be best applied in populations and to determine their impact on improving the health of the population.

In this chapter, the characteristics of different kinds of intervention that may be used in disease control programmes are reviewed. How each type of intervention is implemented is outlined, and the implications of these implementation strategies for the design, conduct, and interpretation of field trials are discussed. The nature of an intervention will determine the way in which it can be evaluated in a field trial. Some interventions which are applied to individuals can be evaluated through the random allocation of individuals to the intervention or the 'control' arms. Other interventions are applied to groups of individuals, such as households or whole communities, and the group should therefore be the unit of randomization.

2 Types of intervention

Interventions can be classified into two broad categories: (1) preventive interventions are those that prevent disease from occurring and thus reduce the incidence (new cases) of disease, and (2) therapeutic interventions are those that treat, mitigate, or postpone the effects of disease, once it is under way, and thus reduce the case fatality rate or reduce the disability or morbidity associated with a disease. Some interventions may have both effects.

2.1 Preventive interventions

2.1.1 Vaccines

Vaccines are administered to individuals, usually before they have encountered the infectious agent against which the vaccine is targeted, in order to protect them when they are naturally exposed to the agent. Many are among the most cost-effective interventions, because, after a single dose or a series of doses of the vaccine, an individual may acquire long-term protection against the agent. They work by inducing a variety of immune mechanisms, through the humoral and/or cellular immune systems. The immunological responses and associated immunological memory induced by vaccination confer protection from later infections, though a booster vaccination may be necessary if the interval between the original vaccination and exposure to the agent is long. Most vaccines have to be administered before the infectious agent is encountered naturally, and thus field trials of such vaccines will involve the enrolment of healthy individuals and often involve infants or very young children—though the vaccine may be given at a later age if the age of natural infection is at later ages, for example, for most sexually transmitted infections (STIs), or if a new infectious agent, to which no one has been previously exposed, enters a community such as a new strain of influenza.

Not all vaccines are targeted at persons without previous exposure to the infectious agent. For example, there is substantial research to develop vaccines against parasitic diseases. The mode of action of some of these vaccines is to prevent parasitic proliferation within the host after invasion (and hence curtailment of disease), and some vaccines against vector-borne diseases are even targeted to prevent replication of the forms of the infection in the vector, so that onward transmission to humans is prevented.

For infectious diseases that affect both high-income countries (HICs) and LMICs, the first trials of new vaccines are usually conducted in HICs. This is because currently most new vaccines are developed and produced in HICs (though this situation is changing), and it is generally accepted that at least early clinical studies should be conducted in the country of vaccine manufacture. However, the results of trials in HICs may not be directly applicable to LMICs for a variety of reasons such as differing prevalences of other infections or of nutritional deficiencies, which might interfere with the mode of action of the vaccine. Thus, there will often be a need for further trials of the vaccine in LMICs, even if efficacy has been established in HICs. In addition, there has been increased focus in recent years on the development of vaccines against infectious agents that only, or almost only, occur in LMICs, such as malaria or visceral leishmaniasis, or where the overwhelming disease burden is in such countries, such as tuberculosis (TB) or HIV infection. For vaccines against these agents, the first major field trials to assess efficacy are likely to be conducted in LMICs.

2.1.2 Nutritional interventions

Food and nutrition are major determinants of human health and disease. Particularly in low-income countries and deprived populations in middle-income countries, under-nutrition remains a major cause of disease. Severe malnutrition, such as kwashiorkor or marasmus, is life-threatening, but milder forms of malnutrition are major risk factors that adversely influence the susceptibility to, and the outcome of, many infectious and other diseases, as well as cognitive development. In addition to calorie and protein deficiencies, specific deficiencies in micronutrients, such as iron, folate, zinc, iodine, and vitamin A, may be important determinants of severe diseases. Trials to address these problems may involve the regular provision of high-protein/calorie diets or supplementation to individuals with specific micronutrients, involving repeated visits to the same persons over several years, the frequency of administration depending on the nature of the supplement(s). Other trials, often with the intervention being applied at a community level, may involve food fortification (for example, iron, iodine, vitamin D) and experiments to change agricultural practices or eating or food preparation habits to increase the intake of particular micronutrients.

2.1.3 Maternal and neonatal interventions

A mother's health and well-being during pregnancy and around the time of delivery, including access to appropriate care, are critical determinants of maternal mortality and neonatal and child health in the early years of life, and possibly for much longer. Preventive interventions before or during pregnancy include family planning, treatment of infections, such as syphilis and malaria, good nutrition, including micronutrients, good antenatal monitoring and care, and access to skilled care at the time of delivery and post-partum. Trials of maternal interventions may involve both community-based studies, with the early identification of pregnancies and the instigation of preventive interventions to avoid pregnancy complications, or may be hospital- or health centre-based, directed at improving the performance of the health system in caring for women during and after pregnancy and at the time of birth.

Interventions directed to the neonate are also important, such as exclusive breastfeeding and care practices, such as 'kangaroo mother care', a method of care of pre-term infants, involving infants being carried, usually by the mother, with skin-to-skin contact.

2.1.4 Education and behaviour change

Some interventions directed at preventing disease are based solely upon changing human behaviour (for example, anti-smoking campaigns or campaigns to promote breastfeeding). Nearly all health interventions must have an associated educational component for their effective deployment, but the extent of educational effort required ranges from the provision of simple information (for example, when and where a clinic for immunization will be held) to efforts at increasing understanding (for example, of the importance of male circumcision for the prevention of HIV) and to attempts to change lifestyles (for example, diet or sexual habits). Education to increase knowledge and impart new skills may be necessary but is rarely sufficient to induce behaviour change. Individuals must also have the capacity, willingness, and motivation to act on the knowledge and to use the skills. The design and implementation of an educational intervention, and other 'complex' interventions (Craig et al., 2008), will usually need to be researched through careful investigations in the community, using the kinds of methods discussed in Chapters 9 and 15.

Examples of educational components of disease control programmes include:

- educating children or mothers about the causes of the disease, such as diarrhoea, and how to prevent it
- promoting adherence to long-term treatment such as for HIV infection or TB
- developing effective participation in programmes that:
  - need broad coverage to maximize the effects of immunization or drug distribution
  - require people to recognize disease symptoms for early treatment
  - necessitate active co-operation in home improvements or insecticide programmes
  - involve direct action and responsibility in deploying vector, or intermediate host, traps
  - need community efforts for environmental improvements such as developing and maintaining improved water supplies or better disposal methods for faeces.

Organizing trials of behaviour change interventions are among the most challenging, and there are few examples illustrating the design of replicable interventions that achieve lasting behavioural change in the context of a trial. For example, changing tobacco smoking behaviour at a population level required decades of concerted, multifaceted campaigns. However, attempts to reduce diarrhoeal diseases and respiratory infections through the promotion of hand-washing with soap have produced encouraging results.

2.1.5 Environmental alterations

Alterations to the environment directed at reducing the transmission of infections are central to the control of many infectious diseases, particularly those that are transmitted through water, such as cholera, or through the faecal–oral route such as many gastrointestinal infections. Environmental interventions to reduce human faecal and urine contamination include latrine construction, provision of sewage systems, clean water supplies, and protected food storage. Other environmental interventions tackle indoor or outdoor air pollution or involve the disposal of contaminants such as pesticides or heavy metals. Many of these interventions require substantial educational efforts and lifestyle changes. They are also interventions that typically have to be applied to whole communities, rather than to individuals in a community, so that, in trials, the unit of randomization is the community or, in some instances, the household.

2.1.6 Vector and intermediate host control

Some major communicable diseases in developing countries depend on vector and intermediate hosts for their transmission. For different infections, the vectors include mosquitoes, tsetse flies, triatomine bugs, sandflies, ticks, and snails. There are a wide variety of control measures to reduce transmission of these infections through attacking the vectors or the reservoirs of infection. Most interventions require a good understanding of the vector or intermediate host, its life cycle, and the environmental conditions that it requires to propagate infections. Control measures may include the application of insecticides or larvicides, new or improved selective biological agents against disease vectors, engineering techniques for reducing vector habitats, community involvement in eliminating vector breeding sites and in deploying traps, housing and screening improvement for reducing human–vector contact, and strategies involving combinations of methods with, for example, the objective of reducing or delaying insecticide resistance. For many of these methods, intermediate process indicators, such as reduction in vector density, can be used for the assessment of impact, but it is often also necessary to determine the impact of the measures on the health status of the population. For example, for malaria, many different approaches to vector control have been used, based upon attacking the mosquito in various stages of its life cycle. These include control of breeding sites to reduce vector density by drainage and waterway engineering and application of specific larvicides and biological agents; the use of mosquito netting, screens, and repellents for personal protection from bites; aerosol distribution of insecticides to reduce adult mosquito densities; and different approaches to killing adult mosquitoes, through either spraying residual insecticides, such as with dichlorodiphenyltrichloroethane (DDT), on the internal walls of houses where mosquitoes rest after a blood meal or through the use of insecticide-treated bednets (ITNs) that kill and/or repel mosquitoes seeking a blood meal. These different approaches require quite different study designs. Residual insecticide on the walls of houses offers relatively little direct protection to those in the treated household, as the mosquitoes take up the insecticide while resting *after* a blood meal. The protection is to those in other households whom these mosquitoes would have bitten for their next blood meal. To reduce transmission in high transmission areas, virtually all households in the neighbourhood must be sprayed. The higher the intensity of transmission, the more difficult it is to achieve sufficient coverage. The use of ITNs, developed as an intervention against malaria over the last two decades, leads to reductions in transmission, clinical disease, and overall childhood mortality. Trials of these kinds of intervention often involve communities, rather than individuals, as the unit of randomization. These trials are especially challenging to design, because some vectors, such as mosquitoes, may have a flight range that may lead to the 'contamination' of intervention communities, with vectors coming in from outside of the community.

2.1.7 Drugs for the prevention of disease

Drugs or other interventions may be used for the prevention of infection (prophylaxis) or disease consequent on infection. An example of the former would be isoniazid prophylaxis to HIV-infected individuals to reduce their risk of TB, and of the latter, the treatment of HIV-infected individuals with antiretroviral drugs to slow the progression of their disease. Sometimes, the use of drugs for prophylaxis or to reduce disease progression does not involve individual diagnosis, but community or group diagnosis is needed to identify groups that should receive the treatment. For example, mass administration of anti-helminthic treatment to schoolchildren is sometimes administered in this way. Whether requiring specific diagnosis or not, therapeutic or preventive agents are usually taken on an individual basis, though sometimes agents can be distributed to everyone in a community through the water supply (for example, fluoride against dental caries) or in food (for example, historically, diethylcarbamazine for filariasis and chloroquine for malaria in medicated salt). Mass treatment of school-age children in areas highly endemic for the infection with an anti-schistosomal drug every year or two may be sufficient to virtually eliminate serious disease consequences of infection with *Schistosoma mansoni*.

Prophylaxis may be aimed at preventing or limiting infection, particularly in those at high risk for a limited period of time (for example, anti-malarials taken by those who are temporarily visiting malaria-endemic areas). The value of such an approach is limited by the duration of action of the agent (which determines the frequency with which it must be taken), by adverse reactions, and sometimes by the role of the intervention in stimulating the development of drug-resistant organisms. For some purposes, prophylaxis may be used by permanent residents of endemic areas (for example, anti-malarials in pregnancy).

Drugs also may be used prophylactically for treatment of preclinical infection (for example, during the incubation period before the onset of symptoms, as for the *gambiense* type of trypanosomiasis) or for treatment of subclinical infection (for example, ivermectin against onchocerciasis, and praziquantel against schistosomiasis).

Strategies for the use of such interventions include the mass treatment of entire populations or the targeted treatment of identifiable subgroups (such as school-age children) in areas where the infection is highly prevalent. Generally, such treatment is applied for the benefit of the individuals treated, but the objective may also be to reduce the transmission of the agent in the community more generally. When the prevalence is very high and the treatment is cheap, treating all those in a defined population may be more cost-effective than screening the whole population and then treating only those found infected.

2.1.8 Injury prevention

Injuries are major causes of death and disability, especially in LMICs. They disproportionately affect the young and have a large economic impact on society. For children and young people, road traffic accidents, drowning, fires, poisoning, interpersonal violence, and war are leading global causes of serious injuries, but often these are not considered 'health problems' and are not sufficiently integrated into public health thinking. Yet there are many potential interventions that might lead to reductions in deaths and disabilities from injuries, such as traffic calming or infrastructural changes to separate pedestrians from fast-moving vehicles to reduce motor vehicle injuries, and improving the security of water sources to reduce drowning accidents; there is great need for more trials of interventions directed at reducing injuries.

2.2 Therapeutic interventions

2.2.1 Treatment of infectious diseases

The mechanism of action of a drug used for disease control will influence the design of field trials to evaluate its impact. Most drugs employed against infectious disease are used to kill or inhibit the replication or spread of the pathogen in the host. Strategies for disease control that use such agents may involve case detection (which requires an appropriate case definition and a diagnostic method), followed by treatment that is designed to reduce morbidity and mortality. Often, the public health success of this approach depends critically upon case finding, and, for diseases such as TB and leprosy, it depends also on case holding, i.e. being able to follow and treat each patient at regular intervals over sufficient time to eliminate the agent from the individual. Case finding and treatment may also reduce transmission of an agent if cases are the main reservoirs of infection, if case detection methods locate a high proportion of prevalent cases, and if the treatment is sufficiently effective.

2.2.2 Surgical and radiation treatment

RCTs of surgical and radiation treatments are usually done as clinical trials; field trials of these interventions are relatively uncommon. However, procedures, such as cataract extraction or simple inguinal hernia repair, are examples of where field trials have been usefully undertaken. In general, the only distinctive feature that may set these apart, in terms of study design, from other field trials is the issue of 'blinding' (see Chapter 11, Section 4). For some forms of surgery, 'sham' operations have been used in clinical studies and perhaps could be considered in field trials. In general, however, randomized trials of these procedures will have to be conducted without blinding.

2.2.3 Diagnostics to guide therapy

The efficient treatment of most diseases requires first that they be accurately diagnosed. Often the diagnosis is made on the basis of clinical symptoms and signs, but the imprecision of this method for many conditions is increasingly recognized. There is an urgent need for new, or improved, sensitive and specific diagnostic tests for many infectious and chronic diseases, that are both simple to use and cheap. For example, intervention strategies that depend upon case finding and treatment usually require suitable diagnostic tests. Specific studies may be necessary to measure the specificity, sensitivity, and predictive values of different diagnostic tests, as these properties will impact on the likely effectiveness of a case finding and treatment intervention. For example, the development and widespread introduction of rapid diagnostic tests for malaria, to replace microscopy or the presumptive treatment of fever, has been an important innovation in malaria control and has also focused attention on the need for improved diagnostic methods and appropriate treatment of non-malarial fevers.

Field trials to evaluate the performance characteristics of diagnostics are not discussed specifically in this book, other than in the context that they may be incorporated as part of an intervention strategy to improve the control of a specific disease. The design of studies to evaluate the properties of diagnostics has been discussed elsewhere (Peeling et al., 2010).

2.2.4 Control of chronic diseases

Chronic conditions may have an infectious aetiology (for example, HIV, TB) or may have environmental or other causes (for example, cardiovascular diseases and many cancers). Many chronic diseases, once diagnosed, may not be curable, but they can be controlled by a combination of education/behaviour change interventions, plus regular, often daily, use of pharmaceuticals. The nature of the clinical care required is often more complicated than required for acute conditions, such as diarrhoea and pneumonia, which, once diagnosed, usually require a single course of treatment. Interventions for chronic disease often must include screening of communities to identify cases; assessment of each case for the stage of the disease and possible attendant complications that are likely to require a variety of laboratory tests; and developing a long-term treatment and assessment plan. The treatment of such conditions often requires long-term monitoring, with a dependence on reliable laboratory results and a system to track the clinical and laboratory findings within a single individual over time. Trials of such interventions must often be conducted over several years, or even decades, to completely assess treatment efficacy.

2.3 Other forms of intervention

2.3.1 Legislation, legal action, taxation, and subsidies

Enforcement of anti-pollution laws, food labelling, and legal restrictions have an important role to play in public health. Behaviour may be strongly influenced by legal restrictions, and increasing prices through taxation have been shown to be effective in reducing tobacco and alcohol consumption, for example. However, it is difficult to design randomized trials of such interventions, because the interventions usually have to be implemented at the national level, making it very difficult to identify a suitable control group.

There has been increasing interest recently in providing various types of subsidies to individuals to change their health-related behaviour (often known as conditional cash transfers). Examples include incentives for children to remain in school, or to health care providers to provide services of at least a certain minimum quality (performance incentives). Some of these interventions have been evaluated through RCTs, and there is further scope for using such approaches.

2.3.2 Health systems interventions

Increasing recognition of the importance of interventions that operate at health systems level, such as policy implementation, financing, educational reform, and strengthening of leadership, management, and governance, has led to a variety of health sector training programmes, organization changes, decentralization and devolution, and various incentives and personnel policies. Most of these efforts have been introduced on a system-wide basis, with little thought about the value of rigorous assessment. But, with adequate planning, rigorous evaluation of these kinds of interventions should be possible through randomized trials, especially by making use of the 'stepped wedge' approach of a phased introduction of measures in different communities over a period of time (Brown and Lilford, 2006). Many health systems research studies may be considered as implementation research, and most could be considered as complex interventions, as discussed in Sections 2.3.3 and 2.3.4.

2.3.3 Implementation research

Within the context of field trials, implementation research does not aim to develop new interventions but focuses on optimizing the delivery of existing interventions that have previously been shown to be efficacious when implemented well. Implementation research explores the challenges of how best to implement research findings in the real world and how to contextualize interventions for specific settings. Hence, an example of an implementation research trial was one where a comparison was made of the costs and effectiveness of health workers delivering antiretroviral therapy to patients who attend a central clinic or hospital, compared with lay workers delivering the antiretrovirals to patients in their homes and only referring them to the clinic if they reported problems on a screening questionnaire (Jaffar et al., 2009).

A general reference on implementation research is Werner (2004).

2.3.4 Complex interventions

The design of a trial to evaluate the efficacy of a new vaccine or drug is relatively straightforward, in the sense that there are many past examples of such evaluations to draw upon when planning a new study. However, the evaluation of some interventions, such as the deployment of a new procedure in the health service or in public health practice, may involve consideration of several interacting components, including, for example, educational components and behavioural change. Such interventions pose special problems for evaluation, and these kinds of intervention have been called 'complex'. Many of the extra problems relate to the difficulty of standardizing the design and delivery of the interventions, their sensitivity to features of the local context, the organizational and logistical difficulty of applying experimental methods to service or policy change, and the length and complexity of the causal chains linking intervention with outcome.

In 2000, the UK Medical Research Council published a *Framework for development and evaluation of RCTs for complex interventions to improve health* to help researchers and research funders to recognize and adopt appropriate methods. These guidelines were updated and revised subsequently and can be downloaded from the Internet (<http://www.mrc.ac.uk/documents/pdf/complex-interventions-guidance>).

Box 2.1 is reproduced from the guidelines and summarizes the steps in developing and evaluating trials involving complex interventions.

Box 2.1 The development–evaluation–implementation process

Developing, piloting, evaluating, reporting, and implementing a complex intervention can be a lengthy process. All of the stages are important, and too strong a focus on the main evaluation, to the neglect of adequate development and piloting work, or proper consideration of the practical issues of implementation, will result in weaker interventions that are harder to evaluate, less likely to be implemented, and less likely to be worth implementing.

Developing an intervention

Questions to ask yourself include: Are you clear about what you are trying to do—what outcome you are aiming for, and how you will bring about change? Does your intervention have a coherent theoretical basis? Have you used this theory systematically to develop the intervention? Can you describe the intervention fully, so that it can be implemented properly for the purposes of your evaluation and replicated by others? Does the existing evidence—ideally collated in a systematic review—suggest that it is likely to be effective or cost-effective? Can it be implemented in a research setting, and is it likely to be widely implementable if the results are favourable?

If you are unclear about the answers to these questions, further development work is needed, before you begin your evaluation. If you are evaluating a policy or a service change as it is being implemented, rather than carrying out an experimental intervention study, you still need to be clear about the rationale for the change and the likely size and type of effects, in order to design the evaluation appropriately.

Piloting and feasibility

Questions to ask yourself include: Have you done enough piloting and feasibility work to be confident that the intervention can be delivered as intended? Can you make safe assumptions about effect sizes and variability, and rates of recruitment and retention in the main evaluation study?

> **Box 2.1 The development–evaluation–implementation process (continued)**
>
> ## Evaluating the intervention
>
> *Questions to ask yourself include*: What design are you going to use, and why? Is an experimental design preferable, and, if so, is it feasible? If a conventional parallel group RCT is not possible, have you considered alternatives such as cluster randomization or a stepped wedge design? If the effects of the intervention are expected to be large or too rapid to be confused with secular trends, and selection biases are likely to be weak or absent, then an observational design may be appropriate. Have you set up procedures for monitoring the delivery of the intervention and overseeing the conduct of the evaluation?
>
> Including a process evaluation is a good investment to explain discrepancies between expected and observed outcomes, to understand how the context influences outcomes, and to provide insights to aid implementation. Including an economic evaluation will likewise make the results of the evaluation much more useful for decision makers.
>
> ## Reporting
>
> *Questions to ask yourself include*: Have you reported your evaluation appropriately, and have you updated your systematic review? It is important to provide a detailed account of the intervention, as well as a standard report of the evaluation methods and findings, to enable replication studies or wider-scale implementation. The results should ideally be presented in the context of an updated systematic review of similar interventions.
>
> ## Implementation
>
> *Questions to ask yourself include:* Are your results accessible to decision makers, and have you presented them in a persuasive way? Are your recommendations detailed and explicit?
>
> Strategies to encourage implementation of evaluation findings should be based on a scientific understanding of the behaviours that need to change, the relevant decision-making processes, and the barriers and facilitators of change. If the intervention is translated into routine practice, monitoring should be undertaken to detect adverse events or long-term outcomes that could not be observed directly in the original evaluation, or to assess whether the effects observed in the study are replicated in routine practice.
>
> Reproduced with permission from Medical Research Council, *Developing and evaluating complex interventions: new guidance*, Copyright © MRC, available from <http://www.mrc.ac.uk/complexinterventionsguidance>. This box is distributed under the terms of the Creative Commons Attribution Non Commercial 4.0 International licence (CC-BY-NC), a copy of which is available at http://creativecommons.org/licenses/by-nc/.

3 Evolution of new intervention products and sequence of study phases

Many intervention products, and especially drugs and vaccines, are likely to originate from basic research in laboratories. Such products must go through a long series of tests, before they can be considered for use in the kinds of field trials that are the focus of this book. Before any human use, a new product will be tested in the laboratory for its activity and toxicity in various *in vitro* and animal test systems. If it successfully passes through these stages, studies of safety, toxicity, and activity may be conducted in a small number of human volunteers, with careful clinical monitoring. A series of further studies, each including increasing numbers of subjects, must be carried out before a new product can be introduced for widespread use. Trials in humans usually go through a series of sequential 'phases' of progressively increasing size to establish first the safety and mode of action and then, in later phases, the efficacy against the target disease(s) and safety in a larger number of subjects.

3.1 Clinical studies: Phases I to IV

Phase I studies are exploratory first-in-human trials and may involve the administration of small, then larger, doses of the study product to a small number of healthy human subjects (ten to 50) to gather preliminary data on the product's pharmacokinetics (where the product and its metabolites go within the body and in what concentrations) and pharmacodynamics (what the drug does in the body). These studies can help to establish the dosage and frequency that are safe and necessary to have an effect. These trials are designed to make an initial assessment of the safety and tolerability of the drug or vaccine in a small number of, usually healthy, volunteers.

Phase II trials are conducted for products that have shown no significant safety problems in Phase I trials. They involve progressively larger numbers of participants (for example, initially tens of subjects, but later studies may involve 100s) and are designed to assess how well the intervention works (therapeutic drugs would involve studies in patients, whereas vaccines would be assessed for immunogenicity in healthy volunteers), as well as to check for safety in a larger number of healthy volunteers (vaccines) or in patients (therapeutic drugs). Phase II trials may also be designed to evaluate what doses and the number of doses of the intervention should be given, and what the intervals should be between doses. Usually, a product will be evaluated in a number of different Phase II trials, evaluating its performance under different circumstances, for example, a malaria vaccine might be initially trialled in adults but then tested in progressively younger groups until tested in the final target population of infants.

Phase III trials aim to provide a definitive assessment of the efficacy of the intervention against the primary outcome(s) of interest. They also provide safety data in a larger group of subjects. These trials usually involve large numbers of individuals (e.g. 1000–3000 or more) and are studies that are conducted to produce the evidence of efficacy and safety required to submit a product to a licensing authority. For this reason, they are sometimes called 'pivotal' trials.

Phase IV studies are conducted after the intervention has been shown to be efficacious in Phase III trials and are conducted to assess the safety and effectiveness of an intervention when used under routine health service conditions, or close to these conditions (rather than in the special circumstances of a controlled trial). Where they involve a regulated product, such as a drug or vaccine, they are usually post-registration or post-licensure studies. Safety issues that are important, but which arise in a relatively small proportion of individuals, may only become apparent through Phase IV studies, once there is widespread use of an intervention. Phase IV studies sometimes take the form of randomized trials where the safety and effectiveness are assessed by comparing the results of administering the product to some individuals or communities, but not to others (allocated at random). However, such trials may be difficult to conduct, once a product has been licensed by the national regulatory authority, and then non-randomized assessments must be made, such as through 'before versus after studies' or case-control investigations. Many trials of strategies of how best to use drugs or vaccines can also be considered as Phase IV studies, such as a comparison of intermittent preventive therapy (IPT) using anti-malarial drugs given to all young children, compared to teaching their mothers to recognize and treat their children if they have possible falciparum malaria.

The main focus of the book will be on large-scale Phase III trials conducted 'in the field' (i.e. outside clinical facilities), but there is also a specific chapter on Phase IV studies (see Chapter 22).

Although similar terms are often used for the 'phase' of trials conducted to test the effectiveness or efficacy of interventions that do not use an investigational product, such as behaviour change interventions or incentives, these have much less well-defined, or universally agreed, phases, and it is not uncommon for the first RCT of such an intervention to be the equivalent of a Phase III trial of a drug or vaccine.

3.2 Registration of new interventions

Legal registration procedures are mandated in most countries before a drug or vaccine can be put into general use, and these procedures normally require documentation of the safety and efficacy of the intervention, based on RCTs involving many hundreds of subjects. Further guidance on the rules and regulations for assessing the safety and efficacy of products for use in human beings can be found at the website of the US Food and Drug Administration (<http://www.fda.gov>).

3.3 'Proof of principle' trials

The purposes of field trials may change as experience with an intervention accumulates. Sometimes, particularly in early trials of a new intervention, the purpose of the study is analytic to demonstrate an effect or to establish a principle, with little consideration as to whether the intervention is practicable at the population level for disease control. An example might be the use of a malaria vaccine that must be administered monthly to be effective. Such studies are sometimes called 'explanatory' or 'proof of principle' trials (Schwartz and Lellouch, 1967). Once an effect against the disease under study has been demonstrated, there might then be greater impetus to develop new formulations of the intervention or different schedules that would be more practicable for application in a disease control programme. Subsequent, and generally larger, trials are conducted, in which the purpose is to establish the benefit of an intervention applied under the circumstances of general use. These studies are often called 'pragmatic' trials (Schwartz and Lellouch, 1967).

3.4 Trials of intervention delivery strategies

Although new products developed through basic science research may serve as the impetus for field trials, some interventions or intervention strategies are developed directly as a result of field studies and experience such as a vaccine strategy for smallpox eradication and the use of tsetse fly traps for the control of trypanosomiasis transmission. Thus, trials may be needed not only of the product itself, but also of the way that product is used or delivered. Trials like these would involve intervention 'packages' which might include, for example, the same drug or vaccine, but provided with different educational approaches or delivery methods. Sometimes, an intervention that has been shown to be effective must be added into an ongoing disease control programme that involves other kinds of interventions. For example, it is expected that, when effective malaria vaccines become available, they will be added to other malaria control methods, based on a combination of vector control, case finding, and treatment strategies. Further studies of how best to integrate these interventions into an overall strategy will have to be worked out. In addition, policy and planning decisions about disease control will have to be guided by appropriate cost-effectiveness analyses.

References

Brown, C. A. and Lilford, R. J. 2006. The stepped wedge trial design: a systematic review. *BMC Medical Research Methodology*, **6**, 54. Available at: <http://www.biomedcentral.com/1471-2288/6/54/>.

Craig, P., Dieppe, P., Macintyre, S., Michie, S., Nazareth, I., and Petticrew, M. 2008. Developing and evaluating complex interventions: the new Medical Research Council guidance. *BMJ*, **337**, a1655. Available at: <http://www.bmj.com/content/337/bmj.a1655>.

Jaffar, S., Amuron, B., Foster, S., *et al.* 2009. Rates of virological failure in patients treated in a home-based versus a facility-based HIV-care model in Jinja, southeast Uganda: a cluster-randomised equivalence trial. *Lancet*, **374**, 2080–9. Available at: <http://www.ncbi.nlm.nih.gov/pmc/articles/PMC2806484/>.

Peeling, R. W., Smith, P. G., and Bossuyt, P. M. 2010. A guide for diagnostic evaluations. *Nature Reviews Microbiology*, **8**, S2–6. Available at: <http://www.nature.com/nrmicro/journal/v8/n12_supp/full/nrmicro1522.html>.

Schwartz, D. and Lellouch, J. 1967. Explanatory and pragmatic attitudes in therapeutical trials. *Journal of Chronic Diseases*, **20**, 637–48.

Werner, A. 2004. *A guide to implementation research*. Washington, DC: Urban Institute Press.

Chapter 3

Reviewing the literature

1 Introduction to reviewing the literature 19
2 Systematic reviews 20
   2.1 Defining the question 21
   2.2 Identifying relevant literature 22
      2.2.1 Electronic searching 22
      2.2.2 Reviewing abstracts 25
      2.2.3 Reviewing full articles 26
      2.2.4 Hand searching 26
      2.2.5 Flow chart of search strategy 26
   2.3 Descriptive synthesis of studies 26
   2.4 Assessing risk of bias in the studies 29
   2.5 Quantitative synthesis of results 30
      2.5.1 Forest plots 30
      2.5.2 Examining heterogeneity 31
3 Software available for systematic reviews and meta-analyses 32
4 Reporting findings from systematic reviews 32

1 Introduction to reviewing the literature

Systematic reviews are increasingly recognized as an essential step in health care research. They are a method designed to produce an objective, unbiased, up-to-date summary of available evidence. In this chapter, an outline is given of the methods used to systematically review the medical literature and to assess the risk of bias in the identified studies. Results from a systematic review may be summarized as a narrative or a summary estimate produced from a quantitative meta-analysis. In either case, systematic reviews are usually a necessary step in preparing to conduct intervention trials and in setting the results of trials into context.

Before embarking on an intervention trial, it is essential to review what is already known about the questions to be addressed in the trial. The most objective way to do this is to conduct a systematic review of all similar studies that have been published previously on the topic. Such a review should enable an assessment to be made of whether (1) sufficient evidence for the effect of the intervention already exists, or (2) there is a clear scientific rationale for an effect of the intervention, but there is insufficient evidence that the intervention works in practice, or (3) there is an insufficient rationale for an intervention effect. If the review of the published evidence supports (1) or (3), then there may be little justification for conducting a (further) trial. Furthermore, funding agencies may require a systematic review to provide evidence that a new trial is justified, and some journals (including, for example, the *Lancet* (Clark and Horton, 2010)) now require authors to include, in papers reporting the results of a trial, a summary of the findings from a recent systematic review, in order to put their trial into context, or to report their own up-to-date systematic review. For example, before proposing a trial of a new school-based behaviour change intervention to reduce the incidence of HIV infection, it would be essential to review the literature on the effectiveness of previous school-based interventions, and also to review the literature on the rationale underpinning the mechanism by which such an intervention might be expected to be effective.

A proposed trial is worthwhile if the conclusions from a systematic search of the literature provide a strong rationale that the proposed intervention will work, but there is currently insufficient evidence to know how effective, if at all, it is likely to be in the target population for the trial. In addition to wasting time and resources, a trial of an intervention which has already been proven effective may be considered unethical, as participants in the control arm would not receive a beneficial intervention, and conducting a further trial may delay scale-up of the intervention to those who would benefit from it.

In this chapter, we describe methods for conducting systematic reviews of epidemiological studies (including observational studies as well as intervention trials) to judge whether a new intervention trial is justified. We also include sections on assessing the risk of bias in studies and on providing a narrative and quantitative summary of the findings.

Systematic reviews are not trivial undertakings, and not all investigators will have the time or resources to conduct the kind of review that we outline in this chapter. Ideally, other investigators will have conducted a recent review, and it will be possible to utilize their findings. For example, an agency such as the World Health Organization (WHO) might have commissioned a review in order to assist them in setting priorities for disease control or to highlight important areas for research. Those planning to conduct a trial might not need to conduct their own systematic review but could build on the previous work. However, even if an investigator is not going to undertake their own review, it is important that they understand how such reviews are conducted and indeed can assess the quality of published systematic reviews. This chapter should facilitate this.

The insights that a systematic review can give to the reviewers on the effects of an intervention and the quality of previous studies are invaluable. It is highly recommended that all those conducting trials participate in at least one systematic review fairly early in their careers!

2 Systematic reviews

Reviewing the literature can be a daunting task. The volume of information available through published papers, or the Internet, is vast and constantly expanding. Given the volume of literature available, an 'ad hoc' review of the literature is subject to substantial biases if only some studies are included, since the studies that are found this way may well not be representative of all the relevant studies. The best way to ensure an objective and unbiased review of the literature is to conduct a review that follows strict guidelines to minimize bias in selecting and interpreting reported studies.

> **Box 3.1 The five basic steps in a systematic review**
>
> 1 Defining the question.
> 2 Identifying relevant studies in a predefined, systematic way.
> 3 Assessing the quality of each relevant study.
> 4 Summarizing the evidence.
> 5 Interpreting the findings.

The basic steps in a systematic review are shown in Box 3.1.

In this chapter, we provide a brief overview of each of these steps. Further details are given in published guidelines, such as the *Cochrane handbook for systematic reviews of interventions* (Higgins and Green, 2008) and the PRISMA (Preferred Reporting Items for Systematic Reviews and Meta-Analyses) guidelines (<http://www.prisma-statement.org>) (Liberati et al., 2009), and books on systematic reviews in health research (Egger et al., 2001, Glasziou, 2001, Khan, 2003).

2.1 Defining the question

The first step in a systematic review is to define the research question. A structured approach for framing the question is useful—the PICOS approach (Population; Interventions (or Exposure); Comparison; Outcomes; Study design) (Higgins and Green, 2008) is used by both Cochrane and PRISMA.

For example, a systematic review summarized the evidence of the effectiveness of behavioural interventions to prevent HIV infection among young people in sub-Saharan Africa (Napierala Mavedzenge et al., 2011). The review question was structured, using the PICOS approach, as follows:

Population: Among young people aged 10–24 years in sub-Saharan Africa . . .

Intervention/exposure/comparison: . . . does exposure to an intervention focusing on reducing HIV risk behaviours, relative to no or minimal intervention, . . .

Outcomes: . . . reduce the risk of HIV, STIs, or pregnancy . . .

Study design: . . . when evaluated through experimental or quasi-experimental study designs?

A second example, used in this chapter, is a systematic review of the evidence that the use of chewing substances (such as smokeless tobacco or betel nuts) is associated with cardiovascular disease (CVD) in Asia (Zhang et al., 2010). In this case, the question was structured as follows:

Population: Among people in Asian countries . . .

Intervention/exposure/comparison: . . . does exposure to chewing substances, relative to not chewing them, . . .

Outcomes: . . . increase the risk of CVD . . .

Study design: . . . when evaluated through observational epidemiological studies?

Previous systematic reviews had examined this question in the United States of America (USA) and Sweden, but there was no synthesis of the evidence from Asia. If strong evidence for an association was found, this could lead to the development and evaluation of an intervention directed at reducing betel chewing in these populations.

Once the research question is identified, a detailed protocol should be prepared for the review. This will include definition of the search strategy and the planned analyses. There are plans to develop an international register of systematic reviews, led by the Centre for Reviews and Dissemination (<http://www.york.ac.uk/inst/crd/index.htm>), which will enable researchers to register their review protocol. This will extend the register developed by the Cochrane Collaboration (<http://www.cochrane.org>), which was established in 1993 to promote systematic reviews of health care interventions. Researchers undertaking reviews under the Cochrane Collaboration are required to register the protocol for their review in advance, and the review is peer-reviewed before publication. However, many systematic reviews are undertaken outside of the Collaboration and may not currently be registered.

2.2 Identifying relevant literature

The most time-consuming step of a systematic review is to identify studies which address the defined review question. The aim is to have a search strategy which is highly sensitive (i.e. there is a very high probability of including relevant studies), specific (i.e. there is a high probability of excluding non-relevant studies), and precise (i.e. the proportion of studies retrieved which are relevant is high) (Jenkins, 2004).

The first step in defining the search strategy to identify published papers is to set inclusion and exclusion criteria, based on the review question (Table 3.1). Ideally, searches should include papers published in any language (to be fully inclusive and to avoid possible publication bias of those with positive findings being more likely than those with negative findings to be published in English language journals). RCTs are generally regarded as the gold standard for providing evidence of the impact of an intervention, and it is essential to review previous RCTs of similar interventions. However, if there have been few relevant RCTs, non-randomized trials and observational studies should also be reviewed. The initial search may be limited to published papers, but sometimes it is important to include the 'grey' literature (conference abstracts, technical reports, and discussion papers). This is because some completed studies are never published in peer-reviewed journals, and studies are often less likely to be published there if they do not find an effect of the intervention. Inclusion of unpublished studies may therefore reduce bias. However, unpublished studies are difficult to identify and have not undergone peer review, so they may be of poorer quality and insufficient information may be provided to contribute usefully to a review.

2.2.1 Electronic searching

Three commonly used electronic medical databases are MEDLINE (available freely via PubMed at <http://www.ncbi.nlm.nih.gov/PubMed>), Embase (<http://www.embase.

2: SYSTEMATIC REVIEWS   23

Table 3.1 Inclusion criteria: example for the systematic review of behavioural interventions to prevent HIV infection among young people in sub-Saharan Africa

PICOS component (see text)	Inclusion criteria	Exclusion criteria
Population	Young people aged 10–24 years. In studies with a wider age range, there must be an analysis of the impact of the intervention in young people (10–24 years) or, at least, in part of that age range. In sub-Saharan Africa. Based in a school, and/or health facility, and/or geographically defined community.	Study population not representative of a general population of young people (for example, young sex workers). Fewer than 100 people in the study.
Intervention/exposure	Behavioural intervention focused on one or more of the following: (i) improving sexual and reproductive health skills and behaviour (ii) reducing the risk of sexually transmitted diseases (STDs) (iii) reducing unintended pregnancies (iv) increasing utilization of health services for treatment of STIs and/or behaviours related to more appropriate service utilization.	
Comparison	No or minimal behavioural intervention.	No suitable comparison group (for example, non-randomized study with post-intervention data only). No adjustment for differences between groups that might bias the findings.

continued

Table 3.1 (continued) Inclusion criteria: example for the systematic review of behavioural interventions to prevent HIV infection among young people in sub-Saharan Africa

PICOS component (see text)	Inclusion criteria	Exclusion criteria
Outcome	At least one of the following measured:	Measured less than 3 months after the intervention starts.
	(i) prevalence or incidence of HIV infection	
	(ii) prevalence or incidence of another STI	
	(iii) prevalence or incidence of pregnancy (measured by laboratory test or clinically observed)	
	(iv) reported sexual and reproductive health behaviour (including treatment-seeking behaviour).	
Study design	Published in 2005–2008 (because an earlier systematic review had covered the period up to the end of 2004).	
	Randomized and non-randomized epidemiological studies which included a contemporaneous comparison group or a before–after/time series analysis in the intervention group only.	

com>), and CENTRAL (Cochrane Central Register of Controlled Trials, <http://www.cochrane-handbook.org>). A comprehensive search strategy requires each of these databases to be searched (Higgins and Green, 2008). However, these databases have a North American/European bias, and, for studies in LMICs, it is worth also searching other relevant databases such as LILACS (Latin American Caribbean Health Sciences Literature), African Healthline, GlobalHealth, and Popline. In addition, there are many subject-specific databases, such as PsychInfo (for psychology and related behavioural and social sciences), as well as Internet search engines such as Google Scholar. It may also be useful to search conference databases and trial registries to identify additional papers.

Strategies can be used to identify both free-text words in the database and controlled terms (called MeSH in MEDLINE, i.e. medical subject headings) that are used as keywords. Search strategies need to include the key terms in the review question and use the Boolean operators (such as 'AND', 'OR', 'NOT') to produce a search that is both sensitive and specific to the research question. The search strategy used for the example of chewing substances and CVD in Asia is given in Box 3.2.

Box 3.2 Example of a search strategy for evidence of an association between chewing substances and CVD, ischaemic heart disease, or cerebrovascular disease in Asia

We searched PubMed (up to July 2010), using the terms: ('cardiovascular diseases' [MeSH] OR ('cardiovascular' [All Fields] AND 'diseases' [All Fields]) OR 'cardiovascular diseases' [All Fields] OR 'cerebrovascular disorders' [MeSH] OR ('cerebrovascular' [All Fields] AND 'disorders' [All Fields]) OR 'cerebrovascular disorders' [All Fields] OR 'stroke' [MeSH] OR 'stroke' [All Fields] OR 'mortality' OR death*) AND ('betel quid' OR 'betel-quid' OR 'betel nut' OR 'betel nuts' OR 'areca nut' OR 'areca nuts' OR 'paan' OR 'pan' OR 'snuff' OR 'snus' OR 'gul' OR 'gutka' OR 'khaini' OR 'loose leaf' OR 'maras' OR 'mawa' OR 'mishri' OR 'naswar' OR '*Areca catechu*' OR 'tooth powder' OR 'shammah' OR 'tobacco chewing gum' OR 'zarda' OR 'tobacco, smokeless' [MeSH] OR 'smokeless tobacco' OR 'chewing tobacco' OR 'non-smoking tobacco') AND ('cohort studies' [MeSH] OR 'cross-sectional studies' [MeSH] OR 'case control studies' [MeSH] OR ('cohort' [TI] AND stud* [TI]) OR (case* [TI] AND control* [TI]) OR 'prospective' OR 'retrospective' OR 'cross-sectional' OR 'cross sectional'), which yielded 1006 potentially relevant references. We adapted the searching strategy for a second search in ISI Web of Science (updated 19 July 2010) and found another 739 references. We identified all observational studies, including cohorts, case-control studies, and cross-sectional studies, provided that they explored the association between ever using chewing substances and the occurrence (incidence or mortality) of CVD and reported the strength of the associations with a quantitative risk estimate. There was no limitation on the language, study year, or publication status.

Text extract reproduced from Zhang, L. N. et al., Chewing substances with or without tobacco and risk of cardiovascular disease in Asia: a meta-analysis, *Journal of Zhejiang University Science B*, Volume 11, Issue 9, pp.681–9, Copyright © Zhejiang University and Springer-Verlag Berlin Heidelberg 2010. This box is not covered by the Creative Commons licence terms of this publication. For permission to reuse please contact the rights holder.

Often the reviewers will already know about some key published studies. It is useful to check that all of these have been identified by the electronic database search. If not, a careful review of the search strategy may establish the reason for this, and the search can be amended accordingly.

2.2.2 Reviewing abstracts

The search strategy commonly identifies several thousands of potentially relevant papers. The next step is for two reviewers to independently read through the abstract of each paper and define it as being potentially relevant or not. At this stage, it is recommended to err on the side of caution, i.e. include as 'potentially relevant' if the relevance is unclear from the abstract. The two reviewers should then compare their results and reconcile any differences by discussion, further reference to the abstracts, or a third reviewer independently reading the abstract.

2.2.3 Reviewing full articles

Full copies of all papers, the abstracts of which were considered to be potentially relevant, should be obtained (electronically, from libraries, or by emailing the author). They should be reviewed by the two reviewers who independently assess whether or not each paper meets each of the inclusion/exclusion criteria. Discrepancies should be resolved as for the abstracts.

2.2.4 Hand searching

The next step in the search strategy is usually to review the reference lists of all the eligible studies identified from the electronic database search, to identify any studies that were missed by that search but have been referenced in the eligible papers.

Previous review papers should also be read to check that no known papers have been omitted. Finally, it is legitimate, though sometimes time-consuming, to include unpublished studies which can be identified through colleagues or contact with the investigators of unpublished studies, for example, identified through Internet searches or trial registers. It is also important to identify ongoing studies, where possible, as these may be included in updates of the review.

2.2.5 Flow chart of search strategy

The template for a flow chart summarizing the search results is given in Figure 3.1. In the example of behavioural interventions among young people in sub-Saharan Africa, a total of 1173 papers were identified from the electronic databases, of which 137 were deemed potentially relevant after review of their titles and abstracts, and full-text articles were obtained. After excluding those not meeting the inclusion criteria, the final review included 40 papers, representing 23 studies (as sometimes the results of one study were reported in more than one paper) (Napierala Mavedzenge et al., 2011). For the example of chewing substances and CVD in Asia, 1756 publications were identified from electronic databases, of which only six were eligible for inclusion in the analysis of CVD (Zhang et al., 2010).

2.3 Descriptive synthesis of studies

When the eligible papers have been identified, a data extraction form should be completed for each study, which contains fields enabling a detailed description of the study design and of the results. For example, descriptive elements would include the PICOS components, as discussed in Section 2.1. The results should focus on the pre-specified outcomes in the review protocol and would include outcome measures, definition of exposures/interventions, measures of effect, and 95% confidence intervals (CIs). The form should be pilot-tested on a few sample papers and revised, as appropriate. Two reviewers then read each paper in detail independently, summarize the paper on to the data extraction form, and appraise the risk of biases. A common shortcut, which is permissible, is that one reviewer completes the data extraction form and the

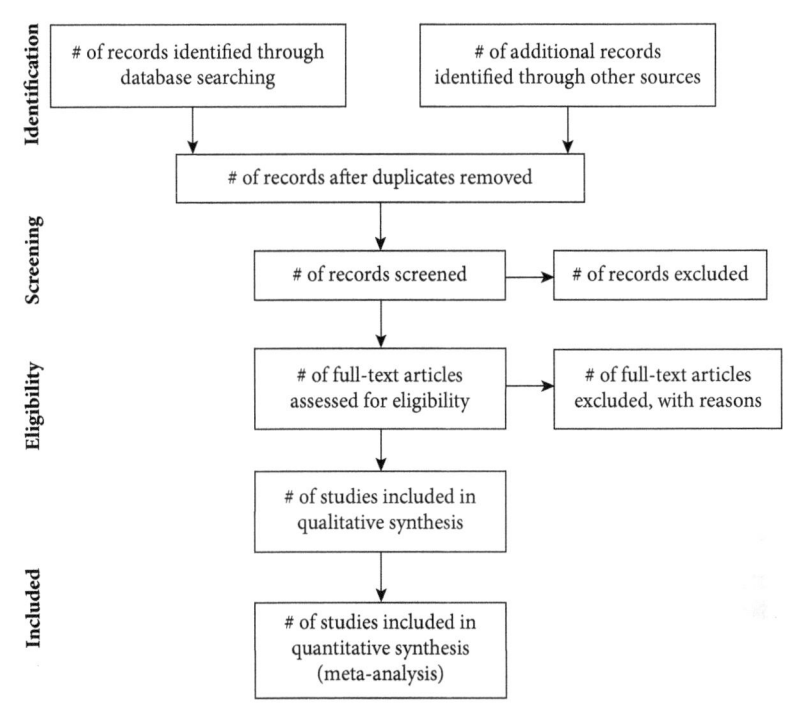

Figure 3.1 Flow diagram of study selection process.

From Moher et al., Preferred reporting items for systematic reviews and meta-analyses: the PRISMA statement, *PLoS Medicine*, Volume 6, Issue 7, e1000097, Copyright © Moher et al. 2009. This figure is reproduced from an open-access article distributed under the terms of the Creative Commons Attribution License, which permits unrestricted use, distribution, and reproduction in any medium, provided the original author and source are credited.

other then checks and edits it, with the final version based on a discussion of any discrepancies.

The next step is to begin to summarize the evidence from the eligible studies as a whole. All reviews should include a descriptive table of the included studies, which summarize the study population, intervention, comparison, outcome, and study design. One of the 23 studies that were identified in the review of behavioural interventions among young people is summarized in Table 3.2.

In the table that summarizes the results of each study, all the primary and secondary outcome measures should be included. For a binary outcome, this would include the proportion with the outcome among the exposed and unexposed groups, the appropriate measure of effect (e.g. risk ratio (RR), rate ratio (RR), or odds ratio (OR)), and 95% CI. For continuous outcomes, the mean, standard deviation in the exposed and unexposed, plus the effect measure (e.g. standardized mean difference) should be given.

Table 3.2 Description of one of the studies included in the systematic review of youth interventions against HIV infection in sub-Saharan Africa

Study, location, and programme	Type of intervention and setting	Target population, primary objectives, comparison, and study outcomes	Intervention description	Study design
United Republic of Tanzania, MEMA kwa Vijana	**Schools:** Teacher-led. Curriculum-based sexual and reproductive health education. **Health facility:** Interventions to facilitate youth friendliness of service providers, linked to interventions in the community and in other sectors (schools), to promote acceptance and utilization	**Target population:** Persons aged 12–19 years in rural areas. **Primary objectives:** Delayed sexual initiation, increased condom use, decreased number of sexual partners, and increased use of health services, especially for sexual and reproductive health services. **Comparison arm:** Current (very limited) sexual and reproductive health education in schools, and no additional interventions within health facilities or in the wider community. **Study outcomes: Primary:** HIV incidence; HSV2 prevalence. **Secondary:** pregnancy (by test and self-reported); prevalence of other STIs (by test and self-reported); knowledge and attitudes related to sexual and reproductive health issues; self-reported sexual risk behaviours, including sexual debut during trial follow-up, use of condoms, number of sexual partners, use of health services if reported a potential STI.	In-school teacher-led and peer-assisted programme. Covered refusal, self-efficacy, self-esteem, STI/HIV, sexuality, contraception, social values, respect, gender. Used drama, stories, and games. Also included interventions to make government health services more youth-friendly, youth condom promotion and distribution, and limited community-wide interventions. Ten to 15 lessons per year over 3 years.	Cluster randomized trial. Ten intervention clusters, ten control clusters.

Adapted with permission from *Journal of Adolescent Health*, Volume 49, Issue 6, Napierala Mavedzenge et al., HIV prevention in young people in sub-Saharan Africa: a systematic review, pp. 568–86, Copyright © 2011 Society for Adolescent Health and Medicine. Published by Elsevier Inc. All rights reserved. <http://www.sciencedirect.com/science/journal/1054139X>. This table is not covered by the Creative Commons licence terms of this publication. For permission to reuse please contact the rights holder.

2.4 Assessing risk of bias in the studies

Once the description of each study is completed, an evaluation should be conducted of the extent of potential bias and error that may have arisen, either from the design or the analysis of each of the original studies. The main aim of this is to guide interpretation of the findings of the review. In some cases, it may be decided to exclude a study which is flawed to the extent that the results are considered likely not to be valid. Alternatively, a sensitivity analysis might be conducted to evaluate how the summary results differ if results from more flawed studies are included or excluded.

There are several methods for assessing the risk of bias, including checklists or 'quality score' scales. The recommendation of the Cochrane Collaboration and the PRISMA guidelines is to use a 'domain-based evaluation', in which critical assessments are made for domains such as blinding of participants and generation of the random sequence (for randomized studies) (Higgins and Green, 2008). For observational studies, there are additional possible sources of bias. For example, in case-control studies, check should be made on the external validity of case selection, the choice of control group, and adjustment for confounding factors.

Table 3.3 summarizes some of the sources of potential bias in RCTs and observational studies.

The assessment of potential biases should be tailored to the research question. For each review, there should be consideration of whether one potential bias is more important to the interpretation of findings than others. For example, if an outcome is

Table 3.3 Methods for assessing risk of bias in RCTs and observational studies

Source of bias	Definition	Assessment for RCTs	Assessment for observational studies
Selection bias	Systematic differences between the comparison groups	Generation of random allocation	Selection of exposed/unexposed
		Allocation concealment	Selection of cases/controls
Performance bias	Systematic differences in the care provided (apart from intervention)	Blinding of participant and provider	Systematic differences in those exposed and unexposed
		Misclassification of exposure	Misclassification of exposure
Attrition bias	Systematic differences between the comparison groups in withdrawals from the study	Intention-to-treat analysis	Differing follow-up rates between exposed and unexposed (or participation rates in cases and controls)
		Outcome data not available for all participants	
Detection bias	Systematic difference in outcome assessment	Blinding of those evaluating outcome	

measured objectively (for example, mortality), then blinding of those evaluating the outcome is not going to be very important. In contrast, if loss to follow-up is high and associated with the outcome, then this could cause substantial bias.

A table summarizing the risk of bias in each study should be completed independently by two reviewers, and any differences reconciled by discussion or reference to a third reviewer. Summarizing the results can be done in different ways—some authors rank the studies in order of quality; others divide them into those with low, medium, or high risk of bias. These decisions should be taken independently of the results of the studies, if possible, before examining the results, and the reviewers need to decide which studies (if any) will be taken forward to a quantitative meta-analysis of findings.

2.5 Quantitative synthesis of results

2.5.1 Forest plots

Following the descriptive analysis and assessment of risk of bias, it may or may not be appropriate to conduct a formal meta-analysis that quantifies the overall effect of the intervention. If, for example, the study populations, interventions, and reported outcomes differed substantially, the authors may decide to focus on describing the studies, their results, applicability, and limitations in a narrative review, rather than produce a quantitative summary. This was the case for the systematic review of interventions in young people in sub-Saharan Africa (Napierala Mavedzenge et al., 2011).

In other cases, it might be useful to summarize the data quantitatively. A first step for this is to produce a graph, called a forest plot, which displays the measure of effect (e.g. OR) for each study, together with a horizontal line denoting the CI. Before constructing such a graph, it is important to consider whether the results from the different studies are indeed measuring the same effect and are comparable to each other. For example, a smoking cessation intervention may have a different effect in pregnant women than among teenage girls. In such cases, it would be beneficial to present results stratified by subgroups, in whom effects might be expected to differ. As with all analyses, these subgroups should be defined in advance and included in the review protocol. For example, in the review of chewing substances in Asia, it was decided a priori to stratify by geographical region, to minimize confounding due to the presence or absence of tobacco in chewing substances, as this was thought to differ between regions.

In this example, the six eligible studies included five cohort studies and one case-control study. The forest plot is shown in Figure 3.2. The solid vertical line indicates a relative risk (RR) of one, representing no association between the exposure and outcome. In this example, all six studies had a RR greater than one, indicating an increased risk of CVD among individuals who used chewing substances, and the 95% CI did not include one for four of these studies, indicating strong evidence of an association. The forest plot also includes an overall (summary) estimate of the RR. This is a weighted average of the effects from each of the studies.

There are two main methods of obtaining the summary measure of an intervention effect. In a 'fixed-effects' model, it is assumed that the true effect of exposure (or the intervention) is the same in each study, any variation between studies being solely due to chance. In contrast, a 'random-effects' model may be used, in which the true

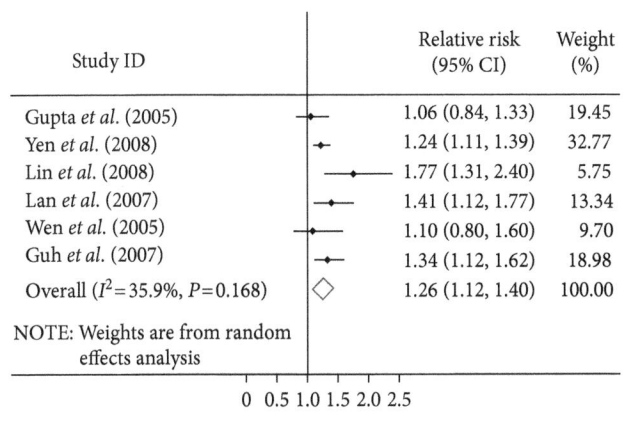

Study ID	Relative risk (95% CI)	Weight (%)
Gupta et al. (2005)	1.06 (0.84, 1.33)	19.45
Yen et al. (2008)	1.24 (1.11, 1.39)	32.77
Lin et al. (2008)	1.77 (1.31, 2.40)	5.75
Lan et al. (2007)	1.41 (1.12, 1.77)	13.34
Wen et al. (2005)	1.10 (0.80, 1.60)	9.70
Guh et al. (2007)	1.34 (1.12, 1.62)	18.98
Overall (I^2=35.9%, P=0.168)	1.26 (1.12, 1.40)	100.00

NOTE: Weights are from random effects analysis

0 0.5 1.0 1.5 2.0 2.5

Figure 3.2 Forest plot for the association of exposure to chewing substances and risk of CVD in Asia.

Reproduced from Zhang, L. N. et al., Chewing substances with or without tobacco and risk of cardiovascular disease in Asia: a meta-analysis, *Journal of Zhejiang University Science B*, Volume 11, Issue 9, pp. 681–9, Copyright © Zhejiang University and Springer-Verlag Berlin Heidelberg 2010, with permission from Springer and Springer Science and Business Media. This image is not covered by the Creative Commons licence terms of this publication. For permission to reuse please contact the rights holder.

effect of exposure for the individual studies are assumed to inherently vary (e.g. due to differences in the populations or residual confounding factors). In a random-effects model, the weights allow for this between-study variation, as well as the random variation.

In Figure 3.2, a random-effects model was used, and the weights for each study are given on the right-hand side of the forest plot. The overall (summary) estimate is RR = 1.26, with a 95% CI of 1.12–1.40. Note that this summary estimate is more precise (i.e. has a narrower CI) than any one of the individual studies. By undertaking a systematic review and meta-analysis, the reviewers can now report that there is strong evidence that, in these populations, exposure to chewing substances was associated with an increased risk of CVD of around 26%, compared with non-users.

2.5.2 Examining heterogeneity

The effect sizes of individual studies will inevitably be different from each other, but it is important to assess whether this difference is likely to be due to random variation (i.e. the true underlying effect will be the same) or to real differences in underlying effect sizes in the individual studies. It is therefore essential to examine the consistency of the effects and to quantify the heterogeneity (or difference) in effect sizes between studies. Several measures are available for this, one of which is the I^2 statistic (Higgins et al., 2003). This statistic is the percentage of total variation across studies that is due to heterogeneity, rather than chance. A value of I^2 of 0% indicates no observed heterogeneity, and larger values indicate increasing heterogeneity. The principal advantage of the I^2 statistic is that it does not depend on the number of studies included in the meta-analysis and so can be used even for meta-analyses containing relatively few studies, which typically have low power to detect heterogeneity using other measures.

In our example, the value of I^2 is 35.9%, with a p-value of 0.17, indicating little evidence of heterogeneity. The reviewers were therefore justified in presenting the summary estimate. If, in contrast, the I^2 statistic suggests evidence of heterogeneity, for example if I^2 was 70%, further exploration of the causes of heterogeneity would be needed, for example by undertaking (pre-specified) subgroup analyses. If there was no longer evidence of heterogeneity within subgroups, this would indicate that the stratifying characteristics were an important source of heterogeneity, and results should be presented within subgroups, rather than overall.

3 Software available for systematic reviews and meta-analyses

Systematic reviews involve managing large quantities of information. There are various software packages available which can be used to prepare systematic reviews. For example, the Cochrane Collaboration produces a freely available program called RevMan which is a Windows-based software package designed to enter reviews in the Cochrane format. This includes an analysis module (MetaView) for quantitative summaries.

Results of searches from electronic databases can also be automatically downloaded into a reference manager software package, such as EndNote, and, from there, exported into database packages, such as Excel, for review and assessment of abstracts. Standard statistical packages, such as Stata, include modules for meta-analyses.

4 Reporting findings from systematic reviews

There are several guidelines for reporting results of a systematic review. The most recent are the PRISMA guidelines (<http://www.prisma-statement.org>) which are given in Table 3.4 (Moher et al., 2009). These include a full description of the rationale for the review, the research question, methods used, and analyses. Reviewers will then need to summarize their main findings, including the strengths and limitations of the review, the strength of the evidence for each main outcome, and the relevance to different population groups.

Finally, the results of the systematic review need to be assessed for their implications for policy and future research. One system to assist with interpreting results of systematic reviews is the GRADE system (Grading of Recommendations Assessment, Development, and Evaluation) (Guyatt et al., 2008). This gives guidelines as to whether results from a systematic review provide 'strong' or 'weak' evidence. This includes not only results of a systematic review, but also an evaluation of the balance between desirable and undesirable effects, and whether the intervention represents a wise use of resources.

Table 3.4 PRISMA guidelines for systematic reviews and meta-analyses

Section/topic	#	Checklist item	Reported on page #
TITLE			
Title	1	Identify the report as a systematic review, meta-analysis, or both	
ABSTRACT			
Structured summary	2	Provide a structured summary, including, as applicable: background; objectives; data sources; study eligibility criteria, participants, and interventions; study appraisal and synthesis methods; results; limitations; conclusions and implications of key findings; systematic review registration number	
INTRODUCTION			
Rationale	3	Describe the rationale for the review in the context of what is already known	
Objectives	4	Provide an explicit statement of questions being addressed with reference to participants, interventions, comparisons, outcomes, and study design (PICOS)	
METHODS			
Protocol and registration	5	Indicate if a review protocol exists, if and where it can be accessed (for example, Web address), and, if available, provide registration information, including registration number	
Eligibility criteria	6	Specify study characteristics (for example, PICOS, length of follow-up) and report characteristics (for example, years considered, language, publication status) used as criteria for eligibility, giving rationale	
Information sources	7	Describe all information sources (for example, databases with dates of coverage, contact with study authors to identify additional studies) in the search and date last searched	

continued

Table 3.4 (continued) PRISMA guidelines for systematic reviews and meta-analyses

Section/topic	#	Checklist item	Reported on page #
Search	8	Present full electronic search strategy for at least one database, including any limits used, such that it could be repeated	
Study selection	9	State the process for selecting studies (i.e. screening, eligibility, included in systematic review, and, if applicable, included in the meta-analysis)	
Data collection process	10	Describe method of data extraction from reports (for example, piloted forms, independently, in duplicate) and any processes for obtaining and confirming data from investigators	
Data items	11	List and define all variables for which data were sought (for example, PICOS, funding sources) and any assumptions and simplifications made	
Risk of bias in individual studies	12	Describe methods used for assessing risk of bias of individual studies (including specification of whether this was done at the study or outcome level) and how this information is to be used in any data synthesis	
Summary measures	13	State the principal summary measures (for example, risk ratio, difference in means)	
Synthesis of results	14	Describe the methods of handling data and combining results of studies, if done, including measures of consistency (for example, I^2) for each meta-analysis	
Risk of bias across studies	15	Specify any assessment of risk of bias that may affect the cumulative evidence (for example, publication bias, selective reporting within studies)	
Additional analyses	16	Describe methods of additional analyses (for example, sensitivity or subgroup analyses, meta-regression), if done, indicating which were pre-specified	

Table 3.4 (continued) PRISMA guidelines for systematic reviews and meta-analyses

Section/topic	#	Checklist item	Reported on page #
RESULTS			
Study selection	17	Give numbers of studies screened, assessed for eligibility, and included in the review, with reasons for exclusions at each stage, ideally with a flow diagram	
Study characteristics	18	For each study, present characteristics for which data were extracted (for example, study size, PICOS, follow-up period), and provide the citations	
Risk of bias within studies	19	Present data on risk of bias of each study and, if available, any outcome level assessment (see item 12)	
Results of individual studies	20	For all outcomes considered (benefits or harms), present, for each study: (a) simple summary data for each intervention group, (b) effect estimates and confidence intervals, ideally with a forest plot	
Synthesis of results	21	Present results of each meta-analysis done, including confidence intervals and measures of consistency	
Risk of bias across studies	22	Present results of any assessment of risk of bias across studies (see item 15)	
Additional analysis	23	Give results of additional analyses, if done (for example, sensitivity or subgroup analyses, meta-regression) (see item 16)	
DISCUSSION			
Summary of evidence	24	Summarize the main findings, including the strength of evidence for each main outcome; consider their relevance to key groups (for example, health care providers, users, and policy makers)	
Limitations	25	Discuss limitations at study and outcome level (for example, risk of bias) and at review level (for example, incomplete retrieval of identified research, reporting bias)	

continued

Table 3.4 (continued) PRISMA guidelines for systematic reviews and meta-analyses

Section/topic	#	Checklist item	Reported on page #
Conclusions	26	Provide a general interpretation of the results, in the context of other evidence, and implications for future research	
FUNDING			
Funding	27	Describe sources of funding for the systematic review and other support (for example, supply of data); role of funders for the systematic review	

From Moher et al., Preferred reporting items for systematic reviews and meta-analyses: the PRISMA statement, *PLoS Medicine*, Volume 6, Issue 7, e1000097, Copyright © Moher et al. 2009. This table is reproduced from an open-access article distributed under the terms of the Creative Commons Attribution License, which permits unrestricted use, distribution, and reproduction in any medium, provided the original author and source are credited.

References

Clark, S. and Horton, R. 2010. Putting research into context—revisited. *Lancet*, **376**, 10–11.

Egger, M., Smith, G. D., and Altman, D. G. 2001. *Systematic reviews in health care: meta-analysis in context*. London: BMJ Books.

Glasziou, P. 2001. *Systematic reviews in health care: a practical guide*. Cambridge, New York: Cambridge University Press.

Guyatt, G. H., Oxman, A. D., Vist, G. E., *et al.* 2008. GRADE: an emerging consensus on rating quality of evidence and strength of recommendations. *BMJ*, **336**, 924–6.

Higgins, J. and Green, S. P. 2008. *Cochrane handbook for systematic reviews of interventions* [Online]. Oxford: Wiley-Blackwell. Available at: <http://tectutorials.com/Resources/AHRQ%20Modules/UoCTrainingMaterials/CochraneHB/booktext.pdf>.

Higgins, J. P., Thompson, S. G., Deeks, J. J., and Altman, D. G. 2003. Measuring inconsistency in meta-analyses. *BMJ*, **327**, 557–60.

Jenkins, M. 2004. Evaluation of methodological search filters—a review. *Health Information & Libraries Journal*, **21**, 148–63.

Khan, K. S. 2003. *Systematic reviews to support evidence-based medicine: how to review and apply findings of healthcare research*. London: Royal Society of Medicine Press.

Liberati, A., Altman, D. G., Tetzlaff, J., *et al.* 2009. The PRISMA statement for reporting systematic reviews and meta-analyses of studies that evaluate health care interventions: explanation and elaboration. *PLoS Medicine*, **6**, e1000100.

Moher, D., Liberati, A., Tetzlaff, J., Altman, D. G., and Group, P. 2009. Preferred reporting items for systematic reviews and meta-analyses: the PRISMA statement. *PLoS Medicine*, **6**, e1000097.

Napierala Mavedzenge, S. M., Doyle, A. M., and Ross, D. A. 2011. HIV prevention in young people in sub-Saharan Africa: a systematic review. *Journal of Adolescent Health*, **49**, 568–86.

Zhang, L. N., Yang, Y. M., Xu, Z. R., Gui, Q. F., and Hu, Q. Q. 2010. Chewing substances with or without tobacco and risk of cardiovascular disease in Asia: a meta-analysis. *Journal of Zhejiang University SCIENCE B*, **11**, 681–9.

Chapter 4

Trial design

1. Introduction to trial design 38
   1.1 Planning a trial 38
   1.2 Ethical considerations in designing a trial 39
   1.3 Trial governance 40
2. Definition of trial objectives 40
   2.1 The idea for a trial 40
   2.2 Trial purpose 41
   2.3 Specific objectives of the trial 42
   2.4 Subsidiary objectives of the trial 42
3. Selection of interventions 43
   3.1 Intervention characteristics required 43
   3.2 Number of interventions compared 44
   3.3 Combined interventions 45
   3.4 Choice of comparison intervention 46
   3.5 Complex interventions 47
4. Allocation of interventions within the trial 47
   4.1 Randomization and 'blindness' 47
   4.2 Unit of application of the interventions 48
   4.3 'Stepped wedge' design 51
   4.4 Other approaches to allocation of the interventions 52
5. Choice of outcome measures and trial duration 54
6. Trial population 56
   6.1 Criteria for selection of trial population 56
   6.2 Inclusion and exclusion criteria 57
   6.3 The size of the trial population 57
   6.4 Compliance 58
7. Implementation 59
   7.1 Community acceptance 59
   7.2 Feasibility studies and pilot testing 59
   7.3 Staff recruitment, training, and retention 59
   7.4 Field organization 60
8. Data handling 60
   8.1 Data collection 60
   8.2 Data processing 60
9. Quality control 60
   9.1 The intervention 61

9.2 **Follow-up** 61
   9.3 **Assessment of trial outcomes** 62
   9.4 **Other field and laboratory procedures** 62
10 **Analysis, monitoring, and reporting** 62
   10.1 **Planning the main analyses** 62
   10.2 **Analyses during the trial** 62
   10.3 **Data and Safety Monitoring Committee** 63
   10.4 **Analysis methods** 64
   10.5 **Reporting results** 64
   10.6 **Further studies** 64
11 The 'SPIRIT' checklist for standard protocol items for clinical trials 65

1 Introduction to trial design

Trials should be designed to produce unambiguous estimates of the effects of interventions, which are precise enough for public health planning. A common goal of all intervention studies, including trials, is to evaluate the effect of a specific intervention (or a specific package of interventions) applied in a specific manner to a well-defined population. In the trial design, the major issues will be: (1) the nature of the intervention, the strategy for its implementation, and the natural size of the unit at which the intervention is applied (for example, individual, household, school, village, district); (2) the likely effects, including possible adverse effects, and how they should be measured; and (3) the comparisons that need to be made with other interventions.

In most LMICs, disease control is the responsibility of the Ministry of Health (MOH). Therefore, wherever possible, the Ministry should be involved in the planning and monitoring of trials, and the results must be made available in such a way that they are of direct relevance to national disease control activities (see Chapter 23). As the Ministry is often the implementing agency for interventions in public health programmes, it is generally desirable that independent investigators actually conduct the trials of interventions.

This chapter gives an overview of the main factors to consider in the development and implementation of health intervention trials in LMICs.

1.1 Planning a trial

The trial planning process is a major exercise which starts, and which should be largely completed, before any field activities have taken place, other than initial feasibility studies and small-scale pilot investigations (see Chapter 13). The planning process should encompass all aspects of the trial, from formulation of detailed objectives, based on the initial idea, through preparation for all field activities, collection of data, and analysis of results, to their publication, dissemination, and potential use in disease control. The plan should also try to anticipate the form of any studies that will follow, depending on the possible different outcomes of the trial.

Detailed planning is necessary for several purposes. First, information on the trial will be required by local and national administrations for them to review as part of the trial approval process. A similar description will be required by any agency that is going to review the proposal for funding. The detail required in such grant applications varies greatly from agency to agency. Some require a comprehensive document with full details of all trial procedures, while others put quite a small upper limit on the size of any application they are prepared to review. It is usually more time-consuming to prepare the former kind of application, but the latter kind may present a more formidable challenge, because, in relatively few words, the investigators have to present convincing evidence that they have considered and worked out all issues that would have been included in the longer type of application. Advice on the preparation of grant applications is given in Chapter 8.

A second reason for detailed planning at the start of an investigation is that possible problems must be anticipated in advance and solutions thought through, in order to reduce the likelihood of the trial falling behind schedule or having to be radically changed or abandoned, due to problems that could have been foreseen and avoided. Commonly, funding agencies require a section on potential risks to the trial, in which the investigators are asked to specify what could go wrong and the consequences this would have for the trial. It is rare to be able to predict all potential problems, but the more that have been considered in advance, the smaller the chance of catastrophe.

Realistic estimates must be made of the resources needed (for example, for transport, staff salaries, allowances, items of equipment) and the likely trial duration, including the time to analyse and report the trial, in order to be able to calculate the required budget for the trial. Underestimating the support needed may jeopardize some of the objectives, which may have to be revised or abandoned in the middle of the trial, whereas overestimating the cost may prejudice the funding agency against agreeing to support the trial. It is tempting to underestimate costs in the hope of increasing the chance of funding, but this may be self-defeating and, in any case, will often be picked up by the experienced investigators asked to review the trial proposal by the funding agency. The time it will take to conduct and analyse a trial is also often underestimated, particularly for trials where implementation of the intervention, or package of interventions, is not directly under the control of the evaluators but depends instead on the MOH or other partners. Advice on the preparation of budgets is given in Chapter 18.

In the present chapter, the steps to be included in the trial plan are discussed in the approximate order that they would arise, from the formulation of objectives through to the eventual publication, dissemination, and use of the findings. In the remaining chapters, specific issues relevant to the planning process are reviewed in greater detail, and cross-references are given in this chapter, where appropriate.

1.2 Ethical considerations in designing a trial

Ethical considerations impinge on many aspects of the design and conduct of trials and are discussed fully in Chapter 6. Briefly, any research investigation that involves human subjects should be submitted for ethics committee review. Intervention trials in some communities in LMICs may pose specific ethical dilemmas. The dogma that an investigator 'should treat everyone in the trial as though they were a member of his or her own family' is both difficult to apply and often inappropriate in situations of extreme poverty, in which some trials in LMICs will take place. Related issues concern the responsibility that an investigator has to those who live in the same community as the trial subjects but who, for whatever reason, are not included in the trial, and what happens regarding the public health use of an intervention after a trial has shown an intervention to be efficacious. Very commonly, an investigator must walk a tightrope, balancing his or her responsibilities to the individuals in the trial with those related to the potential of the interventions being evaluated to improve public health. The MOH knows these problems well, as they are implicit in any allocation of the health budget between the various potential preventive and curative services, but, commonly, the officials allocating the routine health budget are several steps removed from the individuals and communities that their decisions will affect. The field trial researcher usually has to face these issues directly. There are no simple solutions to these problems. It is important that each research study is subject to strict ethical review, with due attention to the specific conditions in and under which it will be conducted.

1.3 Trial governance

Since the first edition of this book was published, there has been a much greater emphasis on trial governance and quality control (QC) in trials. There are now extensive international guidelines on the governance of clinical trials, in which the roles of bodies, such as the trial 'sponsor', the principal investigator (PI), the trial Steering Committee, and the Data and Safety Monitoring Committee (DSMC), are discussed and defined. These aspects are considered in more detail in Chapter 7.

2 Definition of trial objectives

Once an idea for a trial has been formulated, it will be necessary to detail the specific objectives of the trial. To do this, the researcher will need to find out what has already been done regarding the evaluation of the intervention or interventions of a similar kind. This may involve meeting or corresponding with those undertaking similar studies, and it will almost invariably involve conducting a systematic literature review to find out what has been published that is relevant (see Chapter 3).

With this background information, the objectives of the trial can be formulated. These should include the overall aim or purpose of the trial, such as 'to evaluate the efficacy of a specific microbicide gel for the prevention of HIV infection in women' or 'to measure the impact of a breastfeeding promotion strategy on the incidence of diarrhoeal diseases in infants'. The specific objectives give more detailed statements of the particular questions that the trial is designed to answer, or the hypotheses that it will test. Finally, a list of subsidiary objectives may be given which relate to issues which are not central to the overall objectives but about which information will also be gathered while the trial is in progress.

2.1 The idea for a trial

One of the most creative phases of the planning of a trial is the selection of the subject area of the research and the formulation of the specific questions that will be addressed. A major motivation for most successful researchers is that they are doing something that they really enjoy and are researching questions about which they feel passionate. Their motivation may come from scientific curiosity about the causes or treatment or control of a particular disease, or about the effects of a specific intervention, or their concern may be to explore different ways that health or social systems can improve the public health. The field researcher may be motivated by working directly with people in their communities and be stimulated by the challenges posed by working in remote or difficult situations, outside of the hierarchy that may exist, for example, in a hospital environment.

The development or refinement of an idea for a field trial should take place in interaction with others at local, national, and possibly international levels. The research activity must not only be acceptable to the population in which it will be undertaken, but also to those who will authorize it nationally and to those who will fund it. Most good ideas for field research on the control of a disease that is of public health importance are likely to attract support.

Field research likely to receive the highest priority, both nationally and internationally, is that directed at control of diseases of greatest public health importance. An important preliminary to the development of a research proposal on a specific disease or condition may be a survey in the local community to determine the importance of the disease of interest. Such local data might be presented side by side with estimates of the global burden of disease attributable to the condition being studied.

The progress of science (and of public health) is not only dependent on groundbreaking first trials that show that a new intervention can be effective in one context. Progress also requires the replication of such trials in different settings to determine whether the findings from the original trial may be generally applicable. Replications of trials of bacille Calmette–Guérin (BCG) vaccination against TB and leprosy and of rotavirus vaccines, for example, have shown substantial variations in the efficacy of the vaccines in different parts of the world. This is even more important for effectiveness trials of interventions that are delivered through routine services where results may show important variations from one location to another, due to contextual differences. Although sometimes disparagingly called 'me too!' trials, such confirmatory (or otherwise!) trials are very important for the assessment of the public health usefulness of an intervention in a specific context.

A trial may either test for superiority or for equivalence. The choice will depend on the nature and effectiveness of the comparison intervention and has important implications for the choice of trial size (see Chapter 5). For example, if the aim is to test whether a new drug for the treatment of visceral leishmaniasis is more effective than the standard drug treatment, this will require what is called a 'superiority' trial. However, it could be that the new drug is much cheaper or is thought to have fewer side effects. If this was confirmed in a field trial, it would be likely to be adopted even if it was no more effective than the standard drug, so a trial that is designed to test for 'non-inferiority' or 'equivalence' would be appropriate.

2.2 Trial purpose

The statement of the purpose of a trial (termed 'goal' by some agencies) should convey to the reader the type of intervention, or package of interventions, to be evaluated (without details of how it will be applied, dose, and so on) and the endpoints against which the impact will be measured, without necessarily specifying the magnitude or precise nature of the impact expected or which the trial will be designed to detect. It may also include a description of the ways in which the results of the trial may influence public health policy and contribute to scientific knowledge. For example, in a trial of the use of the drug ivermectin against onchocerciasis, the statement of the purpose might be 'to assess the impact of mass treatment with ivermectin on the transmission of onchocerciasis and to measure any side effects in those treated with the drug'. For a trial of a new vaccine against the blood stages of the malaria parasite, the purpose may be 'to measure whether a *Plasmodium falciparum* asexual blood stage vaccine reduces episodes of clinical malaria'. For a trial to test the effect of cash payments conditional on girls either staying in, or returning to, secondary school on their risk of HIV infection, the purpose might be 'to assess whether educational conditional cash transfers reduce acquisition of HIV infection in girls'. Finally, for the example of the equivalence trial of a new drug for visceral leishmaniasis treatment, the purpose might be 'to test whether the new drug is at least as effective as the standard treatment for treatment of visceral leishmaniasis'.

2.3 Specific objectives of the trial

In the specific objectives (called specific aims by some agencies), a quantitative statement should be made regarding the size of the effect of an intervention that a trial is designed to detect and the precision with which the effect will be measured. Such specifications are necessary in order to calculate how large a trial should be, using the methods described in Chapter 5. The nature of the intervention should be given in more detail than in the statement of purpose (for example, dose and frequency of administration), and the endpoints of the trial clearly stated. They should also include a specification of the size of the trial and detail the population in which the intervention will be applied. For the example of the trial of ivermectin against onchocerciasis, the specific objectives would include a statement of the size of the impact on transmission which the trial would have a reasonable chance of detecting and the frequency with which adverse reactions of different kinds would have to occur to be detected in the trial, while, for a malaria vaccine, a more detailed description of the formulation of the vaccine would be required and statements included on the magnitude of the true effects on the incidence of malaria that the trial would be very likely to detect as being statistically significant. Finally, for the conditional cash transfer trial (see Section 2.2), the specific objectives should state the size of payment, to whom it will be given (for example, to the girl herself, her parents, or some combination of the two), the age range of the girls in the trial, and the size of effect on HIV incidence that the trial would have a reasonable chance of detecting.

The proper specification of the specific objectives is crucial to a successful trial. They should include a concise, but detailed, description of the intervention to be evaluated, the outcome(s) of interest, and the population in which the trial will be conducted. The more specific and detailed the objectives are, the clearer it will be how to design a study to meet them. It is crucial to set appropriate objectives, and it is worth spending time to get these both correct and unambiguous.

2.4 Subsidiary objectives of the trial

In the context of many trials, there will be secondary endpoints which will be measured in the trial but which are not the prime purpose for which the trial is conducted.

Also substudies may be included, having subsidiary objectives, such as the comparison of various serological tests or the analysis of genetic markers and their correlation with disease. It may be decided to add other objectives on to an intervention trial which do not relate to the main objectives. In the trial of ivermectin against onchocerciasis, for example, the impact on some other parasitic diseases might be assessed.

To increase the plausibility of trial findings, it is important to document changes in intermediate outcomes, which are directly related to the outcomes of principal interest, whenever this is possible. This requires laying out an 'impact model' (see also Chapter 15), describing how the intervention is expected to lead to the major outcome being studied. For stand-alone biological interventions, these models tend to be quite simple. For example, a trial of the effect of periodic vitamin A supplementation on child mortality should document that the vitamin A status improved in children receiving the supplement, but not in the comparison group. Impact models for non-biological interventions are often more complex. For example, in the conditional cash transfer trial, the impact on retention in secondary school and school achievement grades or the impact on reported sexual risk behaviours or on the incidence of other STDs or of pregnancy could also be studied, as well as the primary endpoint of HIV incidence. Impact models are essential for deciding which intermediate indicators must be measured.

The introduction of an intervention may also provide a special opportunity for determining particular key factors in the pathogenesis of disease. For example, trials of ivermectin, a microfiliaricide, against *Wuchereria bancrofti* may provide evidence for the role of microfilaria, as compared to that of adult worms, in the pathogenesis of lymphatic filariasis disease. Decisions to add on studies of this kind should not be taken lightly, as they will invariably need additional commitment of resources and may involve the trial population in additional inconvenience. They may thus have a negative impact on the primary objectives, perhaps by overstretching the trial team's technical or managerial resources, and the final 'cost' to the trial may be much greater than it appeared to be in purely monetary terms.

Once a large field trial is successfully under way, it is not unusual for the trial organizers to be approached by other investigators who wish to graft on additional procedures to answer questions of interest to them. There may be considerable value in utilizing the same trial for multiple purposes, but full consideration should be given to the extra work that this will entail, especially for key members of the research team, and to other possible harmful effects such as upsetting the rapport between the trial team and the trial population.

3 Selection of interventions

3.1 Intervention characteristics required

Several criteria should guide the suitability of candidate interventions to be evaluated in a large-scale field trial. The intervention, or package of interventions, should usually be one that could be introduced into a national or regional disease control programme (though this criterion might not apply for 'explanatory' or 'proof of principle' trials—see Chapter 2, Section 3.3). The dose (when applicable) should be 'optimal'. Evidence would usually be required from smaller preliminary studies (sometimes called Phase I and II trials, particularly with respect to trials of drugs and vaccines) that the intervention is relatively safe and produces a convincing intermediate response, such as a good antibody response to a vaccine or a change in self-reported sexual behaviour for an intervention to prevent unwanted pregnancies.

When an intervention has to be repeated several times to be effective (for example, micronutrient supplements), there should be evidence that the interval between each intervention is appropriate. For some interventions, the concept of dose is meaningless, such as the application of a diagnostic or screening test. Corresponding relevant evidence would then be required that the test is adequate (for example, previous studies indicating that it had good sensitivity, specificity, and predictive values). For continuous or repeated treatments, similar considerations apply to the duration of treatment. For example, with vitamin supplementation, the duration required will depend on whether the outcome of interest is the reversal of the acute effects of severe deficiency or of the chronic effects of more moderate deficiency. In addition to being safe and giving promise of being efficacious, the intervention must be acceptable to those to whom it is directed, relatively easy to deliver, and, at least eventually, of sufficiently low cost that it could be incorporated into the national disease control strategy if it is proved to be effective within the field trial.

3.2 Number of interventions compared

The choice of the number of different interventions to compare in a field trial is likely to be determined not only by the number of competing alternatives, but also by the implications the choice has on the size of the trial. This, in turn, is dependent on the frequency with which the outcome of interest occurs. 'Rare' outcomes require large trials (as discussed in Chapter 5). For example, in a trial of leprosy vaccines in South India, it was planned that each 'arm' (one of the alternative intervention assignments) included in the trial would require around 65 000 trial participants, in order for the trial to have the desired statistical power to detect effects that would be of public health importance (Gupte et al., 1998). Clearly, in this situation, a decision to add another arm would have had enormous cost and logistic consequences.

If the outcome is common, however, trials to compare more than two interventions may be undertaken more readily. For example, if seroconversion following vaccination is the outcome of interest, it may be straightforward to compare multiple vaccines or vaccination strategies in a single trial.

It is important to note, however, that many researchers try to build too many comparisons into a trial. There is often a tendency to divide groups after the sample size has been calculated or to plan comparisons within groups, without going through the appropriate computations (as given in Chapter 5).

Comparisons within a single trial can always be made with much greater confidence than those between trials. Thus, if drug A is found to be 50% more effective than a placebo in one trial and drug B is found to be 50% more effective than a placebo in another trial, it will not necessarily be possible to conclude that A and B are equally effective, as the circumstances in which the two trials were conducted will not have been identical. A further trial may be necessary for a direct comparison of A and B. If the need for this trial could have been anticipated in advance, it would have been more efficient to conduct one trial involving both drugs A and B and a placebo. A trial like this may be more complex to organize and would probably have to be substantially larger than either of the '2-arm' trials but would still tend to be smaller than the sum of the two trials.

When two interventions are being compared to a control intervention, and in situations where it would be possibly appropriate to apply both interventions to the same individual (or community), an efficient way of comparing both interventions with the control arm in the same trial is to design it as a 'factorial' trial. In such trials, some individuals receive the control intervention, others receive one or other of the new interventions, and some receive both interventions (typically 25% in each of four groups) (Montgomery et al., 2003). Although not commonly used, this design is very efficient, unless there is 'interaction' between the two interventions, i.e. the effect of both interventions applied at the same time is different from the simple sum of the separate effects of each of the interventions. Ayles et al. (2008), Awasthi et al. (2013a), and Awasthi et al. (2013b) are examples of the design of such trials.

3.3 Combined interventions

For some diseases, there are several possible interventions that may reduce the disease impact on a population. For example, interventions against malaria include destruction of mosquito breeding sites, spraying of residual insecticide, personal protection measures (for example, use of bed-nets and repellents), drug prophylaxis, and drug treatment, and trials might be designed to evaluate each of these interventions individually. A malaria control programme may choose to use more than one intervention at the same time and may wish to evaluate the impact of the 'package' of interventions, rather than the individual components of it. In such a case, the trial might compare an integrated strategy incorporating several different interventions applied simultaneously with a control group in which only the routine interventions that were previously available would be applied.

Several trials of this kind have been conducted for the prevention of HIV. For example, a recent trial in Tanzania tested the effectiveness of a package of interventions targeted to young people. Those in the intervention group received HIV prevention education in school; health workers in their local health facilities were given special training and support to try to make their facilities more 'youth friendly'; new suppliers who were thought to be particularly attractive to young people were trained and supported to sell condoms, and annual 'youth health weeks' were organized in their local communities (Ross et al., 2007). The advantage of this kind of trial is that it allows the testing of a package on interventions that might reasonably be expected to have a greater impact than any single component of the package. However, if no effect is seen, then although it may be reasonable to conclude that no one of the components of the intervention (at least, as applied in the trial) would have been effective on its own, it is necessary to think carefully about whether the existence of several concurrent interventions might have diluted the effect of one component on its own, or even that one component might have counteracted the effect of another. Another disadvantage is that, if an effect is demonstrated, it is not possible to be sure of the contribution to the overall result of each of the various components of the intervention.

3.4 Choice of comparison intervention

The best way to evaluate an intervention is to compare its effect with that of another intervention in the same population at the same time. Whenever possible, the allocation of individuals or groups of individuals to the different interventions should be 'at random' (see Section 4.1 and Chapter 11). In general, the intervention that is the current 'best' should be used as the comparison, but the choice of the 'control' intervention is not always straightforward and may involve difficult ethical considerations (see Chapter 6). When no effective intervention is known, the comparison must be with a group in which 'no intervention' is made; ideally, a placebo should be administered in order to preserve 'blinding' (see Section 4.1). For example, before the development of ivermectin no effective and safe treatment for onchocerciasis existed. Thus, placebo-controlled trials of the drug were ethically acceptable, at least until the beneficial effects of ivermectin had been established. For most tropical diseases, however, some kinds of intervention already exist and may already be deployed by the health services or by a control programme in the area where a trial is planned. Only in very rare circumstances would it be ethical to withdraw these existing interventions for the purposes of a trial. A more complex issue is with respect to the extent to which they should be introduced in the context of a trial. It is known that regular prophylaxis with anti-malarial drugs reduces morbidity from malaria, for example, so would it be necessary to give this intervention to all those in the 'control' arm of a malaria vaccine trial, even though, in normal circumstances, very few, if any, of them would otherwise have been on prophylaxis? Indeed, would it even be ethical to withhold prophylaxis from those who would be receiving a malaria vaccine whose efficacy was unknown? The optimistic reader will seek a definitive answer to these questions in Chapter 6! Unfortunately, the search will be in vain, as there are no general definitive solutions to problems such as this; each situation has to be considered on its own merits, taking full account of the circumstances in which a particular investigation is planned. However, in Chapter 6, key principles are outlined that should be used when making such judgements.

In a leprosy vaccine trial in Venezuela, the new leprosy vaccine consisted of a mixture of BCG and killed *Mycobacterium (M.) leprae* bacilli. When the trial was designed, a choice had to be made between using BCG for the control arm (the efficacy of BCG alone against leprosy in Venezuela was unknown at the time) or using a placebo. BCG was chosen, even though doing this might reduce the chance of showing a protective effect (as BCG alone may have been protective). The inclusion of a third, placebo, arm would have allowed the protective effect of BCG alone to be evaluated, but the incidence of leprosy was too small for a third arm to be feasible within the trial. The major purpose of the trial that was conducted was therefore to evaluate whether a leprosy-specific vaccine (i.e. one which included *M. leprae* bacilli as well as BCG) was more effective than a non-specific vaccine (in this case, BCG). If the comparison had been with a placebo instead of BCG, any effect due to BCG could not have been distinguished from that due to the addition of *M. leprae* bacilli to the vaccine. In a larger trial of the same vaccine that was conducted in India, it was possible to include a placebo arm (Gupte et al., 1998).

The use of a placebo may be very important to derive an unbiased measure of effect (see Section 4.1 and Chapter 11, Section 4), but it requires careful ethical justification, and thought must be given to whether particular circumstances might lead to treatment being offered to participants, irrespective of their trial arm. In a placebo-controlled trial of vitamin A supplementation in Ghana, for example, the objective was to determine if a reduction of child mortality was produced by supplementation. As eye signs of vitamin A deficiency are effectively treated by vitamin A supplements, all in the trial were monitored for such signs and treated immediately if such signs were detected, even though this was likely to reduce the power of the trial to detect an impact of vitamin A supplementation on mortality.

A related issue concerns trials which do not test new interventions as such but evaluate new ways of delivering existing interventions. In a cluster randomized trial in Bangladesh, the Integrated Management of Childhood Illness (IMCI) strategy promoted improved ways of delivering interventions such as antibiotics for pneumonia, oral rehydration therapy, and vaccines; these interventions were also available from routine services in comparison areas. It was judged ethical not to change routine practices in the comparison areas, because these reflected what was already in place in the country as a whole (Arifeen et al., 2009).

3.5 Complex interventions

The design of a trial to evaluate the efficacy of a new vaccine or drug is relatively straightforward, in the sense that there are many past examples of such evaluations to draw upon when planning a new trial. However, the evaluation of some interventions, such as the deployment of a new procedure in the health service or public health practice, may involve consideration of several interacting components, including, for example, educational components and behavioural change. Such interventions pose special problems for evaluation, and these kinds of intervention have been called 'complex'. Many of the extra problems relate to the difficulty of standardizing the design and delivery of the interventions, their sensitivity to features of the local context, the organizational and logistical difficulty of applying experimental methods to service or policy change, and the length and complexity of the causal chains linking intervention with outcome. See Chapter 2, Section 2.3.4 and the associated Box 2.1 for further discussion.

4 Allocation of interventions within the trial

4.1 Randomization and 'blindness'

Once a potential intervention has been shown to be safe and acceptable for use in humans and the dose schedule established, trials should be conducted to evaluate quantitatively the benefit attributable specifically to the intervention under trial, compared to some other intervention, while attempting to exclude the confounding effect of other variables. The best way to exclude the potential effects of other factors—both those already known to be confounders and also those that are confounders but are not known to be so—is to base allocation decisions as to which intervention is applied to a particular individual, or group, on a random process. Incorporation of randomization into the trial is an extremely important design issue (see Chapter 11).

The randomized intervention trial is as close to a rigorous scientific experimental study involving human beings as it is possible to achieve ethically. The main study design features of a randomized trial are:

1. to avoid bias in assignment to the alternative interventions, all eligible trial participants should be assigned at random to the alternative treatment groups. This involves two steps; the first is selecting participants on the basis of the pre-established criteria for eligibility, and the second is the randomization procedures should ensure that each eligible participant has the same chance of receiving a particular intervention procedure

2. to avoid bias in the assessment of the trial endpoints, whenever possible, the person(s) assessing the outcome measures should not know to which intervention group the participant was assigned (i.e. the assessor should be 'blind' to the intervention group)

3. to avoid bias in the behaviour or reporting by the participant, whenever possible, the participant should also be 'blind' (i.e. the intervention group assignment should not be known by the participant).

If neither the assessor nor the participant is aware of the intervention allocations, the trial is said to be 'double-blind'. If only the assessors (or, more rarely, only the participants) are aware of the allocations, the trial is called 'single-blind'. For situations in which there is no known effective treatment or preventive method, a placebo of some sort must be used if double-blinding is to be assured. The 'double-blind' approach is the key to the elimination of bias in the assessment of the impact of an intervention, and, wherever possible, a 'double-blind' design should be used. Sometimes it is not possible because of the nature of the intervention procedure, for example, where participation in health education sessions is being compared to no intervention, or where cervical surgery is being compared to drug treatment for cervical cancer. But even if the providers of the intervention must know the assignments, the person who assesses the trial outcome should be kept 'blinded', if feasible. The more clearly defined and objective the outcome to be measured, the less critical it becomes to ensure blinding of the assessor. For example, as long as there is complete ascertainment of all deaths in all arms of the trial, blindness is unlikely to be important in a trial with mortality as the endpoint. Similarly, the less likely a patient is to be influenced by knowledge of which intervention they have received, the less important their blinding is.

4.2 Unit of application of the interventions

Different interventions can be applied either to an individual or groups of individuals, such as everyone in a family or household, everyone working in a particular company, or everyone in the community. The unit for randomization should usually vary in parallel with this. The choice of the unit for application of the intervention depends upon the nature of the intervention, the administrative method for its application, and the purpose for which the intervention is being applied. In statistical terms, the most efficient design, in most circumstances, is to use the individual as the unit of application, and this should be the design of choice, unless there is good reason for household or community (group) application and randomization. There are four main reasons for applying an intervention to a group, rather than by individual.

First, group allocation is appropriate when, by its nature, the intervention must be applied to everyone in the group such as all those living in a geographical area, workplace, school, or community. Examples include most environmental alterations and many vector control interventions. It also applies to many educational or health promotion interventions which, although they can be delivered at individual level, are likely to spill over or 'contaminate' other individuals living in the same community.

Second, it may be logistically easier to administer the interventions to groups, rather than on an individual basis. Sometimes it is administratively simpler and/or more acceptable to randomize by household or village, rather than by individual. Furthermore, with individual randomization of medications, for example, there may be a risk of individuals sharing medications within households or villages.

Third, if the purpose of applying the intervention is to reduce transmission of infection by a parasite, for example, the appropriate unit of application would be the 'transmission zone', i.e. the area in which people (and, where appropriate, vectors and intermediate hosts) may be interacting and sharing a common pool of parasites. Factors of importance in defining such zones may include the flight range of vectors and the movements of people, vectors, and intermediate hosts. To reduce interchange ('contamination') among transmission zones, it may be useful to have intervening buffer zones that are not involved in the trial. For many diseases, however, the size of the transmission zones may be difficult to determine and may vary over time.

Some interventions may be applied to individuals, but with the expectation that there may be an effect on transmission, through applying them to a high proportion of individuals in the community, that goes beyond the effect that would be achieved directly within the individuals who received the intervention (for example, through 'herd immunity'). The extent of coverage required to produce such effects depends upon the epidemiological circumstances, the presence of other control measures, and the type of intervention being introduced. For example, the use of a malaria vaccine to reduce the transmission of malaria in parts of Africa where the disease is 'holoendemic' may require so near to complete coverage that such a purpose would not be seriously considered. However, in other parts of Africa where the disease is much less prevalent, achieving high coverage with a highly effective vaccine might be sufficient to interrupt transmission.

For some types of intervention procedures, when the procedure itself provides individual benefit, such as ivermectin in the treatment of onchocerciasis, a further important issue is whether reduction of transmission provides a benefit, in addition to the individual reductions of morbidity/mortality. Trial designs to demonstrate this additional benefit are likely to be complex.

A fourth reason for applying interventions to a group or community as a unit would be for trials involving an intervention of already proven efficacy in individuals, but for which the delivery may be more effectively carried out on a group or community basis. The trial might consist of a comparison of different delivery systems. Generally, the end result desired in this type of trial is based upon cost-effectiveness criteria. Here the question would be whether it is possible to achieve a greater disease reduction for a given expenditure (or alternatively the same disease reduction for less expenditure) by use of a community-based distribution system than by the usual individual distribution methods. Many types of community-based distribution systems require community participation studies. The basic principles involved in community participation studies and in cost-effectiveness studies are described in Chapters 9 and 19, respectively.

When group randomization is adopted, the efficiency of the design can be improved by ensuring that the groups allocated to the different intervention arms are as similar as possible with respect to risk factors for the outcomes of interest, in the absence of the intervention. In other words, there is 'balance' between the risks of the outcomes of interest between the trial arms. When there are large numbers of units to be allocated, randomization itself will ensure comparability, but usually when communities or other groups are the units to be randomized, the number of units is relatively small, and randomization may leave considerable differences between the groups in the different arms. Attempts can be made in the analysis to allow for these differences, but the persuasiveness of the results may be reduced if the conclusions depend upon extensive statistical manipulation of the trial results. A more efficient approach to increase the comparability of the groups in the different arms is to stratify the groups into 'blocks' having similar underlying pre-intervention risks of the disease outcome in question and to randomize within each block. Stratification should be either in terms of variables which are strongly related to the risk of the outcome under study or in terms of this risk itself. For example, in trials of interventions against malaria in which villages are to be randomized, the villages might be stratified according to their pre-trial malaria prevalence or incidence rates, if such information is available, and the randomization done within each of these strata. An extreme type of stratification is when each 'block' includes the same number of groups (for example, villages) as there are arms of the trial, with each village within each 'block' having similar malaria rates. One village in each block is then randomly allocated to each intervention (see also Chapter 11, Section 3).

An alternative to stratification, when the number of available units for simple randomization, or even for stratification, is too small, is known as 'constrained' or 'restricted' randomization. Assume there are 20 villages to be randomized. All possible combinations of ten versus ten villages are evaluated, and only those combinations with good baseline comparability between the two sets of villages are selected. Next, one of the shortlisted combinations is chosen at random, and one of the two sets of ten villages is randomly selected to become the intervention group (Moulton, 2004). An example of the use of this approach is given in Sismanidis et al. (2008). See also Chapter 11, Section 3.3.

Often, good information on the distribution of the outcome measures will not be available in the trial population. In such circumstances, baseline studies to obtain the required information should be considered. Sometimes, as an alternative, surrogate measures must be used (i.e. measures which are thought to correlate closely with the outcome measures of principal interest). In the absence of detailed data on the population, geographical proximity and socio-economic level may be used as stratification characteristics. Thus, if a small geographical area is chosen as the randomization unit, the total trial area would be divided into regions containing a small number of relatively homogeneous units and, within each region, an equal number of units allocated to each treatment arm.

4.3 'Stepped wedge' design

The issue of the ethics of randomization is presented in acute form in situations where previous studies, perhaps using short-term endpoints or a more intensive intervention than is feasible on a population basis, indicate that the intervention is likely to be beneficial. Withholding the intervention from those in one of the treatment arms for the duration of the trial may then be argued to be unacceptable. Also, some individuals or organizations have an inherent, if irrational, distrust of randomization, worrying that it is 'experimentation' (which of course it is!) or even 'treating humans like laboratory animals'. Such positions can make it impossible for a straightforward RCT design to be accepted. An approach that can be adopted in this situation is the phased introduction of the intervention on a group-by-group basis, until the entire target population is covered. In order to avoid bias, the order in which the groups are given the intervention should be randomized and the number of groups should not be too small—at least six, preferably many more. This approach was first used in The Gambia to evaluate the long-term effects of vaccination against the hepatitis B virus (HBV) (The Gambia Hepatitis Study Group, 1987). A recent example of this design was a trial in Ghana to evaluate the impact on child mortality of treating fever using anti-malarials, with or without also treating with antibiotics (Chinbuah et al., 2012). Other examples are given in Brown and Lilford (2006).

The trial design is illustrated in Figure 4.1. This type of design has been called a 'stepped wedge' design. The power of this approach, compared to a simple allocation

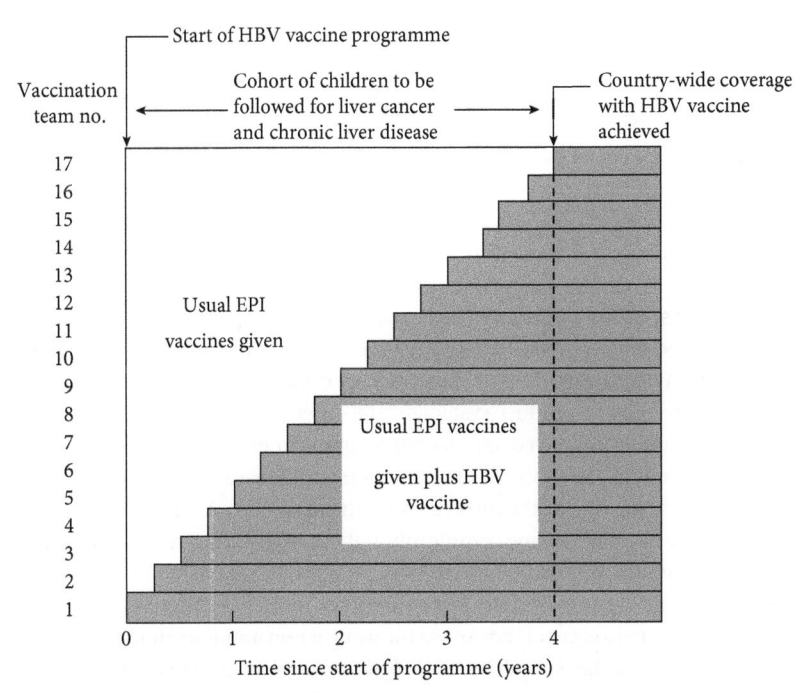

Figure 4.1 The 'stepped wedge' trial design used to evaluate the impact of hepatitis B vaccination on liver cancer rates in The Gambia.

of groups to one or other treatment arms, is of the order of 75–80%, depending on the number of groups. The same considerations apply to stratification and blocking, as in the static allocation designs.

In the trial in The Gambia, hepatitis B vaccine was introduced into the routine child vaccination programme over a period of 4 years. The order in which the different vaccination teams (there were 17 at the time the trial was planned) began to use the vaccine was random. At the end of 4 years, there was a cohort of children who had received the vaccine and a cohort who had not. These cohorts are being followed to compare the incidence rates of liver cancer and chronic liver disease. At the end of the 4 years, all vaccination teams had started vaccinating children, so subsequent cohorts of children were vaccinated. This phased introduction of the intervention mimicked the way in which many public interventions are introduced, but the key feature of the random order of the introduction of the intervention across the 'clusters' (in this case, vaccination teams) brought the crucial benefit of reducing the potential for the trial producing biased results.

4.4 Other approaches to allocation of the interventions

The allocation of interventions to individuals based on a random scheme is the best approach to rigorously exclude the potential biasing effects of other factors. However, non-randomized designs are often used. For example, a common approach is the 'before–after' or 'pre–post' design, in which the incidence or prevalence of the disease under study is compared before and after the intervention has been applied, and an attempt is made to attribute any difference to the effect of the intervention. This approach has important limitations as it may be wrong to assume that, in the absence of the intervention, the disease rate would have remained the same. Many diseases, and especially those of parasitic or infectious origin, vary greatly in incidence and severity from year to year and place to place, for reasons that are incompletely understood. Certainly variations in climate (for example, temperature and rainfall) can have profound effects. Some diseases show marked declines (or increases) over time in some communities (for example, TB and malaria), and sometimes these cannot be predicted in advance, or even related to any obvious specific factor. 'Before and after' evaluations of interventions in such situations may be very misleading. Also, it is not uncommon that the methods used to ascertain the trial outcomes change over time, either in terms of the actual data collection method or the person or organization doing the data collection changes, and the two produce systematically different results.

Another commonly employed approach is to apply an intervention in one community, and not in another, and to attribute any difference in disease rates between the two communities as being due to the intervention. This also may be very misleading, as a change may have occurred in one community, but not in the other, for reasons that had nothing to do with the intervention. Random, rather than purposive, allocation of the intervention to one of the two communities does not make any difference to this.

The commonest reason that is advanced for using a non-random allocation between intervention groups is for simplicity of design and administrative ease. Approaches like these also seem easier to explain to officials and to gain public acceptance. The rationale for randomization is difficult to communicate, even to other scientists, but the arguments in favour of randomization, as outlined in Section 4.1, are extremely strong, and failure to accept this approach has frequently led to studies from which erroneous conclusions have been drawn.

There are, however, situations in which allocation cannot be made on a randomized basis. There are occasions when the benefits of an intervention appear so clear that a properly randomized trial cannot be contemplated, or when the intervention or package has already been subjected to randomized trials and is being scaled up under routine conditions. The value of the intervention then has to be assessed by comparison of the situation before and after its introduction, or by the use of case-control studies after the intervention has been introduced (Smith, 1987). Although before vs after studies suffer from the major limitations described earlier in this section, the plausibility of the trial's conclusions can be increased by trying to rule out alternative reasons why the changes might have occurred (Bonell et al., 2011; Victora et al., 2004). First, if possible, data should be collected on more than one occasion, both before and after the intervention is introduced (sometimes called a time-series study). This allows checking that the outcome of interest was not already declining at the same rate prior to the start of the intervention, and that any decline after the intervention was introduced was consistently present, rather than only there at one time point. Second, a comparison should be made with time trends in disease rates in neighbouring populations where the intervention or package of interventions has not been delivered, and/or in the country or region of the country as a whole. Third, the sharpness with which changes in disease rates take place should be consistent with what might be reasonable to expect from the intervention and related to the speed with which the intervention is introduced over the entire population. Fourth, knowing and recording possible confounding variables in the before and after periods or in the populations being compared in a non-randomized study may also aid interpretation of differences. For example, in a study in which an objective is to reduce transmission of lymphatic filariasis by treating the human population with antifilarial drugs, monitoring the vector population for changes in density and infectivity might be undertaken.

While acknowledging these exceptions to the use of randomization as the basis of allocation, such studies do not have the rigour of a randomized design, and any conclusions drawn from them must be viewed with some caution. It is reasonable to think of there being a hierarchy of evidence from intervention studies, with (1) well-designed and well-conducted RCTs providing the strongest evidence, followed by (2) quasi-experimental studies, in which there is a similar contemporaneous comparison group, but the receipt of the intervention has not been allocated randomly, and then (3) non-experimental designs, in which there is no similar, contemporaneous comparison group such as the before–after, time-series, or after-only designs outlined earlier in this section. Formal guidelines have been developed by the GRADE working group (Guyatt et al., 2008) (<http://www.gradeworkinggroup.org>) to rank the quality of evidence on the effect of an intervention, based on different kinds of study, ranging from the RCTs, which are judged to provide the highest quality of evidence (if properly conducted), through to other kinds of study, providing lower-quality evidence, including observational studies. The WHO has now adopted these guidelines and attempts to undertake a formal grading of the quality of the evidence, with respect to policy recommendations they make regarding specific interventions. The main focus of this book is on RCTs.

5 Choice of outcome measures and trial duration

For many interventions, there will be a range of outcomes that could be affected and which might be of interest to study (see also Chapter 12). Nutritional supplements, for example, might affect any or all of the following:

1 biochemical measures
2 short-term acute consequences of deficiency
3 the consequences of chronic deficiency
4 mortality due to the specific causes of death that the intervention is intended to rectify
5 total (all-cause) mortality.

In determining which outcome is of the greatest importance for the trial, consideration must be given to whether:

1 the outcome is of clinical or public health importance
2 the probable effect on that outcome is large enough to be of clinical or public health interest
3 it can be accurately measured.

A substantial impact on total and age-specific mortality rates is always of public health importance, and systems can usually be set up to ensure that they are well recorded (even though such systems often require considerable input if they are not already in place), but they are unlikely to be sufficiently affected by most interventions to enable effects to be detected with studies of manageable size. Mortality from the specific causes that the intervention is designed to reduce should be more greatly affected, of course, but is usually much more difficult to measure accurately. In most low-income settings, routine reporting of births and deaths by medically certified cause of death is not available or is very incomplete and therefore potentially misleading. In these circumstances, measuring cause-specific mortality rates will require interviews with close relatives or friends of the deceased to try to ascertain the signs and symptoms preceding death, so that an attempt can be made to assign a likely cause of death. Such interviews are known as 'verbal autopsies'. The International Network for the Demographic Evaluation of Populations and Their Health in Developing Countries (INDEPTH) has produced model verbal autopsy questionnaires (<http://www.indepth-network.org>). Using total mortality as the trial outcome, however, will dilute the effect that might be seen if specific causes were examined, since the variation in deaths due to the unaffected causes is included. The choice may have to be made between setting up special mechanisms to collect high-quality information on the cause of each death or to allow for a dilution of the observed effect by increasing the size of the trial. It should be stressed that, for conditions that are life-threatening, mortality is an important outcome to evaluate and, wherever possible, should be a primary trial outcome, but this generally has substantial implications, with respect to the size of the trial.

Short-term outcomes are clearly attractive in that, if used as the outcome on which the design is based, the trial size will be smaller and the duration shorter than if mortality were to be used. The danger is that the short-term measure in itself may not be of principal public health importance, and the effect of the intervention on that outcome may not correlate well with the effect on more serious conditions. There is, for example, little point in measuring an antibody response to infection if it bears no or little relation to the risk of disease. Conversely, in the relatively rare situations where it is known that a short-term outcome is highly correlated with an outcome of greater public health consequence (and is effectively a surrogate measure of the more important outcome), it will be more efficient to focus the trial on the surrogate outcome.

In most circumstances, the appropriate outcome for determining the duration and size of the trial would be the most serious consequence of the specific condition at which the intervention is aimed. However, it is not always feasible to use such outcomes in a trial. For example, in a trial of a new measles vaccine in a HIC where death in someone who has measles illness is rare, the onset of measles illness might be a sensible trial endpoint, rather than death from the disease or total mortality. In contrast, in a country where a relatively high proportion of children with measles die, death from measles might well be the outcome of choice. If mechanisms for establishing accurate diagnosis were inadequate, total mortality might even be considered (especially as measles vaccine may reduce the risk of death attributable to diseases other than measles).

Even in trials where total or cause-specific mortality are the primary trial endpoint, short-term 'intermediate' outcomes should also be collected as valuable secondary monitoring and explanatory outcomes, as laid out in the impact model. They provide information, as the trial progresses, as to whether the trial is on target to meet its primary goals and, if it is not on target, should help to identify what remedial action might be required. Also, if the trial does not find a significant impact on its primary outcome, the 'upstream' outcomes may help provide an explanation for why. For example, in a trial of the impact of insecticide-treated nets on malaria mortality, it would be important to also measure net coverage and use, and data on the incidence of malaria illness and age-specific prevalence of malaria parasitaemia by trial arm. When short-term outcomes are used in this way, any assumptions about the natural history of the disease should be clearly thought through and stated in the trial protocol.

Definition of the primary trial outcome will have consequences for the duration of the trial. Prior information should be available on the time needed for the intervention to affect the outcome. In some situations, such as the prevention of liver cancer in adult life by hepatitis B vaccination in the first year of life, the final outcome measure may not be observed for several decades. The need for monitoring of intermediate outcomes (such as the hepatitis B carriage rate) then becomes even more important.

The choice of trial duration is critical for interventions whose impact does not increase linearly over time. For example, the impact of a health education programme in schools to reduce sexual risk taking might be relatively small, until a high proportion of the students have become sexually active. But even then, the impact might be small, until both the students and their sexual partners (who might be several years older or younger) had been through the programme. And finally, the impact may reach a 'tipping point' when enough people had been exposed to the programme to change general social and sexual norms in the population as a whole. However, the choice of trial duration is complicated by the fact that few funding agencies are keen to fund research projects that last more than 3–5 years. A common strategy is to apply for initial funding for a 3- to 5-year trial that will be able to measure the intervention's impact on important intermediate outcomes but is large enough to measure the impact on the primary trial outcomes if continued into a second trial follow-up phase, with the application for further funding based on the results of the first phase.

A final and important point to stress in this section is that it is essential that attention is given to monitoring the severity and frequency of adverse effects of an intervention. In their desire to assess the effectiveness of an intervention, investigators often do not pay sufficient attention to finding and documenting adverse effects, which may require additional effort and resources. In most situations, the future applicability of the conclusions drawn from a trial will involve an assessment of the balance between positive and negative (adverse) effects.

6 Trial population

6.1 Criteria for selection of trial population

The criteria for selection of the population to be included in the trial depends primarily upon what condition the intervention is directed against and upon the purpose of the trial. In general, the population will be chosen from an area in which there is high incidence of the condition of interest, because the higher the incidence of the primary trial outcome, the smaller the study population for the trial has to be. Exceptions are when the purpose of the trial is to determine the efficacy under special epidemiological circumstances or in special population groups such as in pregnant women.

Good community and governmental co-operation and participation are also key factors in the successful conduct of a trial. The trial area should be accessible at the times surveys are to be conducted (for example, during the rainy season). Well-qualified and experienced field teams should be available or be able to be recruited. In addition, access to high-quality clinical and laboratory facilities may be necessary for the trial. If required, entomological, behavioural science, economic, and other appropriate disciplinary expertise should be available. Planning the trial will be much simplified if baseline data are already available in the trial area.

If the trial design involves the repeated follow-up of members of the study population over several years, as will be the case for many intervention trials, it is important to select a location for the trial in which substantial migration into, or especially from, the area is unlikely to occur. Migration rates in excess of 10% per year are not uncommon in many rural areas and may be considerably higher in urban or peri-urban settings. Unless the trial is conducted within a demographic surveillance population, migration rates may well not be known in advance, so a rapid survey of a sample of the proposed trial population may be useful to determine if a reasonable proportion of the population have been resident in the area for several years.

The choice of trial population may affect the external validity of the trial results. For example, many micronutrient trials are carried out in areas with high prevalence of the specific deficiency. The health impact from supplementation in such areas is likely greater than what would be expected in areas where micronutrient deficits are less frequent, which may represent the majority of areas where supplements will be used in the future.

6.2 Inclusion and exclusion criteria

In general, the trial population should be chosen to represent the group that would be the target for the intervention in a potential future public health programme, if the intervention is found to be effective within the trial. Care should be taken to define the target population. To the extent feasible, those included should be the persons for whom benefit is likely to be the greatest, and those excluded should be the persons for whom benefit is likely to be minimal or indeed who may be harmed. Specific inclusion and exclusion criteria should be developed for the trial. For example, because the major morbidity and mortality associated with malaria in a holoendemic area are seen in infants and young children, these groups are likely to be the focus of a major field trial of a malaria vaccine in such an area, though older children and adults might be used in preliminary studies to test the safety of the vaccine in those who already have some immunity or may be the focus of a vaccine trial where malaria transmission is much less intense.

In early trials of an explanatory nature, special groups at high risk may form the trial population, either to maximize the potential effect, to ensure good compliance, or to facilitate the logistics. Valuable information concerning the potential of the intervention can result, but the extent to which the results can be extrapolated to the general population may be limited.

Exclusion criteria need to be carefully considered so as to eliminate subjects who may be put at greater risk by the intervention or who have underlying conditions that may interfere with the assessment. Exclusion criteria should be stated explicitly and unambiguously, before the trial begins. It is usual to exclude from trials those who are seriously ill, those who are very old, those who are very young, and pregnant women, unless any of these are the specific target group for the intervention. These groups are excluded either because it is considered that they are unlikely to derive benefit from the intervention, or if they are thought to be more likely to be susceptible to possible adverse effects of the intervention, or they are likely to suffer adverse events (AEs) which might incorrectly be associated with the intervention if they are included. Ascertaining pregnancy is difficult, especially in its early stages, without specific testing, and, in some trials, this may not be feasible. Sometimes all women of childbearing age are excluded from trials, if it is thought that damage may be caused by the intervention to the fetus. Against this must be balanced the potential benefit that the excluded groups may receive from the intervention. Also, if pregnant women or children, for example, have been excluded from a trial that shows the intervention to be effective, resulting public health programmes may consider it is inappropriate for them to receive the intervention, in case there are unforeseen risks to them or because the safe and optimal dosage of any drugs involved are not known. As a result, it may be appropriate to include them in later 'bridging' trials, with careful monitoring of pregnancy outcomes.

6.3 The size of the trial population

Attention needs to be given to the required size of the trial, in terms of the precision of the effect estimates and of the power to detect important differences. These aspects are discussed in detail in Chapter 5. It is important to allow for the loss of power that results from group randomization if such a design is adopted (see Chapter 5, Section 6).

For interventions that are likely to be given to large numbers of individuals, if they are subsequently introduced into disease control programmes, there are strong arguments in favour of designing trials of the interventions to also be large not only to pick up any rare side effects, but also to obtain a relatively precise measure of their expected impact.

6.4 Compliance

Conclusions from a trial will be based on a comparison of the outcome measures adopted for the trial in those allocated to the alternative intervention arms of the trial. Only a certain proportion of those allocated to a particular intervention will receive that intervention effectively. Effective delivery of an intervention requires both that the provider carries out the intervention procedure correctly and that the trial participants co-operate in the desired fashion. In field trials, the provision of the intervention will usually be under the control of the investigator, but a successful trial also requires the compliance of the participants, who are not under the control of the investigator, and will depend on the understanding and co-operation of the community involved. Hence, the strong emphasis in this manual on the importance of communication and feedback between the investigating team and the participating communities has a pragmatic, as well as an ethical, basis.

In most trials, however, some participants will not fully comply, and the intervention procedure either will not be carried out or it will not be done in an effective manner. For trials to determine the public health value of an intervention (pragmatic trials), some degree of non-compliance may give a more realistic measure of effectiveness than a tightly controlled trial in which every effort is made to ensure that the intervention is effectively delivered, but for explanatory studies, in which an important objective may be to determine the maximum effect possible, every effort should be made to keep compliance high. Wherever possible, the degree of compliance should be continually monitored, at least on a sample basis. This might be done, for example, by doing urine or blood analyses to check that the expected drug or nutritional supplement has actually been ingested. For intervention measures that are administered sequentially over time or on a continuing ongoing basis, repeated specimens should be taken. In a trial to measure the impact of introducing improved water supplies, for example, it will be important to measure the proportion of the target population who actually access the improved water source. This is particularly relevant in trials in which a health effect is mediated through a change in behaviour, as is the case in a breastfeeding promotion trial with morbidity or mortality as endpoints. Documenting compliance with counselling—assessed through changes in feeding practices—is essential.

A further aspect of compliance that is sometimes overlooked is that those in the 'control' arm of a trial, who are allocated to routine care or placebo, may adopt the test treatment under study. For example, if health centres in some villages are allocated to receive an intervention, such as offering voluntary medical male circumcision or improved STD treatment, while those in other villages serve as controls, people in the control villages may go to the health centres in the intervention villages to obtain the intervention. Monitoring for the possible occurrence of this latter form of non-compliance (sometimes called 'contamination') is important. Care should also be taken in the construction of the different treatment groups to minimize the opportunity for such contamination. In the circumcision example, ensuring there is clear geographical separation of villages in the different arms of this trial by leaving a 'buffer zone' would be one means of minimizing contamination.

7 Implementation

7.1 Community acceptance

Critical to the conduct of a successful trial is that the trial population co-operates during the conduct of the trial and takes up the intervention offered. They must feel a part of the trial and perceive it to be for the benefit of their community. To ensure these aspects will require careful planning and investigation before the trial starts, including appropriate discussion with, and explanation to, community leaders and potential participants. Feedback and interaction should be continued throughout the course of the trial. These aspects are discussed in several chapters, and especially in Chapters 6 and 9 and part of Chapter 15.

7.2 Feasibility studies and pilot testing

Unless the acceptability and feasibility of implementing the intervention and the evaluation procedures that will be used in the trial have already been tested locally, it is usually wise to conduct a smaller feasibility study in advance of the main trial. The feasibility study may only include some aspects of the trial, such as the acceptability and feasibility of delivering the intervention, or the feasibility of enrolling trial participants or of administering a questionnaire or collection and testing of laboratory specimens. Whether or not such a feasibility study has been conducted, it is essential that all the trial procedures are tested together in a pilot study, exactly as they will be applied in the actual large-scale field trial. However, the pilot study should be conducted on a much smaller number of participants and with enough time for the trial procedures to be modified in the light of the findings. Feasibility studies and pilot studies are discussed in detail in Chapter 13.

7.3 Staff recruitment, training, and retention

The dedication and commitment of the staff employed to conduct a field research project are essential. This will involve their careful selection, training, and then support. They must understand the importance of their role in the trial and how it relates to that of others. The importance of high-quality work must be emphasized, and this must be monitored throughout the trial (see Section 9 and Chapter 16). Trials of long duration present the additional challenge of keeping staff motivated and performing at adequate levels of quality and avoiding excessive turnover. Open and frank discussions with staff are essential, and benefits, such as regular increases in salaries over time, may help motivation and retention.

7.4 Field organization

All aspects of field procedures should be planned in advance, and potential problems and solutions anticipated (for example, in case of staff sickness or vehicle, computer, or laboratory equipment failure). The trial design must reflect not only what is ideal, but also what can be done, given the constraints under which the trial must be conducted. These aspects are considered in detail in Chapters 16 and 17. Issues relating to mapping and conducting a census of the trial area are covered in Chapter 10.

8 Data handling

8.1 Data collection

A necessary part of most trials will be the collection of baseline (pre-intervention) data. These will include identification information on participants, such as name, age, sex, place of residence, and information on other factors that may influence the risk of occurrence of the outcome measures under study in the trial. Although randomization of a large enough number of individuals, or clusters of individuals, should result in an approximately equal distribution of all the important characteristics between trial arms, such baseline data, which should ideally include all known confounders, can be used to check that this balance has actually occurred in practice. And if it has not, then it can also be used to adjust for such imbalances in the trial analyses.

In addition, it may be important to collect general baseline data on the population where the trial is being carried out. These may include not only the epidemiological characteristics of the population, but also the socio-economic, cultural, political, health services, nutritional, and other relevant characteristics. Such contextual factors may be essential to interpreting whether the trial's results can be generalized to another setting.

Additional data will be collected during the course of the trial to monitor the application of the interventions and to record information on the outcomes of interest. The conduct of a population census is described in Chapter 10, and methods to obtain high-quality data at the start of a trial and during its course are described in Chapter 14. Obtaining data using social or behavioural methods is outlined in Chapter 15, and for measuring the costs of the interventions is outlined in Chapter 19. Of crucial importance in any trial is the proper measurement of the incidence of endpoints against which the intervention is designed to protect, and these aspects are discussed in Chapter 12.

8.2 Data processing

Methods of coding, entering, and then managing computerized data collected in a trial are described in Chapter 20.

9 Quality control

In most intervention studies, members of the population are invited to participate, the intervention is applied, perhaps repeatedly, and the population is kept under surveillance, until the final trial outcomes are recorded. The quality of each step in this process must be monitored. The two major reasons, which hardly need stating, are first to ensure that each operation is being performed to an acceptable standard, and second to identify areas where attention is required. A third reason is to be able to ascertain, at the end of a trial that failed to show anticipated effects, the possible reasons for failure. The damage done by a misleading 'negative' result can be serious. The following are major aspects of quality control (QC) that need attention.

9.1 The intervention

Regular monitoring of the delivery of the intervention should be an integral part of the design to ensure that there is no change in the quality, as a trial goes on. For example, in a vaccination trial, continual review would be needed of the quality of the vaccination techniques being used by fieldworkers and of the quality of the vaccine(s) used in the intervention. For example, the potency of each batch of vaccine used should be assayed, together with monitoring of the maintenance of any required cold chain. Particularly relevant for trials where the intervention includes case management or counselling is monitoring the quality of these procedures through regular observation of a sample of provider–client interactions.

Short-term endpoints may be used for monitoring the quality of the intervention. At the individual level, repeated surveys of physiological measures of response to the intervention will provide an assessment of whether an effective intervention agent has been delivered. Examples would be antibody levels against a vaccine or levels of a micronutrient in serum. In trials including provider–client interactions, exit interviews with clients can be used to monitor their understanding of the advice that was provided. Such evaluations may have to be done or be evaluated by an independent trial monitor to ensure that those who will assess the main endpoints in the trial are kept blind—whenever possible—to the identity of those in intervention and control groups.

9.2 Follow-up

For many intervention studies, the endpoints of interest may not emerge until a lengthy period after the start of the intervention. It may not be necessary to keep the entire trial population under active observation, and this is often not feasible (for example, cases might be detected, as they report to clinics, rather than by conducting periodic surveys of the trial population), but it is essential that the trial is designed in such a way that losses to the trial population (for example, cases who do not go to clinics) will not distort the conclusions. The follow-up rate should be monitored, in order to identify potential problems at an early stage (for example, disgruntlement in a particular village or to identify a fieldworker whose work quality is declining). If possible, the reasons that individuals are lost to follow-up should be ascertained. Some losses may be inevitable, such as participants who die or who move out of the trial area, while it may be possible to take remedial action to prevent others such as participants who withdraw their participation or who are temporarily absent but could be found by repeated visits to their homes. The baseline characteristics of those who are lost to follow-up should be compared with those of participants who remain in the trial, and this information should be analysed to assess any effect that the losses might have on the interpretation of the results of the trial.

9.3 Assessment of trial outcomes

Mechanisms have to be established to ensure that the quality of information on all the trial outcomes is acceptable. Ongoing monitoring is required to establish that the data on trial outcomes are maintaining acceptable quality and that no biases are present in the way outcomes are recorded in different treatment arms. Attention needs to be paid to inter-observer variation in the assessment of the outcomes and changes that may occur in this variation, as the trial progresses.

9.4 Other field and laboratory procedures

QC should pervade all field activities, and the question as to how high quality is to be achieved and maintained should be addressed specifically for all activities. This is discussed in most of the chapters that follow, and specifically in Chapter 16, Section 7.

Laboratory procedures should be subject to constant scrutiny, and 'blind'-coded duplicate samples or known positives or negatives should be introduced into the workload regularly to monitor performance.

In interview surveys, a proportion of respondents should be re-interviewed by a second interviewer, blind to the results of the first interviewer, to check on the repeatability of the responses. If the questionnaire is long, the re-interviews might focus on a subset of key questions, rather than repeating the full questionnaire, in order to avoid undue demands on participants.

It is important that all involved in the trial accept and understand the need for constant checking and re-checking. This is both so that any sanctions that are taken for repeated poor performance do not come 'out of the blue', but, more importantly, as a way of encouraging all trial staff to maintain high quality at all times, because they know that errors will be spotted reasonably quickly. On the other hand, errors are bound to occur, and their detection should usually result in support and, where necessary, additional training, with reprimands being reserved for where there is evidence of dishonesty or continual carelessness. Incentives or rewards to encourage high-quality work may be worthwhile.

All members of the field team are, and must be made to feel, important contributors to the research project. Feedback of results and progress should be continuous and frequent, so that they can appreciate where their contribution fits into the overall project. Neglect is a great stimulus to poor-quality work.

10 Analysis, monitoring, and reporting

10.1 Planning the main analyses

The main analyses that are expected to result from the trial should be developed in some detail, with the use of dummy tables. Such an exercise is a great help when planning the trial, as it helps clarify exactly what data are actually needed and highlights redundant data. All specific objectives should be tied to planned analyses.

10.2 Analyses during the trial

Analysing relevant data from a trial, as they accumulate during the trial, is an important way of monitoring the satisfactory progress of a trial. Administrative analyses of the numbers of participants recruited each day or week and of the data collected by different fieldworkers are important for QC. A running tally should be kept of the numbers of participants experiencing the various trial endpoints to verify that the estimates of incidence rates used to plan the size of the trial were appropriate. Ideally, the investigators will be blind with respect to which interventions have been allocated to which participants, but differences between the different interventions might be analysed by a data and safety monitoring committee (as discussed in Section 10.3). Other aspects of interim analyses are discussed in Chapter 5, Section 7.1 and Chapter 7, Section 4.1.3.

Increased reliance on the use of smart phones or personal data assistants (PDAs) to record data when interviewing participants facilitates real-time data quality checks and analyses. Considerable ahead-of-time preparation and planning, however, are necessary, in order to programme devices to be able to produce such analyses regularly.

Interim reports, based on such ongoing analyses, may be required during the course of a trial by national authorities and by the trial's funding agency, in order to check that the original proposal is being adhered to and that the assumptions underlying the trial design were correct.

10.3 Data and Safety Monitoring Committee

For large trials, it is advisable for the investigators to set up an independent DSMC. Such a committee generally has access to selected unblinded data during the course of a trial and, for example, will conduct analyses to monitor whether there are an unacceptable number of adverse events (AEs) associated with an intervention. In such circumstances, the committee may recommend changes to the design of the trial or, in more extreme cases, that the trial be stopped, either temporarily or permanently.

The DSMC might also be charged with conducting interim analyses of the trial with respect to the primary endpoint, so that if the efficacy of intervention is substantially lower or substantially higher than expected, changes to the trial design, including early stopping, might be recommended.

The roles and functioning of DSMCs are discussed in Chapter 7. The most important function is usually to hold the randomization code for the trial and to monitor the results of the trial, both in terms of effectiveness and safety, as they accumulate. If there is evidence of a substantially increased risk of adverse reactions associated with any of the interventions under study, the committee would have the power to advise the Trial Steering Committee to stop further recruitment. Similarly, if evidence accumulates that one intervention is substantially better than the others (or one is substantially worse), the committee would usually recommend that the trial be ended or that at least one of the trial arms is discontinued. In blinded trials, a major advantage of these functions being undertaken by an independent committee is that the investigators can remain blind to the randomization codes, which is an important way of ensuring unbiased assessment of the trial endpoints. But, even where the trial is not blinded, it still has the considerable advantage of ensuring that the recommendation of stopping or continuing a trial is as objective as possible, because stopping a trial early usually has considerable logistic implications and may not be popular with the investigators, staff (who may even need to be laid off early), or participants.

The circumstances in which a trial will be prematurely ended should be carefully considered when the trial is being designed, and the DSMC should be party to such discussions. It will not be possible to predict all possible situations that may cause a decision to be taken to end a trial, but this should be done to the extent possible. In particular, there should be consideration as to how large a difference may be apparent between the interventions, with respect to their impact on specific endpoints, before it is decided to end the trial. In some circumstances, it may be important to go on beyond the point where statistical significance is reached. These issues are discussed in Chapter 5, and there are also ethical considerations which are discussed in Chapter 6.

The DSMC might also set up independent QC checks on trial procedures and, for example, may arrange to review the diagnoses of all cases of the diseases of interest arising in the trial (which should be done, of course, 'blind' to knowledge of the randomization codes).

The committee usually works on a pro bono basis and does not have auxiliary staff. If its activities will require QC checks or diagnostic reviews, it may be necessary to budget for these activities when preparing the protocol.

In some trials, the DSMC may consist of one person, sometimes called the 'clinical monitor'.

10.4 Analysis methods

The analysis of a large field trial will usually be a complex undertaking and will usually require the involvement of a professional statistician, sometimes under supervision of a senior statistician or epidemiologist. It is not feasible in a manual of this kind to detail all of the analysis methods that it might be appropriate to employ in different trials. However, in Chapter 21 an outline is given of the main methods of analysis that are likely to be employed. It is included as it summarizes relevant methods that are not covered as comprehensively in the most basic epidemiological texts or books on medical statistics.

10.5 Reporting results

Once a field trial has been completed and the results analysed, it is essential that the results and their implications are made available to the scientific community, to those who participated in the trial, and to those responsible for designing and implementing regional and national disease control strategies. These aspects are discussed in Chapter 23.

10.6 Further studies

Many trials will provoke questions amenable to further research. One example might be if a trial of a hookworm vaccine shows that it provokes good specific antibody- and cell-mediated immune responses and reduces the incidence of infection by 80% but is associated with prohibitive adverse reactions, further studies may well be needed to explore which antigens are causing the adverse reactions and whether removing these will also reduce the vaccine's effectiveness against hookworm.

Alternatively, if a trial of traffic-calming measures in one city shows that they are highly effective in reducing road traffic accidents, questions may well arise on how best to implement similar measures in other settings and/or to monitor the effectiveness of such interventions when implemented on a wide scale and over a long period of time. Such studies are often called Phase IV studies, as they evaluate interventions in real-world settings after the Phase III trial has been completed. These are discussed in Chapter 22.

11 The 'SPIRIT' checklist for standard protocol items for clinical trials

Nearly all intervention trials will need to have a protocol developed, which serves as the basis for trial planning, conduct, and reporting. Before a trial starts, it is recommended or, in many cases, required that the protocol is deposited in a trial register (see Chapter 7, Section 5). Until recently, there has not been specific guidance as to exactly what items should be included in such a protocol. However, such guidance has recently been published (Chan et al., 2013a; Chan et al., 2013b) as a component of the EQUATOR project (Enhancing the QUAlity and Transparency Of health Research) (<http://www.equator-network.org/>). The publications include a 33-item checklist, the so-called SPIRIT (Standard Protocol Items: Recommendations for Intervention Trials) 2013 checklist, which is reproduced in Table 4.1. This gives a useful outline of how a trial protocol might be organized, bearing in mind the issues we have discussed in this chapter. Readers should refer to the SPIRIT website (<http://www.spirit-statement.org/>) for the most recent version.

Table 4.1 The SPIRIT 2013 checklist: recommended items to address in a clinical trial protocol and related documents*

Section/item	Item no.	Description
ADMINISTRATIVE INFORMATION		
Title	1	Descriptive title identifying the study design, population, interventions, and, if applicable, trial acronym
Trial registration	2a	Trial identifier and registry name. If not yet registered, name of intended registry
	2b	All items from the World Health Organization Trial Registration Data Set
Protocol version	3	Date and version identifier
Funding	4	Sources and types of financial, material, and other support
Roles and responsibilities	5a	Names, affiliations, and roles of protocol contributors
	5b	Name and contact information for the trial sponsor
	5c	Role of study sponsor and funders, if any, in study design; collection, management, analysis, and interpretation of data; writing of the report; and the decision to submit the report for publication, including whether they will have ultimate authority over any of these activities
	5d	Composition, roles, and responsibilities of the coordinating centre, steering committee, endpoint adjudication committee, data management team, and other individuals or groups overseeing the trial, if applicable (see item 21a for data monitoring committee)

continued

Table 4.1 (continued) The SPIRIT 2013 checklist: recommended items to address in a clinical trial protocol and related documents*

Section/item	Item no.	Description
INTRODUCTION		
Background and rationale	6a	Description of research question and justification for undertaking the trial, including summary of relevant studies (published and unpublished) examining benefits and harms for each intervention
	6b	Explanation for choice of comparators
Objectives	7	Specific objectives or hypotheses
Trial design	8	Description of trial design, including type of trial (for example, parallel group, crossover, factorial, single group), allocation ratio, and framework (for example, superiority, equivalence, non-inferiority, exploratory)
METHODS: PARTICIPANTS, INTERVENTIONS, AND OUTCOMES		
Study setting	9	Description of study settings (for example, community clinic, academic hospital) and list of countries where data will be collected. Reference to where list of study sites can be obtained
Eligibility criteria	10	Inclusion and exclusion criteria for participants. If applicable, eligibility criteria for study centres and individuals who will perform the interventions (for example, surgeons, psychotherapists)
Interventions	11a	Interventions for each group with sufficient detail to allow replication, including how and when they will be administered
	11b	Criteria for discontinuing or modifying allocated interventions for a given trial participant (for example, drug dose change in response to harms, participant request, or improving/worsening disease)
	11c	Strategies to improve adherence to intervention protocols and any procedures for monitoring adherence (for example, drug tablet return, laboratory tests)
	11d	Relevant concomitant care and interventions that are permitted or prohibited during the trial
Outcomes	12	Primary, secondary, and other outcomes, including the specific measurement variable (for example, systolic blood pressure), analysis metric (for example, change from baseline, final value, time to event), method of aggregation (for example, median, proportion), and time point for each outcome. Explanation of the clinical relevance of chosen efficacy and harm outcomes is strongly recommended
Participant timeline	13	Time schedule of enrolment, interventions (including any run-ins and washouts), assessments, and visits for participants. A schematic diagram is highly recommended (see figure at <http://annals.org/article.aspx?articleid=1556168>)

Table 4.1 (continued) The SPIRIT 2013 checklist: recommended items to address in a clinical trial protocol and related documents*

Section/item	Item no.	Description
Sample size	14	Estimated number of participants needed to achieve study objectives and how it was determined, including clinical and statistical assumptions supporting any sample size calculations
Recruitment	15	Strategies for achieving adequate participant enrolment to reach target sample size

METHODS: ASSIGNMENT OF INTERVENTIONS (FOR CONTROLLED TRIALS)

Allocation:

Section/item	Item no.	Description
Sequence generation	16a	Method of generating the allocation sequence (for example, computer-generated random numbers) and list of any factors for stratification. To reduce predictability of a random sequence, details of any planned restriction (for example, blocking) should be provided in a separate document that is unavailable to those who enrol participants or assign interventions
Allocation concealment mechanism	16b	Mechanism of implementing the allocation sequence (for example, central telephone; sequentially numbered, opaque, sealed envelopes), describing any steps to conceal the sequence, until interventions are assigned
Implementation	16c	Who will generate the allocation sequence, who will enrol participants, and who will assign participants to interventions
Blinding (masking)	17a	Who will be blinded after assignment to interventions (for example, trial participants, care providers, outcome assessors, data analysts), and how
	17b	If blinded, circumstances under which unblinding is permissible and procedure for revealing a participant's allocated intervention during the trial

METHODS: DATA COLLECTION, MANAGEMENT, AND ANALYSIS

Section/item	Item no.	Description
Data collection methods	18a	Plans for assessment and collection of outcome, baseline, and other trial data, including any related processes to promote data quality (for example, duplicate measurements, training of assessors) and a description of study instruments (for example, questionnaires, laboratory tests), along with their reliability and validity, if known. Reference to where data collection forms can be found, if not in the protocol
	18b	Plans to promote participant retention and complete follow-up, including list of any outcome data to be collected for participants who discontinue or deviate from intervention protocols
Data management	19	Plans for data entry, coding, security, and storage, including any related processes to promote data quality (for example, double data entry; range checks for data values). Reference to where details of data management procedures can be found, if not in the protocol

continued

Table 4.1 (continued) The SPIRIT 2013 checklist: recommended items to address in a clinical trial protocol and related documents*

Section/item	Item no.	Description
Statistical methods	20a	Statistical methods for analysing primary and secondary outcomes. Reference to where other details of the statistical analysis plan can be found, if not in the protocol
	20b	Methods for any additional analyses (for example, subgroup and adjusted analyses)
	20c	Definition of analysis population relating to protocol non-adherence (for example, as randomized analysis) and any statistical methods to handle missing data (for example, multiple imputation)
METHODS: MONITORING		
Data monitoring	21a	Composition of Data Monitoring Committee (DMC); summary of its role and reporting structure; statement of whether it is independent from the sponsor and competing interests; and reference to where further details about its charter can be found, if not in the protocol. Alternatively, an explanation of why a DMC is not needed
	21b	Description of any interim analyses and stopping guidelines, including who will have access to these interim results and make the final decision to terminate the trial
Harms	22	Plans for collecting, assessing, reporting, and managing solicited and spontaneously reported AEs and other unintended effects of trial interventions or trial conduct
Auditing	23	Frequency and procedures for auditing trial conduct, if any, and whether the process will be independent from investigators and the sponsor
ETHICS AND DISSEMINATION		
Research ethics approval	24	Plans for seeking research ethics committee/institutional review board (REC/IRB) approval
Protocol amendments	25	Plans for communicating important protocol modifications (for example, changes to eligibility criteria, outcomes, analyses) to relevant parties (for example, investigators, REC/IRBs, trial participants, trial registries, journals, regulators)
Consent or assent	26a	Who will obtain informed consent or assent from potential trial participants or authorized surrogates, and how (see item 32)
	26b	Additional consent provisions for collection and use of participant data and biological specimens in ancillary studies, if applicable
Confidentiality	27	How personal information about potential and enrolled participants will be collected, shared, and maintained, in order to protect confidentiality before, during, and after the trial

Table 4.1 (continued) The SPIRIT 2013 checklist: recommended items to address in a clinical trial protocol and related documents*

Section/item	Item no.	Description
Declaration of interests	28	Financial and other competing interests for principal investigators for the overall trial and each study site
Access to data	29	Statement of who will have access to the final trial dataset and disclosure of contractual agreements that limit such access for investigators
Ancillary and post-trial care	30	Provisions, if any, for ancillary and post-trial care, and for compensation to those who suffer harm from trial participation
Dissemination policy	31a	Plans for investigators and sponsor to communicate trial results to participants, health care professionals, the public, and other relevant groups (for example, via publication, reporting in results databases, or other data sharing arrangements), including any publication restrictions
	31b	Authorship eligibility guidelines and any intended use of professional writers
	31c	Plans, if any, for granting public access to the full protocol, participant level dataset, and statistical code
APPENDICES		
Informed consent materials	32	Model consent form and other related documentation given to participants and authorized surrogates
Biological specimens	33	Plans for collection, laboratory evaluation, and storage of biological specimens for genetic or molecular analysis in the current trial and for future use in ancillary studies, if applicable

* Reproduced with permission of the SPIRIT group. It is strongly recommended that this checklist be read in conjunction with the SPIRIT 2013 Statement (Chan et al., 2013a), in order to fully understand the scope and context of the checklist. It is important to note that this is a minimum list of items, and certain trial protocols may warrant the inclusion of additional items. This table is distributed under the terms of the Creative Commons Attribution Non Commercial 4.0 International licence (CC-BY-NC), a copy of which is available at http://creativecommons.org/licenses/by-nc/4.0/.

References

Arifeen, S. E., Hoque, D. M., Akter, T., *et al.* 2009. Effect of the Integrated Management of Childhood Illness strategy on childhood mortality and nutrition in a rural area in Bangladesh: a cluster randomised trial. *Lancet*, **374**, 393–403.

Awasthi, S., Peto, R., Read, S., *et al.* 2013a. Vitamin A supplementation every 6 months with retinol in 1 million pre-school children in north India: DEVTA, a cluster-randomised trial. *Lancet*, **381**, 1469–77.

Awasthi, S., Peto, R., Read, S., *et al.* 2013b. Population deworming every 6 months with albendazole in 1 million pre-school children in north India: DEVTA, a cluster-randomised trial. *Lancet*, **381**, 1478–86.

Ayles, H. M., Sismanidis, C., Beyers, N., Hayes, R. J., and Godfrey-Faussett, P. 2008. ZAM-STAR, The Zambia South Africa TB and HIV Reduction Study: design of a 2 × 2 factorial community randomized trial. *Trials*, **9**, 63.

Bonell, C. P., Hargreaves, J., Cousens, S., *et al.* 2011. Alternatives to randomisation in the evaluation of public health interventions: design challenges and solutions. *Journal of Epidemiology & Community Health*, **65**, 582–7.

Brown, C. A. and Lilford, R. J. 2006. The stepped wedge trial design: a systematic review. *BMC Medical Research Methodology*, **6**, 54.

Chan, A. W., Tetzlaff, J. M., Altman, D. G., *et al.* 2013a. SPIRIT 2013 statement: defining standard protocol items for clinical trials. *Annals of Internal Medicine*, **158**, 200–7.

Chan, A. W., Tetzlaff, J. M., Gotzsche, P. C., *et al.* 2013b. SPIRIT 2013 explanation and elaboration: guidance for protocols of clinical trials. *BMJ*, **346**, e7586.

Chinbuah, M. A., Kager, P. A., Abbey, M., *et al.* 2012. Impact of community management of fever (using antimalarials with or without antibiotics) on childhood mortality: a cluster-randomized controlled trial in Ghana. *American Journal of Tropical Medicine and Hygiene*, **87**, 11–20.

Gupte, M. D., Vallishayee, R. S., Anantharaman, D. S., *et al.* 1998. Comparative leprosy vaccine trial in South India. *Indian Journal of Leprosy*, **70**, 369–88.

Guyatt, G. H., Oxman, A. D., Vist, G. E., *et al.* 2008. GRADE: an emerging consensus on rating quality of evidence and strength of recommendations. *BMJ*, **336**, 924–6.

Montgomery, A. A., Peters, T. J., and Little, P. 2003. Design, analysis and presentation of factorial randomised controlled trials. *BMC Medical Research Methodology*, **3**, 26.

Moulton, L. H. 2004. Covariate-based constrained randomization of group-randomized trials. *Clinical Trials*, **1**, 297–305.

Ross, D. A., Changalucha, J., Obasi, A. I., *et al.* 2007. Biological and behavioural impact of an adolescent sexual health intervention in Tanzania: a community-randomized trial. *AIDS*, **21**, 1943–55.

Sismanidis, C., Moulton, L. H., Ayles, H., *et al.* 2008. Restricted randomization of ZAMSTAR: a 2 × 2 factorial cluster randomized trial. *Clinical Trials*, **5**, 316–27.

Smith, P. G. 1987. Evaluating interventions against tropical diseases. *International Journal of Epidemiology*, **16**, 159–66.

The Gambia Hepatitis Study Group 1987. The Gambia Hepatitis Intervention Study. *Cancer Research*, **47**, 5782–7.

Victora, C. G., Habicht, J. P., and Bryce, J. 2004. Evidence-based public health: moving beyond randomized trials. *American Journal of Public Health*, **94**, 400–5.

Chapter 5

Trial size

1 Introduction to trial size 71
2 Criteria for determining trial size 72
   2.1 Precision of effect measures 72
   2.2 Power of the trial 73
   2.3 Choice of criterion 73
   2.4 Trials with multiple outcomes 74
   2.5 Practical constraints 75
3 Size to give adequate precision 76
   3.1 Comparison of proportions 76
   3.2 Comparison of incidence rates 77
   3.3 Comparison of means 78
4 Size to give adequate power 79
   4.1 Comparison of proportions 80
   4.2 Comparison of incidence rates 83
   4.3 Comparison of means 85
5 More complex designs 86
   5.1 Two groups of unequal size 86
   5.2 Comparison of more than two groups 87
   5.3 Factorial designs 88
   5.4 Equivalence and non-inferiority trials 88
6 Interventions allocated to groups 89
   6.1 Cluster randomized trials 90
   6.2 Stepped wedge trials 92
7 Other factors influencing choice of trial size 93
   7.1 Allowance for interim analyses 93
   7.2 Allowance for losses 94
8 The consequences of trials that are too small 94
9 Computer software for sample size calculations 95

1 Introduction to trial size

One of the most important factors to consider in the design of an intervention trial (or indeed in the design of any epidemiological study) is the choice of an appropriate trial size to answer the research question. Trials that are too small may fail to detect important effects of an intervention on the outcomes of interest or may estimate those effects too imprecisely. Trials that are larger than necessary are a waste of resources and may even lead to a loss in accuracy, as it is often more difficult to maintain data quality and high coverage rates in a large trial than in a smaller one.

The choice of an appropriate trial size may be based on either the precision of outcome measures desired or the power of the trial wanted. In Section 2, there is a discussion of the criteria used to make this choice. In Sections 3 and 4, procedures are given for calculating trial size requirements in the simplest case where two groups of equal size are to be compared. More complex designs are considered in Section 5. Special methods are necessary when the interventions are allocated to groups (for example, communities, schools, or health facilities), rather than individuals, and these are described in Section 6. Following this, in Section 7, two other factors that may influence the choice of trial size are discussed—first, the need to allow for interim analyses of the results (see Section 7.1), and second, the effects of losses to follow-up (see Section 7.2). In Section 8, the consequences of trials that are too small are discussed. Computer programs can be used to carry out sample size calculations, and these are briefly discussed in Section 9.

The procedures described in this chapter should be regarded as providing only a rough estimate of the required trial size, as they are often based on estimates of expected disease rates, subjective decisions about the size of effects that it would be important to detect, and the use of approximate formulae. However, a rough estimate of the necessary size of a trial is generally all that is needed for planning purposes. More comprehensive reviews of methods for the determination of trial size requirements are available (Chow et al., 2008; Machin, 2009), but the methods given in this chapter should be adequate for most purposes.

Readers who are not familiar with methods for the statistical analysis of trial data and, in particular, with the concepts of confidence intervals (CIs) and significance tests may find it helpful to read Chapter 21, Section 2, before embarking on this chapter, which is placed here because of the importance of considering trial size requirements at the design stage of a trial.

A principal objective of most intervention trials is to *estimate the effect* of the intervention on the outcome or outcomes of interest. Any such estimate is subject to error, and this error has two main components: bias and sampling error. Possible sources of *bias* and ways of avoiding them are discussed in Chapters 4, 11, and 21. The second component *sampling error* arises because the trial data come from only a *sample* of the population. This second component of error is the focus of this chapter. Sampling error is reduced when the trial size is increased, whereas bias generally is not.

2 Criteria for determining trial size

2.1 Precision of effect measures

To select the appropriate sample size, it is necessary to decide how much sampling error in the estimate of the effect of the intervention is acceptable and to select the sample size to achieve this precision. When the data are analysed, the amount of sampling error is represented by the width of the *confidence interval* around the estimate of effect. The narrower the CI, the greater the *precision* of the estimate, and the smaller the probable amount of sampling error. When designing a trial, it is necessary therefore to decide the width of an acceptable CI around the chosen intervention effect. Having made this decision, the method to select the required trial size is given in Section 3.

2.2 Power of the trial

An alternative approach is to choose a trial size which gives adequate *power* to detect an effect of a given magnitude. The focus is then on the result of the *significance test* which will be conducted at the end of the trial. The significance test assesses the evidence against the *null hypothesis*, which states that there is no true difference between the interventions under comparison. A *statistically significant* result indicates that the data conflict with the null hypothesis and that there are grounds for rejecting the hypothesis that there is no difference in the effects of the interventions under study on the outcomes of interest.

Because of the variations resulting from sampling error, it is never possible to be certain of obtaining a significant result at the end of a trial, even if there is a real difference. It is necessary to consider the *probability* of obtaining a statistically significant result in a trial, and this probability is called the *power* of the trial. Thus, a power of 80% to detect a difference of a specified size means that, if the trial were to be conducted repeatedly, a statistically significant result would be obtained four times out of five (80%) if the true difference was really of the specified size. The power of a trial depends on the factors shown in Box 5.1.

The power also depends on whether a one-sided or two-sided significance test is to be performed (see Chapter 21, Section 2.3) and on the underlying variability of the data. How the power may be calculated for given values of these parameters is explained in Section 4.

When designing a trial, the objective is to ensure that the trial size is large enough to give high power *if the true effect of the intervention is large enough to be of public health importance*.

2.3 Choice of criterion

The choice of which criterion (precision or power) should be used in any particular trial depends on the objectives of the trial. If it is known unambiguously that the intervention has some effect (relative to the comparison (control) group), it makes little

---

Box 5.1 The power of the trial depends on:

1 The value of the true difference between the study groups, in other words, the true effect of the intervention. The greater the effect, the higher the power to detect the effect as statistically significant for a trial of a given size.
2 The trial size. The larger the trial size, the higher the power.
3 The probability level (p-value) at which a difference will be regarded as 'statistically significant'.

sense to test the null hypothesis; rather the objective may be to estimate the magnitude of the effect and to do this with some acceptable specified precision.

In trials of new interventions, it is often not known whether there will be any impact at all of the intervention on the outcomes of interest, and what is required is 'proof of concept'. In these circumstances, it may be sufficient to ensure that there will be a good chance of obtaining a significant result if there is indeed an effect of some specified magnitude. It should be emphasized, however, that, if this course is adopted, the estimates obtained may be very imprecise. To illustrate this, suppose it is planned to compare two groups with respect to the mean of some variable, and suppose the true difference between the group means is D. If the trial size is chosen to give 90% power (of obtaining a significant difference with $p < 0.05$ on a two-sided test) if the difference is D, the 95% CI on D is expected to extend roughly from 0.4 D to 1.6 D. This is a wide range and implies that the estimate of the effect of intervention will be imprecise. In many situations, it may be more appropriate to choose the sample size by setting the width of the CI, rather than to rely on power calculations.

2.4 Trials with multiple outcomes

The discussion in Sections 2.1 to 2.3 concerns factors influencing the choice of trial size, with respect to a particular outcome measure. In most trials, several different outcomes are measured. For example, in a trial of the impact of insecticide-treated mosquito-nets on childhood malaria, there may be interest in the effects of the intervention on deaths, deaths attributable to malaria, episodes of clinical malaria, spleen sizes at the end of the malaria season, PCVs at the end of the malaria season, and possibly other measures.

Chapter 12, Section 2 highlights the importance of defining in advance the *primary* outcome and a limited number of *secondary* outcomes of a trial. In order to decide on the trial size, the investigator should first focus attention on the primary outcome, as results for this outcome will be given the most weight when reporting the trial findings, and it is essential that the trial is able to provide adequate results for this outcome. The methods of this chapter can then be used to calculate the required trial size for the primary outcome and each of the secondary outcomes.

Ideally, the outcome that results in the largest trial size would be used to determine the size, as then, for other outcomes, it would be known that better than the required precision or power would be achieved. It is often found, however, that one or more of the outcomes would require a trial too large for the resources that are likely to be available. For example, detecting changes in mortality, or cause-specific mortality, often requires very large trials. In these circumstances, it may be decided to design the trial to be able to detect an impact on morbidity and accept that it is unlikely to be able to generate conclusive findings about the effect on mortality. It is important to point out, however, that, if a trial shows that an intervention has an impact on morbidity, it may be regarded as unethical to undertake a further, larger trial to assess the impact on mortality. For this reason, it is generally advisable to ensure that trials are conducted at an early stage in which the outcome of greatest public health importance is the endpoint around which the trial is planned. This issue is discussed further in Chapter 6.

Sometimes, different trial sizes may be used for different outcomes. For example, it might be possible to design a trial in such a way that a large sample of participants are monitored for mortality, say by annual surveys, and only a proportion of participants are monitored for morbidity, say by weekly visits.

If it is not feasible to design the trial to achieve adequate power or precision for the primary outcome, the trial should either be abandoned or a different primary outcome should be adopted.

2.5 **Practical constraints**

In practice, statistical considerations are not the only factors that need to be taken into account in planning the size of an investigation. Resources, in terms of staff, vehicles, laboratory capacity, time, or money, may limit the potential size of a trial, and it is often necessary to compromise between the results of the trial size computations and what can be managed with the available resources. Trying to do a trial that is beyond the capacity of the available resources is likely to be unfruitful, as data quality is likely to suffer and the results may be subject to serious bias, or the trial may even collapse completely, wasting the effort and money that have already been expended. If calculations indicate that a trial of manageable size will yield power and/or precision that is unacceptably low, it is probably better not to conduct the trial at all.

A useful approach to examine the trade-off between trial size (and thus cost) and power is to construct *power curves* for one or two of the key outcome variables. Power curves show how power varies with trial size for different values of the effect measure. Figure 5.1 shows power curves for malaria deaths in the mosquito-net trial discussed in Section 2.4, assuming that equal numbers of children are to be allocated to the intervention and control groups and statistical significance is to be based on a two-sided test

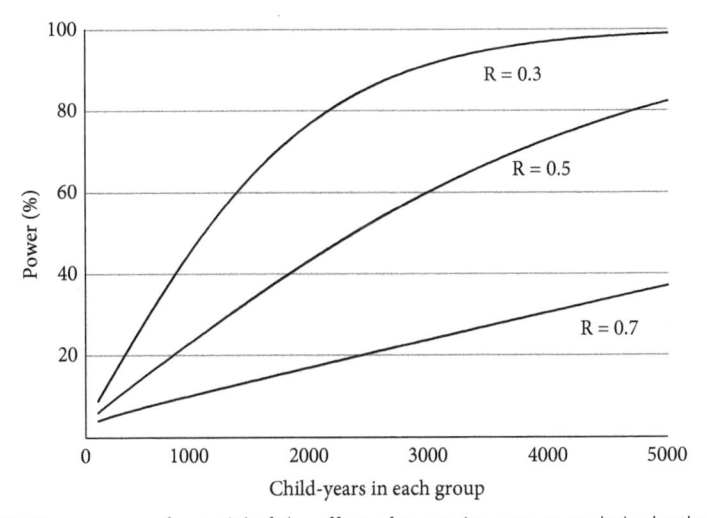

Figure 5.1 Power curves for a trial of the effect of mosquito-nets on malaria deaths.

Malaria death rate in the control group assumed to be 10/1000/year. R, relative rate in the intervention group. Assumes equal-sized groups, two-sided test, and significance $p < 0.05$.

at the 5% level. *R* represents the rate ratio of malaria deaths in the intervention group, compared to the control group, so that $R = 0.3$ represents a reduction in the death rate of 70%. The assumptions used to construct these curves are described in Section 4. The curves indicate that, if 1000 children were followed for 1 year in each group (making 2000 children in all), there would be about a one in two chance of obtaining a significant result (power = 50%), even if the reduction in the death rate was as high as 70%. A trial five times as large as this would have a good chance (about 80%) of detecting a reduction in the death rate of 50% or more but would be inadequate (about 40%) to detect a 30% reduction in the death rate.

3 Size to give adequate precision

This section describes how the trial size is determined if the aim is to obtain an estimate of the outcome of an intervention with a specified level of precision. The simplest case to consider is where just two groups of about the same size are to be compared (for example, the outcome of an intervention compared with that of a control group, or the comparison of outcomes of two interventions). More complex designs are discussed in Section 5. The methodology varies according to the type of outcome measure; the comparison of proportions, incidence rates, and means are considered in Sections 3.1 to 3.3.

3.1 Comparison of proportions

In this section, outcomes are considered that are *binary* (yes or no) variables. This includes cumulative incidence or *risk*, for example, the proportion of children experiencing at least one episode of clinical malaria during the follow-up period. It also includes examination of the *prevalence* of some characteristic, for example, the presence of a palpable spleen in a survey conducted at the end of the trial.

Suppose the true proportions in groups 1 and 2 are p_1 and p_2, respectively, giving a risk ratio (relative risk) of $R = p_1/p_2$. The approximate 95% CI for *R* extends from R/f to Rf where, in this case, the factor *f* is given by:

$$f = \exp\{1.96\sqrt{[(1-p_1)/(np_1)+(1-p_2)/(np_2)]}\}$$

where *n* is the number of children in each group, and *f* is commonly called the *error factor*.

The required value of *f* is chosen, and rough estimates are made of the values of p_2 and *R* to enable the number required in each group *n* to be calculated as:

$$n = (1.96/\log_e f)^2 + \{[(R+1)/(Rp_2)]-2\}$$

where $\log_e f$ is the *natural logarithm* of *f*.

For example, in the mosquito-net trial, one of the outcomes of interest is the prevalence of splenomegaly (the proportion of children with enlarged spleens) at the end of the trial. Prior data from the trial area suggest that, in the control group, a prevalence of approximately 40% would be expected. Suppose the intervention is expected to roughly halve the prevalence, so that $R = 0.5$, and an estimate of *R* is wanted to within about ±0.15. This suggests setting f to about 1.3 (because then the upper 95% confidence limit on R is $Rf = 0.5 \times 1.3 = 0.65$, which is 0.15 above $R(=0.5)$), and thus $n = (1.96/\log_e 1.3)^2 \{[1.5/(0.5 \times 0.4)] - 2\} = 307$. so that around 300 children would need to be studied in each group.

3.2 Comparison of incidence rates

Suppose a comparison of two groups is required, with respect to the rate of occurrence of some defined event over the trial period. Suppose the true incidence rates are r_1 and r_2 in groups 1 and 2, respectively, where each rate represents the number of events per person-year of observation. The rate ratio R (sometimes called incorrectly the relative risk, instead of the relative rate) of the incidence rate in group 1, compared to the incidence rate in group 2, is given by $R = r_1/r_2$ (see Chapter 21, Section 5 for methods of analysis for the comparison of rates). If the total follow-up time for those in each group is y years (for example, y persons are each followed for 1 year, or $y/2$ are each followed for 2 years), each group is said to experience y person-years of observation. The expected numbers of events in the two groups will be $e_1 = yr_1$ and $e_2 = yr_2$, respectively. When the results are analysed, the approximate 95% CI for R is expected to extend from R/f to Rf where:

$$f = \exp\{1.96\sqrt{[(1/e_1) + (1/e_2)]}\}.$$

To decide on the necessary size of the trial, make a rough estimate of the likely value of R, select the precision that is required by specifying a value for f, the error factor, and calculate:

$$e_2 = (1.96/\log_e f)^2 [(R+1)/R].$$

The trial size is then fixed so that the expected number of events in group 2 during the trial period is equal to the calculated value e_2. The expected number of events in group 1 will be Re_2.

It should be noted that these methods are only appropriate in the situation where each individual can experience only one event during the trial period or where the number of individuals experiencing multiple events is very small. If most individuals experience at least one event and many experience two or more, it is preferable to define a *quantitative* outcome for each individual, representing the number of events experienced during the trial period, and to use the methods described in Section 3.3.

Example: in the mosquito-net trial, suppose the trial groups are to consist of children aged 0–4 years and that the death rate associated with malaria in the trial area for that age group is estimated to be roughly 10 per 1000 child-years. If group 1 is the intervention group (treated bed-nets) and group 2 is the control group (no protection), R represents the ratio of the intervention and control death rates. Suppose R is expected to be about 0.4, corresponding to a reduction in the death rate of 60%. Suppose also that f is selected to be equal to 1.25, so that the 95% CI for R is expected to extend from $(0.4/1.25 = 0.32)$ to $(0.4 \times 1.25 = 0.50)$. In other words, it is desired to estimate the protective efficacy to within about 10% of the true value (i.e. 50–70% around the estimated efficacy of 60%). Then:

$$e_2 = [1.96/\log_e(1.25)]^2 (1.4/0.4) = 270.$$

To expect 270 deaths in the control group, it would be necessary to observe an estimated 27 000 child-years $[= 270/(10/1000)]$. This could be achieved by following 54 000 children for 6 months, or 27 000 children for 1 year, or 13 500 for 2 years, and so on, assuming an expected death rate of ten per 1000 child-years in each of these scenarios. The magnitude of the required trial size (27 000 child-years of observation *in each group*) illustrates that, when rare events are being studied, very large samples are needed to obtain a precise estimate of the impact of an intervention.

3.3 Comparison of means

Quantitative outcomes may be analysed by comparing the means of the relevant variable in the intervention and control groups. This could be the mean of the values recorded at a cross-sectional survey, for example, the mean weight of children in the trial at the end of the trial. Alternatively, it could be the mean of the changes recorded between baseline and follow-up surveys, for example, the mean change in weight (or weight velocity, i.e. the change in weight divided by the time between the two measurements) among the children in the trial.

Suppose the true means in groups 1 and 2 are μ_1 and μ_2. These would generally be compared in terms of the difference in the means, $D = \mu_1 - \mu_2$. The 95% CI for D is given by $D \pm f$, where:

$$f = 1.96\sqrt{\left[\left(\sigma_1^2 + \sigma_2^2/n\right)\right]}$$

where σ_1 and σ_2 are the standard deviations of the outcome variable in the two groups.

An acceptable value of f is chosen; values of σ_1 and σ_2 are selected, and the required number in each group is calculated as:

$$n = (1.96/f)^2 \left(\sigma_1^2 + \sigma_2^2\right).$$

An estimate of the standard deviation of the outcome variable is often available from other studies. It is usually reasonable to assume that the standard deviation will be roughly similar in the two trial groups. If no other estimate is available, a rough approximation can be obtained by taking one-quarter of the likely range of the variable.

Example: In the mosquito-net trial, another outcome of interest is the PCV, or haematocrit, measured in blood samples taken from the children at the end of the trial. From previous data, the mean PCV in the control group is expected to be about 33.0, with a standard deviation of about 5.0 (the normal range is about 33 ± 10, and it has been assumed that the normal range covers four standard deviations (i.e. ± 2). An increase in mean PCV in the intervention group of between 2.0 and 3.0 is expected, and it is required to estimate the difference D between the two groups to within about 0.5, so that $f = 0.5$. Assuming that the standard deviation is about 5.0 in both groups:

$$n = (1.96/0.5)^2(5.0^2 + 5.0^2) = 768.$$

4 Size to give adequate power

The alternative approach to setting trial size is based upon selecting the trial size to achieve a specified *power*. In order to do this, the following must be specified:

1. What size of difference, D, between the two groups would be of clinical or public health importance? The trial size will be chosen so it would have a good chance of detecting this size of true difference, i.e. there would be a good chance of obtaining a statistically significant result, thus concluding that there is a real difference between the two trial arms. *D* is the *true* difference between the two groups, not the estimated difference as measured in the trial. Very small differences are generally of no public health importance, and it would not be of concern if they were not detected in the trial. The general principle, in most cases, is to choose *D* to be the *minimum difference* which would be of public health relevance and therefore be important to detect in a trial. Note that 'detecting' *D* means that a significant difference is obtained, indicating that there is some difference between the two groups. This does not mean that the difference is estimated precisely. To ensure a precise estimate is obtained, the approach of Section 3 should be used.

2. Having specified *D*, the investigators must decide how confident they wish to be of obtaining a significant result if this were the true difference between the groups. In other words, the power is set for this value of *D*. Note that, if the true difference between the groups is actually larger than *D*, the power of the trial will be larger than the value set. The required power is specified in the calculations by choosing the corresponding value of z_2, as shown in Table 5.1. Commonly chosen values for the power are 80%, 90%, and 95%, the corresponding values of z_2 being 0.84, 1.28, and 1.64. It would generally be regarded as unsatisfactory to proceed with a trial with a power of less than 70% for the primary outcome, because that means that one would have a more than 30% chance of 'missing' a true difference of *D*.

3. The significance level must also be specified for the comparison of the two groups under study. This is entered into the calculations in terms of the parameter z_1. The commonest choice for the required p-value is 0.05, corresponding to a z_1 of 1.96. Alternative values might be 0.01 or 0.001, corresponding to z_1 values of 2.58 or 3.29, respectively. It is assumed throughout this chapter that *two-sided* significance tests are to be used (see Chapter 21, Section 2.3). A significance level of 0.05 is assumed in the numerical examples, unless otherwise stated.

4. In addition, certain additional information must be specified, which varies according to the type of measure being examined. This may be a rough estimate of the rates or proportions that are expected, or an estimate of the standard deviation for a quantitative variable. Note that, if these quantities were known exactly, no trial would be needed! Only rough estimates are required.

Table 5.1 Relationship between z_2 and % power (numbers in the body of the table show power corresponding to each value of z_2)

z_2	\multicolumn{10}{c}{First decimal place of z_2}
	0.0	0.1	0.2	0.3	0.4	0.5	0.6	0.7	0.8	0.9
−3.0	0.1	0.1	0.1	0.0	0.0	0.0	0.0	0.0	0.0	0.0
−2.0	2.3	1.8	1.4	1.1	0.8	0.6	0.5	0.3	0.3	0.2
−1.0	15.9	13.6	11.5	9.7	8.1	6.7	5.5	4.5	3.6	2.9
−0.0	50.0	46.0	42.1	38.2	34.5	30.9	27.4	24.2	21.2	18.4
+0.0	50.0	54.0	57.9	61.8	65.5	69.1	72.6	75.8	78.8	81.6
+1.0	84.1	86.4	88.5	90.3	91.9	93.3	94.5	95.5	96.4	97.1
+2.0	97.7	98.2	98.6	98.9	99.2	99.4	99.5	99.7	99.7	99.8
+3.0	99.9	99.9	99.9	100.0	100.0	100.0	100.0	100.0	100.0	100.0

Note: for example, $z_2 = -0.7$ corresponds to a power of 24.2%.

Having specified these values, the formulae or tables given in Sections 4.1 to 4.3 can be used to calculate the required trial size.

It is often useful, however, to proceed in the opposite direction, i.e. to explore the power that would be achieved for a range of possible trial sizes and for a range of possible values of the true difference D. This enables the construction of *power curves*, as illustrated in Figure 5.1. Formulae for this approach are also given in Sections 4.1 to 4.3.

4.1 Comparison of proportions

The trial size required in each group to detect a specified difference $D = p_1 - p_2$, with power specified by z_2 and significance level specified by z_1, is given by:

$$n = [(z_1 + z_2)^2 \, 2p(1-p)] / (p_1 - p_2)^2$$

where p is the average of p_1 and p_2.

For 90% power and significance at $p < 0.05$, this simplifies to:

$$n = [21 p(1-p)] / (p_1 - p_2)^2.$$

Table 5.2 shows the required trial size for a range of values of p_1 and p_2 for 80%, 90%, or 95% power.

To calculate the power of a trial of specified size, calculate as follows, and refer the value of z_2 to Table 5.1.

$$z_2 = \left(\sqrt{\{n / [2p(1-p)]\}}\right)(|p_1 - p_2|) - z_1.$$

Example: assume that the spleen rate in the control group of the mosquito-net trial is around 40%. To have very high power (say 95%) of detecting a significant effect if the

Table 5.2 Sample size requirements for comparison of proportions

Smaller prop. p_1	\multicolumn{11}{c}{Difference $D = p_2 - p_1$}
	0.05	0.10	0.15	0.20	0.25	0.30	0.35	0.40	0.45	0.50	0.55	0.60
0.05	435	141	76	50	36	28	22	18	15	13	11	10
	583	189	102	67	48	37	30	25	21	18	15	13
	719	233	126	83	60	46	37	30	26	22	19	16
0.10	686	200	101	63	44	33	26	21	17	14	12	10
	919	268	135	84	59	44	34	28	23	19	16	14
	1134	330	166	104	72	54	42	34	28	24	20	17
0.15	906	251	122	74	50	37	28	22	18	15	13	10
	1212	336	163	98	67	49	38	30	24	20	17	14
	1497	415	201	122	83	60	46	37	30	25	21	18
0.20	1094	294	139	82	55	40	30	24	19	16	13	11
	1464	394	186	110	74	53	40	31	25	21	17	15
	1808	486	230	136	91	66	50	39	31	26	21	18
0.25	1250	329	153	89	59	42	31	24	19	16	13	11
	1674	441	205	119	79	56	42	32	26	21	17	14
	2067	544	253	147	97	69	52	40	32	26	21	18
0.30	1376	357	163	94	61	43	32	24	19	16	13	10
	1842	478	219	126	82	58	43	33	26	21	17	14
	2274	590	270	156	101	71	53	40	32	26	21	17
0.35	1470	376	170	97	63	44	32	24	19	15	12	10
	1968	504	228	130	84	58	43	32	25	20	16	13
	2430	622	282	160	103	72	53	40	31	25	20	16
0.40	1533	388	174	98	63	43	31	24	18	14	11	
	2052	520	233	131	84	58	42	31	24	19	15	
	2534	642	287	162	103	71	52	39	30	24	19	
0.45	1564	392	174	97	61	42	30	22	17	13		
	2094	525	233	130	82	56	40	30	23	18		
	2586	648	287	160	101	69	50	37	28	22		
0.50	1564	388	170	94	59	40	28	21	15			
	2094	520	228	126	79	53	38	28	21			
	2586	642	282	156	97	66	46	34	26			
0.55	1533	376	163	89	55	37	26	18				
	2052	504	219	119	74	49	34	25				
	2534	622	270	147	91	60	42	30				

continued

CHAPTER 5: TRIAL SIZE

Table 5.2 (continued) Sample size requirements for comparison of proportions

Smaller prop. p_1	\multicolumn{12}{c	}{Difference $D = p_2 - p_1$}
	0.05	0.10	0.15	0.20	0.25	0.30	0.35	0.40	0.45	0.50	0.55	0.60
0.60	1470	357	153	82	50	33	22					
	1968	478	205	110	67	44	30					
	2430	590	253	136	83	54	37					
0.65	1376	329	139	73	44	28						
	1842	441	186	98	59	37						
	2274	544	230	121	72	46						
0.70	1250	294	122	63	36							
	1674	394	163	84	48							
	2067	486	201	104	60							
0.75	1094	251	101	50								
	1464	336	135	67								
	1808	415	166	83								
0.80	906	200	76									
	1212	268	102									
	1497	330	126									
0.85	686	141										
	919	189										
	1134	233										
0.90	435											
	583											
	719											

Shown in the body of the table are the sample sizes required in each group to give the specified power.*

* Upper figure: power, 80%; middle figure: power, 90%; lower figure: power, 95%. Using a two-sided significance test with $p < 0.05$. The two groups are assumed to be of equal size.

intervention reduces the spleen rate to 30% (so that $p = 0.35$), the number of children required in each group is given by:

$$n = \left[(1.96 + 1.64)^2 (2 \times 0.35 \times 0.65)\right] / (0.3 - 0.4)^2 = 590.$$

If the true risk ratio is R and we wish to power the trial, such that the lower confidence limit on the risk ratio will be greater than or equal to R_L, where R_L is the lowest acceptable efficacy (say, for whether or not to implement the intervention in a public health system, i.e. we need to be sure that the efficacy is at least R_L), the required sample size is:

$$n = (z_1 + z_2)^2 \left[(1 - p_1)/(p_1) + (1 - p_2)/(p_2)\right] / \left[\log_e(R/R_L)\right]^2.$$

4.2 Comparison of incidence rates

For a specified difference $D = r_1 - r_2$ and values of z_1 and z_2, representing the required significance level and power, the required number of person-years in each group is given by:

$$y = \left[(z_1 + z_2)^2 (r_1 + r_2)\right] / (r_1 - r_2)^2$$

where r_1 and r_2 are the expected rates per person-year in the two groups. A rough estimate of the average of the two rates is therefore required, i.e. $\left[(r_1 + r_2)/2\right]$. For 90% power and significance at $p < 0.05$, this formula simplifies to:

$$y = \left[10.5(r_1 + r_2)\right] / (r_1 - r_2)^2.$$

An alternative, but equivalent, formula gives the number of events required in group 2, the control group, in terms of the rate ratio R, for which the specified power is required:

$$e_2 = \left[(z_1 + z_2)^2 (1 + R)\right] / (1 - R)^2.$$

This formula was used to construct Table 5.3, which shows the number of events needed in group 2 to detect a rate ratio of R with 80%, 90%, or 95% power. The total number of events needed in both groups can be calculated as $e_2(1 + R)$. Since this can be computed without specifying the assumed rates in the two trial groups, this provides a particularly helpful approach when the rates are uncertain. Thus, in an *endpoint-driven trial*, we can specify the number of events that need to be observed to reach the required power, after which recruitment or follow-up may be terminated.

To calculate the power for a given trial size, compute:

$$z_2 = \left\{\sqrt{\left[n/(r_1 + r_2)\right]}\right\} \left(|r_1 - r_2|\right) - z_1$$

where $|r_1 - r_2|$ is the absolute value of the difference between the two rates.

Refer the resulting value of z_2 to Table 5.1 to determine the power of the trial.

Example: Assume, in the mosquito-net trial, that the death rate from malaria in the control group is 10/1000 child-years, so that $r_2 = 0.010$. Eighty per cent power is wanted to detect a significant effect if the true rate in children with bed-nets is reduced by 70% to $r_1 = 0.003$. The number of child-years of observation required in each group is given by:

$$y = \left[(1.96 + 0.84)^2 (0.003 + 0.010)\right] / (-0.007)^2 = 2080.$$

The power curves shown in Figure 5.1 were constructed using the same assumption concerning the death rate in controls. For example, with $y = 2000$ and a rate ratio of $R = 0.7$ (corresponding to a death rate of 7 per 1000 child-years in the intervention group), giving a power of 18% (Table 5.1):

$$z_2 = \left\{\sqrt{\left[2000/(0.007 + 0.010)\right]}\right\} \left(|0.007 - 0.010|\right) - 1.96 = -0.93.$$

These formulae are used to ensure that there is a high probability of rejecting the null hypothesis if the true effect is of the assumed size. However, this may still mean

Table 5.3 Sample size requirements for comparison of rates

Relative rate R*	Expected events in group 2 to give[+]		
	80% power	90% power	95% power
0.1	10.6	14.3	17.6
0.2	14.7	19.7	24.3
0.3	20.8	27.9	34.4
0.4	30.5	40.8	50.4
0.5	47.0	63.0	77.8
0.6	78.4	105.0	129.6
0.7	148.1	198.3	244.8
0.8	352.8	472.4	583.2
0.9	1489.6	1994.5	2462.4
1.1	1646.4	2204.5	2721.6
1.2	431.2	577.4	712.8
1.4	117.6	157.5	194.4
1.6	56.6	75.8	93.6
1.8	34.3	45.9	56.7
2.0	23.5	31.5	38.9
2.5	12.2	16.3	20.2
3.0	7.8	10.5	13.0
5.0	2.9	3.9	4.9
10.0	1.1	1.4	1.8

Numbers in the body of the table are expected number of events required in group 2 to give specified power if relative rate in group 1 is R.
* R, ratio of incidence rate in group 1 to incidence rate in group 2.
[+] Using a two-sided significance test with $P < 0.05$. The two groups are assumed to be of equal size.

that the lower confidence limit for the effect size is close to the null, and this may provide insufficient evidence to recommend widespread adoption of the intervention. A larger sample size will be needed to ensure that the lower confidence limit exceeds a given value.

Suppose the assumed value of the rate ratio is R and that we wish to power the trial so that there is a high probability that the CI excludes a value R_L corresponding to the lower limit of efficacy desired. Then the required sample size is given by the formula:

$$y = (z_1 + z_2)^2 (1/r_1 + 1/r_2) / [\log_e(R/R_L)]^2.$$

Example: In the mosquito-net trial, we found that 2080 child-years were required in each trial group to reject the null hypothesis with 80% power if the true rate ratio R was

0.3, corresponding to an efficacy of 70%. Now suppose we wish to ensure that there is an 80% chance that the lower 95% CI for the efficacy exceeds 30%, corresponding to $R_L = 0.7$. Applying the formula, we obtain the following, demonstrating the substantial increase in sample size that this would necessitate:

$$y = (1.96 + 0.84)^2 (1/0.010 + 1/0.003) / [\log_e (0.3/0.7)]^2 = 4732.$$

4.3 Comparison of means

The trial size required in each group to detect a specified difference $D = \mu_1 - \mu_2$, with power specified by z_2 and the significance level specified by z_1, is given by:

$$n = [(z_1 + z_2)^2 (\sigma_1^2 + \sigma_2^2)] / (\mu_1 - \mu_2)^2$$

where σ_1 and σ_2 are the standard deviations of the outcome variable in groups 1 and 2, respectively.

For 90% power and significance at $p < 0.05$, this simplifies to:

$$n = 10.5 (\sigma_1^2 + \sigma_2^2) / (\mu_1 - \mu_2)^2.$$

To calculate the power of a trial of specified size, calculate the following, and refer the value of z_2 to Table 5.1:

$$z_2 = \{\sqrt{[n / (\sigma_1^2 + \sigma_2^2)]}\} (|\mu_1 - \mu_2|) - z_1.$$

Estimates of σ_1 and σ_2 may be obtained from previous studies or from a pilot study. If appropriate values cannot be determined, an alternative is to dichotomize the continuous outcome variable and use the sample size formulae for comparison of proportions given in Section 4.1. This will give a conservative estimate of sample size, as it ignores some of the information, but will ensure an adequate sample size in the face of uncertainty regarding the standard deviations.

Example: In the mosquito-net trial, the mean PCV in the control group at the end of the trial is expected to be 33.0, with a standard deviation of 5.0. To have 90% power of detecting a significant effect if the intervention increases the mean PCV by 1.5, the number of children required in each group is given by:

$$n = [(1.96 + 1.28)^2 (5.0^2 + 5.0^2)] / (1.5)^2 = 233.$$

Suppose it turns out that only 150 children are available for study in each group. The power in these circumstances is given by the following, corresponding to a power of about 74%:

$$z_2 = \{\sqrt{[150 / (5.0^2 + 5.0^2)]}\} (|1.5|) - 1.96 = 0.64.$$

A summary of the various formulae that have been given for calculating the trial size requirements for the comparison of two groups of equal size is given in Table 5.4.

Table 5.4 Summary of formulae for calculating trial size requirements for comparison of two groups of equal size

Type of outcome	Formula	Notation	Section in text
A: Choosing trial size to achieve adequate precision			
Proportions:	$n = (1.96/\log_e f)^2 \{[(R+1)/(Rp_2)] - 2\}$	n = number in each group	3.1
		R = prop. in group 1/prop. in group 2	
		Gives 95% CI from R/f to Rf	
Rates:	$e_2 = (1.96/\log_e f)^2 [(R+1)/R]$	e_2 = expected events in group 2	3.2
		R = rate in group 1/rate in group 2	
		Gives 95% CI from R/f to Rf	
Means:	$n = (1.96/f)^2 (\sigma_1^2 + \sigma_2^2)$	n = number in each group	3.3
		σ_i = SD in group i	
		D = mean in group 1 − mean in group 2	
		Gives 95% CI of $D \pm f$	
B: Choosing trial size to achieve adequate power			
Proportions:	$n = [(z_1 + z_2)^2 2p(1-p)]/(p_1 - p_2)^2$	n = number in each group	4.1
		p_i = proportion. in group i	
		p = average of p_1 and p_2	
Rates:	$y = [(z_1 + z_2)^2 (r_1 + r_2)]/(r_1 - r_2)^2$	y = person-years in each group	4.2
		r_i = rate in group i	
Means:	$n = [(z_1 + z_2)^2 (\sigma_1^2 + \sigma_2^2)]/(\mu_1 - \mu_2)^2$	n = number in each group	4.3
		σ_i = SD in group i	
		μ_i = mean in group i	

$z_1 = 1.96$ for significance at $p < 0.05$.
Power 80%, 90%, 95%
$z_2 = 0.84, 1.28, 1.64$.

5 More complex designs

5.1 Two groups of unequal size

Sections 3 and 4 considered the simplest situation where the two groups to be compared are of equal size. Sometimes, there may be reasons for wishing to allocate more individuals to one group than to the other. For example, if an experimental drug is very expensive, it may be desired to minimize the number of patients allocated to the

Table 5.5 Trial size necessary to achieve approximately the same power in a trial with two groups, one of which contains k times as many individuals as the other

k	n_1	n_2	$n_1 + n_2$
1	n	n	$2n$
2	$0.75n$	$1.5n$	$2.25n$
3	$0.67n$	$2.0n$	$2.67n$
4	$0.62n$	$2.5n$	$3.12n$
5	$0.60n$	$3.0n$	$3.60n$
10	$0.55n$	$5.5n$	$6.05n$
100	$0.50n$	$50.0n$	$50.50n$

drug, and so the trial may be arranged so that there are two or three patients given the old drug for every patient given the new drug. In order to maintain the same power as in the equal allocation scheme, a larger total trial size will be needed, but the number given the new drug will be smaller. Conversely, in a trial of a new vaccine, it may be decided to allocate twice as many participants to the vaccinated group as are included in the placebo group, in order to increase the size of the safety database for the new vaccine, before it goes into public health programmes.

Let the size of the smaller of the two groups be n_1, and suppose the ratio of the two sample sizes to be k, so that there will be kn_1 individuals in the other group ($k > 1$). Then, to achieve approximately the same power and precision as in a trial with an equal number n in each group, n_1 should be chosen as:

$$n_1 = n(k+1)/(2k).$$

Examples are shown in Table 5.5 for various values of k. Notice that the number allocated to the smaller group can never be reduced below half the number required with equal groups. Little is gained by increasing k beyond 3 or 4, since, beyond this point, even a substantial increase in n_2 achieves only a small reduction in n_1.

5.2 Comparison of more than two groups

Field trials comparing two groups (for example, intervention and control, or treatment A and treatment B) are by far the commonest. However, in some trials, three or more groups may be compared. For example, in a trial of a new vaccine, there may be four trial groups receiving different doses of the vaccine. It is unusual for field trials to have more than four groups, because of logistical constraints or trial size limitations.

It is suggested that, in designing a trial with three or more groups, the investigator should decide which pair-wise comparisons between groups are of central interest. The methods of Sections 3 and 4 can then be used to decide on the trial size required in each group. Where there is one control group for comparison with several intervention groups, it is likely that the main pair-wise comparisons will be between each intervention group and the control group. Note, however, that direct comparisons between the intervention groups may then be inadequately powered, since, if each of the interventions has some effect, differences between the intervention groups may be smaller than when each is compared with the control group.

5.3 Factorial designs

As discussed in Chapter 4, Section 3.2, some trials are designed to look simultaneously at the effects of two interventions, using a *factorial design*. In a 2×2 factorial trial of two interventions A and B, for example, participants are randomly allocated between four trial groups receiving A only, B only, both A and B, or a control group receiving neither intervention. If the effects of A and B can be assumed independent, so that the effect of A is the same in the presence or absence of B and vice versa, then this trial design allows us to measure the effects of the two interventions for roughly the price of a single two-group trial measuring the effect of one intervention.

Under these conditions of independence, the main change to the calculation of sample size for a 2×2 factorial trial is that the expected outcome in the intervention and control groups for intervention A has to be adjusted for the expected effect of intervention B. This is explained with an example.

For example, suppose we are interested in the effects of iron supplements (intervention A) and anti-malarial prophylaxis (intervention B) on anaemia during pregnancy. Suppose that the prevalence of anaemia in the control group that receives neither A nor B is expected to be 30%, that each intervention is expected to reduce the prevalence proportionally by 20%, and that these effects are independent. Then the expected prevalences in the four arms of the trial will be: control—30%; A only—24%; B only—24%; A+B —19.2%. In this factorial trial, the effect of intervention A will be estimated by comparing the prevalence between groups A+B and B only, and between group A only and the control group. The overall prevalence in the two groups given intervention A will be $21.6\%[=(24+19.2)/2]$, and in the two groups not given A $27\%[=(30+24)/2]$. Since the difference in prevalences is slightly smaller than in a simple two-group trial, the total sample size will be somewhat larger for the factorial design.

In some factorial trials, we may wish to look explicitly at whether the effects of the two interventions are independent. This requires a test for *interaction* or *effect modification*, since we are interested in whether the effect of A, for example, differs according to the presence or absence of B. Testing for interaction generally requires a much larger sample size than a simple comparison of two groups. As a rough guideline, the total sample size for a 2×2 factorial trial would need to be multiplied by at least four to detect a substantial interaction (of similar size to the main effects of the interventions) between the effects of two interventions.

5.4 Equivalence and non-inferiority trials

In most field trials, the objective is to determine whether a new intervention is *superior* to a control intervention, for example, an existing intervention. In some cases, however, we may wish to demonstrate that a new intervention is *equivalent*, or at least *not inferior*, to an existing intervention. For example, suppose the current treatment for some condition is known to be highly effective, but it is also expensive and has some unpleasant side effects. Now suppose that a new treatment has been developed which is less costly and has fewer side effects. This would probably be considered for implementation, as long as it is as effective as the old treatment. In this case, we may decide to conduct an *equivalence trial* aimed at determining whether the two treatments have similar efficacy.

For a full discussion of such trials, the reader is referred to Blackwelder (1982) or Wang and Bakhai (2006). However, a simple example is given to illustrate the required sample size calculations.

Example: Suppose that the current treatment for TB has a cure rate of around 90% but requires a prolonged course of treatment. A new shorter-course regimen has been developed which would have advantages, in terms of cost, convenience, and adherence. We wish to carry out a trial to determine whether the cure rate for the short-course regimen is *equivalent* to that of the current regimen. We would usually do this by defining a lower limit for the cure rate, below which we would no longer consider the treatments to be 'equivalent'. If we set this at 85%, the trial would need to be powered to demonstrate that the difference in cure rates is no more than 5%. The null hypothesis is now that the new treatment is *inferior* to the old treatment, and we power the trial to reject this null hypothesis and declare equivalence of the two treatments if the new treatment has a cure rate that is not inferior to the standard treatment by more than the specified 5%.

Modifying the first equation in Section 4.1 appropriately, we need n patients in each group, where:

$$n = \left[(z_1 + z_2)^2 \, 2p(1-p)\right] / D^2.$$

In this equation, p is the expected cure rate of 90% in both groups, assuming equivalence, and D is the acceptable margin of inferiority, which is 5% in this example. Thus, for 90% power and a two-sided significance test with p = 0.05, we have:

$$n = \left[(1.96 + 1.28)^2 \times 2 \times 0.90 \times 0.10\right] / 0.05^2 = 756.$$

In general, large sample sizes are needed to test equivalence.

6 Interventions allocated to groups

The methods described in Sections 3 to 5 all assume that individuals are to be the units of allocation. In other words, the trial groups will be constructed effectively by making a complete list of the individuals available for the trial and randomly selecting which individuals are to be allocated to each trial group. As explained in Chapter 4, Section 4, however, many field trials are not organized in this way. Instead, groups of individuals are allocated to the interventions under study. These groups are often called *clusters* and may correspond to communities, for example, villages, hamlets, or defined sectors of an urban area; institutions such as schools or workplaces; or patients attending a particular health facility.

Trials in which communities or other types of cluster are randomly allocated to the different arms of the trial are known as *cluster randomized trials*, and sample size calculations for such trials are presented in Section 6.1. *Stepped wedge trials* are a modified form of cluster randomized trial and are discussed in Section 6.2.

6.1 Cluster randomized trials

If clusters are randomly allocated to the different trial arms, the cluster should also be used as the unit of analysis, even though assessments of outcome are made on individuals within clusters (see Chapter 21, Section 8). For example, suppose the mosquito-net trial is to be conducted as follows. A number of villages (say 20) are to be randomly divided into two equal-sized groups. In the ten villages in the first group, the entire population of each village will be given mosquito-nets, while the second group of ten villages will serve as controls. The analysis of the impact of mosquito-nets on the incidence of clinical malaria would be made by calculating the (age-adjusted) incidence rate in each village and comparing the ten rates for the intervention villages with the ten rates for the control villages. This would be achieved by treating the (age-adjusted) rate as the quantitative outcome measured for each village and comparing these, using the unpaired t-test or the non-parametric rank sum test (see Chapter 21, Section 8). If analysing proportions, rather than incidence rates, the principle is the same—the (age-adjusted) proportion would be treated as the quantitative outcome for each cluster.

When allocation is by cluster, the trial size formulae have to be adjusted to allow for intrinsic variation between communities. Suppose first that incidence rates in the two groups are to be compared. The required number of clusters c is given by:

$$c = 1 + (z_1 + z_2)^2 \left[(r_1 + r_2)/y + k^2(r_1^2 + r_2^2) \right] / (r_1 - r_2)^2.$$

In this formula, y is the person-years of observation in each cluster, while r_1 and r_2 are the average rates in the intervention and control clusters, respectively. The intrinsic variation between clusters is measured by k, the *coefficient of variation* of the (true) incidence rates among the clusters in each group, and is defined as the standard deviation of the rates divided by the average rate. The value of k is assumed similar in the intervention and control groups, so that the *relative variability* remains the same following intervention.

If proportions are to be compared, the required number of clusters is given by:

$$c = 1 + (z_1 + z_2)^2 \left[2p(1-p)/n + k^2(p_1^2 + p_2^2) \right] / (p_1 - p_2)^2.$$

In this formula, n is the trial size in each community; p_1 and p_2 are the average proportions in the intervention and control groups, respectively; p is the average of p_1 and p_2, and k is the coefficient of variation of the (true) proportions among the clusters in each group.

An estimate of k will sometimes be available from previous data on the same clusters or from a pilot study. If no data are available, it may be necessary to make an arbitrary, but plausible, assumption about the value of k. For example, $k = 0.25$ implies that the true rates in each group vary roughly between $r_i \pm 2kr_i$, i.e. between $0.5r$ and $1.5r$. In general, k is unlikely to exceed 0.5.

Example: Suppose the mosquito-net trial is to be conducted by allocating the intervention at the village level. The incidence rate of clinical malaria among children before intervention is 10 per 1000 child-weeks of observation, and the trial is to be designed to give 90% power if the intervention reduces the incidence rate by 50%. There are about 50 eligible children per village, and it is intended to continue follow-up for 1 year, so that y is approximately 2500 child-weeks. No information is available on between-village variation in incidence rates. Taking , the number of villages required per group is given by the following, so that roughly seven villages would be needed in each group:

$$c = 1 + (1.96 + 1.28)^2 \left[(0.01 + 0.005)/2500 + 0.25^2 (0.01^2 + 0.005^2) \right] / (0.01 - 0.005)^2 = 6.8.$$

Note that this would give a total of 17 500 child-weeks of observation in each group, compared with 6300 child-weeks if individual children were randomized to receive mosquito-nets. Figure 5.2 shows the number of villages required in each group, depending on the child-weeks of observation per village and the value of k.

The effect of group allocation on the total trial size needed will depend on the degree to which individuals within a cluster are more likely to be similar to each other than individuals in a different cluster for the outcome measure in the trial. If there is no heterogeneity between clusters in the outcome of interest, in the sense that the variation between the cluster-specific rates or means is no more than would be expected to occur by chance, due to sampling variations, the total trial size will be approximately the same as if the interventions were allocated to individuals. For most outcomes, however, there will be real differences between clusters, and, in these circumstances, the required trial size will be *greater* than with individual allocation. The ratio of the required trial sizes

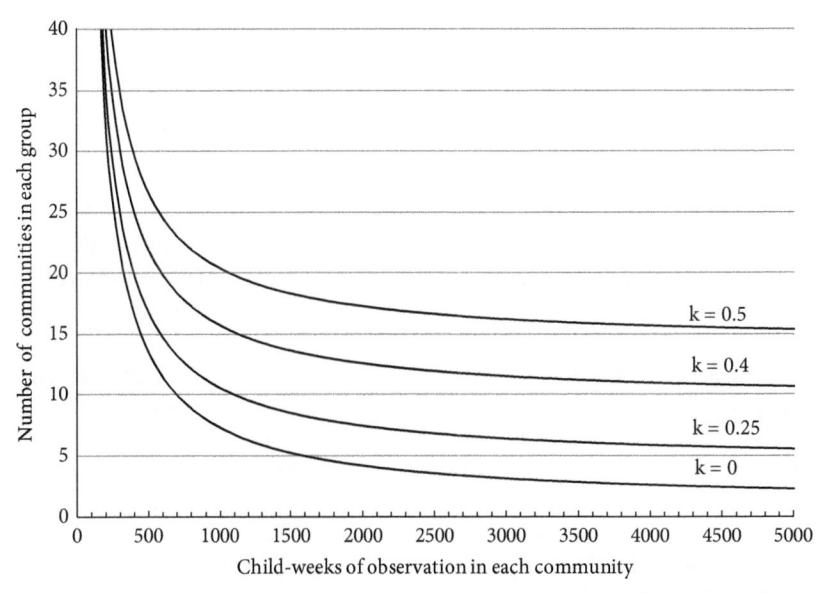

Figure 5.2 Number of communities required in each group in a trial of the effect of mosquito-nets against clinical malaria.

with cluster and individual allocation is sometimes called the *design effect*. Unfortunately, no single value for the design effect can be assumed, as its value depends on the variability of the outcome of interest between clusters and on the sizes of the clusters, and so it is recommended that the required sample size is estimated explicitly.

Note that, even if the calculations suggest that less than four clusters are required in each group, it is preferable to have at least four in each group. With so few units of observation, the use of non-parametric procedures, such as the rank sum test, is generally preferred for the analysis, and a sample size of at least four in each group is needed to have any chance of obtaining a significant result when this test is used.

It may be possible to reduce the required number of communities by adopting a matched design. For example, this can be done by using the baseline study to arrange the clusters into pairs, in which the rates of the outcome of interest are similar, and randomly selecting one member of each pair to receive the intervention. However, it is difficult to quantify the effect of this approach on the number of clusters required. To do this, information is required on the variability of the treatment effect between communities and on the extent to which the baseline data are predictive of the rates that would be observed during the follow-up period in the absence of intervention, and this information is rarely available. With a paired design, at least six clusters are required in each group in order to be able to obtain a significant difference using a non-parametric statistical test.

Further information on sample size calculations for cluster randomized trials is given in Hayes and Bennett (1999) and Hayes and Moulton (2009).

According to the number of child-weeks of observation in each community and the extent of variation in rates of clinical malaria between communities (k is the coefficient of variation of the incidence rates; see text). The average incidence rate of clinical malaria in the absence of the intervention is assumed to be ten per 10 000 weeks of observation, and the trial is required to have 90% power to detect a 50% reduction in the incidence of malaria at the $p < 0.05$ level of statistical significance.

6.2 Stepped wedge trials

The *stepped wedge* design was introduced in Chapter 4, Section 4.3 and is a modification of the cluster randomized trial, in which all clusters commence the trial in the control group. The intervention is then introduced gradually into the clusters in random order, until, at the end of the trial, all the clusters are in the intervention group.

A consequence of the stepped wedge design is that, at most time points during the trial, there will be unequal numbers of clusters in the intervention and control groups. This means that, when secular trends are accounted for by comparing intervention to control groups at each step, a stepped wedge trial can have lower power and precision than a standard cluster randomized trial of the same size, in which the numbers of intervention and control clusters are equal throughout. When there is zero intra-cluster correlation, the trial will need up to 50% more clusters. To adjust for this, the number of clusters has to be multiplied by a correction factor which depends on the number of 'steps' in the stepped wedge design. If there are five steps, the correction factor is 1.3, rising to approximately 1.4 for numbers of steps between 10 and 20. When intra-cluster correlation is large enough, the gain in efficiency that can be made by taking advantage of the pre–post information on each cluster can overtake this factor, making a stepped wedge trial more efficient than a parallel trial. To be conservative, however, it may be best to inflate the number of clusters.

Example: In the mosquito-net trial discussed earlier, the sample size calculation showed that we needed seven clusters in each arm or a total of 14 clusters. If we now propose to carry out this trial using a stepped wedge trial, a conservative correction would be to multiply this number by 1.4, giving 20 clusters. For example, this might be implemented with ten steps over a 5-year period, providing nets to two randomly chosen clusters each half year.

7 Other factors influencing choice of trial size

7.1 Allowance for interim analyses

It is sometimes desirable to incorporate interim analyses into the trial plan, involving review of the results at (say) 6-monthly or annual intervals. If an interim analysis indicates that there is already strong evidence of the superiority of one of the interventions under study, the trial can be terminated in order that participants are no longer subjected to an intervention which is known to be inferior. The incorporation of interim analyses may be particularly valuable if the trial is planned to continue for several years, with the gradual accumulation of cases of the outcome of interest, or if individuals or communities are entered into the trial sequentially.

There are also disadvantages in carrying out interim analyses, however. If the trial is terminated early, because the intervention appears to be beneficial, there may be no opportunity of detecting any long-term effects of the intervention, including how efficacy changes with time or long-term adverse consequences of the intervention. Also, although a significant effect of the intervention may be demonstrated, the precision of the estimate of effect may be too low to be of much value.

If, after careful consideration, it is decided that interim analyses are to be conducted, these need to be planned in the trial design. It is necessary to employ a more stringent significance level for each analysis (interim and final) to maintain the same overall level of significance.

Details of the implications of interim analyses are given by Geller and Pocock (1987). As a rough guide, the following approach is suggested. It is rarely advantageous to plan for more than three or four interim analyses. It is recommended therefore that, for trials planned to continue for 2–4 years, the trial plan should include no more than two interim analyses (plus the final analysis). To compensate for this, the maximum trial size (i.e. the maximum person-years of observation if the trial proceeds to completion) should be increased by about 15%. A stringent significance level of $p = 0.01$ should be used at each interim analysis to decide whether or not the trial should be terminated. This means that, if the trial proceeds to completion, an *unadjusted* $p < 0.04$ would correspond to an *adjusted* $p < 0.05$ if the interim analyses are taken into account, i.e little power has been lost in performing the interim analyses.

7.2 Allowance for losses

Losses to follow-up occur in most longitudinal studies. Individuals may be lost, because they move away from the trial area, they die from some cause unrelated to the outcome of interest, they refuse to continue with the trial, they are away from home at the time of a follow-up survey, or for some other reason.

Losses like these are of concern for two reasons. First, they are a possible source of *bias*, as the individuals who are lost often differ in important respects from those who remain in the trial. Second, they reduce the size of the sample available for analysis, and this decreases the power or precision of the trial.

For these reasons, it is important to make every attempt to reduce the number of losses to a minimum. However, it is rarely possible to avoid losses completely. The extent of the problem will vary, according to circumstances, but, as a rough guide, in a longitudinal trial of a rural community with 2 years of follow-up, losses of around 20% would not be unusual.

The reduced power or precision resulting from losses may be avoided by increasing the initial sample size, in order to compensate for the expected number of losses. For example, if sample size calculations suggest that 240 subjects are required and a 20% loss rate is expected, the sample size should be increased to 300 (because 80% of 300 gives 240). It is important to stress that sample size inflation only deals with the problem due to the reduction in the size of the sample available for analysis; it does not solve any potential problems due to bias. So, even if the sample size has been inflated to allow for losses to follow-up, it is still necessary to strive to minimize losses, in order to avoid bias.

8 The consequences of trials that are too small

The methods outlined in this chapter for selecting an adequate sample size have been available for many years, but it is probably not an exaggeration to state that the majority of intervention trials are much too small. Although there is an increasing awareness of the need to enrol a large enough sample, this chapter is concluded by discussing the consequences of choosing a sample size that is too small.

First, suppose that the intervention under study has little or no effect on the outcome of interest. The difference observed in a trial is likely therefore to be non-significant. However, the width of the CI for the effect measure (for example, the relative risk) will depend on the sample size. If the sample is small, the CI will be very wide, and so, even though it will probably include the null value (a zero difference between the groups, or a relative risk of 1), it will extend to include large values of the effect measure. In other words, the trial will have failed to establish that the intervention is unlikely to have an effect of public health or clinical importance. For example, in the mosquito-net trial, suppose only 50 children were included in each group, and suppose the observed spleen rates in the two groups were identical at 40%, giving an estimated relative risk of $R = 1$. The approximate 95% CI for R would extend from 0.62 to 1.62 (see Section 3.1). A relative risk of 0.62 would imply a very substantial effect, i.e. a reduction in spleen rate from 40% to 25%, and this small trial would be unable to exclude such an effect as being very unlikely. If the sample size in each group were increased to 500, the 95% CI would extend only from 0.86 to 1.16, a much narrower interval.

Suppose that the intervention does have an appreciable effect. A trial that is too small will have low power, i.e. it will have little chance of giving a statistically significant difference. In other words, there is little chance to demonstrate that the intervention has an effect. In the example, if the true effect of the intervention is to reduce the spleen rate from 40% to 25%, a sample size of 50 in each group would give a power of only 36%. A total of 205 children would be needed in each group to give 90% power (Table 5.2). Even if a significant difference is found, the CI on the effect will still be very wide, so there will be uncertainty at the end of the trial whether the effect of the intervention is small and unimportant, or very large and of major importance.

The conduct of trials that are too small has consequences extending beyond the results of the specific trial. There is considerable evidence that trials showing large effects are more likely to be published than those showing little or no effect. Suppose a number of small trials of a specific intervention are conducted. Because of the large sampling error implied by small sample sizes, a few of these trials will produce estimates of the effect of the intervention that are much larger than the true effect. These trials are more likely to be published, and the result is that the findings in the literature are likely to overestimate considerably the true effects of interventions. This publication bias is much smaller for larger trials, because a large trial showing little or no effect is more likely to be published than a small trial with a similar difference.

9 Computer software for sample size calculations

Most of the formulae given in this chapter are simple enough to do by hand, with the aid of a simple calculator. However, computer software is also available to carry out some of these calculations. This can be particularly helpful when a large number of calculations need to be carried out, for example, to explore sample size requirements for different outcomes or under different assumptions, or to produce power curves. Most statistical packages have some provision for sample size calculations. Here we mention three packages which readers may find helpful when planning field trials.

The *sampsi* command in Stata allows the user to obtain the required sample size for the comparison of means or proportions. Alternatively, if the chosen sample sizes are entered, the user can determine the power that these will provide. The command allows for different sample sizes in the two trial arms. The sample size formulae used by this package differ slightly from those presented in this book, but the results should be quite similar in most cases.

The POWER and GLMPOWER procedures in the statistical analysis program package SAS can handle sample size calculations for a range of situations, including survival analysis, as can the PASS module (a trial version of which is available at <http://www.ncss.com>).

A variety of free sample size calculators may be found on the Internet. These include the program PS which is described by Dupont and Plummer (1990) and available at <http://biostat.mc.vanderbilt.edu/wiki/Main/PowerSampleSize>); and Open Epi which can be downloaded from <http://www.openepi.com/Downloads/Downloads.htm>.

Table 5.6 gives a spreadsheet which facilitates the calculation of the required size (number of clusters) for a cluster randomized trial, using the formulae given in Section 6 (as in Hayes and Moulton, 2009).

96 | CHAPTER 5: TRIAL SIZE

Table 5.6 Spreadsheet calculation of the number of clusters required in an unmatched cluster randomized trial. Table 5.6 shows the calculations, for some example situations, for (a) comparison of proportions and (b) comparison of rates. Formulae are given which allow the calculation of required trial size for any (unmatched) cluster randomized trial in an Excel spreadsheet

(a) Comparison of proportions

Significance level	Power	z_1	z_2	$(z_1+z_2)^2$	p_1	% reduction	p_2	Person-years per cluster	k	# clusters per arm	Rounded up
A	B	C	D	E	F	G	H	I	J	K	L
0.95	0.80	1.96	0.84	7.85	2.0%	50%	1.0%	500	0.25	8.08	9
0.95	0.80	1.96	0.84	7.85	3.0%	50%	1.5%	500	0.25	6.51	7
0.95	0.80	1.96	0.84	7.85	4.0%	50%	2.0%	500	0.25	5.73	6
0.95	0.90	1.96	1.28	10.51	2.0%	50%	1.0%	500	0.25	10.48	11
0.95	0.90	1.96	1.28	10.51	3.0%	50%	1.5%	500	0.25	8.38	9
0.95	0.90	1.96	1.28	10.51	4.0%	50%	2.0%	500	0.25	7.33	8
0.95	0.80	1.96	0.84	7.85	2.0%	50%	1.0%	250	0.25	12.71	13
0.95	0.80	1.96	0.84	7.85	3.0%	50%	1.5%	250	0.25	9.57	10
0.95	0.80	1.96	0.84	7.85	4.0%	50%	2.0%	250	0.25	8.01	9
0.95	0.90	1.96	1.28	10.51	2.0%	50%	1.0%	250	0.25	16.68	17
0.95	0.90	1.96	1.28	10.51	3.0%	50%	1.5%	250	0.25	12.48	13
0.95	0.90	1.96	1.28	10.51	4.0%	50%	2.0%	250	0.25	10.38	11

(b) Comparison of rates

Significance level	Power	z_1	z_2	$(z_1+z_2)^2$	r_1	% reduction	r_2	Person-years per cluster	k	# clusters per arm	Rounded up
A	B	C	D	E	F	G	H	I	J	K	L
0.95	0.8	1.96	0.84	7.85	0.050	50%	0.025	300	0.25	6.46	7
0.95	0.8	1.96	0.84	7.85	0.050	45%	0.028	300	0.25	7.99	9
0.95	0.8	1.96	0.84	7.85	0.050	40%	0.030	300	0.25	10.18	11
0.95	0.8	1.96	0.84	7.85	0.050	35%	0.033	300	0.25	13.44	14
0.95	0.8	1.96	0.84	7.85	0.050	30%	0.035	300	0.25	18.57	19
0.95	0.8	1.96	0.84	7.85	0.050	50%	0.025	300	0.20	5.58	6
0.95	0.8	1.96	0.84	7.85	0.050	45%	0.028	300	0.20	6.86	7
0.95	0.8	1.96	0.84	7.85	0.050	40%	0.030	300	0.20	8.68	9
0.95	0.8	1.96	0.84	7.85	0.050	35%	0.033	300	0.20	11.39	12
0.95	0.8	1.96	0.84	7.85	0.050	30%	0.035	300	0.20	15.65	16

Excel expressions:
C = NORMSINV(1− (0.5*(1 − A))); D = NORMSINV(B)
K = 1 + E*((F*(1 − F)/I) + (H*(1 − H)/I) + (J*J)*((F*F) + (H*H)))/((H − F)^2)
L = INT(K) + 1

It is fairly straightforward to set up a spreadsheet, for example, in Excel, to apply any of the formulae given in this chapter. The freeware computer package Epi-Info has a useful component, called StatCalc, for calculating sample sizes for simple trials.

References

Blackwelder, W. C. 1982. 'Proving the null hypothesis' in clinical trials. *Control Clinical Trials*, **3**, 345–53.

Chow, S.-C., Shao, J., and Wang, H. 2008. *Sample size calculations in clinical research*, 2nd ed. New York: Chapman & Hall/CRC Press, Taylor & Francis.

Dupont, W. D. and Plummer, W. D., Jr. 1990. Power and sample size calculations. A review and computer program. *Control Clinical Trials*, **11**, 116–28.

Geller, N. L. and Pocock, S. J. 1987. Interim analyses in randomized clinical trials: ramifications and guidelines for practitioners. *Biometrics*, **43**, 213–23.

Hayes, R. J. and Bennett, S. 1999. Simple sample size calculation for cluster-randomized trials. *International Journal of Epidemiology*, **28**, 319–26.

Hayes, R. J. and Moulton, L. H. 2009. *Cluster randomized trials*. Boca Raton: Chapman & Hall/CRC.

Machin, D. 2009. *Sample size tables for clinical studies*. Oxford: Wiley-Blackwell.

Wang, D. and Bakhai, A. 2006. *Clinical trials : a practical guide to design, analysis, and reporting*. London: Remedica.

Chapter 6

Ethical considerations

1 Introduction to ethical considerations 99
2 Widely accepted ethical principles concerning research on human subjects 100
 2.1 Scientific merit 101
 2.2 Equitable selection of subjects 101
 2.3 Voluntariness 102
 2.4 Informed consent 102
 2.5 Confidentiality 105
 2.6 Coercion 105
 2.7 Review and approval by ethics committees 106
 2.8 Useful guidance documents 108
  2.8.1 Operational guidelines for ethics committees that review biomedical research 108
  2.8.2 International conference on harmonisation/WHO good clinical practice standards 108
  2.8.3 The Declaration of Helsinki—ethical principles for medical research involving human subjects 108
  2.8.4 International Ethical Guidelines for Epidemiological Studies 109
  2.8.5 The ethics of research related to health care in developing countries 109
  2.8.6 Consolidated Standards of Reporting Trials (CONSORT) 109
  2.8.7 Extending the CONSORT statement to randomized trials of non-pharmacologic treatments 109
  2.8.8 Other useful background documents 109
3 Special issues in field trials in low- and middle-income countries 110
 3.1 Obtaining communal and individual consent 110
 3.2 Potential benefit and the risk of harm 111
 3.3 Incentives 112
 3.4 Standard of care 112
 3.5 Choice of 'control' interventions 113
 3.6 Choosing the primary endpoint 114
 3.7 Duration and size of a trial 114
 3.8 Monitoring safety during a trial 116
 3.9 Special ethical issues in cluster randomized trials 117

3.10 Reporting and feedback of results 117
3.11 What happens after the trial? 118
3.12 Special ethical issues in Phase IV (post-licensure) studies 118

1 Introduction to ethical considerations

For any research investigation involving human subjects, there must be careful consideration of ethical issues that may arise in the planning, conduct, and reporting of the study. With very few exceptions, such research is not permitted unless the study has been approved by at least one formal ethics review committee (ERC). All research funding agencies require approval of the research by the appropriate ERC(s) before they will confirm an award for an intervention study. Often ethical review will be required from more than one such committee, for example, by both an institutional and a national ethics review committee, and/or in each of the countries involved in a trial. The ethics committee(s) will not only review the study protocol but usually will require full details of the study plan and procedures and will usually have specific application forms that must be completed. They may require payment of an administration fee for considering an application, irrespective of the outcome of the application. The committee will pay particular attention to informed consent documents and how consent to take part in the research will be obtained from potential study participants. Any significant changes in the study plan, either before it starts or during the conduct of the study, such as adding new objectives, extending the trial catchment area, or adding/removing inclusion or exclusion criteria, require approval by the ERC.

It is important that the ethical aspects of a research study are considered from its inception; for that reason, this chapter is placed early in the book. An underlying philosophy in this chapter is that it is difficult, and often inappropriate, to lay down ethical rules that apply to all studies in all places; each study should be judged in the context of the circumstances in which it will be conducted. A study judged unethical in one place might be considered ethical in another, and both of these might be 'correct' judgements.

Most ethical issues arise from conflicts between competing sets of values. For example, the medical practitioner is dedicated to the provision of the best medical care for an individual who is his or her patient. However, this dedication may be in direct conflict with that of the public health professional whose goal is to achieve maximum health benefits in a community with the limited resources available, which may entail restricting resources available to any one patient. Consuming large amounts of resources on one patient may deprive others of benefit. The appropriate balance between benefit for the individual and benefit for the community depends very much on the particular situation. The conflict is most obvious in situations of poverty and deprivation—just those conditions in which most field trials are conducted in LMICs. Those conducting field trials of interventions against diseases associated with poverty are likely therefore to be faced with especially difficult ethical dilemmas. Resolution of such dilemmas often depends upon where the investigators place their horizon of responsibility. If they consider their responsibility is confined to the participants in a trial, then some studies to resolve important public health issues might be viewed as unethical. But to assess the likely public health impact of an intervention in the wider community, it may be important to continue a trial beyond the point when it is established that one intervention is superior to another, in order to obtain a better estimate of the magnitude of the beneficial effect. Knowledge of the extent of benefit is needed, in order to make an informed decision about whether the benefit is sufficient to introduce the intervention on a widespread basis, especially if it is more expensive than the intervention that is currently available. If the investigators consider their responsibility is extended to the entire population, then they may regard it as unethical to stop a trial before a reasonable estimate of that benefit is obtained.

It is important to recognize that the primary purpose of an intervention trial is not to benefit the specific participants in the trial, but rather to obtain information about the effects of the intervention that will inform decisions about whether the intervention should be introduced on a widespread basis. Although trial participants may derive benefit, for example, they might receive better medical care in the trial than they would with the normal medical services, this is incidental to the main purposes of the trial.

Although intervention trials are not conducted with the prime aim of benefiting those in the trial, investigators have a specific responsibility for participants in a trial and must ensure that they are not harmed as a consequence of taking part in the trial and might derive some benefit. In so far as is possible, at a minimum, participants in a trial should be placed in no worse a situation than would have been the case had they not participated in the trial. It is, of course, not always possible to guarantee this, as sometimes there may be unexpected adverse events associated with an intervention, but it is important to minimize the possibility of harm to trial participants.

There is sometimes a conflict between what is best for the 'future population' and what is best for those participating in a trial. Such conflicts may pose serious ethical dilemmas, for which there are few 'cookbook' solutions. Each situation has to be considered individually and preferably during the planning of the trial, so that potential ethical issues can be thought through in advance and, where necessary, guidance can be sought from properly constituted ethics committees. This issue is discussed further in Section 2.

It is not the purpose of this chapter to provide comprehensive guidance on all of the ethical considerations that must be considered in designing and conducting a field trial. Substantial sets of ethical guidelines have been published by a number of international bodies, and we give reference to these in the chapter, especially in Section 2.8. Rather we highlight some of the basic ethical principles related to randomized trials in Section 2 and then focus on some of the particularly difficult, and sometimes controversial, issues that arise in field trials in LMICs.

2 Widely accepted ethical principles concerning research on human subjects

The ethical principles related to medical research involving human subjects were summarized in the Declaration of Helsinki. This declaration was first formulated in 1964 and has subsequently been debated and revised a number of times, most recently in 2008 (World Medical Association, 2008). While some parts of the declaration remain hotly debated, the basic principles are generally accepted. They were reproduced and further elaborated with special reference to LMICs by the Council for International Organizations of Medical Sciences (CIOMS) (Council for International Organizations of Medical Sciences, 2009). The main principles are the following.

2.1 Scientific merit

To be ethical, research must have scientific merit, preferably in the judgement of an independent scientific committee, rather than only by the researchers themselves. This assessment will generally be made in the peer review process employed by funding agencies. The methods of the research should be appropriate to the aims of the research, and results from any relevant previous or ongoing research should be taken into account in its design. Over the last decade or so, there has been much greater insistence by research funding bodies and ethics committees, as well as research journal editors, that some kind of systematic review of prior research on a topic is conducted before further research on the topic is planned. This is to avoid unnecessary duplication of research where a new study needlessly addresses research questions that have been effectively answered previously. An outline of how to conduct systematic reviews is given in Chapter 3. Anyone proposing a trial should also review the clinical trial registers (see Chapter 7, Section 5), so that they are aware of trials that are already under way which might be addressing similar issues.

The investigator is also obliged to design and conduct the research in such a way that the results from the study are likely to provide answers to the questions being addressed. This includes attention to the appropriate size and duration of the study, as well as to other aspects of its design. For example, a study that is too small to address properly the principal research question may be deemed to be unethical. Furthermore, for research concerning interventions, achievement of the trial objectives must be linked, directly or indirectly, to some kind of action that is expected to lead to improved health for the population, or future population, of which the trial participants are in some way representative. Not all research findings will have immediate health consequences for the population, but the research should be on the pathway that is expected to lead ultimately to such benefit.

2.2 Equitable selection of subjects

The potential benefits of research and the risks and burdens associated with the research should be distributed equitably among communities and among individuals within communities. The economically and socially deprived are often at the highest risk of disease. There is, on the one hand, an imperative to ensure that the appropriate research is conducted in such groups and, on the other hand, an imperative to ensure that they are not exploited in research that will mainly benefit the more wealthy and privileged. For example, it would generally be deemed unacceptable to conduct a trial of an expensive treatment in a deprived group, unless it was expected that the cost of the treatment was likely to be reduced in the immediate future to a level that could be afforded by the community or that, even if there was no reduction in cost, the treatment would at least be made accessible to those in the community in which the trial was conducted, should it be found to be efficacious. Such treatment should not be restricted solely to those who had participated in the trial but should also be provided to those in similar circumstances in the community. Whether the 'community' is the local population in the trial area or a much larger, possibly national, group will often be an important aspect to consider before a trial is started.

2.3 Voluntariness

Voluntariness implies that individuals and communities enrol, continue, or withdraw from the study of their own free will, with full knowledge of the consequences of their participation or withdrawal. They should not be forced or coerced by investigators, officials, family, or friends, enticed by financial or other rewards. Nor should their decisions be constrained by socio-economic or political conditions. The principle of voluntariness is a key component of the informed consent process. Voluntariness, however, applies only as far as community leaders, adult individuals, or legal guardians of children are at liberty to make free choices. In some LMICs, researchers must take extra efforts to understand, for example, the influence that unequal gender relations might have on voluntariness and design information and procedures to minimize this influence. Illiteracy is another factor that may influence voluntariness when the information channels for the study favour those who can read over those who cannot. Any monetary compensation for participants' time or transport fares should be of a level that does not interfere with their freedom of choice, i.e. it should be sufficient to cover the actual costs, but not be an undue inducement to participate in the study (see Section 3.3). Particular attention should be paid to thanking potential participants who want to participate in a trial but are excluded because they are found not to meet the inclusion criteria.

2.4 Informed consent

It is now an established principle that 'informed consent' must be obtained from all participants in a medical or social research investigation on human subjects. Where the participant is not able to give informed consent for themselves, it is usually acceptable to request this from their parent or legal guardian.

Each potential participant should be given a comprehensive explanation as to why the research is being conducted, why they are being invited to participate, what possible benefits, risks, and burdens may arise for them personally as a result of participating in the research, and what benefits are expected to accrue to them and to the community as a result of the research. Translating these goals into a set of procedures that will be used to convey this information in a specific study is often challenging. Special problems arise with respect to field trials in LMICs, commonly involving large numbers of subjects, in obtaining assurance that all individuals are properly informed about these aspects.

Often, a research funding body or ERC will require the use of a consent form that participants must sign in the presence of a witness. The form must give full details of the study, with respect to the aspects outlined in Sections 2.1 to 2.3. It is becoming more widely recognized, however, that, in some societies, the insistence on obtaining a witnessed signature, or thumbprint, on such a form may not guarantee that the consent was fully informed, especially in communities where many are not literate. Moreover, in some societies, the requirement to sign a consent form may actually cause undue fear and anxiety, as when people in the local culture would typically sign or mark documents only in connection with legal transactions such as transferring property or if they were to be arrested. The ethical review process may include an option to request a waiver of signed consent, provided that certain other protective conditions are met. With or without the collection of a signature, what is most important is the *consent process,* through which study personnel have a conversation with prospective participants to make sure that they understand all the key points of information, have an opportunity to ask questions, and understand that they are free to say 'no'. It is *always* the investigator's responsibility to ensure that subjects are properly informed of the potential risks and benefits of participation in a study. It is common practice, in some trials, to include a short 'test' to check that the potential study participant has understood the key information before they are asked to sign the consent form, with the opportunity to receive further explanation of points that they do not fully understand.

Lema et al. (2009) conducted a systematic review on consent procedures in clinical trials in Africa and reported that consent often was not truly voluntary; consent procedures are difficult to implement, due to cultural factors and low literacy, and local ethical review committees may be weak or ill-equipped. These findings are reinforced by a study of informed consent for HIV testing in South Africa that found that, although all women had given informed consent for the testing, they were coerced in direct and indirect ways into providing consent, and many felt they did not, in fact, have a choice (Groves et al., 2010). It is therefore very important that investigators endeavour to ensure that consent is truly informed and non-coercive.

Special provisions must be made for potential participants who are not competent to provide informed consent such as children or patients who are comatose. Such persons require an advocate who is legally and morally responsible for decisions taken on their behalf. Even when the advocate provides consent, the subject should have the right to refuse, if he or she is able to, but, in practice, it may be difficult, for example, for a young child to exercise that right. In general, research procedures should not be conducted on children, unless they have already been demonstrated to be safe in adults and, if appropriate, efficacious in adults also.

The information provided to potential participants to obtain consent for taking part in a trial would be expected to include that listed in Box 6.1.

The checklist in Box 6.1 was drawn up in the context of trials in HICs, but the same principles apply for trials in LMICs. In the latter, however, it may be necessary to go to some lengths to give the required explanations and in ways that will be comprehensible in the context of the local attitudes and beliefs in the communities in which the trial will be undertaken. Often investigators will first meet with community leaders to explain the trial and to seek permission to conduct the investigation. This might be followed by community meetings at which the trial investigators explain the trial and the procedures to be followed and then answer any questions. After that, potential participants

Box 6.1 Information that should be provided to potential participants to seek consent for taking part in a trial

1 A statement that the study involves research, an explanation of the purposes of the research and the expected duration of the subject's participation, a description of the procedures to be followed, and identification of any procedures which are experimental.
2 An explanation of why the subject has been asked to participate in the trial.
3 A description of any reasonably foreseeable risks or discomforts to the subject.
4 A description of any benefits to the subject or to others which may reasonably be expected from the research.
5 A disclosure of appropriate alternative procedures or courses of treatment, if any, that might be advantageous to the subject.
6 A statement describing the extent, if any, to which confidentiality of records identifying the subject will be maintained.
7 For research involving more than minimal risk, an explanation as to whether any compensation and an explanation as to whether any medical treatments are available if injury occurs and, if so, what they consist of or where further information may be obtained.
8 An explanation of whom to contact for answers to pertinent questions about the research and research subjects' rights and whom to contact in the event of a research-related injury to the subject.
9 A statement that participation is voluntary, that refusal to participate will involve no penalty or loss of benefits to which the subject is otherwise entitled, and that the subject may discontinue participation at any time without penalty or loss of benefits to which the subject is otherwise entitled.

Additional elements of informed consent

When appropriate, one or more of the following elements of information shall also be provided to each subject.

1 A statement that the particular treatment or procedure may involve risks to the subject (or to the embryo or fetus, if the subject is or may become pregnant) which are currently unforeseeable.
2 Anticipated circumstances under which the subject's participation may be terminated by the investigator without regard to the subject's consent.
3 Any additional costs to the subject that may result from participation in the research.

> **Box 6.1 Information that should be provided to potential participants to seek consent for taking part in a trial (continued)**
>
> 4 A statement that significant new findings that arise during the course of the research which may relate to the subject's willingness to continue participation will be provided to the subject.
> 5 The approximate number of subjects involved in the study.
>
> Adapted from U.S. Food and Drug Administration, Code of Federal Regulations, Title 21, Section 50.25, 2013, available from <http://www.fda.gov>. This box is not covered by the Creative Commons licence terms of this publication. For permission to reuse please contact the rights holder.

might be given further information, often in written form, that they can take home and discuss with neighbours, friends, and others advisors in the community, before they are asked to provide informed consent. Although key steps of the informed consent process should usually be done face-to-face, it is sometimes effective to get a prospective participant to watch a video or listen to an audio message that explains aspects the study. And sometimes photographs or diagrams can be very useful to supplement a verbal explanation.

2.5 Confidentiality

The confidentiality of all information collected in a research investigation must be maintained and only released to others with the explicit consent of all those concerned. The proportion of individuals who agree to participate in a study, especially one in which sensitive information is being collected (for example, whether or not an individual is infected with HIV), may be increased if careful explanations are given as to how confidentiality will be maintained and who within the study team will have access to such information. In many studies, it will be appropriate to identify individuals on record forms by a code number only, with the list linking names to the codes being kept separately in a secure place, with access limited to only those who must be able to link trial data back to specific individuals.

2.6 Coercion

In general, there are fewer legal and institutional safeguards to protect the rights of individuals in LMICs than there are in most HICs. When research workers are employed by, or identified with, the state authorities or with those who provide medical care, there is a danger that they might be tempted to exploit this position, with greater or lesser degrees of subtlety, to coerce subjects to participate in a study. Coercion and deception, even when rationalized as being for the 'greater good', are unacceptable. Full and open explanations of all study procedures, with the explicit understanding that participation is voluntary and those who decline will not be penalized, may be time-consuming, but this is the only acceptable approach.

2.7 Review and approval by ethics committees

Most research investigations must go through several levels of scientific and ethical review to assess their acceptability. The number of levels will depend on the nature of the research, national regulations, and from which agencies support for the research is being sought.

All ethical review bodies will require that each individual participant in a study is provided with sufficient information on potential risks and benefits to enable them to make an informed decision on whether or not to participate. Illiteracy and differing cultural concepts of health and disease do not alter the basic requirements for informed consent. If permission to approach and recruit individual members of the population has been obtained by virtue of a communal decision, individual informed consent is still necessary, and the research worker and the ethics committee must assure themselves that there is no coercion on individuals to participate. The principles that consent must be given by each individual, rather than assumed, and that all prospective participants have the right of refusal must be regarded as the minimal safeguards.

As well as being acceptable to individual participants, a trial may be reviewed at a community level through either a formal or an informal review committee. In addition, there may be local and national ethical and scientific review bodies to satisfy. If funding for a study is sought from an international agency, there may be a further level of ethical review. For example, research proposals submitted to the WHO are reviewed by the WHO Research Ethics Review Committee (WHO ERC). The committee will only review proposals that have first been approved by national and, if appropriate, local ethics committees. Given all these potential steps, it is very important that investigators allow sufficient time for research and ethics approval. Although many are much faster, it is not uncommon for some ethics committees to take as long as 6 months to review a proposal.

In the case of multicountry studies, it is common that the ethics committees review a master protocol and then subsequently individual or country-specific protocols. The latter are needed to describe how the master protocol was adapted to local reality and resources. The review of protocols for additional study sites is usually more straightforward, given that the main ethical and methodological issues of the study have already been reviewed. In some cases, a centralized ethics committee has been used to review multicentre studies, but generally ERCs are reluctant to delegate responsibility for review to a committee outside of their own country.

Ethics committees should be properly constituted and operating under defined standard operating procedures (SOPs) (see first reference in Section 2.8). Their main role is to ensure that ethical principles, as established by universal guidelines, are applied in the research and the rights, safety, well-being, and confidentiality of participants are protected. The committee review should focus on ethical and quality assurance aspects of the protocol, addressing its relevance, risks (physical, psychological, social, economic), and potential benefits. In some cases, the trial does not bring immediate benefit to the participants, but the knowledge generated will be for the benefit of broader society. In local committees, the inclusion of members representing the group of patients or communities under study enables a better understanding of the social and cultural aspects involved. Ideally, the members of ethics committees comprise a multidisciplinary group with experience in research and should include lay persons who can bring a non-medical perspective to the review. As the focus of review is on fairness and ethical issues, in most cases, there is no need for all members to be knowledgeable about the medical or scientific aspects. However, it is also helpful that a medical or scientific member be available to explain in more detail the rationale or concept for the procedures to be carried out and products to be administered.

The protocol should include copies of case report forms, examples of questionnaires to be used, as well as a model of informed consent in the committee's working language and in the local language, as it is going to be applied. Social sciences methodologies, such as focus group discussions, or in-depth interviews, also require proper description and a list of the topics that will be covered in the protocol.

It is common that, before approval, the ethics committee requests additional information or description of procedures not fully detailed in the protocol, so investigators should endeavour to be comprehensive in their initial application. The queries or deliberations of the ethics committee are transmitted by the secretary to the PIs or sponsor, who should submit a revised version of the protocol with amendments and clarification, following the instructions of the committee. The more complete and detailed the protocol is, the less time will be required for reviewing. However, very often, a resubmission is needed, and the investigator should allow for time for clearance.

Some ethics committees require reports during a trial to ensure compliance with procedures and to evaluate any protocol deviations or to follow up AEs. Serious adverse reactions occurring during a trial that are considered related to the intervention should be reported to the ethics committee, and the balance between risks and benefits should be continually reassessed by the investigators (or by the Data and Safety Monitoring Board, (DSMB) on behalf of the investigators; see Chapter 7, Section 4). Frequency and procedures for reports and review of trial operations and data are laid down by the committee on a case-by-case basis.

Ethics committees pay special attention to studies involving vulnerable individuals, and the protocol should ensure that there is no undue inducement to participate. Vulnerable individuals, according to Good Clinical Practice (GCP) guidelines (International Conference on Harmonisation, 1996), are individuals whose willingness to volunteer in a clinical trial may be unduly influenced by the expectation, whether justified or not, of benefits associated with participation or of a retaliatory response from senior members of a hierarchy in case of refusal to participate. Other vulnerable subjects include children (commonly defined as all those below 18 years of age, but this varies between countries), patients with incurable diseases, persons in nursing homes, unemployed or impoverished persons, patients in emergency situations, ethnic minority groups, homeless persons, nomads, refugees, prisoners, and those incapable of giving consent. In some countries, there are special regulations regarding research involving indigenous populations.

Before initiating a trial, the investigator should have written approval of the protocol, written informed consent documents, subject recruitment procedures, and any other written information to be given to participants. The investigator is responsible for complying with the study protocol that was approved by the ethics committee and agreed by the sponsor and regulatory authority (if appropriate).

A clinical trial legal and financial liability insurance, which is compulsory in some countries, provides the participants and sponsor financial protection against specific contingencies such as death, disability, or other health-related complications that may occur from the participation in a trial. In most cases, liability is product-related, and lawsuits against pharmaceutical companies have increased over the years, as more careful pharmaco-epidemiological studies have been able to identify adverse effects of new products when used in a large number of people or over a long period of time. Some ethics committees will not review a protocol without having a copy of the clinical trial insurance certificate.

2.8 Useful guidance documents

Research involving human subjects is conducted in countries with widely varying socio-economic, health, and research ethics infrastructure. However, irrespective of where the research is conducted, for the ethics infrastructure to be effective, it must have officially recognized regulations or guidelines, a system for oversight and monitoring, and well-functioning research ethics committees. Many LMICs lack laws or regulations governing ethics in research and face the challenge of deciding which international guidelines to use. These guidelines are increasing in number, are not harmonized, and require interpretation or adaptation to local circumstances. Many ethics committees also face the challenge of ensuring adequate ethical review of research protocols.

The following is a selection of the most important guidance documents.

2.8.1 Operational guidelines for ethics committees that review biomedical research

These were produced by the WHO Tropical Diseases Research Programme in 2000. They set out operational guidelines for ethics committees, in order to facilitate, support, and ensure quality of the ethical review of biomedical research in all countries of the world. Targeted for use by national and local bodies, these guidelines define the role and constituents of an ethics committee and detail the requirements for submitting an application for review. The review procedure and details of the decision-making process are provided, together with necessary follow-up and documentation procedures. They can be downloaded from <http://www.who.int/tdr>.

2.8.2 International conference on harmonisation/WHO good clinical practice standards

This document (International conference on harmonisation, 1996) provides a unified standard for the European Union, Japan, the USA, Australia, Canada, the Nordic countries, and the WHO. Thus, any country that adopts this guideline technically follows this same standard.

2.8.3 The Declaration of Helsinki—ethical principles for medical research involving human subjects

The Declaration of Helsinki is a statement of ethical principles for medical research involving human subjects, including research on identifiable human material and data.

It was adopted in 1964 and has since undergone several amendments, including one in 2008 (available at <http://www.wma.net/en/30publications/10policies/b3/17c.pdf>.

2.8.4 International Ethical Guidelines for Epidemiological Studies

In 2009, the CIOMS published its revised guidelines (Council for International Organizations of Medical Sciences, 2009). The book contains ethical guidance on how epidemiologists—as well as those who sponsor, review, or participate in the studies they conduct—should identify and respond to the ethical issues that are raised by the research process. The book can be ordered from WHO through e-mail: cioms@who.int.

2.8.5 The ethics of research related to health care in developing countries

This book was produced in 2002 (Nuffield Council on Bioethics, 2002) and updated in 2005 (Nuffield Council on Bioethics, 2005). It defines the ethical standards for health care research in LMICs (<http://www.nuffieldbioethics.org/research-developing-countries>).

2.8.6 Consolidated Standards of Reporting Trials (CONSORT)

CONSORT 2010 provides a checklist of information to include when reporting a randomized trial. It includes a flow diagram of the process through the phases of a randomized trial. Diligent adherence to these guidelines facilitates clarity, comprehensiveness, and transparency of reporting (Schulz et al., 2010).

2.8.7 Extending the CONSORT statement to randomized trials of non-pharmacologic treatments

The CONSORT statement has been extended to address specific issues that apply to trials of non-pharmacologic treatments and behavioural intervention (Boutron et al., 2008).

2.8.8 Other useful background documents

- *The Belmont report: ethical principles and guidelines for the protection of human subjects of research* (<http://www.hhs.gov/ohrp/humansubjects/guidance/belmont.html>)
- *The common rule, title 45 (public welfare), code of federal regulations, part 46 (protection of human subjects)*, subparts A–D; *The international ethical guidelines for biomedical research involving human subjects. (CIOMS)* (<http://www.hhs.gov/ohrp/humansubjects/guidance/45cfr46.html>)
- Canada: *Tri-council policy statement: ethical conduct for research involving humans* (<http://www.pre.ethics.gc.ca/pdf/eng/tcps2/TCPS_2_FINAL_Web.pdf>)
- Indian Council of Medical Research: *Ethical guidelines for biomedical research on human participants* (<http://icmr.nic.in/ethical_guidelines.pdf>)
- Finally, see the very useful international compilation of human subjects protections maintained by the US Office for Human Research Protections (OHRP) (<http://www.hhs.gov/ohrp/international/index.html>).

3 Special issues in field trials in low- and middle-income countries

Trials of an intervention should be undertaken only when there is uncertainty about the balance of potential benefit and potential harm, with respect to the intervention. The assessment of the extent of such uncertainty will be a critical factor in deciding whether or not it is justifiable to conduct a trial. If one trial provides good evidence of a beneficial effect, further trials of the same agent or procedure, even under very different epidemiological circumstances, will be more difficult to justify than if the first trial had not been conducted. Only if there are good reasons to believe that the results might be different under these different circumstances would further trials be indicated, and indeed a case could be made that it would be unethical not to conduct a further trial in such circumstances.

In communities which are poor and deprived and whose inhabitants may be at substantial risk of premature death and serious disease from many causes, the balance between the potential benefits of an intervention and the risk of harm may be different from that which might apply in a more privileged community. For example, a higher level of vaccine-related adverse effects might be acceptable in a trial of a vaccine against a disease that was responsible for many deaths and considerable disability in a community than would be acceptable in a study in a community in which the disease was rarely fatal and rarely caused severe disability.

In general, it is easier to persuade those who are sick than those who are well to participate in a medical research investigation. Field trials of preventive measures often involve those in the latter category and, unlike most clinical trials, take place in the community, rather than in a clinic or hospital. The task of obtaining consent for the conduct of a study in such a setting involves some special issues discussed in Section 3.1.

3.1 Obtaining communal and individual consent

In communities in many LMICs, decisions about participation in a particular project may be taken initially at a communal level. The permission of community leaders needs to be sought for a research investigation to take place in their community. Only once such approval has been granted is it appropriate to seek approval at a household, and then an individual, level. Thus, permission to conduct a research project may be obtained first through trusted and respected community leaders, rather than through individual community members or through the heads of households. Although such procedures may seem strange and be unnecessary in many HICs and might even be regarded as challenging the right of an individual to make autonomous decisions, they are part of the cultural norm in many other societies.

In a clinical trial conducted in a hospital or clinic setting, the investigator may be able to take considerable time to explain the nature of the trial to each participant, as usually the total number of subjects in a study is relatively small. Field trials of some interventions (for example, vaccines) may be large, sometimes involving thousands, or even tens of thousands of participants, and it is more challenging to explain the trial in detail to all participants. Some of the potential methods for informing potential participants about the study have been outlined in Section 2.4. It is important to note that obtaining 'communal consent' does not dispense with the need to also seek and gain individual informed consent. However, those from whom communal consent is sought should be able to represent properly the participants and to protect their interests. In reality, judgements about whether or not to participate in a research investigation depend greatly on the level of trust that investigators enjoy in a community. If a participant trusts an investigator to protect their interests, then they are more likely to agree to take part in the research. Participants will generally expect community leaders to protect their interests also and thus the importance of communal consent, as well as individual consent.

Before a community is approached regarding the possible participation of members of the community in a trial, it will usually be necessary to seek permission from the relevant local health authority, including those responsible for the medical care of the population. Subsequently, the initial approach to a community is likely to be best made to those recognized as leaders in the community. Generally, field trials are likely to be carried out by, or in direct co-operation with, the Ministry of Health and local health authorities. In such circumstances, it will usually be appropriate for discussions with community leaders to be initiated by such authorities, or at least to include their active participation. The extent of such discussions, and precisely who within a community should be involved, depends on the nature of the intervention that is to be studied. Most communities are heterogeneous, and sometimes there are factions within a community that have their own leaders whose co-operation must be sought. The people may not recognize those who are considered as the 'official' leaders, and others must be brought into discussions. Public notices and public meetings may also be useful.

It must be re-emphasized that obtaining communal consent for a study does not relieve investigators of their responsibility to explain the study procedures and the potential risks and benefits to those individuals who are being invited to participate, and those individuals must also be informed and be aware that they are free to refuse to participate or to withdraw from the investigation at any time without penalty of any kind.

It is also important to stress that consent to participate in a research investigation is not a one-off event in which the ethical requirements are satisfied, for example, once a signature is appended to the informed consent document. Consent to participate in a trial requires an ongoing dialogue between investigators and participants from the start of a trial through to its end. Investigators must take pains to keep participants informed of the progress of a trial, unexpected developments, and other findings, possibly from parallel studies that may impact on the trial.

3.2 Potential benefit and the risk of harm

The simple Hippocratic caveat 'do no harm' is not a sufficient guide to ethical decisions concerning trials of interventions. The introduction of a new intervention requires the demonstration of benefit. Furthermore, since almost any intervention procedure involves some risk of harm, albeit usually small, it is necessary to assess in intervention trials the balance of benefits against risks. In general, ethical review committees are disinclined to approve studies in which healthy persons will be exposed to more than very small risks in the context of a research investigation. Thus, it may be unacceptable to carry out a trial using a vaccine associated with serious side effects, even if it offers protection against a disease that is more serious than the side effects. For example, if one person dies as a result of vaccination for every ten persons who are saved from dying, it is unlikely that such a product would be used, even though the 'public health' balance appears to be in favour of the vaccine. More weight is given to harm that results from a deliberate medical intervention than is given to the harm done by the 'natural' disease against which the intervention protects. Furthermore, legal concerns of litigation may sometimes be given greater weight than would seem appropriate from a strictly public health viewpoint.

A proposed research investigation should be viewed within the context of the overall problems facing the community in which it is to be conducted. The community should have a reasonable expectation of benefiting from the research in both the short and long term. The effects of the conduct of a field trial in a community may be immediate and evident or may be quite subtle. Even the mere presence of the research workers in a community may have side effects (for example, increased cash flow, availability of transport to other centres), and the impact of such effects should be considered in planning the research.

The possibility of long-term harm must be considered, even if there are short-term benefits.

3.3 Incentives

In some circumstances, it may be reasonable to provide direct incentives as an encouragement to participation in a research project. If this is done, it must be recognized that there may be a fine line between compensating individuals for time and income lost as a result of participation in the study and 'bribing' subjects to take part. It may be considered reasonable to give a small snack after a blood sample has been taken, or to repay bus or taxi fares to participants who travel to a research centre, or to give simple medications for minor ailments, but monetary payments to encourage individuals to participate in a trial that are greater than the wages they forego or the expenses they incurred will usually be viewed as a form of undue inducement. It is difficult to lay down any absolute rules as to what is acceptable, and it is necessary to review each situation on its merits in the local context. The level of compensation to be offered will generally be considered carefully by the local ERC, whose concern will be that the level proposed does not constitute undue inducement for individuals to participate in the research.

3.4 Standard of care

There are two aspects of standard of care that have been much debated in the context of trials in LMICs. The first is with respect to the choice of the control intervention against which the effects of some new intervention is to be compared. This is discussed in Section 3.5. The second is the standard of medical and other care offered to all the participants in a trial. When a trial is conducted in a poor community, the resources available for the trial (including additional medical personnel) may enable the standard of medical care to trial participants to be greatly improved over what would be available in the absence of the trial. Some such improvements may be essential for the scientific purposes of the trial such as improving the diagnostic facilities for detection of the disease that is the primary focus of the trial. However, the extent to which the general medical care provided to trial participants should be enhanced will need to be carefully considered in the context of each specific trial. Introducing improvements that cannot be sustained beyond the duration of the trial may, in the long run, be damaging to local communities or provoke unrealistic expectations of the local medical services. To the extent possible, improvements implemented during a trial should be designed so that they can be maintained with the resources available to the local medical service after the trial. This may involve specific training of local staff, introducing improvements in the routine medical records system, rather than setting up a parallel system, or ensuring a regular supply of drugs and other treatments that could be maintained by the local medical service after the trial. Inevitably, however, there will be some enhancements that are introduced that may be difficult to maintain after the trial. The aim should be that these are not disproportionate. In general, the provision of health care for a community is the responsibility of the national or local health services, and the research should neither usurp nor undermine existing services. It is essential therefore that the organizers of a field trial develop and maintain close links with those responsible for the normal provision of health care. Discussion of these aspects is an essential component of the submission for permission to conduct the trial to the local ethics committee.

3.5 Choice of 'control' interventions

The Declaration of Helsinki states that 'the benefits, risks, burdens and effectiveness of a new intervention must be tested against those of the best current proven intervention'. Using this principle, comparison with a placebo is acceptable only if there is no convincing evidence that any intervention is effective. This principle of comparing a new intervention with the best current proven intervention seems reasonable at first sight, but it has given rise to much controversy. The controversy has centred on global 'best' interventions that are neither currently available nor likely to become available to the population in which the trial is being conducted, either because of their cost or because of the feasibility of implementing the intervention (for example, radiotherapy for conditions in countries in which there is little or no provision for such treatment). The 'purists' hold that, if the global 'best' intervention is not included as the control arm, then the trial is unethical and should not be conducted. The pragmatists, who often have experience of conducting trials in LMICs, hold that this position is itself 'unethical', as it prevents research investigations that may lead to important public health benefits in deprived populations. There is no space to expand on these arguments in detail here, but the issue is discussed at some length in other publications (for example, Council for International Organizations of Medical Sciences, 2009; Nuffield Council on Bioethics, 2002; Rid et al., 2014). The view of the pragmatists, including ourselves, is that, if an effective intervention is known, but its cost is beyond that which would make it feasible to introduce it into the local health care system (and there is little prospect that the cost can be reduced by means such as shifting production of pharmaceuticals to generic manufacturers), then it may well be acceptable to exclude it from consideration as a possible comparison intervention in a trial. In some circumstances, it may be acceptable to try to test a new intervention that might be, at best, equivalent to an existing intervention or may even be inferior to it if, for example, it is cheaper or simpler to apply, or more stable, or associated with fewer adverse reactions, or is more acceptable to the community than the existing intervention. In such circumstances, the purpose of the trial might be to show that the efficacy of the intervention was 'equally good or not much worse than' the existing intervention.

3.6 Choosing the primary endpoint

The choice of the primary endpoint for a trial, which will usually determine the necessary minimum size and duration of the trial, will generally depend on scientific, rather than ethical, considerations. Generally, the most important endpoints, in terms of assessing the impact of an intervention, will be in the reduction of severe disease or death. However, in a trial with either of these as the primary endpoint, there may be less severe outcomes, which occur with greater frequency than the severe forms of disease. The benefits of the intervention against these, often chosen as secondary, endpoints may become apparent, before sufficient cases of the more severe primary trial outcome have accumulated to reliably assess the impact of the intervention on the primary outcome. For example, in a trial of a vaccine to measure the impact of the vaccine on the incidence of severe malaria (primary trial outcome), the impact on milder malaria (secondary trial outcome) may be apparent much sooner than the impact on severe disease. Having demonstrated impact on the secondary trial outcome, some may argue that it is unethical to continue the trial, because there is no longer 'equipoise' between the effects of the control and the new intervention. There is no simple answer to such debates, but it is very important that careful consideration is given to such possibilities at the time the trial is designed, so that a clear decision can be taken at that stage, rather than being taken 'on the hoof' when the situation emerges. Sometimes, this may result in some secondary outcomes not being measured so as to avoid the potential problem! Alternatively, the decision may be taken not to break the allocation code for secondary trial outcomes until the end of the trial, or the interim results may be made available only to the DSMC, and not to the trial investigators. Alternatively, the prior decision may be taken to continue the trial until the numbers necessary to satisfy the primary trial outcome have been achieved, because of the public health importance of knowing the impact on severe disease or death. These aspects should be clearly presented to the relevant ethics committees when they consider the trial. Also relevant is what feedback will be given to trial participants of results that become available during the conduct of the trial, so that they can assess whether or not they wish to withdraw from the trial.

3.7 Duration and size of a trial

In field trials, it may be necessary to establish the efficacy of the intervention not only in the population as a whole, but also in special subgroups. This may involve the measurement of efficacy in persons of certain ages or for persons with underlying or associated conditions such as malnutrition. It will also be necessary to determine the duration of efficacy and to have a reasonably precise estimate of the degree of efficacy.

It may be argued therefore that the appropriate point at which to stop a trial should be when sufficient evidence has been collected to support, or reject, the introduction of the intervention by the health services generally, rather than at the point when the difference in response in intervention and control groups is first established beyond reasonable doubt. For many interventions, it is important to establish both the degree and the duration of protection. Thus, a trial might be continued beyond the point at which protection is first established to determine if there is long-lasting protection. For example, it may be established in the first 6 months of a malaria vaccine trial that the vaccine is protective, but, to be of public health value, it may be necessary to demonstrate that long-lasting protection is achieved. This may necessitate continuing the trial for at least 2 or 3 years with the maintenance for this period of an unvaccinated group or of a group whose members had received an inferior vaccine. In some circumstances, this will be considered acceptable, but, in others, it will not. Again, each situation must be considered on its own merits, and much will depend on how far the investigators extend their horizon of responsibility, with respect to the public health use of the intervention they are evaluating.

Often, the most important outcome in a trial may not be observed until a considerable time after the intervention has been applied, but there may be intermediate outcomes against which the intervention is also assessed. For example, a vaccine may produce a good antibody response long before any protection against disease is shown. Demonstration of efficacy against the intermediate outcome (antibody response) might be considered grounds for ending a trial if it is reasonable to assume that the effect observed on the intermediate outcome would necessarily carry over to the more distant trial outcome (protection against disease), even though efficacy against that outcome had not been formally demonstrated. What is 'reasonable to assume' is often a matter of considerable debate, and the ethics of continuing a trial, once protection against intermediate endpoints has been established, must be argued in the particular circumstances surrounding a trial. Immunological measures which are thought to correlate with protection against clinical disease may not so do. For example, in one trial in which this aspect was examined, the protection that BCG conferred against TB did not correlate well with the induction by the vaccine of sensitivity to a tuberculin skin test (D'Arcy Hart et al., 1967), even though it was possible to put forward plausible immunological arguments for believing that such a correlation should exist.

An example of the ethical difficulties that may arise is provided by trials of malaria vaccines. Early treatment with appropriate anti-malarials is normally curative for falciparum malaria, and, in a trial, it would be unethical to withhold such treatment from those with clinical malaria. Yet the main purpose of such a vaccine is the prevention of death from malaria, not of infection, nor even the prevention of minor malaria illness. Indeed, it is conceivable that there may not be a good correlation between the protection of a vaccine against the last two outcomes and the protection against death as the outcome. The dilemma is that, in most of Africa where malaria continues to kill hundreds of thousands of children annually, medical services are not adequate to provide the level of curative care that would be provided in a trial, nor are they likely to be so in the near future. Because malaria is a treatable disease and effective treatment should be made available to all those who are diagnosed with malaria during a trial, it is likely that mortality from malaria in a trial would be at a very low level—too low to allow this to be a primary outcome in a reasonably sized trial—and therefore the primary outcome may have to be either clinical malaria or severe disease (which may also be at a lower level, because of the treatment and care provided in the context of the trial). The assumption would have to be made that any efficacy demonstrated against clinical malaria and/or against severe disease would be likely to carry over into the prevention of malaria mortality. It may not be possible to address the impact on mortality until the vaccine is in public health use, and assessment might be made through specially set-up surveillance or Phase IV studies (see Chapter 22). Such studies may be set up to be very large, such that it would only be realistic to leave the treatment of cases of malaria to the existing system of medical care.

There are very strong reasons for conducting early trials of a new intervention to assess the impact of the intervention against the outcomes which are of greatest public health importance, rather than starting with trials against intermediate outcomes, if, by studying intermediate outcomes, further trials against more important outcomes may be compromised. Sometimes, knowledge from other studies may be sufficient to be confident that, if effects are demonstrated against intermediate outcomes, then impacts on more important outcomes will necessarily follow, but all too often, such an assumption is not warranted.

There are strong reasons for conducting very large trials of interventions that are likely to be used on large numbers of people in the future if the interventions are effective, much larger than would initially seem necessary to achieve only a statistically significant difference in outcome. The results of very large trials, if the trials have been adequately managed, can be much more convincing and are more likely to lead to the implementation of the intervention in disease control programmes than are the results of small trials.

Again, part of the dilemma relates to where the investigator places the horizon of responsibility. If the view is taken that the investigator, by taking on the responsibility of a field study, also takes on responsibility to provide full medical care of the subjects under study, then a study of a malaria vaccine with prevention of death as the endpoint could not be undertaken. If the view is taken that the horizon of responsibility extends to all those who are at risk of dying from malaria, including those who would not be included in the trial but who may benefit eventually from the vaccine, then a trial might be conducted with death as an endpoint, but the design of such a trial would be challenging!

3.8 Monitoring safety during a trial

All clinical studies require safety monitoring throughout the duration of the trial and, in some cases, for a defined period after the completion of the study. Investigators are responsible for the detection and reporting of adverse events or serious adverse events and to the sponsor, the ethics committee, and regulatory authorities, according to the time period and procedures specified in the protocol (see Chapters 7 and 12).

The ethics committee should review a study when serious and unexpected adverse events related to the conduct of a study or study product are reported, as the events may affect the benefit/risk balance of the study. Refer to the *International conference on harmonisation guideline for clinical safety data management: definitions and standards for expedited reporting* for more detail (<http://www.ema.europa.eu/docs/en_GB/document_library/Scientific_guideline/2009/09/WC500002749.pdf>).

3.9 Special ethical issues in cluster randomized trials

In addition to ethical issues common to all randomized trials, additional ethical concerns can arise in cluster or group randomized trials (Edwards et al., 1999).

Most ethical issues specific to cluster trials are related to: (1) the legitimacy of informed consent when sought at group level, (2) the potential conflicts between individual autonomy vs group consent, and (3) the differential benefit that one cluster may have over another in some trials.

Most of the issues concerning informed consent in cluster randomized trials are discussed in Section 3.1. These include the identification of different levels at which consent can, or should be, sought and who has the legitimacy to determine whether researchers may approach groups or communities.

A potential issue in cluster randomized trials is when the request for individual consent is obtained after randomization and allocation of the cluster to the intervention or control arm of the trial. This should not cause an ethical concern per se, but it could lead to bias in the nature of the consent in the different intervention groups and thus be of scientific concern.

3.10 Reporting and feedback of results

At the completion of an investigation, there is a responsibility to inform the community in which a trial has been conducted of the results of the study in such a way that its members can understand the implications of the findings. Indeed, such feedback should be ongoing, as the research progresses. Not only is it important ethically that participants should be kept informed of the progress of the research, but, if this is done, it is also likely to encourage their continued participation. The procedures to ensure this feedback takes place should be planned from the start of an investigation.

There is also a responsibility to feed back the results of the research to the relevant local or national health services and disease control programmes, so that these groups can assess the implications of the findings for their own activities.

These issues are discussed in greater detail in Chapter 23.

The anonymity of participants in a trial should always be respected, and there should be no danger that any of them will be identified through any publication of the results of a trial. The same rights of confidentiality should be considered for communities, as well as for individuals. It will sometimes be appropriate to keep the identity of the community anonymous, particularly if sensitive issues are discussed, such as hygiene practices or sexual or other practices that are sometimes condemned by other cultures (such as female genital cutting, infanticide, or anal sex). Sometimes, it is not possible to disguise a particular location, and, in some circumstances, it may be important that the community be identified to aid interpretation of the study results. Indeed, communities are sometimes proud to be associated with a particular research programme, and the name of the community or place may be used as the title of the project (for example, the Garki malaria project (Molineaux and Gramiccia, 1980)).

3.11 What happens after the trial?

The closure of a trial presents special challenges, especially when the intervention group receives significant improvements in the quality of care, while the control group receives usual care, which, in many LMICs, will be suboptimal care or even no care. The challenges are even greater when the intervention has been shown to be successful. Should the benefits of the intervention be sustained in the study group and, if so, how and with whose resources? Should the intervention be extended to the control group (at the minimum), and possibly to the whole community in which the trial was conducted? If yes, how and with whose resources? These are often difficult questions and should be addressed from the inception of the trial, and the implications included in any discussions with the trial funder and trial sponsor. How they are tackled will depend on the setting, the nature of the intervention, the strength of the health system, and the availability of other partners working the study area. If the intervention can be mainstreamed into the health or other services of the community, this should be explored with the relevant decision makers. If, for example, the intervention concerns children and there is a United Nations Children's Fund (UNICEF) programme in the area that can help to extend it to the communities, these alliances should be established. If there is an opportunity for the local health administration to apply for a local, regional, or international grant to help extend the intervention, the trial team should help with preparing this grant. If the trial team plans to take responsibility for extending the intervention, appropriate funding and timelines should be reflected in the project plan and budget.

3.12 Special ethical issues in Phase IV (post-licensure) studies

Phase IV studies with drugs and vaccines are needed to evaluate effectiveness, long-term safety, and potential drug interactions. For safety surveillance, or pharmacovigilance, a system should be in place for collecting, monitoring, and evaluating information from health care providers and patients on AEs that may be associated with medications and biological products. These issues are discussed in greater detail in Chapter 22.

Ethical concerns, as well as quality of data, should be carefully examined in relation to the physician's relationship with the sponsors, marketing of products, incentives, and biased observations. Special informed consent is not always needed when the intervention under study is already part of the routine public health system. However, if participants are asked for more detailed follow-up than would usually be required, to answer specific questionnaires or to perform additional examinations, special informed consent for research may be needed and ethical review of the Phase IV study protocol required.

Post-licensing studies are also used to explore new routes, formulations, and new or modified indications or drug associations of a registered product. In the case of evaluation for a new indication for a known product (label extension studies), the development protocols and ethics review should follow the same path as for a new product.

References

Boutron, I., Moher, D., Altman, D. G., Schulz, K. F., Ravaud, P., and CONSORT Group. 2008. Extending the CONSORT statement to randomized trials of nonpharmacologic treatment: explanation and elaboration. *Annals of Internal Medicine*, **148**, 295–309.

Council for International Organizations of Medical Sciences (CIOMS). 2009. *International ethical guidelines for epidemiological studies* [Online]. Geneva: CIOMS. Available at: <http://www.ufrgs.br/bioetica/cioms2008.pdf>.

D'Arcy Hart, P., Sutherland, I., and Thomas, J. 1967. The immunity conferred by effective BCG and vole bacillus vaccines, in relation to individual variations in induced tuberculin sensitivity and to technical variations in the vaccines. *Tubercle*, **48**, 201–10.

Edwards, S. J., Braunholtz, D. A., Lilford, R. J., and Stevens, A. J. 1999. Ethical issues in the design and conduct of cluster randomised controlled trials. *BMJ*, **318**, 1407–9.

Groves, A. K., Maman, S., Msomi, S., Makhanya, N., and Moodley, D. 2010. The complexity of consent: women's experiences testing for HIV at an antenatal clinic in Durban, South Africa. *AIDS Care*, **22**, 538–44.

International Conference On Harmonisation. 1996. *Technical requirements for registration of pharmaceuticals for human use: guideline for good clinical practice E6(R1)* [Online]. Available at: <http://www.ich.org/fileadmin/Public_Web_Site/ICH_Products/Guidelines/Efficacy/E6/E6_R1_Guideline.pdf>.

Lema, V. M., Mbondo, M., and Kamau, E. M. 2009. Informed consent for clinical trials: a review. *East African Medical Journal*, **86**, 133–42.

Molineaux, L. and Gramiccia, G. 1980. *The Garki Project: research on the epidemiology and control of malaria in the Sudan Savanna of West Africa* [Online]. Geneva: World Health Organization. Available at: <http://garkiproject.nd.edu/static/documents/garkiproject.pdf>.

Nuffield Council On Bioethics. 2002. *The ethics of research related to healthcare in developing countries* [Online]. London: Nuffield Council on Bioethics. Available at: <http://nuffieldbioethics.org/wp-content/uploads/2014/07/Ethics-of-research-related-to-healthcare-in-developing-countries-I.pdf>.

Nuffield Council On Bioethics. 2005. *The ethics of research related to healthcare in developing countries: a follow-up discussion paper* [Online]. London: Nuffield Council on Bioethics. Available at: <http://nuffieldbioethics.org/wp-content/uploads/2014/07/HRRDC_Follow-up_Discussion_Paper.pdf>.

Rid, A., Saxena, A., Baqui, A. H., *et al.* 2014. Placebo use in vaccine trials: recommendations of a WHO expert panel. *Vaccine*, **32**, 4708–12.

Schulz, K. F., Altman, D. G., and Moher, D. 2010. CONSORT 2010 statement: updated guidelines for reporting parallel group randomised trials. *PLoS Med*, **7**, e1000251. Available at: <http://www.plosmedicine.org/article/info%3Adoi%2F10.1371%2Fjournal.pmed.1000251>.

World Medical Association. 2008. *Declaration of Helsinki: ethical principles for medical research involving human subjects* [Online]. World Medical Association. Available at: <http://www.wma.net/en/30publications/10policies/b3/17c.pdf>.

Chapter 7

Trial governance

1 Introduction to trial governance 120
2 The trial sponsor 121
3 Steering committee 122
4 Data and Safety Monitoring Board 122
    4.1 The functions of a Data and Safety Monitoring Board 124
        4.1.1 Monitoring the conduct of the trial 124
        4.1.2 Monitoring the safety of trial participants 124
        4.1.3 Conducting interim analyses 125
        4.1.4 Modification of trial procedures and other advice 126
        4.1.5 Reporting to the sponsor 126
    4.2 Composition and appointment of the Data and Safety Monitoring Board 127
    4.3 The Data and Safety Monitoring Board charter 128
5 Trial registration 129

1 Introduction to trial governance

Since the first edition of this book was published in 1991, there has been a very large increase in the number of field trials of health interventions being conducted in LMICs and, in parallel with this expansion, an increasing number of regulations and guidelines put in place to govern the conduct of clinical trials. Most of these regulations have been developed in the context of clinical trials in HICs, particularly with respect to the evaluation of new drugs and vaccines, but there is a strong expectation, and in many instances a requirement, that these regulations are followed, no matter where a trial is conducted.

A particularly important development occurred in 1990 when representatives of regulatory authorities and pharmaceutical companies in Europe, Japan, and USA agreed on scientific and technical aspects of drug registration. Guidelines were developed from their deliberations called 'The International Conference on Harmonisation of Technical Requirements for Registration of Pharmaceuticals for Human Use', commonly known by the initials 'ICH'. Since then, ICH has evolved, in response to the increasingly global nature of pharmaceutical development, with the mission to achieve greater harmonization in the planning, conduct, and reporting of trials to ensure that safe, effective, and high-quality medicines are developed and registered in the most resource-efficient manner (<http://www.ich.org>).

In this chapter, we highlight aspects of trial design and conduct that have evolved significantly in recent years, particularly with respect to the role of the sponsor, the functioning of steering committees and data safety and monitoring boards (DSMBs) and requirements for trial registration.

2 The trial sponsor

Whenever a field or clinical trial is conducted that involves human participants, it is necessary that an individual, or more commonly an institution, has legal responsibility for the trial, ensures that the trial is conducted properly, according to a defined protocol, and has overall responsibility for the management and financing of the study. This person, or institution, is known as the *sponsor* of the trial. While, in principle, the PI of a trial may act as the sponsor, for legal reasons most institutions prohibit members of their staff from taking on this role and insist that there is institutional sponsorship. In the case of the trial of a new pharmaceutical product, the sponsor is usually the company that is developing the product. With respect to trials of licensed products or trials that do not involve specific products (for example, hygiene interventions), the sponsor would generally be the agency that is funding the trial or the research institution or university of those conducting the trial. Many funding agencies are not prepared to act as the sponsor for the studies they fund, unless those conducting the study are directly employed by the agency, and, in such cases, the institution employing the PI will generally take on the role of sponsor. In such situations, the sponsor is not responsible for financing the trial directly but does have responsibility for arranging that the funds needed to conduct the trial to a high standard are available from the funding agency and for administering the grant. The sponsor also has legal liability for any harm that might arise during the conduct of the trial.

The sponsor must ensure that the trial meets all relevant standards and regulations and must ensure that arrangements are put in place for carrying out the trial, for monitoring that it is being conducted properly, for meeting all required ethical standards (see Chapter 6), and for reporting the results of the trial at the end of the study. The sponsor also has responsibility for ensuring the safety and well-being of participants in the trial and for ensuring that treatment and care are available, usually free of charge, for any trial participants who are harmed as a consequence of their involvement in the trial.

Usually, sponsors will delegate different elements of their responsibility to the trial's PI, steering committee, or DSMB, but the sponsor remains ultimately accountable for all aspects of the governance of the trial, whether or not some components have been delegated.

For clinical trials of drugs and vaccines and, in some cases, also for other interventions, national regulatory authorities usually require that the sponsor has insurance or indemnity for any potential liabilities of the sponsoring institution and the investigators in the trial. Whether or not this is required, it is a good idea, as the cost of any legal action taken against the trial could be considerable. The regulations will also often require that the sponsor ensures that the trial conforms to GCP (see Chapter 16), for which guidelines have been also produced by ICH (International Conference on Harmonisation, 1996).

The PI of a trial is accountable directly to the sponsor. Furthermore, although any reports from a steering committee or DSMB are formally to the sponsor, the sponsor may delegate responsibility for receiving and acting upon such reports to the PI. Similarly, the sponsor has the formal responsibility for liaison with those who have an oversight responsibility for the trial, such as the funding agency and relevant ethics committees. Formally, therefore all communication between these bodies and, for example, the trial steering committee or the DSMB, and vice versa, should be through the sponsor.

3 Steering committee

It is common in large trials, particularly multicentre trials, for a steering committee to be set up, to which the PI reports and from which the PI may seek guidance or authorization, with respect to aspects of the conduct of the trial. These will include any significant protocol amendments, which will also usually have to be approved by the ethics committees which approved the original protocol for the trial. There is no obligation on an investigator to set up such a committee (unless required by the funding agency), and, for smaller trials, a steering committee may be considered unnecessary. Such a committee should usually consist of senior investigators in the trial, together with appropriate independent experts.

The role of a trial steering committee is to provide overall supervision of the trial and ensure that it is being conducted in accordance with the principles of GCP and the relevant regulations. The trial steering committee should agree the trial protocol and any protocol amendments and provide advice to the investigators on all aspects of the trial. The steering committee often has responsibility for approving the analytic plan for a trial (see Chapter 21, Section 3)—see also the ICH guidelines on statistical principles for clinical trials (International Conference on Harmonisation, 1998). The committee will usually have some members who are independent of the investigators, and, in particular, the chairperson should be independent. Decisions about continuation or termination of the trial or substantial amendments to the protocol are usually the responsibility of the trial steering committee, advised by the DSMB (see Section 4).

The trial steering committee is distinct from a trial management group, which normally includes those individuals responsible for the day-to-day management of the trial such as the PI, statistician, trial manager, and data manager. The role of the management group is to monitor all aspects of the day-to-day conduct and progress of the trial to ensure that the protocol is adhered to and to take appropriate action to safeguard participants.

4 Data and Safety Monitoring Board

For trials of interventions that may entail the possibility of significant harm, as well as benefit, to participants, the trial sponsor should establish a DSMB—sometimes termed a committee (DSMC), a Data Monitoring Board (DMB) (or Committee (DMC)), or Independent Data Monitoring Committee (IDMC). The DSMB is independent of those conducting the trial and separate from the ethics review committee (ERC) to monitor the safety of the trial, while it is being conducted. Not all trials will require a DSMB, but listed in Box 7.1 are the types of trial for which WHO has recommended that it would be considered desirable to set up such a committee (World Health Organization, 2005).

> **Box 7.1 WHO recommendations for the types of trial for which a DSMB is relevant**
>
> - Controlled studies with mortality and/or severe morbidity as a primary or secondary endpoint.
> - Randomized controlled studies focused on evaluating clinical efficacy and safety of a new intervention intended to reduce severe morbidity or mortality.
> - Early studies of a high-risk intervention (risk of non-preventable, potentially life-threatening, complications; or risk of common, preventable AEs of interest (especially adverse drug reactions)), whether or not randomized.
> - Studies in the early phases of a novel intervention, with very limited information on clinical safety or where prior information raises concern regarding potential serious adverse outcomes.
> - Studies where the design or expected data accrual are complex or where there may be ongoing questions with regard to the impact of accrued data on the study design and participants' safety, particularly in studies of a long duration.
> - Studies where the data justify an early termination such as the case of an intervention intended to reduce severe morbidity or mortality, which might turn out to have adverse effects or lack of effect, resulting in increased morbidity or mortality.
> - Studies carried out in emergency situations.
> - Studies which involve vulnerable populations.
>
> Reproduced with permission from the World Health Organization, *Operational Guidelines for the Establishment and Functioning of Data and Safety Monitoring Boards*, Copyright © World Health Organization on behalf of the Special Programme for Research and Training in Tropical Diseases 2005, available from <http://whqlibdoc.who.int/hq/2005/TDR_GEN_Guidelines_05.1_eng.pdf>. This box is not covered by the Creative Commons licence terms of this publication. For permission to reuse please contact the rights holder.

A DSMB will usually be set up for trials which are double-blind, in which the investigators and sponsor do not know which intervention individual participants have received, but the DSMB will have access to the randomization code, which it can break during the course of the trial for specific reasons, including safety concerns or interim analyses (see Section 4.1.3). For trials where the intervention allocation is not blinded, the investigators and the sponsor can assess on a continuous basis if there is an excess of AE s in one of the intervention arms of a trial. Even so, it is usually a good idea to have a DSMB, as this committee may take the responsibility for advising the PI, steering committee, and sponsor on critical decisions, such as whether to stop a trial because of adverse effects or signs of failure of the intervention during the course of a trial. Although members of DSMBs are often not paid for their services, a budget will still be required to cover their meetings and any visits they may need to make to the trial site(s).

In this section, we outline the functions and responsibilities of a DSMB, the selection of members, the major issues with which it has to deal, and lines of reporting to those involved in the trial.

4.1 The functions of a Data and Safety Monitoring Board

The prime function of the DSMB of a trial is to safeguard the welfare of participants in the trial. A key aspect of this is to monitor the occurrence of adverse events (AEs) by trial arm and to recommend action to the investigators in the event of finding evidence of harm. In 'blinded' trials, the DSMB will be the only group to have access to the randomization codes during the conduct of the trial, so that, if necessary, they can ascertain which intervention an individual participant received. The DSMB may also be called upon to 'break the code' for a trial at pre-specified time points to make a recommendation as to whether or not a trial should be stopped prematurely because of 'overwhelming efficacy' or 'futility'.

4.1.1 Monitoring the conduct of the trial

An important aspect of safeguarding the welfare of trial participants is to check that trial procedures are being followed, according to the protocol, and there are no significant deviations from the trial plan. If there is a trial steering committee, responsibility for monitoring trial conduct will lie principally with that committee, and the DSMB should receive reports from the steering committee—often the chair of the DSMB attends all or part of the steering committee's meetings. However, if there is no steering committee, then the responsibility for monitoring trial conduct falls more heavily on the DSMB. Usually, this function is satisfied by the DSMB receiving detailed reports from the investigators on the progress and conduct of the trial at each DSMB meeting, but DSMB members may also make visits to the trial sites. Day-to-day monitoring of trial procedures, including data collection, is often provided by clinical trial monitors (see Chapter 16, Section 7.2) who should report regularly to the sponsor. If there are issues of concern, the sponsor has responsibility for reporting these to the DSMB, through the steering committee if there is one. Clearly, monitoring the conduct of a trial can be a major undertaking, and exactly what part the DSMB is expected to play in this should be detailed in the DSMB Charter (see Section 4.3).

4.1.2 Monitoring the safety of trial participants

Different kinds of AE should be reported to the DSMB on an 'immediate' or regular basis, the frequency depending on the seriousness of the AE.

Any serious AEs (SAEs) (see Chapter 12) that are judged by the investigators to be likely to have been due to the intervention ('potentially intervention-related SAEs') should be reported very quickly to the DSMB, within a few days of their occurrence or their first notification to the trial investigators. Similarly, any deaths among trial participants, whether or not judged related to the intervention, should be immediately reported to the DSMB. As much relevant detail as possible should be provided to the DSMB about the nature and circumstances of the death or SAE, along with a cumulative update of all such events. Deaths and potentially intervention-related SAEs would normally be reported to the sponsor at the same time as being reported to the DSMB.

When such events are reported, the chair of the DSMB should communicate with members to ascertain if any members consider the events are sufficiently serious and linked to the intervention that they require further investigation or, in extreme cases, might require that the trial is paused or terminated. If major changes to the conduct of the trial are suggested, the committee would generally meet by telephone conference or have a face-to-face meeting.

For SAEs that are not considered by the investigators to be directly related to the intervention, the DSMB should be informed of these on a regular basis, possibly monthly, depending on the size of the trial. At regular meetings of the DSMB, the accumulated SAEs should be considered. They should be classified by the type of SAE (for example, by hospital admission diagnosis), when they occurred in relation to the application of the intervention, and whether they affected participants in the intervention or control group. Displaying data by intervention and control groups requires breaking the code, and this is usually done either by an independent statistician (i.e. not one of the investigators, but a statistician contracted by the sponsor to perform the analyses) or by a statistician on the DSMB. Ideally, the tabulations should be presented to the DSMB by trial arm, without specifying what each arm has received intervention or control, and they should consider whether they are concerned by the size of any relative excess of events in any of the trial arms. Only if the answer to this question is 'yes' should they ask which arm was which. This procedure is adopted to avoid unnecessarily exposing the DSMB to unblinded data, unless there is good reason for concern, and to avoid their being biased in their assessment of the distribution of SAEs by knowing which arm any excess is in.

For more minor AEs, such as a minor local reaction to a vaccine or mild nausea, the DSMB can be presented with analyses of these on an occasional basis, though usually this should happen at least once a year. Again, they should initially be presented without identification of what each arm has received. Data on AEs are usually presented for information, rather than action, though occasionally action might be considered if there is a substantial excess of AEs in the intervention arm.

4.1.3 Conducting interim analyses

In some trials, a plan is made to examine interim efficacy results before the trial's expected end date. There are two main reasons for doing this. First, if the intervention proved much more effective than anticipated, then there might be grounds for terminating the trial early on the basis of 'overwhelming efficacy', such that it might not be considered ethical or necessary to continue with a control arm. Such analyses and their timing should be clearly specified in the trial protocol, as should the circumstances in which the results would lead to a recommendation to terminate the trial. In other words, the 'stopping rule' should be predefined. Second, the DSMB might recommend stopping a trial because of 'futility' if the interim results show a difference in study outcomes between the intervention group and the control group which is much less than expected if the intervention is effective and it is clear that, even if the trial is continued until its planned end, it is very unlikely to show an important difference in the rates of the primary outcome between the two groups. Again, such analyses should be planned in advance of starting the trial, and the stopping rules specified in the trial protocol. The

DSMB has responsibility for conducting these analyses, because they require breaking the code of the trial; if the decision is to continue the trial, the investigators have not been compromised by knowing either the interim results or which participants were allocated to which intervention. In such circumstances, the DSMB should not be tempted to share the interim results with the investigators but should merely tell them to carry on as planned. Having an independent DSMB is very valuable if a decision needs to be made about stopping a trial early, because this usually has considerable logistic and funding implications and may not be popular with the investigators, staff (who may even need to be laid off early), or participants.

Another common reason for conducting an 'interim' analysis is if the incidence of the primary outcome in the trial is less than anticipated or if recruitment to the trial is slower than expected. In such circumstances, it may be clear that the funds for conducting the trial will be exhausted before the planned number of participants or outcome events has been achieved. The investigators may then wish to seek further support from the funding agency to complete the trial. That agency may well request an interim analysis to know if the results to date already show the one arm of the trial to be convincingly superior to the other(s) or, conversely, whether there is little difference between the results in the different arms of the trial and collecting further data is unlikely to produce a convincing result, so it would be futile to extend the trial.

4.1.4 Modification of trial procedures and other advice

During the course of a trial, there may be a need for the DSMB to recommend modifications to the study, because of considerations of patient safety such as eligibility criteria, dosages, treatment duration, and/or concomitant therapy. When there is a trial steering committee, the DSMB would normally propose these recommendations to that committee (as representing the sponsor).

In the absence of a trial steering committee, investigators may well turn to the DSMB for advice on other aspects of the conduct of the trial. The DSMB is a useful source of independent unbiased advice, especially as it will often include persons with substantial trial experience.

4.1.5 Reporting to the sponsor

After each meeting of the DSMB, minutes should be drawn up relating to confidential and non-confidential parts of the meeting. In the non-confidential parts of a meeting, the trial investigators or their representatives may be present, in order to update and inform the committee on the progress of the trial, any deviations from planned procedures, and any AEs among trial participants. Confidential (closed) parts of the meeting will be restricted to DSMB members and may involve looking at data from the trial on outcome measures or AEs, unblinded with respect to the intervention arms. The minutes of this part of the meeting should be kept securely and confidential to the DSMB members until the end of the trial, at which time they should be given to the sponsor.

At the end of each of its meetings, the DSMB should draw up a report to the sponsor. This is often short and along the lines of 'We have reviewed the safety and other data from the trial and find no evidence of a safety concern that would lead us to suggest any change to trial procedures at this time'. However, if discussion of the trial data does cause the DSMB specific concerns and leads them to suggest specific changes to the conduct of the trial, these should be conveyed to the sponsor. The most extreme advice would be to halt the trial, but other advice might suggest, for example, changes to trial procedures, such as more frequent reporting of SAEs to the DSMB, more careful follow-up of a subset of participants, or changing diagnostic methods.

Sometimes, the investigators or sponsor will seek specific advice from the DSMB on aspects of trial procedures. For example, in some trials, the DSMB, or a subset of its members, may be asked to classify suspected cases of the disease of interest, according to levels of diagnostic certainty (without knowledge of which intervention they received)—though, depending on its composition in terms of expertise, this role might also be assumed by the steering committee or contracted to other independent experts (sometimes referred to as an 'endpoint committee').

It is important to note that the normal line of responsibility for reporting the deliberations of the DSMB is from the chair of the DSMB to the sponsor, and the responsibility for liaising with investigators and ethics committees lies with the sponsor. Sometimes, the sponsor will delegate this role to the trial steering committee, so that the DSMB reports directly to that committee. However, the DSMB should not report directly to the trial investigators, unless delegated to so do by the sponsor.

4.2 Composition and appointment of the Data and Safety Monitoring Board

The membership of a DSMB is usually decided by the trial sponsor, or the sponsor may delegate this task to the PIs or to the trial steering committee. Persons invited to join a DSMB are typically independent experts in the area of study of the trial, either working in the same field or in a related discipline, who have no personal or professional involvement with the intervention being tested, in that they will not profit either professionally or financially, according to the outcome of the trial. That is, the membership should be persons who are considered to be unbiased experts. Persons with strong views about the relative merits of the interventions under test would generally be considered unsuitable for DSMB membership. Those invited to join the committee should usually be familiar with, or have experience of, the conduct of RCTs. The chair of the committee should certainly have such experience and ideally should have experience of previous service on a DSMB.

The size of a DSMB will vary, according to the size and complexity of a trial and the likelihood that any of the trial interventions or procedures may cause significant harm to participants. The minimum size is three, and it is rare to have more than ten members, though the DSMB of large multicentre trials may approach that upper limit. The typical composition of a DSMB is outlined in Box 7.2.

In multicountry trials, it is common to have DSMB members drawn from at least some, if not all, of the countries included in the trial. Whether or not (lay) community members or advocates are included as members varies between trials. The inclusion of such members may help bring to the DSMB the perspectives of the population under study. Such members should not be participants in the trial, but the member could be someone with the disease or condition under study or a close relative of such an individual. For example, it has been common to include such persons in trials of HIV vaccines, but practice varies in trials of other interventions, and often lay members are not included.

> **Box 7.2 Typical composition of a DSMB**
>
> - At least one clinician with knowledge of the disease(s) under study.
> - A biostatistician knowledgeable about statistical methods for clinical trials and, if interim analyses are to be conducted, knowledgeable about the specific issues related to sequential analysis of trial data.
> - At least one clinician or scientist familiar with the kinds of intervention(s) under test and their possible adverse effects.
> - Others who bring special expertise to the committee relevant to the intervention or its application such as toxicologists, epidemiologists, and clinical pharmacologists.
>
> It is possible for a single individual to cover more than one of these skill areas.

For 'high-profile' trials of interventions, or with study procedures that might be controversial or have unusually high risks, the DSMB might include a medical ethicist knowledgeable in the design, conduct, and interpretation of clinical trials.

Anyone appointed to a DSMB must be prepared to respect the strict confidentiality of the discussions that take place within the committee and of the data that the committee may be given access to. They may also require training, for example, in the principles of GCP. Such training is now widely available either online (which is often free) or face to face.

Generally, members of a DSMB are not paid, but they may be recompensed for loss of earnings, travel, and other expenses incurred as a consequence of DSMB membership. However, in some industry-sponsored trials, members may be paid a fee for their participation.

Before an individual is appointed to a DSMB, it is important that they are given the opportunity to study the trial protocol, so that they fully understand the purposes of the trial and how it will be conducted. Often they will also be given the opportunity to suggest changes to the protocol—especially related to issues such as reporting of AEs and trial stopping rules. Once more, it is important to stress that their advice should go to the sponsor and the trial steering committee, and not directly to the investigators.

4.3 The Data and Safety Monitoring Board charter

In many trials, a specific 'charter' is drawn up by the sponsor that details exactly the terms of reference and responsibilities of DSMB members. The charter should take account of the particular needs of the trial and the questions it is addressing. It should detail the relationship between the DSMB and the sponsor, investigators, steering committee, ethics committees, and others with responsibilities in the study. It also gives details of how meetings will be organized, how often they will take place, how many members constitute a quorum, and how confidential and non-confidential minutes will be produced, distributed, and stored securely until the end of the trial. All members of the DSMB will be required to sign the charter at the time of their appointment. Guidelines are available on drawing up a DSMB charter (DAMOCLES Study Group, 2005).

5 Trial registration

Until relatively recently, there were no comprehensive sources of information about ongoing clinical trials. Not infrequently, trials would be started and would be prematurely ended with knowledge of their conduct known only to those closely associated with the trial if the findings were not published in the medical literature. Other trials were completed, but their results were never reported for various reasons, including that the investigators or sponsors did not like the findings of the trial! Other investigators might start a new trial, ignorant of the fact that a trial addressing essentially the same question was already under way or had even been completed but not yet published. Those conducting systematic reviews (see Chapter 3, Section 2) would be aware of the published literature but would be ignorant of such unpublished trials. It has been well documented that trials that show a 'positive' outcome are more likely to be published than those that do not, and thus the published literature may constitute a biased sample of all of the evidence related to the effects of a specific intervention.

In the 1990s, it was proposed that registers should be set up, in which those conducting trials should be required to record their trial before the first participant was enrolled into it. The record should consist of basic information about the trial (Box 7.3). This recommendation was given teeth in 2005 when the International Committee of Medical Journal Editors (ICMJE), which comprises the editors of many of the major journals that publish papers on the results of trials, made it a requirement for publishing that the trial should have been properly reported to a public clinical trials register before any participant was enrolled into the trial (<http://www.icmje.org>). Initially, the requirement covered only randomized clinical trials, but it has been subsequently expanded to include 'any research study that prospectively assigns human participants or groups of humans to one or more health-related interventions to evaluate the effects of health outcomes', so that Phases I and II trials and non-randomized intervention studies, as well as Phase III RCTs, are included.

Several coordinated trial registries have been set up, so that any individual trial is issued a unique number which is recorded in the International Standard Randomised Controlled Trial Number Register (<http://www.controlled-trials.com/isrctn>). Trials are only eligible for publication by ICMJE journals if they have been registered in one of the following registries:

- <http://www.anzctr.org.au>
- <http://clinicaltrials.gov>
- <http://www.isrctn.org>
- <http://www.umin.ac.jp/ctr/index.htm>
- <http://www.trialregister.nl/trialreg/index.asp>
- <http://eudract.ema.europa.eu> (new registrations after 20 June 2011), or
- any of the primary registries that participate in the WHO International Clinical Trials Portal (see <http://www.who.int/ictrp/network/primary/en/index.html>). This includes the Pan African Clinical Trials Registry (<http://www.pactr.org>). This registry enables African trial registration for those who do not have reliable access to the Internet.

Box 7.3 (Minimal) information that is required when registering a clinical trial

- Title of the trial.
- Acronym for the trial (if there is one).
- Study hypothesis/trial objective, i.e. what question(s) is the trial design to address.
- Ethics committee approval—which committees and when approved
- Study design—individual or cluster, whether or not randomized, double-blind, etc.
- Countries of recruitment.
- Disease/condition/study domain—nature of study population and diseases of interest.
- Inclusion criteria for participation in trial.
- Exclusion criteria for participation in trial.
- Anticipated trial start date.
- Anticipated trial end date.
- Current status of trial—ongoing, waiting ethics approval, etc.
- Patient information material—is information about the trial publicly available and where?
- Target number of participants.
- Description of the interventions (for example, name, dose, duration).
- Primary outcome measures.
- Secondary outcome measures.
- Sources of funding.
- Trial website (if there is one).
- Publications.
- Name and contact details for PI and, where different, of person(s) responsible for providing information about the trial to the public and the scientific community.
- Name and contact details for sponsor.

References

DAMOCLES Study Group. NHS. Health Technology Assessment Programme. 2005. A proposed charter for clinical trial data monitoring committees: helping them to do their job well. *Lancet*, **365**, 711–22.

International Conference On Harmonisation. 1996. *Technical requirements for registration of pharmaceuticals for human use: guideline for good clinical practice E6(R1)* [Online].

Available at: <http://www.ich.org/fileadmin/Public_Web_Site/ICH_Products/Guidelines/Efficacy/E6/E6_R1_Guideline.pdf>.

International Conference On Harmonisation. 1998. *Statistical principles for clinical trials* [Online]. Available at: <http://www.ich.org/fileadmin/Public_Web_Site/ICH_Products/Guidelines/Efficacy/E9/Step4/E9_Guideline.pdf>.

World Health Organization. 2005. *Operational guidelines for the establishment and functioning of data and safety monitoring boards.* Available at: <http://whqlibdoc.who.int/hq/2005/TDR_GEN_Guidelines_05.1_eng.pdf>.

Chapter 8

Preparing grant applications

1 Introduction to preparing grant applications 132
2 Grant awarding agencies 133
    2.1 Understand the remit 133
    2.2 Early contact 133
3 Grant types 134
    3.1 Project and programme grants 134
    3.2 Personal fellowships 134
    3.3 Special initiatives 134
4 Grant awarding process 135
    4.1 Peer review 135
    4.2 Funding committees 135
    4.3 Competitive process 136
5 Developing the proposal 136
    5.1 What is the problem, and why should it be studied? 136
    5.2 What information is already available? 138
    5.3 What are the objectives of the research? 138
    5.4 How will relevant information be collected and analysed? 138
    5.5 Community engagement plan 139
    5.6 Who will do what and when? 139
    5.7 What are the risks? 139
    5.8 What resources are needed? 140
    5.9 How will the project be supervised and administered? 140
    5.10 How will results be disseminated? 140
    5.11 How will the application be presented to funding agencies? 141
6 Responding to referees 141
7 Funding decision 142
8 Common problems in grant applications 143
9 Roles and responsibilities 143
10 Further advice 144

1 Introduction to preparing grant applications

Research funding agencies want to support outstanding researchers to conduct cutting edge studies to advance knowledge that contributes to the solution of health problems. Applicants for grants must convince the funding agency that they are high-quality scientists whose research proposal addresses important question(s) and that the studies planned will deliver the answer(s) on time and within budget. Research proposals have many common elements, but, in intervention trials involving human subjects, some critical aspects, such as ethical, legal, and social issues, must be addressed particularly carefully in the grant application. Determination, good planning, and meticulous attention to details are essential for a successful application.

2 Grant awarding agencies

There are many national and international funding agencies that include intervention trials in their funding portfolio. These include, but are by no means limited to, the WHO Tropical Diseases Research Programme, the European and Developing Countries Clinical Trials Partnership, the Bill and Melinda Gates Foundation, the UK Medical Research Council, the US National Institutes for Health, the Wellcome Trust, the Volkswagen Foundation in Germany, and the French Institut National de la Santé et de la Recherche Médicale (INSERM). The pharmaceutical industry and several non-governmental public–private partnerships created in the last decade have partnered with academic institutions in the development of new drugs and vaccines for LMICs, including supporting clinical trials. In addition, some government development agencies, such as United States Agency for International Development (USAID) and UK Department for International Development (DFID), also support studies on the evaluation of public health interventions.

2.1 Understand the remit

All funding agencies have their own specific remits and priorities. Even for intervention trials, some agencies have specific programmes for particular diseases or will only support certain kinds of study. It is imperative to be familiar with the remit of the agency to which a funding application is planned and to understand what they expect from supporting a research proposal; otherwise, a lot of unnecessary time can be wasted by applicants.

Many funding agencies will ask why they, rather than some other group, should support a specific trial. For example, for a trial of a new vaccine that has been developed by a pharmaceutical company, a likely question is why the company is not providing the support, as it will stand to benefit if the vaccine is found to be efficacious.

2.2 Early contact

Those wishing to conduct a specific trial must decide on the most suitable funding agency to approach for support. One sure way of ensuring that a particular funding agency is an appropriate recipient of an application is to make early contact. Most agencies have detailed information on their websites where information about the forms of support offered, the application process, and deadlines for applications are available. Where there is uncertainty, it is always a good idea to contact individual officers in the agency. They usually welcome an early opportunity to discuss a potential applicant's plans, and they will suggest the best way to submit a grant application. Importantly, they will advise if the agency is unlikely to support a particular application (for example, because the topic is outside of their remit or priorities). Such information early in the process of seeking a grant may be invaluable. A common mistake is to leave the preparation of an application and contact with the grant agency until close to a deadline. Plan ahead, and leave plenty of time for discussions with the grant agency's officers and to prepare an application. A rushed application is almost always a poor one. Many funding agencies will offer to look at an outline application, sometimes known as a letter of intent or a concept note, to advise on whether or not it is within their remit or how it might be modified to better fit their funding schemes.

3 Grant types

The type of support needed for an intervention trial depends on the personal and institutional circumstances of the applicants. For example, an applicant in a tenured position in an academic institution may not require salary support but just need direct and indirect research project costs for equipment, staff, materials, and administrative costs. If the principal applicant is not in a salaried position, salary support will be needed, in which case, for some funding agencies, a fellowship may be an appropriate avenue of support.

3.1 Project and programme grants

In the parlance of many funding agencies, a *project grant* is for a specific piece of work to answer just one or two specific questions, usually for a period of about 3 years. It may be, for example, a clinical trial to test the safety of a drug in its early development phase. A *programme grant* is for a larger, more complex set of studies to answer several related questions and is often for 5–7 years. A clinical trial may sometimes form part of an application for programme grant support. Some agencies may not support project or programme grants but only fellowships, or vice versa, so it is important to check this early.

Once a grant has been awarded, in most cases, funds are released on a yearly basis, taking into account technical progress and financial implementation. Estimating the cost of a project can be a very complicated exercise, especially with respect to indirect costs associated with the study. These aspects are discussed in Chapter 18.

3.2 Personal fellowships

Personal fellowships are for researchers who do not have a salaried, tenured, or substantive 'permanent' position. Fellowship applicants request for their personal salary, in addition to partial or complete research costs. Many agencies have programmes to support scientists throughout their career, from the Masters/PhD stage through one or more intermediate phases where they establish their independence, and finally to senior levels.

3.3 Special initiatives

Investigators should be on the lookout for special initiatives such as calls for support to conduct a trial on a particular topic. When there is a special initiative, research proposals are competing within a smaller specified area of science, and applicants are likely to be reviewed by people who work in roughly the same subject area.

It is not unusual that large clinical trials are conducted as a collaborative effort. For example, vaccine trials might have to be conducted in multiple sites and countries where there are significant differences in population structure, host genetic factors, public health systems, environment, and prevalence of co-infections. In this case, it may be important to collaborate and coordinate approaches to more than one funding agency.

4 Grant awarding process

4.1 Peer review

Nearly all funding agencies subject applications for support to some form of independent peer review. Usually, this will take the form of soliciting comments on the proposal from scientific experts. Some will be selected for their expertise in scientific areas included in a proposal, while others may be chosen for their broad experience to give a generalist perspective. Thus, the application should include a balance of appropriate details and a broader vision, as the familiarity of those conducting the review with the subject area may vary.

Most agencies do not reveal the identity of independent reviewers, so that they provide frank objective comments, including for applications from persons they know or are known by. Agencies sometimes solicit suggestions from applicants as to who might review a proposal, although they may choose not to use anyone suggested. On rare occasions, applicants request that certain individuals not be asked to review their application. This may be because of potential conflicts of interest or because the applicant considers that the individuals may not be objective. Funding agencies do try to take such requests into consideration in their choice of reviewers.

Most agencies allow applicants to see the anonymized reviews or extracts from them, in which reviewers will usually highlight strengths and weaknesses of a proposal. These comments may be sent either after a funding decision has been made or to applicants requesting a response before the funding decision is made. Policies vary from agency to agency. If applicants are given the opportunity, they should always respond carefully and concisely to criticisms or suggestions made by referees, as both the referees' reports and the response to them will be considered by the panel that makes the final funding decision (see Section 6).

It is common that the review process is conducted in two stages. Some agencies recommend that the applicants first submit a 'letter of intent' that gives a brief description of the proposed research. The agency will then advise whether or not it falls within their remit and will advise whether or not a full proposal should be prepared. Changes that would improve the proposal's chances of being supported might also be suggested. One of the purposes of this two-stage approach is to allow the funding agencies to reduce the number of full proposals reviewed, so they can focus on the most promising ones. If an opportunity is given for submission of a letter of intent, applicants should make use of this before preparing a full proposal.

4.2 Funding committees

Decisions whether or not to fund applications are usually made or recommended by an advisory committee. In some funding schemes, applicants may be asked to attend for an interview, as part of the proposal review process. Members of these committees will have expertise in the general area of all the proposals they have to deliberate on. The identities of members of funding committees are usually made available, and it is a good strategy, especially if an interview is involved, for an applicant to read some of their recent work to try to guess some of the issues on which they are likely to focus in their questioning. The detailed discussions that funding committees have, in order to come to a decision on a specific application, are usually strictly confidential. The funding agency will usually convey an appropriate summary of the discussions, if relevant, to applicants. This is particularly useful if an application has been rejected, as a summary of the reasons for rejection may help the development of an improved proposal for the same or another funding agency. Most funding agencies regard it as highly inappropriate for applicants to have direct contact with members of funding committees regarding the application, and members are instructed specifically not to discuss applications outside committee meetings. Whenever a proposal is being reviewed where a member of the committee has a potential conflict of interest, they are usually asked to leave the room. Examples include where the individual or someone from their institution is involved in the proposal.

Funding agencies endeavour to support the best proposals where the research question, the timeliness of the study, the ability of the scientists involved, and the potential impact of the results all come together to make a compelling case for support of the proposal. In a proposal for an intervention trial, applicants should think carefully about how their study will stand out among potentially competing proposals. Whatever the area, the applicant needs to convey that the proposed study is important and timely and has achievable goals.

Most field trials are conducted in partnerships between research institutions and public health systems. For this reason, it is very important to have a clear definition of roles, responsibilities, and complementary expertise of the parties involved. How any ethical or legal issues related to potential consequences of the study will be handled should be carefully explained.

4.3 Competitive process

Obtaining grants is a highly competitive process. All agencies receive far more applications than they are able to fund, so a rejection does not necessarily mean that the proposal was weak. The decision on whether to resubmit a revised proposal to the same or another agency should take the feedback into account. Sometimes, but not always, the funding agency's officer administering the application may be willing to give advice on this.

5 Developing the proposal

When developing the proposal, it is wise to follow a systematic approach. In Box 8.1, a 10-step chronological, algorithmic approach is summarized that might be helpful for less experienced grant writers.

5.1 What is the problem, and why should it be studied?

The first step is to define clearly the *primary research question* to be addressed by the trial. Next, articulate why it is important and how the knowledge or evidence

Box 8.1 A 10-step guide to preparing a grant application

1 What is the problem, and why should it be studied?
   - Primary research question
   - Why is it important?
2 What information is already available?
   - Literature review
3 What are the objectives of the research?
   - Purpose of the trial
   - Specific objectives
4 How will the information be collected and analysed?
   - Study design
   - Data collection methods; sampling; data processing
   - Study size—what criteria and assumptions?
   - Data analysis methods
   - Ethical, legal, and social issues
5 Who will do what and when?
   - Work plan with a timetable
   - Human resources; collaborations; training
6 What are the risks?
   - Contingencies. Is there a 'plan B'?
7. What resources are needed to carry out the research?
   - Budget
   - Justification
8 How will the project be supervised and administered?
   - Identification of advisors and planning for trial administration
   - Trial governance, including data and safety monitoring and trial steering committees, if relevant
9 How will results be disseminated?
   - Plan for utilization of research; identification of potential users of results
   - Data and sample archiving, access, and availability
10 How will the application be presented to funding agencies?
   - Submission forms; deadlines
   - Attention to detail; presentation

derived from the trial will contribute to addressing one or more health problems. Many proposals fail because too many questions are being asked and the proposal is unfocused.

5.2 What information is already available?

A good, but brief, *literature review* of what has already been done in the research area is an important element of any grant proposal. It demonstrates that the applicant has looked at the relevant publications to identify gaps and opportunities in the field on which the study is based. Wherever possible, past work should be summarized in the form of a systematic review, as discussed in Chapter 3. This stage should also include a review of any relevant registered trials that have not yet been completed.

5.3 What are the objectives of the research?

The title of a proposal is the first thing that the reader sees. After identifying the research question, produce a title that gives the reader a clear idea of what it is hoped to discover. Respect any word limits imposed by the funder.

The next step is to formulate the aims and specific objectives. These vary, according to the nature of the study. For a straightforward trial, for example, comparing the effects of two drugs, it may be relatively simple to state the aim. It may simply be to show whether drug A is superior to drug B in curing a specific disease in an individually randomized controlled trial.

In more complex studies, it may be necessary to articulate a general aim, followed by a list of specific objectives, some of which may include sub-objectives. Sometimes, several sequential steps may need to occur. In vaccine studies, for example, the immune status of the target population may need to be assessed first to select the target group for vaccination, and, before that, immunological assays may need to be developed, or tested and evaluated in the specific target population for the trial.

5.4 How will relevant information be collected and analysed?

The study design is a major component of a trial. Whether it should be placebo-controlled, double-blind, stratified, cluster randomized, etc. depends on many factors. State why a particular approach is necessary, and, if apparently superior designs have not been chosen, state why not. Many of these issues are discussed in Chapter 4.

The data to be collected and how they will be analysed must be described. If any of the data are to be from a sample of trial participants, the sampling technique needs to be explained and justified. Describe how the data will be processed and what statistical tests will be used in the analysis. Discuss any ethical, legal, and social issues that could arise from the specimen or data collection, storage, and dissemination. For example, it is important to describe informed consent processes for the trial population, what examinations will be performed on participants, and who will be responsible for their health care during the trial. Issues related to the taking, storage, and analysis of biological specimens should be addressed. If there are no previous published data to guide study design, will existing preliminary data or a pilot study be important? These issues are dealt with in detail in other chapters.

5.5 Community engagement plan

The proposal should include a description of how the community will be engaged in the planning and conduct of the trial (see Chapter 9). This should include a brief description of any formal structures, such as a Community Advisory Board (CAB), and other mechanisms that will be used to solicit the trial community's support and advice and to keep them fully informed of the trial's progress and results.

5.6 Who will do what and when?

The *work plan* is important to show in a logical way what aspects of the trial will be done and when. If a trial is 'high risk', this should be because the topic being studied is intellectually and conceptually challenging, not because it has been inadequately planned.

For nearly all trials, certain steps need to be conducted first, before others can proceed. A 'Gantt chart' is a helpful tool for project planning and presenting the proposed work plan, especially if there are complex dependencies among several components. Gantt charts are used to illustrate a project schedule, indicating in a graphical way start and end dates of specific components and activities to show how the individual tasks are sequenced.

It is important to identify specific milestones in the planning, conduct, and analysis of the trial and if strategic decisions will need to be made and when, such as whether the trial should continue or be stopped, given defined developments or outcomes.

Typical intervention trials involve large teams of people such as recruiters, interviewers, nurses, clinicians, laboratory technicians, public health officials, data management staff, statisticians, collaborators, and consultants. These have to be carefully managed, and their work budgeted for. In many cases, additional training may be needed. How the trial team will be managed and the work will be coordinated should be summarized in the proposal.

5.7 What are the risks?

In any research undertaking, there is a chance that the objectives will not be achieved because of unexpected changes in circumstances. It is a good strategy to have contingency plans to cover areas where there are such potential risks. While it is impossible to anticipate all risks, list the known ones. Do not wait until reviewers point them out. It shows awareness and preparedness to alter plans without jeopardizing the main aims of the proposal. A good risk management plan would anticipate potential issues and corresponding solutions to prevent delays, increased cost, or poor quality to the study data. An example of a potential, and not uncommon, risk would be that the trial recruitment rate will be slower than anticipated. Potential ways of dealing with this could include close monitoring, so that remedial action can be taken early, using conservative recruitment estimates or planning recruitment at times in the year when the population in most accessible, for example. Contingency plans are particularly important in high-risk research. Identify the potential pitfalls, and describe how plans will change if they arise. For example, what is the alternative strategy if it proved impossible to conduct the trial in one of the trial populations?

5.8 What resources are needed?

Some funding programmes invite proposals that must cost less than a specified amount, and it is necessary to design a study that fits within that budget limit. Whether or not there is a specified budget limit, much thought needs to be given to the budget. On the one hand, an inflated budget could render a proposal uncompetitive if equally strong proposals cost less. On the other hand, an under-budgeted trial may not be completed, and the results will be unpublishable. Be honest about what is needed. Discuss with the officer at the funding agency if guidance is required.

Funding agencies usually provide a list of costs that are eligible to be included in a grant application, i.e. costs that they are prepared to cover. It is important to study the conditions carefully. Salaries must be commensurate with qualifications, fairness, and compatible with local contexts. If equipment is being requested, maintenance costs may need to be factored in. In intervention trials, other costs associated with medical treatment and social care may have to be included. Some agencies do not fund institutional overheads or limit them to a maximum percentage of the total budget, so it will be necessary to check that these are acceptable to the applicant's institution in advance. Institutional contributions could be important to show their commitment to the trial.

Sometimes, it is possible to leverage donations of drugs or supplies from pharmaceutical companies—these can lower the overall costs and make a proposal more cost-effective to funders. If the specific proposal is linked to other projects, provide detail of what is already funded, and be clear about how much funding is being sought and how much will come from other sources. The key message is to cost the trial carefully, and justify all the costs requested.

5.9 How will the project be supervised and administered?

The grant application should demonstrate, for the conduct and analysis of the trial, that the trial team either has all the necessary skills and experience or will have access to the appropriate expertise. This may include aspects of trial governance and monitoring of GCP and Good Clinical Laboratory Practice (GCLP) (see Chapters 16 and 17). It may be possible to delegate some of the trial procedures to specialist clinical research organizations (CROs). These units often have specialists in clinical trials to run certain aspects of a trial such as GCP or GCLP monitoring procedures.

Unless the trial is small, it is worth considering setting up a trial steering committee to guide and support the organization and monitoring of trial activities and guide its development, as the trial progresses. The steering committee should include members that represent a broad range of perspectives relevant to trial management. The steering committee also has the task of working with the DSMC to monitor progress and results without compromising the study design, especially in blinded studies (see Chapter 7).

5.10 How will results be disseminated?

The results of intervention trials are generally expected to contribute to the formulation of health policies and practice. It is important to think about how the results of a trial might be used. Including policy makers and officials from the public health sector in the early planning and design stages of a trial, and keeping them informed during the conduct of the trial, can lead to a faster adoption of trial results into policy and practice after the trial. Funding agencies like to see a quick impact for their funds, so specific provision for this in the application can be an advantage (see also Chapter 23).

Intervention trials, by their nature, often produce very large amounts of personal data and biological specimens. Specimen and data storage and access may present complicated ethical and legal issues. Who owns the specimens and data, who can see the personal data, how long the information and specimens should be kept, how the storage will be paid for, etc. are all pertinent questions. Funding agencies often require open access to data after the end of a trial, and the investigators may have to explain in their application how they will manage this requirement, taking into account confidentiality issues.

5.11 How will the application be presented to funding agencies?

Most funding agencies have detailed instructions on the application process available on their Internet sites. Read the instructions carefully, and contact staff at the funding agency if anything is not absolutely clear.

Meeting deadlines is important. Sometimes, funding committees meet only once a year, and, if the deadline is missed, it may be a year before another submission can be made. Do not aim to submit just before the deadline—allow time, and submit ahead of the deadline. Sometimes, funding organizations need clarification if something is not clear in the application. Submitting early allows these issues to be sorted out, before the funding committee meets.

Do pay attention to details. Answer all the questions in the application form. For good presentation, make sure the proposal reads easily, for example, by minimizing the use of abbreviations and acronyms. Avoid technical jargon where unnecessary, and supply clear definitions of any technical terms that must be used. The proposal should be clear and succinct, free of contradiction or 'leaps of faith', and readily understood by scientists outside the immediate field of the investigator. Pay careful attention to its structure, ensuring it is logically ordered and argued. The aims and objectives of the proposal should be clearly defined at the start. Most space should be given to study design and methods. Use flow diagrams and figures where these will help the reader.

Allow time to go through the form several times. Make sure the final application is free of errors (spelling, typing errors, grammar, etc.), so as not to distract the reader. A carelessly put together application is often interpreted to indicate a careless investigator. It is valuable to have one or more colleagues, who have not been involved in writing the proposal, to review it before submission, as they will often pick up inconsistencies and errors that the investigator has missed simply through being too familiar with the proposal.

6 Responding to referees

Many funding agencies allow applicants to respond to referees' comments before the applications are considered by the funding committee. It is critical to make full use of the opportunity. Referees may have considerable experience in the field of the proposed research, and it is important to consider carefully their remarks and suggestions. Challenge comments that appear to be incorrect, preferably citing a reference. However, if suggestions are made that might improve the design of the study, consider carefully how the study might be modified to address the concerns, and include these in the response that will go to the funding committee. The length of the response allowed to referees' comments is usually limited, so be precise and concise.

7 Funding decision

Members of funding committees will usually have to read a large number of proposals in a relatively short period of time, and thus it is important that grant applications are written clearly and unambiguously to facilitate rapid understanding. Brevity, precision, and clarity therefore have great merit! The length of the grant application should be the minimum necessary to demonstrate the competence of the investigator and of the appropriateness and importance of the study proposed. It should never exceed the limits set by the funding agency. Reviewers will usually be annoyed, rather than impressed, with information, however erudite, that is not directly relevant to the research that is being proposed.

In reviewing a grant application, reviewers and committee members will be looking for the answers to some key questions, which are summarized in Box 8.2.

Box 8.2 Key questions that reviewers and funding committee members will consider when reviewing a grant application

1. What are the research questions that will be addressed by the proposed study?
2. Why is it important that this research be carried out? How will the study contribute, directly or indirectly, to the advancement of public health?
3. Are the applicants familiar with previous work in the area of the research, and does the study proposed build on and complement that work?
4. Have the applicants done preliminary or pilot studies that demonstrate the feasibility of the proposed research?
5. What is the research design, and how will it be implemented? Is the design appropriate?
6. Are the estimates of the impact of the intervention reasonable? Is the size of the study correct to detect an impact of the magnitude expected? Is the expected impact of the intervention of public health importance?
7. Is the time schedule for the work appropriate?
8. How much will the research cost? Are the costs justified?
9. Have the applicants considered the possible obstacles they might encounter in conducting the research and devised ways of overcoming these?
10. Have the applicants assembled the right team to do the research? What is their track record in research of this kind? Are their training and experience appropriate?

8 Common problems in grant applications

The amount of detail to include on the trial design is a tricky one to get right. Some forms allow only a limited space, so care is required to provide the key details concisely but clearly articulated, so that reviewers can make an informed judgement. Standard methodologies can be simply referenced. A common fault is that applicants do not discuss obvious potential problems or limitations with their study design and just hope that they will not be picked up by reviewers. This strategy rarely works, and it is better to show awareness of the issues and explain how they will be addressed.

A list of common problems in grant applications is given in Box 8.3.

9 Roles and responsibilities

Expect a response from funding agencies in a timely manner. Most funding agencies will inform applicants of the date by which a decision will be made on an application. Remember that the reason for rejection may not be due to obvious flaws in the proposal

Box 8.3 Common problems with grant applications

- Poorly formulated objectives.
- Too ambitious—trying to address too many questions in one study.
- Insufficient attention to previous literature on the research question.
- Poorly identified target population.
- Poor research design—inadequate attention to what specific research question is being addressed.
- Insufficient explanation of why it is important to answer this question and what impact it may have on public health practice.
- No data, preliminary results, or pilot studies to support the feasibility of the proposed approach.
- Inadequate description of the study design and procedures—derivation of sample size is often done poorly (consult a statistician!).
- Analysis methods not specified sufficiently in relation to the main objectives.
- Inadequate description as to who is doing what and when; lacking a detailed timetable for the research.
- Insufficient attention to quality and quality control.
- Inadequate allowance for data entry and analysis—often arrangements for analysis of data are not addressed at all in a proposal, other than that it will all go into a computer!
- Inadequately justified budget.
- Poorly structured; hard to follow the logic; inconsistencies.

but may just be that the application was not competitive, compared to others considered by the funding committee.

Remember that a successful application is only the start. Funders are interested in the progress of the project. They should be informed of any major findings, especially if there are going to be publications or if the results are controversial or groundbreaking. Funders may wish to publicize these, and they often have the resources to do so effectively.

Funding agency staff are usually prepared to offer advice on grant issues, and keeping them informed of important developments in a timely manner is advisable, for example, unavoidable delays to a study, changes to the study design, extension requests, etc. If delays are anticipated, it is much better to notify the agency early, so they are not wrong-footed but can work with you to mitigate the impact of these delays. For example, given sufficient notice, they may be able to revise the trial budget to allow money to be spent later than was originally agreed.

10 Further advice

There are numerous sources of general advice on how to write a successful research grant proposal such as a book by Gitlin and Lyons, 2008. Some are even produced by specific funding agencies such as the Medical Research Council of South Africa (<http://www.mrc.ac.za/researchdevelopment/researchgrant.pdf>). Clearly, it is a smart move to read such advice if you are applying to an organization that provides it!

Reference

Gitlin, L. N. and Lyons, K. J. 2008. *Successful grant writing : strategies for health and human service professionals*. London: Springer.

Chapter 9

Community engagement

1 Introduction to community engagement 145
2 Planning and initiating community engagement 146
   2.1 Defining communities and aims of engaging communities 146
   2.2 Preliminary investigations in study communities 147
   2.3 Setting up Community Advisory Groups or Boards 149
3 Engaging community stakeholders 151
   3.1 Engaging national and regional administrations 151
   3.2 Engaging district health teams and health providers 151
   3.3 Engaging community leaders 152
   3.4 Working with the wider community 153
   3.5 Roles of front-line research staff in community engagement 153
4 Strategy and content of information for communication 155
5 Sustaining community engagement 156

1 Introduction to community engagement

The impetus to conduct trials of major public health interventions will often be from research centres or universities, in collaboration with the Ministry of Health (MOH). The intervention trial team will usually select the communities which they consider are most suitable for the conduct of a trial. The active and continued engagement with people within these communities is essential for the successful execution of the field trial. This chapter aims to provide practical guidance to researchers on ways of approaching community engagement in trials in LMICs, including identifying some common pitfalls.

The terms 'community' and 'engagement' attract debate and controversy around their meanings and the social, ethical, and political implications of their application in development and biomedical research practice. These aspects will not be explored in detail in this chapter but are discussed elsewhere (Participants in the Community Engagement Consent Workshop, 2013). The present chapter should also be read in conjunction with Chapters 6 and 15, as understanding of the ethical responsibilities of researchers working in LMICs underpins the overall importance of community engagement and the planning of its components (see Chapter 6), and community engagement is essentially a social endeavour, with many overlaps with social and behavioural research approaches and methods (see Chapter 15).

For the purposes of this chapter, community engagement will be defined as the process of the trial team working collaboratively with the community on all aspects of the study which affect the community and its well-being. Overall, engagement should typically involve continuous mutual learning and communication between researchers and a range of community members before and during a trial and after a trial ends.

2 Planning and initiating community engagement

2.1 Defining communities and aims of engaging communities

The overarching goal of community engagement is to create and maintain mutual understanding and trust between researchers and the communities in which the trial takes place. Community engagement is supportive of many different aspects of good science and ethics in research. Examples are fostering broad support for research activities, facilitating good informed consent processes, encouraging sustained participation, reducing risks of rumours and loss of trust, and making falsification of information less likely. From a community perspective, engaging with the trial team can help to ensure that the benefits of participation by community members outweigh the costs to them and supports their autonomy (i.e. informed, uncoerced decision making) within the trial. But community engagement is also seen as a good in itself, in demonstrating the trial team's respect for the community and what has been described as 'cultural humility' (Participants in the Community Engagement Consent Workshop, 2013).

As a first step, it is important to establish clearly who 'the community' is, or communities are, in relation to the trial and who the leaders or representatives of those communities are. In many instances, the community will be defined, at least initially, by the trial team and may thereby be relatively artificial. Often, trial communities are defined as all those living within a particular geographical area, but, for some trials, the community may be a social or an activity-based group such as intravenous drug users or sex workers. Defining communities is not necessarily straightforward. For example, what are the relevant communities for trials whose participants are regular migrants (for example, people who move seasonally between two geographical locations in pursuit of employment) or for trial participants who are selected at their place of work, such as factory workers, who live within wider social and geographical communities? In many trials, researchers have to engage with several communities and several different types of communities. If problems arise in relation to the trial in any one community, this may slow, or in extreme cases, jeopardize the conduct of the whole trial.

When the participants in a trial are selected from a specific subgroup of the population, such as a particular occupational group, or people who share a particular behaviour, such as men who have sex with other men, careful thought needs to be given to which aspects of the community engagement will apply only to the social community that the trial participants come from, and which will apply to the wider community from which they are drawn. For example, in a trial in Tanzania, women who worked in specific locations, such as bars, restaurants, and guesthouses, were invited to participate in an HIV prevention trial, because they were at relatively high risk of HIV infection. It was decided that the reason why this 'high-risk' occupational group had been selected for the trial would not be discussed explicitly in community engagement activities with the wider geographical community and their representatives. It was also decided that community engagement structures (such as the representatives of the trial's CAB and its subgroups) would be drawn from trial participants and that communication with the wider geographical community would be kept to a minimum to avoid further stigmatization of women from these occupations (Shagi et al., 2008). In Kenya, a similar approach was adopted for a study working with men who have sex with men, but, over time, members of the wider geographical community became concerned that researchers were promoting homosexuality; following protests and media attention, far greater attention was placed on communication with the wider community.

While the overarching goals for community engagement have been described earlier in this section, this must be followed by defining the specific objectives of community engagement with each of the specific trial communities. These objectives will help to define the overall strategy, in relation to who should be involved, how, throughout and after the trial, and what methods and resources will be needed for the community engagement process.

Both the trial and community engagement activities will inevitably have implications and impacts which are not expected or intended. Community engagement can never be a prefabricated and entirely predictable set of activities that could apply to different settings; rather it needs to be seen as a dynamic and an ever-changing set of negotiated relationships (Lavery et al., 2010). The objectives and activities identified at the outset may need to be modified over time, in response to emerging issues and shifting priorities over the course of the trial. For this reason, community engagement must not be seen as an entirely linear process, nor its effectiveness evaluated as though it were.

2.2 Preliminary investigations in study communities

As early as possible, even during the process of identifying the communities, the trial team should work together with community leaders and local experts to begin to develop a strategy for achieving and sustaining community engagement throughout the trial. Many of the specific issues to be considered will depend upon the nature of the intervention and the kind of participation anticipated from the community, so it is important to contextualize planning to the specifics of the trial. The aim is to develop as close a partnership as possible between the trial team and all relevant communities in all aspects of the trial's design, implementation, interpretation, and dissemination. To achieve this, sustained two-way channels of communication must be created that facilitate regular exchange of information between community stakeholders and the trial team. The formation of a specific CAB, in some cases with representation from several Community Advisory Groups (CAGs), is one means of supporting this ongoing communication and is discussed in more detail in Section 2.3. Given some of the recognized problems with CABs, many trials engage with several CAGs, without one overall CAB. For simplicity, we shall use CAB/G to represent both concepts in the rest of this chapter.

Figure 9.1 outlines the main steps involved in engaging communities with the many activities involved in a field trial.

Preliminary studies and participatory planning processes can reduce the risk of potential pitfalls by accommodating the perspectives and preferences of different

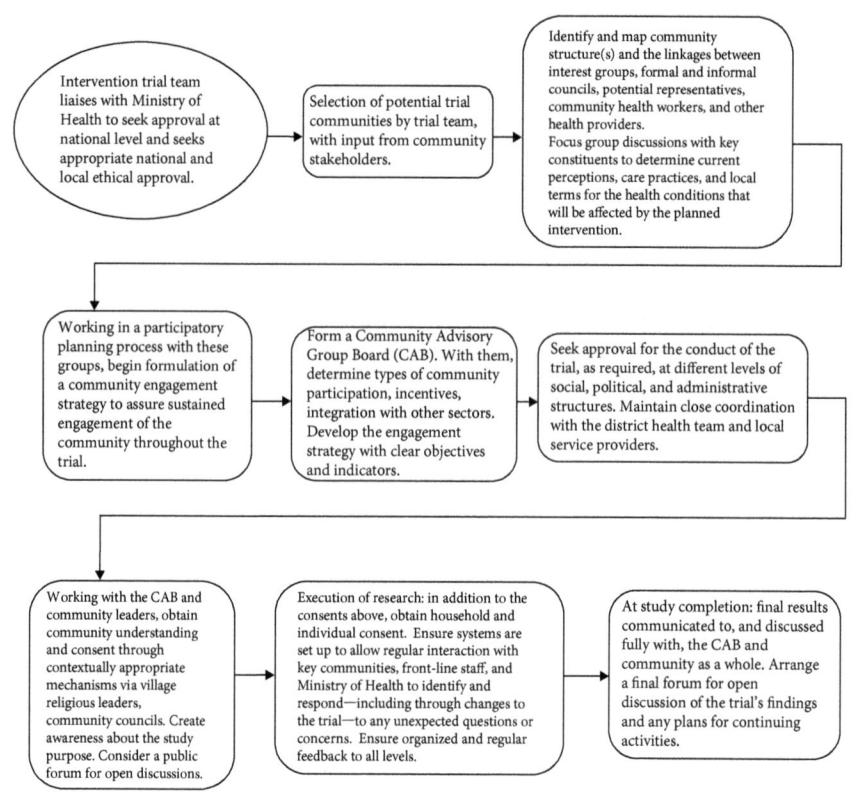

Figure 9.1 Community engagement for an intervention trial.

[Flowchart description:]

- Intervention trial team liaises with Ministry of Health to seek approval at national level and seeks appropriate national and local ethical approval.
- → Selection of potential trial communities by trial team, with input from community stakeholders.
- → Identify and map community structure(s) and the linkages between interest groups, formal and informal councils, potential representatives, community health workers, and other health providers. Focus group discussions with key constituents to determine current perceptions, care practices, and local terms for the health conditions that will be affected by the planned intervention.
- → Working in a participatory planning process with these groups, begin formulation of a community engagement strategy to assure sustained engagement of the community throughout the trial.
- → Form a Community Advisory Group Board (CAB). With them, determine types of community participation, incentives, integration with other sectors. Develop the engagement strategy with clear objectives and indicators.
- → Seek approval for the conduct of the trial, as required, at different levels of social, political, and administrative structures. Maintain close coordination with the district health team and local service providers.
- → Working with the CAB and community leaders, obtain community understanding and consent through contextually appropriate mechanisms via village religious leaders, community councils. Create awareness about the study purpose. Consider a public forum for open discussions.
- → Execution of research: in addition to the consents above, obtain household and individual consent. Ensure systems are set up to allow regular interaction with key communities, front-line staff, and Ministry of Health to identify and respond—including through changes to the trial—to any unexpected questions or concerns. Ensure organized and regular feedback to all levels.
- → At study completion: final results communicated to, and discussed fully with, the CAB and community as a whole. Arrange a final forum for open discussion of the trial's findings and any plans for continuing activities.

---

community members, as far as possible, and can provide some accountability. Various ethnographic and participatory methods can be used to explore community characteristics to ascertain the local relevance of the diseases under study and to facilitate the participation of community members in the proposed trial. Some of these methods are described in more detail in Chapter 15. Participatory rural appraisal (PRA) and participatory learning and action (PLA) methods may be particularly helpful (Chambers, 2008). Of particular note, exploration of views around aspects of trials that are unfamiliar to community members are likely to need methodological approaches, based on participatory forms of information sharing and discussion to generate meaningful engagement.

Deciding who should speak for the community, based on accurate knowledge of local interest groups and their likely representativeness, can be an essential, but difficult, step, given the likely range of different interests. Errors at this stage can damage the relationship of the trial team with the community. It may be useful for the trial team to listen to multiple community voices. It should also be recognized that some communities may simply not be interested in a trial as it is planned, or at all. A common failing in planning is for researchers not to recognize the complexity of, and dynamics between, various interest groups in a community and to assume that the official community authorities, such as government administrators or traditional leaders, accurately represent the views of all groups within the community. If the trial requires active involvement of, for example, the poorest and least educated, a careful investigation of who could best represent their views will be important. These complexities and dynamics are also reflected within and between extended families and households, such that the views of the least empowered (often young mothers) may be particularly difficult to ascertain and take into account.

In relation to understanding community perceptions and practices relevant to the trial, researchers can draw on preliminary participatory planning processes, including local experts and community representatives and leaders. It may be easy for researchers to overlook important differences between their own health beliefs and practices and those of community members, in ways that can have major practical and ethical implications for the conduct of the trial (including the engagement of the community in, or its rejection of, the trial and any future research). For example, in some areas where infection with *Schistosoma haematobium* is endemic, some people regard blood in the urine as a normal part of a child's development, so an intervention that prevents this may be unpopular, unless this belief is taken account of in planning the intervention. Differences in health beliefs and practices are also likely to exist across the community, making them less easy for researchers to recognize and generating the need for flexibility in the way research is implemented. The preliminary investigations undertaken to explore community perceptions and practices can also begin to sensitize communities in a positive way to the future research. In some situations, these early investigations will reveal that more focused and detailed social science or multidisciplinary studies are needed to explore particular issues (see Chapter 15).

There is a growing body of work documenting experiences with community engagement from many different settings (for example, Cheah et al., 2010; Gikonyo et al., 2008; Marsh et al., 2010, 2011; Reddy et al., 2010; Shubis et al., 2009). These studies illustrate how community engagement and input, particularly where well planned, can improve consent procedures and promote better understanding of the purposes of research among study participants. However, they also illustrate the complexity of doing community engagement well (it can never be an easily ticked off checklist!). It is also important to recognize that community engagement can sometimes lead to unexpected, and sometimes unwanted, outcomes such as raised expectations among community members, confusions about the roles of community members, and conflicts within communities (Angwenyi et al., 2013). These studies illustrate the importance of thinking about community engagement goals, activities (for example, roles of different boards or committees), and monitoring and responding to issues and ideas, as they arise.

2.3 Setting up Community Advisory Groups or Boards

An important initial step to facilitate community engagement in a trial is often the establishment of a CAG or CAB. The exact form of a CAG/B is likely to vary, depending on the context of the trial, but each one is generally made up of representatives of the trial community and serves as a liaison body between the trial team and local communities. Investigators can liaise with the CAG/Bs to ensure there is a clearly articulated engagement strategy which has defined objectives and appropriate approaches to assess effectiveness. Issues of governance, such as the degree of responsibility and formality of the CAG/Bs and their relation to other district and community organizations, must be worked out, according to the specific needs of the trial and circumstances of the community. One engagement approach, adopted by a long-term international research programme in Kenya, has been to have regular interactions with a relatively large network of local residents put forward as representatives by their own communities. This network is consulted on a range of studies for a fixed period of time (Kamuya et al., 2013).

The primary role of a CAG/B is to provide input to study planning, including early stage advice on the acceptability of planned research and how to maximize this, and continuous advice throughout the study, including:

- practical study arrangements for transport, follow-up, informed consent, and assent processes at individual and community levels, reimbursements, and study compensations and benefits
- consideration of the potential issues and sensitivities associated with the trial in the context in which it will be conducted. For example, past or current exposure to research programmes or interventions may have an adverse or a positive effect on the planning for a future trial. Knowledge and understanding of this history is an important topic to discuss in the early stages of engagement. Since some of these sensitivities and issues are likely to emerge during the course of the trial, rather than being anticipated at the start, the advice of a CAG/B throughout the trial is likely to be important
- identification of important people and groups to involve in the trial, for what purpose, and at what stage in the conduct of the trial. Examples include those to consult on study design, the 'gatekeepers' whose support must be sought, those to assist in creating awareness of the study within the community, and those best placed to provide feedback from the various interest groups about the research activities.

While working through CAG/Bs has been shown to strengthen research relationships and ethical practice, challenges include defining which communities should be represented, selecting representatives as CAG/B members, ensuring clarity in roles and adequate training to fulfil those roles, facilitating appropriate motivation of members, moving beyond tokenism or window dressing, and avoiding politicization. These challenges are most likely for small groups or boards with long-standing, highly formalized structures. A specific set of tensions have been identified around the potentially conflicting dual functions that some CABs have of both advancing the research and protecting the community.

Given these issues and the overall importance of seeking community inputs to trial planning and conduct throughout the trial, it will generally be important for researchers to seek actively to understand the views of a wider range of community members. This will involve the use of a range of different community engagement mechanisms and require the skills of experienced community liaison staff. In complex or controversial situations, social science research methods can help to understand, and sometimes to build on, wider community views to support decision making on appropriate research practice.

Taken together, creative engagement of community stakeholders and champions who have local knowledge and expertise, through CAG/Bs and other formal and informal mechanisms, is important for establishing community rapport and trust, implementing the research, and ensuring community involvement and counsel throughout the execution of the research.

3 Engaging community stakeholders

3.1 Engaging national and regional administrations

Appropriate regard must be paid to the local and national social, political, and administrative structures and procedures. It is important to determine in which order the various preliminary contacts should be made (Figure 9.1).

At the national level, research investigators must comply with appropriate administrative, political, and research consent procedures. These may include obtaining consent from national research councils, ethics committees, and civil society interest groups. With increasing community-based efforts in many LMICs in recent years, many different groups may be active at the research site. Their activities may compete with, or enhance, the proposed research operations. Where other groups are operating in the study area, it is important to create strategic alliances with the programme implementers to ensure their support and cooperation for the various elements of the study. However, investigators must exercise caution, especially if tensions exist between different groups in the communities, as allying the trial to such a group may adversely impact the trial's community partnerships. Religious organizations are often powerful advocates, favoured by the communities, but may be strongly opposed to some intervention strategies or to each other, so it is important to think carefully and act strategically, in terms of how the trial team approaches and relates to them.

3.2 Engaging district health teams and health providers

Generally, research trials are conducted at the sub-national level and therefore require close coordination with local authorities and ongoing programmes and activities at that level. Investigators should seek opportunities for leveraging the interest, advice, and support of the local health authorities, including building synergy between research and routine health care programmes and services, as far as possible. An early meeting with the local health management team(s) for the area covered by the trial (in this book, referred to as the district health management team(s) (DHMTs)) should be arranged to discuss the planned trial, review the specifics of the interventions to be tested, and explore opportunities for partnership in planning and execution. Depending on the relevance of the trial for international and national policy, it may be important to have early discussions with the DHMT on ways in which the new intervention could best be integrated with ongoing programmes if the trial were to show a beneficial effect of the intervention under study. The involvement of MOH health care providers in the research will help align operations, prevent conflict in services and scheduling, and facilitate their perceptions of transparency, so they do not feel threatened or intimidated by the trial. Their endorsement is critical, as study participants are likely to consult them for advice or to alleviate their fears about possible adverse outcomes of the intervention. Physical integration of research activities within routine health service facilities can also provide opportunities to develop local health system infrastructure, with further positive effects on these key relationships, as well a provide long-term benefits to the community.

The DHMT can also foster community partnerships between the researchers and informal networks of opinion leaders, potential champions, and service providers such as traditional birth attendants, community health workers, and community health councils. Inclusion of influential traditional healers in the community engagement process may also help, since they will be consulted by some community members and are often highly influential within the community. Endorsements from the DHMT and other health care providers trusted by the communities can facilitate subsequent engagement within the communities.

3.3 Engaging community leaders

A multi-pronged, multi-stage strategy may be essential to explore and identify appropriate community leaders from the communities and to ascertain their willingness to support the planned trial activities. Community advocates from the private or public sector, including health providers from the local health facility or district hospital, or researchers who have previously worked in those sites can facilitate the identification of these formal and informal community leaders. They may include village leaders, traditional healers, religious leaders, traditional birth attendants, leaders of women's clubs, farmers' clubs, midwives, or others. The first consultation may involve discreet enquiries to determine these power structures and the level of influence and trust that they have among the community members. Usually, there are multiple leaders, and a CAG/B could include members from among these, with representatives from each community segment that is relevant to the trial—political, geographic, religious, and socio-economic.

Appropriate formative research methods, such as key informant interviews, focus group discussions, and observation (see Chapter 15), can be applied to appreciate local norms and to guide effective and appropriate protocols for community engagement. The best ways of providing the information on the purpose of the trial, potential benefits and risks, roles and expectations within the trial, how best to detect and address potential AEs, etc. can be established through dialogue with key informants within the community. This may be particularly important if the health problem being addressed is a community priority and a placebo arm is part of the study design. If community volunteers are to be engaged for enrolment of trial participants, follow-up, distribution of interventions, or data collection, their recruitment, oversight, and norms for remuneration should be discussed with community representatives, where possible (for example, CAG/Bs or other established mechanisms), as these can be complex (Molyneux et al., 2013). Community representatives can also help with the design of appropriate household and participant consent procedures. Concepts, such as trial 'blinding' and randomization, are not likely to be readily understood by community members, so the investigators should work with community representatives to establish how best to communicate these ideas to potential participants, using local illustrations and rationale.

The duration of this process will depend on the past exposure of the community to research trials, the complexity of the trial or trial-related issues, and the trial team's pre-existing knowledge of the community. In isolated communities, with poor linkages to health personnel or other public entities, the process may need to be longer and require more rigorous dialogues with the community leaders to ensure that locally appropriate ways of interacting are not violated. Some traditional practices may require tokens of appreciation. For example, in some societies, it is appropriate to give a community leader a small gift at the commencement of a formal visit. In others, the norm is for 'visitors' to be given a small gift. These local practices must be within research norms and should not unduly influence participation or compliance. Cultural and language barriers should be considered in approaching the leaders and decision makers in communities. Locally employed community liaison staff, other front-line research staff, and local representatives might assist in selecting a respected advocate who speaks the local dialect or language, where needed.

3.4 Working with the wider community

It is often important and useful for community liaison staff or researchers to introduce the study to the wider community, from which participants may be drawn, at public meetings organized in conjunction with community leaders or representatives. In some situations, CAG/B members or other community representatives may play an important role in this introduction, including explaining the expectations from the community of the trial team and describing the characteristics of the potential participants who will be recruited. Community representatives or leaders must have a reasonable level of understanding of the technical and ethical aspects of the study to take on this initial introduction, since there are risks of important (often inadvertent) misrepresentation.

Early on, it may be sufficient to provide a general introduction to the trial, along with some details of the benefits and potential risks associated with participation. A transparent process should be adopted to solicit questions and to address concerns truthfully. It is critically important to establish mechanisms to ensure that there is a continuing dialogue and interchange between the community and the researchers throughout the trial, and regular meetings with representative groups (such as a CAG/B or community leaders) and periodic open meetings with the community should usually be a part of this process.

Initial public meetings can be used to begin the process of recruitment in some situations by inviting interested individuals or families to attend follow-up meetings that will feed into later informed consent processes.

3.5 Roles of front-line research staff in community engagement

With respect to the engagement of the trial team with the community, it is very important to consider the range of formal and informal interactions that front-line staff (fieldworkers, research assistants, community facilitators, counsellors, health workers) have with trial participants, their families, and the wider community from which participants are drawn. Front-line staff often come from the communities involved in the research and have the greatest amount of formal and informal interaction about the trial (i.e. engage the most) with community members. In mediating between the often very different priorities and concerns of well-resourced research institutions and relatively poor communities without good access to affordable quality health care, front-line staff are not simply neutrally observing and adhering to formal, externally derived ethical rules. Instead, they play a crucial, and often under-recognized and under-supported, role in 'doing ethics' in the field, for example, negotiating tensions between benefits approved in protocols with participants' and communities' needs and demands (Kamuya et al., 2013). In establishing and maintaining interactions and relationships between study participants, non-participants in a community, and research staff, front-line workers also have a central role in the success and quality of the science itself.

Front-line research staff vary enormously in how embedded they are in the communities of a trial, and how embedded they are has differing implications for their social relationships and associated practical and ethical strengths and dilemmas. At one end of the spectrum, staff may continue to live in their own homes and neighbourhoods over the course of the trial, and, at the other end, they may not live in any of the specific study communities but be employed to work across a large geographical area and travel out to work in trial communities every day. There should be careful consideration at the outset of a trial of how different strengths and challenges, related to how closely each member of the trial team is related to the trial community, might be balanced across a team. Where a trial is employing new staff in areas of few opportunities for paid employment, this can be a highly contentious issue. It can be helpful, where possible, to introduce systems that are open and transparent (as opposed to being solely based on, for example, community leader recommendations).

Also important is ensuring careful participatory training and interactions with front-line staff from the outset and throughout the trial. These interactive sessions should be two-way—staff should feel free to make supervisors and PIs aware of gaps in their own understanding, challenges that they face, and ideas on how to strengthen research, and researchers should share their perceptions, understanding, and knowledge of the requirements for trial success. This open, respectful two-way exchange will help the senior researchers to learn about local priorities and concerns and how to respond to these in a way that balances local needs and priorities with trial and (inter)national requirements, while, at the same time, maximizing the understanding and ownership of key trial issues among front-line staff, and hence their ability to communicate these effectively with the trial community. Training and supportive supervision sessions are likely to need to include information on what a trial is and how the rights of participants are protected in trials, benefits to local communities from this trial, and what happens when the trial ends. Role plays and demonstrations, based on local knowledge and experience, can help to develop a range of strategies for field staff to cope with both expected and unexpected scenarios.

In some scenarios, such as discussion of highly sensitive topics or where there are interactions with very vulnerable communities, it may be important to ensure that fieldworkers have access to counsellors. Where trials or research programmes are large or long-term, it may be important to professionalize this cadre of staff, including establishing systems by which such workers can, if performing well, advance their careers and increase their remuneration. This may include giving such staff training opportunities.

4 Strategy and content of information for communication

Appropriate communication strategies and content should be designed and developed for different community audiences, depending on the nature of the information to be conveyed in the trial (also see Chapter 23). Depending on the specific requirements of the trial, these strategies may need to operate at several levels of the trial community, including communication with individuals, specific target groups, or the wider public. For example, community engagement can feed into, and overlap with, consent processes, which are discussed in Chapter 6 and are a clearly key activity in any trial (Participants in the Community Engagement Consent Workshop, 2013). All communication activities must use culturally appropriate methods and take into consideration the target audience's beliefs and norms, numeracy and literacy skills, power structures, gender issues, and other community dynamics that may differ from those of the trial team. Special issues may arise related to the collection of blood, urine, or stool specimens (see Chapter 17, Section 2).

Participatory methods, using visual aids, can be used to illustrate and simplify scientific concepts related to the trial. Community health workers, traditional birth attendants, and other community health care providers with established credibility may sometimes be appropriate people to communicate with community members at various levels throughout the trial. But their motivation, training, other activities, and sustained engagement will need to be managed in collaboration with other community representatives (Angwenyi et al., 2013). Forms of participatory theatre, song, and dance can be effective in introducing new studies in contexts where these are established and valued means of communication. In some settings, radio, roadshows, and mobile phone messaging have been used to communicate with communities about research (Ndebele et al., 2012).

While much of the content of the information to be conveyed will depend on the details of the trial, it will be important in all cases to emphasize general information on the nature of research, including the voluntary nature of participation and the confidentiality of any information provided by the participants. Given common public concerns about safety in intervention trials, it may also be helpful to give a basic explanation of international and national research review processes for all studies and, for trials of drugs and vaccines, the trial phases, so that the current study is widely seen in this context. CABs and front-line staff can provide good support in assessing the appropriateness and comprehensibility of information included in messages and materials to support communication about the trial.

5 Sustaining community engagement

The initial discussions with the community leaders will provide insights for developing good strategies for sustained community engagement. Intervention studies evaluating medical products or vaccines will require close monitoring, and therefore continuous surveillance and frequent engagement with a CAB and other community members. AEs, often unpredictable, may worry local communities, harm the reputation of the trial and its parent research institutions, and damage the credibility of the researchers. Such events need to be appropriately managed. Effective management and reporting mechanisms, with clearly defined protocols, should be established as part of wider community engagement strategies. Informal meetings and fora can be held periodically to engage community members about their perspectives of the trial and to address any concerns in a timely manner. Frequent two-way information flow between the investigators, front-line staff, CAGs, other representative groups, and individual community members can foster trust, ensure sustainability, and enhance management oversight.

In long-term field trials, even if excellent procedures have been established to incorporate the ideas of community members and to respond to concerns at the outset, new expectations may evolve over time, and perceptions may change. Good sustained community engagement mechanisms should ensure that the trial team is aware of these issues, and it will be necessary to work with the front-line staff and representative groups to decide how best to address them.

Some trials may involve community members in substantial inconvenience. If procedures are time-consuming, participants may become fatigued and their initial enthusiasm may wane. Generally, it is important to discuss what time of day, or what time of year, is most convenient for the community members. Sometimes, compensating individuals, in the form of money or food, for time lost from work or other activities may be warranted, and, in some cultures, it may be considered appropriate to compensate the participant if a blood sample is taken. However, this could be a disastrous practice in some settings, as it may fuel commonly held rumours that blood is being bought and sold by researchers. Various strategies have been adopted by researchers to ensure culturally appropriate compensation for trial participation such as through the provision of health care services. These strategies need careful thinking through for each trial, ideally with community input. Mechanisms for referral to appropriate health care and compensation if harm does occur are key elements of trial protocols and could be informed by community representatives. All benefits must be viewed carefully from an ethical standpoint, with the aim of ensuring that people are compensated appropriately, but intra-family and community conflicts are minimized, and individuals are not 'coerced' to participate in the study against their will (Molyneux et al., 2012). See Chapter 6 for further discussion of these issues.

Consideration of the frequency and nature of feedback of results is important in all trials and must be considered from the outset. It is important to distinguish between feedback of individual and of overall (aggregate) trial results.

For individual test results, a common reason for a participant to refuse to provide a second blood sample is that no information was provided regarding the result of tests on the first sample. Sometimes, this problem may be avoided by conducting some laboratory tests on site. For example, haemoglobin, rapid tests for malaria, and tests for a large number of other conditions can be performed in the field. Rapid diagnostic tests for malaria, for example, can be done on the spot, and immediate treatment can then be provided, if indicated. Where this is not possible, individual results can be fed back to participants, and the practical and health implications of doing so for individuals and the research team may need careful deliberation and clear communication with both trial participants and the wider trial community.

For overall trial results, it is important to keep local health workers and the DHMT informed of the progress of the trial and of the results, as they accumulate and at the end of the trial. Newsletters or district and provincial meetings can be used to communicate the results to them. At the completion of the trial, the final results of the study should be communicated to, and discussed with, the participants and the trial community as a whole. The implications for the community should be discussed with them, as well as with all the authorities involved. Such feedback is essential, not only from an ethical point of view, but it may also pave the way for co-operation in future research activities and for sustained health-seeking behaviour on the part of the community members. For example, research on the feedback of findings from a malaria vaccine trial in Kenya showed that sharing of aggregate findings was very much appreciated and that the inclusion of individual results in feedback sessions reassured participants of trial safety and helped ensure that positive results of the trial were not over-interpreted. Feedback sessions also offered an opportunity to explain key information and respond to emerging community questions and ultimately re-evaluate and re-negotiate trial relationships and benefits (Gikonyo et al., 2013).

References

Angwenyi, V., Kamuya, D., Mwachiro, D., Marsh, V., Njuguna, P., and Molyneux, S. 2013. Working with Community Health Workers as 'volunteers' in a vaccine trial: practical and ethical experiences and implications. *Developing World Bioethics*, **13**, 38–47.

Chambers, R. 2008. *Revolutions in development inquiry*. London: Earthscan.

Cheah, P. Y., Lwin, K. M., Phaiphun, L., *et al.* 2010. Community engagement on the Thai-Burmese border: rationale, experience and lessons learnt. *International Health*, **2**, 123–9.

Gikonyo, C., Bejon, P., Marsh, V., and Molyneux, S. 2008. Taking social relationships seriously: lessons learned from the informed consent practices of a vaccine trial on the Kenyan Coast. *Social Science & Medicine*, **67**, 708–20.

Gikonyo, C., Kamuya, D., Mbete, B., *et al.* 2013. Feedback of research findings for vaccine trials: experiences from two malaria vaccine trials involving healthy children on the Kenyan Coast. *Developing World Bioethics*, **13**, 48–56.

Kamuya, D. M., Marsh, V., Kombe, F. K., Geissler, P. W., and Molyneux, S. C. 2013. Engaging communities to strengthen research ethics in low-income settings: selection and perceptions of members of a network of representatives in coastal Kenya. *Developing World Bioethics*, **13**, 10–20.

Lavery, J. V., Tinadana, P. O., Scott, T. W., *et al.* 2010. Towards a framework for community engagement in global health research. *Trends in Parasitology*, **26**, 279–83.

Marsh, V. M., Kamuya, D. M., Mlamba, A. M., Williams, T. N., and Molyneux, S. S. 2010. Experiences with community engagement and informed consent in a genetic cohort study of severe childhood diseases in Kenya. *BMC Medical Ethics*, **11**, 13.

Marsh, V. M., Kamuya, D. K., Parker, M. J., and Molyneux, C. S. 2011. Working with Concepts: The Role of Community in International Collaborative Biomedical Research. *Public Health Ethics*, **4**, 26–39.

Molyneux, S., Kamuya, D., Madiega, P. A., Chantler, T., Angwenyi, V., and Geissler, P. W. 2013. Field workers at the interface. *Developing World Bioethics*, **13**, ii–iv.

Molyneux, S., Mulupi, S., Mbaabu, L., and Marsh, V. 2012. Benefits and payments for research participants: experiences and views from a research centre on the Kenyan coast. *BMC Medical Ethics*, **13**, 13.

Ndebele, P. M., Wassenaar, D., Munalula, E., and Masiye, F. 2012. Improving understanding of clinical trial procedures among low literacy populations: an intervention within a microbicide trial in Malawi. *BMC Medical Ethics*, **13**, 29.

Participants in the Community Engagement Consent Workshop. 2013. Consent and community engagement in diverse research contexts. *Journal of Empirical Research on Human Research Ethics*, **8**, 1–18.

Reddy, P., Buchanan, D., Sifunda, S., James, S., and Naidoo, N. 2010. The role of community advisory boards in health research: divergent views in the South African experience. *SAHARA Journal*, **7**, 2–8.

Shagi, C., Vallely, A., Kasindi, S., *et al.*; Microbicides Development Programme. 2008. A model for community representation and participation in HIV prevention trials among women who engage in transactional sex in Africa. *AIDS Care*, **20**, 1039–49.

Shubis, K., Juma, O., Sharifu, R., Burgess, B., and Abdulla, S. 2009. Challenges of establishing a Community Advisory Board (CAB) in a low-income, low-resource setting: experiences from Bagamoyo, Tanzania. *Health Research Policy and Systems*, **7**, 16.

Chapter 10

Censuses and mapping

1 Introduction to conducting censuses and mapping 159
2 Uses of maps and censuses in intervention trials 160
3 Preparations for a census 160
   3.1 Planning 160
   3.2 Pre-testing 162
   3.3 Recruitment and training of field staff 162
   3.4 Mapping 162
4 Enumeration 166
   4.1 Organization of enumeration of households 166
   4.2 Definition of dwelling units 167
   4.3 *De facto* and *de jure* populations 167
   4.4 Ensuring completeness of the census 168
   4.5 Numbering and identifying individuals 169
   4.6 Household or individual forms within a census? 170
   4.7 Coding relationships 171
   4.8 Names and addresses 173
   4.9 Ages 174
   4.10 Other identifying information 179
5 Processing of census data 180
6 Post-enumeration checks and quality control 180
7 Keeping the census up to date: demographic surveillance 180

1 Introduction to conducting censuses and mapping

In nearly all intervention trials, it will be necessary to compile a register of individuals included in the trial. The register should include sufficient identification information on each person to enable participants to be followed over time, with minimal possibility of confusing one individual with another. To assemble a suitable group for inclusion in a trial, it may be necessary to enumerate (i.e. count and identify) all the members of a geographically, or otherwise, defined population or a specific subgroup of it (for example, children aged less than 5 years). Such a population enumeration (census) may serve as a sampling frame to select a representative subset of the population or may be used to assess how representative the study group is of the whole population, if some individuals refuse to participate, or are not included, in the trial for other reasons.

Identification and follow-up of the members of a population and selecting a sample of them will usually be easier if a map is drawn of the area, marking individual homes and prominent topographical features. Mapping may also be valuable in planning the logistics of fieldwork and in studying the epidemiology of a disease, for example, to determine if cases of a disease tend to occur near water courses or in some other non-random fashion geographically.

Mapping and enumeration of a population are not always necessary, but often such information collected at the start of a trial is vital to its successful conduct. For example, in a leprosy vaccine trial in Venezuela, the trial group was defined as the household and other close contacts of prevalent leprosy cases (Gupte, 1999). The prevalent cases were distributed over a very wide area, in which most of the population were not included in the trial. It was necessary to enumerate the household and other contacts of prevalent cases, but it would have been inappropriate to enumerate the entire population or to map the locations of all households, other than was necessary to be able to find the contacts during the course of the trial. Conversely, in a malaria chemoprophylaxis study in The Gambia, an attempt was made to include all children in a defined area, and detailed mapping and enumeration were undertaken to facilitate the conduct of the study (Jukes et al., 2006).

In this chapter, guidelines are given on mapping and on ways of compiling a population register to facilitate long-term follow-up of the participants in a trial. Resources, including tools and advice on doing this in LMICs, are available from INDEPTH (<http://www.indepth-network.org>).

2 Uses of maps and censuses in intervention trials

A map of the trial area and a population enumeration (census) provide:

- a sampling frame for the selection of those in the target population who will be included in a trial
- denominators for the computation of morbidity and mortality rates
- baseline population characteristics, which may affect the impact of an intervention and which can also be monitored for changes during the study
- a basis for planning the logistics of the fieldwork, for example, which households should be visited by one fieldworker and in which order or to demarcate clusters within a cluster randomized trial
- a means for studying factors that affect disease rates. Age, sex, and place of residence affect the risk of many diseases, and information on these and other factors that may influence exposure or susceptibility to disease, or which may influence its outcome, should be recorded at the start of a trial.

3 Preparations for a census

3.1 Planning

Early in the planning of a census, it is important to ascertain what information already exists about the population, either in national censuses or from local or national surveys that may have been conducted previously. In planning a census, it is important to seek the active collaboration of the community, generally through the community advisory board (CAB) and the local health services, using the special knowledge these groups are likely to have on the local population (see Chapter 9). This will also enable them to get to know their area better, and they may wish to use the information collected in the census for the benefit of the population, while the trial is in progress and after it has finished. Indeed, if local health workers and community leaders are not involved in the planning, they may be antagonistic to the study and may transmit these feelings to the study population.

In some populations, local administrative offices maintain up-to-date lists of tax payers that may give a good indication of the size of a population (or may not if large numbers of people avoid registering for tax collection!). Lists of voters or of residents may also be available through local administrative offices. Health or other surveys may also have been conducted previously. Gathering this information will entail visits to the study area, to government statistical offices, and possibly to universities or other institutions that may have organized specific surveys.

Useful data are usually available from national censuses, generally undertaken every 10 years. In the planning of a trial, census data may be used to select a suitable area such as a group of contiguous villages whose population is of adequate size for the trial. Often, however, the information in a national census is out of date or may be inaccurate. For example, a population census for a trial in Ghana found that the study census numbers matched those of the recent national census very well, except in one area that had applied to become a separate district where the national census numbers were roughly 50% higher than those in the study census! From a national census, it will usually be possible to obtain data for an area regarding the distribution of the population, with respect to age, sex, ethnic group, household size, and population density, though this may require a specific request to the census bureau. Estimates of mortality, fertility, and migration rates may also be available. Migration rates may be especially useful to estimate potential losses to follow-up in a longitudinal study.

For detailed planning and conduct of a trial, a special enumeration will usually be necessary. The population may be enumerated at the same time as the intervention is being started or as a separate exercise in advance. The decision regarding which to use will depend on the specific circumstances of the trial. In the rest of this chapter, the census is assumed to take place shortly prior to the start of the intervention, but the basic principles of enumeration are similar whenever it is conducted.

The initial census may be the first formal contact that most members of a population have with the trial team, though it should have been preceded by liaison of the trial organizers with local officials and local leaders (discussed in Chapter 9). The enumeration exercise provides an opportunity to explain the aims, objectives, and procedures to be used in the trial. For example, an information sheet or newsletter might be left with each household explaining key issues, announcing community meetings where the trial will be explained in more detail, and giving contact details for further information.

Although adequate time needs to be allocated for enumeration and mapping, these tasks should be conducted fairly rapidly to minimize the amount of migration, including from one house to another house within the study area, during the course of the census. The aim of a census is to enumerate the resident population as completely as possible, so the timing of the census is often very important. In areas where there is seasonal migration, the census might be planned for a period when most people are at their normal residence, and, in some populations, trading seasons and market days should be avoided. It may also be important to avoid the rainy season when areas may be inaccessible or the harvest season when people may spend most of the day away from their homes working in their fields. In urban areas, weekends may be the best time for surveys, since, during the week, a high proportion of people may be at work. The time of day may also be important. In some areas, it has been found best to conduct a census after dark, when people have returned from work, but this may not be acceptable or safe in other settings.

It is tempting to try to collect as much information as possible about the study population during the initial census such as information on education or fertility histories. In the interests of speed, however, it is usually preferable to collect such information in a separate round of interviews after the initial census.

Once they have been entered into a computer, data from the census may be used for printing questionnaires, lists of children, and so on, which will aid subsequent surveys (see, for example, Schellenberg et al., 2001).

To conduct a census, a house-to-house enumeration is necessary in most populations. In densely populated villages, with only a few items of data being collected for each individual, a fieldworker going from house to house might be expected to complete census schedules for about 200 people in a day. The number of households this will comprise will depend upon the population structure. In less densely populated areas or with a longer census schedule, 50 persons a day might be a realistic target (see also Chapters 14 and 20).

3.2 Pre-testing

The design and testing of questionnaires, including their pre-testing and pilot testing, whether developed for use with pen and paper or on mobile electronic devices such as mobile phones, tablet computers, or PDAs, are discussed in Chapters 13 and 14. This process will involve several steps, from initial drafting and pre-testing to pilot testing under field conditions on, say, between 50 and 200 households. Field testing will provide an opportunity to train and evaluate the performance of staff and may assist in the identification of those suitable to become supervisors for the main enumeration.

3.3 Recruitment and training of field staff

Guidelines for the recruitment of staff are given in Chapter 16. Training in census techniques is a good way of introducing staff to field research methods. Following instructional 'classroom' sessions, trainees should practise conducting a small census themselves.

3.4 Mapping

While a population census can be conducted without a detailed map being drawn, for many trials, especially large ones, or when the trial will last several years, they will greatly benefit from maps being drawn of the study area. These can be used for planning and conducting an initial census, for subsequent house-to-house surveys, and/or for following up participants, but also for displaying trial results and for spatial analyses.

The type and accuracy of mapping will depend on how maps are to be used, but there are two main types: paper maps (either official or hand-drawn) and digital maps.

The simplest mapping is the use of existing maps from Departments of Lands and Surveys (or their equivalents) and from special sources such as the Army, Agriculture Departments, Tourist Offices, and the Central Statistics Office (for example, maps that were specially drawn for a national census). These maps may provide enough information for the trial to be carried out without the need for further mapping. More likely, they will form the initial starting point for additional mapping.

While existing paper maps and hand-drawn maps may supply all the information required, digital maps provide far better functionality. For example, if looking at the relationship between a population and a water source or access to services, distances can be calculated quickly and easily, using digital mapping software.

Digital maps do not need to be expensive or complicated, and modern Internet mapping sites (for example, <https://maps.google.com> or <http://www.openstreetmap.org>) may provide maps of sufficient resolution to identify individual houses, streams, and tracks. Where data are missing, a global positioning system (GPS) device can be used to record the location of each household, uploading this information to a computer. These Internet mapping packages allow simple maps to be produced but have very limited scope for spatial analysis. If any spatial analysis is going to be carried out or in order to provide more flexibility with the mapping, dedicated mapping software is required. There is an increasing amount of both commercial and open source or freeware mapping software available such as ARCGIS (<http://www.esri.com>), MapInfo (<http://www.mapinfo.com>), and Quantum GIS (<http://www.qgis.org>).

GPS devices use signals from at least three satellites orbiting the earth to give the longitude and latitude of the hand-held device. The accuracy of the positioning depends upon the number of satellites from which a signal can be received and the strength of their signals. Usually, the accuracy is to within 20 metres, but, in open areas, with single-storey buildings or huts, it can be to within less than 10 metres, while, in areas with poor satellite coverage or where it is heavily forested, it can be worse than 50 metres. There are many ways to collect GPS data, including specific GPS receivers, data loggers, and modern mobile phones. The choice of which to use depends on how the GPS data are to be collected and used. If GPS data will be collected at the same time as other survey data, a GPS-enabled data logger may be most efficient. However, if the mapping is to be done as a separate exercise, dedicated GPS receivers are more cost-effective. Most GPS receivers can store several hundred 'waypoints' (for example, households or other points of interest for the map), which can be uploaded into computers at the end of each day's work. The cost of a simple GPS receiver is around $100. Commonly used systems are produced by Garmin (<http://www.garmin.com>), Magellan (<http://www.magellangps.com>), and Trimble (<http://www.trimble.com>).

When either paper or digital maps are obtained, the information recorded may be incomplete or inaccurate, and it should be checked in the field. Names of villages may have changed or they may be known by different names locally, and villages and households may have been abandoned or been newly formed if the maps are not recent. Checks, and alterations as necessary, should be made on the positions of roads and tracks, health facilities, schools, official offices, markets, churches, mosques, bars, shops, hotels, boreholes, and other locally important features.

CHAPTER 10: CENSUSES AND MAPPING

In field trials, the first time that a map is likely to be needed is for planning the baseline survey. In longer-term field trials where houses will be revisited, individual houses are usually mapped. It is good practice to assign a code number to each house on the map. This may consist of a location (for example, village), code (for example, village BS), and a number to indicate the house within that location (for example, BS374). If it is locally acceptable, the number can be painted on the house or fixed to a board (take care: numbers painted on mud walls may be washed off in the rains or painted over, and boards with numbers can be taken down and moved by the residents to a new house!). This helps to ensure that each house is only mapped once and as a quick check on arrival at a house.

The numbering system should be designed to take account of the local family structures and their living arrangements. For example, in studies in some parts of Africa, the same number might be assigned to all houses that comprise a 'compound' where extended family members live. This is not always straightforward to do and is discussed further in Section 4.2.

Figure 10.1 shows part of four trial clusters of a large vitamin A trial in the Kintampo area of central Ghana (Kirkwood et al., 2010). The map was produced using ARCGIS software and shows roads, paths, schools, a hospital, a market, a refuse site, and two communal latrines, along with the location of each compound (identified with a 4-digit number).

Once each house or compound has been mapped and assigned a code, fieldworkers can use either a printed or digital map to locate the households that they need to visit. If small numbers of fieldworkers are involved, the list of households to be visited can be uploaded

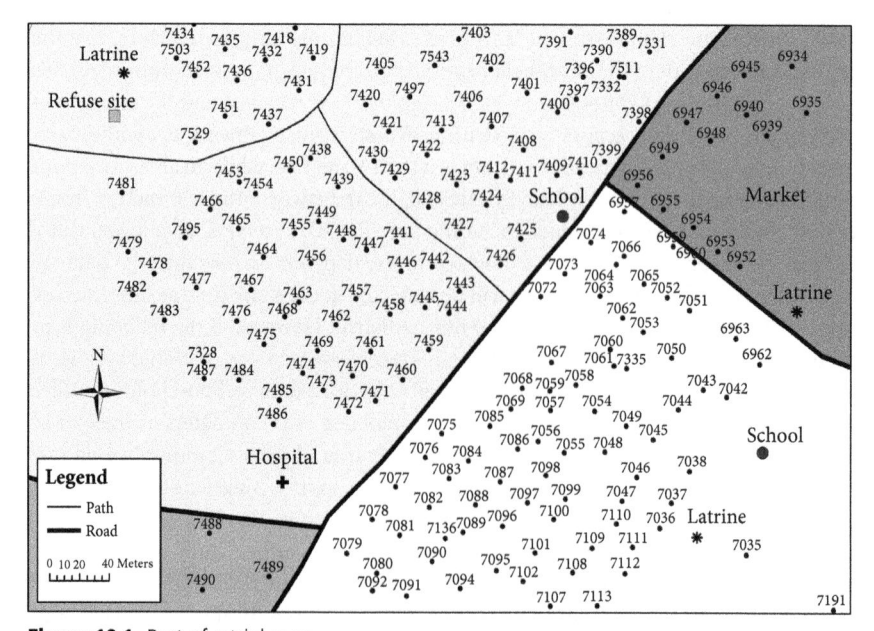

Figure 10.1 Part of a trial map.

Reproduced courtesy of C. Grundy, B. Kirkwood, and S. Owusu-Agyei. This image is distributed under the terms of the Creative Commons Attribution Non Commercial 4.0 International licence (CC-BY-NC), a copy of which is available at http://creativecommons.org/licenses/by-nc/4.0/.

into a GPS receiver, and a 'GO TO' function used to direct the fieldworker to the location of the house. While these methods may not be exact, they can save large amounts of time.

Once a census has been carried out, the combination of the map and household population data can be used to delineate trial clusters or fieldwork areas. If the households have been mapped digitally, there are functions to allow this to be done manually or using an automated method. Users simply specify the number of people required in each cluster, and either the user or the computer will group houses together to form clusters or groups of the appropriate size. Once fieldwork starts, maps can be printed out, as required, or displayed on a hand-held computer to report on progress.

Maps are also very useful for dissemination of trial results and for community engagement. Because they can display data in a visually striking way, maps, if used well, can have a much bigger impact than other methods of displaying results such as tables or text. They can also be used at routine staff meetings during the trial, such as to display which areas still need to be surveyed or to highlight where unusual results have been recorded.

In many field trials, only simple mapping is required, but the more data that are available, the more spatial analyses can be carried out. The two commonest ways maps are used in analysis are spatial overlays and for calculation of distances. Many health outcomes have a spatial relationship to a risk factor, for example, schistosomiasis to water sources, or malaria to swamps, elevation, and climate. Here, the 'exposure' to these risk factors can be calculated, using Geographical Information System (GIS) software. This requires two geographical datasets: one for the population data and one for the risk factor data. Often, the risk factors, such as rivers and lakes, are collected as part of the mapping process. In other cases, datasets of vegetation type, rainfall, and elevation are available online or from satellite images. In simple cases, these 'layers' can be overlaid to link the population to the risk factor, for example, what the elevation, mean daily temperature, or annual rainfall at the location of each house is. If useful, the results from a regression analysis of such overlays can then be fed back into the computer mapping software to produce risk maps. There are very good examples of such risk maps for infectious diseases such as soil-transmitted helminths, trachoma, or malaria, for which global atlases have been produced (<http://www.thiswormyworld.org>, <http://www.trachomaatlas.org>, <http://www.mara-database.org>).

The other spatial analysis that is commonly used is for calculating distances, for example, from a house to the nearest river or to the nearest health facility. This type of analysis is widely used to investigate access to services. An example of this in a multisite community-based social mobilization trial related to HIV counselling and testing in South Africa is given in Chirowodza et al. (2009).

Computer mapping and spatial analysis are increasingly being used in trials, and the methods available are constantly being improved and refined. For example, satellite imagery is increasingly being used to plan surveys, as this does not require someone to physically visit and locate each house, in order to create the map. It is possible to use the images provided by sites, such as Google Earth, to mark the location of each structure in the trial area. Once all structures are marked, these can either form the basis for a full survey or a random selection of structures can be selected and surveyed. In some cases, the approximate population can be estimated by multiplying the number of structures by a population per structure estimate. These methods currently tend to be used by research groups with relatively advanced GIS expertise but will increasingly be used more widely, as user-friendly software packages are developed.

4 Enumeration

A census of the population may be conducted after, or at the same time as, mapping. The census will involve the collection of information on the composition of each household and demographic, and possibly other, data on each household member.

4.1 Organization of enumeration of households

A combination of speed and accuracy is required in the conduct of a census. It is useful to draw a flow chart of the data collection and processing operations. Simple examples of such charts are shown in Figure 10.2 for collection of data on paper or on an electronic device.

(a) Data collected on paper

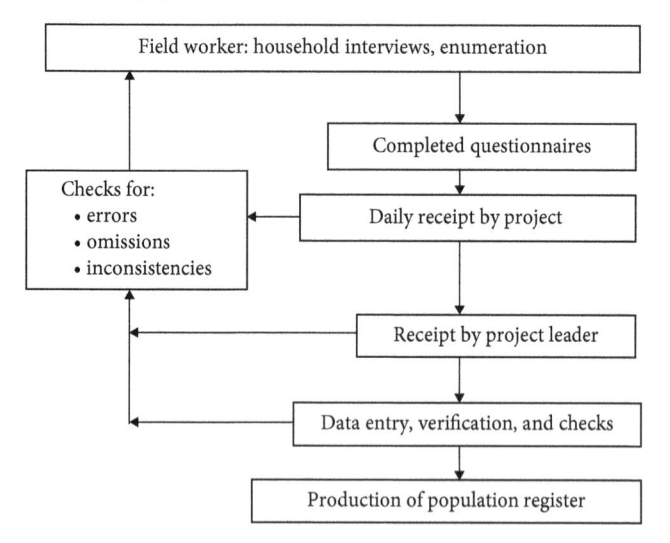

```
Field worker: household interviews, enumeration
    ↓
Completed questionnaires
    ↓
Checks for:        ← Daily receipt by project
 • errors
 • omissions
 • inconsistencies
    ↓
              Receipt by project leader
    ↓
              Data entry, verification, and checks
    ↓
              Production of population register
```

(b) Data collected on a digital device

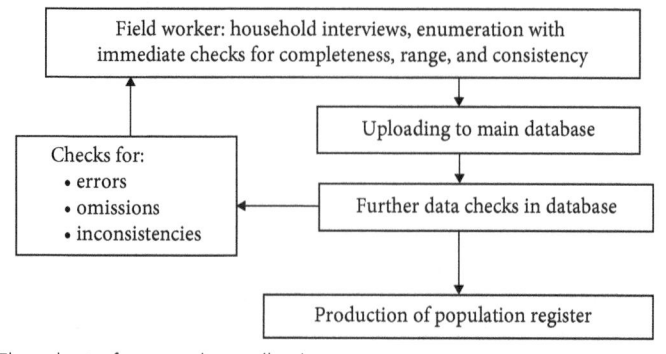

```
Field worker: household interviews, enumeration with
immediate checks for completeness, range, and consistency
    ↓
Uploading to main database
    ↓
Checks for:        ← Further data checks in database
 • errors
 • omissions
 • inconsistencies
    ↓
Production of population register
```

Figure 10.2 Flow chart of census data collection.

A field manual is essential and should include a checklist of equipment that the interviewers will need to take with them each day (see Chapter 16).

4.2 Definition of dwelling units

The definition of a village and a household (or compound) within a village will vary, depending on the location of the trial. Villages generally share the same leaders, although the inhabitants may be dispersed over a wide area. In parts of Africa, for example, in the Sahel zone of West Africa, a compound is a cluster of households fenced or partitioned off from other compounds and may have features, such as a well or latrine, which all the households of a particular compound share. In parts of Asia, such as in parts of Borneo and Indonesia, several households live together in a single building called a 'longhouse'.

A household is usually defined as a nuclear or extended family group, whose members usually eat together (the 'from the same cooking pot' definition of a household). The exact definition of a household should be decided before mapping and enumeration begin and clearly defined in the field manual. Households can be spread over several buildings, or several households may share the same building. There are no uniquely correct ways of defining households, compounds, or dwellings, but, in any particular study, it is important that clear definitions are agreed for all of the different terms to be used in describing people's living arrangements. New investigators in an area should find out what systems others have used who have worked in the same area, and whether or not these worked satisfactorily.

4.3 *De facto* and *de jure* populations

Before conducting a census, it is necessary to decide which individuals will be registered as members of the study population. The two commonest options are the so-called *de facto* and *de jure* populations. The *de jure* population comprises the 'normal residents' and includes individuals who usually live in a particular household but who may be absent during the enumeration. The *de facto* population consists of those who slept in the household the night before the census. In national censuses, it is usual to enumerate the *de facto* population, but, for the purpose of most intervention trials, the *de jure* population is the most appropriate. In some cultures, the definition of household membership may be difficult to specify. Some individuals may live in one household but spend a significant amount of time in another household either within or outside the study area. These individuals may be incorrectly enumerated twice, unless care is taken to assess the unique 'normal' domicile of each person. When using a *de jure* enumeration, each resident's status can be recorded as 'absent' or 'present'. This will give some indication of the degree of temporary migration and would allow the calculation of the *de facto* population from the *de jure* census. Similarly, fieldworkers will have to distinguish between 'temporary' visitors and those who will remain for a long time. It may be difficult to obtain such information reliably, as respondents may inform a fieldworker that a temporary visitor is 'permanent' if it is thought that some benefit may derive from this. The definition of who is a normal resident will depend upon the objectives of the trial. It is important to decide upon a period of time that a person should have been in or out of a community to be considered as having migrated in or out. In general, a clear and full definition is required as to who should be considered as a resident, especially in long-term studies that may involve multiple census updates. The definitions should be clearly stated in the field manual.

4.4 Ensuring completeness of the census

As houses may be empty at the time the interviewer calls or some residents may be away, the interviewer may have to rely upon proxy reporting in some instances. If a house is empty, arrangements should be made to call back at a time when someone is likely to be there. Whenever possible, all households reported as being empty should be revisited, ideally later the same day, by a supervisor or another interviewer. This helps to avoid interviewers reporting remote households as being empty to reduce their workload.

Information about the composition of the household is best elicited if there is a standard order in which information is sought about individuals (discussed in Section 4.5). In a simple census, it is not necessary that the information on all members of a household should be given by a single respondent, nor that the interviews are held privately, unless sensitive information is also being collected. Whenever there is some lack of certainty, respondents can be encouraged to consult others in the household or compound to provide information. It is useful to specify in advance who would be regarded as an acceptable informant in a household. For example, for information on young children, the list, in order of preference, is often first the mother, second another adult female relative living in the household, and third the father.

Whether or not a respondent is willing to co-operate in the study may depend on the initial impression an interviewer makes and on the respondent's understanding of the reasons for the census. Co-operation may be poor if the study subjects suspect that the information collected may be used to their disadvantage (for example, for tax collection). Involvement of local leaders and the CAB, if one is set up, may be critically important in obtaining co-operation (see Chapter 9). The interviewers should introduce themselves properly to the respondents, explain the purpose of the study, and assure them that any information given will be regarded as confidential. It may be necessary to reassure them, specifically, if appropriate, that the information will not be made available to the local administration for compiling lists of taxable adults. If those in a household refuse to participate, the field supervisor should be informed, and, with input from the CAB, the reasons for their refusal investigated as soon as possible. An initial refusal should not be taken as final. Individuals may be unwilling to collaborate merely because they have not properly understood the objectives of the trial or have not appreciated the potential benefits to them. However, the right of an individual not to participate in a survey should always be respected. If more than a small proportion of individuals refuse to participate, the generalizability of the trial findings may be compromised. Discussions should be held with village leaders if it appears that such problems are developing, in order to ascertain the reasons and to seek suitable remedies.

If data are collected using mobile phones or PDAs, these should be synchronized with computers, and the data uploaded each day. Whether the data have been collected on paper or electronically, at the end of each day, all completed forms should be carefully checked by the interviewers and, whenever possible, also by a supervisor for errors or omissions, so that these may be corrected either immediately or on the following day, before the team moves on to another area. Plans should be made to revisit any household that could not be enumerated, because of the absence of eligible informants or because the house was empty.

4.5 Numbering and identifying individuals

One purpose of a census is to allocate a unique identification number to each member of the population. This number will remain assigned to the individual for the duration of the trial, since it may be used to link information on an individual from different sources, such as from interviews, clinical examinations, and laboratory studies, and also on different occasions such as baseline, interim, and final surveys. Therefore, the person's identification number must never be changed or reallocated to any other individual, even if they die or move either within or outside the study area. There are several different ways that are commonly used to allocate identification numbers. As an example of one such system, suppose, in village B, the first compound is numbered 01. Within compound 01, the first household is numbered 01, and the household head is given the number 01 within the household. Thus, this individual has the unique identification number B010101, plus a check digit (see later within this section and Box 10.1). (Note that such a numbering system assumes there are fewer than 27 villages

---

Box 10.1 Method of assigning check digit to six-digit number

Suppose the trial number consists of a six-digit number, and it is desired to add a one-digit check number that will guard against transcription errors (such as reversing the order of two digits or recording one digit incorrectly). The number will take the form of:

	d1	d2	d3	d4	d5	d6	c
(Prime	11	7	5	3	2	1)	

The first six prime numbers are shown below the digits of the trial number. The check digit c is calculated by multiplying each digit by the corresponding prime, summing the results, and the *last* digit of the result is taken as the check digit. Thus, for example, we would have:

Trial number		Trial number with check digit
467913	4 × 11 + 6 × 7 + 7 × 5 + 9 × 3 + 1 × 2 + 3 × 1 = 153	4679133
476913	4 × 11 + 7 × 7 + 6 × 5 + 9 × 3 + 1 × 2 + 3 × 1 = 155	4769135
567913	5 × 11 + 6 × 7 + 7 × 5 + 9 × 3 + 1 × 2 + 3 × 1 = 164	5679134

Source: based on methods supplied W. Meade Morgan (personal communication).

in the study, fewer than 100 compounds in every village, fewer than 100 households in every compound, and fewer than 100 persons in every household (see also Chapter 20, Section 5).) If this identification system is used, a separate record should also be kept of the location of this individual at each study visit. If, for example, this same individual is currently within their original household, their current household will be B0101 plus a check digit. However, if they have moved to household 28 within compound 17 of village K, then their identification number will still be B010101 plus a check digit, but their current household will be K1728 plus a check digit.

Alternatively, numbers might be allocated in a simple continuous sequence to each member of the trial population, without building codes for village or household into the number. An advantage of this system is that forms can be pre-numbered before they are taken to the field, and the number allocated to an individual is simply that on the form that is filled in for them.

Whichever system is used, it is important to supplement the number with a check digit or character to aid the detection of transcription errors. These work by using a formula whereby any number can only correspond to one character or digit. If the number is transcribed wrongly, then the check digit or character will not match. One source for check digit systems is available at <http://code.google.com/p/checkdigits>. A simple method of generating check digits to guard against common transcription errors (such as reversing the order of two digits or recording a digit incorrectly) is given in Box 10.1.

In addition to, or instead of, the check-digit system, the practice in some trials is to record, for data linkage purposes, both an individual's identification number and the first few, say five, letters of their name. Checks are made that both of these items match, before any linkage procedures are undertaken. However, this system does require that an individual does have a name with an explicit spelling. Sometimes, people use several different names and are not consistent about how they are spelt, so we recommend using a check digit.

4.6 Household or individual forms within a census?

After mapping the study area and assigning numbers or codes to villages, compounds, and households, the household and/or individual census survey forms can be marked with household identification numbers. Whether all members of a household should be recorded on one form or on separate individual forms will depend on the way in which the survey is organized, the amount and degree of standardization of the data collected on each individual, and the design of the data processing system. Sometimes, both a household form and individual forms will be required—the former to collect basic demographic information on all members of a household, and the latter to record more detailed information on some, or all, members of the household.

If the census is being conducted at the same time that other procedures are being undertaken on the study subjects, it may be best to use individual forms, in addition to household forms, as otherwise it may be necessary to wait until a complete household has been registered before other procedures can start. If household sizes are large, this may lead to significant delays for those following the interviewers, especially at the start of each day.

Survey form number |__| of |__|					
Village name _____ |__|__|		Interviewer code |__|__|		
Compound Head _____ No. |__|__|		Date|__|__|__|__|__|__|		

Hhold	Person	Names	Relat.	Sex	Birth date	Resid.
|__|__|	|__|__|		|_____|	|__|	|__|__|__|__|__|__|	|__|
|__|__|	|__|__|		|_____|	|__|	|__|__|__|__|__|__|	|__|
|__|__|	|__|__|		|_____|	|__|	|__|__|__|__|__|__|	|__|
|__|__|	|__|__|		|_____|	|__|	|__|__|__|__|__|__|	|__|
|__|__|	|__|__|		|_____|	|__|	|__|__|__|__|__|__|	|__|
|__|__|	|__|__|		|_____|	|__|	|__|__|__|__|__|__|	|__|
|__|__|	|__|__|		|_____|	|__|	|__|__|__|__|__|__|	|__|
|__|__|	|__|__|		|_____|	|__|	|__|__|__|__|__|__|	|__|
|__|__|	|__|__|		|_____|	|__|	|__|__|__|__|__|__|	|__|
|__|__|	|__|__|		|_____|	|__|	|__|__|__|__|__|__|	|__|
|__|__|	|__|__|		|_____|	|__|	|__|__|__|__|__|__|	|__|
|__|__|	|__|__|		|_____|	|__|	|__|__|__|__|__|__|	|__|
|__|__|	|__|__|		|_____|	|__|	|__|__|__|__|__|__|	|__|
|__|__|	|__|__|		|_____|	|__|	|__|__|__|__|__|__|	|__|
|__|__|	|__|__|		|_____|	|__|	|__|__|__|__|__|__|	|__|
|__|__|	|__|__|		|_____|	|__|	|__|__|__|__|__|__|	|__|
|__|__|	|__|__|		|_____|	|__|	|__|__|__|__|__|__|	|__|
|__|__|	|__|__|		|_____|	|__|	|__|__|__|__|__|__|	|__|
|__|__|	|__|__|		|_____|	|__|	|__|__|__|__|__|__|	|__|
|__|__|	|__|__|		|_____|	|__|	|__|__|__|__|__|__|	|__|

Comments:
_____
_____
_____
_____
_____
_____

Figure 10.3 A census schedule.

Figure 10.3 is an example of a simple household form to collect basic demographic information. General issues related to production and coding of questionnaires and forms are considered in Chapters 14 and 20.

4.7 Coding relationships

Interviewers should be instructed regarding the order in which individual household members should be registered, as a systematic approach is less likely to lead to omissions.

In polygamous households, it would be usual to begin recording with the male household head (if there is one), followed by his first wife, and all her children living in the household; his second wife and her children; and so on. Next might be any brothers of the household head, each followed by their wives and children, as for the head. Unrelated individuals, such as lodgers and employees, might be recorded last. Relationships between different household members may be coded so that, in so far as possible, everyone is linked to one or two others in the household in a simple way, using as close a relationship as is possible. Codes for brother, sister, mother, and so on should only be used when wife, son, or daughter cannot be used to describe a relationship. To the extent possible, terms such as granddaughter, grandson, grandmother, grandfather, niece, nephew, uncle, aunt, and cousin, should be avoided. An example of a coding system for relationships that was used in a vaccine trial in Uganda (Smith et al., 1976) is given in Box 10.2. Two alternatives to this procedure may be better in some circumstances—either everyone is related to the household head or detailed records are made of the name of each individual's mother and father (even if they are dead or do not live in the household).

In some societies, it may be very difficult to ascertain the precise relationship between individuals. For example, no apparent distinction may be made between children and nephews/nieces—both the father and uncle might refer to them as his children. So long as this is appreciated it may cause little confusion, but it may be very important if, say, genetic studies are being conducted.

Box 10.2 Example of instructions for coding relationships

Coding of relationships

In this column, write down the relationship of the individual to the other persons in the household. Since each person will be entered against a person number (the second item in the columns), the relationship can conveniently be expressed by reference to these numbers, for example, 'Wife of 01' or 'Son of 01 and 02'.

The following abbreviations may be used:

Head of household	H	Sister	SR
Wife	W	Grandson	GS
Son	S	Granddaughter	GD
Daughter	D	Grandfather	GF
Mother	M	Grandmother	GM
Father	F	Other blood relative	R
Brother	BR	Unrelated	X

> **Box 10.2 Example of instructions for coding relationships (continued)**
>
> Example: A household consists of the head, his two wives, and five children, three by his first wife and two by his second, and also his mother, and an unrelated visitor and her child. These would be coded as follows.
>
> | Person number | Person | Code |
> |---|---|---|
> | 01 | Head | H |
> | 02 | Wife 1 of household head | W01 |
> | 03 | Child 1 (M) of household head and his wife 1 | S01,02 |
> | 04 | Child 2 (F) of household head and his wife 1 | D01,02 |
> | 05 | Child 3 (M) of household head and his wife 1 | S01,02 |
> | 06 | Wife 2 of household head | W01 |
> | 07 | Child 1 (F) of household head and his wife 2 | D01,06 |
> | 08 | Child 2 (M) of household head and his wife 2 | S01,06 |
> | 09 | Mother of household head | M01 |
> | 10 | Visitor | X |
> | 11 | Child 1 (M) of visitor | S10 |

4.8 Names and addresses

The most important way of identifying an individual will be through his or her names, and these must be recorded with special care. Interviewers must be instructed how to spell names, including those given by semi-literate individuals. It is important to try to record all of the names of a person, including nicknames, as it is not uncommon, in some cultures, for individuals, and especially children, to employ different names in different situations. The most frequently used names should be recorded first. In some areas, confusion may arise, as many people have the same names, especially in cultures in which the first-born males or females are always given a set name or in which they are always named after their grandmother or grandfather. In some societies, very young children are not named until some time after birth, and, until this time, they may have to be recorded as 'unnamed'. In some cultures, young infants are not thought to be part of society, and specific questioning may be necessary to elicit information, even about their existence.

In addition to the names, the complete addresses of study participants should be recorded. In some instances, this will be just the name of a village, but, if there is some system of subunits within a village, then this also should be recorded. Often, it will be useful to record the name of the local leaders or elder who have some responsibility in the area in which a participant resides, though it should be remembered that this person may change during the course of a study.

4.9 Ages

In some societies, it takes only a few seconds to elicit an individual's age or date of birth through a simple question, but, in others, these are very difficult to obtain, as individuals do not know their age or date of birth and this information has no special significance to them. The importance of collecting accurate information on ages or dates of birth will depend upon the objectives of the trial.

Accurate dates of birth may not be necessary for all age groups, and those in age groups not pertinent to the trial may not have their specific age recorded at all (for example, but just be recorded as ≥50 years). In some trials, however, accurate estimates of dates of birth may be needed for all age groups. It is generally better to record the date of birth, rather than the age at last birthday, as the latter will change during the course of a trial. During the census, field staff can convert ages to dates of birth, using a simple application on a PDA or mobile phone or transcription tables (relating ages to years of birth), which should be included in their manual. Protocols and methods of estimating dates of birth, such as those described in this section, should be an integral part of the interviewers' training and be included in their field manual. Even if the study area does not have universal civil registration of births, various other sources of information may be available. For children, health cards and the mother's antenatal card may be a good source of information. However, one should remember that, for children who were born at home and not taken to a health facility immediately after birth, they may be less accurate. Mothers can be questioned as to how many days or weeks old the child was when taken to the health facility. Antenatal cards should have dates of delivery or, if not, when the mother was seen and the estimated gestational age. In the absence of any documentation, various other methods of estimating dates of birth of a child have to be employed.

Developmental characteristics, such as the ability of the child to place the right arm over the head to touch the left ear (roughly possible from age 5 years onwards), the ability to sit upright unaided, walking, talking, and so on, can all be used to estimate the developmental age, and hence the approximate date of birth of young children.

Older children are more difficult to age by means of physical and developmental characteristics, due to variations in growth patterns. Age may be inferred from their grade in school or the grade in which they would be if they went to school. However, some educational systems make pupils repeat grades if they are thought unsuitable for higher grades, or a child may start school late.

If the interviewers can accurately age one child, the 'index child' method can be used. The mother is asked about her other children in relation to this child. For example, the fieldworker might ask questions such as: 'Before Ebrima, did you deliver a live birth? Is that child here? How many rainy seasons passed before you became pregnant again?'. With such information on the birth interval, the preceding child's date of birth may be estimated. Similarly, procedures can be used for the following child's date of birth and all her other children.

To estimate the month of birth, calendars can be constructed. The calendar will list the months of rains, dry season, and so on. Religious or cultural festivals, such as Ramadan, Easter, or Christmas, can be included for recent years. For example, a mother might be asked if her child was born in the rains and, if so, whether at the beginning, middle, or end of the rains. At set times of the year, members of the village will be ploughing, planting, sowing, weeding, or harvesting different crops. An example of part of a monthly event calendar that was used in a study in Ghana is given in Box 10.3 (D. A. Ross, personal communication).

Children whose dates of birth are accurately known can be used as index children to estimate the dates of birth of children in other neighbouring households.

Having estimated the ages of all members of a household, the fieldworker should look at all the family together to assess if the ages are plausible, bearing in mind any infant or childhood deaths, stillbirths, or abortions.

The age of adult women can be estimated in several ways. Although age at menarche varies between women, a question about whether the woman had reached menarche before a certain event of known date can give a rough estimate of their date of birth (though, in many cultures, it may be difficult to discuss). Similarly, age at marriage may be, or may have been, fairly uniform for women in some societies, and women can also be asked if they married early or late, compared to their contemporaries. But when 'marriage' is deemed to have occurred must also be elicited, as, in some societies, the marriage process involves numerous stages.

Given an estimated age at first marriage, birth histories can be elicited to estimate a woman's current age. Under conditions of natural fertility, on average, approximately 2.5, 1.5, 1.0, and 1.0 years elapse between births, which are respectively, a live birth that was weaned, a live birth that died in infancy, a stillbirth, and an abortion. This method assumes no infertility, spouse separation, or use of contraception. In areas where these conditions are common, different assumptions have to be made.

Historical event calendars are one of the most commonly used methods to estimate ages. This method is especially useful where societies have a predominantly oral tradition. Historical event calendars require much effort to develop, and, before doing this, it is worth finding out if they already exist in government census departments or elsewhere. If they do not, a calendar can be created, with the assistance of local members of staff, teachers, and community leaders. The calendar should include all the major national historical events, and their dates, and all outstanding local events such as major bush fires, murders, drownings, deaths of religious and political leaders, wars, droughts, floods, famines, and so on. If an individual can remember an event and can estimate how old he or she was (for example, just married, just started school) at the time of that event, their date of birth can be estimated. This method is time-consuming and should be pilot-tested before use. It may be decided that it is too slow and cumbersome to be of use or there may be too few significant events that can be dated that individuals will remember for the method to be used. To be most useful, it is necessary to construct calendars which focus on local, rather than national, events and which are particular to a relatively small geographical area.

An example of an event calendar that was used in the same vitamin A trial in northern Ghana, that was referred to in Box 10.3, is given in Box 10.4 (D. A. Ross, personal communication).

The age of adult men can also be estimated using event calendars, but there are fewer cross-checks, such as menarche or parity, to confirm the approximate date of birth. Even in traditional societies living in rural areas, adult males may have dated documentation, such as voting cards, military service papers, and other official papers, which may include age information. As for children, if the age of some adults can be

---

Box 10.3 Example of part of a monthly calendar of local events used in the Ghana Vitamin A Supplementation Trial (VAST)

SEPTEMBER

Specific dates: none

Farming:	Harvesting of groundnuts, cowpeas, and maize starts
	Harvesting of sweet potatoes, peas, and wet-season rice starts
General:	Heavy rains continue (*Duliu*)
	Drumming and other loud noises banned
	Beginning of the school year

OCTOBER

Specific dates: 1 to 31 'Rosary'

Farming:	Harvesting of groundnuts, cowpeas, maize, sweet potatoes, *pesa*, and wet-season rice ends
General:	Rains slackening off
	Season of abundant food (*Womodaabu Ch'ana*)
	Ban on drumming and other loud noises is lifted

NOVEMBER

Specific dates: 1 All Saints; 2 All Souls

Farming:	Late millet harvest
	Construction of dry-season gardens starts
	Coccidiosis disease (*Choguru*) tends to start in fowls
General:	Harmattan (dust-laden wind from the north) starts
	Cutting of '*sange*' and grass starts
	Firewood collecting season starts
	Frog hunting season starts
	School Nov/Dec exams start

Box 10.3 Example of part of a monthly calendar of local events used in the Ghana Vitamin A Supplementation Trial (VAST) (continued)

DECEMBER

Specific dates: 19 *Feok* Festival in Sandema; 25 Christmas Day; 26 Boxing Day; 27–29 *Fao* Festival in Navrongo; 31 Anniversary of the 31 December Revolution

Farming: Dry-season tomatoes and other vegetables start to become available

Collection of kapok starts

Harvest of ebony fruits starts

Gathering of millet stalks starts

Storing of grain

Domestic animals allowed to move about freely again

General: Harmattan continues

Making of bricks and repairing of houses start

Bush fire season starts

Hunting season starts

Many Northerners start to move South, looking for farm work

Christmas school holidays start

Source: data courtesy of D. A. Ross (personal communication).

Box 10.4 Example of part of a calendar of local events used in Ghana Vitamin A Supplementation Trial (VAST)

1900 (approx.)	◆ War with Zabog people from Burkina Faso
1906	◆ Founding of the Catholic Mission in Navrongo (by Father Oscar Morin)
1908	◆ First Kassenas enrolled for Catechism training
1913	◆ Baptism of the first Kassenas in Navrongo
1916	◆ First conscription of local people into the British army for the First World War
1918	◆ Collection of mats from each household for roofing of houses for British people to stay in
1919	◆ Bad plague of locusts

Box 10.4 Example of part of a calendar of local events used in Ghana Vitamin A Supplementation Trial (VAST) (continued)

1977	♦ Introduction of First Phase of Junior Secondary Schools
1978	♦ Achaempong overthrown by General Akuffo (5 July)
	♦ Change of currency notes (50 cedi note added)
1979	♦ J. J. Rawlings first came to power (4 June)
	♦ Shooting of Colonel Felli and others by firing squad
	♦ Elections for the Third Republic (Hilla Liman elected)
1981	♦ PNDC revolution (31 December)
1983	♦ Year of drought, bush fires, caterpillars, and food shortages
1984	♦ Bumper harvest
	♦ Cancellation of all O- and A-level results throughout West Africa
1985	♦ Major dust storm, when it was dark all day (13 March)
	♦ 25th anniversary celebrations of Navrongo Secondary School (Navasco) and Notre Dame Secondary School
	♦ Start of the Mamprusi/Kusasi War in Bawku
	♦ Fighting between Saboro and Wusungu started (Nov–Dec)
1986	♦ Good harvest
	♦ Heavy rain storm which destroyed part of the Bolgatanga–Navrongo road
1987	♦ Introduction of Second Phase of Junior Secondary Schools (September)
	♦ Ritual murder of an old man in Navrongo
1988	♦ Start of armyworm invasion (June)
	♦ Ordination of three local men to the RC priesthood in Navrongo (23 July)
	♦ The bodies of three Kassenas who had been killed in a road traffic accident in Nigeria were brought back (August)
	♦ Very heavy rain storm and floods with many houses destroyed
	♦ President J. J. Rawlings' visit to Sandema (15 December)
	♦ First *Navro Fao* Festival celebrations for many years (27–29 December)

Source: data courtesy of D. A. Ross (personal communication).

determined accurately, that of others may be estimated in relation to those of known age by asking if any of them attended circumcision ceremonies together, grew up together, played together, or went to school together. If not, perhaps they did so with the older brothers or sisters of the index individuals, and so on. Interviewers must review their data to check that the age information derived is plausible. If data are collected digitally, such checks can be made automatically on entry and time-consuming errors avoided. For example, a woman born in 1935 could not have had a child in 1942; in many societies, it is very unlikely that a woman would be 10 years older than her husband, and birth intervals of less than 9 months are uncommon and those of less than 7 months are not possible. Interviewers and supervisors must be trained to check for such inconsistencies.

Well-known problems with age reporting are age 'heaping' and 'shifting'. Age heaping refers to terminal digit preference—the tendency for ages to be recorded as 10, 20, 30, 40 years or 25, 35, 45 years, and so on. Interviewers should be made aware of this during their training. However, there are examples where such training resulted, at the end of the census, in there being too few individuals with ages ending in 0 or 5! Such effects may be of no great consequence for older adults, for whom precise age estimation is rarely necessary. Age shifting is more difficult to detect and is commonest where age is a criterion of social status. Individuals may falsify their ages, so that they will appear to interviewers to have higher 'age status'. Conversely, women who have not yet married may falsify their age downwards, as may young men who wish to avoid taxes or military draft. In Muslim communities, the ages of women may be especially difficult to estimate, as women may be secluded and the men may respond on their wives' behalf.

4.10 Other identifying information

In some countries, a full name and date of birth are usually sufficient to identify a person. In many others, this will not be enough, but the addition of the individual's parents' names, place of residence, and their relationships to other household members is likely to be sufficient. Individuals may be issued with an identity number by the state or with a social security number that they keep throughout life, and these should be recorded, whenever possible. For trials involving adults, it may be worthwhile to take photographs of all those registered and give each person a laminated photo–ID card that also includes their trial number, with a copy of their photo kept in the trial records. In some trials, involving long-term follow-up of large populations, hand-, foot-, or fingerprints may be used to check identities. This last method was used in a large BCG trial against TB in South India (Tuberculosis Prevention Trial Madras, 1979), and also in a large study to assess whether vaccination with hepatitis B vaccine shortly after birth protects against liver cancer in adult life (The Gambia Hepatitis Study Group, 1987). There are now several commercially available digital print scanning and reading devices that can be used for this; some are combined with hand-held digital data entry devices that can be used for the completion of census and other forms in the field.

5 Processing of census data

Most censuses involve the collection of substantial amounts of data. It is important to plan how these data will be processed, before the study is started. Usually, it will be desirable that the information is either entered electronically on collection into a PDA, tablet computer, or mobile phone or is entered into a computer shortly after it is collected, so that a large backlog of work does not accumulate. Rapid data entry and checks for transcription errors are especially important if the information collected at the census is to be used to produce forms for the recording of additional procedures to be performed on the trial participants shortly after the census. Furthermore, once the information is in a computer, consistency checks can be conducted, and errors or queries referred back to the relevant fieldworkers. Such feedback should occur as soon as possible after the original information has been collected.

In recent years, there have been major advances in computer systems and transmission of digital information, enabling the collection, processing, and checking of data virtually anywhere, eliminating many of the bottlenecks that, until quite recently, so slowed analysis of trial data in LMICs. Nevertheless, data management is a major task in all field trials and requires a well-defined data management strategy, as discussed in Chapter 20. The design of the recording system may need to allow for changes in the composition of the study population over time, due to in-and-out migration, and for movement between households within the population. It is usually desirable to seek help and guidance from an experienced statistician or data analyst for these aspects. This should be done at the start, rather than in the middle, of a study.

6 Post-enumeration checks and quality control

As discussed in Chapter 20, SOPs should be drawn up for QC at all stages of a trial, and, since the mapping and census are usually the first major field data collection stages of a trial, it is usually these steps that require the most preliminary pre-testing and pilot testing of all procedures, including post-enumeration checks and QC. After the census, the list of the population can be checked against other sources of information on the population. For example, school attendance records can be compared to the eligible age bands in the census, and the information collected can also be compared with other census data from the Central Statistics Office or elsewhere. Population pyramids can be drawn to see if there are any unusual features such as age heaping or disproportionate numbers of individuals at certain ages. Sex ratios can be checked, though one must allow for selective migration of certain age groups and of males or females.

7 Keeping the census up to date: demographic surveillance

In some trials, the enumeration of the population at the start of the study is all that is required, and there is no reason to monitor the population 'continuously' for births, deaths, and migration. In other trials, however, a system of registration of vital events may be required. This is usually known as demographic surveillance. A good source of advice on how to do this is available at <http://www.indepth-network.org>.

After the initial census and when the intervention has started or been applied, follow-up surveys may be required to assess the effects of the intervention. For diarrhoeal or respiratory illness episodes, weekly or twice-weekly visits may be required, whereas, for deaths, annual or quarterly surveys may be adequate. These visits provide an opportunity to update the census by ascertaining births, deaths, address changes, and migration into or out of the study area.

Maintaining an up-to-date population database in this way is a major undertaking. It requires good organization, especially in areas with substantial migration such as in peri-urban slums. For example, in a study carried out in southern Brazil, one half of the families with young children changed address within 2 years (Barros et al., 1990). It may be difficult to conduct long-term follow-up studies in such populations.

A census is relatively easy to update if a computer listing is available, either on paper or on a digital device, which gives the names of the residents in each household at the previous survey, with appropriate spaces for updating information (for example, see Stephens et al., 1989). Pregnant women should be noted, so that, in the next survey, enquiries may be made about the outcome of that pregnancy. Maps should be updated, marking any new or abandoned houses. To obtain reasonable information on births and deaths, the maximum interval between surveys should not exceed a year and preferably will be less—ideally every 3–6 months.

The recording of deaths occurring in the population is usually of special interest. Information on these may be obtained by employing 'village informants' to notify the trial investigators when deaths occur. Information may also be available through health facilities, religious institutions, or cemetery records. Usually, it will be necessary to supplement this information with periodic re-surveying of the population if complete ascertainment of such events is required. Deaths tend to be missed, unless specific questions are asked about each individual who was registered in the last round of the fieldwork, and stillbirths, neonatal, and infant deaths may well be missed, unless full demographic surveillance with frequent survey rounds is employed. Such questioning must be done with sensitivity, and the responses may need to be interpreted in the light of any local taboos against speaking of the dead.

References

Barros, F. C., Victora, C. G., and Vaughan, J. P. 1990. The Pelotas (Brazil) birth cohort study 1982–7: strategies for following up 6,000 children in a developing country. *Paediatric and Perinatal Epidemiology*, 4, 205–20.

Chirowodza, A., Van Rooyen, H., Joseph, P., Sikotoyi, S., Richter, L., and Coates, T. 2009. Using participatory methods and geographic information systems (GIS) to prepare for an HIV community-based trial in Vulindlela, South Africa (Project Accept-HPTN 403). *Journal of Community Psychology*, 37, 41–57.

Gupte, M. D. 1999. Vaccine trials in leprosy—Venezuela, Malawi and India. *International Journal of Leprosy and Other Mycobacterial Diseases*, 67, S32–7.

Jukes, M. C., Pinder, M., Grigorenko, E. L., et al. 2006. Long-term impact of malaria chemoprophylaxis on cognitive abilities and educational attainment: follow-up of a controlled trial. *PLoS Clinical Trials*, 1, e19.

Kirkwood, B. R., Hurt, L., Amenga-Etego, S., *et al.* 2010. Effect of vitamin A supplementation in women of reproductive age on maternal survival in Ghana (ObaapaVitA): a cluster-randomised, placebo-controlled trial. *Lancet*, **375**, 1640–9.

Schellenberg, J. R., Abdulla, S., Nathan, R., *et al.* 2001. Effect of large-scale social marketing of insecticide-treated nets on child survival in rural Tanzania. *Lancet*, **357**, 1241–7.

Smith, P. G., Revill, W. D., Lukwago, E., and Rykushin, Y. P. 1976. The protective effect of BCG against Mycobacterium ulcerans disease: a controlled trial in an endemic area of Uganda. *Transactions of the Royal Society of Tropical Medicine and Hygiene*, **70**, 449–57.

Stephens, J., Alonso, P. L., Byass, P., and Snow, R. W. 1989. Tropical epidemiology: a system for continuous demographic monitoring of a study population. *Methods of Information in Medicine*, **28**, 155–9.

The Gambia Hepatitis Study Group. 1987. The Gambia Hepatitis Intervention Study. *Cancer Research*, **47**, 5782–7.

Tuberculosis Prevention Trial Madras. 1979. Trial of BCG vaccines in south India for tuberculosis prevention. *Indian Journal of Medical Research*, **70**, 349–63.

Chapter 11

Randomization, blinding, and coding

1 Introduction to randomization, blinding, and coding 183
2 Randomization schemes for individual participants 185
   2.1 Unrestricted randomization 185
   2.2 Restricted randomization 186
      2.2.1 Small block sizes 187
      2.2.2 Larger block sizes 187
   2.3 Stratified randomization 188
3 Randomization schemes for community or group-based interventions 189
   3.1 Matched-pairs design 189
   3.2 Stratified design 189
   3.3 Constrained randomization design 190
4 Blinding 193
5 Coding systems 194
   5.1 Individual allocations 194
   5.2 Group allocations 195

1 Introduction to randomization, blinding, and coding

As discussed in Chapter 4, the random allocation of participants in a trial to the different interventions being compared is of fundamental importance in the design of investigations that are conducted to produce the highest-quality evidence of any differences in the effects of the interventions. Only if the units to which the interventions are applied (for example, individuals, households, or communities) are randomized between the interventions under study and the study is of a sufficient size is it possible to be confident that differences in the outcome measures of the trial among those in the different intervention groups are due to the effects of the interventions, rather than to underlying differences between the groups. Randomization should ensure that any potential confounding factors, whether known or unknown, are similarly distributed in each of the intervention groups and therefore cannot bias the comparisons of outcome measures between the groups.

Randomization, if done properly, eliminates the possibility of subjective influence in the assignment of individuals to the different intervention groups. Sometimes 'pseudo-randomization' methods are employed in trials for reasons of convenience such as alternate assignment of the different interventions to successive trial entrants or allocation based upon the date of birth or date of entry (with, say, one intervention being assigned to those reporting on even dates and another to those reporting on odd dates). However, proper randomization is superior to any systematic method of allocation, and these other methods should be avoided, unless there are very compelling reasons for using them. With systematic allocation, it is possible for the investigator, and sometimes the participant, to know in advance the group to which a participant will be allocated, and this may introduce conscious or unconscious bias into the allocation procedure. For example, such knowledge may affect the investigator's judgement as to whether or not an individual is eligible for entry into a particular trial. For this reason, it is essential that the randomization is done (or the randomization allocation is revealed to the investigator) only *after* it has been ascertained both that an individual is eligible for entry into a trial and also that he or she is prepared to participate in the trial, no matter which intervention is assigned.

As Schulz (1995) pointed out, the success of randomization depends on two interrelated processes. The first entails generating a sequence by which the participants in a trial are allocated between intervention groups. To ensure unpredictability of that allocation sequence, it should be generated by a random process. The second process *allocation concealment* shields those involved in a trial from knowing upcoming assignments in advance, so that investigators cannot change who gets the next assignment, potentially making the comparison groups less equivalent and thus biasing the measurement of the effects of the intervention.

In this chapter, various ways are described in which interventions may be randomly assigned among trial participants. The simplest method, if there are two intervention groups, is by using a procedure which is equivalent to tossing a coin to decide the allocation for each individual unit. This can either be done literally, or an equivalent procedure may be simulated using a table of random numbers or by using a computer to generate random numbers, as described in Section 2.1. In large trials, the use of such a simple randomization procedure is highly likely to ensure that there are nearly equal numbers of units allocated to the different intervention groups and the distribution of potentially confounding factors will be similar in all groups. However, if the total number of units in a study is small, such an assignment procedure may result by chance in the compositions of the different intervention groups being markedly different with respect to factors that may affect the outcome measures in the trial, or markedly unequal numbers of participants may be recruited to each intervention group. Such imbalance may arise by chance as, for example, it is possible that, if a coin is tossed ten times, it will come down heads, say, only twice. In fact, the chance that it will come down exactly heads five times and tails five times is only about 25%. For trials involving several hundreds of participants or more, any such imbalance is likely to be small and can be taken into account in the analysis of the trial. In a small trial, imbalance may make the trial more difficult to interpret, and it is advisable to design the randomization procedure to ensure balance. For this purpose, 'restricted' or 'blocked' randomization (see Section 2.2) can be used to ensure balance in group sizes. Blocked randomization also helps to achieve balance on time sequence and, in multicentre trials, study site.

Stratum-matched designs (see Section 2.3) can be employed to produce balance in the composition of the groups, with respect to those variables on which the matching is based.

The techniques described in Sections 2 and 3 may be used whether the intervention is assigned to communities or to individuals. However, when communities are randomized, as in cluster randomized trials, the number of randomization units (communities) may be relatively small (often 20 or less), and more sophisticated methods of randomization have been devised to reduce sources of potential bias in the allocation of interventions in such trials. These methods are summarized in Section 3.

Whenever possible, intervention studies should be both randomized and *double-blind*, i.e. neither the participants nor the investigator should know to which group each participant has been allocated. This guards against biases that may result from knowledge of the intervention affecting the way an individual behaves, is treated, or is monitored during the trial, or assessed during, or at the end of, the trial. Blinding is discussed in Section 4. In Section 5, there is a discussion of coding systems for recording intervention allocation that may be used in trials.

2 Randomization schemes for individual participants

2.1 Unrestricted randomization

Simple random allocation of individuals between the different intervention groups is carried out most conveniently by using a computer. For example, in Microsoft Excel, the instruction '= RANDBETWEEN(1,3)' will produce a random number between 1 and 3, i.e. each of the numbers 1, 2, or 3 has an equal chance of being generated. The equivalent of tossing a coin is = RANDBETWEEN(1,2). Some calculators also have a key which generates a random number on the display (usually a decimal number between 0 and 1, so that, for example, the equivalent of coin tossing would be to allocate a number less than 0.5000 as 'heads' and a number 0.5000 or greater as 'tails').

In large trials, it is common for a centralized randomization system to be used. When an investigator has decided that a participant meets the entry criteria for a trial, and the participant has given informed consent to be randomized to one of the trial interventions, the investigator telephones, or sends a text, to a central office to give the identification details for the participant, and the office then tells, or texts, the investigator to which intervention the participant has been randomly assigned or, in the case of a double-blind trial, the code for the intervention that should be administered to the participant. Systems are now commonly used whereby this process has been automated and does not require an individual to answer the telephone in the central office or for a similar automated procedure to be followed over the Internet. The advantage of this method of intervention assignment is that there is no way in which the investigator can influence the randomization procedure, and if, for example, the investigator decides not to allocate an intervention to a participant after knowing the random assignment, there is a central record of this.

For investigators who cannot set up access to a procedure for remote randomization, a frequently used alternative procedure is for a set of opaque, sealed, and numbered envelopes to be prepared, containing the intervention allocations (or possibly even the actual interventions if these are, for example, drugs). The envelopes are opened in numerical sequence, as each new person is entered into the trial. Entry criteria must be checked and eligibility satisfied before an envelope is opened, in order to exclude the possibility that the decision to accept a subject into the trial is influenced by the knowledge of the group to which he or she would be allocated. For large trials, the use of envelopes may be too cumbersome. Coding systems and alternative procedures appropriate for use in the case of 'double-blind' designs are discussed in Section 5.

Where the study product (for example, drug, vaccine) package is individually numbered and labelled (and randomization has been done before the numbering and labelling and where there is an indistinguishable placebo or control intervention), randomization may simply be achieved by registering each new recruit and assigning them the number on the product package.

In some circumstances, it may be better to design the randomization system, such that it is completely transparent to participants that a random allocation process is being used. A trial may be more acceptable if the trial population is involved in the randomization procedure. For example, in a trial in Ghana, the allocation of insecticide-impregnated bed-nets was randomized, such that, in some communities, all households received a bed-net immediately and, in other communities, the distribution of nets was deferred until a later time (Binka et al., 1996). At a public meeting involving all of the trial communities, the name of each community was written on a slip of paper. All the slips were put in a bucket, and a child was asked to draw some of the slips from the bucket to determine which communities received the bed-nets first. By using this procedure, it was apparent that the allocation was random and that no favouritism was operating. The fairness of the procedure was demonstrated to the population by the fact that, by chance, the community in which the area chief resided was not selected for early bed-net allocation (much to the surprise of the population)! (Fred Binka, personal communication.)

Unrestricted randomization is often employed in large trials, as it is likely that any imbalance between the intervention groups with respect to risk factors for the occurrence of the outcomes of interest will tend to even out. Furthermore, it is possible to adjust for any residual imbalance during the analysis of the study without important loss of statistical power.

2.2 Restricted randomization

Although an unrestricted randomization procedure should lead to approximately equal numbers of participants in each group, this is not guaranteed. For example, there is more than a 5% chance that, if 20 participants are allocated to one of two groups at random, six or fewer may be allocated to one group, and 14 or more to the other. A better balance is achieved by using a 'restricted randomization' procedure, also called 'blocked randomization' or 'randomization with balance'. This procedure ensures equal numbers in each group, after there have been a fixed number of allocations. For example, the allocation procedure might be designed in blocks of ten, such that, in every ten allocations, five are to one group and five to the other. The total number of intervention groups must be a multiple of the size of the blocks.

In order to minimize the possibility that an allocation can be deduced from previous allocations, the block size should not be too small (in particular, it should not be two!), and, if possible, it should not be known to the investigator responsible for the administration of the interventions. Indeed, as far as possible, those giving the interventions should not be aware that blocking has been carried out, or, if the block size is a fixed number, the person giving the intervention would know in advance what the intervention allocation of the last individual or group in the block would be. Another safeguard is to use several different block sizes for allocating interventions in a trial. For example, in a trial with two arms, the block size might be varied, at random, between eight, ten, and 12.

Two different procedures for carrying out restricted randomization are described in Sections 2.2.1 and 2.2.2, one appropriate for small block sizes and the other appropriate for larger block sizes, say eight or more.

2.2.1 Small block sizes

If two interventions, say A and B, are to be allocated using a block size of, say four, it is possible to list all the different possible combinations of the allocations that will yield two As and two Bs. This is illustrated in Table 11.1. A number is allocated to each combination, and a random number is chosen to select a particular allocation.

The selection of each random number (between 1 and 6) generates four intervention allocations. Thus, if the random numbers 4, 5, and 1 are generated, these yield a list of twelve intervention allocations (to be assigned to participants in sequence) (Table 11.2).

2.2.2 Larger block sizes

Listing all possible combinations of allocations within a block becomes unmanageable, as the block size increases. For example, with a block size of ten, there are 252 different possible combinations, each yielding five participants in each of two intervention groups A and B. An alternative approach is necessary therefore. Suppose the block size is to be 12 and six allocations are to be made to group A and six to group B. Random numbers between 1 and 12 are generated, until six different numbers in that range have been generated (numbers that duplicate a previous one are ignored). Algorithms

Table 11.1 Example of allocation rule for a block size of four, with two intervention groups A and B

Allocation	Corresponding random number
AABB	1
BBAA	2
ABAB	3
BABA	4
ABBA	5
BAAB	6

Table 11.2 Example of random allocation to two groups using a block size of four

Block number	1	2	3
Random number	4	5	1
Allocation sequence	BABA	ABBA	AABB

are easily available on the Internet to generate such random numbers. (For example, at <http://www.random.org/integers>, it is straightforward to generate X random integers between Y and Z where the user inserts values for X, Y, and Z.) Thus, we might request six random numbers between 1 and 12 and obtain 1, 2, 4, 7, 11, and 12. Then, the first, second, fourth, seventh, eleventh, and twelfth participants within the block are allocated to one of the interventions, say A, and the other participants to B. The complete sequence for the block of 12 is shown in Table 11.3.

A similar procedure, with a different set of random numbers, is used to allocate interventions in the next block (i.e. 13 to 24), and so on.

In general, it is better to choose block sizes which are not too large, in order to reduce the risk of a long sequence of individuals being allocated to the same intervention. A maximum block size of 12 is suggested.

2.3 Stratified randomization

If different subgroups of participants, say males and females, have different background rates of disease, it may be desirable to design the allocation procedure such that the interventions are equally divided in each subgroup. This may be achieved though 'stratified' randomization. The population is stratified, for example, by sex or by age group, and the allocation of the interventions is carried out separately in each stratum.

Stratification may be based on more than one factor. For example, there may be a separate allocation of interventions in each of a number of different age–sex groups. The greater the number of strata, the more complex the organization of the randomization is; in general, the number of strata should be kept small. Separate randomization lists will have to be maintained for each stratum. This may be achieved by using different sets of coloured envelopes, packages, or sticky labels for each stratum.

Stratified randomization should be considered if it is known that there are large differences in disease risk between different groups of individuals in a trial (or in response to treatment in the case of a therapeutic trial) and if it is possible to place individuals in strata corresponding to different levels of risk prior to entry to the trial. The objective of stratification is to try to include in each stratum those at similar risk of disease (or response to treatment) and to randomize between interventions separately within each stratum. In multicentre trials, randomization is often stratified on study site.

Table 11.3 Example of random allocation to two groups using a block size of 12

Participant	1	2	3	4	5	6	7	8	9	10	11	12
Intervention	A	A	B	A	B	B	A	B	B	B	A	A

3 Randomization schemes for community or group-based interventions

As discussed in Chapter 4, trial designs have been increasingly employed in recent years, in which the unit of allocation of the intervention is a community or group, rather than an individual. These cluster randomized trials may involve the randomization of communities that can be quite large; consequently, the number of communities that can be included in a trial is often relatively small and may be of the order of 20 communities or fewer. If a method of simple unrestricted randomization is used to allocate interventions to communities, there is a reasonably high chance that there may be differences between the two groups of communities, unrelated to the interventions, that may bias the measurement of the effects of the intervention. It is common therefore to employ some method of restricted randomization in the allocation of interventions to communities (see also Chapter 4, Section 4.2).

3.1 Matched-pairs design

A matched-pairs design is a special case of stratified randomization, in which the strata are each of size two. Communities are matched into pairs, the pairs being chosen so that the two communities in a pair are as similar as possible with respect to potential confounding variables; in the absence of any intervention, the two communities would be expected to have similar incidence rates of the disease or other outcome under study. One member of each pair is assigned at random to one intervention group and one to the other. Similar matching procedures can be employed when there are more than two intervention groups. For example, with three groups, matched triplets would be employed.

Recent research on the design of cluster randomized trials has indicated that, although matched-pairs randomization remains a valid study design, other methods of randomization, such as stratified randomization or constrained (restricted) randomization, discussed in Sections 3.2 and 3.3, may generally be more appropriate design strategies (Hayes and Moulton, 2009). The major reason for this is because, if a trial is designed as a matched-pairs study, then it must be analysed as such. In technical terms, pairing reduces the number of 'degrees of freedom' that are available in the statistical comparison of the outcome measures in the intervention and comparison communities, compared to an unmatched design. This has little consequence if the number of communities is large, but, if the number is small, as is typically the case, then matching reduces the statistical power of a trial to detect an intervention effect of a given size (unless the matching factors are very closely correlated with the outcome).

3.2 Stratified design

For the reasons outlined, unrestricted randomization in a cluster randomized trial may lead to imbalance with respect to potential confounding factors between the different comparison arms of the trial, unless the number of clusters is very large. Pair matching of communities is one way of attempting to overcome this problem to ensure better balance between the arms of the trial, but this strategy may be associated with a substantial loss of statistical power. An intermediate alternative is to adopt a *stratified*, rather than a matched-pairs, design. A stratified design involves the grouping of communities into a number of strata, based on the expected rate of disease in the absence of the intervention. For example, in a study on malaria, communities with high transmission intensity would be put into the same stratum, and those with low transmission intensity would be put into a different stratum. The communities within each stratum are then randomly allocated between the different intervention arms of the trial.

In practice, it is often challenging to decide which communities should go into the same stratum. If there are baseline rates available for the disease under study from surveillance or from a previous study, then these may provide a reasonable guide as to the expected rates in the different communities in the absence of the interventions. However, the rates of some diseases may vary substantially from year to year, and what happened in the past may not be a very good guide for what will happen in the future. Quite commonly, such rates are not available, and the investigator has the alternative of conducting a pre-trial study to estimate disease rates in each community or, based on ecological and epidemiological considerations, of making some estimate of what the rates might be. The first of these options adds to the cost of the study, whereas there may be considerable uncertainties regarding the utility and accuracy of the second approach. A fuller discussion of these issues is given in Hayes and Moulton (2009).

A stratified design is associated with less loss of statistical power than a matched-pairs design and will assist in making the communities in the different arms of the trial more comparable with respect to potential confounding factors. There may still remain some imbalance with respect to these factors, but it is possible to adjust for this in the analysis of the trial, provided, of course, the relevant confounding factors have been measured. Methods for the analysis of cluster randomized trials and the adjustment for confounding factors are beyond the scope of this book and will generally require the input of a specialist statistician.

Hayes and Moulton (2009) suggest that, in practical situations, it is likely that the use of three or four strata will provide most of the advantages provided by pair matching, such that communities can be very accurately paired with respect to expected disease rates during the trial. With respect to the choice of the number of strata, these authors suggest that there should be no more than two strata if there are six or fewer clusters per arm, and no more than three strata if there are 7–10 clusters per arm.

3.3 Constrained randomization design

A further method of controlling for confounding is to adopt a method known as *constrained* or *restricted* randomization. Consider a trial to be conducted in 12 communities, six of which will be allocated to the intervention under test, the remaining six serving as control communities. Using a simple unrestricted randomization design, six communities would be selected at random to receive the intervention, and the other six would serve as controls. By chance, it might happen that the six intervention communities all turn out to be close to a major highway, and the six control communities are all more distant from the highway. If the disease we are studying might be related to proximity to the highway (for example, HIV infection rates show this characteristic in some situations), then we may be rather unhappy with this particular selection of intervention communities, as there would be a priori reasons for believing there would be differences in disease rates, irrespective of the effect of the intervention we wanted to test. In these circumstances, we might reject the initial random selection of communities and select another set of random numbers to determine which our intervention communities are. While this strategy may not seem unreasonable, it is clearly dangerous to allow an investigator to override a randomization procedure if he or she does not like the result!

Constrained randomization designs aim to exclude from consideration random allocations that result in unsatisfactory imbalance between communities in the intervention and control arms. In the study already outlined, involving 12 communities, there are 924 possible different allocations of which communities comprise the six in which the intervention will be applied. Conceptually, we could imagine examining each of these possible allocations and deciding which of them we would be happy with and which would cause us concern. Suppose there were, for example, 400 for which there seemed to be a reasonable balance of confounding factors between the putative intervention and control communities. We could restrict our consideration of possible allocations to these 400, and choose one of these at random to be the one that was actually used in the trial. This is the basic principle of the constrained or restricted randomization design.

Examining all 924 possible allocations would be a considerable undertaking and would be even more difficult if the total number of communities was more than 12. It is therefore necessary to seek some more automated method of deciding which randomizations are acceptable. In practice, what is done is to define some key variables for which we wish to achieve reasonable balance across the intervention and control arms. These key variables are then compared in each of the possible randomizations, and a rule is set up to exclude a randomization if the difference between the key variables in putative intervention and control arms is more than some specified amount. Thus, the selection of 'acceptable' randomizations can be programmed into a computer, so that the selection is done automatically once the acceptability criteria for balance between the intervention and control communities have been defined.

The procedure described as a modification of simple unrestricted randomization can also be incorporated into a stratified design, so that there is a selection of acceptable possible randomizations within each stratum.

Both stratification and restricted randomization can be used to achieve good balance (avoid confounding), but stratification *also* aims to reduce between-cluster (within-stratum) variation, and hence to increase power and precision.

An example of the use of restricted randomization in the design of a trial of an adolescent sexual health intervention carried out in Tanzania (Hayes et al., 2005) is given in Box 11.1.

Box 11.1 Use of restricted randomization in a community randomized trial of an adolescent sexual health intervention in Tanzania

In this trial, carried out to evaluate the impact of a multi-component sexual health intervention on HIV and other adverse outcomes among adolescents in Tanzania, the 20 rural study communities were grouped into three strata, based on their expected risk of HIV infection (Hayes et al., 2005). There were six communities in the low-risk stratum, eight in the medium-risk stratum, and six in the high-risk stratum.

There is a total of 28 000 ways of assigning half the communities in each stratum to the intervention arm and half to the control arm. Because the total number of communities is quite small, not all of these 28 000 allocations would provide a good balance of key characteristics across treatment arms. Restricted randomization was therefore used to achieve an acceptable balance by applying the following criteria:

- mean HIV prevalence in each treatment arm within 0.075% of overall mean
- mean prevalence of *Chlamydia trachomatis* (CT) infection in each treatment arm within 0.1% of overall mean
- two of the 20 communities were close to gold mines, and one of these was to be allocated to each treatment arm
- even distribution of intervention communities across the four administrative districts in which the trial was carried out.

HIV and CT prevalence were based on an initial survey of young people carried out in each study community. Prevalences of HIV and CT (also an STI) were assumed to be correlated with sexual behaviour in the study communities and therefore to be predictors of the risk of acquiring HIV infection during the trial. HIV prevalence is often increased in mining communities, and it was important to ensure that one mining community was allocated to each treatment arm. Finally, ensuring an even distribution of intervention communities across districts helped to ensure that the trial was acceptable to local leaders.

A computer program was used to check each of the 28 000 possible allocations against the balance criteria, and 953 allocations satisfied the criteria and were listed. One of these was chosen randomly at a public randomization ceremony.

Source: data from Hayes, R. J., et al., The MEMA kwa Vijana project: design of a community randomised trial of an innovative adolescent sexual health intervention in rural Tanzania, *Contemporary Clinical Trials*, Volume 26, Issue 4, pp. 430–42, Copyright © 2005 Elsevier Inc. All rights reserved.

4 Blinding

Whenever possible, neither the participants nor the investigators should know to which intervention group each participant belongs until after the end of the trial. Such 'double-blind' designs (both the investigator and the participants are blind to the knowledge of who have received each intervention) eliminate the possibility that knowing to which intervention an individual is allocated may affect the way the individual behaves, is treated, or is monitored during the trial, or the way an individual is assessed at the end of the trial. Sometimes, a double-blind trial is not possible, and a 'single-blind' design might be used, in which the investigator knows to which group a participant belongs, but the participant does not.

'Blinded' designs are especially important when those in one of the groups under comparison are given an intervention that is expected to have no effect on the outcome of interest. To maintain blindness in these circumstances, a placebo should be used, if possible, which should look and smell as similar as possible to the intervention itself (and have a similar taste if it is being given orally). Sometimes, an identical-looking placebo cannot be obtained, and, in these circumstances, the investigator and the participants should be kept blind to which treatment is the active one. While this may be the best that can be done in some trials, it is generally undesirable. Either the participants or the investigator may form a view as to which the active treatment is (possibly erroneously), and this may affect differentially the amount of other care given to the participants or the likelihood that a participant reports apparently beneficial or harmful effects. For example, there is evidence that the colour of a tablet may affect the perceived action of a drug and seems to influence the effectiveness of a drug in some situations (de Craen et al., 1996).

For some interventions, it may be possible to preserve blindness in the initial phase of a trial, but this may be more difficult later. For example, in placebo-controlled studies of ivermectin against onchocerciasis, it was found that some participants were able to guess that they had received an active drug, rather than a placebo, because of the effect of ivermectin on other helminth infections, such as *Ascaris*, through the passage of worms in their stools, whereas those receiving placebo rarely experienced this effect. In placebo-controlled trials of BCG vaccination, most of those who have received BCG develop a lasting scar, whereas those who have received placebo do not. The possible bias that this might induce in the assessment of whether or not a participant developed leprosy, following vaccination, was overcome in a trial in Uganda by covering the vaccination site with sticking plaster for all participants before each clinical examination (Brown and Stone, 1966).

For some intervention trials, in which the unit of randomization is the community, the use of a placebo is straightforward and is no different, in principle, from the situation for an individually randomized trial. This was the case, for example, in a cluster randomized trial to assess the impact of regular vitamin A supplementation on child mortality. Those in the control communities received supplementation with an inert liquid that was administered in such a way that it was indistinguishable from the administration of vitamin A (Ghana VAST Study Team, 1993). For some interventions, however, a suitable placebo may be impossible to find.

What would be a suitable placebo for an improved water supply and sanitation programme in a village, for example?

5 Coding systems

In some circumstances, it may be necessary to break the intervention code for an individual. This might arise, for example, if a severe adverse event becomes manifest and the treatment for it may be influenced by knowledge of what intervention the individual received. The coding system which is used to record which individuals received which intervention should be designed, such that, if it is necessary to break the code for one individual, the blindness of the investigator, with respect to the interventions received by other trial participants, should be preserved. For example, if one intervention is coded A and the other B, breaking the code for one individual effectively breaks the code for all participants (if the investigator knows who has received A and who has received B). The use of a single code for each intervention is generally a poor design. It is better to have a unique code for each participant and to have a separate list linking participant numbers with the intervention allocated, or to have only a very small number of participants sharing the same code number. For example, in a BCG trial in South India for tuberculosis prevention, ampoules (each containing several doses of vaccine) were packed in boxes of three. Each box held three vials containing one of two different vaccine doses or a placebo preparation. The three ampoules were randomly coded 1, 2, and 3. The vaccine received by a participant was coded in the trial records by a combination of the box number and the ampoule number (Tuberculosis Prevention Trial Madras, 1979). If it had been necessary to break the vaccine code for an individual, it would only have been broken for those participants who received vaccine from the same ampoule in the same box.

The randomization list should usually be prepared in advance of the trial, and the codes assigned by someone other than the PI. If the intervention is a drug or a vaccine, the manufacturer may agree to supervise the packaging and coding, but the allocation procedure should be overseen, and the code should be held during the trial by a disinterested party. Often, the code is held by the data safety and monitoring committee (see Chapter 7, Section 4). It is also worth checking, for a random sample of the drugs or vaccines, that the codes are correct and errors have not been made in the packaging.

5.1 Individual allocations

Suppose two interventions are to be allocated between 200 individuals. A good coding scheme would be to choose 100 random numbers between 1 and 200 and allocate these codes for intervention A, say, and allocate the other 100 for intervention B (there may also be some 'blocking' within the total group of 200, say in blocks of size ten; see Section 2.2). When an intervention is allocated to the 127th patient in the trial, they would be given the drugs in envelope number 127, and this would be noted in their trial record. A master list of the interventions corresponding to each number would be kept in a secure place by a third party not directly connected with the trial. If it were necessary to break the code for an individual patient, the third party could do this without revealing any of the other codes to the investigator. Only at the end of the trial would the list be released to the investigator for the analysis of the results of the trial.

5.2 Group allocations

If a trial involves many thousands of participants, it may be logistically too complicated to allocate a separate treatment code number to each participant, though this will depend upon the circumstances, and, in some cases, having thousands of individual codes poses no problem. An alternative approach is to use a fixed, but not too small, number of codes for the different interventions. If there are N participants in the trial and C codes for the interventions, then breaking the code for one participant would break the codes for N/C in total. For example, the coding system used for a vaccine trial in Venezuela is given in Box 11.2. In this trial, 998 different codes were used (499 for one vaccine and 499 for the other) for about 30 000 participants. Breaking the code for one individual would break it for about 30 others (Convit et al., 1992).

A simpler system might be required if participants had to be given the same intervention on a number of occasions. A method that was used in a trial of ivermectin against

---

Box 11.2 Assignment of check letter for three-digit vaccine code

The coding system described was that used in a leprosy vaccine trial conducted in Venezuela (Convit et al, 1992). Randomization was to one of two vaccines.

The vaccine vials were labelled with a number between 1 and 998. A total of 499 of these numbers were allocated at random for one vaccine, and the other 499 for the other vaccine. A check letter was added to each number, so that transcription errors would stand a high chance of being detected. The code was devised, such that every possible permutation of the same three digits in a number had a different check letter, as illustrated:

001A	010B	100C			
002D	020E	200F			
.					
.					
009M	090N	900P			
010B—already allocated—see line 1					
011R	101S	110T			
.					
.					
123W	132X	213Y	231A	312B	321C
124D	142E	214F	241G	412H	421J
etc.					

> **Box 11.2 Assignment of check letter for three-digit vaccine code (continued)**
>
> In some countries, number 1 and number 7 are distinguished clearly when written, as it is the custom for the number 7 to have a horizontal stroke put through it. In other countries, however, this is not the custom, and there is a danger that these numbers will be confused. In such cases, it would be advisable to change the check coding system, such that, if a 1 is confused with a 7, or vice versa, the check letter will enable the error to be detected. Thus, the system outlined might be modified, as indicated:
>
> | | | | | | | | | |
> |---|---|---|---|---|---|---|---|---|
> | 001A | 010B | 100C | 007D | 070E | 700F | | | |
> | 002G | 020H | 200J | | | | | | |
> | 003K | . | . | | | | | | |
> | . | | | | | | | | |
> | . | | | | | | | | |
> | . | | | | | | | | |
> | 011R | 101S | 110T | 017V | 071X | 107Y | 170A | 701B | 710C |
> | 077D | 707E | 770F | | | | | | |
> | 012G | etc. | | | | | | | |
>
> Source: data from Peter Smith (personal communication).

onchocerciasis in Sierra Leone was to allocate 20 codes for ivermectin or placebo treatments (A, B, C, D, and so on) (Whitworth et al., 1991). The drugs were taken to the field in 20 tins, with the code letters on them (ten of which contained ivermectin, and ten contained placebo tablets), and participants were allocated to one of the 20 codes at random. If a participant was allocated, say to code E, then each time they were treated, the dose was taken from tin E. About 1000 patients were included in the trial, so that breaking the code for one individual would have also broken it for 1000/20 = 50 others. A similar system was used in a trial of a pneumococcal vaccine in The Gambia, which involved many thousands of participants, and each participant was scheduled to receive three doses of the vaccine at different times (Cutts et al., 2005).

With either individual or group allocations, it is helpful if the intervention codes are on removable sticky labels that can be affixed to an individual's form, thus minimizing the likelihood of recording errors. Where possible, the coding system should be devised so that transcription errors in recording may be detected. How this was achieved in the leprosy vaccine trial in Venezuela is illustrated in Box 11.2. More commonly now, bar codes are used to identify interventions in trials using drugs or vaccines, and, provided that suitable computer systems are set up, this should eliminate the possibility of transcription errors.

References

Binka, F. N., Kubaje, A., Adjuik, M., *et al.* 1996. Impact of permethrin impregnated bednets on child mortality in Kassena-Nankana district, Ghana: a randomized controlled trial. *Tropical Medicine and International Health*, **1**, 147–54.

Brown, J. A. and Stone, M. M. 1966. B.C.G. vaccination of children against leprosy: first results of a trial in Uganda. *BMJ*, **1**, 7–14.

Convit, J., Sampson, C., Zuniga, M., *et al.* 1992. Immunoprophylactic trial with combined Mycobacterium leprae/BCG vaccine against leprosy: preliminary results. *Lancet*, **339**, 446–50.

Cutts, F. T., Zaman, S. M., Enwere, G., *et al.* 2005. Efficacy of nine-valent pneumococcal conjugate vaccine against pneumonia and invasive pneumococcal disease in The Gambia: randomised, double-blind, placebo-controlled trial. *Lancet*, **365**, 1139–46.

De Craen, A. J., Roos, P. J., Leonard De Vries, A., and Kleijnen, J. 1996. Effect of colour of drugs: systematic review of perceived effect of drugs and of their effectiveness. *BMJ*, **313**, 1624–6.

Ghana VAST Study Team. 1993. Vitamin A supplementation in northern Ghana: effects on clinic attendances, hospital admissions, and child mortality. *Lancet*, **342**, 7–12.

Hayes, R. J., Changalucha, J., Ross, D. A., *et al.* 2005. The MEMA kwa Vijana project: design of a community randomised trial of an innovative adolescent sexual health intervention in rural Tanzania. *Contemporary Clinical Trials*, **26**, 430–42.

Hayes, R. J. and Moulton, L. H. 2009. *Cluster randomized trials*. Boca Raton, Fla.; London: Chapman & Hall/CRC.

Schulz, K. F. 1995. Subverting randomization in controlled trials. *JAMA*, **274**, 1456–8.

Tuberculosis Prevention Trial Madras. 1979. Trial of BCG vaccines in south India for tuberculosis prevention. *Indian Journal of Medical Research*, **70**, 349–63.

Whitworth, J. A. G., Gilbert, C. E., Mabey, D. M., Maude, G. H., Morgan, D., and Taylor, D. W. 1991. Effects of repeated doses of ivermectin on ocular onchocerciasis: community-based trial in Sierra Leone. *Lancet*, **338**, 1100–3.

Chapter 12

Outcome measures and case definition

1 Introduction to outcome measures and case definition 199
2 Types of outcome measures 200
　2.1 Primary, secondary, tertiary 200
　　2.1.1 Primary outcomes 200
　　2.1.2 Secondary and tertiary outcomes 201
　　2.1.3 Other variables which are not study outcomes 201
　2.2 Clinical case definitions 201
　　2.2.1 Physician-based case definitions 201
　　2.2.2 Laboratory-based case definitions, including any diagnostic procedure 202
　　2.2.3 Lay worker-based case definitions 203
　　2.2.4 Case definitions using secondary data sources 203
　　2.2.5 Standardization 203
　　2.2.6 Inclusion and exclusion criteria 204
　2.3 Death and verbal autopsies 204
　2.4 Non-clinical case definitions 205
　2.5 Proxy measurements as study outcomes 206
　　2.5.1 Behavioural changes 206
　　2.5.2 Transmission reduction 206
　2.6 Adverse events 207
3 Factors influencing choice of outcome measures 208
　3.1 Relevance 209
　3.2 Feasibility 209
　3.3 Acceptability 209
　3.4 Opportunity for add-on studies 210
4 Variability and quality control of outcome measures 210
　4.1 Reproducibility 210
　4.2 Sensitivity and specificity 211
　4.3 Bias 213
　4.4 The Hawthorne effect 214
　4.5 Quality control issues 214

1 Introduction to outcome measures and case definition

Field trials of health interventions are designed to assess the impact of one or more interventions on the incidence, duration, or severity of specified diseases, or on intermediate variables or risk factors considered to be closely related to these measures of disease (for example, hygiene behaviours for diarrhoeal diseases, reduction in density of parasite vector, reduction of indoor air pollutants for pneumonia, or reduction of salt intake for hypertension). The measures chosen to assess the impact of the interventions are called the *outcome* measures in the trial (or the trial *endpoints*). Such measures should be defined at the time the trial is designed and should be specified in detail in the study protocol. The outcomes should be compared between those in the different intervention groups and should be measured in a consistent way during the course of the trial in the different groups. Clear definitions are also necessary, so that the measures can be replicated in other trials and meaningful comparisons made between trials. Failure to pay sufficient attention to the precise definition of the primary outcome measures at the start of a trial may lead to confusion in interpreting the results or can even invalidate them.

As discussed in Chapter 4, Section 5, several different outcome measures may be employed in a trial. It is important to decide which is of most interest (primary outcome), as this has major design implications, particularly in terms of the study size and duration. Trials may have other outcomes (secondary or tertiary) that may be important to measure, although they will generally not determine the size of the trial. In Table 12.1, there are some examples of primary and secondary outcomes for trials of different interventions.

In this chapter, different types of outcome measures are reviewed in Section 2, and factors influencing the selection of these are discussed in Section 3. The importance of standardizing measurements between different observers is stressed in Section 4.1,

Table 12.1 Examples of primary and secondary outcomes for trials of different interventions

Intervention trial	Primary outcome(s)	Secondary outcomes	Comment
Phase III trial of 9-valent conjugate pneumococcal vaccine in The Gambia (Cutts et al., 2005)	◆ First episode of radiological pneumonia	◆ Clinical or severe clinical pneumonia ◆ Invasive pneumococcal disease ◆ Invasive pneumococcal disease due to serotypes in vaccine ◆ All-cause hospital admissions ◆ All-cause mortality	The main purpose of the trial was to evaluate the public health impact of the vaccine. First episodes of radiological pneumonia were reduced by 37% (and all-cause mortality by 16%—not a primary endpoint in the trial). Highest efficacy was expected against invasive pneumococcal disease due to serotypes in the vaccine, but the aetiology of most cases of pneumonia is difficult to establish.

continued

Table 12.1 (continued) Examples of primary and secondary outcomes for trials of different interventions

Intervention trial	Primary outcome(s)	Secondary outcomes	Comment
Cluster randomized trial to assess the impact of an adolescent sexual health intervention in Tanzania (Ross et al., 2007)	◆ Incidence of HIV infection ◆ Prevalence of herpes simplex type 2 (HSV 2) infection at end of trial	◆ Six biological measures (for example, syphilis and gonorrhoea prevalence at end of trial) ◆ Five behavioural endpoints (for example, use of condoms during sexual intercourse) ◆ One attitudinal endpoint ◆ Three knowledge endpoints (for example, how HIV is transmitted)	The intervention was designed to reduce HIV incidence through behaviour change brought about by sexual health education. A substantial number of secondary outcomes were included to facilitate understanding of the main results. This was important, as the intervention was shown to substantially improve knowledge, reported attitudes, and some reported sexual behaviours but had no consistent impact on biological outcomes.
Trial of intermittent treatment of infants for malaria and anaemia control at time of routine vaccinations in Tanzania (Schellenberg et al., 2001)	◆ First or only episode of clinical malaria	◆ Multiple malaria episodes ◆ Fever episodes ◆ Severe anaemia ◆ Admissions to hospital ◆ Outpatient attendances	This was a test of a new approach to malaria control by administering anti-malarial drugs routinely to infants attending clinics for vaccination. Clinical malaria was reduced by 59%, and severe anaemia by 50%

and there is a discussion of how the results of a trial may be influenced by poor sensitivity or specificity in the outcome measures in Section 4.2. Finally, ways of avoiding bias and maintaining quality control (QC) in case ascertainment methods are reviewed in Sections 4.3 and 4.5.

2 Types of outcome measures

2.1 Primary, secondary, tertiary

2.1.1 Primary outcomes

Primary outcomes are the most important outcomes of the study, the ones that determine its design and the study size. They represent the main reason the trial is being conducted. Normally, a trial has only one primary outcome, so, for each main question in the development of a new drug, vaccine, or intervention, one specific trial is usually conducted. However, more than one primary outcome may be selected in some trials, provided the design and sample size allow it and if measuring them in the study does not substantially add to the cost or complicate the design or conduct of the trial. For example, Phase I or II clinical trials usually have several primary outcomes (such as the safety of a new drug or vaccine, evaluated through a series of clinical outcomes, as well as the immunogenicity of the vaccine or pharmacodynamics of the drug). Phase III or IV trials have fewer primary outcomes, and often only one. Primary outcomes need careful definition prior to the start of the trial (indicator, instrument to be used, measurement to be taken, values which will be considered as a positive or negative result, which laboratory will be used, etc.); these should be agreed upon among investigators, sponsors, and any regulatory agencies overseeing the trial.

2.1.2 Secondary and tertiary outcomes

Trials often have additional important outcomes, but these are not usually used to determine the trial design and sample size. They are included as secondary or tertiary outcomes to be measured in the trial. These outcomes may not be statistically conclusive, since the trial may not have been designed with the power to evaluate them, but they can be very useful to generate further hypotheses and guide future trials. Because of their importance in justifying future studies, these additional outcomes also need careful definition and measurement and should be fully specified in the protocol, since extra resources often are needed to measure and evaluate them.

2.1.3 Other variables which are not study outcomes

Often, trials have other variables measured in the study not directly related to the study outcomes. Variables, such as age, gender, educational or socio-economic level, and nutritional status, may be used to evaluate potential effect modifiers or confounders to the study outcomes. These variables also need to be defined and considered at the beginning of the study, so they may be included in any pilot investigations.

2.2 Clinical case definitions

2.2.1 Physician-based case definitions

In some trials, outcomes are based on a clinical diagnosis by a physician, without any type of laboratory confirmation. For example, pneumonia may be diagnosed by auscultation in a trial evaluating the impact of an intervention designed to reduce indoor air pollution. This type of outcome is subjective, and interpretation may vary among doctors, and even among experienced specialists. Nevertheless, in many clinical trials, physician-based clinical diagnosis determines the main outcome of the study, since no alternatives exist. For many diseases, standardized criteria for defining a 'case' have been established by experts. The International Classification of Diseases (World Health Organization, 2010; see also <http://www.who.int/classifications/icd/en>), which is revised about every 10 years, provides a basis for coding all diseases in a systematic way and is widely used for clinical and epidemiological research.

If standardized criteria for a 'case definition' have not been developed for the disease under study, a suitable definition should be established before the trial starts. For infectious diseases, there is often the need to distinguish between infection and disease, since clinical manifestations of infections may vary widely, from subclinical to overwhelming disease. For many trials, the main outcome of public health interest may be those infections that are severe or fatal. Careful definitions of these types of clinical categories are important, and, if available, the criteria used in other studies should be used to facilitate comparability across studies. The physicians charged with making diagnoses in the trial should discuss and agree the criteria they will be using to make a diagnosis and should compare their diagnoses on a range of patients prior to the start of the trial and at periodic intervals throughout the trial (see Section 2.2.5). Cases may also be classified as suspected, probable, or definite, using clinical and/or laboratory criteria.

In some populations, the conduct of a clinical examination may be problematic. Physical examinations are virtually always highly personal and may raise sensitive issues concerning individual dignity. In those populations when privacy is required, a third person in the examination room is often important, both to reassure the patient and to provide protection against possible charges of misconduct. In the case of children, the mother's presence should normally be requested; for the examination of women, a nurse and an appropriate family member may be needed, even when the examiner is a woman. If there are local codes of behaviour that cover such circumstances, these must be adhered to.

2.2.2 Laboratory-based case definitions, including any diagnostic procedure

Commonly, a clinically defined study outcome involves the combination of a clinical assessment with the support of a confirmatory laboratory, or other diagnostic, procedure. For example, the clinical diagnosis of malaria may be supported by a positive identification of the parasite in the blood, or the diagnosis of dengue fever in a subject with 48 hours of elevated temperature with a positive immunoglobulin M or viral antigen present in the blood, as detected by polymerase chain reaction, or the clinical diagnosis of pneumonia with a confirmatory chest X-ray. All these diagnostic procedures need careful definition, including the technique, machine, or equipment to be used, reference values considered normal for the study population, and the level at which they will be considered abnormal. It is important to describe, in the protocol, how the test or procedure will be conducted and whether a reference laboratory will be used to validate the site laboratory or procedure—also, how procedures used by laboratory personnel to interpret results will be standardized and how monitoring for QC will be done. Some diagnostic results are also affected by subjectivity such as reading the results of a chest X-ray. In such cases, protocols have been developed to try to standardize the diagnosis, such as establishing defined criteria for each type of pathology in advance, having two independent, blinded radiologists read all X-ray films, with a third radiologist reading all films where there were disagreements, with their result used as the tiebreaker. Similar procedures have been developed to read blood smears for malaria. All these options have important consequences on the trial logistics and cost, so careful consideration needs to be given to them when designing the trial and selecting its study outcomes. Issues concerning laboratory tests of relevance to diagnosis in field trials are outlined in Chapter 17.

2.2.3 Lay worker-based case definitions

Some trials use lay workers (fieldworkers) to measure a study outcome. Examples of such trials are diarrhoeal diseases where prevalent diarrhoea might be defined as three or more liquid or semi-liquid stools passed in a 24-hour period, as reported by the mother or the child's caretaker to a fieldworker, or hygiene behaviours observed by fieldworkers in spot household checks during a hand-washing intervention trial. These types of outcomes are usually captured in questionnaires or study forms. Interviewing techniques and questionnaire design are discussed in Chapter 14.

Fieldworkers may also measure a clinical indicator such as the body temperature or respiratory rate. Because of the high cost of using physicians, in many trials, lay workers or paramedical workers are trained to assess clinical signs and symptoms. When using lay workers or professional fieldworkers, such as nutritionists, auxiliary nurses, or nurse technicians, it is essential to train them and standardize the methods they use, in order to assure uniform implementation of these procedures in the field throughout the study, with good supervision and QC procedures.

2.2.4 Case definitions using secondary data sources

In some trials, such as in phase IV trials, existing surveillance systems may be used to define a study outcome. These secondary data sources, in which trial outcomes are not measured directly by study staff, will have the limitations intrinsic to the quality of the existing surveillance system. Examples of such study outcomes are post-marketing passive surveillance of vaccine or drug-related SAEs, such as hospitalizations of any type, after the introduction of the intervention into general use. They could also be used to evaluate the efficacy of a new vaccine or intervention on an important outcome which, for reasons of cost or ethics, could not be measured in a phase III trial such as the impact of a new vaccine on mortality.

2.2.5 Standardization

All study outcomes to be used in a clinical trial need to be properly standardized. When an outcome requires physicians, other professionals, or lay workers to measure it, standardization usually requires predefined exercises, with the use of an expert to act as the 'standard' against which the group is compared, defining differences which will be considered acceptable as part of the precision of the study. These standardization exercises could be done with real patients or mock subjects who may be trained actors. The use of videos showing different types of patients, which all participants evaluate independently, is a very useful exercise to help standardize them against the 'standard' observer. Standardization of this sort is not easy; it requires resources, time, and, in many cases, patients or volunteers willing to be examined by multiple persons. Ideally, the same set of samples, films, blood smears, subjects, or videos would be evaluated again by the same individual in a random order, under code, to allow the calculation of intra-observer reproducibility. All these procedures need to be carefully described in operating manuals and recorded, so they can be reviewed by investigators, collaborators, or regulatory agencies. In studies that last for several years, it is important to re-standardize observers every 6 to 12 months or if any observer needs to be replaced, to assure that the quality of the study is maintained.

2.2.6 Inclusion and exclusion criteria

An important component of an outcome definition is the description of the inclusion and exclusion criteria for the subjects to be evaluated in the trial. Ideally, the trial results should be able to be generalized to the whole population in which the intervention will be used. Under ideal circumstances, nobody should be excluded from the trial. However, for ethical, logistic, or analytical reasons, most trials establish stringent inclusion and exclusion criteria to exclude certain persons from participation. These criteria could be established on the basis of factors such as age, gender, literacy, being healthy or not, not affected by chronic diseases different from the study outcome, or not affected by other conditions such as abnormal baseline laboratory results. All these criteria need careful evaluation and discussion not only within the research team and the sponsor of the trial, but also with the ethics committees, the regulatory agencies overseeing the trial, and the communities in which the trial will take place, to assure that the trial results can be generalized to the intended population. It is common practice to exclude persons who are very sick from a trial (unless, of course, the trial intervention is directed at such persons). This is done because early deaths, or other SAEs in such persons, may occur independently of the trial intervention but may complicate interpretation of the effects of the intervention.

Signing a written informed consent form is now a standard inclusion criterion in most clinical trials (see Chapter 6). However, such a requirement will select a subgroup of the population who accept to sign such a form and participate in the study, generating a potential selection bias. To measure how strong that bias may be, it is important to register all eligible subjects who were considered as potential participants in the trial, indicating the reasons for refusal for those who did not enter into the trial.

2.3 Death and verbal autopsies

Preventing deaths (or severe disabilities) is one of the most important public health outcomes of any type of treatment or preventive intervention. It is the most important outcome in driving disease control policies and the introduction of new interventions or treatments into the population, once they have been found to be safe and effective. These types of outcomes have the heaviest weight in terms of disability-adjusted life-years (DALYs), when undertaking cost-effectiveness analyses of new drugs or interventions (see Chapter 19). Therefore, trials designed to evaluate these outcomes are very important. But, for many reasons, they may be difficult and costly to conduct, and, in many cases, they may not be feasible or ethical to do. Counting deaths in the conduct of a trial is a very sensitive issue, particularly in developing countries with poor health systems. It may create moral issues or generate political tension that may stop the trial. Therefore, few trials are done with these important outcomes, despite their major importance. However, those trials that are done with this endpoint and which demonstrate that an intervention significantly reduces mortality are most likely to influence a policy decision on a more widespread introduction of the intervention.

When deaths or severe disability are chosen as study outcomes, several problems emerge, depending on the setting where the study is conducted. In many LMICs, the quality of vital registration systems is poor or they are non-existent, precluding their use. Therefore, methods are needed to identify deaths, as well as to establish causes of death. In LMICs, the most commonly used method to ascertain causes of death are 'verbal autopsies'. A verbal autopsy is a structured interview, conducted with the relatives of the deceased person, with the intention to reconstruct the series of events that led to the death (or severe complication or disability). Standard verbal autopsy questionnaires have been developed (World Health Organization, 2012). Such 'autopsies' should be conducted neither too soon after the death (to avoid asking questions when relatives are still very upset by the death) nor too long after the death (to avoid recall bias). This interview is then analysed in a standardized way, either by physicians or using a computer algorithm, to classify the likely cause of the death, following a predefined set of criteria (Lopez et al., 2011).

The reliability of verbal autopsy methods varies according to the cause of death, as some causes of death may be confused because signs and symptoms in the illness leading up to death may be similar. The usefulness of verbal autopsies is also dependent on the culture of the population under surveillance. It is essential to pilot-test the (translated) questionnaire to assure that appropriate local words are used to ascertain signs or symptoms of the causes of death.

In many populations, there could be a wide range of reasons why deaths may not be reported, and therefore special care should be taken to ensure that ascertainment is as complete as possible. This becomes crucial when the study outcome is death in the perinatal period, since an important proportion of live births that die in the minutes or hours after birth could be either missed or wrongly reported as stillbirths. In some trials, members of the study community may be hired as local informants to report any deaths. Other techniques include enumerating all members in a community and checking for the absence of any of them in frequently conducted cross-sectional surveys. Special attention should be paid to households for which all members are absent during one of these follow-up surveys, because the death of an adult may lead to dissolution of a household or migration of household members. Enquiries should be made with neighbours in such circumstances. Training and standardization of interviewers are essential. The frequency of surveillance will be a critical decision in designing trials with mortality outcomes, since a long recall period (such as 1 year) may miss deaths, particularly of children or infants; but each additional surveillance round will be expensive.

2.4 Non-clinical case definitions

Non-clinical case definitions can also be used in trials such as quality of life in trials of the use of chemotherapy for advanced cancer, antibiotic use in children in settings where they are available without prescription, satisfaction of users of a health service, and economic outcomes (costs) which are discussed in Chapter 19. They also may include outcomes that come directly from patients about how they feel or function in relation to a health condition and its therapy (so called *patient-reported outcomes*), without interpretation by health care professionals or anyone else. For these case definitions, instruments that have been developed previously or that are created especially for the trial need to be validated, in order to have valid and comparable results.

2.5 Proxy measurements as study outcomes

Some trials may select outcome measures that are associated with the outcome of interest such as reported risky sexual behaviour, which are either easier to measure, cheaper, or more socially acceptable. Those outcomes are called 'proxy' measurements of the outcome of interest. Such measures, however, may be subject to invalidity and bias (for example, misreporting, differential degrees of desirability bias between trial arms).

2.5.1 Behavioural changes

A behaviour thought to be critical to reduce the disease of interest might be selected as a study outcome. For example, in a study to investigate the effectiveness of a health education campaign to promote the use of latrines, where the ultimate objective was to reduce diarrhoeal disease, the frequency of use of latrines might be measured. Sometimes, health-related behaviours may be measured by direct observation.

Changes in knowledge or attitudes are sometimes an important initial step before a behaviour is changed, which, once changed, should reduce the risk of the disease of interest. Knowledge or attitudes can be assessed with reasonable reliability, using questionnaires or other interview methods, but observational studies may be required to determine if behavioural changes have actually occurred. For example, in a study to investigate the effectiveness of a health education campaign to promote the use of latrines, it may be relatively straightforward to assess, after the campaign, whether individuals have a better knowledge of why using latrines is desirable, but observational studies, before and after the campaign, may be necessary to ascertain whether or not the frequency of use of latrines had actually changed, let alone whether behavioural change led to a reduction in the incidence of diarrhoea. Similar issues arise with respect to the evaluation of a hand-washing intervention campaign. Further studies may then be needed to determine whether the changed behaviour has led to a reduction of diarrhoeal diseases.

Some trials have the incidence of a self-reported behaviour as one of their outcomes. For example, in evaluating the effectiveness of sexual behaviour change interventions, it is not possible to observe sexual behaviours directly, so self-reported behaviours are frequently recorded. But such measures are very open to desirability bias where the respondent reports the behaviour that they think the investigator would judge to be the desirable one. Furthermore, the desirability bias may be differential between the trial arms. For example, if the intervention group has been encouraged to reduce their number of sexual partners and always use a condom, while the control group has not, the intervention group may be more likely to over-report these 'desired' behaviours at follow-up. Self-reported behaviours, though sometimes the only practical outcome for a trial, are potentially misleading and should be avoided, at least as the primary outcome measure in a trial, if at all possible.

2.5.2 Transmission reduction

The purpose of interventions, based on vector control or environmental alteration, may be to reduce or interrupt transmission of the infectious agent of interest. Generally, the first priority is to determine whether the intervention has accomplished the immediate changes intended. For example, in trials in which insecticides are applied to reduce vector populations in order to reduce the transmission of some infectious agent, the first step would be to determine the impact of the intervention on the vector population. If the vector population is little affected, it may be reasonable to conclude that any impact on human disease is unlikely. However, if there is a reduction in vector population, it may be erroneous to conclude that the human disease load will also fall. A further study to determine the impact on disease may be required. Similarly, if interventions are being evaluated that may reduce indoor air pollution as a measure against respiratory disease, it may be best to focus initial studies on the assessment of changes in pollution levels, before assessing the impact on respiratory diseases. Usually, it will be more efficient to carry out trials to monitor the impact on disease only after there is evidence of an effect on the vector or on the agent against which the intervention is directed.

In order to assess a change in transmission, any, or all, of several different outcomes may be used:

- incidence of infection or disease
- prevalence of infection or disease
- severity of disease
- intensity of infection (for example, for helminths)
- intensity of infective agent in the vector.

Any changes to these different outcomes will happen at different intervals after the intervention is in place, and may require studies over time to measure the overall study impact. For instance, in an onchocerciasis control programme, the first evidence that an intensive larviciding of *Simulium damnosum* (black fly) breeding sites is having an effect may be a dramatic drop in fly-biting rates in the intervention area. Over the next several years, there may be a steady fall in the intensity of microfilarial infections among those living in the endemic area, but only after some years might it be possible to detect evidence of a fall in the prevalence of infection, and later still an impact on blindness rates which is the major adverse health consequence of onchocercal infection.

2.6 Adverse events

An important outcome of all trials is to assess the safety of the intervention under evaluation (for example, of a new drug or vaccine). Adverse events (AEs) are defined as any untoward clinical or laboratorial medical occurrence in a patient or clinical investigation subject, related or not to the use of an intervention in a trial. Serious AEs (SAEs) are defined as any events that are life-threatening or result in death. They include patient hospitalization or prolongation of existing hospitalization, events that result in persistent or significant debilitation or incapacity, and congenital anomalies and birth defects. All SAEs should be reported immediately to the sponsor (or the DSMB on behalf of the sponsor), followed by detailed written reports (see Chapter 7). Usually, two types of study outcomes are defined: (1) the active, prospective evaluation of a set of predefined potential AEs known or suspected to be associated with the type of drug, vaccine, or product under evaluation, and (2) recording all clinical or laboratory abnormalities, expected or not, that occur in study subjects during a specified time period or throughout the conduct of the trial, by active or passive surveillance, which may reveal an adverse consequence previously not known to occur with the drug, vaccine, or product under evaluation. For both types of safety outcomes, criteria must be developed to assess the severity, as well as the incidence of AEs associated with the drug, vaccine, or product under evaluation. Severity can be measured by the magnitude of a laboratory or clinical test abnormality, or by the subjective perception on how much the AE altered the function or quality of life of the individual. For instance, a reaction at the site of injection of a vaccine could be graded as mild if only a colour change is noted with mild pain, without induration and without any restriction on the arm or leg movement; moderate if, in addition to colour change of the skin, induration is noted and there is some restriction of movement; and severe if the subject cries out or winces if the area is touched and the arm or leg cannot be moved without pain. In many studies, a diary card may be provided to the study subject or, in case of children, to the mother or caretaker to record these reactions during a 7- or 14-day period after the administration of a vaccine or during the drug therapy. To aid measuring an injection site reaction, a ruler may be provided to the subject. And to standardize the measurement of temperature, a digital thermometer may be provided as well. Study subjects or children's mothers or caretakers need to be appropriately trained in using these study cards and instruments. In addition to its severity, these reactions are usually classified as unrelated, unlikely to be related, or possibly related to the intervention under evaluation. The criteria used for this classification may include proximity of the event to the administration of the intervention (for instance, a rash developing within 20 minutes of an injection would most likely be classified as possibly related), the unusualness of the clinical event (a disease which normally occurs in that age group or a complication expected to happen in the disease under study), or even the subjective interpretation of the investigator. Whatever criteria are used should be stated. The incidences of AEs, graded by the severity and likelihood of being related to the interventional product, are later compared between the study group exposed to the intervention and the control group (using placebo or an active comparator) to assess statistically if AEs of different kinds were or were not associated with the drug, vaccine, or product.

All safety measurements need careful definition in the study protocol, study forms to record them, using standardized measurements and codes to register them, and active monitoring of their occurrence. Most trials require those AEs that are considered serious to be individually reported to the sponsor and to an ethics review board, to the regulatory agency overseeing the trial, and to an independent DSMB for their careful evaluation during the conduct of the trial, to allow the possibility for the trial to be stopped or modified before its completion if it is suspected that SAEs are associated with the drug, vaccine, or product under investigation.

3 Factors influencing choice of outcome measures

The choice of the outcome measures in a specific trial largely depends on the purpose of the trial and how relevant, feasible, and acceptable the measures will be in a particular study population. Furthermore, the choice may be constrained by economic, logistic, or ethical considerations.

3.1 Relevance

Interventions are generally designed to reduce disease and/or to promote health. The outcome measures chosen should reflect these objectives as fully as possible, but, when intermediate variables are used, rather than those of main interest, care must be taken to choose variables of direct relevance to the main outcome. This is not always straightforward. For example, it may be decided to assess the impact of a vaccine by measuring the proportion of individuals who develop antibodies to the vaccine. This may be reasonable if it is known that there is a high correlation between the development of antibodies and protection from clinical disease. For many diseases, however, this relationship has not been established, and it would not be warranted to base conclusions regarding protection against disease simply on antibody determinations.

A health education intervention may be designed to change behaviour to reduce disease risk, but, as discussed in Section 2.5.1, asking individuals if they have changed their behaviour may give a measure of impact that correlates poorly with true changes in the risk of disease. Are individuals responding truthfully? Are they doing what they say they do? Even if behaviour changes, is this associated with a lowering in the incidence of disease?

The outcome variable measured should be as close as possible to the outcome of main interest. While this may seem an obvious suggestion, it may have major impact on the design of a study. For example, if the prevention of death is of prime interest, then, whenever possible, this should be made the endpoint of the trial. To do so might require an increase in the size of the trial from hundreds to thousands, or even tens of thousands, of individuals. Such a large trial might be difficult to find funding for, and there may never be an adequate test of whether the intermediate variables measured are acceptable surrogates for effects on mortality.

3.2 Feasibility

To be successful, a trial must be designed to have achievable objectives. A trial which has mortality as the endpoint, but which is too large to be successfully completed, may be of less value than a well-designed smaller trial aimed at assessing the impact on some intermediate endpoint such as severe disease. There must often be a compromise between relevance and feasibility. It is pointless to set unachievable goals, even if they look attractive in the objectives section of a proposal. Also, it may be of little value to measure the effect of an intervention on an outcome measure which is only distantly related to the measure of prime interest. The outcome measures selected will be much influenced by the resources available for the trial, the availability of skilled personnel, and the necessary laboratory support to diagnose cases of disease. In many large trials, every individual in the study population may have to be screened for disease or infection in a relatively short time. With such time constraints, some individuals may be misdiagnosed. The consequences of reductions in diagnostic sensitivity and specificity are discussed in Section 4.2.

3.3 Acceptability

The acceptability of the measurement of an outcome variable to the study population is critical to the successful conduct of a trial. For example, the recording of birthweights may not be possible in a population that allows only close relatives to have access to a mother for a few days or weeks after the child's birth. Taking venous blood samples or repeated blood samples is unpopular in many societies. If the method for measuring the outcome involves pain or inconvenience to the participants, it may be necessary to modify or abandon it. An outcome, of which the assessment involves a long interview with participants at a time when they would otherwise be planting crops or taking care of their household chores, may be unacceptable; it may either have to be abbreviated or carried out at a more convenient time.

3.4 Opportunity for add-on studies

Some trials offer the opportunity to measure outcomes that are not directly related to the objectives of the original study itself. These opportunities can be exploited by researchers to answer questions with minimal additional funding. For example, a diarrhoeal surveillance study might be carried out within a clinical trial in which a cohort of healthy children is being followed over time. However, it is very important that the add-on study does not interfere with the original study outcome measure. Such additions should be considered at the beginning of the study and should have a separate study protocol. It is also important to inform sponsors, participants, and all stakeholders of the original trial of the coexistence of the proposed add-on study. Such investigations will usually require separate ethical approval and informed consent.

4 Variability and quality control of outcome measures

4.1 Reproducibility

The extent to which different observers will make the same diagnoses or assessments on a participant and to which observers are consistent in their classifications between participants may have an important influence on the results of a trial. Clearly, it is desirable to choose outcome measures for which there is substantial reproducibility and agreement among observers, with respect to the classification of participants in the trial.

For objective outcome measures, variations between observers, or by the same observer at different times, may be small and unlikely to influence the results of a study. For outcome measures requiring some degree of subjective assessment, however, such variations may be substantial. The likely degree of such variations will influence the choice of outcome measures, as it will be preferable to select those measures that have the smallest inter- and intra-observer variations, yet still give valid measures of the impact of the intervention.

Variation among observers is often much greater than expected, for example, in the reading of a chest X-ray to assess whether there is evidence of pneumonia. If a study involves several observers, pilot studies should be conducted, in order to measure the extent of the variation and then to seek to standardize the assessment methods to minimize the variation. With suitable training, it is usually possible to reduce the variation between observers substantially.

For some outcomes, independent assessment by two observers should be routine, with a third being called in to resolve disagreements. It may be costly to screen the whole trial population in this way, but a common approach is to have all suspected cases of the disease of interest examined by a second observer, mixed in with a sample of those not thought to have the disease. Sometimes, it is possible to have the observer examine the same individual twice, but these examinations may not be independent, unless the survey is large and the observer does not remember the result of the first assessment.

It is important to make every effort to reduce variability to the maximum extent possible. Having done so, however, it is also critical to know the extent of the remaining 'irreducible' variability for purposes of analysis. The purpose of trials is usually to demonstrate the effect of an intervention or to compare differences between interventions. Knowledge of the inherent variability in diagnostic procedures is essential for this demonstration, and the best way of assessing this is through replicate measures. It is especially important to take account of between-observer differences when communities are the units of randomization in a field trial. Differences between observers may produce biases if different observers are used in different communities. In such situations, it is better to organize the fieldwork so that the workload within each community is split among different observers and differences between the observers are not confounded with the effect of the intervention.

4.2 Sensitivity and specificity

The choice of an appropriate definition of a 'case' in a field trial will be influenced by the sensitivity and specificity associated with the diagnostic criteria. *Sensitivity* is defined as the proportion of true cases that are classified as cases in the study. *Specificity* is the proportion of non-cases that are classified as non-cases in the study. A low sensitivity is associated with a reduction in the measured incidence of the disease. This decreases the likelihood of observing a significant difference between two groups in a trial of a given size. In statistical terms, it reduces the *power* of the study (see Chapter 5, Section 2.2). If the incidence of the disease in both the intervention group and the comparison group will be affected proportionately in the same way, as is often the case, it does not bias the estimate of the relative disease incidence in the two groups, though the absolute magnitude of the difference will be less than the true difference. Thus, in the context of a vaccine trial, because protective efficacy is assessed, in terms of relative differences in incidence between groups, the estimate of protective efficacy will not be biased, but the confidence limits on the estimate will be wider than they would be using a more sensitive case definition. In theory, the reduction in power associated with low sensitivity can be compensated for by increasing the trial size.

In general, a low specificity of diagnosis is a more serious problem than a low sensitivity in intervention trials. A low specificity results in the disease incidence rates being estimated to be higher than they really are, as some participants without the disease under study are classified incorrectly as cases. Generally, the levels of inflation in the rates will be similar, in absolute terms, in the intervention and comparison groups, and thus the ratio of the measured rates in the two groups will be less than the true ratio, though the difference in the rates should be unbiased. Thus, in vaccine trials, for example, the vaccine efficacy estimate will be biased towards zero, though the absolute difference in the rates between the intervention and control groups will not be biased (unless there is also poor sensitivity). Increasing the trial size will not compensate for the bias in the estimate of vaccine efficacy.

In algebraic terms, suppose the true disease rates are r_1 and r_2 in the two groups under study, the true relative rate R is r_1/r_2, and the true difference in disease rates D is $r_1 - r_2$. If sensitivity is less than 100% (but specificity is 100%), and only a proportion k of all cases are correctly diagnosed, the measured disease rates in the two groups will be kr_1 and kr_2; the measured relative rate will be $kr_1/(kr_2) = R$; and the measured difference in disease rates will be $kr_1 - kr_2 = k(r_1 - r_2) = kD$ (which will be less than D). If specificity is less than 100% (but sensitivity is 100%), and the rate of false diagnoses is s, the measured rates in the two groups will be $(r_1 + s)$ and $(r_2 + s)$; the measured relative rate will be $(r_1 + s)/(r_2 + s)$ (which will be less than R); and the measured difference in disease rates will be $(r_1 + s) - (r_2 + s) = D$.

To measure the sensitivity and specificity of the diagnostic procedures used in a trial, it is necessary to have a 'gold standard' for diagnosis (i.e. it is necessary to have a diagnostic procedure that determines who really is a case and who is not). Sometimes, this is not possible, and, even if definitive diagnostic procedures exist, it may be necessary to use imperfect procedures in a field trial for reasons of cost or logistics. In this situation, if an assessment is made of sensitivity and specificity, it is possible to evaluate the consequences for the results of a field trial, and possible even to correct for biases in efficacy estimates due to the use of a non-specific diagnostic test. Unfortunately, in many situations, there is no 'gold standard', and so the sensitivity and specificity of the diagnostic methods used remain uncertain. For example, there is no universally agreed definition of a case of clinical malaria. Most would agree that the presence of parasites in the blood is necessary (unless a potential case has taken treatment before presenting to the study clinic), and many would agree that the presence of fever associated with parasitaemia increases the likelihood of the disease being clinical malaria, but it is also possible that the fever is due to other causes, rather than the parasitaemia being the cause of the fever.

The bias induced by a low specificity of diagnosis is most severe for diseases that have a low incidence. A good example of this is provided by leprosy, which is both difficult to diagnose (in the early stages) and also of low incidence. Consider a vaccine trial in which the true disease incidence in the unvaccinated group is ten per thousand over the period of the trial, and the true efficacy of a new vaccine against leprosy is 50%, i.e. the true disease incidence in the vaccinated is five per thousand over the period of the trial. If the sensitivity of the diagnostic test used for cases is 90%, but the specificity is 100%, the observed disease incidences would be $10 \times 0.9 = 9.0$ and $5 \times 0.9 = 4.5$ per thousand, respectively. Thus, the estimate of vaccine efficacy is correct (50%). The power of the study is reduced, however. To achieve the power that would be associated with a 'perfect' test, the trial size would have to be increased by about 11%.

On the other hand, if the specificity of the diagnostic test is as high as 99% and the sensitivity is 100%, the observed disease incidences would be ten true cases + $(990 \times 0.01 = 9.9)$ false cases = 19.9 per thousand in the unvaccinated group, and five true cases + $(995 \times 0.01 = 9.95)$ = 14.95 per thousand in the vaccinated group. Thus, even with a test with 99% specificity, the estimate of vaccine efficacy is reduced from the true value of 50% to 25%. If the specificity of the test were 90%, the expected estimate of vaccine efficacy would be only 4%.

In vaccine trials, the sensitivity and specificity of the diagnostic test are of consequence in different ways at different times in the trial. When individuals are screened for entry to the trial, it is important that the test used should be highly sensitive, even if it is not very specific, as substantial bias may be introduced if undiagnosed 'cases' are included in the trial and included in the vaccinated or unvaccinated groups. If the vaccine has no effect on the progression of their disease and they are detected as cases later in the trial, a false low estimate of efficacy will result. Thus, individuals whose diagnosis is 'doubtful' at entry to the trial should be excluded from the trial. Conversely, once individuals have been screened for entry into the trial and they are being followed for the development of disease, a highly specific test is required to avoid the bias illustrated in the preceding paragraph.

In situations where there may be no clear-cut definitions of a case (for example, early leprosy or childhood TB), studies of intra- and inter-observer variation may be undertaken, using various definitions of the disease. The definition that shows the least disagreement between observers and gives maximum consistency within each observer may be the appropriate one to use in a trial, but the investigator should be aware of the potential for bias if the specificity of the diagnostic procedure is less than 100%.

4.3 Bias

The most powerful way to minimize bias in the assessment of the impact of an intervention is through the conduct of a double-blind randomized trial. If these two aspects are built into a trial, an effect of an intervention is not likely to be observed if there is no true effect. However, as pointed out in Section 4.2, if the specificity of the diagnosis for the outcome of interest is poor, the estimate of the efficacy of an intervention, measured in relative terms, may be biased towards zero, even in a properly randomized double-blind investigation.

It is highly desirable that the person making diagnoses in a trial is ignorant of which intervention the suspected cases have received. If the diagnosis is based on laboratory tests or X-ray examinations, blindness should be easy to preserve. In some circumstances, it may be possible to determine from the results of a laboratory test which intervention an individual has received, as the test may be measuring some intermediate effect between the intervention and the outcome of prime interest (for example, an antibody response to a vaccine). In such cases, those making diagnoses in the field should not be given access to the laboratory results. For example, in placebo-controlled studies of praziquantel against schistosomiasis in communities where the infection is common, those who had received the active drug would be easily detected by a rapid reduction in egg counts in stool or urine samples following treatment. If the outcome of main interest is morbidity from the disease, then the egg count information should be kept from those making the assessment of morbidity. It would generally be inappropriate to use measures of antibody level to make diagnoses of disease following vaccination, if the vaccination itself induced antibodies indistinguishable from those being measured. Similarly, tuberculin testing should not be part of diagnostic procedures for TB in studies of the efficacy of BCG vaccination, as the vaccine alters the response to the test.

If the diagnosis of disease is based on a clinical examination, it may be necessary to take special precautions to preserve blindness. An example is given in Chapter 11, Section 4, with respect to a BCG trial against leprosy, in which all participants had the upper arm area, where BCG or placebo was injected, covered during the clinical examination, since BCG leads to a permanent scar. Even if the participants know which intervention they had, it is important to try to keep this knowledge from the person making any diagnoses. Thus, participants might be instructed not to discuss the intervention with the examiner, and the examiner would be similarly restricted. Such a procedure is obviously not fail-safe, but great efforts should be made to preserve blindness, if at all possible, especially if the diagnosis is made on subjective criteria.

If randomization in a trial is by community, rather than by individuals, it may be especially difficult to keep examiners ignorant of the intervention an individual received. Sometimes, ways can be found of doing this, for example, by conducting surveys for disease by bringing all participants to a clinic outside the trial communities. If communities are randomized to receive an improved water supply or not, one outcome measure of interest might be the incidence of scabies infection. It may be difficult to avoid the possibility of the diagnoses of scabies being influenced by the observer's knowledge of whether or not the participant was in a village with an improved water supply. In such a case, it may be best to seek other measures of impact, based upon objective criteria or laboratory measures, or to take photographs of the relevant body parts and have these assessed objectively and 'blind' to intervention group.

4.4 The Hawthorne effect

Trials that require active home visits by study personnel during the surveillance period to evaluate the effect of an intervention may be affected by an indirect effect of the home visits on the study objective, even when not intended. The presence of a study member in a subject's home may have a positive effect on the health status of the subject, since it may, for example, stimulate better health behaviour of the subject or improve hygiene practices in the house or better health care utilization. In studies with such effects, rates of illnesses or of severe illness may be reduced in both study arms—an indirect effect known as the 'Hawthorne effect' (named after a study in the 1930s in the USA at the Hawthorne Works, in which it was documented that worker behaviour changed as a consequence of them being observed). This effect reduces the power of the study and may make it inconclusive. There is no easy way to control for it, so, if such a Hawthorne effect is expected in a field trial, the sample size may need to be increased to maintain statistical power.

4.5 Quality control issues

The sensitivity and specificity of the diagnostic procedures employed in a trial should be monitored for the duration of the trial, as they may change as the study progresses. Such changes may be for the worse or for the better. With experience, diagnostic skills may improve, but also, as time passes, the staff may become bored and take less care. It is important that the field staff are aware that their performance is being continuously monitored. If this is done, then anyone who goes 'off the rails' can be steered back or removed from the study, before much harm is done. Such monitoring is important for both field and laboratory staff.

The methods used to monitor the quality of diagnostic procedures may include the re-examination of a sample of cases by a supervisor or a more highly trained investigator and, for the laboratory, may be done by sending a sample of specimens to a reference laboratory and by passing some specimens through the laboratory in duplicate, in a blinded fashion, to determine if the differences between results on the same specimen are within acceptable limits (see Chapter 17, Section 5).

If the disease under study is relatively rare, it may be difficult to measure sensitivity based on small numbers of individuals being examined twice. While it will be possible to check if specificity is poor (a high proportion of those classified as cases are wrongly diagnosed), checks on sensitivity may involve the examination of thousands of individuals twice to determine if cases are being missed. Fortunately, in most trials, specificity is of more critical importance than sensitivity, although the relative importance can change as the survey goes on, as discussed in Section 4.2.

References

Cutts, F. T., Zaman, S. M., Enwere, G., *et al.* 2005. Efficacy of nine-valent pneumococcal conjugate vaccine against pneumonia and invasive pneumococcal disease in The Gambia: randomised, double-blind, placebo-controlled trial. *Lancet*, **365**, 1139–46.

Lopez, A. D., Lozano, R., Murray, C. J. L., Shibuya, K. 2011. Verbal autopsy: innovations, applications, opportunities improving cause of death measurement. *Population Health Metrics*, **9**, 128–254.

Ross, D. A., Changalucha, J., Obasi, A. I., *et al.* 2007. Biological and behavioural impact of an adolescent sexual health intervention in Tanzania: a community-randomized trial. *AIDS*, **21**, 1943–55.

Schellenberg, D., Menendez, C., Kahigwa, E., *et al.* 2001. Intermittent treatment for malaria and anaemia control at time of routine vaccinations in Tanzanian infants: a randomised, placebo-controlled trial. *Lancet*, **357**, 1471–7.

World Health Organization. 2010. *International statistical classification of diseases and related health problems*, 10th revision, Volume 2, instruction manual [Online]. Geneva: World Health Organization. Available at: <http://www.who.int/classifications/icd/ICD10Volume2_en_2010.pdf>.

World Health Organization. 2012. *Verbal autopsy standards: the 2012 WHO verbal autopsy instrument* [Online]. Geneva: World Health Organization. Available at: <http://www.who.int/healthinfo/statistics/WHO_VA_2012_RC1_Instrument.pdf>.

Chapter 13

Preliminary studies and pilot testing

1 Introduction to preliminary studies and pilot testing 216
2 Preliminary studies 216
   2.1 Purposes 216
   2.2 Design of preliminary studies 218
3 Pilot testing 220
   3.1 Purpose 220
   3.2 Design of the pilot test 220

1 Introduction to preliminary studies and pilot testing

The time between the idea for an intervention trial and first entering participants into the trial is usually long, generally at least a year and often several years. Even when funding for a trial has been obtained, which, in itself, may take a year or more, there is often much work to do before the first participant can be enrolled into the trial. This chapter outlines the kinds of investigations and studies that may be carried out before starting the main trial to try to maximize the possibility that the trial will be conducted successfully. We divide these into two kinds of study. First are *preliminary studies* to develop different aspects of the trial procedures or to collect data to facilitate the planning and conduct of the trial. Second are *pilot studies* which are tests of the full trial procedures on a small sample of potential participants to make sure, in so far as is possible, that any problems with the conduct of the trial will be identified, so that procedures can be changed before the full trial starts.

Though often very useful, no specific type of preliminary study is invariably essential, whereas a pilot study should always be planned, though such studies can range from a relatively brief testing of the intervention and its evaluation that lasts a week or less through to an extensive period of testing and refinement of the intervention and evaluation methods that spans several months, or even a year or more.

2 Preliminary studies

2.1 Purposes

Preliminary studies are often conducted to refine the intervention and evaluate its acceptability, feasibility, cost, and uptake. For example, prior to a large field trial of a multi-component intervention that aimed to improve adolescent sexual and reproductive health in Tanzania, a preliminary study was carried out to test and refine the intervention. The main cluster randomized trial was planned to involve about 10 000 adolescents in over 120 schools, with an initial follow-up period of 3 years. A preliminary study was conducted to develop and refine the intervention methods that would be used to train and support teachers and class peer educators who would deliver the in-school sexual and reproductive health education intervention to be used in the trial (Obasi et al., 2006).

Preliminary studies may be needed to provide local up-to-date data, in order to calculate or confirm the sample size required for the main trial. For example, before embarking on a field trial of a malaria vaccine that will be evaluated for its effect in reducing the incidence of clinical cases of malaria, a preliminary study may be required to obtain estimates of the incidence of cases of malaria in the study population, probably spanning a complete year, in order to allow for seasonal variation in transmission. The outcome from such preliminary studies provides the data necessary for designing the size of the main trial. It is commonly found in trial design that investigators are over-optimistic about the likely frequency of outcome events in their trial population. Consequently, after a preliminary (baseline) study, the size of the main trial needs to be increased. Sometimes, the reverse happens, but not so commonly! In so far as is possible, the baseline study should be conducted under similar conditions to those that will hold in the main trial. Thus, for example, if insecticide-impregnated bed-nets are to be distributed to all children participating in a trial of a malaria vaccine, as may be required for ethical reasons, this should be done for the baseline studies to avoid overestimating the likely incidence of malaria in the trial population (Leach et al., 2011).

In some cases, preliminary investigations may even show that the proposed study population will not be suitable. A trial of a vaginal microbicide gel to prevent HIV transmission among women in Ghana was based upon an assumption of an annual transmission rate of HIV in the trial population of 5% a year. Baseline studies were not conducted to verify this assumption, and, once the trial had started, it was discovered that the actual transmission rate was only about 1% a year. Thus, an expensive trial had to be abandoned, because of a lack of statistical power (Peterson et al., 2007). Had it been known, before the trial started, that it should have been five times as large, it perhaps would never have been started.

Preliminary studies may also be needed to estimate how long it will take to enrol the target number of trial participants, the proportion of participants who are likely to be lost to follow-up, the best interval to have between follow-up visits, and the overall duration of the trial.

Other preliminary studies are helpful to refine the design of specific methods for use in the process and/or impact the evaluation within the main trial, and to evaluate their acceptability, feasibility, and cost. For example, will taking blood specimens, skin snips, or self-administered vaginal swabs be feasible and acceptable? Can the cold chain be maintained for vaccines or specimens that need to be kept cold, and for how long, since this will govern how frequently they need to be taken to or from the field research team? How many staff will be required, and how much will it cost, to carry out and collect data and specimens from 60 participants a day, for example?

It will also be necessary to explore the likely community acceptance of the trial (see Chapter 9), staff training needs, and other logistic requirements related to field and laboratory activities, data management, and study clinics. Some of these data may have already been collected in studies previously conducted by the trial team or by others, but, in other circumstances, special preliminary studies are required.

Many preliminary studies can be small and quick such as a qualitative study to ask potential trial participants to review a draft information sheet for clarity and acceptability. On the other hand, others may take over a year such as a study to check the incidence of a seasonal disease that must cover at least one 12-month period.

An example of a relatively large preliminary study conducted prior to a trial was the feasibility study for a multicentre trial of the impact of a vaginal microbicide on HIV incidence among women at high risk of acquiring sexually transmitted infections (STIs) that was conducted in four East and Southern African countries (McCormack et al., 2010). The main trial was planned to be conducted over several years at a likely cost of tens of millions of pounds, so it was crucial to ensure, prior to starting the main trial, that the sample size was right and that the methods planned for all aspects of the trial were both feasible and acceptable. Within the Tanzanian site for the trial, for example, a preliminary study was designed (Vallely et al., 2007). This lasted more than a year, to:

- identify the population groups to invite to participate in the trial
- work out how best to deliver the intervention and related clinical services
- evaluate the likely acceptability of the microbicide gel
- test and refine the study methods and instruments
- estimate the incidence of the primary (HIV) and secondary (STIs, reported use of the microbicide gel) outcomes for the main trial, and
- estimate the costs of each of the activities needed for the trial.

2.2 Design of preliminary studies

The design and methods used for preliminary studies should be tailored to address the specific issues and questions to be answered. Often, both qualitative and quantitative methods will be required, drawing upon social and behavioural sciences, and economic, epidemiological, laboratory, statistical, and community development approaches. Usually, a preliminary study will be relatively short term and inexpensive, in comparison to the main trial. Ideally, the main trial should be started soon after the preliminary study to avoid the situation changing between the two. This frequently raises the question of whether preliminary studies should be built into the funding proposal for the main trial, or whether they should be the subject of one or more separate preliminary funding proposals. If the latter approach is adopted, there may be a delay between the preliminary investigations and funding being secured for the main trial. A reasonable approach might be to present the design of the main trial to the funding agency, but acknowledging that preliminary studies will be necessary to confirm some of the assumptions in the proposal such as disease incidence rates. The funding for the main trial might then be made conditional on the results of the preliminary investigations. If the preliminary studies indicate that additional funding will be required for the main trial, for example, because the sample size has been underestimated, then the agency may wish to reconsider the proposal. The best strategy will often depend on the work that has been done in the past and the degree to which the results of the preliminary studies might affect the size, duration, or cost of the trial. Further details on some of the social and behaviour science methods that can be used within preliminary studies can be found in Chapter 15.

It is usually best to conduct the preliminary studies in the same general population, but in different individuals (or clusters) from those who will be involved in the main trial.

A preliminary study for the in-school intervention component of the Tanzanian adolescent sexual and reproductive health trial mentioned in Section 2.1 was conducted over a period of about 6 months in five schools that would not be included in the subsequent trial but that were conveniently located close to the offices of the research institution coordinating the trial. Teachers and class peer educators were selected and trained to deliver the in-school sessions and were then observed actually teaching the sessions to evaluate the session quality and how long it took to teach each session. The study identified misunderstandings and that there were some topics that the teachers obviously felt uncomfortable teaching, for example. Researchers also interviewed the teachers, peer educators, school headteachers, some of the students, and their parents to get their impressions of each session and the course as a whole and their suggestions for improvements. In the course of this preliminary study, many lessons were also learned about the resources that would be needed, the best ways to select the teachers and peer educators, and how to gain the trust of the local education department, school authorities, local religious leaders, students, and their parents.

The feasibility study in the Tanzania site of the microbicide trial mentioned in Section 2.1 involved conducting a rapid assessment and mapping of bars, guesthouses, restaurants, shops, sellers of local brew, and wayside food sellers, and enumeration of the number of women working in them to identify the potential numbers that could be invited to join the subsequent trial. A group of these women were invited to join a preliminary longitudinal cohort study which would receive all the proposed trial procedures, except being given either the microbicide or placebo gel. The procedures included setting up study clinics that the women were asked to attend on a quarterly basis and the regular monitoring of the outcomes that were proposed for the trial, including tests for HIV and other STIs, pregnancy, and reported sexual behaviours. The opportunity was taken to conduct comparisons of alternative ways of collecting data on self-reported sexual behaviours (including face-to-face interviews and use of pictorial diaries kept by the women) and of testing various alternative methods for interacting and exchanging information with women participants, their representatives, the owners and managers of the institutions in which they worked, community leaders, and relevant local officials. Discussions and negotiations were held with health facilities where women were referred for clinical care beyond the scope of the trial team themselves. The feasibility study also allowed detailed preparations and negotiations with national and international regulatory authorities.

Pre-testing of procedures for data and specimen collection and analysis should always be part of the preliminary studies for a trial. For example, any information sheet or questionnaire should be translated and back-translated if it is to be administered in a different language from the original in which it was designed. If it is going to be administered in several different languages, this can take a considerable amount of organization and time. The document should be pre-tested by administering it to a small number of volunteers. This will usually reveal problems with the order or clarity of information or questions, or with the coding of answers. Clearly, enough time must be left to act on the lessons learned during the pre-testing, and it may be necessary to pre-test several sequential versions of an information sheet or data collection form, before it is considered ready for pilot testing. More details on questionnaire design are given in Chapter 14.

3 Pilot testing

3.1 Purpose

Every field trial should be preceded by a pilot study (also known as a pilot test) prior to launching the main trial. This should test, on a small scale, all the study procedures, including the selection of eligible potential participants, their enrolment, recording the required data, specimen collection (if applicable), supervision systems, quality control, and data processing. If the trial involves multiple data collection rounds, where either staff or procedures change between rounds, it is a good idea to pilot test the procedures before each round.

3.2 Design of the pilot test

The design of the pilot study should be as similar as possible to the design of the procedures in the main trial, and the population selected to take part should be representative of the trial population (though not part of it). In a drug or vaccine trial, the actual interventional and comparison products (for example, drug or vaccine or placebo) might be administered, and procedures tested for monitoring immediate outcomes and responding to any potential AEs. However, sometimes, only the standard comparison product or placebo is used in the pilot study, as those included in the pilot study might not be included in the long-term safety monitoring that would be present in the main trial. For example, only the placebo gel was used in the pilot test for the microbicide trial described in Sections 2.1 and 2.2. For other types of intervention, such as the combination of in-school sexual and reproductive health education, training of health workers and youth condom promoters, and community-wide supportive activities that were evaluated within the trial that was also mentioned in Sections 2.1 and 2.2, the interventions were pilot-tested in separate communities.

Usually, it is best to conduct the pilot study in individuals or a cluster that will not be included in the main trial, in order to avoid having to go back to the same individuals to collect similar data in the main trial. In a multi-round trial, the same specific individuals or clusters might participate in the pilot test that precedes each data collection round. This has logistic advantages. The field teams will get to know the community in which the pilot tests are conducted, facilitating logistics such as where to conduct the survey, where to stay overnight, and who the best local people are to ask to help introduce the study to householders or to help find people who do not come forward for the trial. It also has the technical advantage that the individuals and communities involved in subsequent rounds of the pilot test will have had similar prior exposure to the procedures to those in the main trial population.

The pilot study can often be linked to staff training. For example, in a multi-round field trial of vitamin A supplementation in children, staff received a specific training course that covered all the field data collection methods that would be used in the subsequent trial round. This course lasted a total of 2 weeks and included both classroom and practical training. During the first week, the practical training included 'mock interviewing' their colleagues and role plays, in which one interviewer asked questions of the trainer, while all the field interviewers entered the answers into the questionnaire. The pilot test was carried out early in the second week, so that any necessary changes could be made to the procedures, or even to the data collection forms, in time for the interviewers and their supervisors to be brought up to speed on the modifications before the end of the 2-week training period.

Every step in the field trial processes should be tested in the pilot study. Importantly, the pilot test of data and specimen collection procedures must allow enough time for the pilot data to be entered on to computers, 'cleaned', and analysed, so that these systems can also be checked for functionality. Similarly, whenever possible, any specimens collected during the pilot test should be processed, so that, at a minimum, it is possible to check that the specimens have been collected and transported correctly and are in good condition. In addition, enough time must be allowed between the completion of the pilot test and all its checks, for revisions to be made to the instruments and procedures if they are needed. All too often, inexperienced trial managers do not allow enough time for this and hope that no changes will be needed or are then under pressure to ignore indications from the pilot test that improvements would be desirable.

Sometimes, investigators are tempted to use the results from a small, time-limited pilot test to predict whether the sample size that was calculated for the main trial will be sufficient. While a small pilot test can give rise to worries about recruitment rates and suggest ways of increasing these, pilot studies will usually not have been designed with sufficient numbers or duration to give a precise enough estimate of trial outcomes to make it sensible to attempt to use it to test sample size calculations. Given very wide CIs around the outcome estimates that are likely in a small pilot test, such projections may be very misleading. If there is a need for checks on the assumptions used in the trial sample size calculation, these should be tested within a preliminary study, as described in Section 2.2.

References

Leach, A., Vekemans, J., Lievens, M., *et al.* 2011. Design of a phase III multicenter trial to evaluate the efficacy of the RTS,S/AS01 malaria vaccine in children across diverse transmission settings in Africa. *Malaria Journal*, **10**, 224.

McCormack, S., Ramjee, G., Kamali, A., *et al.* 2010. PRO2000 vaginal gel for prevention of HIV-1 infection (Microbicides Development Programme 301): a phase 3, randomised, double-blind, parallel-group trial. *Lancet*, **376**, 1329–37.

Obasi, A. I., Cleophas, B., Ross, D. A., *et al.* 2006. Rationale and design of the MEMA kwa Vijana adolescent sexual and reproductive health intervention in Mwanza Region, Tanzania. *AIDS Care*, **18**, 311–22.

Peterson, L., Nanda, K., Opoku, B. K., *et al.* 2007. SAVVY (C31G) gel for prevention of HIV infection in women: a Phase 3, double-blind, randomized, placebo-controlled trial in Ghana. *PLoS One*, **2**, e1312.

Vallely, A., Shagi, C., Kasindi, S., *et al.*; **Microbicides Development Programme.** 2007. The benefits of participatory methodologies to develop effective community dialogue in the context of a microbicide trial feasibility study in Mwanza, Tanzania. *BMC Public Health*, **7**, 133.

Chapter 14

Questionnaires

1 Introduction to questionnaires 224
2 The questions 225
   2.1 Relation to study objectives, content, and duration 225
   2.2 Development of questions 226
   2.3 Types of question 229
      2.3.1 Historical recall 229
      2.3.2 Open and closed questions 230
   2.4 Validation 230
   2.5 Translation 231
3 The questionnaire 231
   3.1 Length 231
   3.2 Order of questions 232
   3.3 Layout 233
   3.4 Coding 233
4 The interviewers 234
   4.1 Selection 234
   4.2 Training 235
   4.3 Standardization 235
   4.4 Interviewers' manual 236
5 Data capture 237
   5.1 Pen and paper 237
   5.2 Electronic 237
6 The interview 238
   6.1 Who, where, and when 238
   6.2 Non-response 239
Appendix 14.1 Options for recording responses on a questionnaire 240
Appendix 14.2 Pre-coded responses which are mutually exclusive 241
Appendix 14.3 Pre-coded responses which are not mutually exclusive 242
Appendix 14.4 Questions with a 'skip' instruction 242
Appendix 14.5 Recording of multiple items of information for direct computer entry 243
Appendix 14.6 'Open' questions 244
Appendix 14.7 Questions for self-completion by the respondent 245
Appendix 14.8 Questionnaires on a mobile phone 246
Appendix 14.9 Collecting geolocation data on a mobile phone 247
Appendix 14.10 Recording a laboratory test result on a mobile phone 248

1 Introduction to questionnaires

The collection of information by asking questions of members of the study population is likely to be a component of any health intervention trial. Such information may be relatively simple and straightforward to collect (for example, a census of the study population in which the name, age, and sex are recorded for the members of each household in the study area) or may be very difficult to elicit reliably from respondents (for example, beliefs about the causes of illness or details of income or sexual behaviour). The focus of this chapter is on quantitative surveys, in which data are collected by asking the same questions to multiple members of the study population. The responses are recorded in a standardized way, either on paper or electronically, and analysed later. Qualitative approaches to investigate the beliefs, attitudes, and practices of members of a study population, such as anthropological studies based on participant observation, in-depth interviews, or focus group discussions, are discussed in Chapter 15. In this chapter, we discuss key issues related to the methods of collection of quantitative survey data. The selection, training, standardization, monitoring, supervision, and support of the interviewers to ensure that they do a good job of collecting the data are discussed in Chapter 16.

The commonest approach to the collection of quantitative survey data is through face-to-face interviews where an interviewer asks each of the questions and records the participant's answers, either on paper or electronically. The major advantages of this method are that the participants do not need to be literate and will usually be familiar with this approach. However, it is relatively labour-intensive, since each participant has a questionnaire administered by an interviewer on a one-to-one basis.

In literate populations, questionnaires may be 'self-administered', i.e. either a paper questionnaire is distributed to study participants that they are asked to complete themselves or the participant is given an electronic device such as a computer (desktop, laptop, tablet, PDA) or mobile phone on which they read each question and enter the answer. These methods can be 'audio-assisted' where the participant can listen to each question being read out and select the answer from a list. Such approaches have been successfully used with semi-literate participants where the participants can listen to the pre-recorded questions and possible answers and only need to be able to identify and select the answer code (such as A, B, or C) (Langhaug et al., 2010).

The basic principles of planning and designing self-administered questionnaires are similar to those for the interviewer-administered questionnaires. Interviews of several respondents at the same time (group interviews or focus group discussions) are discussed in Chapter 15, Section 3.3.

In addition to asking questions, an interviewer may carry out observations. For example, questions about the use of bed-nets could be supplemented by inspection, and observations on their location and state of repair. Similarly, the participant may be asked to demonstrate how they do something. For example, in a study of diarrhoea, they might be asked to show how they would prepare oral rehydration salts or how they wash their hands.

The methods outlined in this chapter are most appropriate when information on a relatively small number of well-defined subject areas is required, for which the responses to enquiries are either numerical (for example, number of pregnancies) or may be classified into a small number of different categories (for example, current feeding mode of an infant). Even simple items of information may be difficult to elicit accurately, unless adequate research has been conducted to find out how questions should be asked and phrased in the study community. The methods described in Chapter 15 to obtain such background information are relevant here.

In a particular trial, the study subjects may be visited and interviewed once only or, more commonly, several times. Simple cross-sectional surveys provide an example of the former. An example of the latter would be the collection of regular information on child morbidity from the mothers of study children through weekly or fortnightly interviews such as might be used for the evaluation of the efficacy of a vaccine against diarrhoeal disease. The first interview might be more extensive, with a shorter list of questions asked at each subsequent visit. Intervention trials often involve an initial cross-sectional survey, followed by periodic surveys of either the same or different individuals from the trial population, the frequency of which will be determined by the nature of the outcome variables under study.

In this chapter, the different components of a questionnaire survey are reviewed. The formulation and validation of questions to be included are considered in Section 2. Section 3 deals with the construction of the complete questionnaire; Section 4 deals with the interviewers, their selection, training, and standardization; Section 5 discusses the alternative ways of 'capturing' the data, using pen and paper or electronic methods, while Section 6 discusses factors relating to the actual interview.

As with most aspects of field research, there is no satisfactory substitute for experience to know how to formulate and administer a questionnaire satisfactorily. The inexperienced investigator would be well advised to seek guidance of those who have previously conducted surveys in the study area, if possible, as well as searching for examples of questionnaires that have been extensively validated in similar contexts such as national censuses and Demographic and Health Surveys (DHS). Those with social science, statistical, and data processing skills are also likely to make important contributions. A recently updated guide to questionnaire construction and question design is Woodward and Chambers (2012).

2 The questions

Quantitative data may be collected in field trials by a series of questions asked of the respondents that are compiled into a questionnaire. Additional quantitative data may be obtained by direct observation (for example, of what the house's roof is made of or of whether a male has been circumcised), measurement (for example, weight), or after taking a tissue sample (for example, haemoglobin level). This section will cover issues related to data that are collected through questions.

2.1 Relation to study objectives, content, and duration

The questions to be included in a questionnaire should be developed to relate directly to the objectives of the study. Usually, at least an outline questionnaire will be drawn up in parallel with the formulation of the protocol for the trial. Most grant review committees expect to see such an outline in the trial funding application.

Questionnaires must be realistic, both in terms of content and length. For example, it may not be possible to obtain valid data on highly sensitive questions such as illegal or stigmatized behaviours through a structured questionnaire.

When a questionnaire survey is being planned, it will often seem attractive to add questions that do not relate directly to the objectives of the study but which may be of interest for other reasons (see also Chapter 12, Section 2.1). As a general rule, this temptation should be resisted, as lengthening interview schedules is likely to lead to a higher non-participation rate, and time devoted to questions of peripheral interest may be at the expense of time on more important questions, with a consequent lowering of the quality of the information collected on the latter. It is good practice to go through a draft questionnaire, specifying which objective or important trial outcome each question will contribute to, with the aim of deleting any which cannot be clearly justified on these grounds. Nonetheless, in some circumstances, it may be desirable to ask other questions if this increases the likelihood of participation in the survey or serves to divert attention away from the main questions, in order to reduce the chance of biased responses. For example, it may be more acceptable to ask questions about sexual behaviour in the context of a more general behavioural survey than to include only questions that concern sexual behaviour. Similarly, if particular adverse effects are expected from an intervention, it will usually be best to also include questions about effects thought to be unrelated to the intervention, as this may help identify any biases in response between intervention and control groups that are not directly attributable to the intervention.

Few respondents will be willing to complete a questionnaire that takes more than 20–30 minutes, and, even if they do, the quality of responses may well decline if the respondent gets bored or tired. In general, it is best if a questionnaire can be kept to less than 30 minutes, though this can sometimes be extended if it includes a variety of different activities, such as answering questions about photographs or scenarios or taking physical measurements, rather than only questions and answers.

2.2 **Development of questions**

A plan for the development of the questions to be included in a questionnaire survey is given in Box 14.1, and Box 14.2 gives a checklist of points that should be considered in drafting questions.

Increasingly, standardized questionnaires are being developed and shared. These draw on questionnaires and interviews that have been conducted in many countries and studies, and often the questions and responses have been translated into many different languages. An example of this is the Economic and Social Research Council (ESRC) question bank (<http://www.surveynet.ac.uk/sqb>), which has hundreds of survey questionnaires in it. With the advent of standards for data documentation (see <http://www.ddialliance.org>), searching and browsing for questions on particular themes will be easier and more extensive. While it is unlikely that complete questionnaires can be copied for new trials, it is important to utilize the resources and knowledge from previous studies to avoid making the same mistakes and to build on existing knowledge.

Box 14.1 Checklist for the development of a questionnaire

1. Define the information that is required from the questions. Some items of information may only require a single question, such as name or sex, while others require a series of questions such as socio-economic status or episodes of illness in the past week.

2. Formulate draft questions. Attention to the wording of questions is important, as slight variations may result in different responses. For example, 'Where do you normally seek help when your child has diarrhoea?' vs 'Where did you seek help when your child last had diarrhoea?'. Box 14.2 gives a checklist of points that should be considered in drafting questions. In general, it is a good idea to search for, and to critically review, how others have asked specific questions, especially if these questions have been formally validated.

3. Informally test the questions. This may involve trying them out on different members of the study team and discussing them with those knowledgeable of the study area, including residents. It may be necessary to base someone in the community under study (ideally, someone with anthropological or social science skills) to investigate how different questions will be perceived to find out if there are taboos regarding certain topics, if there are local words for some illnesses or conditions, and the extent to which these correspond to the investigator's definitions (for example, many communities have special words for measles, night blindness, sexual intercourse, depression, or lethargy). The investment warranted for such qualitative studies will depend upon local sensitivities regarding the items on which information is required and the degree to which each question is critical for the trial. For example, it will require less work to find out how to ask questions about breastfeeding practices than to formulate appropriate questions on aspects of sexual behaviour. As a result of such investigations, the original draft questions may have to be modified. Some may even have to be abandoned if research indicates that valid information is unlikely to be elicited through a questionnaire survey.

4. Prepare a first draft of the questionnaire for pilot testing.

5. Translate each question into the language(s) of the study population, followed by independent back-translation by someone who does not know the original questions, with reconciliation of any discrepancies—ideally followed by further independent translation and back-translation (see Section 2.5).

6. Prepare a draft instruction manual for interviewers and their supervisors (see Section 4.4).

7. Pilot-test the questionnaire in field conditions, preferably in an area adjacent to the study area and using the interviewers who will work on the main survey (see Chapter 13).

> **Box 14.1 Checklist for the development of a questionnaire (continued)**
>
> 8 Analyse the experience in the pilot test and the data collected.
> 9 Reformulate the questionnaire, with further translation and back-translation of any amended questions, followed by further pilot testing, especially if important changes have been made to questions related to primary or secondary trial outcomes.
> 10 Finalize the questionnaire for the main survey, along with the instruction manual for interviewers (see Section 4.4).

> **Box 14.2 Checklist of points to consider when drafting questions**
>
> 1 Keep wording informal, conversational, and simple. Avoid words longer than three or four syllables.
> 2 Avoid jargon and sophisticated language; assessing understanding at the pre-test and pilot test stages is essential. The wording of all questions must be appropriate to the educational, social, and cultural background of the respondents.
> 3 Check the cultural relevance to the respondents of concepts used. Ensure mutual understanding between the interviewers and the respondents, paying attention to cultural and educational differences.
> 4 Avoid long questions, but vary the length of questions to avoid administration of the questionnaire becoming repetitive and boring for the interviewer or interviewee.
> 5 It may be necessary to define a term or a concept before asking about it. If the definition is short, it can be included in the question, but otherwise it is better given separately before the question is asked.
> 6 Avoid leading questions that may bias the respondent to a particular answer (for example, 'Do you think the improved clinic arrangements are better?').
> 7 Avoid open questions beginning 'Why?'.
> 8 Avoid negative questions (for example, 'Do you not think . . .'—in some cultures, the answer 'no' indicates 'I do not think . . .'; in other cultures, the answer 'yes' indicates 'Yes, I do not think . . .'!).
> 9 Where possible, avoid hypothetical questions, as some respondents will find these difficult to answer (for example, 'If the bus fare was less, would you come to the clinic more often?').
> 10 Keep to a single subject for each question. For example, do not say 'Do the cost and times of the clinic prevent you going?'.

> **Box 14.2 Checklist of points to consider when drafting questions questionnaire (continued)**
>
> 11 Pay particular attention to sensitive issues. Review the inclusion of very sensitive ones. If they are to be retained, pay very careful attention to the wording, and consider the use of indirect approaches. Think carefully about their position within the questionnaire (see Section 3.2).
>
> 12 Check the adequacy of the lists of responses to 'closed' (see Section 2.3.2) questions. For example, ensure a food list covers most things normally eaten in the community concerned. It is usually a good idea to include an 'other (specify)' category, unless you are sure that every possible answer is in the list (such as male and female for gender). But it is also important that only a relatively small proportion of responses (definitely less than 10%) end up being in the 'other (specify)' category. This should be checked in the pilot test, with additional categories being added for the commoner responses that were initially in the 'other (specify)' category.
>
> 13 Never include an 'other' category without asking the respondent to specify what the response was—as in 'other (specify)'—and leave space for the respondent or interviewer to write the specific answer next to this code.

2.3 Types of question

Information may be sought on opinions or facts through a questionnaire. The distinction between the two is not always clear, but, in general, the collection of data on the latter is easier to plan. Local sensitivities will influence the reliability with which either kind of information may be obtained. For example, in some cultures, it is considered unlucky to count your children, so asking a parent 'How many children do you have?' may be too direct an approach.

2.3.1 Historical recall

Information may be sought about the present (for example, 'Does your child have fever now?') or about the past ('Did your child have an episode of fever in the last month?'). The advantage of asking about the present situation is that responses are not susceptible to memory lapses, and furthermore they will usually be more amenable to validation (see Section 2.4). The reliability of historical information decreases the further back in time the question relates to, and is influenced greatly by the importance of the event to the person (also referred to as its salience). Thus, deaths will be remembered better than hospital admissions, which, in turn, will be remembered better than illness episodes not requiring hospital admission. To obtain reliable information on mild, or even moderately severe, fevers, diarrhoea, or respiratory infections, the recall period probably should not exceed a week. The implication of this for longitudinal studies in which these outcomes are of interest, is that at least weekly surveys of the study group will be necessary to collect reliable information.

2.3.2 Open and closed questions

A 'closed' question is one that allows only a defined set of answers which have been anticipated and categorized in advance (for example, 'Do you own a radio?' 0 = No; 1 = Yes). Replies to an 'open' question can take any form and should, whenever possible, be recorded in the respondent's own words (for example, 'What were the symptoms your child had before being taken to the health facility?'). It is possible to ask a question with a closed list of responses in an open way, with the answer being assigned to one of a previously compiled list of codes held by the interviewer (for example, 'What did you eat yesterday?', with a list of types of food on the questionnaire for the interviewer to tick off those mentioned). This may produce a different response from asking closed questions about each of the items on the list. Reading out the list will remind the respondent of the possibilities but may also tend to produce affirmative answers as a gesture to 'please' the interviewer or because the respondent is embarrassed to admit that they have not eaten a high-status food such as meat. If the information is sufficiently important, both approaches can be used, the list of unmentioned possible answers being read out after initial responses are recorded without such prompting. The two responses should be recorded separately. For example, against each category, there could be three options: '0 = No'; '1 = Yes, unprompted'; '2 = Yes, prompted'. An analogy is medical history taking where questions about specific signs and symptoms might be asked after an initial neutral enquiry such as 'What is the problem today?'.

In preliminary qualitative investigations, open questions are likely to be preferred to determine the full range of possible responses. As a general rule, however, for questions that are to be administered in a large survey, closed questions are better, as it is very tedious and time-consuming to go back to code the open answers subsequently. It is important that they are the 'right' closed questions, of course. This requires careful research and the avoidance of the premature administration of a questionnaire that may be simple to administer, code, and analyse but which does not provide the information required to meet the study objectives.

2.4 Validation

The principles underlying the validation of a questionnaire are similar to those for validating a diagnostic test. The objective is to determine to what extent the answers given to a question correspond to the 'true' situation. Problems arise if there is no independent way of ascertaining what is 'true'. If a mother is asked 'Does your child have fever now?', the temperature of a child might be measured independently, and the response to the question *validated* against the direct measurement (by defining temperatures above some limit as 'fever'). It will usually be impossible to validate the responses to a question such as 'Did your child have fever yesterday?'. If a 'gold standard' exists, i.e. a means of obtaining an independent measure of the true response, the *sensitivity* and *specificity* of a given question can be assessed. The *sensitivity* of the question is the proportion of true positive responses that are reported as positive (for example, the proportion of all children with a current fever who are reported as having fever by their mother). The *specificity* is the proportion of true negative responses where the question produces a 'negative' response (for example, the proportion of all children without a current fever who are classified as not having a fever by questioning their mother).

The relative importance of sensitivity and specificity in intervention trials is discussed in Chapter 12, Section 4.2.

If there is no 'gold standard', other characteristics of the responses to questions must be evaluated to assess their usefulness in a particular survey. A minimal requirement for a question should be that the respondent gives the same answer to the same question at different times if the circumstances have not changed (i.e. responses should be 'repeatable'). Also, if different interviewers administer the same question to the same person, the same answer should be obtained (i.e. responses should be 'reproducible'). Repeatability and reproducibility are not a guarantee of validity, of course. The question 'Do you beat your spouse?' might be answered consistently over time to the same interviewer and reproducibly to different interviewers, but it may still be a very poor way of detecting spouse beaters! Also, a man might consistently report that his wife is his only sexual partner, even if this is not the case.

If a question fails to induce consistent answers, either within or between interviewers, it may be because of a fault in the question or in the interviewers or be due to the respondent deliberately varying their responses for some reason. For example, the respondent might reason that, 'if I am being asked the same question a second time, this must be because they didn't like my first answer, so I'd better change it'!

2.5 Translation

It will often be necessary to translate the questionnaire into local languages. Such translation should be undertaken with care and attention to detail, as it is easy for the sense of a question to be changed, sometimes substantially, by the translation process. For example, apparent differences in responses to a question asked to those in different language groups may be due entirely to variations in the translation processes. Words for some illnesses or concepts may not exist in a language, and this may necessitate major changes in the wording of questions. An apparently equivalent word may exist, but it may be used in a different way and cover a narrower, or wider, range of conditions. For example, there may be several local words used to describe acute respiratory infections, one of which corresponds closely to what we mean by pneumonia. Conversely, difficulties may be encountered when one local word is used to encompass several different conditions. In studies of meningitis in The Gambia, for example, there was difficulty in finding terms to distinguish between a 'floppy' and a 'stiff' neck (B. Greenwood, personal communication).

Once a questionnaire has been translated into a local language, it should be independently back-translated into the original language. Comparing the original text with the back-translated text will indicate possible areas of confusion where attention to the original translation will be required.

3 The questionnaire

3.1 Length

Adequate time must be allowed for the interviewer to solicit the correct responses to all the questions included in a questionnaire. The time that an interview will take may be difficult to estimate and may depend on the inherent interest of the subject matter to respondents, as well as the amount of time they can spare. The likely duration of an interview can be evaluated during pilot testing. Neither the interviewer nor the respondent should feel under time pressure to complete the interview. Also, the questionnaire should be long enough to allow the required information to be collected, but without unduly inconveniencing the respondent. The work schedule of interviewers should be planned, such that they are not tempted to hurry through interviews. In general, it is not a good policy to pay interviewers according to the number of interviews completed, unless it is certain that this will not compromise quality. Sufficient time must be allocated to allow the interviewer to explain why the survey is being conducted, to emphasize the importance of truthful responses, and to reassure the respondent regarding the procedures undertaken to ensure the confidentiality of any information divulged in the interview.

Interviews lasting an hour or more are rarely feasible in the context of a large-scale survey; usually, it is more realistic to aim for a maximum of around 30 minutes per interview. Respondents may not complete an interview that is too long, and this may be particularly problematic if crucial questions are towards the end of the questionnaire. Problems of compliance may also grow, as the interviewers' reputations go before them. Brevity is especially important if repeated follow-up questionnaires are planned.

It is a good practice to have the interviewers record the time that each interview starts and finishes. This is one way of checking how interviewers spend their days (though it is obviously susceptible to manipulation), and, more importantly, it provides a measure, for example, of whether different degrees of attention are being given to those in the intervention or control groups, with a consequent possibility of bias.

3.2 Order of questions

The initial questions in an interview will seek to verify the identity of the respondent (to ensure the correct person is being questioned) and to collect basic demographic information (for example, age, sex, marital status). The most sensitive questions should usually be asked in the second half of the questionnaire. This is done to give the interviewer time to establish a rapport with the respondent and also so that, if the respondent should be upset by the questions and withdraws from the interview, at least this happens after most other information has been collected (though such questions should have been weeded out during pilot testing). However, it is usually best not to have the most sensitive questions last, to avoid the respondent ending the questionnaire with these at the top of their mind. Questions which are not judged to be sensitive should tend to be asked in their order of importance (to the study objectives), the most important ones being asked first, to minimize the losses due to any premature cessation of an interview.

Responses to some questions may condition the responses to other questions, and this should be taken into account in their ordering. For example, a question asking if the respondent is generally 'well', which produces a 'yes' response, may bias questions about specific illnesses if the respondent feels obliged to justify their overall 'wellness'. If the interest of the study is in specific diseases, it might be better to focus on these first, before questions about general health.

Some questions may seek to obtain the same information in different ways as a validation procedure. If this is done, the questions should not be too close together in the questionnaire.

3.3 Layout

A questionnaire should be able to be used in the field with, at most, infrequent reference to manuals or instructions. It should provide the interviewer with sufficient information to conduct the interview smoothly and without difficulty, after suitable training (see Section 4.2). At the same time, it should not be a bulky document, as this may alarm the respondent (in terms of the time they think it will take to complete), and it may add to the problem of paper storage (see Section 5). Instructions to interviewers may be distinguished from questions to respondents by printing them in a different typeface (for example, italics). Each interviewer should be issued with an interviewer's manual (see Section 4.4), which contains information to supplement instructions to interviewers on the questionnaire itself. Interviewers should be instructed to consult their manual if they are uncertain about how to ask a question or how to record responses or carry out any other procedure.

It is especially important that the initial introduction the interviewer gives a respondent is clear and consistent from interview to interview. It is common for the text of this introduction to be printed at the start of the questionnaire. Usually, interviewers will be instructed to ask questions exactly as they are written in the questionnaire. This is an important way to achieve greater reproducibility and standardization between interviewers.

Whether printed on paper or on an electronic device, the questionnaire should be well designed. If paper is being used, the size and quality should be chosen to suit field conditions. Cards are often easier to work with in the field than paper sheets but may be unsuitable if more than one is required for an interview and they are also bulky to carry around. The layout of the questionnaire should be sufficiently spaced to allow those with large handwriting to record all the required information. If whether or not a question is asked depends on the response to a previous question, this should be indicated on the questionnaire with clear instructions and appropriate 'branch and skip' explanations (see Appendix 14.4). If the questionnaire is being administered from an electronic device, it is essential that such branches and skips have been correctly pre-programmed (see Section 5.2).

All questions should be assigned a number. For questions that are repeated several times, such as questions about each of a mother's children, a tabular layout can be used (see Appendix 14.5), but this should be designed with care, as such a layout puts more demands on the interviewer, or on the respondent if the questionnaire is self-completed.

To facilitate later checking and coding, it may be useful to include, on the questionnaire, the names that variables are going to be assigned for computer processing (see Section 3.4). These are often typed in capital letters and placed just to the right of the coding boxes on the questionnaire.

3.4 Coding

Coding is discussed in detail in Chapter 20, Sections 5.4 and 7.3, and only a few points pertinent to questionnaire design are covered here. Coding is the process of converting the recorded answers to questions into a numerical or alphabetical code. The answers may be numeric (for example, age) or be the replies to closed questions. For closed questions, there are two possible ways of coding, depending upon whether only one answer, out of the list of possible responses, can be given or whether several are possible. Examples of the former are any 'yes/no/don't know' answers or answers to questions such as relationship to the head of household (for example, wife, child, brother, or sister, etc., where only one answer is allowed). An example of where several answers on the list are possible for a single respondent is a question about food consumed on the previous day. In the first case, the possible responses are each given a code, usually a letter or a digit, and a respondent's answer is coded accordingly. In the second, each possible response must be coded for the answer 'no' or 'yes' (often coded as '0' or '1', respectively, or as 'N' or 'Y') or 'don't know' (if applicable) (often coded as '9'), and the codes for each of them will make up the respondent's reply.

It is important to allow codes for 'don't know', rather than leaving the code blank. On paper questionnaires, answers to questions that are skipped (i.e. which are not relevant) are normally left blank during the interview. It may be convenient to leave the codes blank as well, or a specific code for 'not applicable' (for example, '8') can be used. The choice depends on data processing requirements (see Chapter 20). With lists of possible responses, a category 'Other (specify)' is often included and needs to have its own code. There should be space on the questionnaire to write or type in the actual reply, but, as mentioned in Box 14.2, the pre-testing and pilot work should ensure that the 'Other (specify)' category is uncommonly used for a reply.

Appendices 14.1 to 14.10 give some examples of different ways of designing a questionnaire and examples of different types of questions.

4 The interviewers

4.1 Selection

Interviewers should be selected with careful attention to the tasks they will be expected to perform. They must be seen by the respondents as individuals who can be trusted to keep sensitive and confidential information to themselves. They must be of pleasant disposition, and be well-mannered, well-dressed, reliable, and punctual. They must not make promises to respondents that they do not honour (for example, if they say they will return on a given day they must do so or, at least, send a message in advance to explain and apologize if they cannot). The study investigator must attempt to assess whether potential interviewers have these characteristics during initial selection processes, which should include written tests and interviews.

In general, contracts of employment for interviewers should include a probationary period, during which their suitability is further assessed and at the end of which a decision about longer-term employment is made. In some countries, it is possible to offer initial contracts solely for the training period. If so, the trial can select more interviewers that are needed and train them. This has two considerable advantages. It gives the trial team much more time for a detailed assessment of their character and performance than is possible through a short written test and interview, and also it is possible to select the best potential interviewers at the end of the training period, which should have included actual pilot testing of their tasks in the field. Other interviewers who have performed satisfactorily can be put on a waiting list, so that they could be offered the job at a later date, without the need for a full training course if one or more interviewers drops out or falls sick. Even after this, there must be provision for removing an interviewer from fieldwork if their performance is unsatisfactory.

If possible, interviewers should speak the same language as the respondents; otherwise, interviews will have to be conducted through interpreters, which is usually unsatisfactory (for the reasons outlined in Section 2), although it is sometimes unavoidable.

The sex, age, and normal place of residence of an interviewer may be important. For example, in some societies, male interviewers are less likely to get reliable information from women and may even not be allowed by local custom to interview them at all. If interviewers clearly belong to the health services, replies may be biased towards support for those services. Well-educated interviewers may not be best for interviews with less educated respondents; substantial differences in social status between interviewer and respondent should be avoided. Young interviewers may not be regarded as reliable or trustworthy recipients of sensitive information by adults but may be best able to elicit sensitive information from other young people. Also, sometimes sensitive information may be more readily given to a stranger than to a member of the same community, provided the respondents are assured of confidentiality.

The most skilled and reliable interviewers are not always the most intelligent or highly educated. Indeed, highly educated interviewers may be more likely to become bored with repeated administration of the same interview schedule, especially if they do not see a clear and feasible career path by which they can progress, for example, to being a supervisor or to getting the opportunity for further training.

4.2 Training

The training of interviewers might initially be done as a group exercise, with classroom-type teaching. This must be supplemented with practical exercises. These might consist of one interviewer administering the survey questionnaire to the trainer (or another interviewer or someone else), while others look on, followed by a critical evaluation and discussion of the interview with the group. The person acting as the respondent should not be expected to answer any sensitive questions honestly but can make up plausible answers.

The draft interviewers' manual (see Section 4.4) should be used extensively in the training process, so that, by the end of training, the interviewer should be familiar with all aspects of the manual and know which parts to consult for advice on queries about particular questions or aspects of field procedures. Also, the training process usually reveals aspects of the manual that need revision or further clarification.

Only after interviewers have been through a preliminary training course should they be allowed to try out interviews in the community. Initially, such interviews might be done by pairs of interviewers, in the presence of a trainer, with detailed 'post-mortems' being conducted after each interview or series of interviews. The training process will merge with the processes of standardization (see Section 4.3) and validation (see Section 2.4) and should be continually reinforced throughout the trial through supervision visits and meetings, and, when necessary, refresher training courses.

4.3 Standardization

As discussed in Section 2.4, an interview must be both repeatable and reproducible. Standardization of interview technique within and between interviewers is necessary for reproducibility. Interviewers must be trained to follow instructions on the questionnaire, as well as all other instructions, exactly. This extends to asking all questions exactly as written, if this is appropriate. As well as questions, the introduction to the interview, explanations and definitions made to the respondent, and transition statements that explain a change of subject of the questions should be said as written. The points in the interview to use probes and prompts to get the respondent to reply more fully should also be clearly specified.

Standardization may also apply to the place and time of interviews. For example, interviews conducted in a home and health centre will, in many circumstances, produce different responses.

It is not realistic, however, to insist on interviewers being merely reading and transcription 'machines'. They must have some leeway to add extra explanations and guidance when it is clear that a respondent does not understand a question or a definition. Interviewer training should cover this and detail the extent to which this is permissible. However, stress should be placed on following the written wording, whenever possible.

Standardization needs a certain degree of regimentation, and this can act against rapport and personal contact. Since the wording of questions is laid down in advance, it is important to ensure that it is friendly and does not alienate the respondent. If different interviewers are getting different responses to the same questions, it is important to investigate why. For example, one of the interviewers may be deviating from the interview schedule and giving undue emphasis to part of a question. Different interviewers attempting to collect the same information from one respondent at different times will normally be a part of the validation procedures (see Section 2.4).

No matter how well interviewers are trained and standardized against each other, it is as well to assume in the design of a survey that some differences will exist in the responses obtained by different interviewers. This will influence the way different interviewers are deployed for fieldwork. Not only is it important to record on the interview schedule who conducts each interview, so that differences between interviewers can be analysed, but also interviewers should be deployed in a 'balanced' way, so that interviewer differences are not confounded with other differences of potential interest. For example, in an intervention trial, each interviewer should question similar numbers of subjects from the intervention and control groups. The worst situation would be for one interviewer to question those in the intervention group and another interviewer to question those in the control group.

4.4 Interviewers' manual

An interviewers' manual should be developed for use during the field survey. This should be reviewed during the training programme for interviewers and revised, as necessary. Careful version control will be needed to ensure that the current versions of the manual and questionnaire match each other. The manual should give detailed instructions regarding how individuals are to be selected and approached for inclusion in the study and for each specific interview, and it should detail any special instructions regarding each question in the questionnaire and how the responses should be entered. It should include guidance on how to deal with unusual situations and how to code unusual responses. It should also outline what checks are to be conducted on completed questionnaires and how and when completed questionnaires should be submitted for data processing and analysis.

During the conduct of fieldwork, regular meetings should be held of interviewers to discuss the progress and queries. When new problems arise, the solutions should be incorporated into the field manual, so that there is consistency in dealing with the problem in the future and a permanent record is kept of the solution adopted. The manuals held by each interviewer should be updated regularly, and the text should be kept electronically to facilitate this. Again, careful version control is essential, and any changes to the manual (or questionnaire) should be documented in the trial diary (see Chapter 16).

5 Data capture

Traditionally, data, whether from interviewer-administered or self-completion questionnaires, have been entered initially (captured) on to paper, but there is increasing use of electronic data capture. The latter has many advantages and has become more generally feasible, as the sizes, prices, and robustness of suitable electronic devices have improved.

5.1 Pen and paper

The major advantages of data capture by pen and paper are that it involves relatively little capital expenditure and does not require interviewers to be familiar with using an electronic device. Also, if an interviewer detects some specific problem with a question or an answer code, they can easily make a note of this in the margin of the paper form and move on to the next question. However, if many questionnaire forms are being used, the paper becomes bulky and heavy to transport and store. Paper forms can easily be damaged by rain, insects, or other animals, and a further step of data entry on to computers causes extra expense and delays and can result in transcription errors (see Chapter 20). Some projects scan the data from the paper form into a computer or fax the data to a central data management facility for subsequent scanning or manual data entry. Such methods require relatively high-quality scanners or fax machines and that the questionnaires are completed neatly, using standardized writing styles to avoid transcription errors.

5.2 Electronic

Electronic data capture involves either the interviewer or the respondent entering the responses directly into an electronic device. This allows electronic range and consistency checks to be done at the time of data capture when it is still possible for the interviewer or the respondent themselves to correct a mistake or misunderstanding that leads to an 'impossible' response. Even in most rural areas of low-income countries, electronic devices, and especially mobile phones, are now widespread, so using them for data capture is now rarely likely to faze respondents, though this must be checked in preliminary pre-testing and pilot studies.

Some electronic devices incorporate GPS (see Chapter 10), so that the coordinates of a household or other interview location can be recorded, and the device can even be used to guide the interviewer to the same location subsequently. Many electronic devices also incorporate an audio function, so that the respondent can listen to the questions and answer options through a loudspeaker or earphones. It is also possible to allow the respondent to have the question repeated, and, if necessary, they can be allowed to go back to correct an earlier answer.

Data captured onto one electronic device can be easily transferred to another. It is essential that all such data are kept confidential through password protection and, when applicable, encryption.

Until recently, initial hardware, software, and programming costs prohibited the widespread use of electronic data capture in field trials in LMICs, but there are now cheap smartphones that are capable of displaying a substantial questionnaire and capturing data in a way that is very simple for interviewers or respondents to use. There is also free user-friendly software that can be programmed by non-specialists for questionnaire design and data capture (for example, <http://opendatakit.org>).

Although electronic data capture has major advantages over traditional pen and paper approaches, it is important to allow sufficient time for someone on the team to fully familiarize themselves with the hardware and software to be used and for electronic questionnaire development and careful testing. All programming 'bugs' need to be ironed out before fieldworker training starts, and procedures need to be carefully tested and rechecked during training and in any pilot test. Unlike with a paper questionnaire, a problem with the programming of an electronic questionnaire can result in it being impossible for an answer to be entered or for the respondent to move on to the next question, being made to skip questions they should have answered, and even for whole batches of data being lost, for example, during data transfer. Furthermore, during the early stages of transferring from using paper questionnaires to electronic devices, all investigators, data managers, and fieldworkers must become fully familiar with the new method and device, and someone must be immediately available to solve any unexpected problems that arise (see Chapter 20, Section 5 for further details). During the transition period from a team using pen and paper to electronic data capture, it is often a sensible precaution to give the interviewers paper versions of the questionnaire as a backup, in case there is some unexpected problem which makes the electronic version unusable, at least during the pilot test and perhaps the first few days of the main survey. This is particularly important if the interviewers will be a long way from the trial's coordinating centre.

Some examples of using mobile phones to capture different kinds of data are given in Appendix 14.8, Appendix 14.9, and Appendix 14.10.

6 The interview

As much as possible, a face-to-face interview should approximate to a conversation between the interviewer and respondent and must not be an interrogation. Good rapport between the two is vital, and the onus is entirely on the project team to ensure this.

6.1 Who, where, and when

In studies of children, the best informant regarding their health or behaviour is likely to be their mother or guardian. Only as a last resort should someone else be interviewed for this purpose. This may necessitate repeated visits to a household, until the mother or guardian is at home. Other than for children, proxy informants should be avoided, if possible.

The choice of the place of interview will be influenced by logistic considerations and the nature of the information to be collected. Usually, the place will have to be chosen for the convenience of the respondent, rather than for that of the interviewer. Privacy will be easier to ensure in a hospital or a clinic than in a village setting, but special arrangements may be made to ensure greater privacy in a village. For example, an interview might be conducted slightly away from the house under a shady tree. If interviews are to be conducted in homes, as far as possible, the time should be chosen to fit the convenience of the residents. If possible, they should be consulted, or at least informed, in advance regarding when an interview will be scheduled. Preliminary investigations, before the main survey, should be made to ascertain when the most convenient time will be for most participants. In rural communities, during planting or harvesting seasons, evening interviews may be preferred. But, if interviews take place after dark, poor lighting may be a problem, and attention to clear printing and a well-spaced layout for the questionnaire becomes even more important (as well as the provision of torches and batteries to interviewers). In some areas, security after dark may also be a significant problem, and interviewing at that time may be inadvisable.

6.2 Non-response

Steps that can be taken to ensure data completeness within a single questionnaire are discussed in Chapters 16 and 20. Here, we discuss the problem of non-response where a trial participant is either not seen or refuses to take part in the trial or in a particular data collection 'round' or survey.

Non-respondents in a study are rarely representative of the rest of the study population. They are a self-selected group, and thus their exclusion will usually introduce bias into the results of a survey, but the degree to which that has occurred is not usually directly measurable. Thus, if a high proportion of the target population for interviews are not interviewed, the valid interpretation of the results from those who are interviewed, and in particular the generalization of these results to the whole community, may be open to serious question. Therefore, great care must be taken to ensure that the response rate is high. This may be achieved in several ways. First, the questions included in the questionnaire should be thoroughly tested in a pilot study, so that any that a significant proportion of respondents cannot, or will not, answer adequately are eliminated. Second, an appropriate explanation of the survey should be given to study participants in advance, and any false suspicions they have about the motives or intentions of the investigators must be dispelled. Third, interviewers must be selected who are persistent, yet polite, and who will probe for a correct response to a question and not accept a 'don't know' response too readily. Fourth, interviewers must be instructed to call back repeatedly if a house is empty or a respondent is away, before abandoning an interview. Their work schedule should take into account the need for such return visits.

Systems should be put in place to monitor the non-response rate within a trial on an ongoing basis, so that steps can be taken to attempt to decrease this, before it is too late. The non-response data should be disaggregated by the interviewer, the trial team, and other important groupings, where appropriate, such as language, location, etc., and all outliers investigated carefully. For example, in a trial of human papillomavirus vaccination within schools, it was discovered that the non-response rate was substantially higher for one field team than for the other. This turned out to be due to the way the team members were introducing themselves and the trial within the schools—something that could be changed, and the problem was quickly solved.

Even in the most well-conducted surveys, a 100% response rate is rare. Indeed a 100% response rate should be viewed with some suspicion! As much information as possible should be obtained about non-respondents, where necessary from proxy informants, so that the characteristics of non-responders for which information is available (for example, age and sex) may be compared with that available on responders. This may give clues to the extent of possible biases resulting from their exclusion.

References

Langhaug, L. F., Sherr, L., and Cowan, F. M. 2010. How to improve the validity of sexual behaviour reporting: systematic review of questionnaire delivery modes in developing countries. *Tropical Medicine & International Health*, **15**, 362–81.

Woodward, C. A. and Chambers, L. W. 2012. *Guide to questionnaire construction and question writing*. Ottawa: Canadian Public Health Association.

Appendix 14.1 **Options for recording responses on a questionnaire**

There are many ways in which the responses to a question can be recorded within a questionnaire. Three of the commonest ways are shown in Figure A14.1.

				CODE FOR COMPUTER
(1)	Q27	Do you usually listen to the radio every day? (CIRCLE RESPONSE)	No........0 Yes.......1	|__|
(2)	Q27	Do you usually listen to the radio every day? (No = 0; Yes = 1)		|__|
(3)	Q27	Do you usually listen to the radio every day? (No = N; Yes = Y)		|__|

Note: Using option (1), the response would usually be coded in the box on the far right-hand side, either at the end of the day or at the end of the interview, so that the interviewer can check that the question was not missed, and, if it was, ask it again. The data entry clerk would only look at the boxes when entering the data into the computer. Using options (2) or (3), the interviewer codes directly into the boxes with no intermediate step. Whichever system is used, it is advisable to adopt and use the same system throughout all questionnaires to avoid confusing the interviewers.

Figure A14.1 Three alternative options for recording the response to a single question (face-to-face interview using pen and paper).

Appendix 14.2 **Pre-coded responses which are mutually exclusive**

If there are multiple potential responses to a question, but these are mutually exclusive, so only one answer is permitted, then it is possible to use a layout as in Figure A14.2.

		CODE FOR COMPUTER
Q49	What is the main source of drinking water for members of your household?	
	(*CIRCLE ONE RESPONSE*)	|___|___|
	Piped into residence..01	
	Piped into yard or plot......................................02	
	Public tap...03	
	Well with hand-pump..04	
	Well without hand-pump...................................05	
	River, spring, surface water................................06	
	Tanker truck or other vendor..............................07	
	Rain water..08	
	Other (specify)..09	
	Not known..99	

Note: A special code has been allocated for 'Not known'—in this case, 99. It is good practice to use a standard code for answers such as 'Not applicable' (such as serial 8s (8 or 88 or 888…)) or 'Not known' (such as serial 9s (9 or 99 or 999…)). In this example, it would also be possible to subdivide and add further codes for the 'Other' responses at the analysis stage. This would require that all the questionnaires coded '09' were re-examined, and the responses given new codes such as 10, 11, 12, and so on. Such re-coding is time-consuming, and it is usually better to try to ensure during the pilot study that all, or almost all, the responses will fall into the specific coded categories to avoid having to do such later re-coding.

Figure A14.2 Design of a question with multiple, mutually exclusive responses (face-to-face interview using pen and paper).

Appendix 14.3 **Pre-coded responses which are not mutually exclusive**

If there are multiple potential answers to a question, but these are not mutually exclusive so multiple responses are permitted, then each option must have its own response (for example, Yes/No) within the questionnaire (Figure A14.3.).

	CODE FOR COMPUTER
Q33 Which of the following items does your household own? (ENTER NO = 0 OR YES = 1 FOR EACH ITEM)	
Radio...	|__|
Television...	|__|
Sewing machine.............................	|__|
Bicycle..	|__|
Motorcycle......................................	|__|
Car..	|__|
Tractor..	|__|

Figure A14.3 Design of a question with multiple responses that are not mutually exclusive (face-to-face interview using pen and paper).

Appendix 14.4 **Questions with a 'skip' instruction**

Some questions on a questionnaire may not be applicable for some respondents, based on their answers to earlier questions. Although it is possible to design the questionnaire so that a special 'Not applicable' code is allocated for any such questions, an alternative is to design the questionnaire to allow the respondent to skip such questions. An example is given in Figure A14.4.

		CODE FOR COMPUTER
Q39	Have you ever given birth to any children who were born alive? NO = 0 → GO TO Q42 YES = 1→ GO TO Q40	|__|
Q40	How many of these children are still alive?	|__|__|
Q41	How many of these children are dead?	|__|__|
Q42	Is your mother still alive? (NO = 0; YES = 1)	|__|

Figure A14.4 Design of a sequence of questions which allow questions that are not applicable to be skipped by appropriate respondents (face-to-face interview using pen and paper).

Appendix 14.5 Recording of multiple items of information for direct computer entry

Sometimes, one needs to ask a series of questions about each person in a group (for example, household). In such situations, the questions series might be structured in a table, as shown in Figure A14.5.

Q93	\multicolumn{5}{l}{For all your children who were born alive, give the following details (starting with the first born):}
Child number	Name	Alive (1) or dead (2)	Sex (1 = Male; 2 = Female)	Age* Years	Months
01		|_|	|_|	|__|__|	|__|__|
02		|_|	|_|	|__|__|	|__|__|
03		|_|	|_|	|__|__|	|__|__|
04		|_|	|_|	|__|__|	|__|__|
05		|_|	|_|	|__|__|	|__|__|
06		|_|	|_|	|__|__|	|__|__|
07		|_|	|_|	|__|__|	|__|__|
08		|_|	|_|	|__|__|	|__|__|
09		|_|	|_|	|__|__|	|__|__|
10		|_|	|_|	|__|__|	|__|__|

IF NUMBER OF CHILDREN IS DIFFERENT FROM TOTAL NUMBER RECORDED IN Q40, PROBE AND RECONCILE.

* IF DEAD, GIVE AGE AT DEATH.

RECORD AGE IN *COMPLETED* YEARS AND MONTHS.

IF LESS THAN 1 MONTH, RECORD AS '00' YEARS AND '00' MONTHS.

Figure A14.5 Design of a form to record a series of questions about children born to the same woman (face-to-face interview using pen and paper).

Appendix 14.6 **'Open' questions**

Although open questions should be avoided if possible in questionnaires, as collating and post-coding such questions can be very time consuming in large studies, occasionally it is essential to have an open question. An example is given in Figure A14.6.

Q82 What do you do when your child has diarrhoea?
     (RECORD MOTHER'S RESPONSE)
     (PROMPT: DO YOU INCREASE OR DECREASE FLUID INTAKE?)
     (PROMPT: IF YOU SEEK HELP, WHO DO YOU GO TO FIRST?)

     _____
     _____
     _____
     _____
     _____

Note: The prompts are included, so that the interviewer is asked to enquire about these issues if the mother does not volunteer the information spontaneously.

If the responses to this 'open' question are to be analysed quantitatively, the information must be coded after all the questionnaires have been completed and the full range of different responses has been assessed. If the survey is large, this can be a lot of work, and it is usually better to have explored this in pilot studies, so that as many questions as possible are in the form of 'closed' questions on all questionnaires that will be analysed quantitatively within the main trial.

Figure A14.6 Example of an 'open' question (face-to-face interview using pen and paper).

Appendix 14.7 **Questions for self-completion by the respondent**

Questionnaires can be designed for the respondent to enter their responses directly, rather than this being done by an interviewer. Figure A14.7. gives two examples.

Now we have some questions which are related to having sex. Please be as truthful as possible.
First, we would like to learn/know about the first time you had sex.

---

28. Have you ever had sex? *(tick one box)*
    - ☐ A. Yes
    - ☐ B. No

    If yes, how old were you the first time that you had sex?
    I was _____ years old when I had sex for the first time.

---

29 When you had sex for the first time, what kind of a person did you have sex with? *(tick all boxes that apply)*
    - ☐ A. He/she was a relative of mine.
    - ☐ B. He/she was a student in my school.
    - ☐ C. He/she was another person about my age.
    - ☐ D. He/she was a teacher.
    - ☐ E. He/she was another person I knew who was older than me.
    - ☐ F. He/she was a stranger.
    - ☐ Z. I have not had sex.

Note: Using a self-completion questionnaire, the respondent reads (or listens to) each question and enters the answers themselves. They can be completed, either using pen and paper or onto an electronic device such as a computer or mobile phone. They often give more valid answers than face-to-face interviews conducted by an interviewer, especially for sensitive questions like the ones in this example, which were asked of school-going adolescents. If administered on an electronic device, the questionnaire can also be 'audio-assisted' where the respondent can listen to each question and potential response being read out loud, and can have this repeated as many times as they need. If completed on pen and paper, this can also be done by having a research assistant read out each question and potential response to a group of respondents.

Figure A14.7 Example of questions for self-completion by the respondent (pen and paper).

Appendix 14.8 **Questionnaires on a mobile phone**

Increasingly, questionnaires are being designed so that the responses are recorded directly into an electronic device such as a computer (desktop, laptop, tablet), PDA, or mobile phone. This can be done either by an interviewer or the respondent themselves. An example is given in Figure A14.8., which shows photographs of mobile phone screens showing data on sexual behaviour that has been entered directly into an Android phone using Open Data Kit (ODK) software by three different trial participants.

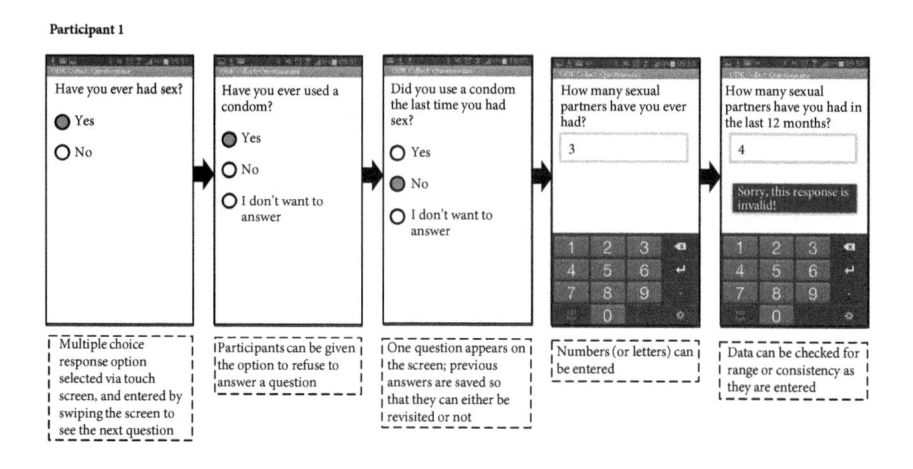

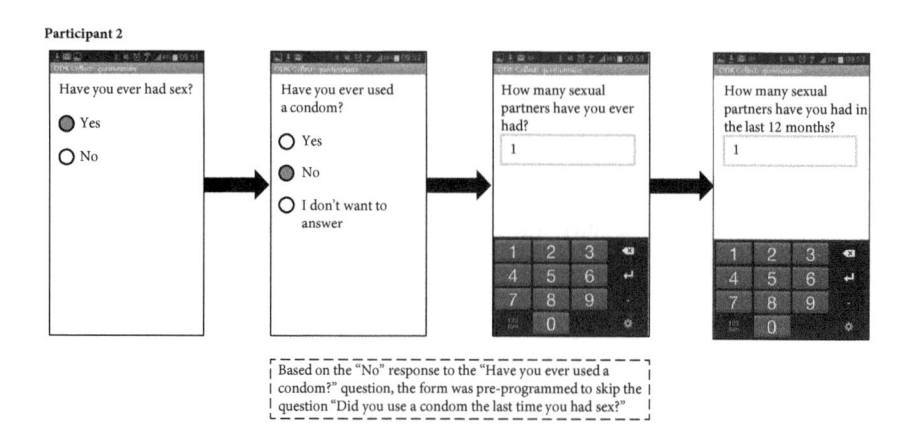

Participant 1

Screen	Content	Note
1	Have you ever had sex? ● Yes ○ No	Multiple choice response option selected via touch screen, and entered by swiping the screen to see the next question
2	Have you ever used a condom? ● Yes ○ No ○ I don't want to answer	Participants can be given the option to refuse to answer a question
3	Did you use a condom the last time you had sex? ○ Yes ● No ○ I don't want to answer	One question appears on the screen; previous answers are saved so that they can either be revisited or not
4	How many sexual partners have you ever had? 3	Numbers (or letters) can be entered
5	How many sexual partners have you had in the last 12 months? 4 — Sorry, this response is invalid!	Data can be checked for range or consistency as they are entered

Participant 2

Screen	Content
1	Have you ever had sex? ● Yes ○ No
2	Have you ever used a condom? ○ Yes ● No ○ I don't want to answer
3	How many sexual partners have you ever had? 1
4	How many sexual partners have you had in the last 12 months? 1

Based on the "No" response to the "Have you ever used a condom?" question, the form was pre-programmed to skip the question "Did you use a condom the last time you had sex?"

Participant 3

Have you ever had sex?
○ Yes
● No

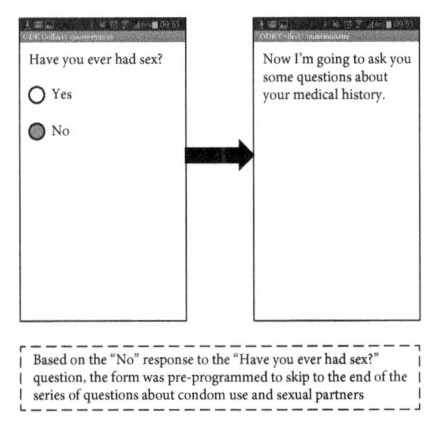

Now I'm going to ask you some questions about your medical history.

Based on the "No" response to the "Have you ever had sex?" question, the form was pre-programmed to skip to the end of the series of questions about condom use and sexual partners

Figure A14.8 Examples of questions answered directly on a mobile phone by three different study participants.

Reproduced courtesy of Zachary Kaufman and Rebecca Hershow, GOAL Trial, South Africa. This image is distributed under the terms of the Creative Commons Attribution Non Commercial 4.0 International licence (CC-BY-NC), a copy of which is available at http://creativecommons.org/licenses/by-nc/4.0/.

Appendix 14.9 Collecting geolocation data on a mobile phone

Electronic devices can be used to collect geolocation coordinates if the device has that facility. Figure A14.9. reproduces photographs of mobile phone screens showing data on the coordinates (geolocation) where a questionnaire has been completed that have been entered directly into an Android phone, using ODK software.

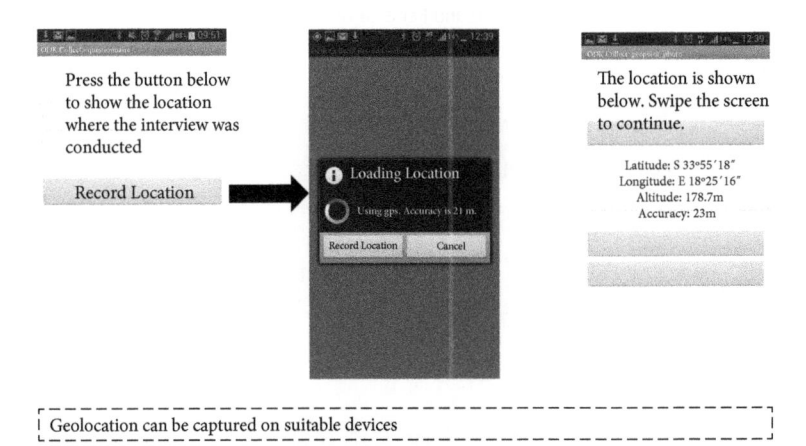

Press the button below to show the location where the interview was conducted

Record Location

Loading Location
Using gps. Accuracy is 21 m.
Record Location | Cancel

The location is shown below. Swipe the screen to continue.

Latitude: S 33°55′18″
Longitude: E 18°25′16″
Altitude: 178.7m
Accuracy: 23m

Geolocation can be captured on suitable devices

Figure A14.9 An example of collecting geolocation data on a mobile phone.

Reproduced courtesy of Zachary Kaufman and Rebecca Hershow, GOAL Trial, South Africa. This image is distributed under the terms of the Creative Commons Attribution Non Commercial 4.0 International licence (CC-BY-NC), a copy of which is available at http://creativecommons.org/licenses/by-nc/4.0/.

Appendix 14.10 **Recording a laboratory test result on a mobile phone**

Electronic devices can be used to collect photographs if the device has that facility. Figure A14.10. reproduces photographs of mobile phone screens showing a photograph of a pregnancy test result that has been taken using an Android phone which will be saved for the record.

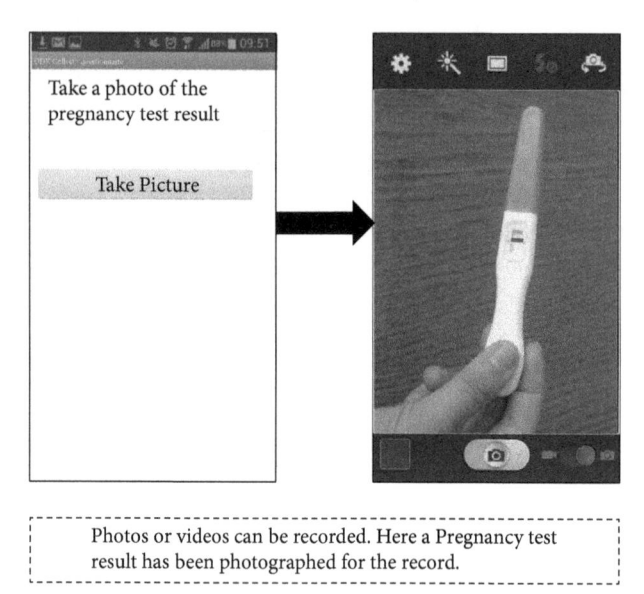

> Photos or videos can be recorded. Here a Pregnancy test result has been photographed for the record.

Figure A14.10 Example of a photograph taken with a mobile phone as part of a questionnaire.

Reproduced courtesy of Zachary Kaufman and Rebecca Hershow, GOAL Trial, South Africa. This image is distributed under the terms of the Creative Commons Attribution Non Commercial 4.0 International licence (CC-BY-NC), a copy of which is available at http://creativecommons.org/licenses/by-nc/4.0/.

Chapter 15

Social and behavioural research

1 Purposes of social and behavioural research in intervention trials 249
  1.1 Formative research to define the intervention package 250
    1.1.1 Fieldwork 251
    1.1.2 Literature review 252
    1.1.3 Developing and pilot testing intervention delivery 254
  1.2 Formative research to adapt the study protocol 255
    1.2.1 Study design and procedures 255
    1.2.2 Consent procedures and measurement tools 257
2 Social and behavioural research in evaluation 257
  2.1 Process evaluation to understand implementation 257
  2.2 Evaluation of pathways of change 259
    2.2.1 Hypothesis testing research 259
    2.2.2 Hypothesis-generating research 259
3 Commonly used methods in social research 260
  3.1 Direct observation 261
    3.1.1 Unstructured observation 262
    3.1.2 Structured observation 262
  3.2 In-depth interviews 263
  3.3 Focus group discussions 264
  3.4 Participatory research 265

1 Purposes of social and behavioural research in intervention trials

Social and behavioural research is often conducted during the design and evaluation of health interventions. In the design phase, 'formative research' is conducted in the community in which the proposed trial is to be conducted to explore the context in which the intervention will be delivered and to examine ways in which the intervention might be optimized. Examples are given later in this chapter. The outcome of such research should help define the content and delivery of the intervention package and ensure that the study protocol takes proper account of local conditions. In the evaluation phase, either during or after a trial, social and behavioural research is often used as part of a 'process evaluation' to understand aspects of the implementation of the intervention, such as in the context of intervention coverage, comparing how the intervention was supposed to be delivered, compared to how it was actually delivered, and to understand 'pathways of change' in the case of behavioural intervention trials (i.e. what the components of the intervention that led to, or did not lead to, behaviour change were).

The methods applied derive from a variety of disciplines, including anthropology, sociology, and psychology. They include both qualitative and quantitative approaches. In Section 3, we outline qualitative methods that are commonly incorporated in the design and conduct of intervention trials. Rather than detailing all possible methods, examples are given of how different methods can be used in the context of such trials.

1.1 Formative research to define the intervention package

All of the component parts of an intervention (the 'intervention package') to be tested in the field trial and the method of delivering the intervention should be clearly defined. To maximize the potential for the intervention package to be effective, it should draw on local priorities and contexts, as well as best practice from elsewhere. With the potential exception of some 'proof of concept' trials, the intervention must have the realistic prospect of being affordable, given the resources available at the household level and to the local health system, either immediately after the trial or in the foreseeable future. It must be acceptable to the community, and it must be feasible for it to be implemented by those charged with delivering the intervention in the trial (e.g. local health workers). If the intervention tested in the trial is poorly designed or does not have the potential to meet these criteria, this greatly reduces the chance that the intervention will be adopted into routine practice at the conclusion of the trial, even if it is found to be effective. To optimize evaluation methods, particularly in the context of 'complex' interventions, the intended mechanisms of effect should be clearly articulated in advance, for example, through a logic model (see Section 1.1.2).

In the context of this chapter, we use the term 'intervention package', rather than simply intervention, to emphasize that, even if the core intervention under evaluation is a single item, such as a vaccine or a drug, it will always be necessary to deliver it as part of an intervention package, which will have a number of different components that have to fit together for there to be a significant effect on the health outcomes of interest. An intervention package can be regarded as composed of the core intervention and complementary activities to promote uptake and use of the core intervention. Varying amounts and types of formative research are required, depending upon the nature of the core intervention and how fully it has already been defined. As discussed in Chapter 2, the core intervention under trial varies widely from products or technologies such as vaccines, drugs, food supplements; behaviours such as hand-washing and exclusive breastfeeding, or care seeking from a health facility in response to danger signs; different methods of delivering or managing health services, such as delivery of services through visits by community health workers to the home, rather than through visits by users of the services to a clinic or dispensary, or different methods of supervision of health workers. Whichever intervention type, it is likely that the intervention and package will require one or more components beyond the core idea or technology.

Formative research to define intervention packages typically involves fieldwork and review of the literature before an intensive period of design and pilot testing of the

1: PURPOSES OF SOCIAL AND BEHAVIOURAL RESEARCH IN INTERVENTION TRIALS | 251

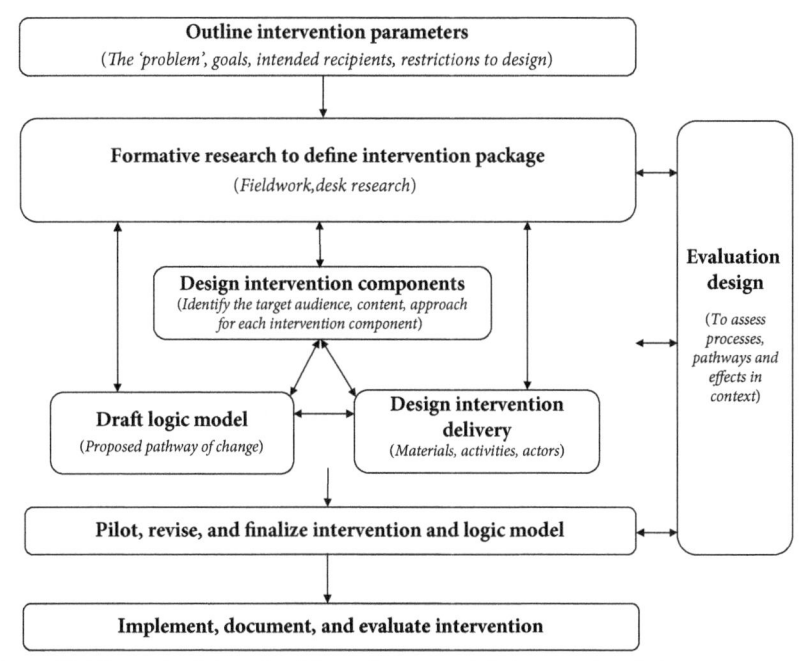

Figure 15.1 Example of the role of formative research in intervention design.

Reproduced courtesy of Claire Chandler. This image is distributed under the terms of the Creative Commons Attribution Non Commercial 4.0 International licence (CC-BY-NC), a copy of which is available at http://creativecommons.org/licenses/by-nc/4.0/.

intervention package. An example of the role of formative research in intervention design is shown in Figure 15.1, which was developed in the context of trials of the delivery of drug treatment interventions against malaria (see <http://www.actconsortium.org>).

1.1.1 Fieldwork

Formative research fieldwork aims to understand the 'problem' that will be targeted by the trial, to gain an understanding of the 'audience' for the intervention and to understand the context in which the intervention will take place. For example, the overdiagnosis of malaria by health workers has been identified as a major problem across malaria endemic countries. Prior to a trial to improve the diagnosis of fevers in northeast Tanzania, anthropological research at hospitals had described how clinicians operated through shared 'mindlines', rather than following clinical guidelines, shaped by perceived patient expectations and norms established with peers and historically in the wider medical community (Chandler et al., 2008). An intervention package designed to improve the diagnosis of malaria would require changing these norms in a manner that would not undermine clinical autonomy. The audience for the trial intervention was defined to be both clinicians and patients at dispensary level facilities. Further qualitative work was carried out with these groups to learn what existing ideas and situations supported the use of diagnostic tests and to discuss how these could be built upon to develop intervention activities and messages that would encourage a change in practice.

Table 15.1 outlines four areas for exploration in formative research: understanding the current policy and operational context of behaviour; understanding current practice in the local context; understanding current perceptions; and understanding whether the population of interest perceives a need for change, and their ideas for how this might be achieved. Each area may be explored, using different methods and with different participants.

The identification of existing practices, ideas, and scenarios upon which to build intervention design is important in formative research. Identifying only barriers to a particular health practice can be limiting in designing an effective intervention. An approach to identify existing beneficial practices is 'positive deviance inquiry', which uses multiple methods. For example, a research group may want to improve child malnutrition by promoting beneficial child feeding behaviours that exist in the community but are only practised by a minority of households. Here, the study team might identify two sets of households with similar levels of material wealth and other characteristics, but with different levels of child nutrition. A small descriptive study, including structured observation of child feeding practices and interviews of various household members, can be carried out to try to identify potentially beneficial behaviours, which might subsequently be confirmed in a larger study with a representative sample. A detailed manual of how to apply this methodology is available (<http://www.positivedeviance.org>) (Sternin et al., 1998).

An important characteristic of the core intervention to be explored at this stage may be its cost. In efficacy trials, the product or intervention is typically provided to research participants, free of change. In trials designed to mimic what might happen when an intervention is introduced into public health practice, a product may be sold to participants, at the cost users will pay when the product eventually is available through routine distribution channels. One major focus of formative research at this stage may therefore be on evaluating not only the acceptability and feasibility of use, but also the willingness to pay for the intervention (see also Chapter 19).

1.1.2 Literature review

In addition to fieldwork, the formative stage of intervention design requires review of previous work. Systematic reviews of evidence of other interventions that have been more and less successful in achieving similar objectives are recommended as a first step (see Chapter 3 and Medical Research Council, 2008). In addition, identification and specification of the theory or theories used to guide the design of the intervention and its delivery are recommended, in order to strengthen the effectiveness of the intervention, as well as to enable evaluations to contribute to wider bodies of theory about 'what works'. This is especially relevant for behavioural interventions. Care must be taken in identifying an appropriate behaviour change theory to ensure that the theory reflects well the situation found locally in formative fieldwork research. Certain cognitive-based models, such as the health belief model, that centre on replacing 'beliefs' with biomedical 'knowledge' and replacing 'myths' with 'truth' have been criticized for taking too little account of the local issues around health, care seeking, and care giving, and not relating these to their social, economic, and political contexts. Even in the absence of the explicit use of theory to guide intervention design, social

Table 15.1 Areas for exploration in formative research for the design of an intervention package to improve the diagnosis and treatment of fevers

Area of exploration	Method	Potential participants and sources	Information gathered
Understanding the context of behaviour and potential for change	In-depth interviews, desktop research	◆ Key stakeholders related to the current behaviour ◆ Policy documents ◆ Historical and anthropological reports	◆ Policy and operational influences on current practice (guidelines, supervision, in-service training) ◆ Feasibility and willingness to implement behaviour change ◆ Existing or previous interventions with similar topics or behaviours
Understanding current practices	Direct observation	◆ Families ◆ Mothers ◆ Drug sellers ◆ Policy makers	◆ How practices are enacted in context, looking at the role of spaces, time, economics, and other priorities in shaping practices
Understanding perceptions of practices	In-depth interviews	◆ Key informants ◆ Patients ◆ Health workers	◆ Prevailing perceptions of practices in the groups of interest ◆ Narratives of experiences of the group of interest, showing meaning interpreted in actions and words of selves and others, social context of behaviour of interest
Understanding priorities and logistics for change	Focus group discussions	◆ Community groups ◆ Patients ◆ Drug sellers ◆ Health workers ◆ District officials	◆ Exploration of perceived need and priorities for change ◆ Generation of ideas for intervention messages and materials ◆ Exploration of readiness for different interventions in context ◆ Identification of social and structural issues to address in a given intervention activity

Reproduced courtesy of Claire Chandler. This table is distributed under the terms of the Creative Commons Attribution Non Commercial 4.0 International licence (CC-BY-NC), a copy of which is available at http://creativecommons.org/licenses/by-nc/4.0/.

science approaches are useful in enabling depiction of the implicit pathway of change (how change will be brought about) and the hypotheses embedded within this. Such a depiction is often termed a 'logic model' or 'theory of change' or 'impact model' and can help to tighten up an intervention design as well as to identify where evaluation activities are required, in order to test hypothesized pathways of change. For a discussion of these aspects, see National Institute for Health and Clinical Excellence (2007).

Figure 15.2 shows a framework for a logic model.

Analysis of the intervention details and the context in which it is implemented is important for the proper interpretation of trial outcomes, so that the applicability of the trial results in other situations can be assessed.

1.1.3 Developing and pilot testing intervention delivery

Once the core intervention is defined, the details of the intervention's delivery require development to promote understanding, acceptance, and utilization of the core intervention, or to improve physical, financial, and cultural access to the core intervention. Details to develop and pilot-test for the effective delivery of the intervention include activities, materials, and 'purveyors' (explained in the following paragraphs).

Activities to accompany a core intervention might include the design of workshops, media spots, or engagements with opinion leaders. When the intervention to be introduced is new to the potential recipients, a small-scale pilot introduction may be carried out. This can help to refine the activities and identify needs for materials and the optimal characteristics of the purveyor(s) who will deliver different components of the intervention package. An example is a pilot feasibility study carried out in rural Zimbabwe to design an intervention to target adolescent sexual health (Power et al., 2004). Teachers were trained in four schools to deliver weekly lessons on reproductive health. Feedback and responses to the materials and delivery were gained through questionnaires, in-depth interviews, focus group discussions, and participant observation with pupils, parents, teachers, and education officers. The research found that the intervention as originally conceived was unlikely to be deliverable because the classroom was

Intervention inputs (resources and activities)	Fidelity, dose, reach of intervention	Enabling conditions	Outputs	Outcomes
Human, financial and material resources needed for the intervention. Specific activities in which the target audience (s) participate, e.g. training activities, workshops, events, requisition of supplies.	Measurable process outputs of the intervention upon which the intended mechanisms of effect rely, e.g. supplies delivered or numbers of target audience attending an event.	Factors amongst recipients and in their environment that are expected to affect the mechanism of effect of an intervention, e.g., political leadership or presence of supporting resources.	Measurable proximal outputs of intervention activities, e.g. knowledge or motivation of a direct or indirect target audience.	Changes that occur in the target audience(s), which can be proximal, e.g., drug use behaviour, patient satisfaction, or distal, e.g., community health indicators.

Figure 15.2 Framework for a logic model of an intervention's pathway of change.

not the appropriate context for delivering the intervention, the school infrastructure was not suitable to deliver the intervention materials, and existing materials were inadequate for the intervention. As a result, substantial changes were made to the design of the intervention prior to formal testing in a large community randomized trial.

Materials for the intervention delivery might include printed instructions and/or a film of how to use the product or how to perform the behaviour; vouchers to be provided to the poor who otherwise could not afford the product; materials for the channels through which the product will be sold or distributed such as pharmacies, shops, and health facilities; and print or audiovisual materials for communication activities such as radio broadcasts, protocols for community meetings, and posters. The development of these materials should draw on best practice in communication science, together with either information already gained from local formative research or participatory research at the design stage. Participatory, or 'action' research, can lead to the development of intervention materials that are more effective and acceptable to end-users. An example is the development of a treatment guideline for the effective case management of malaria in children at home by caregivers (Ajayi et al., 2009). Several forms of modified focus group discussion sessions were undertaken, with ideas depicted in illustrations by a graphic artist. The emerging guideline, in a cartoon format with a local language script, was subject to multiple rounds of pre-testing by end-users, during which edits were made to the pictures and text to increase comprehension and interpretation of the stories. Pre-testing of materials with community members is essential before finalizing them. Images, statements, and even colours can often portray different meanings to different people. To avoid misinterpretation, community members should be shown drafts of materials and systematically asked for their comprehension and interpretation of each element of a poster, video, or audio broadcast. An excellent manual for pre-testing that includes principles for clear communication has been produced for the WHO (Haaland, 2001).

Purveyors are the people who will deliver the intervention. Attention must be given to their selection, training, and supervision. These may include facility-based health workers, community health workers, traditional healers, private and informal sector providers, traditional birth attendants, women's groups, and community or religious leaders. Small-scale studies can be conducted to investigate which type of person might be the most appropriate as the purveyors of the intervention. These might be based on either discussions of hypothetical options with the potential recipients of the intervention or pilot projects to implement one or more alternative options. Examples of projects with a comprehensive package of complementary activities and people to implement these activities in the field were a programme for the social marketing of bed-nets in Tanzania (Schellenberg et al., 2001) and an education and counselling programme on exclusive breastfeeding for HIV-infected mothers in a trial in Zimbabwe (Iliff et al., 2005).

1.2 Formative research to adapt the study protocol

1.2.1 Study design and procedures

Chapter 4 describes decisions to be made regarding study design such as selection of interventions, allocation of interventions and unit of randomization, and method of implementation. Often, such decisions are made far from the study site, and they will always benefit from detailed information about the study site. Formative research conducted to inform the study design may examine different topics, including:

Selection of study site: Typically, there are a number of possible locations at which a trial may be conducted. Requirements of the trial may include enrolment of people with specific characteristics, and long-term follow-up of those enrolled in the trial. The decision on the choice of site may be informed by analysis of existing census data or other datasets, or interviews on community characteristics such as patterns of migration, economic activities, and observation of health programmes already being implemented by local organizations (see Chapter 9).

Randomization: Qualitative data can inform decisions about the unit of randomization (individual, village, cluster of villages, sub-district, etc.) and the boundaries of the units for group randomization. An understanding of the social structure and the social context of the target behaviour is useful for identifying the importance of administrative or social groups. For example, if a target behaviour is known to be habitual to a group and the intervention relies on individuals making changes as part of a group, the unit of randomization should be that group, rather than individuals within the group. Another consideration may be defining boundaries to minimize the potential for contamination, due to interactions between those assigned to different trial arms. Formative research can reveal common interactions and social and logistic boundaries.

Promotion of trial participation: Prior to the start of a trial, its usefulness and the priority given to the research question should be established from the perspective of the hosting communities. If the question or methods are not aligned with local interests, changes to the intervention or evaluation may need to be made (see Chapter 9). Once a trial is launched, it is desirable that a high proportion of those eligible to participate in the trial agree to do so when invited. A high refusal rate may jeopardize the generalizability of the trial findings or may even threaten its viability. Thus, it is important to implement activities to promote understanding and acceptance of the research activities and create the conditions under which truly informed consent is possible. These might include community meetings to discuss why certain communities or persons will receive the intervention, while others will not, and print or counselling materials to explain the risks and benefits of participation. This component may also elicit community input to improve the trial protocol itself, as occurred in the design phase of a clinical trial on the safety and efficacy of antiretroviral and nutrition interventions to reduce post-natal transmission of HIV conducted in Malawi (van der Horst et al., 2009). Qualitative studies were conducted to assess the acceptability of three alternative efficacy study designs and the feasibility of participant recruitment for such study designs.

Participatory methods can be used to engage communities in the design and implementation of the trial interventions. For example, a feasibility study for a microbicide trial in Mwanza Tanzania formed a city-level CAB, with representatives from among the potential trial participants elected from each ward. Through workshops and meetings, both with the CAB and wider groups of potential trial participants, many modifications were made to both the trial design and the study procedures. CAB members expressed concerns about the sale of blood specimens for witchcraft purposes, whether speculae for pelvic examinations would be reused and therefore be unclean, insufficient transport allowances for attending the trial assessments, and delayed reporting of laboratory test results. In response, the study team invited CAB members to observe the preparation and storage of blood specimens and the use of the autoclave in the laboratory, raised the amount for reimbursements, introduced HIV rapid testing, and accelerated the feedback of laboratory results (Shagi et al., 2008; Vallely et al., 2007).

1.2.2 Consent procedures and measurement tools

Obtaining truly informed consent for participation in an intervention trial is very challenging. The researcher's perception of an intervention and its possible beneficial and adverse effects may be very different from those of potential trial participants. Social science investigations conducted in the trial community, prior to designing the informed consent procedures, may give the investigator a much better understanding of how the community is likely to view the proposed trial and will inform the ways in which the trial should be presented to potential participants to facilitate their understanding of both the potential risks and potential benefits and of why the trial is being conducted. Issues around informed consent are discussed further in Chapter 6, Section 2.4.

Social and behavioural research methods can also help inform the design of quantitative outcome measures for the trial. Tasks include formulation of questions and definition of appropriate forms of measurement. Some trials make the mistake of measuring outcomes through open questions, thinking that closed questions introduce bias. In addition to the fact that post-coding of open questions is very time-consuming (see Chapter 20), problems caused by incomplete responses to open questions may outweigh the limitations of closed questions. Also, open questions have lower test–retest reliability, leading to difficulties when pre–post comparisons are made. Nichter et al. (2002) outline a systematic process for informing the design of survey instruments through formative research.

2 Social and behavioural research in evaluation

Social and behavioural research conducted during and after the trial may facilitate understanding and interpretation of the trial results. Two methodological approaches for this purpose are process evaluation (process documentation, process learning) and evaluation of pathways of change.

2.1 Process evaluation to understand implementation

Process evaluation is a term applied to a range of data collection activities conducted during the implementation of a trial to assess, at a minimum, whether the intervention is being implemented according to the study protocol. This is important to document and report, in order to determine whether an intervention's apparent success or failure is attributable to the intervention's concept or theory or to the way it was implemented.

Table 15.2 shows six aspects of process evaluation that have been described by Saunders et al. (2005) to guide data collection activities.

Each of the intervention components and its delivery methods should be subject to a process evaluation, resulting in the documentation of the six aspects in Table 15.2. Data collection may be quantitative, such as the number of subjects who receive an information leaflet, or qualitative such as perceptions of the political agenda behind an information leaflet that affects the 'dose received' of a particular message. Data may be collected through self-completion questionnaires, for example, by trainers who can record the amount of content actually delivered, the relative participation of different members of the group, and their impressions of the level of understanding for the various objectives of the training. Direct observations of activities can also provide an assessment of how well a particular intervention activity was delivered and can provide interpretations of the delivery in context, for example, to note other activities or events occurring at the same time that could support, or conflict with, the trial intervention. Interviews may also be used with both purveyors and intended recipients to understand what was delivered and what was received, and to give an understanding of why some aspects of an intervention may have been more effective than others. The data

Table 15.2 Six dimensions of process evaluation

Fidelity (quality)	The extent to which the intervention was implemented, as planned
Dose delivered (completeness)	Amount or number of intended units of each intervention or component of the intervention that were delivered
Dose received (exposure or adherence)	Extent to which participants actively engage with, interact with, are receptive to, and/or use materials or recommended resources. Can include initial and continued use
Reach (participation rate or coverage)	Proportion of subjects who receive or participate in the intervention; includes documentation of barriers to participation
Recruitment and retention	Procedures used to approach and attract participants at individual or organizational levels; includes maintenance of participant involvement in the intervention
Context	Aspects of the environment that may influence intervention implementation or study outcomes

Adapted with permission from Saunders, R. P. et al., Developing a process-evaluation plan for assessing health promotion program implementation: a how-to guide, *Health Promotion Practice*, Volume 6, Number 2, pp. 134–47, Copyright © 2005 by Society for Public Health Education. Includes data from Steckler, A. and Linnan, L., pp. 1–24, in A. Steckler and L. Linnan (Eds.), *Process evaluation for public health interventions and Research*, Jossey-Bass, San Francisco, USA, Copyright © 2002 by John Wiley & Sons; and Baranowski, T. and Stables, G., Process evaluations of the 5-a-day projects, *Health Education and Behavior*, Volume 27, Number 2, pp. 157–166, Copyright © 2002 by Society for Public Health Education. This table is not covered by the Creative Commons licence terms of this publication. For permission to reuse please contact the rights holder.

collected can be used in the interpretation of the final trial outcomes. The data can be incorporated into final analyses quantitatively, for example, in dose–response or per protocol analyses. The qualitative data can also be used to interpret what any change may be attributable to, in terms of the intervention delivered and received.

Process evaluation can also identify difficulties with implementation that occurred and how these difficulties were addressed.

2.2 Evaluation of pathways of change

In the evaluation of pathways of change, which is particularly relevant for behavioural interventions or multi-component interventions, the researcher aims to establish the relationship between any changes detected in trial outcome data and the intervention package, taking into account contextual factors that may have shaped the intervention and outcome variables. The objectives of an evaluation of pathways of change are to establish plausibility that outcomes are attributable to the intervention and to depict the mechanisms by which an intervention had effect, including identification of contextual factors considered significant in supporting these mechanisms. Two approaches can be taken to understanding pathways of change: hypothesis testing and hypothesis generating. These approaches are complementary and should be considered together to maximize understanding of the trial and generalizability of the results.

2.2.1 Hypothesis testing research

The hypothesis testing approach relies on prior specification of the intended pathway of change, for example, through a logic model. Steps along the pathway can be identified, and the relationships between these steps tested. For example, a multi-component trial in Uganda to enhance the quality of care at rural health facilities included a workshop series on patient-centred services. The hypothesized pathway of change was that health workers would attend the workshops and participate in individual reflection, conceptualization, experimentation, group reflection, and planning in the workshops; would feel motivated and able to change their practice; health worker interactions with care seekers would be more patient-centred; care seekers would detect, and be more satisfied with, this style of communication; and community members would subsequently be more attracted to attending the enhanced health facilities. The study included a process evaluation to document the attendance, participation, and learning, followed by a pathway evaluation to assess communication between health workers and care seekers using audio recordings, care seeker satisfaction with their interactions with health workers, and logs of attendance at health facilities (Chandler et al., 2013a).

2.2.2 Hypothesis-generating research

A hypothesis-generating approach intends to understand 'what happened' from the perspective of the target population, from the time of intervention delivery to outcome evaluation activities. Here, unintended pathways of change can be captured, together with information on factors that affect the delivery, uptake, and use of an intervention in practice, as well as factors that may influence the outcomes of interest in the trial. Unstructured methods are best suited to this task to enable the research team to discover findings that may not have been hypothesized or depicted in the logic model. Project ethnography is one methodological approach to capture what actually happened. Here, an anthropologist, or someone similarly trained, carries out detailed participant observation, for example, working alongside the intervention implementation team for the trial, or even as a member of that team. Analysis of the in-depth data from these observations can provide insights into why and how members of the target community took up, adapted, or ignored different intervention components. Project ethnography can capture interpersonal relationships and power dynamics among the multiple actors involved and provide insights that would have ordinarily been missed. Evans and Lambert (2008) provide an excellent example of the value of project ethnography in illuminating key factors in the successful implementation of an intervention related to HIV. Other methods include in-depth interviews and focus group discussions with implementers, stakeholders, and the target population.

Further information and examples about using social research to carry out formative studies and evaluations of pathways of change in LMICs can be found at <http://www.actconsortium.org/qualitativemethodsguidance>.

3 Commonly used methods in social research

Qualitative research methods commonly used in field trials of health interventions include direct observation, interviews with key informants, focus group discussions, and participatory methods. These relatively open-ended techniques are suitable for exploring how an intervention might be perceived, the priorities of different members of the community, and ways that people view a trial from the perspective of potential participants. These methods are used to provide information relevant to devising intervention components, such as communication strategies, as well as devising trial methods, for example, to ensure recruitment and designing effective and appropriate data collection instruments.

The aim of qualitative research is to understand the perspectives of specific groups of individuals. In doing this, researchers are attempting to learn about the social worlds in which others live: their experiences with specific issues, their points of reference around particular topics, and broader factors that shape these, from local to global, historical, and political economic factors. When studying the world from a social perspective, it is recognized that what people say and do is contingent on the scenario in which words are being spoken and the action taken. Qualitative research attempts to make sense of, or interpret, phenomena in terms of the meanings people bring to them, and qualitative research practice recognizes the role of the researcher in bringing out these meanings. Key concerns in qualitative research are therefore how best to interpret perspectives of others and how to integrate into analyses the subjective nature of this interpretation. Both of these issues are relevant in research to guide intervention development, as well as to evaluate trial outcomes.

When considering methods to interpret others' perspectives, most qualitative research embraces the following four concepts: *explorative flexibility, iteration, triangulation*, and *contextualization*. Although the researcher has specific topics to be explored, it is assumed that new questions will emerge frequently, as the research progresses. Specific techniques and associated data collection methods are refined and modified throughout the research process. A *flexible* approach is adopted whereby unanticipated findings are explored, as new lines of inquiry develop, unproductive forms of data collection are dropped, and new methods developed, without losing sight of the original research objectives. There is an emphasis on in-depth investigation. The same or different key informants and other respondents may be interviewed repeatedly, with each new interview building upon the previous one with increasing refinement and focus. This *iterative* process applies not only to specific methods, but also to the qualitative research process as a whole. Multiple fieldwork strategies may be employed, including one-to-one conversation, as in key informant interviewing, group discussions, and direct observations of actual behaviour. The use of multiple methods in conjunction, or *triangulation*, adds depth to an inquiry of the phenomenon in question. Rather than being a strategy for validation, triangulation adds richness and breadth, enabling a more rigorous exploration of the complexity of a phenomenon, through its multiple representations. Qualitative research may be used to help researchers understand the social, cultural, historic, political, and economic context within which an intervention trial will be conducted. Such *contextualization* is particularly valuable during the initial planning phases and also to help understand unexpected trial findings.

When considering how to integrate the subjective nature of interpretation into analyses, the concept of *reflexivity* is crucial to qualitative research. This requires that the researcher explicitly acknowledges his or her motivations and theoretical positions in relation to a piece of research and makes an effort to reflect and articulate these in decisions made in fieldwork and interpretations. For example, if a researcher feels alignment with ideals of market-led provision of health care, this may affect the way in which they ask questions and interpret responses, which can impact the shape of an intervention developed and the way a trial outcome is interpreted. Being reflexive about political, economic, and theoretical agendas underlying one's own motives for, or implementation of, the research can allow greater transparency, as well as the opportunity to challenge and reconsider these perspectives. Methods for attaining a reflexive stance include keeping reflexive diaries and field-notes and discussing decisions reflexively as a team. This approach has been proposed to be extended beyond qualitative activities to trial conduct in general to promote transparency and encourage more realistic accounts of trial contexts that are often in flux, allowing anticipation of barriers to recruitment and potential sources of bias which can be addressed in trial activities or analyses (Wells et al., 2012).

We have outlined some of the principal qualitative social science research methods. More detailed descriptions of the main qualitative research methods are given by Kielmann et al. (2011) and Bryman (2012). Chandler et al. (2013b) have also produced a compilation of guidance for carrying out qualitative research in the context of health interventions and provide a parallel protocol template document which includes example topic guides and standard operating procedures (SOPs) and a set of training materials for field teams (<http://www.actconsortium.org/resources.php/72/qualitative-methods-for-international-health-intervention-research>).

3.1 Direct observation

Direct observation includes both unstructured and structured observations. These methods are useful for learning about the everyday context relevant to an intervention.

Spending an extended time observing these enables the researcher to appreciate the factors that may be relevant to an intervention, in relation to other priorities in the community and activities and concerns of the group of interest. This may be important for both the development of appropriate interventions and in the interpretation of trial outcomes.

3.1.1 Unstructured observation

Unstructured observation is the cornerstone of ethnography, the classical methodology of anthropology. Ethnographers often undertake *participant observation* when they endeavour to become a functioning member of a community and engage in local activities, watching carefully what others do and how they react to the ethnographer's own behaviour. The purpose is to attempt to view the community from the perspective of a participating member, rather than as an outsider. In many situations, *non-participant observation* is more feasible and can allow for a more systematic description of activities, in which the observer is not directly part of the activity under study. Non-participant observations may concentrate on an individual (for example, a pregnant woman), location (such as the kitchen or a water collection site), or event (for example, a wedding party or a market). The observer attempts to record as much behaviour as possible, including actions, conversations, description of the physical locale, and other relevant features. Focused observations often require some preliminary examination of the activity or location to prepare the observer. For example, the investigator may have a general impression of the interior of a rural house but may not know the kind and quantity of cooking utensils, nor how they are washed or stored. Some research questions require detailed observations on how a procedure is actually carried out. For example, how a mother mixes water with rehydration salts at home for the treatment of diarrhoea or how a health worker interacts with a client and/or carries out a medical procedure. Such observations may be used in the design of questionnaires and to confirm or refine data collected through interviews.

Unstructured observational activities are often carried out together with informal and formal interviews and group discussions. Observations and reviews of discussions are typically recorded in detailed field-notes, following the activity. Analysis is ongoing, often involving a daily review and reflection on occurrences and the way they have been interpreted by the ethnographer. Unstructured observation can be useful at all stages of the research relating to a trial, for example, in understanding how guidelines are used in practice by health workers, in preparation for, or the evaluation of, an intervention to improve clinical practice relating to a particular guideline such as treatment with antimalarial drugs or antibiotics. The rate-limiting step is often the availability of trained researchers to carry out such activities and ongoing analyses.

3.1.2 Structured observation

Structured observations involve the recording of behaviours or the outcomes of behaviours by trained observers, through the use of a pre-coded or partly coded data collection instrument. Structured observation methods can be used for continuous monitoring or for spot checks on a behaviour. These approaches are used when the behaviours that are to be studied in detail have been identified (possibly through unstructured observation), and it is clear what information is needed (for example, time of day, frequency, duration, and types of behaviour).

The researcher observes, as unobtrusively as possible, occurrences of events or behaviours. A dilemma faced by every observer is where to focus attention and what details to record. The data collection instruments are designed to help focus the researcher's attention on matters of greatest relevance to the research question. Predetermined structure limits discovery but assures relevance and consistency. The complexity of structured observation instruments varies. Some studies focus on detailed description of one or two events of interest, breaking them into fine units of activities, noting who performs them where, with what tools, and for how long, as was done in a study of hand-washing practices in Bangladesh reported by Stanton and Clemens (1987). Structured observations can form part of larger ethnographic studies, which has the advantage that the findings can be interpreted in the wider social context, enabling a more careful interpretation to feed into behaviour change interventions. For example, Chandler et al. (2008) conducted an ethnographic study of health workers' treatment of malaria, incorporating structured observations of clinical consultations within a wider study of the over-diagnosis of malaria in Tanzania, informing the design of interventions tested in a 3-arm cluster randomized trial. Unlike most methods described in this chapter, structured observation may yield data amenable to statistical analysis. This holds potential for repeated observations to monitor behaviour change over time.

3.2 In-depth interviews

In-depth interviews usually aim to get a comprehensive understanding of a participant's perspective, in their own words, of the issues under study. Such interviews may take a narrative approach whereby the interviewer aims to hear the 'story' of the participant in a historical perspective, probing for more detail on areas of interest to the research, for example, access to maternal health care services. In-depth interviews may also be used to explore individuals' ideas and concepts about particular issues, with the interviewer asking questions relating to specific topics identified as being of interest to the research objective. In both cases, a topic guide or list of questions may be used, as an aide-memoire, and may include specific questions that have been pilot-tested. The objective is to use this guide to explore the experiences and perspectives of each respondent, as they feel able and willing to explain themselves. Thinking of relevant and useful probing questions is an important skill for the interviewer who must bear in mind the research objective, while engaging with, and pursuing, trains of thought of respondents. They must be able to use new pieces of information to take the interview in previously unplanned, but relevant, directions. A further key skill in interviewing is the ability to create rapport and ensure confidentiality, such that the respondent feels comfortable and confident in expressing their views and experiences.

In-depth interviews take significant time to set up, carry out, transcribe (and translate), and interpret. This means they can usually only be conducted with a few carefully selected individuals. Depending on the objectives of the study, respondents for in-depth interviews may be 'key informants' or individuals selected as representing particular characteristics of interest (for example, mothers who have lost a child, migrants). Key informants, in the context of intervention trials, tend to be of three types: administrators/community leaders or other persons in positions of power, community-based health workers, and individuals in the community with specialized areas of expertise or experience (for example, traditional birth attendants, traditional healers). Key informants are identified through casual inquiry of formal and informal leaders and other pivotal community members, or through more systematic methods such as consensus analysis or social network analysis (Bernard and Ryan, 2010). Informants become 'key', because they are more knowledgeable, co-operative, and accessible than other respondents and often are interviewed on multiple occasions. They serve to inform the investigator about selected aspects of the culture and customs of a community and may be used to provide information throughout the course of the study.

3.3 Focus group discussions

Focus group discussions are a useful method for getting to know shared values and points of reference. Focus groups can also be a good opportunity to generate and test out initial ideas for an intervention, with the ability for group members to offer, modify, or reject ideas for introducing changes relevant to a particular health problem.

In a focus group discussion, a small group of participants (usually six to 12), under the guidance of a facilitator, are encouraged to talk about topics which are thought to be of special importance to the respondents and to the investigation. Topic guides are utilized by the facilitator to stimulate discussions around areas of interest. Participants are selected from specific target groups whose ideas and experiences are germane to the study. Participants in a focus group are best chosen to avoid power differentials that could lead to some individuals dominating the discussion. Generally, participants are of the same sex and age group, but similarity in other characteristics may be important, depending upon the research question. For example, in the case of an evaluation of a trial to improve maternal health services, participants may include those who took up the intervention and those who did not, but they should not also include the health workers (whether from the formal or informal sector) who provide such services. It is important, but difficult, to ensure that participants are comfortable with one another, which may mean a natural grouping, such as a village microfinance group of women which may or may not be desirable as a sampling unit, depending upon the research question and the potential for divulgence of confidential information during the discussion.

For discussions to be productive, the facilitator must have skills in understanding and encouraging positive group dynamics and must be able to keep in mind the research objectives, in order to steer the discussion to maximize time spent on matters that may be relevant to the research question. In addition to the facilitator, it is useful to have an observer who makes notes and is alert for non-verbal cues. This observer may also collect demographic data from participants and ensure they receive refreshments. If possible, a focus group discussion should be tape-recorded and later transcribed in full. However, if it is thought that this would unduly inhibit open discussion, detailed notes should be taken by the observer as close to verbatim as possible.

The number of focus groups held will depend on the number of different relevant groups in the community of interest. Focus group sessions usually last for at least an hour and continue until the facilitator considers that all the participants have expressed their opinions adequately on the topics under investigation. Transcribing and translating focus group discussions can take a considerable amount of time, with transcripts typically running to 50–100 pages. Coding and analysis of such transcripts takes a correspondingly long time. To make the most of this method, it is therefore important to think carefully about sampling, the topics for discussion, and the facilitator's level of experience and familiarity with the research questions.

3.4 Participatory research

Participatory research methods aim to enable change at a local level through a process of sequential reflection and action carried out with and by local people. This is distinct from the other methods outlined in this chapter, which, in a general sense, can be considered to be carried out 'on people.' In participatory research, the focus is on basing research and planning on local knowledge and perspectives, situating power more evenly between researchers and the researched. In their purest form, participatory, or 'action', research approaches do not start out with a specific intervention in mind but aim to respond to local priorities and needs, and aim to empower local bodies to define and develop their own interventions. This is done through a series of facilitated discussions, workshops, planning sessions, and activities. In health research, a number of trials have adopted a form of this approach, by providing a structure within which local actors can define their priorities and intervention methods. An example is the Health Workers for Change programme, a series of six workshops which aimed to address the interpersonal component of quality of care by enabling participants to explore provider–client relations within a gender-sensitive context. This programme was implemented and evaluated in four country contexts, in each of which the intervention played out differently guided by the local participants, and was found to allow difficult issues to be discussed openly, fostered problem solving, and helped health workers to develop practical plans to address problems that could strengthen district health systems (Fonn et al., 2001).

References

Ajayi, I. O., Oladepo, O., Falade, C. O., Bamgboye, E. A., and Kale, O. 2009. The development of a treatment guideline for childhood malaria in rural Southwest Nigeria using participatory approach. *Patient Education and Counseling*, 75, 227–37.

Bernard, H. R. and Ryan, G. W. 2010. *Analyzing qualitative data: systematic approaches*. Los Angeles: SAGE.

Bryman, A. 2012. *Social research methods*. Oxford: Oxford University Press.

Chandler, C. I., Diliberto, D., Nayiga, S., et al. 2013a. The PROCESS study: a protocol to evaluate the implementation, mechanisms of effect and context of an intervention to enhance public health centres in Tororo, Uganda. *Implementation Science*, 8, 113.

Chandler, C. I., Jones, C., Boniface, G., Juma, K., Reyburn, H., and Whitty, C. J. 2008. Guidelines and mindlines: why do clinical staff over-diagnose malaria in Tanzania? A qualitative study. *Malaria Journal*, 7, 53.

Chandler, C. I. R., Reynolds, J. L., Palmer, J., and Hutchinson, E. 2013b. *ACT Consortium guidance: qualitative methods for international health intervention research*. Available at: <http://www.actconsortium.org/qualitativemethodsguidance>.

Evans, C. and Lambert, H. 2008. Implementing community interventions for HIV prevention: insights from project ethnography. *Social Science & Medicine*, **66**, 467–78.

Fonn, S., Mtonga, A. S., Nkoloma, H. C., et al. 2001. Health providers' opinions on provider-client relations: results of a multi-country study to test Health Workers for Change. *Health Policy Plan*, **16** Suppl 1, 19–23.

Haaland, A. 2001. *Reporting with pictures. A concept paper for researchers and health policy decision-makers* [Online]. Geneva: UNDP/World Bank/WHO Special Programme for Research and Training in Tropical Diseases. Available at: <http://www.who.int/tdr/publications/documents/pictures.pdf>.

Iliff, P. J., Piwoz, E. G., Tavengwa, N. V., et al. 2005. Early exclusive breastfeeding reduces the risk of postnatal HIV-1 transmission and increases HIV-free survival. *AIDS*, **19**, 699–708.

Kielmann, K., Cataldo, F., and Seeley, J. 2011. *Introduction to qualitative research methodology* [Online]. London: Department for International Development. Available at: <http://r4d.dfid.gov.uk/PDF/Outputs/HIV_AIDS/qualitativeresearchmethodologymanual.pdf>.

Medical Research Council. 2008. *Developing and evaluating complex interventions: new guidance* [Online]. London: Medical Research Council. Available at: <http://www.mrc.ac.uk/complexinterventionsguidance>.

National Institute for Health and Clinical Excellence. 2007. *Behaviour change at population, community and individual levels* [Online]. London: National Institute for Health and Clinical Excellence. Available at: <http://www.ncsct.co.uk/usr/pub/guidance-on-behaviour-change-at-population.pdf>.

Nichter, M., Thompson, P. J., Shiffman, S., and Moscicki, A. B. 2002. Using qualitative research to inform survey development on nicotine dependence among adolescents. *Drug and Alcohol Dependence*, **68** (Suppl), S41–S56.

Power, R., Langhaug, L. F., Nyamurera, T., Wilson, D., Bassett, M. T., and Cowan, F. M. 2004. Developing complex interventions for rigorous evaluation—a case study from rural Zimbabwe. *Health Education Research*, **19**, 570–5.

Saunders, R. P., Evans, M. H., and Joshi, P. 2005. Developing a process-evaluation plan for assessing health promotion program implementation: a how-to guide. *Health Promotion Practice*, **6**, 134–47.

Schellenberg, J. R., Abdulla, S., Nathan, R., et al. 2001. Effect of large-scale social marketing of insecticide-treated nets on child survival in rural Tanzania. *Lancet*, **357**, 1241–7.

Shagi, C., Vallely, A., Kasindi, S., et al.; Microbicides Development Programme. 2008. A model for community representation and participation in HIV prevention trials among women who engage in transactional sex in Africa. *AIDS Care*, **20**, 1039–49.

Stanton, B. F. and Clemens, J. D. 1987. An educational intervention for altering water-sanitation behaviors to reduce childhood diarrhea in urban Bangladesh. II. A randomized trial to assess the impact of the intervention on hygienic behaviors and rates of diarrhea. *American Journal of Epidemiology*, **125**, 292–301.

Sternin, M., Sternin, J., and Marsh, D. R. 1998. *Designing a community-based nutrition program using the Hearth model and the positive deviance approach* [Online]. Westport, CT: Save the Children. Available at: <http://www.positivedeviance.org/pdf/manuals/fieldguide.pdf>.

Vallely, A., Shagi, C., Kasindi, S., *et al.*; Microbicides Development Programme. 2007. The benefits of participatory methodologies to develop effective community dialogue in the context of a microbicide trial feasibility study in Mwanza, Tanzania. *BMC Public Health*, **7**, 133.

Van Der Horst, C., Chasela, C., Ahmed, Y., *et al.*; Breastfeeding, Antiretroviral, and Nutrition Study Team. 2009. Modifications of a large HIV prevention clinical trial to fit changing realities: a case study of the Breastfeeding, Antiretroviral, and Nutrition (BAN) protocol in Lilongwe, Malawi. *Contemporary Clinical Trials*, **30**, 24–33.

Wells, M., Williams, B., Treweek, S., Coyle, J., and Taylor, J. 2012. Intervention description is not enough: evidence from an in-depth multiple case study on the untold role and impact of context in randomised controlled trials of seven complex interventions. *Trials*, **13**, 95.

Chapter 16

Field organization and ensuring data of high quality

1 Introduction to field organization and ensuring data of high quality 268
2 Manual of field operations and study diary 273
3 Personnel issues 273
4 Physical location and facilities 276
5 Equipment and supplies 277
6 Timetable for field activities 279
7 Ensuring data of high quality 279
    7.1 Regulatory requirements and good clinical practice 280
    7.2 Supervision and data checks 281

1 Introduction to field organization and ensuring data of high quality

The complexity of the organization of a field trial will vary, according to the planned size of the trial population, the frequency of follow-up, the expected duration of the trial, and its location. For example, a trial of the long-term effects of a hepatitis B vaccine in The Gambia involved enrolling a population of 120 000 infants, many of whom lived in remote rural areas, and linking their vaccination status to outcome events measured several decades later (The Gambia Hepatitis Study Group, 1987; van der Sande et al., 2007). Such a trial is a much more complex undertaking than, say, a trial to assess the immunogenicity of a new measles vaccine, involving a few hundred subjects, conducted in or near a major population centre and completed within a year or two.

Whether a trial is small or large, it is important to plan the organization of the trial in detail before starting any substantial field activities. The design of the trial should be reviewed to identify all the procedures and tasks that it is necessary to undertake to meet the study objectives, and the logistics developed to carry out these procedures and tasks in a timely fashion. During this planning, it may become clear that compromises have to be made between what is theoretically desirable and what is logistically possible. For example, in a vaccine trial, it may be of great interest to relate the immune response to vaccination to subsequent protection against disease on an individual-by-individual basis. This would involve collecting a blood sample from all participants before vaccination, shortly after vaccination, and possibly at repeated intervals thereafter. In practice, it may not be feasible to do this in the full trial population, for reasons of cost or because those in the trial population would not accept repeated blood samples being taken. Thus, relating protection against disease to individual responses to vaccination might have to be excluded from the objectives or restricted to a substudy in selected trial participants.

A checklist of some of the most important items that it may be necessary to consider when planning a field trial is given in Box 16.1. Trial investigators should draw up a detailed and specific list tailored to the requirements of their particular trial.

It is important that the field team understands, and is sensitive to, local customs and cultures. This will be facilitated if many of the field team members are recruited from the community in which the trial is to be conducted. The planning for the trial must take into account cultural practices that may affect both the acceptability of the trial and the organizational arrangements for conducting it.

In planning the organization of the trial, it is critical to always keep in mind the overall objectives of the trial, as specified in the study protocol. Detailed planning should start at an early stage, as, once activities get under way, it is easy to 'lose sight of the wood for the trees', unless there is a clear plan of activities to refer to. A checklist that covers some of the most important organizational aspects of field trials is given in Box 16.2.

Box 16.1 A checklist for planning a field trial

1 Proposed trial
- Title
- Purpose
- Type
- Population included: location and numbers involved
- Expected duration of trial
- Persons in charge: both central and field
- Address, phone/fax numbers, website, and e-mail addresses of trial headquarters
- Initiate a field manual and study diary to record all decisions and changes made during planning and conduct of trial (see Section 2)

2 Clearances: legal and ethical
- Local authority (district health officers, local government)
- Police

2 Clearances: legal and ethical (cont.)
- Government—MOH—others, as appropriate
- Local population—informed consent procedures

3 Location
- Climate
- Geographical features
- Maps
- Roads, including routes, distance, and time taken to travel between survey sites in different road conditions
- River conditions
- Airstrips (where relevant)
- Electricity supply
- Mobile phone network coverage
- Internet access

> **Box 16.1 A checklist for planning a field trial (continued)**
>
> 4 Data collection and storage
>   - Type
>   - Regularity
>   - Timing
>   - Method of data collection (for example, pen and paper, electronic)
>   - Logistics
>
> 5 Staff requirements
>   - Functional categories
>   - Number
>   - Existing/new staff
>   - Training and support/supervision requirements
>
> 6 Accommodation
>   - Location (survey team, support group, females/males)
>   - Tents/housing arrangements
>   - Electricity
>   - Water
>
> 7 Supplies
>   - Immediate
>   - Replenishments
>   - Stockpile
>   - Ordering and recording systems
>   - Food/cooking
>   - Water/purification
>   - Fuel (vehicles, electricity generators, cooking, etc.)
>   - Refrigeration
>
> 8 Transportation
>   - Vehicles (for example, cars, motorbikes, bicycles, boats)
>   - Maintenance
>   - Tools (for repairs, but also for digging them out of mud holes, and for emergencies—such as reflective vests and emergency triangles)
>   - Spares
>
> 9 Equipment
>   - Field
>   - Laboratory
>   - Survey equipment
>   - Record forms
>   - Questionnaires
>   - Computer hardware
>   - Computer software
>   - Stationery
>   - Chemicals
>   - Generator
>   - Waterproofing
>   - Photographic equipment
>   - GPS equipment
>   - Electronic data collection equipment (PDAs, tablet computers, mobile phones, etc.)
>   - Tape recorders
>   - Mobile phones
>   - Backup generators (and backups for other vital equipment)
>   - Medical care for staff (for example, drugs and instructions for needle-stick injuries)
>   - Medicines and drugs for participants
>   - Records
>   - Other equipment
>
> 10 Specimens
>   - Receipt and handling (for example, gloves, sharps disposal boxes)
>   - Pick-up schedules
>   - Refrigeration containers
>   - Instruction slips for participants
>   - Labelling and other recording supplies

> **Box 16.1 A checklist for planning a field trial (continued)**
>
> 11 Other
> - Develop field manual
> - Data entry equipment, staff, and systems
> - Other communication equipment (for example, email, Internet, radio)
>
> 11 Other (cont.)
> - Written SOPs for every aspect of the trial
> - Job descriptions, staff contracts, and a human resource manual
> - Bank and accounting systems

> **Box 16.2 A checklist of organizational activities for a field trial**
>
> The activities are listed in the order in which they might be done.
>
> ### Planning
>
> - Define the trial question(s), and work out the implications of these for the planning of the trial.
> - Develop the preliminary study design that includes the purpose and estimates of population size and duration of the trial.
> - Consult with MOH officials at headquarters and district levels.
> - Consult those with relevant experience in local district government, community leaders, and health workers.
> - Visit local communities to discuss the trial, and learn about the local population, their needs and perceptions, and how the proposed trial would fit into their priorities.
> - Choose an appropriate population sample for the trial.
> - Decide which observations and measurements are needed, and standardize the techniques.
> - Conduct preliminary studies (for example, qualitative, feasibility, or validation studies).
> - Design and pilot-test record forms and questionnaires (electronic and/or paper).
> - Make arrangements for staff recruitment, training, and supervision; secure equipment, transport, and finance; arrange accommodation.
>
> ### Organization
>
> - Obtain co-operation from local leaders.
> - Develop a manual of field operations and all specific SOPs.

> **Box 16.2 A checklist of organizational activities for a field trial (continued)**
>
> - Train survey staff.
> - Arrange for laboratory procedures and specimen storage, both short- and long-term.
> - Draw up a daily work plan for all staff.
> - Pilot-test all organizational details.
>
> ### During the fieldwork
>
> - Supervise and provide feedback to all staff to ensure their work is at a high standard throughout.
> - Monitor participant compliance and follow-up with representatives of the trial participants and local leaders if there are problems.
> - Make both scheduled and unscheduled checks on all study procedures.
> - Conduct regular staff meetings for reporting progress, discussion of problems and potential solutions, and for maintenance of morale.
>
> ### Analysis and communications
>
> - At an early stage, develop an analytical plan for each phase or round of data collection, and for the trial as a whole.
> - Enter data into a computer, and then check and analyse it as soon as possible.
> - Make regular checks on the data, preferably daily, to assess quality and completeness.
> - Discuss results and their interpretation with health workers, community leaders, or others (as appropriate) to obtain their feedback and comments.
> - Write a report, incorporating comments on the trial's strengths and limitations, its results, and recommendations for new or improved health programmes.
> - Distribute the report, and discuss the trial's findings and recommendations with relevant local authorities, other organizations, and with local and international media, as appropriate.
> - Disseminate the trial results and policy implications, using multiple dissemination channels—not just the main technical report. The audiences should include study participants and/or their representatives locally, nationally, and internationally, as appropriate, for example, through meetings, newsletters, press releases and/or radio programmes, peer-reviewed journal articles, policy briefs, on the organization's website, presentations at conferences, etc.

> **Box 16.2 A checklist of organizational activities for a field trial (continued)**
>
> - Take steps to try to ensure that appropriate action is taken, based on the trial's outcomes, at international, national, and local levels.
> - Consider evaluating any changes introduced as a result of the trial to estimate their effectiveness.

2 Manual of field operations and study diary

The tasks and procedures necessary to achieve each objective of a trial should be listed. A manual of field operations should be prepared, in which each procedure to be carried out is detailed and each task described fully (for example, step-by-step instructions for the administration and completion of questionnaires, the method to be used for weighing infants, including maintenance procedures for the weighing scales, checklists for equipment, and the materials required for each procedure). Each fieldworker should be given a copy of the manual, or of those parts of the manual that are relevant to their work, and these must be updated if changes are made to procedures, as the trial progresses. The field manual for the trial should not only provide a clear set of rules for actions under different circumstances, but it can also serve as a long-term record of the detailed design aspects of the trial. This latter feature may be of special value in trials of long duration where investigators may change or they may forget previous decisions or the reasons for them.

In addition to the field manual, it is very valuable to maintain a trial diary, in which the progress of the trial is recorded, problems noted, and solutions recorded. This will be useful in maintaining consistency of decisions throughout the trial. These notes may be of value for final reports on the trial, in which documentation of particular events during the course of the trial may be needed (for example, recording exactly when a particular disease epidemic took place or when fieldwork had to stop because of adverse weather conditions or civil disturbance).

To guard against loss and to facilitate the subsequent search for events of interest, it is recommended that the diary is maintained as a computer file with backups, rather than just in a paper notebook. The latest version of the field manual should also be stored electronically, so that it can be updated and modified easily.

3 Personnel issues

Field trials may involve a large number of personnel, often for considerable periods, working under difficult conditions, and the staffing arrangements must be well organized. Each person should know what they have to do and when they have to do it, to whom they should report, and when, where, and how they should do this. A job description should be prepared for each position, incorporating the tasks specified in the field manual. Preparing such job descriptions forces the investigator to work out in advance what each individual will do, and then inform each worker formally what is expected of him or her. The job descriptions specify not only the tasks to be undertaken, but also the workload (for example, the approximate number of thick and thin blood films to be collected per day) and the quality of work expected. The minimum educational levels and training required for each position should also be specified. Personnel for the posts should be recruited and trained for their specific tasks, based on their job descriptions. Training should include an overview of the objectives and flow of the study, research ethics, especially related to confidentiality and relationships with study participants, reporting and supervision systems, personal safety and security, and training on the specific tasks for that position. It may also need to include training related to teamwork and communication skills, and information technology skills (such as the use of laptops, PDAs, mobile phones, or tablet computers for data collection, or the use of GPS devices). Increasingly, it is expected or required that at least relatively senior personnel have received basic training and ideally have been certified in 'GCP' (see Section 7).

It may be beneficial to provide staff with initial training in more than one set of tasks, as this will allow easier transfer of staff between positions, if necessary. Managerial and supervisory activities, with appropriate hierarchical relationships and lines of authority, need to be established. An organizational chart illustrating the lines of authority may be useful. Each staff member should be broadly familiar with the responsibilities of other staff. Staff should be made aware of health and safety procedures, for example, what to do if there is a road traffic accident or an armed robbery or someone has a needle-stick injury (see Chapter 17, Section 8).

The composition of the field team should directly reflect the specific activities they must undertake. It might include, for example, a driver, a registration clerk, one or more interviewers, an assistant to take temperatures and to measure heights and weights or to test eyes, a clinician for physical examinations and the application of any clinical intervention procedures, a laboratory technician to collect blood, urine, or stool specimens for laboratory tests, and a medical or pharmacy assistant or nurse for dispensing medications. A constraint on the size of a field team may be the number of persons who can be accommodated in the trial vehicle, along with the equipment they must use in the field. It will be useful to draw up an organizational plan outlining the activities and functions of the members of such a team, with a diagram showing how the team will operate in the field. This should include a careful, and if possible, pilot-tested, estimate of the average and range of times that each participant is expected to take at each step in the field survey. Ideally, these times should be approximately equal for each step to avoid bottlenecks developing. To achieve this, it may be necessary to have different numbers of workers at individual steps in the participant flow. For example, in a follow-up survey in an adolescent HIV prevention trial in Tanzania, the main survey team of 14 people included two drivers with their vehicles, a team leader, one registration clerk, two male and two female interviewers, a laboratory technician and laboratory assistant, a nurse who supervised young women taking self-administered vaginal swabs, two HIV testing counsellors, and a clinician (who also did dispensing).

Detailed descriptions of the procedures to be followed for each of the activities should be included in the field manual (for example, how the census form should be completed, how the items on the form should be checked, what should be done with the form at the end of the day).

Frequent and effective supervision of field activities is essential for ensuring the collection of high-quality data (see Section 7.2), but also for keeping the fieldwork moving, according to the timetable, for maintaining field team morale, and for preventing the escalation of any disputes or disagreements. Field team leaders have primary responsibility for the activities of their team, and they should regularly report progress and any problems or issues arising to the field supervisors. The field supervisors should, in turn, report to the project coordinator who monitors overall progress of the study and reports to the PIs, government officials, and funders.

Mobile phones are commonly used during supervision of field activities. For example, they might be used by field team leaders to provide supervisors with daily updates which include basic data on the number of participants seen, refusals, and any problems encountered via text messages or phone calls. Supervisors, in turn, can use mobile phones to advise and guide team leaders and to provide field teams with lists of participants or households to interview or re-interview. Prompt transfer and data entry of completed paper questionnaires can aid supervision through providing early and frequent feedback to field teams on data inconsistencies or errors. Wireless transfer of data collected in the field to the central data section, either via the Internet or mobile phones, is increasingly being used and offers increased opportunity for the early identification of problems with data collection or the interpretation of questions by participants. Such data transfer should be encrypted and password-protected to ensure it remains secure and confidential. Timely transfer of field data to the central or field trial office allows databases of the data collected to be kept up to date and delays or other problems can be acted on promptly.

It is essential that checks on data quality are incorporated into routine field procedures. Examples of these are given in Section 7. It is also important to keep a close check on the arrangements for laboratory specimen collection, storage, and shipment back from the field to the base laboratory (see Chapter 17).

As a general principle, the designer of fieldwork procedures should think carefully of everything that could realistically go wrong and put systems in place for what should be done in the event that these problems occur, for example, what should be done if one or more team member falls ill, a vehicle or other piece of equipment, such as a centrifuge or freezer, breaks down, or if a national holiday is declared at short notice. Overcoming such problems may require staff being trained to be able to fill in for each other, there being two of each vital piece of equipment, or the potential for emergency repair or replacement of equipment. The details of what should be done will partly depend on the remoteness of the field work from the trial coordination centre.

Field teams that spend extended periods of time in the field can be prone to internal disputes and disagreements, and the importance of good team dynamics and team leadership should not be underestimated. In some circumstances, movement of staff between teams during the course of the trial can be beneficial, for example, to strengthen a weaker team or to improve team dynamics.

Good financial management is essential for staff morale. Salaries and allowances should be paid on time, and staff provided with medical insurance cover and legal protection against being sued in relation to their trial work. Petty cash should be available when required. A detailed record of expenditures should be kept together with receipts, as a senior staff member will have to account for all funds issued and spent. For large studies, it will be essential to employ an administrator to take care of these aspects, as they may be very time-consuming. Systems must be put in place to prevent fraud, and staff should be made aware of the policies regarding accountability when equipment or supplies go missing or are stolen (see Chapter 18).

4 Physical location and facilities

An issue to be resolved early in the planning of a field trial is whether the study participants should be seen at a central location, at a series of local assembly points, or be visited on a house-to-house basis. The decision will depend upon the procedures to be carried out, the nature of equipment required, the time the study procedures take, the population size, density, and distribution, and the environmental and physical conditions.

A central assembly point may be most efficient for the study team, since more people can be seen in a day than in a house-to-house survey. If heavy or delicate non-portable equipment must be used, then a central assembly point cannot be avoided. Even if some of the data collection or physical or laboratory examinations have to be done at a central location, it is often advisable to conduct the census, and sometimes questionnaire interviews, at the houses of participants.

One advantage of a house-to-house survey is that it is possible to be reasonably sure of being able to compile a list of most of those who are eligible for the trial. Any persons who do not report to a central assembly point can then be identified, and, if necessary, attempts made to find them. Individuals who are not present during the home visit might be able to attend the central assembly point at another time. Tracing those missing can be costly and time-consuming, and decisions about the benefits of doing this, as compared to the time and effort required to visit individual households, need to be considered in the planning phase. Also, the likely magnitude of 'non-response' may need to be estimated during the pilot phase (see Chapter 13). Sometimes, a combination of both approaches may be suitable, whereby someone visits each household to conduct a household census and identifies all potentially eligible individuals who are given an appointment to go to a central location for the actual data collection.

Careful planning of the physical layout for the flow of people from one part of the field station to the next is important. Special attention may have to be given for carrying out the physical examination, in order to ensure both privacy and adequate light. Usually, there is little difficulty about making such arrangements when the examinations are conducted at a central assembly point, but, for more mobile surveys, special arrangements may be necessary, ranging from simple screening under a shady tree to the use of a tent with special lighting.

In addition to whatever arrangements are made for the interviewing, examinations, and specimen collection from study subjects, there are supporting functions that will require physical facilities. These include a headquarters for administration; a room for team training courses, meetings, and review of activities and problems on a daily basis; space for computer processing of data; file storage space; laboratory accommodation;

stores for equipment and supplies; and transport garaging. The various components may be needed at one place or at several places or may need to be mobile.

If the field team must live away from home for long periods, they may be able to obtain local accommodation, but other accommodation might have to be provided (for example, tents). Accommodation and cooking facilities should be arranged in advance, and employment of a cook will save on staff time and improve staff morale (if the cook is good!). Food may need careful storage and cooking, in order to avoid food poisoning. Water for drinking may need to be purified, filtered, or boiled. Refuse disposal and toilets may also be needed.

Where the field teams will use electrical equipment for their activities, a reliable source of electricity will be required. Even if there is a normally reliable local electricity supply, some form of backup supply should be considered. In some cases, using solar power or project vehicles to charge equipment may be sufficient, though it is usually wise to have an additional backup source such as a portable generator. In some places, there will be no local mains electricity, and then it is essential for the team to have their own electricity supply and strongly advisable to have a backup for that too in case of malfunction. Similarly, ease of access to the Internet and the quality and extent of mobile phone network coverage should be taken into account if field teams will be expected to communicate with headquarters in these ways.

5 Equipment and supplies

The major items of equipment and reagents required must be specified in the study protocol. The choice of what technical equipment to buy should be influenced by what the investigators or others in the field have used and whether it has been found to produce valid results and is reliable in the specific field contexts required (and this will include servicing arrangements). The power requirements of electronic equipment should be considered prior to purchase. Some equipment and supplies may need to be pre-ordered from abroad, as they may not be available locally, so considerable pre-planning may be required. This is likely to be particularly relevant for the clinical and laboratory equipment and supplies (see Chapter 17). It may be important to order a basic supply of spare parts at the same time as ordering equipment, if local availability is in doubt. Purchasing of equipment and supplies locally can be open to many kinds of fraud (see Chapter 18), and steps should be taken to ensure not only that a fair price is obtained, but also that the goods are genuine and of high quality.

The field manual should include lists of all the equipment required for each of the trial procedures (for example, record cards, questionnaires, needles and syringes, laboratory supplies) and for the support of those procedures (for example, vehicles, filing cabinets and files, benches, screens, tents). Providing 'packing lists' to individual team members and checking that they have all the items on their list prior to departure from headquarters each day can reduce the number of requests from the field for additional supplies. Systems need to be put in place to ensure that maintenance and quality control of equipment is carried out, according to a standard schedule. Some laboratory equipment will need standardization, validation, servicing, and revalidation (see Chapter 17).

Provision for transport is essential in most LMICs. One of the most expensive items of equipment are trial vehicles, so the decision as to whether to purchase or hire them, and, if purchasing, whether to buy new or second-hand, requires careful consideration and price comparisons. Key issues are not only the capacity, purchase price, or daily hire price, but also fuel consumption, type of fuel and its local availability and price, and vehicle maintenance and reliability. It is a false economy to purchase a cheaper vehicle if it is more liable to break down, losing days of work, while it is repaired or dug out of the mud. It is also important to check whether the funding agency imposes restrictions on which vehicles can be purchased or how vehicles should be disposed of at the end of the trial.

Transporting people and equipment will require careful planning. Extra time should be allowed for possible mishaps. If possible, backup transport should be available in case of emergencies. Maintenance of vehicles and close supervision of their use are essential. Control and discipline of vehicle use are key factors in the conduct of almost all field trials. Particular problems may arise if field staff are issued with vehicles (for example, motorcycles) that they keep at home, rather than return to a central parking place on a daily basis. When staying overnight in the field, all vehicles should be parked overnight in a secure site, such as the guesthouse or hotel where the team are staying where there is a security guard. If necessary, a guard should be hired for this purpose.

Great care should also be taken in hiring drivers, and a practical driving test that includes a section that mimics difficult field conditions should be included. It is important to remember that having a good, safe driver could not only save considerable time wasted through breakdowns or getting stuck in mud, but may also save the lives of field team members. Linked to this, strict rules as to who may and who may not drive the trial vehicles and for what purposes should be specified and enforced.

Maintenance, fuel supply, and the use of vehicles for purposes other than those for which they were intended can pose substantial problems. Careful monitoring of vehicle fuel consumption is essential, as it is not uncommon for drivers to supplement their income through fuel fraud. Common tricks include having an agreement with the fuel supplier that the receipt will show a larger volume of fuel than is actually given, siphoning off fuel, or unauthorized use of the vehicle (for example, as a taxi). Although each such theft only costs the project a relatively small amount, fuel often accounts for a substantial proportion of the non-staff recurrent costs of a field trial, and the losses can quickly add up to a sizeable amount. As well as each vehicle having a logbook with each journey requiring signed authorization by a senior member of staff, other useful techniques for minimizing fuel fraud is to allocate each vehicle to a single driver, with checks on prior fuel consumption carried out whenever the vehicle passes from one driver to another, and regular checks of fuel consumption, with the record being from full tank to full tank.

Illicit exchange of vehicle parts by vehicle mechanics is also not uncommon, either with or without the driver's knowledge. Again, this can be minimized by selecting a reputable garage and, if necessary, marking key vehicle parts. Vehicle theft can jeopardize a field trial, so, where possible, it is very important to fit vehicles with a satellite tracking device, an immobilizer, and a gear-locking device.

Of all vehicles, motor bicycles are the most dangerous. They are often driven by fieldworkers who are young men who enjoy the status that the motorbicycle gives them and may be prone to showing off. Very strict monitoring of their use is essential. All the rules given above should apply to motorbicycle, as well as other trial vehicles, plus all motorbicycle users (drivers and their passengers) should always wear a full-face helmet. Motorbicycles are less stable, particularly in muddy or sandy conditions, when carrying two (or more!) people, rather than one, so this should be avoided, whenever possible.

Loss of other stores and supplies can also be a major problem, particularly due to theft. A staff member at the trial base should be appointed to be solely responsible for all the stores, maintaining inventories and issuing items. Each item issued should be signed for by an individual team member who should also be expected to sign the store inventory book upon return of the item. Transferring equipment between team members in the field should be discouraged and, if necessary, should be accompanied by documentation signed by both team members. Staff should be provided with an SOP for equipment, which includes instructions on the correct use, storage, maintenance, and charging of the equipment. Staff need to know what to do when equipment is lost or stolen or stops working properly. It is advisable to provide field teams with extra backup equipment. If this is not possible, such as for large or expensive laboratory equipment, plans should be in place to deal swiftly with breakdowns.

6 Timetable for field activities

An organizational timetable should be constructed which shows all of the field activities and indicates when each will be undertaken. An example of such a timetable, for a trial of the effect of regular vitamin A supplementation on episodes of diarrhoea and respiratory infections, is shown in Figure 16.1 (Betty Kirkwood, personal communication). The dates for fieldwork may have to be fixed some time in advance. The time required for preparations and pilot testing may overlap with training, but all three must be completed before the start of the main fieldwork. Similarly, analysis and consultations should be completed, before the final report is produced.

The planning of trial activities must take account of climatic and seasonal factors. These may affect access to the trial area (for example, flooding) and the activities of those in the area such as to make them difficult to survey (for example, seasonal migrations for work, working on farms during the planting or harvesting seasons). It may be important to plan activities to take into account market days, local holidays and festivals, and activities of the local medical services (for example, antenatal clinics). Also, adequate plans must be made to allow for staff leave (both annual leave, sickness absences, and compassionate leave such as to attend funerals or to look after a close relative). The timetable should fit into local practices, if possible (for example, in Muslim countries, if most people do not work on a Friday, the trial should be planned to fit in with this).

7 Ensuring data of high quality

To be able to derive reliable and accurate conclusions from a health intervention trial, it is important to ensure that all processes and procedures, at all stages in the conduct of the trial, are performed at high quality. The many steps involved in planning and carrying out trials are described in the other chapters of this book. Here, we focus on the actions needed to ensure that all data collected are of high quality and that this high quality can be demonstrated both to those directly involved in the trial and to

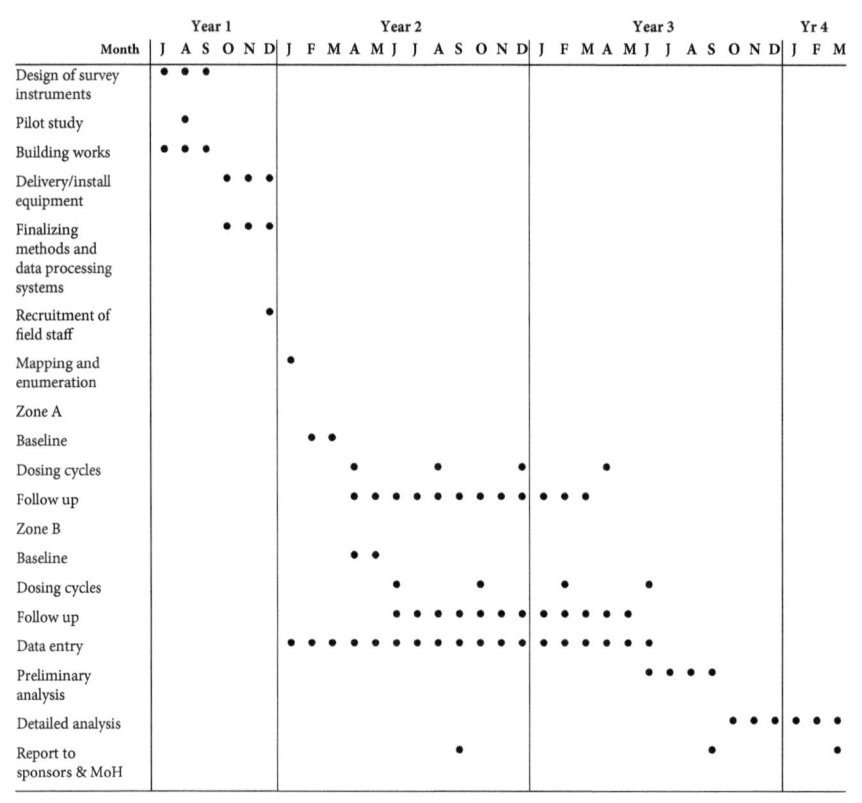

Figure 16.1 Example of an organizational timetable for a field trial.

all those external to the trial but who have responsibilities or interests in relation to the trial. The general principles and some of the terminology that is commonly used related to what is called 'Good Clinical Practice' or 'GCP' will be described, but this chapter is not a GCP manual. Investigators who require formal training in GCP should contact a local internationally accredited institution that offers such training or one of the many internationally accredited online courses that are available from groups such as the Clinical Research Network of the United Kingdom (UK)'s National Institute for Health Research (<http://www.crncc.nihr.ac.uk>) or the OnlineGCP Group (<http://www.onlinegcp.com>).

If high-quality data are to be achieved, the investigator and all of the trial team must accept the need for rigour in the collection of all data and in the checks built into every step of the trial.

7.1 Regulatory requirements and good clinical practice

The ICH (1996) (<http://www.ich.org>) is an internationally accepted set of standards that are intended to apply to all research on human subjects. It is mainly applied in the context of trials of medicinal products, but increasingly there is an expectation that observational epidemiological studies will be conducted to a similar standard. The aim of the guidelines is to ensure the safety and rights of all participants in the research study, while, at the same time, ensuring that the study is likely to achieve valid and reproducible results.

Based on the ICH–GCP guidelines, regulatory bodies, such as the US Food and Drug Administration (<http://www.fda.gov>) and the European Medicines Agency (<http://www.ema.europa.eu/ema>) have set out a rigorous series of procedures and checks that must be followed in clinical trials of new drugs and vaccines to provide the standard of evidence necessary for the licensing of a new product. There is a widespread misconception that all trials (including field trials of social or public health interventions or of alternative delivery mechanisms for licensed drugs or other medical products) must meet all requirements of such regulatory bodies—often called being 'fully GCP-compliant'. This is not the case, and some flexibility is appropriate as to exactly how closely the GCP guidelines are implemented for non-licensing trials (i.e. of an intervention for which a licence is not being sought from a regulatory agency). However, all trials should comply with the basic principles contained within the ICH–GCP guidelines. The basic principles are that all studies involving human subjects should be conducted ethically (including that the interests of participants should be central to the trial design and implementation) and that all data collected should be of high quality and be likely to be valid. Furthermore, the investigators must be able to demonstrate that both these fundamental principles have been met. A trial can comply with the principles of GCP without meeting all the regulatory requirements for the licensing of a new product. This is important, since the full regulatory requirements are very demanding and will greatly increase the cost and human resources required. At an early stage in the planning of any trial, and certainly before any proposal is submitted to a funding agency or ethics committee, the PI and sponsor must make a clear decision as to whether their proposed trial needs to be 'fully GCP-compliant'. As discussed in Chapter 2, many field trials in LMICs do not test investigational products but test the effectiveness of alternative delivery strategies for licensed products, or test interventions that do not include any medicinal products at all, such as trials of health promotion or other public health interventions.

The key individuals and institutions that have responsibility for ensuring that a trial is complying with the principles of GCP have been defined in Chapter 7. The trial sponsor has overall responsibility for all aspects of the trial; the PI has primary responsibility for ensuring that the trial is carried out according to protocol; and the ethics committee (sometimes called the Institutional Review Board (IRB)) has primary responsibility for monitoring the ethical aspects of the trial. To ensure trial data are of high quality, the sponsor 'should determine the appropriate extent and nature of monitoring which should be based on considerations such as the objective, purpose, design, complexity, blinding, size, and endpoints of the trial' (International Conference on Harmonisation, 1996).

7.2 Supervision and data checks

Although, in some large trials, someone is designated to be the overall quality manager, the entire trial team should have data quality at the forefront of their minds. From the start, the investigator should assign quality assurance tasks to the team and build quality assurance (QA) processes into the trial procedures.

The two key principles for obtaining high-quality data are to plan ahead and to check everything. Nothing should be taken on trust, and, while remaining optimistic, it should be assumed that anything that could go wrong might go wrong!

Key issues in data quality are covered in other chapters: clear case definitions and valid measures of all trial outcomes in Chapter 12; preliminary studies and pilot tests in Chapter 13; questionnaire design, selection, and training of fieldworkers in Chapter 14; and some of the checks that can be done on the quality of the data collected are given in Chapter 20. In this chapter, we focus on steps that can be taken once fieldworkers have been deployed at the end of their initial training to ensure both that the data that they collected is of high quality and that this high quality can be demonstrated to external trial auditors. Most of these activities fall under field supervision.

In successful field supervision, prevention is better than cure. A supervision system should be designed not only to detect problems and provoke responses to solve them, but also to prevent problems from occurring in the first place. For example, if fieldworkers know that every piece of data they collect might be checked but have no way to know which pieces will actually be checked, they are more likely to always be careful. Conversely, if the fieldworker knows that only data collected on a Tuesday will be checked, then he or she may be less conscientious on other days.

Also, it is important to institute a system for checking all data collected, and especially data critical for identifying and linking data on the same individual throughout the trial. Examples of checks that should be built into field supervision include checks of completed forms, observation of work, replicated collection of a sample of data, checks without repeated data collection, review of errors detected after data collection, and checks with participants and community representatives.

The record forms that each fieldworker completes should be checked for accuracy and completeness. Because of delays between data collection and entering the data into a computer, if paper forms are used, some preliminary checks should be done before the forms are submitted, while the fieldworker is still in the vicinity of the participant, and before the participant's situation may have changed. When the data are directly entered electronically, checks for data completeness, range, and consistency can be incorporated into the data capture program.

Each fieldworker should receive regular scheduled visits from their supervisor, during which the supervisor observes them carrying out their routine data collection tasks and gives them constructive feedback and a chance to discuss any issues that they have faced. These scheduled visits should be particularly frequent during the early phases of the trial. Observation tests whether the fieldworker knows how to carry out their tasks (competence) and can do so when being observed, and provides an opportunity for the supervisor to identify and correct any problems with their understanding of how the data should be collected. For example, they may have misunderstood how to measure a child's height or may not be asking questions exactly as they are written in the questionnaire. However, it does not show whether they actually do so when they are not being observed (performance) (see later in this section).

Throughout a survey, it is important to monitor the performance of each interviewer and to institute corrective training, if required. One means of quality control (QC) is to organize for a proportion of respondents (selected at random) to be re-interviewed by another interviewer. Discrepancies in the two interviews may identify deficiencies in the interview methods of one or other interviewer. It is not an uncommon experience in large surveys that some interviewers complete some questionnaires without ever having seen the 'respondents'. A good system of checking, supervision, and QC is necessary to prevent this, or at least to detect it soon after it occurs, so that remedial action can be taken.

To check whether the fieldworker actually collects the data correctly when not being observed, unscheduled checks need to be implemented. For example, in a field trial of vitamin A supplementation in northern Ghana, each fieldworker received unscheduled, as well as the scheduled, visits from the supervisor, who would ask permission to sit in on any interview that was happening or about to happen when they arrived and then collect the forms that the interviewer had completed earlier that day. These would be sealed in an envelope in front of the fieldworker. The supervisor would then go back to the previous five households that had been visited that day. In two households, they would merely ask the household whether the fieldworker had actually visited them, conducted an interview with an appropriate person, and taken the appropriate biological specimens from them. This checked that the fieldworker was not fabricating the data. In the other three households, they would request an independent partial re-interview of the trial participant. When they returned to the trial office, the supervisor would then submit their own forms and the original forms collected by the fieldworker, and the data centre would generate a comparison of the two.

Various checks can, and should, be carried out after data collection. For example, all data incompleteness (for example, missing items on the questionnaire) or variables that are out of range (for example, an infant's weight being recorded as 100 grams) or inconsistent (for example, a woman recorded with penile warts or a person recorded with fever in one part of the questionnaire but afebrile in another) should be identified. It is useful for all such errors to be tabulated on a regular basis by the fieldworker and the field team. Such tabulations will show which fieldworkers or field teams have more errors detected. The reasons for these can then be investigated, and steps put in place to rectify them. One method that has been used for this has been to send data queries back to the fieldworker. For example, if a check shows that a participant's height is lower than it was in a previous study round, the fieldworker can be asked to go back to collect that participant's height again. Ideally, the fieldworker should not be told why they are being asked to re-collect the height, let alone what they had entered the height as during their recent visit or during the previous round. In the field trial of vitamin A, this method was extended, so that each fieldworker received some such requests, even when there was no reason to suspect an error in the data. These checks occasionally identified errors that were not detectable by routine range or consistency checks.

Finally, it is important that the trial team has periodic meetings with participants or their representatives and with other members of the trial communities to check that they are happy with the activities of the fieldworkers and their supervisors.

An important principle is that every error or problem that is detected should provoke a response. This is for two reasons. First, if errors are not investigated and acted on, the effort of detecting them is wasted, and also the field staff may interpret this to imply that the importance of data quality is being neglected. Second, since it is never possible to check every piece of data collected, any errors that are detected are likely to be the 'tip of the iceberg'.

The actions taken when errors are detected should not generally be punitive but should include support and further training to help the fieldworker improve. However, if this fails to correct the problem, or if the errors have come about through data fabrication, disciplinary mechanisms should be in place, and ultimately these may need to include termination of employment.

It is important that field staff are aware of all the types of checks that will be conducted on the data they collect. This is partly to avoid their feeling that they have been spied on behind their backs, but also so that they will be encouraged to ensure that all data are collected as well as possible.

It is a good plan to have weekly fieldwork meetings which include reports from individuals, on progress, work accomplished, identified problems and how they were solved, queries, etc. This also provides an opportunity for systematic feedback from the central administration on fieldworker performance, including results of repeat interviews for quality checks. Meetings of this kind may greatly assist in maintaining staff morale and improving the quality of the data collected.

References

International Conference On Harmonisation. 1996. *Guideline for good clinical practice E6(R1).* Available at: <http://www.ich.org/fileadmin/Public_Web_Site/ICH_Products/Guidelines/Efficacy/E6/E6_R1_Guideline.pdf>.

The Gambia Hepatitis Study Group. 1987. The Gambia Hepatitis Intervention Study. *Cancer Research,* **47**, 5782–7.

Van Der Sande, M., Waight, P., Mendy, M., *et al.* 2007. Long-term protection against HBV chronic carriage of Gambian adolescents vaccinated in infancy and immune response in HBV booster trial in adolescence. *PLoS One,* **2**, e753.

Chapter 17

Field laboratory methods

1 Introduction to field laboratory methods 285
2 Sample collection 286
  2.1 Types of specimen 286
  2.2 Handling specimens 287
  2.3 Blood 288
  2.4 Cerebrospinal fluid 289
  2.5 Stool and urine 289
  2.6 Sputum 290
3 Labelling and storage 290
  3.1 Labelling 290
  3.2 Storage 291
  3.3 Aliquoting 292
  3.4 Storage system 292
4 Documentation of laboratory procedures 292
  4.1 Supplies 293
  4.2 Equipment maintenance 293
  4.3 Procedures and staff duties 293
  4.4 Unusual or adverse events 294
5 Quality control and quality assurance 295
  5.1 Reproducibility of test results 295
  5.2 Internal quality control 296
  5.3 External quality assurance 296
6 Accreditation and links between laboratories 297
7 Coding and linkage of results 297
8 Laboratory health and safety 298

1 Introduction to field laboratory methods

Laboratory tests may provide the definitive basis for the measurement of outcome variables in field trials, either directly by demonstration of the presence of the pathogenic agent under study or indirectly by demonstration of a host reaction or of biochemical changes due to the pathogen. They may also provide evidence of the mechanism of action of the intervention, for example, directly by measuring the drug or metabolic by-products or indirectly by measuring an immune response to a vaccine. In addition, they may be used to detect or confirm the presence of adverse reactions and prior exposure to an agent or to antimicrobials.

Rigorous laboratory process is crucial to the generation of good-quality data and may be important to ensure the safety of trial participants. Laboratories participating in trials are expected to adopt the Good Clinical and Laboratory Practice (GCLP) guidelines, which govern the conduct of clinical trials globally (Stevens, 2003; World Health Organization, 2009). GCLP provides a framework covering the spectrum of laboratory studies, from planning to analysis and storage of specimens and archiving of data. The WHO publication documents a set of minimum requirements for laboratory involvement in clinical trials, including the use of standard operating procedures (SOPs), monitoring, quality control (QC), and external quality assurance (QA) arrangements (World Health Organization, 2009).

The organization and operation of a field laboratory for the support of a field trial are different from those of a routine medical laboratory and have become more demanding in recent years. Laboratory accreditation (see Section 6) may be necessary when laboratory data are required for the process of product licensure. In field trials, the emphasis is often on the collection and processing of large numbers of samples, on which only a few specific tests will be performed. Aliquots of samples are usually required, so that different aliquots can be used for different tests, for storage as backup specimens, and for shipment for further analysis. Storage of specimens with computerized records, including electronic monitoring and bar coding, has been introduced, even in field laboratories in rural settings.

General aspects of the setting up and running of a field laboratory are discussed in this chapter. Other literature should be consulted for information on specific laboratory tests and specific laboratory methods. Useful general texts containing relevant information for the operation of a field laboratory and for collecting specimens include Cheesbrough (1987), World Health Organization (2003), and World Health Organization (2009). See also Chapter 16.

2 Sample collection

Accurate laboratory results depend on proper collection, processing, and handling of samples. The method of collection, timing, and handling of samples will be determined by the purpose of the trial and specified in the trial protocol. Careful attention must be given to the quantity and quality of samples, aseptic precautions, and prompt transport of samples and their processing and storage in the laboratory. Advances in technology and analytical chemistry have led to the development and use of direct testing in the field, using point of care (POC) diagnostics, and rapid diagnostic tests (RDTs) have been introduced in some areas.

2.1 Types of specimen

The kinds of specimen that are commonly collected in field trials include:
- specimens from humans, including blood, stool, urine, sputum, skin snips, and other tissue biopsies, and swabs or smears collected from skin or mucosal surfaces

- entomological specimens for studies of vectors, and animal or malacological specimens for studies of intermediate hosts
- food, water, and environmental samples.

In this chapter, we discuss only specimens collected from humans, though many of the issues (such as the use of sterile techniques) apply to the other types of specimen.

2.2 Handling specimens

The collection of samples for laboratory studies will usually involve the steps outlined in Box 17.1.

The procedures for collecting and processing samples must be unambiguously specified, including to where they are to be transported and how they will be labelled. Whenever required, the type of shipment must be specified, for example, in dry ice or liquid nitrogen. If samples are to be transported by air, safe shipment of samples is mandatory, and procedures must follow the International Air Transport Association (IATA) guidance for infectious substances and diagnostic specimens, which detail packaging and shipment methods. Each package must contain a primary and a secondary container, and both of these must be leak-proof to avoid accidental spillage during transport. The whole process must be performed only by trained staff, whose competence has been certified. The regulations governing the transport of potentially hazardous samples are designed to ensure that samples reach their destination in good condition and to eliminate exposure of those handling the shipment to any potential hazard. Prior communication with the recipient and tracking information are vital, in order that shipments can be dealt with promptly on arrival. On occasion, this may require staff to receive the specimens outside normal working hours to avoid the specimens sitting around and deteriorating.

All aspects of the collection, transport, and processing of samples must be pilot-tested. Often, much attention is paid to the proper design and testing of questionnaires, but much less care is taken to finding the most appropriate and culturally acceptable methods for the collection of blood, stool, urine, or tissue samples. Yet, this may be crucial to sustained community involvement and participation (see Chapter 9, Section 5).

Box 17.1 Steps involved in the collection of samples for laboratory studies

1. Collection of specimens from the study participants.
2. Placement in a suitable container.
3. Labelling of the container.
4. Temporary storage at an appropriate temperature.
5. Initial processing (for example, serum separation from whole blood), with appropriate re-labelling.
6. Transport to intermediate or final destination for further processing, testing, and storage.

2.3 Blood

The usual methods by which blood is collected in field surveys are by venepuncture or by finger- or heel-pricks, depending on the nature of the investigations required. If small quantities of blood are required, finger-pricks are usually taken from adults, with heel-pricks more commonly used in infants and young children, whose fingers are very small and whose heels do not yet have calluses. A finger-prick provides an adequate volume of blood for many laboratory tests. Micro-techniques are to be preferred whenever they have acceptable validity, as they either avoid the need for venepuncture altogether or reduce the volume of blood that is needed. Micro-techniques have been, or are being, developed for many assays, and investigations should be conducted before a study starts to find out the latest availability of such techniques (for example, by literature search or contact with those in a central or reference laboratory). It is important to verify that the methods have been adequately validated. Some tests require larger quantities of blood, however, and it will often be necessary to collect blood by venepuncture from at least a sample of the population.

After collection, blood may be separated into several components, including serum, plasma, red cells, and white cells. The separation must be done shortly after the blood has been collected, and it is common for this procedure to be carried out close to where the samples have been collected or in a nearby field laboratory.

A sample of blood taken from a finger-prick may be collected in one of several ways, including:

1 collection into capillary tubes, for example, narrow glass tubes, by capillary action, or microtubes by gentle squeezing of the finger
2 dropping onto a glass slide for direct examination of a blood smear
3 dropping onto strips or discs of absorbent paper (filter paper).

Fingertips are swabbed with alcohol before pricking, and the first drop is wiped off. Sufficient blood can be obtained for two thick, and two thin, malaria smears to do one or two haemoglobin level measurements (for example, with the Haemocue® system or the older haematocrit tubes), to collect 50–100 microlitres of blood in a microtube or Microtainer® for serum, and to place a drop on filter paper (World Health Organization, 2003). Filter paper samples need to be air-dried, before storing with silica gel. Tubes with plasma or serum can be stored on dry ice, in a freezer, or in liquid nitrogen. The amount of plasma or serum recovered from a finger-prick sample will be sufficient to perform serological tests, such as enzyme-linked immunosorbent assay (ELISA) or Multiplex® assays, and is sufficient for the determination of some micronutrients such as vitamin A or zinc (minimum serum requirements of 25–40 microlitres). Establishing volume requirements for the tests to be conducted is a prerequisite.

If repeated blood sampling is to be undertaken from participants during the course of a study, it is likely to be more appropriate ethically, and easier to maintain the cooperation of most study populations, if finger-prick, rather than venous blood, sampling is used. While filter paper samples are satisfactory in many cases, the larger sample volumes from venous sampling are currently needed for some tests (for example, tests for cell-mediated immunity, human leucocyte antigen (HLA) typing, bacterial cultures).

A variety of systems using an evacuated tube, such as Vacutainer® or Vacuette® collection tubes, and blood culture bottles are suitable for this purpose. For repeated sampling, it is also essential to provide feedback to the individuals involved, and to the community if appropriate, about the earlier results (see also Chapter 9).

If multiple types of collection tubes are to be used, the order of draw should be written into the SOP to minimize cross-contamination of tube additives.

Special care in handling and processing samples is needed if any DNA-based work is to be conducted, as the potential for cross-contamination between samples is high. Blood for bacterial cultures is collected by venepuncture and delivered directly into blood culture bottles containing bacterial growth media, before incubation in the laboratory in either a conventional incubator or an automated incubator system such as the BACTEC® series. Blood for immunological and genetic analysis can be collected as whole blood and stored in specialized tubes such as PAXgene™ or Tempus™ or, when only small volumes are available, as spots collected on filter paper for later analysis in a specialist laboratory.

Special precautions should be taken when collecting blood. Disposable gloves should be worn, a sharps box provided, and water and detergent should be available for use by those taking blood. All blood samples should be considered to be potentially infectious, and appropriate handling procedures must be employed to safeguard all those who will come into contact with the specimens during their collection, processing, analysis, or storage (World Health Organization, 2004). Guidelines and drugs should be available for use in the event of a needle-stick injury or blood spillage.

2.4 Cerebrospinal fluid

Collection of cerebrospinal fluid (CSF) requires lumbar puncture, which must be performed by a clinically trained member of staff with prior supervised experience. Using aseptic techniques, CSF should be collected into a sterile container for prompt transfer to the laboratory for biochemical and microbiological analysis. An obviously 'bloody' sample may compromise the laboratory results, especially from biochemical analyses.

2.5 Stool and urine

A summary of different methods that may be used for collecting urine and stool samples, with details of different container types, is given in World Health Organization, 2003. The methods considered for use in a particular survey should be discussed with those knowledgeable of local customs and taboos. In some cultures, sensitivity regarding the collection or public display of stool specimens may be greater than that for blood. A container that is technically appropriate may not be acceptable in a particular study community (for example, due to colour, transparency, or resemblance to a cultural design or pattern). In advance of a survey, the proposed stool and urine containers should be shown to the village leaders, and the proposed methods of sample collection discussed. As with all field procedures, it is important to undertake pilot testing to ensure that the procedures planned will be acceptable (both to the investigator and to the study population).

As stool samples can rarely be collected 'on the spot', it is usually necessary to leave the container with an individual overnight and to arrange to pick up the specimen on the following day. A potential hazard in doing this is that containers may be exchanged between individuals or, for example, one person may provide a sample for the whole family. It is difficult to rule out this possibility, but it is important for fieldworkers to stress the importance of participants adhering to the correct procedures and to be alert to possible problems.

2.6 Sputum

The WHO manual (World Health Organization, 2003) gives a concise description of recommended methods of collecting sputum samples, using different kinds of jars, boxes, and containers, including transport media. Two general points merit special attention:

1. all sputum samples should be considered potentially infectious
2. careful attention should be given to the cold-chain requirements if sputum samples have to be sent to another laboratory for culture.

3 Labelling and storage

3.1 Labelling

Proper labelling of samples is essential. The labelling scheme should be as simple as possible, consistent with the study objectives, and must take due account of the size of containers and how the specimens will be handled, transferred, and stored. In most cases, computer-generated, self-adhesive, pre-printed labels, with the individual identification or code numbers duplicated on data sheets, can speed processing. Also, labels in a variety of materials suitable for differing storage conditions, and with each number duplicated several times, are available commercially. Bar codes for specimen containers that can be read automatically by bar code readers are also available commercially.

The information recorded on a label will vary, according to particular requirements. It may include a unique identification number assigned to a study participant, which is utilized during laboratory processing and which may be linked back to an individual by reference to records kept at the time the sample was taken. In some circumstances, it will be appropriate to include on the label a record of the date of collection, the type of specimen, if not evident, and possibly the location (for example, name of the village). Individual names may also be recorded on the label, but this can create problems with blinding and confidentiality, and often names are not a unique identifier, as several individuals may have the same name.

Containers should usually be labelled using waterproof marker pens (but see item 1 in Box 17.2), writing directly onto the container-labelling area or onto adhesive labels attached to the container. If the container has a cap, the marking should be on the body of the container (and possibly on the cap as well, but never on the cap only). For smaller micro- or capillary tubes, an adhesive label with the identification information on it can be wrapped around a container with the two ends joined, such that they protrude (sometimes known as a 'flag'). Flags can be written on with a waterproof marker pen, and tubes may be stored in labelled envelopes, as they are collected in the field.

> **Box 17.2 Some warnings regarding labelling and storing specimens**
>
> 1 If the transport cold chain includes a stage where samples are frozen in salt–alcohol mixtures, *never* use felt pens (even waterproof ones). Always use ordinarily pencils or pre-printed highly adhesive labels.
> 2 Written numbers and letters must be in a clear and standardized form. For example, 191 looks the same as 161 upside down!
> 3 The methods to be used for collection, storage, and transport of specimens should be thoroughly researched and pilot-tested.
> 4 Special containers and labels are required if samples are to be stored in liquid nitrogen.

If smaller tubes are stored in boxes that are too large for them, staff need to be careful to record and maintain the correct numbering and not to invert or tip the box, so that they can fall out and move around in the box. Packing with cotton wool will help to keep the tubes in place in a box, and tape can be used to secure the lid.

Filter paper can be written on either directly or on the protective cardboard surround.

It is not possible to recommend a single standardized form of labelling for different sample containers that will be appropriate in all circumstances. It will be necessary in a particular study to establish, through field testing, a method that guarantees the reliability of the labelling from the time the sample is first collected, through transportation, processing, analysis, and storage. Using sets of labels with series of identical numbers on them, for coding samples and associated record forms, reduces the chances of labelling errors.

Some warnings regarding labelling and storage are given in Box 17.2.

3.2 Storage

The storage area of a field laboratory should be designed to be adequate for the studies to be conducted. This will require estimation of the rate at which samples will be collected and processed and for how long they must be stored before being transported on to another location (for example, for processing or long-term storage in the base laboratory). Serum and plasma samples should be frozen as soon as possible after separation, and storage in a field laboratory at −20 °C is adequate for most purposes, at least for several weeks, although some tests require immediate storage at −70 °C. The location and positioning of any fridges, freezers, and liquid nitrogen containers need to take account of access, power supply, and consistency of ambient temperature. Specifically designed freezer rooms with conduits to vent air from the freezer exhaust externally are often a good option.

Stool, urine, and tissue samples may be stored under various conditions, using appropriate fixatives and stabilizers; different possibilities are summarized in World Health Organization (2003).

3.3 Aliquoting

Biological samples are easily damaged by repeated freezing and thawing. This can be avoided if samples are divided into small portions (aliquots) before freezing; moreover, this provides a backup sample if problems are encountered during shipping. Ideally, the size of aliquots should be chosen so that there is just sufficient material in each aliquot to perform the tests that will be required at one particular time. This is not always possible, and, in practice, compromise procedures may have to be adopted (for example, on grounds of cost). It is important that the laboratory recording procedures are such that the histories of each aliquot are properly documented (especially recording how many times each one has been thawed and re-frozen), so that any recipient of the samples can be given detailed information about their preparation (for example, whether volumes are precisely measured or are approximate) and subsequent storage.

3.4 Storage system

When large numbers of samples are collected and stored, a storage and record system must be devised that allows the rapid retrieval of particular samples. If this is not done, sorting through large numbers of samples can be a very time-consuming activity. The particular storage system used should be tailored to the design of the specific study. Often, it is appropriate to store samples in batches, according to the date they were collected or frozen, with a record being kept of the contents of each batch. For longer-term storage and/or transport, storage boxes of standardized tube capacities (for example, nine by nine or ten by ten) with coded slots can be used. These boxes can be part of a racking system, for which a detailed inventory can be maintained as part of a computerized laboratory data management system. Generic software systems (some of which are free) are available. These computerized systems are used to record the receipt and storage of samples and can be used to track everything that happens to a sample, from when it was collected until it is disposed of or used up. Two of the most widely used examples are the Laboratory Data Management System (LDMS) and the Laboratory Information Management System (LIMS), though neither of these is free.

4 Documentation of laboratory procedures

There should be clear and explicit documentation of all laboratory procedures as SOPs in the laboratory manual, which should be subject to periodic review. The degree to which the documentation is computer-based will depend on local capacity and, to some degree, on the demands of the sponsors. SOPs will help to ensure reproducibility and will facilitate comparisons with results from other laboratories. Logbooks and records should be made for equipment maintenance, the batches of supplies and reagents used at different times, and for the detailed test procedures and the duties and responsibilities of staff members. Certification of staff competencies can also be included. Specific provision should be made for recording unusual events that may affect the results of a test (for example, power failures and fluctuations—though, in some places, these may not be unusual!).

Depending on the size of the laboratory and the variety of tests and procedures undertaken, the documentation should be arranged in a single or several logbooks that are arranged chronologically (World Health Organization, 2009).

4.1 Supplies

One of the sets of laboratory logbooks should provide information on: the reagents, test kits, laboratory equipment (including brand names), the expiry dates of reagents and test kits, storage conditions, batch or lot numbers, specification sheets, and the relevant re-ordering arrangements (for example, when, how much, and by and through whom). A checklist of itemized activities is important to avoid irregular supplies or shortage of reagents and test kits. Regular, at least monthly, inventories and appropriate documentation of all supplies can help to keep track of expiry dates and check on pilferage. Supplies and reagents that have passed their expiry date should never be used. To avoid this happening, a 'first in first out' system should be used for issuing reagents and supplies, i.e. the reagents or test kits that are closest to their expiry date should always be issued before the ones that are further from their expiry date. Where Internet access is available, the website addresses and e-mail addresses of suppliers should be recorded.

4.2 Equipment maintenance

Regular checks should be made on each piece of equipment to ensure that it is in good working order. Such checks should be recorded and, for key items, publicly displayed. Some of the items that should be checked regularly are listed in Box 17.3.

In laboratories in the tropics where air conditioning is not available, humidity may lead to problems with both equipment and storage of certain sample types (for example, blood stored on filter paper). In these circumstances, storage with silica gel (as a desiccant) in airtight boxes is appropriate, and the silica gel will require regular (monthly) replacement.

Maintenance procedures are usually described in the instruction booklets for the relevant equipment, but these will need to be augmented with details relating to troubleshooting and contacts of qualified staff or engineers. The complete maintenance instructions for each piece of equipment should be incorporated into a dedicated manual, and a logbook with checklists kept for each piece of equipment. Regular maintenance of certain pieces of equipment may be a prerequisite in some studies. It is important therefore that laboratory staff review these logbooks regularly. It is usually a good idea and cost-effective to have a maintenance contract for all major, complex, and expensive laboratory equipment.

4.3 Procedures and staff duties

Laboratory SOPs, detailing step-by-step instructions for individual procedures, should be collected together in a laboratory manual. The author of each SOP and those staff members who have read it and, where appropriate, been trained in it (and who can therefore perform the procedure) should sign the SOP cover sheet. SOPs will specifically detail to whom staff should report and how they should record results, additional observations, mistakes, and other unusual events. These include, for example,

> **Box 17.3 Equipment and maintenance: items that should be regularly checked**
>
> 1. Twice-daily (morning and evening) recording of temperatures of refrigerators, freezers, and cool-rooms, using maxima and minima thermometers and/or digital data loggers where available, should be performed without fail—even on weekends and public holidays! These data should be updated daily on standardized forms to allow easy monitoring of any changes away from the norm.
> 2. Checking on the position of the cap and the level of nitrogen in liquid nitrogen containers.
> 3. Regular and systematic inspection of all items of equipment which require clean lenses (for example, microscopes, spectrophotometers) and checks on focus and adjustment of light sources.
> 4. Periodic checks on the position of centrifuge rotors (tight centre bolts) and regular cleaning. Rotor speeds can be calibrated with an anemometer.
> 5. Many automated pieces of equipment (for example, haematological and biochemistry analysers) will have self-test and self-calibration programmes that run at start-up and shutdown. The results of these runs should be recorded and archived. More elaborate procedures may be required before and after longer periods of storage without use.
> 6. Any regularly used field equipment, such as thermometers, portable haemoglobin machines, and other POC diagnostics, will need to be calibrated periodically and have new batches of reagents checked.
> 7. Regular calibration of routinely used equipment such as balances, pH meters, and variable volume pipettes.

any change of kit or batch number of sera, media, or preservatives. Any changes in assay conditions (for example, changes in incubation time or temperature) will require amendments and updating of protocols, which should be validated by the laboratory supervisor. Staff members involved in distinct sequences of the procedures should be indicated on relevant flow charts, and these should be written into the logbook. A separate staff file, containing details of relevant training and certification, may be warranted in some circumstances.

4.4 Unusual or adverse events

The logbook should be used to keep a record of errors in test procedures (operator- or machine-reported) and in the preparation of reagents, power failures, temperature, and humidity changes that might influence the results of the tests or the quality of stored samples. The remedial action taken and results of the rerun of the test should also be documented.

5 Quality control and quality assurance

QC is an inherent component of any good study and a good laboratory. It is a process of routine checks designed to detect any deficiencies that could compromise the results of laboratory analysis and suggest how these might be corrected. An example would be checks that the laboratory always gets the same result for a split specimen. QC checks should be specified in the laboratory work plan and in SOPs. A useful resource that discusses general laboratory QC issues is Ratliff (2003).

QA is a set of activities aimed at evaluating the accuracy of laboratory analysis and to guide improvements if inaccuracies are detected. QA provided by a resource external to the field laboratory is complementary to QC and should be established to monitor and improve the quality of laboratory procedures and validate the effectiveness of a QC programme. For example, a reference laboratory may supply specimens that are analysed 'blind' with the results compared to those of the reference laboratory and all the other laboratories participating in the same QA scheme.

5.1 Reproducibility of test results

The reliability of laboratory results should be tested by regular checks on their reproducibility. The level of acceptable variation will depend both on the test and study. This information is normally predefined in SOPs, test manuals, and the study protocol. Many test systems have inbuilt controls for this purpose, using standardized reagents of known concentration or quantity. The use of such standard controls is important, but not necessarily sufficient, to monitor the quality of test procedures. Depending on the procedure, samples should be tested in duplicate or re-read by a second technician. The frequency with which such repeats are performed depends upon how well the laboratory is running and how long it has been doing the test. Typically, when a test is first introduced or a new staff member is conducting the test, a high frequency of such checking is appropriate, with a decreased frequency as the procedures become more familiar, assuming the re-tests are showing negligible differences to the original results. In many circumstances, it will be appropriate to ensure that duplicate analyses are done on between 5% and 10% of samples on a routine basis. It is sometimes possible and advisable to seed known positive or known negative samples into test runs, which are labelled in such a way that the laboratory staff running the test cannot spot them. This is particularly important if it is expected that the great majority of samples will either test negative or test positive (for example, seeding a positive result if a long run of negatives is expected). Needless to say, a system will need to be in place to remove these QC test results from the data on the study samples. Where POC diagnostic tests are administered by field staff, it may be essential for a supervisor to review or repeat tests in the field, as results may become less reliable over time.

Reproducibility should be checked within batches, between batches, and from day to day or week to week by the use of appropriate controls. Intra-observer variation can be determined by having duplicate samples processed by the same observer at different times, and inter-observer variation measured by having the same samples processed independently by two different staff members. Inter-product variation is tested by comparing new vs old batches of staining solutions, media, reagents, and so on, on a group of the same samples.

It is essential that immediate remedial action is taken if QC checks reveal a problem.

5.2 Internal quality control

Two types of QC can be distinguished—'internal' and 'external'. Internal QC comprises procedures that are introduced within the field laboratory. External QC involves external monitoring such as the duplicate testing of samples in another reference laboratory to serve as a 'gold standard' or 'blind' measurement in the field laboratory of a set of samples provided by an external reference laboratory.

The essence of internal QC lies in a tight circle of checks, reporting, evaluation, and action. It is essential to have detailed manuals of every procedure, with a checklist to be consulted each time the procedure is run. Well-kept records, with regular review of these by the supervisors, are key elements in QC. Laboratory QC procedures must be an integral part of the work plan for the study.

5.3 External quality assurance

A major reason for external QA programmes is to check the accuracy of test results. Reproducibility can be assessed adequately by internal QC procedures, but checks on accuracy are best done, for many tests, in collaboration with other laboratories. The results from a laboratory may be highly reproducible within that laboratory but might be consistently incorrect. There are a range of external QA programmes which offer both testing of site-generated samples and/or the provision of a panel of samples with known characteristics that are specific for each assay (for example, biochemistry and haematology analysers). If specimens are selected for QA checks after they have been analysed locally and in such a way that the laboratory staff will not know which specimen will be selected, the use of site-generated QA systems are to be preferred to QA that depends on specimens provided by the external laboratory, since the laboratory staff will know which these QA panel specimens are and may take particular care with them.

SOPs need to be developed for the shipping and reception of samples for QA. An investigation request form should accompany samples that are sent, and every effort should be made to ensure that transport conditions are appropriate and the same for all samples (for example, route, packing conditions, and type of container). Attainment of levels of proficiency by the laboratory and its staff may be a prerequisite prior to involvement in some studies; but, after that, external QA activities would be most frequent during training phases and at the beginning of a field study but should continue throughout. If a problem is detected, it is essential that the reason for this is investigated immediately and that this leads to effective remedial action.

The WHO has produced a list of pre-qualified QC laboratories (<http://apps.who.int/prequal/lists/pq_qclabslist.pdf>), and a link to the United Kingdom National External Quality Assessment Service is <http://www.ukneqas.org.uk/content/Pageserver.asp>.

6 Accreditation and links between laboratories

In some cases, a field laboratory may be set up specifically for the conduct of a particular study and may have no regular links with other laboratories. Increasingly, however, there will be links with other laboratories, either as collaborative partners in projects or to provide specialized expertise and analysis. There should be a clear specification in the study protocol of which procedures and checks will be performed at each laboratory, how arrangements will be made for the transport of specimens and supplies between them, and how and which records will be exchanged. Links with an external reference laboratory may be desirable for independent checks, as part of QA procedures (see Section 5.3).

If samples are to be sent to other laboratories for further storage, processing, or analysis (for example, blood, sera, slides), it will be important to give attention to the following points.

1. It is risky to send entire samples to another laboratory or to send all of the samples from one survey or study at the same time. Duplicates should be kept, even when storage facilities are limited, to guard against loss during shipment.

2. Samples should not be sent to another laboratory without a clear agreement as to what analyses will be done and how these will be reported back. It is essential that an SOP defines *who does what, with what, and when*. These arrangements are defined in Material Transfer Agreements (MTAs). An MTA is a contract that governs the transfer of research materials, such as blood or serum samples, between two organizations. The number of samples to be analysed and type of tests should be agreed beforehand, ideally as part of a predefined analysis plan. It is common practice to send samples to another laboratory in such a way that they are analysed 'blind' (for example, no details are sent of which trial arm the samples are from or of the age and sex of the individual subjects). Agreement with respect to publication procedures should also be made, before specimens are sent.

3. The MTA agreed between the field and other laboratories should be part of the study protocol, in which the division of responsibilities should be specified. All parties must also adhere to the provisions of the MTA, in order to participate in the study (for example, local research clearance and ethical clearance).

7 Coding and linkage of results

In order to remove the possibility of bias, staff working in the laboratory should not know which trial arm any sample is from, and it should not be possible for this to be deduced from the labelling system employed. Specimens must be labelled in such a way, however, that each is identified uniquely, and any test results can be linked back to other records of the individual from whom the specimen was taken. While this seems to be stating the obvious, the problems that arise with these aspects of large studies are often substantial. Special care is necessary in longitudinal studies where individuals may be followed for many years, in studies involving many different research groups or laboratories, and in studies where results need to be linked with census information that may be updated over time (for example, individuals may move house, and this may cause problems if the coding system for individuals is too closely linked to a house code). Pre-printed labels are highly advantageous.

Laboratory results will usually be recorded in laboratory books or on specially prepared forms for data entry. Where the machine used for a particular test prints out the results, these should be carefully transcribed on to data forms, preferably using double entry (see Chapter 20, Section 5.1), and the printed output stored. Some machines generate printouts on heat-sensitive paper. In this case, a heat-stable photocopy must be made and stored. Increasingly, electronic record keeping will render these particular storage methods obsolete. Result codes that identify particular problems or features, such as lost and broken samples, technical problems with batches of samples (for example, staining, storage, transport), and the identification of the technicians involved with each test (to check variations between observers) should be used. Errors in readings on some automated machines (for example, values outside the normal range) will be reported or 'flagged' immediately, so that the assay can be repeated, if necessary.

If the study uses laboratory numbers, in addition to individual identification numbers, as is often the case, both numbers should be entered on a computer form for data entry, so that cross-checks and data linkage can be done in the computer.

If multiple laboratory tests are being performed on samples from the trial population, it may be best to wait until all the results have been assembled and collated before entering them into the computer, so that the checking and linkage back to other data on each individual can be done in relatively few steps. This will depend on how the data entry system is organized, but repeated processing of many small sets of data is liable to lead to confusion and may be unnecessarily time-consuming. However, a compromise may be necessary if results are needed in a timely manner for selection for QC or QA checks so that they can be used for the clinical care of the participant.

8 Laboratory health and safety

Detailed attention to health and safety are key aspects of any laboratory. This may be of special importance in some field laboratories, as they may be relatively accessible by the public or have other specific safety risks. It is important therefore to ensure that each laboratory has its own health and safety manual, addressing both general and specific risks, and that this is read by each new staff member or authorized laboratory visitor. A process of evaluation should be instituted to make sure that all the staff understand the health and safety rules, before performing laboratory tasks. If field staff are to collect and perform primary processing of samples, they will need to be made aware of potential risks. Procedures that will need to be covered will include disposal of needles, blood, stool, urine, and sputum samples, and of used reagents, chemicals, and detergents. Usually, all sharps should be disposed of in special sharps containers, which should be returned to the base laboratory for final disposal. Special attention should be paid to precautions concerning the transmission of blood-borne infections such as hepatitis B and HIV, and specific instructions given for what staff are to do if they are inadvertently exposed to potential infection. It should be standard procedure that field laboratories have at least a starter supply of antiretroviral drugs for HIV post-exposure prophylaxis if blood is being collected or processed. This is obviously even more important in high HIV prevalence areas. Adequate personal protective equipment should be made available for the type of samples to be collected.

Safety procedures should be regularly reviewed by laboratory supervisors and all staff concerned. Laboratory safety guidelines are given in World Health Organization (2004).

References

Cheesbrough, M. 1987. *Medical laboratory manual for tropical countries*. London: Tropical Health Technology.

Ratliff, T. A. 2003. *The laboratory quality assurance system: a manual of quality procedures and forms*. Hoboken, NJ: Wiley-Interscience.

Stevens, W. 2003. Good clinical laboratory practice (GCLP): the need for a hybrid of good laboratory practice and good clinical practice guidelines/standards for medical testing laboratories conducting clinical trials in developing countries. *Quality Assurance*, **10**, 83–9.

World Health Organization. 2003. *Manual of basic techniques for a health laboratory* [Online]. Geneva: World Health Organization. Available at: <http://www.labquality.be/documents/ANALYSIS/9241545305.pdf>.

World Health Organization. 2004. *Laboratory biosafety manual* [Online]. Geneva: World Health Organization. Available at: <http://whqlibdoc.who.int/publications/2004/9241546506.pdf>.

World Health Organization. 2009. *Good Clinical Laboratory Practice (GCLP)* [Online]. Geneva: World Health Organization. Available at: <http://www.who.int/tdr/publications/documents/gclp-web.pdf>.

Chapter 18

Budgeting and accounting

1 Introduction to budgeting and accounting 300
2 Budgeting 303
  2.1 Capital costs 304
  2.2 Recurrent costs 305
    2.2.1 Personnel 305
    2.2.2 Consultant or technical advisor costs 305
    2.2.3 Supplies 305
    2.2.4 Travel and per diems 306
    2.2.5 Patient care and participant costs 306
    2.2.6 Other expenses 306
    2.2.7 Indirect costs (institutional overheads) 306
3 Accounting 307
  3.1 Supporting documents 307
  3.2 Books of account 308
  3.3 Reconciliations 309
    3.3.1 Bank reconciliation 310
    3.3.2 Petty cash reconciliation 310
    3.3.3 Trial balance 310
  3.4 Cost codes 310
4 Budget monitoring 310
  4.1 Analysis of expenditure 311
  4.2 Balance sheet 311
  4.3 Cash flow forecast 311
5 Accounts summaries and auditing 311
6 Prevention of fraud and other losses 313
  6.1 Purchasing 314
  6.2 Debtors 315
  6.3 Cash payments 315
7 Glossary of financial terms 317

1 Introduction to budgeting and accounting

This chapter gives a brief introduction to budgeting and accounting requirements and associated methods in the context of field trials. For all but the smallest trials, a trained accountant should be part of the trial team, at least part-time. This chapter is not written for such accountants. Rather its aim is to help non-specialists, such as PIs or trial managers, understand the basics of what budgeting and accounting will be needed in the management of a trial, and why. Though this knowledge is essential for those conducting trials of interventions everywhere, well-qualified support staff who can do much of the checking of budgets and accounts are generally in short supply in LMICs, so the PIs and trial managers may need to do more of this themselves. The chapter does not attempt to cover what would be included in a full textbook on budgeting and accounting. For that, readers are referred to specialist textbooks, some of which are available free online (Walther, 2012). Most budgeting and accounting textbooks are written from the perspective of a profit-making business, but Mango's excellent *Financial management essentials: a handbook for NGOs* (Lewis, 2013) is designed specifically for non-governmental organizations (NGOs) and is also available free. With permission, this chapter summarizes many of the issues discussed in the Mango handbook, and those who want to know more are advised to consult the Mango website (<http://www.mango.org.uk/Guide>).

Like any specialist discipline, accounting has its own 'language'. The 2010 edition of a widely used dictionary of accounting runs to over 400 pages and has more than 3600 entries (Law, 2010). The definitions of some of the most important terms are given in Section 7, and every time a term that is defined in Section 7 is used in the chapter it is written in italics.

All too often, those planning a trial put a great deal of effort into the scientific aspects of trial design, but relatively less effort into ensuring that the *budget* for the trial is adequate. Yet the latter is critical for the success of the trial. Also, once the trial is funded, it is essential that the trial has a well-thought-through budgeting and accounting system, with sufficient checks and balances built into it to ensure that 'leakage' of those hard-won funds will not occur and that funds will be available when and where they are needed, so that the implementation of the trial can flow in a timely and efficient manner. PIs and other researchers do not usually need to do most of these tasks themselves, but they need to ensure that they will be done and know enough to be able to supervise them adequately.

There are four key principles of financial management of project grants:

- use funding for the purpose for which it has been given
- regularly monitor expenditure against the budget
- maintain accurate accounting records
- maintain a good filing and backup system for all financial information.

Keeping track of all purchases, donations, stores, and equipment is usually seen as a task for the accounting staff of an organization. These issues will not be dealt with in detail here, and those who want to know more about them are referred to the relevant sections of Lewis (2013). Monitoring and maintenance of clinical and laboratory supplies raise special issues such as needing to keep careful track of expiry dates and the rigorous use of the 'first in, first out' system of disbursement from the stores. Some of these are discussed in Chapter 17, and others are covered in accounting textbooks (Walther, 2012).

All organizations hosting trials should have a *financial manual* or a set of *financial regulations* that sets out all the financial policies and procedures to be followed.

This may be developed from scratch, but usually it is possible to modify a manual from a similar institution. The manual should cover the procedures that will be used for the tasks listed in Box 18.1. Almost, but not all, of these issues are covered in this chapter. Readers are referred to accounting textbooks for further details (Walther, 2012).

Most trials will operate within an existing organization that already has its own *financial manual* and detailed methods for budgeting and accounting. Where this is the case, the PI, trial manager, and others involved in the trial should obtain a copy of these and make sure that they know the procedures and that they will provide all the information and necessary financial checks and balances. Occasionally, a trial will need to set up its own procedures, either because there is no pre-existing local organization involved

---

Box 18.1 Financial manual

The manual should include instructions and notes relating to the items listed:
- financial accounting
- the *chart of accounts* and *cost codes*
- *budget* preparation and monitoring
- management accounting routines and deadlines
- managing internal risk, for example, delegated authority rules (i.e. who can do what), separation of duties, reconciliation, cash control, physical controls
- procurement and *tendering*
- expense claims
- *storekeeping*
- *asset* management, including vehicle management
- bank and cash handling
- management of exchange rate variations
- payroll procedures and staff *loans/advances*
- staff benefits and allowances
- *internal* and *external audit* arrangements
- how to deal with fraud and other irregularities.

It should also include:
- standard forms
- organization charts (organogram)
- job descriptions.

Adapted with permission from Lewis, T., *Financial management essentials: A handbook for NGOs*, Management Accounting for Non-governmental Organisations (MANGO), Oxford, UK, Copyright © 2014, available from <http://www.mango.org.uk/Guide>. This box is distributed under the terms of the Creative Commons Attribution Non Commercial 4.0 International licence (CC-BY-NC), a copy of which is available at http://creativecommons.org/licenses/by-nc/4.0/.

in the trial or because the trial will need to be run from a new remote office. Here, the PI should seek professional help to set up suitable financial systems but should know enough to ensure that the results meet the standards of good financial practice. The rest of this chapter gives a brief introduction to what these should include.

In this chapter, the focus is on the costs of conducting an intervention trial. In Chapter 19, the focus is on the costs of the intervention itself, as they would be when the intervention is implemented in a public health programme. The time horizon for the research is generally well circumscribed, whereas that for provision of an intervention in a public health system is usually open-ended. This chapter is written from the perspective of accountants, whereas Chapter 19 leans more towards that of economists.

2 Budgeting

The trial *budget* should be prepared as part of the trial planning process and be used throughout the trial as a monitoring tool. Usually, the budget will need to be prepared as part of the grant application. The potential funder will usually have specific instructions for presentation of the budget, but the norm is to have a detailed *budget* and a *budget* justification as an annex to the application. In some cases, a summary *budget* may also be required within the main body of the application.

The costing of research is often an aspect of proposal development that gives inexperienced investigators considerable difficulty, and getting it wrong can have serious consequences. Overestimating the required budget will be viewed poorly by the reviewers and the funding agency and may lead to the proposal being rejected, while under-budgeting may result in resources being exhausted before the study is completed. Some funding agencies may be sympathetic to requests for supplementary funding if there are good reasons, for example, greater than expected inflation or unexpected currency devaluation, but are less sympathetic when investigators have not properly anticipated costs while preparing the original proposal.

It is difficult to give firm guidelines of what may or may not be included in the trial budget. Funding agencies often give specific guidelines. The important points to bear in mind are first that all costs should be justified, in terms of project needs, and second, if it is not asked for, it is unlikely to be given! The essential characteristics of budgets are that they should be:

- *reasonable*. The costs shown should be appropriate for the purposes for which they will be used
- *well-researched*. Actual costs in the past provide a good guide for anticipating future costs for the same or similar equipment or procedures. Several independent quotations (three is the usual minimum) should be obtained for major items of equipment to ensure that the costs quoted represent the best value for money
- *detailed*. All significant costs should be given in detail. 'Fuel and servicing of vehicles $10 000' is inadequate! Even if the funding agency does not require the detail, the appropriate calculations should be done, in order to be able to arrive at an accurate final figure
- *well-justified and explained*. The necessity for each cost should be given. A good general rule is to justify all costs!

Most sponsors of research have specific forms for the *budget,* and they will usually specify what kinds of costs they will and will not cover. For example, some funders expect the institution in which the applicants are based to cover local telephone and postage costs and office accommodation and supplies, or to get the funds for these from the project's *indirect costs* (also called *overheads*) (see Section 2.2.7), while others are happy for these to be included in the *direct costs.* If it is not ruled out by the funder's guidelines, it is best to include as much as possible in the *direct costs.*

A common approach to categorizing costs is to separate them into *capital* and *recurrent* costs (Box 18.2).

Budgets for recurrent costs are usually done each year, whereas planning and budgeting for buildings, vehicles, and large equipment are often done for a 3- or 5-year period. It is critically important, however, to plan for the recurrent costs that will be required to maintain and use buildings, vehicles, and equipment. Generally, capital costs are discounted over the expected lifespan of the equipment or building and depreciated with use over time.

2.1 Capital costs

The purchase, construction, alteration, or renovation of a building is rarely needed for a single field trial, but, if this is required, the amount required would be included as a *capital cost* in the budget.

List each item of equipment required separately, and justify the need for each item. Sometimes, it might be possible to share equipment with another project in the same institution or a neighbouring institution, especially if the equipment is very expensive such as vehicles or major items of laboratory equipment. Estimates for the cost of

Box 18.2 Division of costs into capital and recurrent

Capital costs—relate to investments in items that last for more than a year such as:
- buildings
- vehicles
- equipment
- basic training
- land.

Recurrent costs—relate to those used up in the course of a year and needing regular replenishment such as:
- personnel and other labour (wages, salaries)
- supplies
- building operating and maintenance costs (electricity, water, etc.)
- in-service training (in-service courses for specific skills and knowledge)
- information, education, and communication (IEC) costs.

equipment should be obtained from manufacturers or suppliers and should include shipping and associated insurance costs. Maintenance agreement costs should be included under 'other expenses'. *Depreciation* of equipment must be allowed for, but there are wide variations in what is allowed by funders. Purchase of vehicles is often one of the major equipment costs in a large field trial. If a new vehicle is requested, reasons should be given why any existing vehicles cannot be used. In some places, it may be possible to rent a vehicle commercially, so the costs of rental should be compared with the costs of purchase, and any proposals for purchase should be justified on this basis. Even with a new vehicle, there will be costs to add for fuel, lubricants, servicing, and maintenance, with the maintenance costs increasing with vehicle age. These should be budgeted under recurrent costs.

2.2 Recurrent costs

2.2.1 Personnel

Give details of the names (where known), positions, and roles of personnel to be engaged on the project. Indicate the proportion of time that each person, including the PI, will devote to the project, and calculate the salary cost on a pro rata basis. Estimates should be made separately for each year of the study and should include provision for annual increases in salary, where appropriate. Some grant agencies will not contribute to the salary of the PI but will still expect to know what proportion of their time will be spent on the project. Appropriate amounts should be added to cover staff benefits such as the employer's pension contributions, staff health insurance, cost of living allowances, and housing and leave allowances. Internationally recruited staff usually receive specific additional benefits such as travel costs from their normal country of residence to the project site and back for themselves and their dependants. Staff benefits and allowances may be a considerable proportion (often 25%, sometimes more) of the total gross salary costs to the project. If staff will need to be recruited, or might need to be replaced if they leave before the end of the trial, make an allowance for their recruitment costs.

2.2.2 Consultant or technical advisor costs

Sometimes, it is appropriate to buy in the time of a consultant or technical advisor, rather than hiring them as staff. The grant application should specify the number of days that will be spent on the project by each consultant, together with their daily rate of remuneration and any associated costs such as travel and per diems. The funding agency may have guidelines for the rates of remuneration that they are willing to pay for consultants to a project. The specific contribution that any consultant will make to the project must be justified.

2.2.3 Supplies

Supplies should be itemized in separate categories (for example, stationery and office supplies, communications (such as Internet, postage, phone calls), fuel and lubricants, laboratory supplies) and should be justified in terms of the needs of the project (for example, numbers of each laboratory test to be performed). If the trial requires the use of experimental animals, the PI should seek specific advice in advance on whether the funder will allow this and the specific information they will need in the proposal.

2.2.4 Travel and per diems

Specify the destination of each trip, the number of persons, the mode of transport, and the basis for the costs (most funders will only pay economy air fares). Justification should be given for all travel. Funders have different rules about travel to conferences (some do not allow any, while others allow one or more attendance per year).

Per diem (overnight allowance) costs may be a significant proportion of the budget in field trials, and the rates paid should be based on existing practice of the research institution. These costs should be justified for each member of the project staff to whom they will be paid, in terms of the necessity for spending the specified number of days away from the home institution.

2.2.5 Patient care and participant costs

There are often patient care costs that may be incurred in a trial that are not directly related to the trial intervention. A frequent concern in field trials in LMICs is provision of adequate health care to those in the trial and the degree to which the research project should be responsible for these (see also Chapter 6, Section 3.4 concerning medical and other care offered to participants in a trial).

Reimbursement to participants in a trial for travel or loss of earnings should usually be listed under 'other expenses', but some funders suggest these are put under patient care costs or in a special section.

2.2.6 Other expenses

This section should contain items such as rentals and leases, equipment maintenance (service contracts, repairs), computer charges (if there is not a separate claim for purchase of computers under 'equipment'), publication costs, fees for services related to the project (for example, library searches), office supplies, postage and telecommunication charges (telephone, telex, fax, e-mail), and possible patient care costs (see Section 2.2.5).

For trials of drugs and vaccines and some other interventions, it is strongly advised to include indemnity insurance costs, i.e. insurance for claims against the sponsor for damage that might be done to participants in a trial through the trial procedures.

Not all costs listed above may be allowed by a funding agency, but, if in doubt, it is better to include them in the application (even though the agency may subsequently disallow them!).

2.2.7 Indirect costs (institutional overheads)

There are 'hidden' costs associated with all research. Someone must administer the grant, pay salaries, order supplies, supply heat or air conditioning and light to offices, supply the offices themselves, have them cleaned and maintained, provide security, etc. These costs, called *indirect costs* or 'institutional *overheads*', may be substantial. Such costs may amount to between 20% and 90% or more of the direct costs of the research project, depending on exactly what is included in the direct costs. These *indirect costs* should be added on to the *direct costs* of the research when a grant is submitted to a funding agency. Many institutions in LMICs have been lax about claiming such costs, with the result that scarce core institutional budgets have effectively subsidized specific research projects.

Some funding agencies refuse payment of *overheads* (for example, most United Nations (UN) agencies and charitable foundations), while others will pay them in their own country, but not outside (for example, US Public Health Service). Often, it is possible to directly budget for many of these items (to be listed in the direct costs as rental of office space, cost of utilities, administrative staff support, cost of library searches, etc.), and it is usually advantageous to do so.

It is common for an investigator to underestimate, rather than overestimate, the final costs of a trial, especially if it lasts several years. Though some funders may accept requests for an additional allocation when increases in costs could not reasonably have been foreseen, even this cannot be guaranteed, let alone if something has been forgotten or underestimated in the costing. Whenever possible, avoid cutting corners on a budget in order to fit it to a pre-specified total amount, as underfunding may result in many stressful months in trying to conduct the trial on an insufficient budget. It may be better either to not apply for the grant or to rethink the trial question and design, rather than knowingly under-budgeting the trial from the start.

3 Accounting

All money that is received and spent for the trial must be accounted for in a way that is both truthful and transparent, so it can be checked by an outsider (an 'auditor').

Accounts can either be maintained on an *accruals* or a cash basis. In the *accruals* method, *income* and *expenditure* are attributed to the month they are 'incurred'. For example, an item of equipment may be acquired during February, and so the expenditure for that equipment has been incurred in February, even if the *invoice* is not received and/or the payment made until April. Under the *accruals* accounting method, the cost would be accounted for in February, whereas, under the cash accounting method, it would be accounted for in April, i.e. when the invoice is paid. Some funders require one or the other method, while many leave it up to the grant holder. Clearly, a mixture of both methods should never be used within a single set of accounts.

Accounting records should include four main types of documents: *supporting documents*, *books of account, reconciliations*, and a list of *cost codes*. These will each be discussed briefly in this section, but a fuller description can be found Lewis (2013).

3.1 Supporting documents

These are the original documents that show how the money has been received and spent. They should all have a brief written explanation (a voucher), which has a unique sequential reference number that corresponds to an entry in one of the *books of account* (see Section 3.2).

They include:

- *receipts and receipt vouchers* for all money received. Every *receipt* should be given its own receipt voucher, which should be assigned its own unique sequential reference number, along with the date of the receipt, the name of the person or organization that gave the money, a description of what the payment was for, the amount received, and the accounts or *cost code* (see Section 3.4)

- *receipts and payment vouchers* for all money paid out. These are the equivalent of the *receipts* and receipt vouchers for all money received and should have similar information on them
- *invoices* provided by other organizations or individuals requesting payment. These should be certified and stamped as paid
- *pay-in vouchers* for all money paid into the bank
- *bank statements*
- *journal vouchers*. These are vouchers that record adjustments, for example, if a payment or *receipt* has been entered incorrectly or allocated to the wrong *cost code*. They therefore relate to transactions where no actual cash changes hands, but they explain a change that has been made after an original entry into the accounts was made.

With the above documents on file, it will always be possible to (re)construct a full set of accounts, and they form the basis for the *audit trail*.

Other useful supporting documents include:

- *local purchase orders*. These are vouchers requesting that something be purchased
- *supplier's waybill*. This is a list of goods sent by a carrier (see Glossary, Section 7)
- *delivery notes* (or goods received notes, goods receipt advice). These are vouchers that record any item received by the project such as a piece of equipment or a box of pencils
- *stores requisition vouchers*, bin cards (tally cards), and stores issue notes. These are documents that record all the incomings, outgoings, and the balance of all items kept in the *stores*
- *approvals*. These are specific notes or vouchers approving payments
- *petty cash vouchers*. In order not to have to go to the bank every time a relatively small expenditure is made, it is useful to have *petty cash* in the office. The initial amount (*petty cash float*) for this comes from the bank account, and, under the commonly used 'fixed float method', the *petty cash* is topped up to the same amount when it falls below a preordained threshold. For example, if the *petty cash float* is $100, then it may be reasonable to top it back up to $100 whenever the balance falls below $50. A maximum limit for a single *petty cash* payment should be fixed, with any payments that are larger than this needing to come directly from the bank (for example, be made by cheque). Each payment from the *petty cash* should be backed up by a receipt and a *petty cash* voucher which records similar information to that on a payment voucher. Money that is paid into the project should not be paid into the *petty cash*, but directly into the bank. This is to ensure that it does not just 'disappear' but passes through an externally recorded system.

3.2 Books of account

Various books of accounts should be maintained, covering different aspects of income and expenditure, as follows:

- *cash book* (sometimes called the *bank book*). Rather confusingly, the *cash book* records all transactions that pass through a bank account, but, although '*bank book*' would be the more logical name, '*cash book*' is much more commonly used. Some of the transactions may relate to actual cash, while others will be based on cheques, for example. Every entry in the *cash book* should have a unique transaction number which corresponds to a specific receipt or payment voucher, and the entry itself should also appear on the bank statement, thus allowing cross-checking
- *petty cash book*. The *petty cash book* records all transactions related to the *petty cash* and is the *petty cash* equivalent of the *cash book*. Any *income* to the *petty cash book* should match an *expenditure* in the *cash book*
- *advances ledger*. This records all payments that have been made to anyone in advance. This may be a down payment on a large item of equipment, for example. However, the commonest recipients are members of staff receiving an *advance* on their salary, for example, as a *loan* or to allow them to pay their rent in advance. Usually, the staff member must pay these advances off in monthly instalments by deductions from their pay. The simplest way to keep a record of these *advances* and their repayment is to allocate a page in the *advances ledger* for each person or organization who receives an *advance*, and then the accountant enters each repayment until the *advance* has been fully paid off
- *assets register* (also often known as the *fixed assets register*). The *assets* of the trial are all the buildings or items of equipment that have been purchased by, or been donated to, the trial. The *assets register* should list all of these, along with identifying details such as their make, model, and serial number. Each *asset* should be physically tagged with a unique reference number for identification purposes. The *asset register* should also, at a minimum, include the date and purchase price of each item. It is useful to split the list into major and minor *assets*. Major *assets* are items that are worth more than a specific amount when new (often between $500 and $1000) such as buildings, vehicles, and major items of laboratory equipment. Many funding agencies will want to decide on the disposal of items at the end of the trial that cost the grant more than a certain amount, so, if there are such restrictions, it is sensible to fix the threshold for 'major *assets*' to that amount
- *taxes withheld ledger*. This is a record of any taxes that the project has withheld, in order to pay them to the tax authorities. Examples include staff income tax and other national insurance payments.

3.3 Reconciliations

Reconciliations are undertaken to ensure that the *books of account* and *supporting documentation* are consistent. All too frequently, *reconciliations* either are not conducted or are not carried out frequently enough. Yet this can mean that errors, either due to mistakes or fraud, go unnoticed until a major problem has accrued. *Reconciliations* should be reviewed by a different staff member from the one who did them, in order to provide a check on their validity. This can be a challenge when the number of staff who are either qualified or senior enough to do this are few and over-stretched, but it is asking for trouble not to follow the rule of separation of duties in this regard.

3.3.1 Bank reconciliation

The *cash/bank book* is checked against the bank statement. This should be done at least once a month. In practice, there will almost always be a difference because of delays such as:

- money banked by the project has not yet been shown in the bank's records
- cheques issued by the project have not yet been presented to the bank
- bank charges and interest may have been applied
- errors may have been made by the bank or in recording entries in the *cash/bank book*.

The reasons for any discrepancies should be listed in the *bank reconciliation* report prepared by the project accountant.

3.3.2 Petty cash reconciliation

Petty cash should be counted and reconciled at least weekly (and also on an unscheduled basis from time to time) by someone who is not responsible for handling the petty cash.

3.3.3 Trial balance

Every month, or at least once a quarter, two lists of balances should be drawn up, one of the *debit* balances and the other of the *credit* balances, on all the accounts that relate to the trial. The totals of each list should match. If they do not, then checks need to be made to explain the differences, which should be resolved.

3.4 Cost codes

Cost codes (sometimes called *analysis codes*) identify specific budget lines for each transaction. They allow the accountant to summarize *income* and *expenditure*, according to these budget lines such as personnel costs, travel, or laboratory consumables. It is important to give careful thought to the *cost codes* before the accounts are set up and, if in doubt, to subdivide the cost codes using a tree system, as any later changes to the *cost codes* will require the accountant to go back and recode the relevant vouchers and entries in the *books of account*. For example, if there is only one *cost code* for all travel, but later information is required on how much has been spent for international travel, as opposed to travel within the country, this will not be possible without going back to re-code all the travel *expenditures*.

4 Budget monitoring

Once the budget has been finalized and the necessary funds have been received, the budget acts as the basis for all future *expenditure* and financial reporting for the trial. The *expenditure* should be compared against the *budget* on a frequent and regular basis, such as every 3 months for a trial that lasts more than 1 year, and every month for a trial of a year or less. This process is known as *budget monitoring*. This is an activity that is frequently given too little attention—sometimes with disastrous consequences for the trial. *Budget monitoring* should include *variance analysis* where the difference (*variance*) between the *actual* (past) and *forecast* (future predicted) *expenditure* is compared with the *budget* to see whether there have been, or are predicted to be, any over- or under-spends, either overall or on specific budget line items.

The overall and future *budget* should be reviewed at least once a year to check whether it will still be adequate. If not, it is best to approach the funder early, rather than leaving it till towards the end of the trial when the money is about to run out.

4.1 Analysis of expenditure

Regular analysis of expenditure by *cost codes* is very useful to allow the detection of excessive expenditure on one or more *cost codes*. For example, if the laboratory seems to be getting through an excessive amount of laboratory supplies, this might be because the supplies of another project are being erroneously charged to the trial's account or because the laboratory staff or storekeeper are stealing them. The level of detail provided by the *cost codes* is not usually needed for the summary accounts sent to the funding agency, but it is relatively easy to collapse the *cost codes* down to major budget line items such as all personnel costs or all travel costs.

Funders often have specific rules about *virement* of expenditure between budget line items. Many allow no more than 10% *virement* out of, or into, any budget line item, and some will not allow any *virement* into personnel or into equipment, for example.

4.2 Balance sheet

The balance sheet summarizes the current financial position of the project by showing all its *assets* and *liabilities*. It and the *cash flow forecast* are needed for *budget monitoring*. The *assets* include both *fixed assets* (tangible and likely to last more than 1 year) and current assets (cash or something that could be converted into cash within a year such as a savings account at a bank). *Liabilities* include current or short-term *liabilities* (to be paid within year) and long-term *liabilities* (long-term commitments).

4.3 Cash flow forecast

This shows the expected income and expenditure of the project into the future and is essential to be able to predict when there might be a shortage of funds to be able to meet future expenditure and to take steps to avoid this.

5 Accounts summaries and auditing

Once *expenditure* on the trial has started, the *income and expenditure accounts* will show the *actual* (past) *income* and *expenditure* within the *cash book*, and this should then be summarized periodically (ideally once a month, but at least once every 3 months) by major line items. The *income and expenditure accounts* can then be put into an income and expenditure statement, which will show *actual* (past) and *forecast* (future) *income* and the equivalent for *expenditure*, broken down by period (for example, monthly or quarterly) and by line items. This is used for *budget monitoring*. It is useful to include a column showing the percentage by which the budget has been over- or under-spent (known as a *variance analysis*). The *income and expenditure accounts* and statement are the most useful summary accounts for most time-limited projects such as a trial.

The *balance sheet* summarizes the overall current financial position of a project or institution, taking into account the current market value of *assets*—fixed (for example, buildings, vehicles) and current (cash or savings that are likely to be converted into cash within 12 months). However, for a specific trial, a *balance sheet* is likely to be less useful than the *income and expenditure accounts*, an income and expenditure *forecast*, a list of (major) *assets*, and a *cash flow* report and *forecast* showing when *expenditures* can be expected relative to the *income*, in order to highlight potential periods when there may be a shortfall or when cash may need to be spent to avoid it being lost back to the funding agency.

It is essential that all accounts are subjected to *external audit*. Ideally, this should be done annually as soon as possible after year-end, based on the *annual accounts*. *External audit* is relatively expensive and needs to be included in the budget. Sometimes, the institution has arrangements in place that all their accounts are externally audited each year. Where this is the case, this is usually sufficient, but it is essential that this is checked with the funding agency, which may require a separate project-specific external audit.

Box 18.3 gives a checklist of questions to ask when reviewing financial information in a trial.

Box 18.3 Questions to ask when reviewing financial information

General

- Do the accounts make sense? Do the various figures add up correctly? Do the amounts given in different parts of the accounts match each other?
- Are the amounts given backed up by *supporting documents*?
- Do spot checks of some of the original *supporting documents* match the amounts given in the accounts?

Funding and expenditure

- Are funding and *expenditure* broadly in balance?
- Is there a significant increase or decrease in activity levels from the previous reporting period?
- What is the balance of direct project costs vs administrative and *indirect costs*?
- Is expenditure reasonable for the size and nature of the project?
- Are there any large bills outstanding which could substantially affect the figures shown?
- Are bills paid in a timely manner? If not, *creditors* may refuse to supply the project or the institution as a whole in the future.
- What is the projected year-end balance? Is this satisfactory? If not, what steps need to be taken to change things?

> **Box 18.3 Questions to ask when reviewing financial information (continued)**
>
> **Variances and virement**
>
> - Is the *expenditure* broadly in line with the *budget* (for example, ± 10%)?
> - Is the *income* broadly in line with the *budget* (for example, ± 10%)?
> - Are there any significant *variances* (for example, under-spending as a result of delayed activity plans, or overspending due to *inflation* or unexpected salary increases)? If so, have they been explained satisfactorily?
> - What action is being taken to correct significant *variances*? This might include going back to the funder to get permission for the *budget* to be changed.
> - Are all *virements* within the permitted range? If not, will it be possible to rectify this before the end of the project? If not, has the funder been approached to give their permission?
>
> **Cash flow**
>
> - Is the project owed any large sums of money? Are the project funds expended, borrowed, pledged, transferred, or otherwise used for reasons that are not directly associated with the project? What is being done to retrieve them?
> - Are there any unbudgeted expenses that may occur later in the financial year?
> - Is *income* still expected to come through on time?
> - Are spare cash balances invested to produce the best return? Is any interest being properly accounted for?
> - Has the *income* or *expenditure* been affected by exchange rate movements? Will the funder compensate for these if they were in a negative direction?
>
> Adapted with permission from Lewis, T., *Financial management essentials: A handbook for NGOs*, Management Accounting for Non-governmental Organisations (MANGO), Oxford, UK, Copyright © 2014, available from <http://www.mango.org.uk/Guide>. This box is distributed under the terms of the Creative Commons Attribution Non Commercial 4.0 International licence (CC-BY-NC), a copy of which is available at http://creativecommons.org/licenses/by-nc/4.0/.

6 Prevention of fraud and other losses

One of the duties of the PI in a trial is to ensure that there are systems in place to try to prevent or expose *fraud*. Preventing *fraud* is far better than exposing it after the event, so it is best to put systems in place in advance to check for potential *fraud* and to ensure that all relevant staff know that such checks are going to be carried out, in order to dissuade them from committing *fraud*.

One key mechanism for preventing *fraud* is through the separation of duties. This includes ensuring that a different person has custody of *assets* and cash from the person who does the recording of the related accounting entries. This provides a safeguard against any misuse of funds but also protects the individuals involved from any unfounded or malicious allegation of misuse. Separation of duties may be difficult to achieve where there are a limited number of personnel, but wherever possible:

- staff responsible for ordering goods or services (procurement) should not also have the power to authorize payment for the goods
- staff who raise cheques should not have the authority to sign them
- the *reconciliation* of the bank statement to the *cash/bank book* should be carried out by a different person from the one who writes up the *cash/bank book*. It must always be checked and authorized by a senior member of staff
- staff responsible for selecting and engaging new staff should not also operate the payroll system
- *petty cash* and banking should be checked by a member of staff who does not normally have access to the cash and bank records.

Areas where *fraud* is particularly common include purchasing, *debtors*, and cash payments.

6.1 Purchasing

In many countries, it is possible for the purchasing officer to arrange with the supplier whereby the supplier increases the price of the goods or services and the supplier and the purchasing officer share the mark-up between them. Insisting on three quotations may help avoid this but does not get round the problem if the purchasing officer has a similar arrangement with all three suppliers. A standard way that is used to try to get around this problem is the institution of a Tender Committee which is responsible for the evaluation of tenders from the potential suppliers prior to procurement. However, it is very rare that the members of a Tender Committee have insider information on the real minimum costs of items, and so they usually have to accept the information provided to them by the purchasing officer and can only spot obvious problems such as the purchasing officer recommending a supplier known to be unreliable simply because they have given the lowest quotation. An effective way to get round this problem is to periodically ask a trusted person (for example, from a different organization) to also price out some of the items, and the quotations can be compared with those obtained by the purchasing officer.

A purchasing plan should be made well ahead of time to try to ensure that all purchases are made according to plan. This is both to avoid delays due to late availability of key items, but also to avoid last minute purchases where it is not possible to check for the lowest possible prices. This is particularly important for items that are much cheaper if bought in a large city or imported.

Purchasing of fuel is a specific area that is a common source of *fraud*. Often, it will be a driver who has to purchase the fuel, rather than a professional purchasing officer. In some places, it is possible to get a receipt for more fuel than has actually been put into the vehicle, and the purchaser shares the mark-up with the supplier. Alternatively, some unscrupulous drivers have been known to siphon fuel out of the tank. One way of trying to avoid both of these problems is to allocate each vehicle to a specific driver and insist that the vehicle tank is always, or at least once per month, filled to its maximum capacity. It is then possible to monitor the fuel consumption accurately, i.e. from full tank to full tank. If the driver is made aware that this is going to be done and is given feedback on their vehicle's fuel consumption each month, this can make such *fraud* less likely.

6.2 Debtors

Some of these may be staff who have been given *loans* or *advances*, so that they can make payments on behalf of the trial (such as for overnight accommodation, travel expenses, cash payments to local assistants in the field, etc.). It is sometimes difficult for the accountant to insist on repayment by their friends (or relatives) on the staff, including the accounts staff themselves, or to resist the temptation to do a deal, so that the *loan* is accounted for as an *expenditure* and never recovered. To avoid this, each *debtor* should have a separate account within the *advances ledger*, in which all debts and their repayment are entered. These should be monitored by the accountant and checked by someone else at least once a quarter, so that action can be taken to follow up on debt retrieval.

As far as possible, staff should only be given *advances* or *loans* for specific and exceptional reasons, such as so that they can pay their rent in advance, since many landlords require a deposit that is only returned at the end of the rental period. Unless the *advances ledger* is kept up to date and checked against the payroll each month, *advances* can be very difficult for the accounts department to keep track of, and their repayment makes preparation and checking of the payroll complicated. Outstanding *advances* are difficult to recover at the end of a staff member's contract, especially if the staff member leaves at short notice. Staff have been known to deliberately get as many *advances* as possible just before they leave without notice, knowing that it will probably be too much trouble to pursue them. Where an *advance* is given to cover the purchase of a large item, such as a vehicle or for a rental down payment, it is advisable to require the original receipt for the item or rental agreement to be deposited with the trial office where it must, of course, be stored in a secure place such as in a safe. Where other *advances* are given to staff, it is rarely a good idea to allow these to exceed 1 month's net salary, as this is likely to be recoverable, even if someone leaves their post without giving notice.

6.3 Cash payments

These must always be signed for. Even so, it is relatively easy to either get a friend to sign or to fabricate a signature. It is important therefore that checks are made, such that payments are reasonable and reflect the activities carried out. Many projects insist that all cash payment vouchers are countersigned by a senior member of staff.

Box 18.4 gives a checklist for good financial practice.

Box 18.4 Financial good practice checklist

Budget management

- At least annual *budget* preparation/review.
- Monthly (or at least quarterly) *budget monitoring*, including:
  - *variance analysis*
  - *forecast, balance sheet, cash flow* report.
- Process to manage exchange rate movements.

Accounting records

- Maintain and keep original *supporting documentation* for all financial transactions.
- Maintain *books of account* recording all financial transactions, comprising as a minimum:
  - *cash/bank book* for each bank account
  - *petty cash book*
  - *assets register*.
- Undertake monthly bank *reconciliations*, and investigate any inconsistencies.
- Undertake weekly *petty cash book reconciliations*, and on a surprise basis from time to time, and investigate any inconsistencies.
- Regularly summarize records to feed into *budget monitoring*.
- Use a *cost codes* system.

Financial and related policies and procedures

- Have a written *financial manual* that details the budgeting and accounting procedures that will be used.
- Use standard forms, such as payment vouchers, *receipt* vouchers, *petty cash* vouchers, purchase order forms, travel and subsistence expenses claims, *assets register*, vehicle logs, bank *reconciliations, journal vouchers, advance/loan* applications, *storekeeping* forms such as stock cards/bin cards, goods received vouchers, and stock taking forms.
- Have clear procedures for managing internal risk, including:
  - delegated authority
  - separation of duties
  - cash control
  - physical controls such as having a safe, adequate security, and insurance cover

> **Box 18.4 Financial good practice checklist (continued)**
>
> - Have clear rules and procedures for:
>   - procurement and *tendering*
>   - expense claims
>   - *storekeeping*
>   - *asset* management (including vehicle management)
>   - payroll
>   - tracking for *loans*, *advances*, and repayments
>   - *audit* arrangements.
>
> ## Other policies and procedures
>
> - Governance arrangements, such as a constitution for the organization hosting the trial, with a governing body that meets on regular occasions, procedures for declaring and handling potential conflicts of interest, etc.
> - Staff management arrangements, including for:
>   - recruitment and selection
>   - induction
>   - discipline and grievance
>   - contracts of employment.
>
> Adapted with permission from Lewis, T., *Financial management essentials: A handbook for NGOs*, Management Accounting for Non-governmental Organisations (MANGO), Oxford, UK, Copyright © 2014, available from <http://www.mango.org.uk/Guide>. This box is distributed under the terms of the Creative Commons Attribution Non Commercial 4.0 International licence (CC-BY-NC), a copy of which is available at http://creativecommons.org/licenses/by-nc/4.0/.

7 Glossary of financial terms

Accruals	*Expenditure* incurred in an accounting period that has not yet been paid or *invoiced*. Opposite of *pre-payments*
Actual	*Income* earned and *expenditure* incurred over a given time period
Advance	Funding provided for future *expenditure*, which must be either accounted for or be repaid
Analysis code	Also known as *cost code*. A coding structure which specifies clearly and consistently the type of *income* being received and the type of *expenditure* being incurred
Annual accounts	The financial statements at year end (or each month or quarter) which include an *income and expenditure account* and *balance sheet*. The financial statements require external audit

continued

Asset	Anything that is of value to its owner. Also see *assets register*, *fixed asset*, *fixed assets register*
Assets register	Shortened name for the *fixed assets register*. A list of the *fixed assets* of the organization, usually giving details of value, serial numbers, location, purchase date, etc.
Audit	An independent check on the accounts of the project or organization. An *external audit* is done by a person who is independent of the organization, while an *internal audit* is done by someone from the project's own organization, but by a person who is independent of the management of that particular project
Audit trail	The ability to follow the course of any reported transaction through an organization's accounting systems and *supporting documents*
Balance sheet	Summarizes the current financial position by showing *assets* and *liabilities*
Bank book	Also known as *cash book*. A record of all transactions passing through a bank account
Bank reconciliation	The process of agreeing the entries and balance in the *cash/bank book* to the bank statement entries and balance at a particular date. Acts as a check on the completeness and accuracy of *cash/bank book* entries
Books of account	These detail all financial transactions and normally consist of, as a minimum, *cash/bank book* for each bank account, *petty cash book*, and *assets register*
Budget	Describes an amount of money that a project/organization expects to receive and spend for a set purpose over a given period of time
Budget monitoring report	A report showing actual performance against the *budget* for *income* and *expenditure*, with explanations provided for any significant *variances*. *Budget monitoring* reports are usually prepared at more than one level of detail
Capital expenditure	*Expenditure* which creates a *fixed asset*
Cash flow	The difference between cash received and cash spent in a period
Cash book	Also known as *bank book*. A record of all transactions passing through a bank account
Chart of accounts	A list of all the *cost codes* that are used to analyse transactions in an organization's accounting system
Cost code	Also known as *analysis code*. A coding structure that specifies clearly and consistently the type of *income* being received (for example, grant from the funder) and the type of *expenditure* being incurred (for example, salary costs, vehicle running costs)

7: GLOSSARY OF FINANCIAL TERMS | 319

Credit	A payment into the account
Creditor	A third party that has provided goods or services but has not yet been paid
Debit	A payment out of the account
Debtor	A third party that has been *invoiced* for goods or a service rendered but has not yet paid. Hence, a 'bad debtor' is a third party from whom a debt is very unlikely to be recovered
Delivery note	A voucher recording receipt of an item (i.e. that it has been delivered)
Depreciation	An *expense* recorded in the accounts to reduce the value of a long-term *fixed asset* to reflect the fact that it will be worth less, the older it gets
Direct costs	A cost that is directly attributable to an activity, service, or capital item (for example, purchase of a computer or a flight)
Expected income and expenditure	Expected *income* is usually from the funder. Expected *expenditures* are the anticipated running/recurrent or capital costs. These expected costs will help with *forecasting* at year-end
Expenditure	Money paid out; an amount of money spent
External audit	Check on the accounts by a person who is independent of the organization, usually an accountant with special training to be an auditor
Financial manual (or financial regulations)	A manual containing a full set of financial policies and procedures. These will support financial management
Fixed assets	Items (such as equipment, vehicles, or buildings) that are owned by an organization and are intended for use on a continuing basis in the organization's activities. In practice, this means for more than one accounting period. The cost is usually apportioned (or *depreciated*) over the asset's useful life
Fixed assets register	Sometimes shortened to *assets register*. A list of the *fixed assets* of the organization, usually giving details of value, serial numbers, location, purchase date, etc.
Forecasting	The estimation of the (future) year-end (or next month/quarter) position with regard to *income* and *expenditure*
Imprest	There are two alternative definitions of this term, so it is best avoided. It is sometimes synonymous with *petty cash float*, but it is also sometimes used to mean an *advance*
Income	Money paid in

continued

Income and expenditure accounts	The income and expenditure account includes all *income* generated and *expenditure* incurred over the accounting period and shows the resulting surplus or deficit achieved by the organization for the period. These accounts are usually broken down by *cost codes*
Indirect costs	Also known as *overheads*. A cost which cannot be directly allocated to a specific activity, service, or capital item but which is more general in nature (for example, to cover the utility, insurance, infrastructure, general administrative, management, and governance costs, etc. for the running of an organization)
Inflation	A general increase in prices and consequent decrease in the purchasing power of money
Internal audit	An *audit* that is carried out by the organization that holds the account
Invoice	A written request for payment received from a supplier for specific goods or services
Journal voucher	A voucher that records an entry in the accounts that relates to a non-monetary transaction, for example, for recording a donation in kind or depreciation or to correct a previous error in the accounts
Ledger	A collection of accounts of a similar type such as an *advances* ledger or a 'taxes withheld ledger'
Liability	An amount owed by your organization to others, including *loans*, *accruals*, grants received in advance, and outstanding *invoices*
Loan	Funding provided, which must be repaid
Overheads	Also known as *indirect costs*. A cost which cannot be directly allocated to a specific activity, service, or *capital* item but which is more general in nature (for example, to cover the utility, insurance, infrastructure, general administrative, management, and governance costs, etc. for the running of an organization)
Petty cash	Money kept as cash for making small payments below a certain threshold to save needing to go to the bank to withdraw funds too frequently
Petty cash book	The day-to-day listing of *petty cash* paid in and given out
Petty cash float	A sum of money, set at an agreed level, which is topped up by the exact amount spent since it was last reimbursed, to bring it back to its original level. See also *petty cash* and *petty cash book*

Receipt	A formal record received from a supplier that confirms that a specific amount of money was paid for certain goods or services. Also given to anyone who buys goods or services from the trial
Reconciliation	Checking mechanism which verifies the integrity of an accounting system by comparing account balances to an independent source (for example, a bank statement) or by identifying the individual balances which make up a total account balance (for example, comparing the total of individual *asset* balances to the total of the *fixed asset* account)
Storekeeping	The process for managing *stock*
Stores	A generic term either for *stock* or for the place where the *stock* is kept when not in use
Supporting documents	Original documents to support *income* and *expenditure* (for example, *receipts*, *invoices*, bank statements, *journal vouchers*, purchase orders, *delivery notes*, approvals, etc.)
Tender	An offer made in writing by one party to another to execute specific work, supply certain commodities, etc. at a given cost
Trial balance	A listing of the balances on all the accounts that relate to this specific account, with debit balances in one column and credit balances in another. The totals of each column should match
Variance	Difference between the *budget* and actual amount of *income* and/or *expenditure*. Variances are often described as 'adverse' or 'favourable'
Variance analysis	Part of budget monitoring, looking at the significant variations between the *budget* and *actual income* and *expenditure*, and seeking to explain why they exist and what can be done to rectify the position
Virement	Transfer of funds from one *budget*/budget line to another. If a virement exceeds the threshold that has been pre-agreed with the funder, this will require formal approval from the funder, usually in advance
Waybill	A list of goods sent by a carrier, such as a courier, road haulage, railway, or air-freight company, that states the route that the goods will follow

Adapted with permission from Lewis, T., *Financial management essentials: A handbook for NGOs,* Management Accounting for Non-governmental Organisations (MANGO), Oxford, UK, Copyright © 2014, available from <http://www.mango.org.uk/Guide>. This table is distributed under the terms of the Creative Commons Attribution Non Commercial 4.0 International licence (CC-BY-NC), a copy of which is available at http://creativecommons.org/licenses/by-nc/4.0/.

References

Law, J. 2010. *A dictionary of accounting*. Oxford: Oxford University Press.

Lewis, T. 2013. *Financial management essentials: a handbook for NGOs* [Online]. Oxford: Mango (Management Accounting for Non-governmental Organisations). Available at: <http://www.mango.org.uk/Guide>.

Walther, L. 2012. *Principles of accounting* [Online]. Available at: <http://www.principlesofaccounting.com/>.

Chapter 19
Intervention costing and economic analysis

1 Introduction to intervention costing and economic analysis 323
2 Types of economic analyses 324
   2.1 Cost-effectiveness analysis 325
   2.2 Cost-utility analysis 325
      2.2.1 Disability-adjusted life-years and quality-adjusted life-years 326
   2.3 Cost–benefit analysis 326
3 Framing the analysis 327
   3.1 Perspective 327
   3.2 Range of inputs and outcomes 328
   3.3 Time frame 328
4 Health intervention costs 329
   4.1 Types of costs 329
      4.1.1 Provider costs 329
      4.1.2 User costs 329
   4.2 Approaches to costing 331
      4.2.1 Valuing resource use 331
5 Presentation of results 332
6 Generalizability 333
   6.1 Uncertainty 333
      6.1.1 Sampling uncertainty 333
      6.1.2 Parameter uncertainty 334
   6.2 Policy inferences 334
   6.3 External validity 334
7 Modelling 334
8 Publication of findings 335

1 Introduction to intervention costing and economic analysis

This book is focused on intervention trials in which the effectiveness of some new or modified intervention is compared with a control intervention, which would generally be the currently used intervention for a particular disease or condition. At the end of the study, estimates should be available of the impact of the intervention, compared to the control intervention. However, the decision on whether or not to apply the new intervention in a public health programme will be governed not only by the effectiveness of the intervention, but also by its costs. This chapter gives an overview of the main methods used to assess the costs of health interventions and summarizes the types of economic analyses that can be conducted to assist decisions concerning resource allocation to the deployment of health interventions. Just as the statistical design and analysis aspects of a trial will generally require the involvement of a statistician, from an early stage, in the planning of a trial, similarly it is highly recommended that a health economist be involved from the stage of initially planning the trial to advise on how costs should be measured during the course of the trial and on how these will be used at the end for an economic analysis that may ultimately influence whether or not an intervention is implemented on a widespread basis. The chapter is aimed at those who will be working with economists, in order to help design and conduct the economic aspects of a field trial to collect the appropriate data and to obtain the most useful results from an economic analysis.

In the wider scheme of things, governments have to make decisions about resource allocation between health and all the other sectors such as defence, education, and agriculture. Along with social, political, and logistic considerations, economic analyses should be an important component in decision making about those allocations. In general, economic analysis should take into account the benefits of using resources for a proposed action, compared to the use of those resources for any other purpose. However, such broad considerations are well beyond the scope of the present book! Instead, we focus on the more narrow comparison of the costs and benefits of deploying a new or modified health intervention, compared with the currently used intervention.

2 Types of economic analyses

The main types of economic analyses are cost-effectiveness analysis (CEA), cost-utility analysis (CUA), and cost-benefit analyses (CBA). How the results of these different kinds of analysis are expressed is shown in Table 19.1. CEA and CUA are those most commonly used in the analysis of health interventions. The problem with CBA is that it requires putting a monetary value on a life saved.

Analysis of the costs involved in providing the health interventions under comparison in a trial is needed for all three types of analysis. Measurement of these costs can be made in the context of an intervention study, provided due account is taken of the fact that the costs associated with an intervention in a trial may be different from those which would apply if the intervention was applied in a public health programme. It is important therefore to separate out any trial-specific costs that would not be incurred in more widespread deployment of the intervention. For example, often checks are made in a trial that the intervention has been delivered to participants in the appropriate fashion at an appropriate time. Such checks might not be made, or not be made with the same rigour, in the context of the deployment of the intervention in the routine public health system. However, there may be additional costs in the public health deployment of an intervention that would not be incurred in a trial. For example, drugs

Table 19.1 Types of economic analysis

Type of analysis	Costs	Outcome (effect)	Results expressed as:
Cost	Monetary units (commonly US $)	Not relevant	$ per unit of output (for example, $ per fully vaccinated child)
CEA	Monetary units (commonly US $)	Effect of intervention (for example, cases prevented)	$ per effect (for example, $ per case prevented)
CUA	Monetary units (commonly US $)	Premature mortality and disability averted (measured in DALYs) or healthy life time gained (QALYs)	$ per DALY averted or QALY gained
CBA	Monetary units (commonly US $)	Monetary units (for example, value of a statistical life)	Benefit–cost ratio or net present value (for example, money value of benefits–costs)

DALY, disability-adjusted life-year; QALY, quality-adjusted life-year.

or vaccines for use in a trial are often donated, whereas, for public health use, they may have to be purchased.

2.1 Cost-effectiveness analysis

CEA has been the most commonly employed type of economic analysis used in relation to randomized trials of health interventions. CEA compares the costs to accomplish a specific technical goal by a new method with the costs of the present method such as the costs per case of a particular disease diagnosed by the new method with the costs per case of disease diagnosed using the current diagnostic method, or the costs of the prevention of a death from a given cause by the new intervention compared to the costs of the prevention of a death with the present intervention. Note that it is the incremental cost-effectiveness ratio that captures the value of the new method being examined, i.e. the difference in costs between the new method and the present method, divided by the difference in effects between the new method and the present method. This summary measure thus captures the extra cost per additional unit of effect and begs the question 'is it worth it?'.

2.2 Cost-utility analysis

For CUA, the effects of an intervention are expressed as a measure of 'utility'. Simply, the utility is a measure of the impact of the intervention on the health status of the individual or population, commonly stated as a combined measure of mortality (amount of life lost due to premature death) and morbidity (amount of life lived with disability, weighted according to its seriousness and duration). Commonly used utility measures are the disability-adjusted life-year (DALY) and the quality-adjusted life-year (QALY) (Hyder et al., 2012).

2.2.1 Disability-adjusted life-years and quality-adjusted life-years

The DALY was first given prominence in the *World development report 1993* (World Bank, 1993) and has become the most widely used composite measure of population health in LMICs. It built on earlier work by the Ghana Health Assessment Project Team (1981) who introduced the similar concept of 'amount of healthy life lost', combining measures of the effects of a disease, in terms of life lost both from mortality (expected years of life remaining had the disease not occurred) and from morbidity (severity and duration of disability).

DALYs are calculated by combining the years of life lost (YLL) from premature mortality with the years of life lived with disability (YLD), weighted according to a severity grading. Thus:

$$DALY = YLL + YLD.$$

As originally formulated, the DALY directly incorporated three social value choices: (1) life expectancy values, (2) discount rates for future life, and (3) variable weighting for life lived at different ages. The recent *Global burden of disease report* for 2010, however, has dropped both discounting and age weighting (Murray et al., 2012).

A related measure, the QALY, was introduced in 1976 to provide a guide for individuals to select among alternative tertiary health care interventions (Zeckhauser and Shepard, 1976). The idea was to develop a measure of quality of life that would enable investigators to compare expected outcomes from different interventions, a measure that valued possible health states both for their impact on the quality of life and for their duration. The measure sums the time an individual spends in different health states, using weights on a scale of 0 (in a state equivalent to being dead) to 1 (perfectly healthy) for each health state; it is the sum of arithmetic products of the duration of time spent in a state and a measure of the quality of life in that state. QALYs in modified forms have come into widespread use in the UK (by the UK National Institute for Health and Clinical Excellence), Europe, and the USA (by the US Agency for Healthcare Quality and Research).

Despite distinctly different origins, DALYs and QALYs, with appropriate formulation and comparable parameters, can be considered equivalent indicators to assess intervention utility. However, there are many versions of both DALYs and QALYs, and it is very important to know exactly what is being counted in the study under consideration.

2.3 Cost–benefit analysis

CBA goes a step beyond CEA or CUA and expresses both costs and effects (or utility) of interventions in monetary terms. It directly compares the monetary costs of an intervention with the monetary benefits from the intervention. If the monetary benefits from an intervention exceed the monetary costs, the decision is straightforward in purely economic terms—implement the intervention. For most sectors, other than health, CBA is the standard form of economic analysis, and it lies at the centre of decision making in these sectors. For example, the decision to build a new road would be based on considerations of the cost of building the road, compared to the economic benefits it would bring (which might include reduction of wear and tear on vehicles, increased speed of delivery of people and goods, increase in trade, and also reduction in injuries and deaths from accidents). The aspect that has impeded its use in the health sector is that, in order to use CBA, a monetary value must be placed on human life. Some argue that this is done implicitly in any decision process, but there has been a reluctance to do this explicitly. Nevertheless, it should be recognized that decisions are regularly being taken in both public and private sectors that implicitly do place a monetary value on life. There are several different approaches to valuing human life which may give marked different results (Australian Safety and Compensation Council, 2008; Viscusi and Aldy, 2003), but further discussion is beyond the scope of this book.

Sometimes, a narrower perspective may be taken with respect to CBA. For example, in consideration of whether the public health service should introduce a vaccine against pneumonia, the costs assessed may be limited to those for the health system. If the vaccine reduces the incidence of pneumonia, the costs of delivering the vaccine to the at-risk population could be compared with the reduction of health service costs from fewer cases of pneumonia to treat. If there is a clear benefit, simply based on a CBA that only considers costs spent and saved by the health system, the decision about the introduction of the vaccine may be relatively straightforward. It becomes more complicated if there is not a monetary saving to the health system (for example, it costs more to deliver the vaccine than the saving in health service costs), but there is a reduction in mortality and/or morbidity in the population. In fact, a 'true' CBA requires a comprehensive and comparable range of inputs and outcomes, all expressed in monetary terms and, for fatal diseases, that would include putting an explicit monetary value on human life at different ages.

3 Framing the analysis

For all types of economic analyses, the perspective, range of inputs and outcomes, and the time frame of all components of the interventions and of their effects should be comparable and explicitly stated. The focus of this chapter is on CEA conducted in the context of randomized trials. For purposes of health intervention assessment, we generally take the perspective of society as a whole and attempt a comprehensive consideration of the range of inputs to be costed and of outcomes to be considered that result from the intervention. The time frame will be the period of time over which these inputs and outcomes will be assessed.

3.1 Perspective

Quantification of the economic consequences of disease and the full costs of an intervention can be viewed from different perspectives, for example, an individual, family (household), community, health system, or government (local, district, national). The societal viewpoint examines the economy as a whole. Though, for some purposes, the perspective of the individual and family or of the health system may be appropriate, taking this narrower view can be misleading and lead to erroneous conclusions about the best use of resources from a societal perspective. For example, the cost to the health service of providing access to treatment at a clinic would be much less than the cost of taking the treatment to patients at home. However, the reverse would be the situation for patients. A societal perspective would take both sets of costs into account.

3.2 Range of inputs and outcomes

The economic consequences (costs) of disease are directly related to the type and extent of disability and, for fatal diseases, to the age at death, with loss of expected healthy life that results from the disease. Ideally, all consequences of disease that the intervention addresses should be tracked (and valued), including loss of work, education, and leisure of the patient, family, and friends, emotional stress, fear, and anxiety. To a large extent, these consequences may be subsumed in measures of utility lost from disease (see Section 2.2).

3.3 Time frame

Generally, time factors involved in assessing the costs of interventions are fairly straightforward, whereas the time factors for assessing the outcomes of an intervention may be much more problematic. For example, the costs of adding hepatitis B vaccine to an immunization programme are immediately expended, but the most important consequences of hepatitis B infection include chronic liver disease and liver cancer that occur many years after the initial infection. Adequate assessment of the impact of a hepatitis B vaccine will require continuing observations of the trial populations for very long periods. Usually, the longer term is modelled, rather than measured. Furthermore, since these gains in healthy life will occur in the distant future, some would argue that their value should be discounted in some way. The key issue related to the time frame concerns the differential timing of intervention costs and intervention effects, and this is particularly problematic if these differ between interventions under consideration (for example, comparing measles vaccination with hepatitis B vaccination). Generally, there is a longer gap between a preventive intervention and realization of its effects than there is with treatment interventions. Whatever the nature of differential timing, discounting should be considered to equate future costs or effects to present costs or effects. It is generally accepted that discounting should be applied to costs, but discussions continue concerning whether to discount future effects and, if so, what rate of discounting to apply (Mathers et al., 2006).

Joint costs are those resources that are shared with other interventions or programmes. Costs frequently shared include buildings and their overhead costs such as for maintenance, electricity, and water. Other types of joint costs might include personnel or equipment such as those involved in diagnostic tests that typically are shared among several interventions. In practice, joint costs are estimated by applying some allocation rule related to the use of the resource. For example, personnel costs can be allocated to the intervention on the basis of the proportion of time devoted to it, vehicle costs according to the proportion of the total distance travelled, and building costs by the proportion of the space used. The notion of joint costs is straightforward, but exactly how best to do that is often problematic. Creese and Parker (1994) discuss the allocation of joint costs.

4 Health intervention costs

When planning to obtain cost information in the context of an intervention trial, it is important to plan and budget for the collection of cost data as an integral part of the trial design. While it is usually possible to carry out an economic analysis with retrospective estimation of costs at the end of the trial, this is likely to be less satisfactory than if the cost data are obtained concurrently.

4.1 Types of costs

Two types of costs should be considered in analysing the costs of a health intervention: the costs of providing the intervention (provider costs) and the costs of obtaining it (user costs).

4.1.1 Provider costs

Many kinds of inputs are needed to carry out health interventions. A helpful way to describe and catalogue the inputs required is to plot each step in the intervention process on a flow chart, reviewing all inputs needed (costs) at each step. The Panel of Experts on Environmental Management (PEEM) for Vector Control guidelines (Phillips et al., 1993) provide an excellent framework for estimating both financial and economic costs of an intervention. Financial costs are expenditures on the inputs for the intervention (the usual lay use of the term 'cost'); economic costs are the value of the benefits foregone by employing the resources for the intervention, rather than for something else.

A common approach to categorizing costs is to separate them into recurrent and capital (Box 19.1).

The main categories of cost involved in providing a health intervention are likely to include staff time, provision of drugs or vaccines, laboratory tests, other diagnostics, information and education costs, transport costs, utilities, space or rent costs, equipment, any incentives or reimbursements provided to patients, and other administrative costs, including any indirect costs or 'overheads'. Most of these data can be obtained from the project accountant or the health facility or the health programme itself. It may be worth focusing time and effort to get more precise estimates of costs of the items that account for a large share of the budget. Staff costs are likely to be a major component, and getting as much precision as possible, in terms of the time allocation of different categories of staff and their different salary levels, will be essential. For example, if, in one arm of the trial, the patients are seen by a doctor and, in the other arm, by a nurse, it is important to establish the number of hours and the hourly rate of the two categories of staff. It is also useful to focus on those elements that are likely to differ between arms of the trial; if the trial is comparing a laboratory-intensive intervention with an intervention that depends simply on clinical signs, it will be important to obtain as much precision as possible on the costs of laboratory tests involved.

4.1.2 User costs

The second type of cost data to be collected includes the costs patients and families incur in seeking care or availing themselves of the intervention. Usually, these data can be collected fairly simply through a brief interview with patients. A short questionnaire,

Box 19.1 Categorization of costs into recurrent and capital

Recurrent costs—those used up in the course of a year and needing regular replenishment such as:

- personnel and other labour (wages, salaries)
- supplies
- building operating and maintenance costs (electricity, water, etc.)
- in-service training (in-service courses for specific skills and knowledge)
- information, education, and communication (IEC) costs.

Capital (fixed) costs—investments in items that last for more than a year such as:

- buildings
- vehicles
- equipment
- basic training
- land.

Generally, capital costs are discounted over the expected lifespan of the entity.

using only a few questions, can provide sufficient data to estimate patient costs. PIs are often reluctant to add questions to existing instruments, and even more reluctant to add entire new questionnaires, however brief. But the downside of not collecting patient cost data may be large.

Patient cost elements may include:

- cost of travel to and from a clinic to obtain the intervention
- time of patients and, where relevant, their family for travel to the clinic or intervention site
- other costs incurred—lunch, overnight stay, childcare, etc.
- wages/salary foregone or costs of work not done (for example, on the family farm).

As an example of the importance of estimating patient costs, in a trial in Uganda, HIV-infected patients were randomized to receive home-based or facility-based delivery of antiretroviral therapy. The outcomes (disease progression) for patients in the two arms were similar, but the home-based strategy, which relied on monthly home visits by trained lay workers, used less of the time of doctors and nurses. However, the main difference in cost-effectiveness was due to the costs to patients in obtaining care; the cost of a clinic visit was assessed as, on average, $2.30, which represented about 13% of reported monthly cash incomes for men and 20% for women (Jaffar et al., 2009). Given the disparities in average wealth, this level of expenditure would be approximately equivalent to an average European taking an intercontinental flight every month for a clinic visit!

Saunderson (1995), in an economic evaluation of options for the treatment of TB in Uganda, found that 70% of the cost of tuberculosis treatment was borne by patients themselves. Similarly, Ettling et al. (1991) found that 90% of the costs of seeking treatment for malaria fell on patients, while Needham et al. (1998) found that patient costs of seeking care for tuberculosis in Zambia were prohibitive.

4.2 Approaches to costing

Although categorizing and listing costs of inputs needed for interventions are an important first step, there are three further important aspects of costing that should be considered to ensure comparability and completeness. The first is to examine costs by unit of service (such as days in hospital, outpatient visits, education campaign, or delivery of bed-nets or vaccines to a community). The second is to use a functional approach to costing, such as activity-based costing (ABC), where each specific activity, such as a hospital-based delivery, is costed. This is more useful for understanding the nature of costs than that of a line item that simply lists costs by type of input such as personnel or travel. The third is to annualize all costs for a given population for a given period of time, using depreciation methods for capital expenditures and appropriate discount rates, to bring all costs to the current year value (see Section 3.3).

Functional costing is usually based on a unit of service such as an outpatient visit or a hospital stay. All activities (processes) needed to carry out a unit of service are mapped out by a flow chart; each step in the process is analysed for the inputs used, including personnel time and overhead; a cost schedule is constructed to determine the full costs of each activity; and finally these are summed to determine the costs of that unit of service.

The idea of putting all costs involved in providing a service (intervention) onto a comparable basis of time and population is straightforward, but the details of depreciation and appropriate rates of depreciation for different inputs are beyond the scope of this chapter, and input from a health economist should be sought.

4.2.1 Valuing resource use

Sometimes, unit costs will be estimated from trial centres, but more commonly they are derived from national data. Another option is to use the estimates provided by the WHO-CHOICE programme (<http://www.who.int/choice/en>). WHO-CHOICE has the objective of 'providing policy makers with the evidence for deciding on the interventions and programmes which maximize health for the available resources'. Among the data provided are unit cost estimates for a variety of health services, by country or region; examples include the cost of a hospital bed-day by type of hospital, outpatient visit, and other patient-level costs.

As indicated in Section 1, collection and management of costing data should be planned during the study design phase and linked to the intervention outcome data. As with any prospective study, there should be a plan for ongoing data quality monitoring to address missing and poor-quality data issues immediately. Queries should be managed on an ongoing basis, rather than at the end of the trial, to maximize data completeness and quality and the timeliness of the final analysis.

5 Presentation of results

The incremental cost-effectiveness ratio (ICER) is a common way of summarizing results from a cost-effectiveness study (expressed as the ratio of two differences in costs and in effects of the alternative interventions):

$$\text{ICER} = \{\text{Cost (new intervention)} - \text{Cost (current intervention)}\} /$$
$$\{\text{Effect (new intervention)} - \text{Effect (current intervention)}\}$$

The result can be considered as the cost of the additional effect obtained by switching from current practice to the new intervention. If the differential cost is low enough or the differential effect is large enough, the new intervention is considered 'cost-effective', as compared to the current. If an intervention is considered to be 'cost-effective', it means that local and/or global policymakers believe it is worth paying the amount estimated to produce an additional unit of effect.

Table 19.2 indicates the various ways a new intervention might be compared with the current intervention. Note that the decision is straightforward only if a new intervention is *both* less effective and more costly (or both more effective and less costly).

CEA is sensitive to the choice of interventions being compared. Researchers should consider whether the choices of interventions being compared are really the choice of interest. Clearly, this decision must precede the final design of the trial.

Consider two strategies intended to lengthen life in patients with heart disease. One is 'simple' and cheap (for example, aspirin and beta (β)-blockers) and lengthens life, on average by 5 years; the other is more 'complex', more expensive, and more effective (for example, aspirin and β-blockers plus cardiac catheterization, angioplasty, stents, and bypass), lengthening life, on average, by 5.5 years. Table 19.3 shows the relevant (hypothetical) data.

The incremental cost of the simple intervention is the difference between the cost of that strategy ($5000) and the cost of doing nothing ($0), so the ICER = ($5000 − $0)/(5.0 − 0.0) = $1000/life-year gained. The incremental cost for the complex intervention relative to the simple intervention is the difference between the cost of the complex intervention ($50 000) and the cost of the simple intervention ($5000), so the ICER = ($50 000 − $5000)/(5.5 − 5.0) = $90 000/year gained.

Table 19.2 Cost-effectiveness analysis as an aid to decision making

Effectiveness	Cost	
	New intervention costs more	**New intervention costs less**
New intervention is more effective	CEA needed	Adopt new intervention
New intervention is less effective	Do not adopt new intervention	CEA needed

Table 19.3 Example of the application of cost-effectiveness analysis

Strategy	Additional cost	Incremental cost	Effectiveness (years gained, compared to 'nothing')	Incremental effectiveness	ICER ($/year gained)
Nothing (0)	–	–	–	0.0	–
Simple intervention (S)	$5000	(S vs 0) $5000	5.0	5.0 – 0.0 = 5.0	$1000
Complex intervention (C)	$50 000	(C vs S) $45 000	5.5	5.5 – 5.0 = 0.5	$90 000

Thus, implementation of the simple intervention costs $1000 for every year of life gained, and implementation of the complex intervention, compared to the simple intervention, costs $90 000 for every year of life gained. The decision maker will have to decide between these different options, based upon the resources available and taking into account the years of life that might be gained (and the cost of so doing) by intervening against different diseases (with different interventions). But, in this example, while paying $1000 for an extra year of life seems cost-effective, paying $90 000 for an additional year of life appears to be a less worthwhile use of scarce resources. In practice, comparison is often made to cost-effectiveness 'thresholds', in order to facilitate the interpretation of ICERs. The most commonly used threshold is the gross domestic product (GDP) per capita of the country in question, i.e. if the cost per DALY averted or QALY gained is less than the country's GDP per capita, then the intervention being assessed is considered to be relatively cost-effective and hence worth implementing.

For those who wish to pursue these issues further, Drummond (2005) and Eichler et al. (2004) give a much fuller discussion of CEA.

6 Generalizability

6.1 Uncertainty

Results of economic evaluations in trials are subject to several sources of uncertainty.

6.1.1 Sampling uncertainty

Economic outcomes in trials are usually based on effectively a single sample drawn from the population. In general, there is uncertainty with respect to both costs and outcomes, and this variability should be reflected in CEAs to determine to what extent uncertainty in the estimates might influence the decisions that might be made as a result of the analyses. For example, if an intervention appears to be, on average, cost-effective, but the uncertainty interval includes instances of cost-ineffectiveness, then the confidence with which the intervention can be recommended might need to be tempered. Methods for taking into account uncertainty are not always straightforward and generally benefit from the input of a health economist.

6.1.2 Parameter uncertainty

Uncertainty related to parameter estimates, such as unit costs and the discount rate, should be assessed by the use of sensitivity analysis. For example, if a discount rate of 3% is used, it may be desirable to assess the impact of this assumption by repeating the analysis, but using a 0% or 5% rate. Analysts should evaluate the effect of varying all major cost parameters (such as the proportion of personnel time allocated to the intervention), as this may influence policy decisions.

6.2 Policy inferences

Policy inferences about the adoption of an intervention should be based on the level of confidence that the cost of the intervention for a unit of outcome, for example, a DALY, is affordable, with a threshold, or ceiling, beyond which it would be unacceptable to adopt it. Ranges of ceiling ICERs should be reported, for which the analyst: (1) is confident that the intervention is good value for the cost; (2) is confident that the intervention is not good value; or (3) is unsure that the cost-effectiveness of the two interventions differ from each another sufficiently to make a choice between them based on the ICER alone. Policymakers can then draw inferences by identifying into which of the ranges it falls. The ranges of ceiling ratios where the analyst can and cannot be confident about the value of a new intervention relative to the current intervention can be calculated by the use of confidence intervals (CIs) for the cost-effectiveness ratios, allowing for the various sensitivity analyses done.

6.3 External validity

Some field trials may have low external validity (i.e. they cannot be generalized easily, and the impact of the intervention may be different when applied in a public health setting). The threats to external validity come from:

- inclusion of study sites with access and availability of health care services which are not representative of the wider population that would be targeted in a public health programme
- restrictive inclusion and exclusion criteria (patient population, disease severity, co-morbidities)
- artificially enhanced compliance (for the purposes of the trial).

In such circumstances, it might be possible to test the potential cost-effectiveness of the new intervention in programmatic conditions within sensitivity analyses, after making assumptions about how each of these factors might differ in the routine programmatic situation relative to the situation within the trial.

7 Modelling

The cost-effectiveness measured within the trial follow-up period may be substantially different from what would have been observed with longer follow-up. For example, at the time a phase III trial is completed and a vaccine is licensed, there may still be substantial uncertainty about the duration of protection offered by the vaccine beyond the follow-up period in the trial. Modelling of various kinds can be used to estimate costs and outcomes that would have been observed had follow-up of the trial population been prolonged. This involves projecting costs and outcomes over the expected duration of disease and of the intervention and its effects. This may involve making significant assumptions about the future, for example, the life expectancy of a patient on a given treatment. Any such assumptions should be specified. In general, modelling of costs and effectiveness of interventions is being more widely used to assist in decision making (World Health Organization, 2004) but is beyond the scope of this book.

8 Publication of findings

The impact of a publication on health practice and policy is likely to be strengthened if the results of an economic analysis are included in the main publication from an intervention trial itself. However, constraints on word limits often mean that full details of the economic analysis methods cannot be included. Thus, it is common practice to write a companion paper, in which the data collection method, analytic techniques, and assumptions for the economic analyses are fully presented and discussed. An example of the abstract from such a paper is shown in Box 19.2.

Box 19.2 Cost-effectiveness of improved treatment services for sexually transmitted diseases in preventing HIV-1 infection in Mwanza Region, Tanzania

THE TRIAL: A community-randomised trial was undertaken to assess the impact, cost, and cost-effectiveness of averting HIV-1 infection through improved management of sexually transmitted diseases (STDs) by primary-health-care workers in Mwanza Region, Tanzania.

METHODS: The impact of improved treatment services for STDs on HIV-1 incidence was assessed by comparison of six intervention communities with six matched communities. We followed a random cohort of 12 537 adults aged 15–54 years for 2 years to record incidence of HIV-1 infection. The total and incremental costs of the intervention were estimated and used to calculate the total cost per case treated, the incremental cost per HIV-1 infection averted, and the incremental cost per disability adjusted life-year (DALY) saved.

FINDINGS: During 2 years of follow-up, 11 632 cases of STDs were treated in the intervention health units. The incidence of HIV-1 infection during the 2 years was 1.16% in the intervention communities and 1.86% in the comparison communities. An estimated 252 HIV-1 infections were averted each year. The total annual cost of the intervention was US$59 060, equivalent to $0.39 per head of population served. The cost for each STD case treated was $10.15, of which the drug cost was $2.11. The incremental annual cost of the intervention was $54 839, equivalent to $217.62 per HIV-1 infection averted and $10.33 per DALY saved (based on Tanzanian life

> **Box 19.2 Cost-effectiveness of improved treatment services for sexually transmitted diseases in preventing HIV-1 infection in Mwanza Region, Tanzania (continued)**
>
> expectancy). In a sensitivity analysis of factors influencing cost-effectiveness, cost per DALY saved ranged from $2.51 to $47.86.
>
> INTERPRETATION: Improved management of STDs in rural health units reduced the incidence of HIV-1 infection in the general population by about 40%. The estimated cost-effectiveness of this intervention ($10 per DALY) compares favourably with that of, for example, childhood immunisation programmes ($12–17 per DALY).
>
> Reprinted from the *Lancet*, Volume 350, Issue 9094, Gilson, L., et al., Cost-effectiveness of improved treatment services for sexually transmitted diseases in preventing HIV-1 infection in Mwanza Region, Tanzania, pp.1805–9, Copyright © 1997 Elsevier Ltd All rights reserved, with permission from Elsevier, <http://www.sciencedirect.com/science/journal/01406736>. This box is not covered by the Creative Commons licence terms of this publication. For permission to reuse please contact the rights holder.

References

Australian Safety And Compensation Council. 2008. *The health of nations: the value of a statistical life* [Online]. Available at: <http://www.safeworkaustralia.gov.au/sites/SWA/about/Publications/Documents/330/TheHealthOfNations_Value_StatisticalLife_2008_PDF.pdf>.

Creese, A. and Parker, D. 1994. *Cost analysis in primary health care: a training manual for programme managers* [Online]. Geneva: World Health Organization. Available at: <http://apps.who.int/iris/bitstream/10665/40030/1/9241544708.pdf>.

Drummond, M. F. 2005. *Methods for the economic evaluation of health care programmes*. Oxford: Oxford University Press.

Eichler, H. G., Kong, S. X., Gerth, W. C., Mavros, P., and Jönsson, B. 2004. Use of cost-effectiveness analysis in health-care resource allocation decision-making: how are cost-effectiveness thresholds expected to emerge? *Value in Health*, 5, 518–28.

Ettling, M. B., Thimasarn, K., Shepard, D. S., and Krachaiklin, S. 1991. Economic analysis of several types of malaria clinics in Thailand. *Bulletin of the World Health Organization*, 69, 467–76.

Ghana Health Assessment Project Team. 1981. A quantitative method of assessing the health impact of different diseases in less developed countries. *International Journal of Epidemiology*, 10, 73–80.

Hyder, A. A., Puvanashandra, P., and Morrow, R. H. 2012. Measures of health and disease. In: Merson, M. H., Black, R. E., and Mills, A. J. (eds.) *Global health: diseases, systems and policies*. Burlington, MA: Jones & Bartlett.

Jaffar, S., Amuron, B., Foster, S., *et al*. 2009. Rates of virological failure in patients treated in a home-based versus a facility-based HIV-care model in Jinja, southeast Uganda: a cluster-randomised equivalence trial. *Lancet*, 374, 2080–9.

Mathers, C. D., Salomon, J. A., Ezzati, M., Beg, S., Vander Hoorn, S., and Lopez, A. D. 2006. Chapter 5: Sensitivity and uncertainty analyses for burden of disease and risk factor estimates. In: Lopez, A. D., Mathers, C. D., Ezzati, M., Jamison, D. T., and Murray, C. J. L. (eds.) *Global burden of disease and risk factors* [Online]. Washington, DC: World Bank. Available at: <https://openknowledge.worldbank.org/bitstream/handle/10986/7039/364010PAPER0Gl101OFFICIAL0USE0ONLY1.pdf?sequence=1>.

Murray, C. J., Vos, T., Lozano, R., *et al.* 2012. Disability-adjusted life years (DALYs) for 291 diseases and injuries in 21 regions, 1990–2010: a systematic analysis for the Global Burden of Disease Study 2010. *Lancet*, **380**, 2197–223.

Needham, D. M., Godfrey-Faussett, P., and Foster, S. D. 1998. Barriers to tuberculosis control in urban Zambia: the economic impact and burden on patients prior to diagnosis. *International Journal of Tuberculosis and Lung Disease*, **2**, 811–17.

Phillips, M. R., Mills, A., and Dye, C. 1993. *PEEM Guidelines 3—Guidelines for cost-effectiveness analysis of vector control* [Online]. Geneva: World Health Organization. Available at: <http://www.who.int/water_sanitation_health/resources/peem3/en/>.

Saunderson, P. R. 1995. An economic evaluation of alternative programme designs for tuberculosis control in rural Uganda. *Social Science & Medicine*, **40**, 1203–12.

Viscusi, W. K. and Aldy, J. E. 2003. *The value of a statistical life: a critical review of market estimates throughout the world* [Online]. Cambridge, MA: National Bureau of Economic Research. Available at: <http://lsr.nellco.org/harvard_olin/392>.

World Bank. 1993. *World development report 1993: investing in health* [Online]. Oxford University Press for the World Bank. Available at: <https://openknowledge.worldbank.org/handle/10986/5976>.

World Health Organization. 2004. *Making choices in health: WHO guide to cost-effectiveness analysis* [Online]. Geneva: World Health Organization. Available at: <http://www.who.int/choice/publications/p_2003_generalised_cea.pdf>.

Zeckhauser, R. and Shepard, D. 1976. Where now for saving lives? *Law and Contemporary Problems*, **40**, 5–45.

Chapter 20

Data management

1 Introduction to data management 339
2 Before starting to collect data 340
   2.1 Hardware 340
   2.2 Software 342
   2.3 Personnel 343
   2.4 Data oversight 344
   2.5 Summary 346
3 Planning the data flow 346
   3.1 Database design 346
   3.2 Data cleaning and integrity 348
   3.3 Programming issues 349
   3.4 Standard operating procedures 349
   3.5 Version control 349
   3.6 Confidentiality 350
   3.7 Training 350
   3.8 Pilot testing and database testing 350
4 Data collection systems 351
   4.1 Questionnaires 351
   4.2 Electronic data capture 351
   4.3 Laboratory data 351
   4.4 Clinic data 352
   4.5 Longitudinal data collection 352
   4.6 Quality control 353
   4.7 Future trends 353
5 Managing data 354
   5.1 Data entry 354
   5.2 Data checks 355
   5.3 Data cleaning 357
   5.4 Variable naming and coding 358
   5.5 Data lock 359
6 Archiving 359
   6.1 Interim backups 359
   6.2 Metadata 360
   6.3 Data sharing policy 360
   6.4 Archiving hard copies 361

7 Preparing data for analysis 362
  7.1 Data dictionary 362
  7.2 Creating new variables 362
  7.3 Coding and re-coding 362
  7.4 Merging and linking data 363

1 Introduction to data management

All intervention trials involve the collection and management of data, often in large quantities. In order to get the most out of study data, it is important to have worked through plans for the collection, management, and use of the data early in the planning stages of a trial. Previous editions of the *Toolbox* discussed the role and choice of computers in the management of trial data, but now they are so ubiquitous that there will be few trials in which they are not central to data handling and analysis. Indeed, developments in computing have changed the way that trials are conducted, from the way that data are collected through to the way data are used and disseminated. However, in the processing of data, it is important to remember the 'GIGO' principle 'garbage in, garbage out'! The data used in final data tables are only as good as the data that go into their construction. Thus, while developments in computer hardware and software have made the processing and analysis of data much quicker, it is still necessary to pay careful attention to the way in which the original data are collected and recorded in the field and transferred from one program to another during the data management process. Every instrument used in the study, including questionnaires, laboratory methods, and data management programs, must be properly validated and tested and have good quality control (QC) procedures in place throughout the trial. Great attention to detail is necessary in every step the data take, in the design of data forms, in the recording of data in the field, in transferring the data from paper to the computer (if data are not collected digitally), in the transfer from one software package to another, and in how they are manipulated and managed in computer packages and programs. These data processing aspects are the focus of this chapter. The chapter focuses exclusively on quantitative data.

Section 2 covers some of the data-related issues that should be resolved before the study starts, and Section 3 concerns the planning that should be done for the data flow within the study. Sections 4 to 7 deal with various specific issues related to data flow and data management. This chapter can only give a basic introduction to key issues related to data management. More detailed explanations are available in various books and other resources. The general principles of data management are covered in books by Hernandez (2013), Powell (2006), McFadden (2007), Murrell (2009) (available free via <https://www.stat.auckland.ac.nz/~paul/ItDT/>), Prokscha (2012), and Pryor (2012). Other free online resources are provided for specific data management software, such as Epi-Info (<http://wwwn.cdc.gov/epiinfo>) and EpiData (<http://www.epidata.dk>), or Microsoft Access™ (<http://office.microsoft.com/en-us/access/>) such as for Access 2007 (<http://office.microsoft.com/en-us/access/HA012242471033.aspx>), and there is a useful web-based discussion group for data managers within the Global Health Trials website (<http://globalhealthtrials.tghn.org/community/groups/group/data-management-statistics/topics/290>).

2 Before starting to collect data

All trials need appropriate resources to collect data and information, to check the consistency and quality of the data, and to organize the data into a suitable form for analysis. It is important that all the steps of the trial and the associated data flow are planned before starting the trial, and the resources needed at each step are defined. This section describes the different hardware, software, personnel, and systems needed to process data in a trial. When considering the trial budget, resources must be allocated for all of these aspects, and often components have to be capable of multitasking, for example, computers that can be used for both data entry and administrative functions, and software that can manage different data formats.

There are four components to the description of the data processing for a trial:

1. hardware, i.e. any physical entity used for data processing. This may include computers, printers, and electronic hardware, but also includes paper, pens, and other equipment used to collect, transfer, and archive the data
2. software, i.e. the programs needed to make the hardware manipulate and process the data for the study
3. personnel that are needed for the data processing
4. the systems and organization that must be in place to bring all of the different components together.

2.1 Hardware

The commonest hardware used in a small trial is still paper questionnaires and forms. Much of what is done is recorded on paper, and, at all stages, paper copies are kept as the definitive record. The advantage of using paper is that it is a physical entity, which preserves the data content. The disadvantage is that it is difficult to process and analyse, particularly in large quantities. Data collected or stored electronically are much easier to manipulate and use in a variety of different ways.

If paper systems are used to collect data, it is important to include, in the planning, provision of all the necessary ancillaries for the paper collection such as pens, clipboards, and storage boxes. Management of the paper is also an issue that needs to be thought through to the end of the trial and beyond, with proper filing systems and archives for data storage. Paper systems need to be integrated with the computer hardware and software used in the study, first to do the printing of the questionnaires and other forms, and second to take the data from the forms and input them into a computer package for electronic checking and analysis.

The use of computers to collect, process, and analyse data is ubiquitous nowadays. There are so many different computers, and they are continually getting better and faster that it is impossible to give very specific guidance on which would be best for particular studies. Much depends on the way the data management for the study has been planned and what software the analyst is already familiar with. One way to divide up the many computer hardware options is through the distinction between desktops, laptops, mobile devices, and servers. Desktops are useful for data entry and when there are many people wanting to share a computer for short periods of time, for example, field supervisors who need to input a report at the end of the day. Desktops are also needed for some of the administrative functions, but, in general, it is good to keep the research data physically separate from the administrative computers that the project needs.

Laptops provide comparable computing power to desktops and can be used to collect and manage data in the field, even where mains electricity is not widely available. Smaller devices, such as PDAs or ultra-mobile personal computers (UMPCs) or even 'smart' mobile phones, are easier to use and transport in the field than laptops. With laptops and smaller mobile computing devices, two issues need to be considered; first, the smaller the device, the easier it is to lose or be stolen, and second, these devices have batteries that need recharging and periodically replacing. When purchasing laptops and smaller devices, buying a security cable for each machine, where appropriate, is often a good investment. It is also important to make sure that the person responsible for the computer uses the security cable and the procedures are well known to all, as it only takes a minute to lose large amounts of data if a computer is stolen. If in continuous use, recharging laptops, PDAs, UMPCs, or mobile phones can be a time-consuming task. Long-life batteries can be used to extend the time the machines can be used between charging, and, if mains power is available, recharging can be done at meal breaks and overnight. Otherwise, inverters can be used to charge from car batteries or from solar panels.

PDAs, tablet computers, mobile phones, and other devices can be programmed to accept electronic questionnaires and can also be purchased with GPS software, cameras, bar code readers, and automatic Internet capabilities, with the only drawback being the cost of the extra functions. In general, it is important to specify what is needed for the trial and to avoid expenditure on functions that are not needed.

All but the smallest trials will benefit from having a server, in order to store the data and to manage resources. A server can be a special computer with a large amount of data storage capacity or a standard desktop configured to organize data storage and administrative procedures. However, servers do need to be looked after carefully, with control of the temperature, dust, and humidity in the server room. If the trial operates out of an established institute, it is likely that it will be possible to use the institution's server and network, perhaps through creating a virtual server for the use of the trial. The networking of the server can be through physical cables or could be set up as a simple local area network (LAN) using a wireless router, but note that, while laptops usually have built-in wireless capability, this is often not the case for desktops and PDAs. A good server and network can simplify many operations, such as access to the Internet and sharing of data, and should be high on the list of priorities for all but the smallest study.

Ancillary equipment ('peripherals') is also needed. This may include printers, scanners, photocopiers, cameras, bar code readers, and backup devices. These can be installed and connected to one computer, but a simple network will make it easier for different members of the research team to access the different peripherals. The wider access to the Internet needs to be planned as well. If the Internet service is poor, it may be necessary to have more than one way of accessing the Internet, perhaps through fixed lines or through mobile phone networks.

2.2 Software

In this section, we will not consider general software, such as word processing or antivirus, which are typically available to all computers, but concentrate on the specific options available for data processing. Data processing software comprises specialist packages which facilitate the collection, management, and organization of trial data. They can be used to prepare data for analysis by specialist data analysis packages. We consider three broad categories of software—freeware (free software packages), proprietary software (which must be bought), and open source software—and give some examples of the different packages available, but the choice is wide. The most important consideration is to plan out how the data processing for the trial will be done and to use the appropriate package for each step in the data flow. It should be simple to transfer data from one package to another and is wasteful of time and resources to do any data operation in a package that is not designed for that purpose. In many ways, the selection of the software is more important than the hardware, and good selection can save a lot of time.

For the sort of data that are collected in epidemiological studies and trials, Epi-Info (<http://wwwn.cdc.gov/epiinfo>) is a very useful freeware package which can be used for many types of study. A similar freeware package Epi-Data (<http://www.EpiData.dk>) provides data management, analysis, and transfer capabilities. These packages are easy to learn and use and are ideal for small studies.

For larger studies, it is usually better to use a proprietary software package such as Microsoft Access™ or MS-SQL™. These are easy-to-use software, with good learning materials to help in developing and using the database. These software packages can be used to clean and manage data, and it is easy to transfer data from them to analysis packages. Free, but limited, versions of these software packages are available for those on limited budgets.

Open source software packages are also usually free to the user, and it is possible to access the source code and develop applications that are tailored to specific studies. A challenge, however, is learning how to manipulate the source code and make the software function appropriately for a specific study. Examples include RedCap which is aimed at investigators who do not have access to much computing support but who wish to quickly set up and manage clinical studies, including longitudinal ones, while OpenClinica targets researchers conducting clinical trials that must meet the regulatory requirements of the US Food and Drug Administration. Open Data Kit (ODK) is a suite of open source applications that allow the creation of questionnaires for data collection on Android-enabled mobile devices and facilitate online data management. Force.com is a powerful data management platform, for which a limited number of free licences are provided to non-profit organizations and higher education institutions. All of these packages are free to use and are highly customizable, and all but Force.com can be configured without highly specialized computer programming skills. All four systems are supported by knowledgeable end-user-driven online communities.

2.3 Personnel

The personnel needed for data management will depend on the size of the trial and the computer and software systems being used. For a small study, using paper forms and a simple software package, such as Epi-Info, for data processing, one part-time data manager and one data entry clerk may be sufficient. For larger studies using paper forms, a team of data entry clerks and several data managers might be needed. Although the requirements for data entry clerks can be greatly reduced or eliminated for studies using electronic data capture, skilled data managers and expert programmers may be needed to program some of the collection devices to validate the systems and to design the database.

Successful data management requires a variety of different skills at different times during the study. At the start of the study, except for simple software packages such as Epi-Info, someone with technical skills will be needed to set up the database and write the data check programs. If the study personnel are not skilled in database programming, it may be better to hire a consultant to do it. When the study is under way, staff will be needed to enter data (unless all data are captured electronically), manage data checking, and clean the data on a daily basis. By the end of the study, data files must be prepared for the statistical analysis and report writing, and again buying in the expertise may be appropriate if there are no staff in the team with the necessary skills. Depending on the size of the study, some of these roles may be combined in a single individual, whereas, in larger research groups, individuals may be specialists who work full-time in one area of data management such as database development or writing data checks.

Staff must be recruited before the trial starts to be able to both develop, and be trained in the use of, the data processing systems. It is important to allocate sufficient time for training. Even staff who have previous experience of data management on other studies will need to be trained to use the system being used in the trial and become familiar with the study protocol. The most important attributes for data entry staff are conscientiousness, reliability, and attention to detail. Existing computing skills may be less important, as staff can be trained to use a computer and to enter data. Sometimes, staff who were originally employed to collect data in the field can be trained to be good data entry clerks. This has the advantage that they will be familiar with the kind of data being collected and the forms in use. They will also be aware of the problems that may arise in the collection of data in the field. However, data entry clerks and their supervisors are gradually being reduced in number in many research groups, as they move from collecting data on paper to electronic data capture.

A supervisor is likely to be necessary for every four to six data entry clerks to control the quality of their work, to ensure a proper and equitable distribution and flow of work, and to ensure that all data and forms are correctly processed and stored. The supervisor may be able to do some of the initial data checking and cleaning and take some of the data management tasks from the study data manager. A good way to identify persons who might be trained as supervisors may be to select them from among the data entry clerks, based on their performance and aptitude for this work, although the ability to type data quickly and reliably does not necessarily provide a good indication that an individual will make a good supervisor.

Pilot studies may be necessary to determine how much data can be processed by a data clerk in a day, to know how many such individuals to include in the trial budget. This should be part of the pilot testing, which is covered in more detail in Chapter 13. As the work is repetitive, but requires considerable care, it is advisable to plan that a clerk should not be entering data for more than 5 or 6 hours a day. Data entry may be interspersed with filing tasks to maintain variety in the work.

If a trial is large, substantial numbers of forms may accumulate quickly, and the design of an appropriate filing and tracking system, such that individual forms can be retrieved, if needed, is important. The employment of filing clerks may also be necessary in large trials. Data entry and filing are tasks that need to be done in the same way, day after day. So it is important to devise ways of maintaining staff morale, so as to ensure high-quality work. For larger trials conducted over several years, working out career development structures within the project may be important (for example, the progression from filing clerk or fieldworker to data entry clerk to supervisor). Also, training in new techniques and the use of computer packages may be appropriate. Individuals must be aware that their work is considered important and that its quality is monitored, so that bad work is detected and will need to be corrected, while good work is noticed and rewarded appropriately.

The data management staff must be made to feel that they are an integral part of the project. Appropriate measures should be installed to allow field and data management staff to liaise with each other, so that they consider themselves part of the same team. See Chapter 16 for more details of field operations. Field staff must understand the problems that errors in data collection cause in the processing and analysis of data, and data management staff must appreciate the obstacles to high-quality data collection in the field. Visits by data staff to the field can do much to aid such mutual understanding, as can field staff spending short periods working or observing in the data office.

2.4 Data oversight

No matter how good data systems are, there is always benefit in getting someone outside of the study to look at them to see if they can be improved. The best time for this is before starting to collect real data, in time for the systems to be changed, if necessary. For small studies, this may be a matter of getting a colleague to check the data systems. In larger studies, outside advisors might be hired to look at the data system.

In most clinical trials, the requirements of good clinical practice (GCP) are such that the trial data must be collected and processed, in compliance with the ICH–GCP guidelines (see Chapter 16, Section 7.1). The practical implications of these requirements are that the data management process must be documented, and the computer systems used to collect, store, and process the data must be validated. The regulations governing the management of data from clinical trials can be broadly classified into: (1) clinical data-related; (2) technology-related; and (3) privacy-related. The guiding principle behind all of these regulations is the need to be confident that the data were collected as defined in the study protocol, are from real participants, and can be independently verified. Small studies may not be required to implement GCP, but, for all studies, there should be awareness that good practice and procedures should be in place, ensuring that data systems are checked for errors or oversights.

Compliance with GCP requires that all phases of the data management processes are controlled by standard operating procedures (SOPs). Data management staff must be trained in each process, and training must be documented. ICH–GCP does not require double data entry but requires that processes are in place to ensure that the data in the database accurately reflect what was recorded in the field on questionnaires or through other means.

The computer system used to store and manage the data will need to be validated, which requires a validation plan, user specification, testing, and change control. In the simplest form, an SOP that describes the steps necessary to build, test, and release a database can serve as the validation plan. The database and data entry screens will need to be tested to ensure that they function correctly, and the testing and its results should be documented.

A further requirement of GCP is that all changes that are made to the data in the study database are documented and that the original data are not deleted. This requirement is generally interpreted to mean an electronic audit trail must be created, in which the software system automatically records any changes that are made to the database, including when they were made and who made them. However, there are differences in how the term 'audit trail' is interpreted and implemented and at what stage the audit trail is 'turned on'. Some audit trails may record changes after first entry into the database, others after second entry when data have been verified, and others not until after initial data cleaning is done. Building a database with an electronic audit trail requires specialist skill and knowledge; however, software packages specifically designed for clinical trials, such as OpenClinica, have an audit trail as an inbuilt feature.

In a small trial that does not involve licensing of a pharmaceutical product, it may be possible to document data changes by other means to demonstrate compliance with GCP, for example, keeping a copy of the original database after second entry, a separate database containing all updates to the data, and a paper record of all changes that are made.

GCP also requires that a security system is maintained that prevents unauthorized access to the data. This would generally mean having a separate password to access the database and users having different levels of permitted access, depending on their role in the data management process. Randomization codes (see Chapter 11 for details) should always have restricted access, so that unauthorized staff cannot find out which treatment has been allocated to which participants.

GCP also requires that data are backed up adequately. Even in a study that is not being run to GCP, it is essential to develop a system for regular data backups. Failure to do so may result in the loss of data. Several types of media can be used for backup, including tapes, CDs, or external hard drives. Whatever is used, backup copies should be made regularly (at least weekly and possibly daily), once data entry has started. At least two backup copies of the database should always exist, and periodic 'restores' of the backed up data should be done to verify the data integrity. The copies should be updated regularly and frequently, although it is a good idea to keep some old versions as well, as errors are sometimes found in the more recent ones that make it necessary to restart data entry from a previous copy. Some of the copies should be stored in a geographically separate location in a dry and relatively dust-free environment (for example, in a sealed plastic bag). Complete records should be kept of the data that are stored on all backups, with one copy stored with the backup and at least one other copy stored in a separate place.

2.5 Summary

In this section, emphasis has been given to the need to plan the data system and all its dependencies before starting the trial. This involves planning the hardware and how it will be used, the software and what it needs to be able to do, the personnel, and the data practices. If the data systems are planned and thought through at the beginning of the study, the study progress is less prone to error and easier to operate.

It is useful to make a process flow diagram of the data indicating the people who will handle the data at each point in the flow diagram. Taking the time to highlight the resources needed and the person responsible for each action can make the implementation easier when the study is under way.

3 Planning the data flow

There are many advantages to collecting and storing research data electronically. Electronic storage of data facilitates easy retrieval, simpler generation of study reports, easy exportation to statistical packages, and rapid data sharing. The benefits of electronic storage of data can only be fully realized if the database storing the data is well designed. A poorly designed database leads to poor performance, inefficient data queries, inaccurate and unreliable data, and redundant data that are duplicated in many places, making it difficult to check and clean. This section focuses on the key aspects of the processes in the data flow.

3.1 Database design

Database design is the process of organizing data in such a way that it can be stored and retrieved efficiently. It involves making decisions on how best to model a real-world information system, such as a paper-based data collection system, into a database. It is very unlikely that an analyst can correctly design a system without a full understanding of the key processes and activities involved in the study. This requires researchers spending time with the system developers to ensure that the system developed is what is required.

It is good practice to use a structured approach, referred to as a system development life cycle, when undertaking a database development project. The choice of the methodology is usually influenced by factors such as the complexity of the proposed database, the size of the database and the programming team, cost, time, and criticality of the project. What is important is to get an approach that meets the needs of the project. An overview of the key phases involved in database development is presented, rather than focusing on a specific methodology. These procedures should not been seen as checklists, but rather key processes that can be incorporated in any methodology chosen. The key procedures are:

1 project specification
2 requirements gathering

3   programming and testing
4   database implementation ('going live')
5   database maintenance and change management.

A database project should start by clearly defining what the database will be expected to do. The high-level requirement is defined, which is the mission statement that states the intended goal of the new database. It should not be more than a few lines long. Other critical factors to define at this initial phase are the scope, resources, timelines, hardware, software, and the database team. The scope is the boundary of the system and database, and it states what data and functionality will be included and what will be excluded. It is important that the scope is defined clearly at the start of the database development project, as poor definition leads to ambiguity and poorly defined database requirements. It is also important to choose the hardware and software early, as this may affect some of the design features of the database. The output of this initial phase is a project specification document that defines the objectives, timelines, deliverables, and milestones.

The objective of the next phase is to transform the high-level requirements into more detailed manageable tasks and functions that can be programmed into a software system. The requirements can be gathered by interviewing end-users of the proposed new database, examining the current database, if any, and also looking at existing forms such as questionnaires and reports. It is important to think of what extra functionality is required in the database. Will the data be shared? If so, which specific data will be shared? What are the security and compliance requirements? Have risks been assessed, and the database designed to mitigate the risks? The output of this process is a detailed requirements specification document, describing all the functional and non-functional requirements of the database. It is imperative that requirements are specified correctly and as comprehensively as possible at this phase; otherwise, it could lead to a system that does not meet its intended goal and may necessitate major changes during programming and testing or after the database has gone live.

The third phase involves creating a conceptual design (logical diagram) that shows the different tables that will be required to store the data identified in the first two phases. A good place to start from when generating the list of possible tables and their attributes (data columns) is to look at the current process, if any, used to collect data. There are two possible scenarios—an existing computer system is being converted or modernized or a new system is being built from scratch. In the former scenario, the tables and data entry forms of the existing computer system should be used as a starting point. If there was never a computerized system in place, begin with the existing paper-based data collection forms. If there are none, sketch out the forms, based on the requirements specification document, and discuss the sketches with the research team, and refine them further. Note that, while some of these data entry forms are sketches of what will eventually become data entry screens, others will properly remain in the realms of paper forms and will not necessarily map directly into data entry screens. If new requirements arise, while the conceptual design is being created, add them to the list of requirements that was created in the earlier phase. While sketching out the tables, also review the list of existing and new reports to establish a reasonably definitive list of the reports that the system must produce if it is to satisfy the needs of the users. The objective of analysing the reports is to ensure that the tables sketched out will have all the attributes that are needed to generate the reports. If there are missing attributes or tables, they should be added now. The completeness is important, but it can sometimes be difficult to know if all the reports that are being, or will be, produced or used have been identified. The database developer can proceed to create the physical database when the team considers that the requirements are sufficiently comprehensive.

After the database has been created, a programmer designs the data entry forms and links them to the tables in the database. There are various types of software that can be used to create the electronic data entry forms to capture the data. The choice of the tools and programming language will depend on the technical skills and preference of the team. When the programming phase is done, the database application should be tested. It is recommended that someone other than the programmer who developed it tests the application. Testing is an important phase, because it ensures that the system is validated and verified, a major requirement for GCP compliance. Users have to be trained on how to use the database, before deploying it for actual use. The database application should supplement user training by providing help features where users can access help through the application.

3.2 Data cleaning and integrity

Data cleaning should be an ongoing process, rather than something that is done at the end of the study. The process by which the data will be cleaned should be well thought out, planned, and documented at the beginning of the project, and certainly before any significant volume of data has been collected.

Double data entry is commonly used to minimize data entry errors. In this technique, two different people enter the same record independently, and the two entries are compared against each other. A validated data record is one where both entries are the same (see Section 5.1). It is important to remember, however, that no data entry system can avoid errors that were made by the interviewer using a paper-based questionnaire to record information in the field.

The database application can be programmed to flag inconsistencies in records, either during or after data entry. One approach is to categorize errors as being critical and non-critical. A critical error is one that is so important that systems are put in place to ensure that the data record cannot be saved into the database until the error has been fixed, for example, lack of the respondent's identity code or this being out of the valid range, as this code will be needed to link information in the database. The programmer would write these as checks embedded in the database application, sometimes called 'online checks'. The downside to having too many such checks embedded into the data entry screens is that the users cannot save the data until all the errors have been fixed, which can lead to back-logs. Decisions about what errors will be critical and non-critical should be made early enough, so that these are programmed in the system. Non-critical errors should not stop the user from saving the data record. They would instead be flagged up as data queries and reports for the data manager to follow up, rectify, and update the database.

Another approach is to incorporate data checks in a statistical program, for example, Stata, and run the checks against the data periodically. In the case of a paper-based collection system, periodic monitoring visits can be made to ensure that SOPs are being adhered to. Further checks can be done by taking a random sample of paper forms and comparing them against the corresponding electronic data records.

3.3 Programming issues

Computerized data collection systems are driven by computer programs written by system developers. The resources used to develop these systems can be made more effective if good programming practices are used. Computerized data systems should be documented to a sufficiently detailed level, so that any other system developer could quickly take over the maintenance or extension of such a system. A poorly documented computerized data system makes it very difficult to make changes to the existing system, and it will take a second person longer to figure out what needs to be changed. Even the programmer who wrote the initial program may forget specific technical details after a few months. Investing the effort to document programs, as they are developed, makes them easier to maintain, and changes can be made much more quickly.

Prototyping is an iterative technique used in computer systems development where the programmer designs mock-ups and asks the user to try them out and give feedback. The advantage of prototyping is that the users do not have to wait until the system has been fully developed, before they can try it out.

3.4 Standard operating procedures

SOPs are a set of written instructions detailing how a particular process is carried out. Computer-based systems support trial processes by providing a means of storing, modifying, and retrieving data. The process by which these computer systems are developed and used should be documented and controlled by procedures (SOPs) that ensure that they are adequate, and, where necessary, GCP-compliant. SOPs allow different people to check the procedures and ascertain whether what is done corresponds to what should be done. SOPs are also invaluable for training different people in the tasks that need to be undertaken in the study.

It is usually a good idea to split the SOPs into different categories such as database development, database validation and testing, database implementation and site set-up, and database maintenance/backups/upgrades. SOPs should be written by the person responsible for the task (who knows what should be done) and checked by the person who supervises their work and finally approved by the study PI.

3.5 Version control

The purpose of version control is to keep track of changes made to a computerized system during its development and after it has been implemented. The changes can come from various sources. For example, the users may find errors that need to be fixed when they start using the live system or may request new features or improvements to the system. Also, a change in environment may require a change in the computer system.

For example, a decision to move from Microsoft Access databases to SQL Server databases will require changes to the data entry screens. Another example is a new compliance requirement that requires a certain type of report to be generated by the system.

A requirement for GCP-compliant data management is the use of validated and verified computerized data collection systems. Systems are validated and verified by thorough testing, comparing the database system against the user requirements. A validated and verified system is one that meets its specifications and requirements and that fulfils the purpose it was created for. Any change made to an already validated computer system may introduce new errors. Hence, the process of making changes needs to be done in a controlled environment. Previous versions of the program code are stored in a version control software, for example, Visual SourceSafe, Subversion. The system ought to be tested after making changes to ensure it remains in a validated state, before deploying the updated version. The detailed process for managing and maintaining changes to the system should be written in a version control and change management SOP. It is important that the SOP is adhered to strictly.

3.6 Confidentiality

Information that can be used to identify a person should be stored in a secure database that allows only authorized persons to access the data. Any data that can be used to identify a person, for example, name, address, date of birth, should be kept out of the public domain. Sensitive information should be identified from the onset, so that appropriate controls are put in the database. If the data are to be shared, it is necessary to decide how this will be done and what kind of security checks will be put in place. Technical security mechanisms, such as audit trails, access control using user logins and passwords, and permissions should be supplemented by data-sharing contracts and user training. Encryption should be used when sharing or carrying data on portable devices to ensure that unauthorized users cannot read the data, even if they get hold of the portable device.

3.7 Training

However basic the database system may seem, users should be adequately trained and should fully understand what they are doing. This training may be in the form of professional and in-house training and may involve using a prototype of the database in a pilot scheme. User training logs should be kept as evidence of training.

3.8 Pilot testing and database testing

User acceptance testing and pilot testing are commonly used to verify that the database performs well. In user acceptance testing, the end-users test the new database by entering data, following the SOP, and trying out the functionality provided by the database. The end-users feed back comments to the programmers and study leaders, who can make the necessary changes to the database programs and to the SOP that define how the procedures work. This is very useful, since database issues are identified early and rectified, before data have started being captured. Pilot testing also helps to identify potential issues that may arise when the study systems go 'live'.

4 Data collection systems

In this section, we review some of the ways in which data can be collected from the participants and put into an electronic database.

4.1 Questionnaires

Paper-based questionnaires are often used to capture responses from study subjects, especially in small studies. These will need to be printed, taken to the study site, collated, batched for data entry, stored, and preserved for future reference. The design of questionnaires is discussed in Chapter 14.

4.2 Electronic data capture

Electronic data capture through the use of field computers, PDAs, UMPCs, or mobile phones is increasingly used. Using electronic data capture makes the data available immediately and removes the need for separate data entry, but it increases the need for data quality checks at the time of data collection. Electronic data capture devices need to be programmed to ensure that checks on the data quality are performed at the time of collection, as it is difficult to verify the data afterwards. With electronic data capture, it is easier for additional modules to be administered to a sub-sample of participants. These additional modules can be triggered by specific questions, for example, loops to ask about all the children in the household or about all the medicines taken at the last illness.

Using electronic data capture properly can enable data to be collected quickly and allows for numerous checks of data quality to be built in at the time the data are collected. Open source software exist for many applications, such as openXdata (<http://www.openxdata.org>), OpenEHR (<http://www.openehr.org>), and ODK (<http://opendatakit.org>), with the advantage that source code is available for modifying and adapting them.

Collecting data using mobile phone applications is becoming increasingly common. Mobile phones are relatively cheap, and telecommunications network coverage in most countries makes them available to large sections of the population. Information can be collected remotely, wherever the study subject might be, and the person does not have to be questioned face to face by an interviewer. Mobile phones can also be used to collect repeated data from individuals who may be difficult to locate or who may be in remote locations. Computer programs, such as FrontlineSMS or EpiSurveyor, allow data to be collected through simple text message or through interactive voice response or self-administered questionnaires. In all these cases, the data are stored directly in a central database, following transmission across the telephone network, and are available for processing almost immediately, following collection.

4.3 Laboratory data

Data from laboratory tests are important in many research studies, and it is important to design the stickers, labels, and linking mechanisms, so that samples collected in the field can be linked to the results of the laboratory tests and the other data collected on the same individual. Many laboratories use laboratory data management systems (LDMS), such as LIMS, which automatically download laboratory results into a computer database (see Chapter 17). Alternatively, the results can be entered on to paper or electronic forms, which are later merged into the database.

It is better to use a unique specimen identification number, rather than the individual's study identification number. This is because a single individual may have several specimens of the same type taken during a trial. As a check, the questionnaire number should be written (or a sticky label can be used) on the laboratory form, and a copy of the specimen identification sticker placed on the questionnaire, as well as on the specimen itself. If both the individual's study identification number and the specific specimen identification number are used on both forms, there can be assurance that the samples are correctly matched to the questionnaires when the analysis is done. Bar codes can be used for these laboratory numbers to enable the code to be read automatically by the laboratory equipment (also see Chapter 17).

LDMS must be programmed and managed carefully. Often, several studies use the same laboratory for many different tests. The LDMS must allow a study team to access all the data for their study, but they must not be able to access data from other studies. This requires common protocols and database programs, and good SOPs to ensure that data access is controlled and monitored.

4.4 Clinic data

Data from hospitals and clinics are sometimes used in trials. Patient-level data may be collected by clinicians when they assess, diagnose, and treat patients who are participating in the trial. The clinical data can be collected on a separate dedicated form, from which data are entered into the database later. Alternatively, there may be a trial research assistant in the clinic who enters the data into the computer from clinical records, or an electronic data collection tool may be introduced for use by the clinician, which removes the need for paper forms. With suitable choices for database programming and hardware, such systems can be relatively cheap and cost-effective.

There are several software options for the collection and management of health records from clinics and other health facilities (such as openXdata, openEHR, openMRS). These support data entry at the time the patient is seen by the clinician.

4.5 Longitudinal data collection

Longitudinal data require a system to link individuals within the database with each of the occasions when they are followed up. To do this, personal information, such as the person's names, address, and/or an identity number, needs to be stored in the database and used for subsequent survey visits to make a positive identification of the study subject. In order to make the identification more certain, photographs of the study subjects or fingerprints might be collected. These methods are cost-effective for even small studies, using mobile technology such as PDAs, cameras, and mobile phones.

The first time any individual is seen, sufficient personal information must be collected at the time that they are assigned a unique study identification number, so that unambiguous identification can be made on the second and subsequent visits.

Such personal identifiers must be kept secure and confidential, especially if these can be linked with health information or other sensitive data. However, appropriate information for identifying individuals must be made available to the fieldworkers at follow-up visits, through printed lists or through access to the electronic database, using PDAs, UMPCs, or other mobile computing devices. Links between the study numbers of individuals who belong to the same family or household can be easily stored in relational databases.

4.6 Quality control

In all trials, there is a need to ensure the quality of the data collected. To do this, it is necessary to be able to answer, and show evidence for, the following questions. Are the data a true reflection of the response from the study subjects? Has anyone changed the data and, if so, how? Is there effective QC over the data collection and data management? Are the data correctly matched and linked to the right respondents? (See also Chapter 14.) It is important to build quality checks and audits into the data collection and their subsequent management, in order to have the evidence to answer these questions. These checks fall into four main areas: design, training, supervision, and checking. Data collection should build in design features that allow checks and simplify coding and responses. Training should include a thorough examination of the instructions that all data collectors should know and follow. It should also explain and go over the ways that the data are checked at all levels, so that everyone knows that the process has checks and balances and that mistakes will be found and corrected. Supervision is important and should be supportive and non-threatening, with the objective of building quality and encouraging self-assessment and improvement. Regular tallies should be kept of the number of questionnaires completed, the number of refusals, and the number of errors or mistakes discovered. At the beginning of data collection, daily tallies of these indicators may be needed, but even weekly or monthly tallies may ensure that difficulties with the data collection are picked up early, and re-training given to those who need it.

Audit trails are used to keep track of any changes in the data. While every effort should be made to collect the correct data at the time of the interview or measurement, there will always be times when data need to be changed. Before the advent of computers, data managers used to keep logs of their work in ledger books, recording all the changes made to the database. Now any changes that are made should be documented in the database, which will include a record of the old values and a record of the reason for the change. Computers should never be programmed to make changes automatically. Rather they should be programmed to highlight probable errors, and a data manager can make any necessary changes and record the reasons for each of the changes.

4.7 Future trends

The traditional ways of collecting data through paper-based questionnaires will continue to be needed for some studies, but there are increasingly diverse other methods available. The use of mobile phones for collecting data has grown substantially in recent years. They have the advantage of enabling data to be collected frequently, and at any location or time, but currently are limited in the amount of data that can be collected at any one time.

Computer-assisted self-interviewing is a growth area. The advantages are that questions are standardized and confidential, and many people can be interviewed at the same time. Translations of questions can be made into different languages. The questions can be delivered in many ways, as an audio system for those who cannot read or through pictures and visual choices available through touch-screen technologies.

Online databases have become much more accessible and allow direct data collection into a master database located in the study centre or elsewhere. Mobile phone networks allow instantaneous transmission of data from the field to the data centre where it can be checked against the master database. Based on the data sent to the online database, fieldworkers collecting the data can be given instructions about the data to be collected and new study subjects to interview. These systems are increasingly used by large multicentre studies but will become more applicable to smaller studies where the online database can be linked to other resources, in order to improve the study design or data collection.

5 **Managing data**

Data management is a major task in most intervention trials. The main stages of the data management process are:

1. entering the data into a computer system
2. checking the data for errors and inconsistencies
3. organizing the data into an appropriate form for analysis
4. archiving the data.

Good data management requires a well-defined data management strategy—it is not something that will just happen. The complexity of the data management process will depend on the size and type of study. Attention to data management will greatly reduce the time needed in the analysis stage, because the data will be well organized and consistent and have fewer errors.

5.1 **Data entry**

The process of data entry will usually involve a data manager who designs the data entry screens, while other staff, such as data entry clerks or field staff, do the actual entering of the data. Creating data entry screens is not difficult but requires care. The data entry screen should follow the questionnaire, so automatic skips can be used to follow the skips in the questionnaire, and drop down menus can be used to show the same options as in the questionnaire for individual questions.

If data are being entered from paper-based forms, data entry can be double or single. Double data entry is routinely used to minimize typing errors and to ensure that the data in the database accurately reflect what was recorded on the forms. There are two main techniques used for double data entry. In one method, two data entry clerks independently enter the data without any knowledge of the other's work, and both entries are stored. A program, which may have to be written by the data manager, compares the two entries and identifies any discrepancies. The resolution of the discrepancies is generally referred to as 'verification' and can be done in different ways. In some systems, verification may involve both data entry clerks re-entering the specific data fields where discrepancies were identified and comparing the new entries. More commonly, a third person resolves the discrepancies, by referring to the original forms or questionnaires, and makes a decision as to the correct entry, changing the incorrect entry appropriately. Once the data have been double-entered and no discrepancies between the two entries are identified, the data are considered verified.

In the other method, which is used in specialist data entry programs, such as CSPro, the second person resolves the mismatches at the time of entry. After the first entry is complete, a second person enters the data, and any discrepancies are flagged up immediately, as the data are being entered. The second person must decide what the correct value should be and enter it accordingly. With this method, the second person is generally chosen to be more experienced and is expected to make the final entry, corresponding to what is on the form. This method is quicker but more prone to error than the first method described.

Facilities for double data entry are a feature in some software packages, for example, Epi-Info. In other packages, such as Access, double data entry must be set up when the database is created and would require considerable time and skill. One option is to use a package, such as Epi-Info, for data entry, before transferring the data to a separate package, such as Access, for storage and management.

Single entry of data is relatively rare and not recommended. It should only be considered if there are extensive checking routines, strong supporting processes, and technology in place to identify possible errors. Generally, the cost of doing a second entry of data is less than the costs of the additional data management required to clean the errors that that may remain after just a single entry of data.

The task of entering data should be conceptually separated from the task of analysis. Different software may be used for data entry, data checking, and analysis. The data entry system should be designed to make data entry as simple as possible. Simplifying the keying process will speed the task and make it less error-prone. Ideally, the data entry screens should closely resemble the paper form from which the data are being copied. Questionnaires should also be designed with data entry in mind. The data should be entered as recorded on the questionnaire. No hand calculations or transformation should be done before data entry—these can all be done during the analysis stage.

5.2 Data checks

Most data management time is taken up with checking the study data for errors and inconsistencies and 'cleaning' it. There are three main points to be considered when developing data checks: (1) deciding what will be checked; (2) working out when each check will be used; and (3) specifying how to resolve inconsistencies and errors identified by the checks.

Many software packages have inbuilt facilities for data checking. These automatic check programs can be set up when the database is created and run at different stages of the data management process. Before the check program is created, a specification document should be prepared, defining the data that will be checked and the errors that the program will be designed to catch. This document is usually written by the data manager or statistician, with input from the investigators, and is known as the data validation plan or check specification plan. Generally, the person who sets up the study database will also write the checking program and will be responsible for testing it. The program should be tested on 'dummy' data, before using it on the actual study data, to ensure that it is working correctly. Several 'dummy' questionnaires can be completed with deliberate errors and entered into the database; these can be used as test data for checking purposes.

Data checks can be incorporated into the data entry screens, so that illogical or implausible values are flagged up at the time of entry. Furthermore, the entry screens can be designed, so that they do not allow entry of invalid values, such as an impossible date or a value of '5' for a question that has '1' to '4' as the only possible answers. There are arguments for and against using data checks at the time of data entry. The checks will slow down the entry process, and, with double data entry, it can be argued that the checks are not needed to pick up errors in data entry, but they will pick up some data that have been incorrectly recorded on the questionnaire. If checks are incorporated into the entry screens, they should be designed so as to allow entry of invalid values, if that is what is recorded on the questionnaire. Otherwise, the questionnaire must be put to one side, until the error is resolved, and risks being lost or misplaced, so that it never gets entered in the database. Except for very small studies, it is often better to get the data entered in the database and to run checks to identify any errors afterwards, especially where there are a large number of questions that might need checking. However, interactive checking may be preferable when data are entered by the same field staff who completed the questionnaires earlier in the day. They may be slow typists but, having the interviews fresh in their minds, are more likely to be able to correct errors at the time of entry. However, in this case, it would probably be even better to consider having the data entered at the time of the interview, using electronic data capture methods.

After data entry is complete and the data are verified, an automatic check program is run to identify errors. These checks can include range checks to identify out-of-range or missing values (for example, dates out of the expected range, participant's age outside the range permitted by the study protocol) and cross-checks to identify inconsistencies between values (for example, males who are pregnant). The timing of when these checks are run requires careful consideration—for example, if a check compares data from different visits, the data from both visits must be present for the results to be meaningful.

In a longitudinal study, with repeated data collection visits to each subject, data checks should be run early on and continuously throughout the study. When errors are identified early in the study, it is often possible to uncover misunderstandings in the interpretation of the questionnaire or a flaw in the questionnaire design that was not picked up during the pilot phase. Clarification or further training can prevent those problems from recurring throughout the entire study.

The initial analyses are a continuation of the checking process and should include looking at cross-tabulations of the data to identify inconsistencies, and scatter plots and box-plots to compare groups and identify outlying observations. In large longitudinal trials, interim tabulations of data are recommended as a way of detecting possible data errors. Special checks might be made on observations that are more than two or three standard deviations from the mean. Such observations should be checked individually, as they are not impossible, merely unlikely.

Lastly, it should be noted that discrepancies in data are time-consuming to identify and resolve. The implications for data checks and query resolution should be considered during the questionnaire design stage. Asking for duplicate information in different parts of the questionnaire is one source of unnecessary queries. Queries will also arise if the questionnaire design does not make adequate provision for unavailable responses or permits ambiguous responses. Questionnaires frequently include questions that are deliberately used as cross-checks of other fields. This can be a very good policy when the data are actually different. For example, a check of sex against the subject's pregnancy status provides a reasonable cross-check of whether the person could not possibly be pregnant because they are male. However, problems arise when questions duplicate the same data, for example, a questionnaire that asks to record both the age and birth date. Discrepancies and confusion are bound to be generated when the values do not agree. When designing a questionnaire with requests for repeat information, consideration should be given to the implications for data checking and whether the duplicate information is truly needed.

5.3 Data cleaning

Data cleaning involves raising and resolving data queries that are identified during the data checking process and making the appropriate changes to the database to correct the errors. The aim is to be sure that the data are as of high quality as possible, before they are analysed.

Some data queries can be resolved within the data management group, for example, an obvious error in the year of a visit date. However, most problems will need to be resolved by the field team or the investigator. Commonly, the data management group will send a list of queries to the field team; the team will resolve the queries by writing the correct answer next to each one and return the list to the data management group. Alternatively, corrections can be made to the questionnaire itself. However, it is very important that the original answer is not obscured—instead, it should be crossed through with a single stroke, so that it is still legible, and the new information written on the side. It is good practice (and required for GCP) for the person making the change to initial and date the changes.

After the queries have been resolved, the database should be updated to reflect the corrected information. Some software systems have features to allow changes to the data after query resolution. These changes are usually made through the data entry screens and are recorded in an electronic audit trail. In a system without an automatic audit trail, changes may be made directly to the data tables themselves, although this can be more error-prone than changing the data via the data entry screens.

Correction or editing of data to reflect a resolution generally follows a different path from that of initial entry of the data. Most systems do not support double entry of corrections, so it is good practice to have a visual check of the data after correction to be sure that the change was made correctly. After the changes are made, it is essential to re-run the check program again, since it is possible that the update of the data has caused a new inconsistency to be identified.

In some cases, it may not be possible to obtain a resolution to a query, particularly if it is some time since the data were collected. Some software systems keep an electronic record of the problems identified by the check program, and a code can be entered to indicate that the inconsistency cannot be resolved. Alternatively, the incorrect data can be given a code for 'missing' if the correct answer cannot be obtained. The number of times this is done should be kept as small as possible and should be documented.

It is important to have a single master copy of the database that contains all the data corrections that are made. Even after the data cleaning stage is complete, errors may be detected much later during analysis; these should all be corrected on the master copy, so that it is always up to date. A version control system should be in place to ensure that it is possible to know which version of the database was used for any particular analysis.

5.4 Variable naming and coding

One of the first things to be done, before developing the study database, is to create an annotated questionnaire, containing the names that will be given to different variables and the characteristics of the variables such as numeric or text, the length of the variable (maximum number of characters), and any specific code lists that will be used. Ideally, variable names should provide information about the data being recorded, for example, 'birthwt' for birth weight or 'intdate' for interview date. In a longitudinal study, the same name should be used for those variables that are recorded at every visit. Some studies have used a convention of naming the variables at different visits with a number at the end corresponding with the visit, for example, 'visit_date3' and 'visit_date6' for visits 3 and 6. However, it is generally easier to run data checks and do other manipulations on the data if the variables have exactly the same name at each visit. An additional variable for the visit number should be included to identify the visit.

Some software packages have restrictions on the length of variable names; in particular, some older packages do not allow more than eight characters. A good general rule is to use no more characters than are allowed by the most restrictive (in terms of the number of characters) software package that is likely to be used for the study.

Questions that have categories of answers are best entered as coded values, rather than text (for example, 0 = No, 1 = Yes). These fields have a limited list of possible answers and only present a problem for data management if the field can contain more than one answer or if the answer falls outside the predefined list. When more than one answer is possible (for example, a list of types of contraception ever used), the database design changes from a single field to a series of fields, each of which can hold any of the valid responses from the list (coded yes or no). If an answer occurs that is not on the predefined list, a value for 'other' may be needed. In this case, it is advisable to create an additional database field where the specific response can also be entered as text. If an answer that is not on the list occurs frequently, it may be worth creating a new code for it. New codes may also be needed if the questionnaire design changes during the study or between survey rounds. In these cases, it is essential that the existing code list does not change. Instead, the new codes should be added at the end of the list. The coding of responses to questions is dealt with in more detail in Chapter 14.

Some studies use free-text on the questionnaire and re-code the text into categories at the time of data management. Re-coding variables in this way is generally not recommended, as, if they have been collected and entered, the original data should be found in the final data set. If any re-coding is done after data entry, the new data should be put into a new variable, with a note to indicate how the variable and the codes were defined.

5.5 Data lock

When all the data checks have been run, the queries resolved, and all QC activities are complete, the data are declared 'clean', and the database is 'locked'. This means that no further corrections will be made to the data. In GCP-compliant studies, the trial cannot be unblinded, i.e. the randomization codes made available to the study team and the main analyses cannot be performed, until the database is locked. At this stage, the locked database may be deposited with an independent body, such as the data safety and monitoring committee (DSMC), so that, if there are any later queries about the integrity of the data or changes that may have been made, comparison can be made with the locked set.

Even in studies that are not being run to be fully GCP-compliant, it is useful, at some stage, to make the formal decision that the data are 'closed', and no more corrections will be made. Sometimes, the data can be closed for one analysis, while corrections are ongoing for other data. The purpose of 'closing' the database is to ensure that the data are defined for a stable set of analyses and will not change every time the analysis program is re-run. The closing of the database, or any part of the database, should not be done before all the errors that are correctable have been resolved.

6 Archiving

New data are brought into a data management centre daily, and many different data changes and decisions are made. It is important that these are recorded and documented. If an accident happens (for example, a fire in the data centre), these changes and decisions could be lost and may be difficult to re-create, with potentially serious consequences for the integrity of the trial. This section advises on some of the ways to backup and keep the data, both for short-term protection and long-term use.

6.1 Interim backups

Backups of data are essential and should follow a regular pattern. Backups should not be thought of as an archive of the data, but only as a temporary store of the latest work. The procedure for backup should include times when a complete, full backup is made (perhaps monthly) and times when an incremental or partial backup is sufficient. The backup procedures should be documented in a SOP and agreed with the trial PI. Backups should be automatically scheduled, using a program or backup package, but one person in the study should be given responsibility to check the backup happens as scheduled. If the backup fails for some reason, that person needs to know what to do. At periodic intervals (preferably at least once per month), data should be backed up off-site, which can usually be easily and cheaply done onto an independent website.

What should be backed up? Everything should be kept in a backup, but not everything needs to be kept in every backup. The master database with the study data needs to be backed up regularly and completely. Other data that contribute to the master data should be backed up, and any changes recorded and backed up. Data entry files need to be backed up at least once but, as they should not be changed, may not need to be backed up again. Questionnaires and forms need to be included, as do coding sheets, reports, and correspondence with personnel inside and outside the study. Organization of the study data is important and should probably reflect the organization of the data on the main computer or server, and it should include a directory map to allow someone who is unfamiliar with the structure to find their way around.

An external hard disk is a cheap and easy way to make a backup. These are large enough to store many copies of the data (previous backups should not be deleted), but these external drives can suffer accidents and should not be considered a safe or secure storage of data. It is worth getting programs that will compress, encrypt, time-stamp, and validate the backed-up data to ensure that it does represent a true copy of the data at that time. Backups should not be considered a permanent solution, as technology moves on, and new systems and programs replace old ones. For example, backup data stored on floppy disks from 2000 were no longer readily accessible by computers or programs in 2012. This means that it may be necessary to copy backups onto new hardware/software every few years, before they become obsolete. And the final archived data sets must always be kept accessible on current hardware and software.

6.2 Metadata

An archive of the data is of limited use without the extra information that specifies exactly what the data comprise. These additional pieces of information are called metadata and can include information about the study setting, inclusion and exclusion criteria, the questions asked in any questionnaires, the codes for the variables, and a host of other information. Without such information, the data collected in the study are not interpretable. Note that metadata can include the names of the authorized users of the database and their passwords, as, without this information, it would not be possible to access the database and retrieve the data.

Extensible Markup Language (XML) is a set of rules that allow text, documents, codes, names, and even pictures to be stored in a machine-readable format. This allows the metadata for any study to be added to a repository and enhance the ability of others to use and understand the data. There are a number of XML schemes available, but, whichever is chosen, the metadata should be preserved for future use.

The Data Documentation Initiative (DDI) (see <http://www.ddialliance.org>) takes the storage of data and metadata one step further by defining a set of instructions for the storage, exchange, and preservation of statistical and social science data.

6.3 Data sharing policy

Usually, investigators will not allow sharing of the data from a trial with persons not directly involved in the trial, until the data collection and entry are complete, the trial has been analysed, and the main results published. However, at this stage, others may be interested in accessing the data to undertake further analyses or to combine the data with those from other trials to conduct a meta-analysis (see Chapter 3). Many funding agencies are moving towards insisting on sharing of data as a condition of funding. For example, the Wellcome Trust states that it is 'committed to ensuring that the outputs of the research it funds, including research data, are managed and used in ways that maximize public benefit. Making research data widely available to the research community in a timely and responsible manner ensures that these data can be verified, built upon and used to advance knowledge and its application to generate improvements in health'. Most other major charitable or governmental funding agencies have a similar policy. The US Institute of Medicine published a consultation document in January 2014 on the guiding principles related to clinical trial data sharing (National Research Council, 2014), and their final recommendations in 2015 (National Research Council, 2015). Most large research institutions have a data sharing policy. The data sharing policy will define what data have been collected, stored, and will be made available, and the procedures to be followed for making some, or all, of the trial data available publicly or to selected recipients. Increasingly, the data collected in any trial, especially if it has been funded by a charitable or government agency, should not be thought of as belonging exclusively to the research team or to the director of the institute that conducted the trial but as a public good. After a reasonable period of exclusive access, it is widely accepted that the data should be made available to other researchers, policy makers, and medical authorities to further the advancement of knowledge.

The data sharing policy should be drafted at the start of a trial, as it will influence the way in which data are stored and archived. In particular, consideration must be given to how the strict confidentiality of the identity of the study participants can be preserved in any data that are shared. Furthermore, shared data are only useful if the recipient has a proper understanding of the information being shared. This requires that the data collection and coding systems are carefully documented for possible future onward transmission. This is one reason why metadata are essential.

6.4 Archiving hard copies

Paper copies of data and study procedures need to be kept for some time after the end of a trial. Some funders require these hard copies to be kept for periods in excess of 10 years after the completion of the trial, as the ultimate reference for the study data. Paper copies will need to be sorted and archived in a logical way. Space needs to be obtained for such storage, and protection ensured against fire, theft, and destruction by mould, insects, or other animals. Some studies are experimenting with scanning all documents and preserving the digital images instead of the hard copies, but this needs to be agreed in advance with the regulatory authorities and may not be acceptable to all. If data are collected electronically, the long-term storage of paper forms is no longer relevant. However, this puts even more emphasis on the need for careful and accessible archives of electronic databases, which should always include the original data as entered, as well as any final data sets.

7 Preparing data for analysis

The 'raw materials' for data analysis are the data files created by the data management process. However, the variables, as recorded in the questionnaire and entered into the database as raw data, are not always the ones directly suitable for data analysis. Re-coding and creating of new variables is likely to be necessary. It is generally also necessary to combine information from different data files.

When preparing the data for analysis, it is good practice to create a new data set with a different name to separate it from the original study data. Also, it is advisable to keep a copy of the commands used to prepare the data (either the program that was used or the 'log' files), in case it is necessary to re-create the file from the raw data.

7.1 Data dictionary

The data dictionary is part of the metadata and is the link between the questionnaire and the data files. It typically contains the name and a description of each variable, with additional information such as the data type (for example, numeric or text), coding (for example, 0 = No, 1 = Yes), and the questionnaire section and question number to which the variable relates. The data dictionary is essential for understanding how the data are structured and is used in preparing for data analysis.

7.2 Creating new variables

Sometimes, it is necessary to create a new variable from two or more existing variables, since this new variable may be more meaningful than the ones on which data were collected directly. For example, body mass index (BMI, defined as weight in kilograms/height in metres^2) or weight-for-age may be better markers of nutritional status than weight on its own. Such composite variables may be calculated directly from the raw data or be obtained by comparison with a given standard (as in the case of weight-for-age).

Variables related to time, such as the length of residence or the duration of exposure to a risk factor, present a special case. Depending on the characteristics of the variable and of the population under study, it may be preferable to record relevant dates on the questionnaires and to subtract them during the analysis stage to compute the duration of residence, exposure, etc. These calculations can be done, without difficulty, with any statistical package.

After creating a composite variable, it is useful to check that the distribution of the new variable seems reasonable. It is also appropriate to check the range of the new variable, as data errors may only show up at this stage. For example, negative ages or extreme weights-for-age may result from errors in the date of birth (or date of interview) in the questionnaire, though such errors should have been detected through consistency checks at an earlier stage.

7.3 Coding and re-coding

Before beginning the analysis, it is usually necessary to re-code some variables, so that they can be grouped into categories. Since it is advisable to look at cross-tabulations of data before moving on to regression methods, re-coding is generally needed for quantitative variables. Grouping makes it easier to understand the data and, in particular, to look for non-linear associations. But re-coding may also be necessary for categorical variables with large numbers of categories, or few observations in some categories.

When re-coding quantitative variables, one strategy is to divide the range of the variable into quartiles or quintiles, giving four or five groups with equal numbers of observations in each group. Alternatively, cut-off points may be chosen on the basis of established standards. For example, when grouping age, it is more natural to use 5- or 10-year age bands (for example, 20–29, 30–39, etc.), rather than base the categorization on quartiles. Similarly, there are recognized international cut-points for variables such as BMI (less than 18.5 is considered underweight) or weight-for-age (less than −2.0 is considered stunted). A histogram of the data is often a good way of deciding how to categorize a quantitative variable with no standard cut-points.

With categorical variables, it may be necessary to combine groups if there are very few observations in some groups. When combining groups, an important principle to remember is that, for combining to be appropriate, the risk of the outcome should be similar in each of the combined groups. For example, in a study of child malnutrition, it may not be appropriate to group mothers with no schooling with those with primary school education.

The number of groups to use also depends, in part, on how the variable will be used in the analysis. If the variable is an exposure of interest, where it is planned to examine the pattern of dependence of the outcome on the amount of exposure (for example, a dose–response), it is important to use enough groups to get a reasonable picture of the relationship. For example, to examine the effect of alcohol intake during pregnancy on birthweight, one group might be non-drinkers, and there could be four or five groups for different levels of alcohol intake.

After deciding if and how each variable should be grouped, the different categories should be assigned 'labels' to describe them. These labels should be saved in the data set, which will eliminate the need to return to the questionnaires or code lists during the analysis. When a variable is re-coded, it is important to create a new variable and allocate it a different name, so as to preserve the raw data. Thus, the variable 'AGE' might be grouped and allocated to another variable called 'AGEGP'.

7.4 Merging and linking data

The data required for a particular analysis may need to come from several different data sets (for example, questionnaire data on an individual's recent sexual behaviour may need to be linked to laboratory results, demographic data collected previously, and household-level data on the socio-economic status). If complete data tables are extracted for analysis, merging of the data may be more easily managed in the statistical package used for the analysis.

Many data management packages allow the construction of complex views of the data and can be used to extract merged data for analysis. The data analyst can specify the variables for analysis, and these can be extracted from the database, using standard data management tools, thereby maintaining the confidentiality of the data. It also enables simple data extraction programs to be used at regular intervals for longitudinal data, giving regular snapshots of the data for analysis.

References

Hernandez, M. J. 2013. *Database design for mere mortals: a hands-on guide to relational database design*. London: Addison-Wesley.

McFadden, E. 2007. *Management of data in clinical trials*. Hoboken, NJ: John Wiley & Sons.

Murrell, P. 2009. *Introduction to data technologies*. Boca Raton: Chapman & Hall/CRC.

National Research Council. 2014. *Discussion framework for clinical trial data sharing: guiding principles, elements, and activities*. Washington, DC: The National Academies Press.

National Research Council. 2015. *Sharing clinical trial data: maximizing benefit, minimizing risk*. Washington, DC: The National Academies Press.

Powell, G. 2006. *Beginning database design*. Indianapolis: Wiley Publishing.

Prokscha, S. 2012. *Practical guide to clinical data management*. Boca Raton: CRC Press.

Pryor, G. 2012. *Managing research data*. London: Facet.

Chapter 21

Methods of analysis

1 Introduction to methods of analysis 366
2 Basics of statistical inference 367
   2.1 Types of outcome measure 367
   2.2 Confidence intervals 367
   2.3 Statistical tests 368
3 Statistical analysis plan 369
4 Analysis of proportions 371
   4.1 Confidence interval for a single proportion 371
   4.2 Difference between two proportions 371
   4.3 Ratio of two proportions 372
   4.4 Trend test for proportions 373
5 Analysis of rates 374
   5.1 Risks, rates, and person-time-at-risk 374
   5.2 Confidence interval for a rate 375
   5.3 Difference between two rates 376
   5.4 Ratio of two rates 377
   5.5 Trend test for rates 377
6 Analysis of mean values 378
   6.1 Confidence interval for a mean 378
   6.2 Difference between two means 378
   6.3 Analysis of more than two groups 379
7 Controlling for confounding variables 380
   7.1 The nature of confounding variables 380
   7.2 Adjusting for confounding variables 381
   7.3 Adjusting risks 381
      7.3.1 Overall test of significance 381
      7.3.2 Pooled estimate of risk difference 383
      7.3.3 Pooled estimate of risk ratio 383
      7.3.4 Confidence intervals 384
   7.4 Adjusting rates 384
      7.4.1 Overall test of significance 384
      7.4.2 Pooled estimate of rate difference 385
      7.4.3 Pooled estimate of rate ratio 385
      7.4.4 Confidence intervals 385
   7.5 Adjusting means 387

8 **Analyses when communities have been randomized** 388
      8.1 **Calculation of standardized responses** 389
      8.2 **Non-parametric rank sum test** 390
      8.3 **Tests on paired data** 391
   9 **Prevented fraction of disease** 392

1 Introduction to methods of analysis

This chapter describes simple statistical methods that are likely to be most useful for the basic analysis of intervention trials. Usually, a statistician will be closely involved in the design and analysis of a trial, and the more advanced analytical techniques that they might employ are not covered in this chapter. For more information on such techniques, the reader is referred to statistical texts such as Armitage and Berry (1987), Kirkwood and Sterne (2003), and Rothman et al. (2008). However, the methods presented in this chapter should enable the analysis of the main results of a trial. More advanced statistical techniques usually result in relatively small changes in the estimates of effect sizes through multivariate and associated analyses. Also, armed with the methods in this chapter, the reader should be in a good position to interpret and check the analyses reported in published studies.

The methods that are going to be used to analyse a trial should be considered at the time the trial is set up, so all of the appropriate data are collected and are assembled in a form suitable for the planned analyses. It is a common requirement nowadays for the *statistical analysis plan* to be fully developed, before any blinding in a trial is broken and in advance of a 'frozen' data set being prepared for analysis. Such plans are discussed in Section 3.

The choice of an appropriate method of analysis of a trial depends on the type of outcome measure which is of interest. The different types of outcome measure are discussed in Section 2, which also includes a brief review of the concepts of confidence intervals (CIs) and statistical tests. In Sections 4, 5, and 6, methods are described which are appropriate for the analyses of data in the form of proportions, rates, and means, respectively. RCTs have been recommended as the method of choice for determining the effects of an intervention, because such trials generally avoid the problem of confounding. Sometimes, however, particularly in small trials, there may be differences between the randomized groups, with respect to factors that might affect the outcome of interest, but which are unrelated to the intervention under test. If there has been a proper randomization process, any such differences should rise by chance only. If the trial is large, it is unlikely that there will be any important imbalance in this respect between the randomized groups. In small trials, such chance differences may have a larger effect, and, in such circumstances, it may be important to adjust for any potential confounding due to these chance differences. In addition, where randomization is not feasible, any attempt to draw conclusions about the effects of an intervention must make allowance for possible confounding factors, and simple methods for doing this are described in Section 7. The analysis of trials in which interventions are allocated to groups, rather than individuals, is discussed in Section 8. How the results of a trial may be used to assess the possible public health impact of an intervention is considered in Section 9.

2 Basics of statistical inference

2.1 Types of outcome measure

The appropriate method of statistical analysis depends on the type of outcome measure that is of interest. An outcome in an intervention study can usually be expressed as a proportion, rate, or mean. For example, in a trial of a modified vaccine, an outcome measure of interest may be the *proportion* of vaccinated subjects who develop a protective level of antibodies. In a trial of multi-drug therapy for tuberculosis, the incidence *rates* of relapse, following treatment, may be compared in the different study groups under consideration. In a trial of an anti-malarial intervention, it may be of interest to compare the *mean* packed cell volume (PCV) at the end of the malaria season in those in the intervention group and those in the comparison group.

2.2 Confidence intervals

An estimate of an outcome measure calculated in an intervention study is subject to *sampling error*, because it is based on only a sample of individuals and not on the whole population of interest. The term *sampling error* does not mean that the sampling procedure or method of randomization was applied incorrectly, but that, when random sampling is used to decide which individuals are in which group, there will be an element of random variation in the results. The methods of statistical inference allow the investigator to draw conclusions about the true value of the outcome measure on the basis of the information in the sample. In general, the observed value of the outcome measure gives the *best estimate* of the true value. In addition, it is useful to have some indication of the *precision* of this estimate, and this is done by calculating a *confidence interval* for the estimate. The CI is a range of plausible values for the true value of the outcome measure, based on the observations in the trial. It is conventional to quote the 95% *confidence interval* (also called 95% *confidence limits*). This is calculated in such a way that there is a 95% probability that the CI includes the *true* value of the outcome measure.

Suppose the true value of the outcome measure is ϕ and that this is estimated from the sample data as $\hat{\phi}$. The 95% CIs to be presented here are generally of the form $\hat{\phi} \pm 1.96 \times SE(\hat{\phi})$, where $SE(\hat{\phi})$ denotes the *standard error* of the estimate. This is a measure of the amount of sampling error to which the estimate is susceptible. One of the factors influencing the magnitude of the standard error, and hence the width of the CI, is the sample size; the larger the sample, the narrower the CI.

The multiplying factor 1.96, used when calculating the 95% CI, is derived from tables of the *Normal* distribution. In this distribution, 95% of values are expected to fall within 1.96 standard deviations of the mean. In some circumstances, CIs, other than 95% limits, may be required, and then different values of the multiplying factor are appropriate, as indicated in Table 21.1.

Table 21.1 Multiplying factors for calculating CIs, based on the Normal distribution

CI (%)	Multiplying factor
90	1.64
95	1.96
99	2.58
99.9	3.29

When analysing means, the multiplying factor sometimes has to be increased to allow for additional errors in estimating the standard error (see Section 5).

2.3 Statistical tests

As well as calculating a CI to indicate a range of plausible values for the outcome measure of interest, it may be appropriate to test a specific *hypothesis* about the outcome measure. In the context of an intervention trial, this will often be the hypothesis that there is no true difference between the outcomes in the groups under comparison. (For this reason, the hypothesis is often referred to as the *null hypothesis*.) The objective is thus to assess whether any observed difference in outcomes between the study groups may have occurred just by chance, due to sampling error.

A statistical test is used to evaluate the plausibility of the null hypothesis. The sample data are used to calculate a quantity (called a statistic) which gives a measure of the difference between the groups, with respect to the outcome(s) of interest. The details of how the statistic is calculated vary, according to the type of outcome measure being examined, and are given in Sections 4 to 6. Once the statistic has been calculated, its value is referred to an appropriate set of statistical tables, in order to determine the p-value (probability value) or *statistical significance* of the results. The p-value measures the probability of obtaining a value for the statistic as extreme as the one actually observed if the null hypothesis were true. Thus, a very low p-value indicates that the null hypothesis is likely to be false.

For example, suppose, in a trial of a vaccine against malaria, an estimate of the efficacy is obtained of 20%, with an associated p-value of 0.03. This indicates that, if the vaccine had a true efficacy of zero, there would only be a 3% chance of obtaining an observed efficacy of 20% or greater.

The smaller the p-value, the less plausible the null hypothesis is as an explanation of the observed data. For example, on the one hand, a p-value of 0.001 implies that the null hypothesis is highly implausible, and this can be interpreted as very strong evidence of a real difference between the groups. On the other hand, a p-value of 0.20 implies that a difference of the observed magnitude could quite easily have occurred by chance, even if there were no real difference between the groups. Conventionally, p-values of 0.05 and below have been regarded as sufficiently low to be taken as reasonable evidence against the null hypothesis and have been referred to as indicating a *statistically significant difference*, but it is preferable to specify the actual size of the p-value attained, so that readers can draw their own conclusions about the strength of the evidence.

While a small p-value can be interpreted as evidence for a real difference between the groups, a larger *non-significant* p-value must not be interpreted as indicating that there is no difference. It merely indicates that there is insufficient evidence to reject the null hypothesis, so that there *may* be no true difference between the groups. It is never possible to *prove* the null hypothesis. Depending on the size of the study and the observed difference between the groups under comparison, the CI on the difference provides a range of plausible values in which the true difference might lie, which may include a zero difference.

Too much reliance should not be placed on the use of statistical tests. Usually, it is more important to *estimate* the effect of the intervention and to specify a CI around the estimate to indicate the plausible range of effect than it is to test a specific hypothesis. In any case, a null hypothesis of zero difference is often of no practical interest, as there may be strong grounds for believing the intervention has some effect, and the main objective should be to estimate that effect.

The statistical tests presented here are *two-sided* tests. This means that, when the p-value is computed, it measures the probability (if the null hypothesis is true) of observing a difference as great as that actually observed *in either direction* (i.e. positive or negative). It is usual to assume that tests are two-sided, unless otherwise stated, though not all authors adhere to this convention. A full discussion of the relative merits of one-sided and two-sided tests is given in Armitage and Berry (1987) and Kirkwood and Sterne (2003).

3 Statistical analysis plan

A common mistake in the planning of a trial is to delay consideration of the analyses until the data become available. It is essential that the main analyses that will be undertaken are planned at the design stage, as this provides several major benefits. First, it encourages a clearer understanding of the basic questions to be answered and thus assists with the formulation of clear and specific objectives. For example, in a vaccine trial, a simple comparison of the numbers of cases of the disease occurring over a 5-year period in the vaccinated and unvaccinated groups may answer the question of the magnitude of any protective effect. A comparison of the incidence rates of disease in vaccinated and unvaccinated individuals in the first, second, third, fourth, and fifth years after vaccination can be used to answer a rather different question, namely, whether the protective effect is constant over the 5-year period.

A second benefit of considering the analyses at the design stage is that it necessitates specification of what data need to be recorded. The investigator can check that arrangements have been made to measure and record all variables that will be needed in the analyses. Also, and perhaps as importantly, it may become clear that some variables will not be needed, and these can then be omitted from the study.

The process of planning the analyses may identify also the importance of subgroup analyses. In a vaccine trial, for example, it may reveal a need to assess the efficacy of the vaccine in children vaccinated at different ages. This may have major implications for the choice of sample size, as the need for age-specific estimates of efficacy requires a much larger sample in each age group than would be needed if only an overall estimate of efficacy was wanted.

Finally, advanced planning of the analyses is desirable to ensure that adequate arrangements have been made for data handling, the necessary computer software is available, and sufficient time for data cleaning and analysis has been allowed for in the study schedule.

Prior to any formal statistical analyses of the kinds discussed from Section 4 onwards, it is essential to perform simple tabulations of data and to construct simple diagrams to summarize the information that has been collected. Simple statistical *package* computer programs, such as Epi-Info (<http://wwwn.cdc.gov/epiinfo>) or STATA (<http://www.stata.com>), greatly facilitate doing this. The investigator should use these simple approaches to gain a good understanding of the data collected, before embarking on more complex analyses. These simple analysis methods are not described further in this manual, but they are discussed in most good textbooks on medical statistics (for example, Armitage and Berry, 1987; Kirkwood and Sterne, 2003).

If the results of a trial are to be used for submission to an appropriate authority to grant a licence for a new drug or vaccine, the licensing authorities will require that a *statistical analysis plan* (SAP) is developed as a separate document, to be completed after finalizing the protocol and before the code is broken for who is in the intervention and control groups (if it is a blinded trial). The SAP should contain a technical and detailed description of the principal analyses to be conducted on the trial data, which has more detail than would typically be included in the trial protocol. The plan should include detailed procedures for conducting the statistical analysis of the primary and secondary outcome variables and of other relevant data. Often, the licensing authority will require a copy of the SAP for them to examine and approve in advance of a trial being analysed.

It is good practice to prepare a SAP for any trial, even if the results are not to be used for product licensing. In addition to any necessary review by licensing authorities, the SAP should be reviewed and approved by the trial steering committee and also often by the trial data safety and monitoring committee (DSMC). A formal record should be kept of when the statistical analysis plan was finalized, as well as when the final data set was 'frozen' and when the trial was unblinded.

It is common to develop the computer programs for conducting the SAP in advance of breaking the treatment code. To check that these are working properly, some analysts assign study participants at random to intervention or control groups (irrespective of which group they were actually in) and run the programs on these 'test' data. In this way, they are able to check that the final tables are in an appropriate format to be interpreted, once the code is broken. Conducting such a 'dummy run' analysis generally greatly speeds the analysis and interpretation of the trial, once the data are finalized.

Often, when an analysis is conducted, further analyses will be appropriate and prompted by an initial examination of the study results, rather than being pre-planned in the SAP. Such analyses are often called 'exploratory'. They were not specifically planned in advance but were prompted by examination of the trial findings. Such exploratory analyses are sometimes informative and may suggest new hypotheses, but it is important to distinguish them from the analyses that were included in the SAP, as they were suggested by the data, rather than being planned in advance of the code being broken. It is generally wise to interpret the results of such exploratory analyses with caution.

4 Analysis of proportions

4.1 Confidence interval for a single proportion

Methods appropriate for the analysis of proportions are used when the outcome of interest is a *binary* ('yes/no') variable (for example, the proportion of individuals who develop a disease). The standard error of a proportion p, calculated from a sample of n subjects, is estimated as $\sqrt{[p(1-p)/n]}$. For example, if the prevalence of splenomegaly in a random sample of 200 children from a population is found to be 0.40 (40%) (i.e. 80 had splenomegaly), the standard error (SE) is given by:

$$SE(p) = \sqrt{(0.40 \times 0.60/200)} = 0.035 (3.5\%).$$

The 95% CI for a proportion is given by $p \pm 1.96 \times SE(p)$. In the example, the 95% CI is $0.4 \pm 1.96 \times 0.035$ or (0.33, 0.47), i.e. 33–47%. There is a 95% chance that the true prevalence of splenomegaly in the population from which the sample of 200 was taken was between 33% and 47%.

4.2 Difference between two proportions

Suppose now that the objective is to compare the proportions observed in two groups of individuals, as is typically the case in a trial, comparing outcomes in an intervention and control group. The standard error of the *difference* between two proportions p_1 and p_2, based on n_1 and n_2 observations, respectively, is estimated approximately as:

$$\sqrt{\{\bar{p}(1-\bar{p})[(1/n_1)+(1/n_2)]\}}$$

where $\bar{p} = (n_1 p_1 + n_2 p_2)/(n_1 + n_2)$.

For example, if the proportions to be compared are 90/300 (30%) and 135/300 (45%), the observed difference between the two proportions is −0.15, $\bar{p} = 0.375$, and the standard error of the difference is given by:

$$\sqrt{\{0.375 \times 0.625[(1/300)+(1/300)]\}} = 0.040.$$

The 95% CI for the difference between the proportions is given by $(p_1 - p_2) \pm 1.96 \times SE$. In the example, this gives $(-0.15) \pm 1.96(0.040)$, i.e. (−0.23, −0.07), or −23% to −7%.

To test the null hypothesis that there is no true difference between the two proportions, the data are first arranged in a 2 × 2 table, as in Table 21.2.

In the table, a is the number in group 1 who experiences the outcome of interest. The expected value of a, $E(a)$, and the variance of a, $V(a)$, are calculated under the hypothesis of no difference between the two groups:

$$E(a) = m_1 n_1 / N \qquad (21.1),$$

Table 21.2 Comparison of two proportions

Group	Outcome Yes	Outcome No	Total	Proportion with outcome
1	a (90)	b (210)	n_1 (300)	$p_1 = a/n_1$ (0.30)
2	c (135)	d (165)	n_2 (300)	$p_2 = c/n_2$ (0.45)
Total	m_1 (225)	m_2 (375)	N (600)	

$$V(a) = n_1 n_2 m_1 m_2 / [N^2(N-1)] \tag{21.2}$$

The chi-squared (χ^2) statistic is then calculated. This gives a measure of the extent to which the observed data differ from those expected if the two proportions were truly equal.

$$\chi^2 = (|a - E(a)| - 0.5)^2 / V(a) \tag{21.3}$$

where $|a - E(a)|$ indicates the *absolute* value of $[a - E(a)]$.

The calculated value of χ^2 is compared with tables of the chi-squared distribution with one degree of freedom (df). If it exceeds 3.84, then p < 0.05, indicating some evidence of a real difference in the proportions. If it exceeds 6.63, then p < 0.01, and there is strong evidence of a difference.

In the example, $a = 90$; $E(a) = (225)(300)/600 = 112.50$; and $V(a) = (300 \times 300 \times 225 \times 375)/(600 \times 600 \times 599) = 35.215$. Thus $\chi^2 = (|90 - 112.50| - 0.5)^2 / 35.215 = 13.74$. From tables of the chi-squared distribution, a p-value of 0.0002 is obtained, indicating a difference as large as that observed would be very unlikely to arise by chance if there really was no difference between the two groups.

If any of the quantities $E(a)$, $E(b)$, $E(c)$, or $E(d)$ (for example, $E(b) = m_2 n_1/N$) are less than 5.0 and N is less than 40, the χ^2 test is invalid, and a test called 'Fisher's exact test' should be used instead (Kirkwood and Sterne, 2003).

4.3 Ratio of two proportions

The ratio of two proportions is sometimes referred to as the *relative risk* (R). To construct a CI for a relative risk, the natural logarithm of the estimate of the relative risk is computed (Table 21.2):

$$\log_e(R) = \log_e(p_1/p_2) = \log_e[(a/n_1)/(c/n_2)].$$

Its standard error is estimated by:

$$SE[\log_e(R)] = \sqrt{\{[b/(an_1)] + [d/(cn_2)]\}} \tag{21.4}$$

The 95% CI for $\log_e(R)$ is given by $\log_e(R) \pm 1.96$ SE, and the 95% CI for the relative risk is obtained by taking anti-logarithms.

In the example given in Table 21.2, the relative risk is estimated as $0.30/0.45 = 0.667$, and $\log_e(R) = -0.405$. The $SE[\log_e(R)]$ is estimated as $\sqrt{\{[210/(90 \times 300)] + [165/(135 \times 300)]\}} = 0.109$, and the 95% CI for $\log_e(R)$ is given by $-0.405 \pm 1.96(0.109)$, i.e. $(-0.619, -0.191)$. Taking anti-logarithms, the 95% CI for the relative risk is $(0.538, 0.826)$.

4.4 Trend test for proportions

Sometimes, it is of interest to examine whether there is a trend in a series of proportions associated with different levels of some underlying characteristic. For example, consider the proportion of leprosy patients who report regularly to collect their monthly drug supply from a clinic when the accessibility of the clinic is rated as very poor, poor, fair, or good (Table 21.3).

A 'score' (x_i) is assigned for each kind of clinic, of which the value relates to the level of accessibility. For example, '0' has been assigned to those with 'very poor' accessibility and '3' to those with 'good' accessibility. A test for the trend in the proportions a_1/n_1, a_2/n_2, a_3/n_3, and a_4/n_4 is provided by testing, as a chi-squared with one df, the expression:

$$\chi^2 = N[(N\Sigma a_i x_i) - (A\Sigma n_i x_i)]^2 / \{A(N-A)[(N\Sigma n_i x_i^2) - (\Sigma n_i x_i)^2]\} \quad (21.5).$$

For example, suppose the data are as shown in Table 21.3 (the respective percentages of regular attenders in the four rows are 20%, 30%, 50%, and 60%). The value of χ^2 is:

$$150[(150 \times 125) - (63 \times 245)]^2 / \{63 \times 87 [(150 \times 555) - 245^2]\} = 12.95$$

which is highly significant (p = 0.0003), based on a χ^2 test with one df. It may be concluded therefore that there is strong evidence that the regularity of drug collection increases with the accessibility of the clinic.

Table 21.3 Regularity of collection of drugs by leprosy patients, according to accessibility of clinic

Accessibility of clinic	Collection of drugs		Total	'Score' x_i
	Regular	**Not regular**		
Very poor	a_1 (5)	$n_1 - a_1$ (20)	n_1 (25)	0
Poor	a_2 (12)	$n_2 - a_2$ (28)	n_2 (40)	1
Fair	a_3 (25)	$n_3 - a_3$ (25)	n_3 (50)	2
Good	a_4 (21)	$n_4 - a_4$ (14)	n_4 (35)	3
Total	A (63)	N – A (87)	N (150)	

5 Analysis of rates

5.1 Risks, rates, and person-time-at-risk

The terms 'risk' and 'rate' are often used rather loosely and interchangeably to describe the frequencies of events in epidemiological studies. Usually, this is of no great consequence, but, in some circumstances, the distinction is important and, in particular, may affect the way in which a study is analysed. A *risk* is essentially a proportion, or equivalently a probability. The numerator consists of the number of individuals who experience the event of interest (say, develop the disease) in a defined period. The denominator consists of the total number of individuals who were followed for the defined period, some of whom experienced the event of interest (for example, developed the disease) and the remainder of whom did not (ignoring, for the moment, complications that might arise if some individuals are lost to follow-up). A *rate* takes into account both the number of persons at risk and also the duration of observation for each person. In the simplest case, the numerator is the number of individuals who experience the event of interest during the study period (i.e. the same as the numerator for a risk), but the denominator is expressed as the person-time (for example, person-years or person-days) at risk for the individuals in the study.

For example, if 120 persons are observed for 3 years and 40 of them die at some time during the period, and none are otherwise lost to follow-up, the *risk* of death over the 3 years is estimated as $40/120 = 0.33$, whereas the death *rate* is estimated as 40/(the number of person-years-at-risk). The denominator for the rate calculation is $(80 \times 3) + (40 \times 1.5) = 300$ years, as 80 persons were 'at risk' for the full 3-year period, and 40 were at risk until they died (which, on average, is likely to have been about halfway through the follow-up period if deaths occurred uniformly over the period). Thus, the death rate is $40/300 = 0.133$ per person-year-at-risk (which is not the same as the risk of death during the 3 years of 0.33 divided by 3).

Mathematically, it is straightforward to convert rates to risks, and vice versa, if it may be assumed that the rates are constant over time (see, for example, Breslow and Day, 1980). The reason for discussing the distinction in this chapter is that different methods of statistical analysis are appropriate for risks and rates. As mentioned in Section 4, risks are proportions, and thus the methods described in that section are applicable. Modifications of these methods are necessary for the analysis of rates.

Rates are useful if different individuals in a study have been followed for different periods. This may arise if recruitment to the study population is staggered over time, but follow-up is to a common date, or if individuals are lost to follow-up at different times (for example, because of death, migration, or non-co-operation).

An example of the computation of person-years-at-risk in a large study is given in Table 21.4. In this study, a census was done of the study population on the 1 November each year, and the number of persons remaining at risk was ascertained.

Alternatively, the exact period of follow-up may be known for each subject in the study (if the dates of entry and exit are available for each person), in which case these periods would be summed to derive the total person-years-at-risk.

Another situation in which rates, rather than risks, may be more appropriate is when each individual may be at risk of experiencing the event of interest more than once

Table 21.4 Example of the computation of person-years-at-risk in a large study

	Date	No. of persons under observation	Average of successive numbers	Years of observation	Person-years
	(a)	(b)	(c)	(d)	(c × d)
Start date	1 November 2004	10140			
	1 November 2005	9145	9642.5*	1	9642.5
	1 November 2006	8232	8688.5	1	8688.5
	1 November 2007	7389	7810.5	1	7810.5
	1 November 2008	6281	6835.0	1	6835.0
End date	1 April 2009	5779	6030.0	5/12	2512.5
				Total	35489.0

* If 10140 persons were alive on 1 November 2004, and 9145 of them were known to be alive on 1 November 2005, and if losses to follow-up occurred evenly throughout the year, there would have been, on average, (10140 + 9145)/2 = 9642.5 persons at risk on each day during the first year, hence a total of 9642.5 person-years.

during the study period (for example, an episode of diarrhoea). The incidence rate in the study population would be calculated as the total number of events (for example, episodes of diarrhoea) for those in the study divided by the total person-time-at-risk (which, in this case, would not end at the first episode). Responses such as this can always be converted to a risk by expressing the outcome as the proportion of individuals who experience more than a specified number of events (for example, one or more episodes of diarrhoea), but, in doing this, some information is lost, with a consequent reduction in the power of the study to detect a difference between groups being compared. The analysis of rate data of this kind (where one individual may experience more than one episode of disease) is not straightforward, as the approach depends upon whether it is reasonable to assume that, once an individual has experienced one event, he or she is no more or less likely to experience another event than anyone else in the same intervention group (say, of the same age and sex). Usually, it is not reasonable to make this assumption, as it is frequently found that susceptibility and exposure to disease vary considerably between individuals in ways that cannot be predicted. A simple way out of the analytical problem is to classify individuals, according to whether or not they experienced any events or not. If this is done, the data can either be analysed as a proportion (using the methods given in Section 4) or the individual can be excluded from follow-up for purposes of analysis, from the time the *first* event occurs (i.e. they are not counted as 'at risk' after the first event), and the methods given in Sections 5.2 to 5.5 can be used.

5.2 Confidence interval for a rate

Suppose e is the number of events that occurred during the study period, and the total person-years-at-risk during the period was y. (Note that the period does not have to be measured in 'years'; it could be in, for example, days, weeks, or months.) The event rate (r) is estimated by e/y. For example, suppose 5000 patients who have received a new tuberculosis (TB) vaccine have been followed for 5 years, but, due to losses in follow-up, the total person-years-at-risk is 20 000 (instead of the nearly 25 000 that would have been appropriate if every patient—except the cases whose follow-up period would be counted up to the time they developed TB—had been followed up throughout the 5 years). If the number of new cases of TB that were detected during the follow-up was 80, the estimated incidence rate of TB would be 80/20 000 = 0.0040/person-year, i.e. four per thousand person-years.

The standard error of a rate (r) is, $\sqrt{(r/y)}$ and the approximate 95% CI for the rate is given by $r \pm 1.96\sqrt{(r/y)}$. Thus, in the TB example, the 95% CI for the TB incidence rate is:

$$0.0040 \pm 1.96\sqrt{(0.0040/20\,000)} = 0.0040 \pm 0.0009,$$

i.e. 3.1–4.9 per thousand person-years.

5.3 Difference between two rates

Suppose it is required to compare event rates in two groups, and the number of events and the person-years-at-risk in the two groups are as in Table 21.5.

The standard error of the difference between two rates is given by: $\sqrt{(r_1/y_1 + r_2/y_2)}$, and the 95% CI on the difference is given by $(r_1 - r_2) \pm 1.96$ SE.

Thus, for the example, the 95% CI on the rate difference of the vaccinated, compared to the unvaccinated, group in Table 21.5 is:

$$(0.0041 - 0.0084) \pm 1.96\sqrt{[(0.0041/19\,470) + (0.0084/19\,030)]} = -0.0043 \pm 0.0016$$
$$= -0.0059 \text{ to } -0.0027$$

i.e. −5.9 to −2.7/1000/year.

To perform a statistical test, it is necessary to calculate a test statistic, which may be done along similar lines to those described in Section 4.2. If e_1 is the observed number of events among those in group 1 (say, those vaccinated), then:

$$\text{Expected value of } e_1 = E(e_1) = ey_1/y \qquad (21.7).$$

$$\text{Variance of } e_1 = V(e_1) = ey_1y_2/y^2 \qquad (21.8).$$

Table 21.5 TB incidence rates in vaccinated and unvaccinated groups

	Number of events (new TB cases)	Person-years-at-risk (pyar)	Event rate (TB cases per 1000 pyar)
Vaccinated	e_1 (80)	y_1 (19470)	r_1 (4.1)
Not vaccinated	e_2 (160)	y_2 (19030)	r_2 (8.4)
Total	e (240)	y (38500)	r

Then:

$$\chi^2 = (|e_1 - E(e_1)| - 0.5)^2 / V(e_1) \qquad (21.9).$$

And the value of χ^2 is looked up in tables of the χ^2 distribution, with one df, to assess the p-value.

In the example shown in Table 21.5, $e_1 = 80$; $E(e_1) = 240 \times 19\,470/38\,500 = 121.37$; and $V(e_1) = (240 \times 19\,470 \times 19\,030)/(38\,500 \times 38\,500) = 59.99$.

Thus, $\chi^2 = (|80 - 121.37| - 0.5)^2/59.99 = 27.84$, and p < 0.000001, indicating that the difference is highly unlikely to have arisen by chance.

5.4 Ratio of two rates

In some situations, the *ratio* of two rates will be of greater interest than their *difference*. For example, vaccine efficacy is usually calculated from a ratio. The test of the null hypothesis is identical in the two situations (i.e. the difference is zero, or the ratio is unity), but the CIs are calculated in a different way.

The ratio of two rates, sometimes called the relative risk, but more correctly called the relative rate, is $(e_1/y_1)/(e_2/y_2)$, and the standard error of the logarithm of this ratio is approximated by $\sqrt{[(1/e_1) + (1/e_2)]}$. In the example given in Table 21.5, the ratio of the rates is 0.489 (corresponding to a vaccine efficacy of 51.1%), and the standard error of the logarithm of the ratio is $\sqrt{[(1/80) + (1/160)]} = 0.1369$. The 95% CI of the logarithm of the ratio is given by $-0.715 \pm 1.96(0.1369)$, i.e. -0.983 to -0.447. Thus, the 95% CI for the ratio of the two rates is 0.37–0.64 (or the 95% CI on the estimate of vaccine efficacy is from 36% to 63%, i.e. 100(1−0.64) to 100(1−0.37)).

5.5 Trend test for rates

Directly analogous to the trend test for proportions described in Section 4.4, there is a similar test for a trend in rates. Suppose data have been collected from the time since the start of a study to the first attack of malaria among children of different ages, and it is of interest to test whether the attack rate declines with age. The data may be summarized, as in Table 21.6.

A 'score' has been assigned to each group. In the example, the scores have been taken as the mid points of the different age groups (for example, those aged 1–2 years range in age from 1.00 to 2.99 years).

Table 21.6 Malaria attack rates in children of different ages

Age of children (years)	'Score' x_i	No. with malaria attack (e_i)	Child-weeks-at-risk (y_i)	Attack rate e_i/y_i
1–2	x_1 (= 2.0)	e_1 (30)	y_1 (200)	0.150
3–4	x_2 (= 4.0)	e_2 (20)	y_2 (150)	0.133
5–7	x_3 (= 6.5)	e_3 (10)	y_3 (150)	0.067
Total		e (60)	y (500)	0.120

A test for trend in the attack rates in the three age groups e_1/y_1, e_2/y_2, and e_3/y_3 is provided by testing the expression, as χ^2 with one df:

$$\chi^2 = \left\{\left[\Sigma e_i x_i - [(e/y)\Sigma y_i x_i]\right]^2\right\} \Big/ \left\{(e/y^2)\left[y\Sigma y_i x_i^2 - (\Sigma y_i x_i)^2\right]\right\} \quad (21.10).$$

For example, suppose the malaria attack rates (attacks/weeks-at-risk) were as in Table 21.6, then the value of χ^2 is:

$$\left\{205 - [(60/500)1975]\right\}^2 \Big/ \left\{(60/500^2)[(500 \times 9537.5) - 1975^2]\right\} = 4.91$$

which has an associated p-value of 0.03, and thus there are grounds for believing that, in the study area, the risk of a malaria attack declined with increasing age.

6 Analysis of mean values

6.1 Confidence interval for a mean

If the outcome measure is taken as the mean ($\bar{x}$) of a sample of n observations, for example, the weights of a sample of newborn infants, the standard error of the mean is given by $\sigma/\sqrt{n}$, where σ is the standard deviation of the variable measured (for example, weights of newborn infants) in the population from which the sample of n observations was taken. The 95% CI on the mean is given by $\bar{x} \pm 1.96(\sigma/\sqrt{n})$.

In general, σ (the standard deviation in the population) will not be known but must be estimated, based on the n observations in the sample. Thus, the estimate of σ is subject to sampling error also, and this must be taken into account in the computation of the CI on the mean. This is done by using a multiplying factor in the CI calculation taken from tables of the t-distribution, rather than from tables of the 'Normal' distribution, on which Table 21.1 was based. The value of the multiplying factor will depend on the size of the sample from which the standard deviation was estimated. For example, for 95% CIs, appropriate multiplying factors for sample sizes of 10, 20, 50, and 100 are 2.26, 2.09, 2.01, and 1.98, respectively. (Note that, in using the tables, the values of t are given for different 'degrees of freedom'. In the situation considered here, the degrees of freedom correspond to the sample size minus one, i.e. $n - 1$.) If the sample size is 30 or more, little error is introduced by using the value of 1.96 derived from the normal distribution when calculating 95% CI, rather than the appropriate t-value.

If the estimate of the standard deviation, based on the sample, is s, the 95% CI on the mean is given by $\bar{x} \pm t(s/\sqrt{n})$. For example, if the mean birthweight of 25 infants was 3.10 kg and the standard deviation of the weights in the sample was 0.90 kg, the 95% CI would be given by $3.10 \pm 2.06(0.90/\sqrt{25})$, i.e. 2.73 – 3.47 kg, where the multiplying factor 2.06 is taken from a table of the t-distribution corresponding to 24 df.

6.2 Difference between two means

In a trial, it is very common to want to compare the means of observations in different groups, for example, to compare observations from an intervention group with those from a control group. Suppose that two groups are to be compared and the means

Table 21.7 ESR in an intervention and a control group

	Intervention group ($i = 1$)	Control group ($i = 2$)
Number of subjects (n_i)	10	12
Mean ESR ($\bar{x}_i$)	9.7	6.5
Standard deviation (s_i)	2.41	2.54

are $\bar{x}_1$ and $\bar{x}_2$, respectively, and the corresponding standard deviations observed in the groups are s_1 and s_2. The standard error of the difference between the means is given by $\sqrt{\{s[(1/n_1)+(1/n_2)]\}}$, where s is the *pooled* estimate of the standard deviation, based on the observations from the two groups. s is estimated as:

$$s = \sqrt{\{[(n_1-1)s_1^2 + (n_2-1)s_2^2]/(n_1+n_2-2)\}}.$$

The 95% CI for the difference between the means is given by:

$$(\bar{x}_1 - \bar{x}_2) \pm ts\sqrt{[(1/n_1)+(1/n_2)]}$$

where t is taken from a table of the t-distribution with $(n_1 + n_2 - 2)$ df.

For example, suppose erythrocyte sedimentation rates (ESRs) were measured in an intervention group and in a control group, as shown in Table 21.7. The standard deviation s may be calculated as $\sqrt{\{[(9\times 2.41^2)+(11\times 2.54^2)]/(10+12-2)\}} = 2.48$, and the 95% CI on the difference is given by:

$$(9.7 - 6.5) \pm \{(2.09 \times 2.48)\sqrt{[(1/10)+(1/12)]}\} = 3.2 \pm 2.2 = 1.0 - 5.4.$$

To test the null hypothesis that there is no true difference in the mean ESRs between the two groups, a statistical test must be performed. A test statistic is calculated to assess the probability of the observed results (or more extreme) if there really is no difference between the two groups. The difference of the means divided by the standard error of the difference gives a value of a test statistic that may be looked up in tables of the t-distribution with $(n_1 + n_2 - 2)$ df.

For the example in Table 21.7, the test statistic $= (\bar{x}_1 - \bar{x}_2)/\{s\sqrt{[(1/n_1)+(1/n_2)]}\}$ $= 3.01$. The associated p-value is 0.0035, i.e. if there really is no effect of the intervention on ESRs, the chance of observing a difference in the means as large or larger than that in the study is 0.35% (i.e. not impossible, but rather unlikely!).

6.3 Analysis of more than two groups

If a study involves the comparison of observations in more than two groups, it is necessary to generalize the methods given in Section 6.2. This is straightforward but is beyond the scope of this book, and the reader is referred to standard statistical texts, such as that by Armitage and Berry (1987) or Kirkwood and Sterne (2003), for details. The relevant sections to which to refer are those on 'one-way analysis of variance'.

Of course, it is always possible to use the methods given in Section 6.2 to compare groups, just two at a time. This is a reasonable approach, but some caution must be exercised when interpreting the findings, as the chances of finding at least one pair to be significantly different (for example, p < 0.05) may be substantial, even if there are, in truth, no differences between the groups. To illustrate this, suppose six groups are being compared. In an analysis of variance, the question is asked: 'Considered as a whole, is the variation between the means observed in the six groups more than might be expected to arise by chance if there were no differences in the true means?'. This question may be answered with one statistical test in an analysis of variance, and the null hypothesis may, or may not, be rejected on the basis of this one test. Suppose, however, it was decided to examine all possible pairs of comparisons of the groups. There are 15 possible pairs, and, if a *t-test* was done on each pair, there is a reasonable chance that at least one comparison would be found to be 'p < 0.05' by chance alone, because of the number of different tests that had been performed. There are ways of adjusting the significance levels to allow for this effect, and the reader is referred to standard texts again for a discussion of 'the multiple comparison problem'.

7 Controlling for confounding variables

7.1 The nature of confounding variables

A risk factor for the disease under study that is differentially distributed among the groups receiving different interventions in which the disease incidence is being compared is called a *confounding* factor. Unless the trial is very small, confounding factors are not likely to bias the comparisons between intervention and control groups in randomized trials, as the process of randomization ensures that any such factors, whether known or unknown, will be equally distributed in the different groups (apart from random variation). In studies in which those in the different groups have not been allocated at random, the control of confounding factors is a critical component in the analysis. For example, consider a comparative study of TB incidence in persons who received BCG in a routine vaccination programme and those who were not vaccinated. BCG coverage is often higher in urban areas and, independently of any effect of BCG, those living in urban areas also tend to have a higher incidence of TB because of overcrowding and other environmental factors. In this instance, residential status (rural/urban) could be a confounding factor, and, if it is not taken into account in the analyses, any protective effect of BCG against TB might be underestimated. Consider the hypothetical situation depicted in Table 21.8, which shows the incidence of TB over a 10-year period in BCG-vaccinated and unvaccinated individuals in urban and rural areas.

BCG coverage is appreciably higher in the urban population (80%) than in the rural population (50%). Also, in unvaccinated persons, the incidence of TB is higher in the urban population (20 per thousand over 10 years) than in the rural population (10 per thousand). In consequence, although BCG vaccine efficacy is 50% in both urban and rural areas, the estimate obtained from a comparative study, in which the place of residence is ignored, is only 41%. This difference is due to the confounding effect of the place of residence on the estimate of efficacy (the place of residence being related to both the disease incidence and, independently, to the prevalence of vaccination).

Table 21.8 TB incidence rates by BCG vaccination status and urban or rural residence

BCG vaccination status	Urban			Rural			Both groups		
	Total popn.	TB cases*		Total popn.	TB cases*		Total popn.	TB cases*	
		No.	/1000		No.	/1000		No.	/1000
Vaccinated	16000	160	10	40000	200	5	56000	360	6.4
Unvaccinated	4000	80	20	40000	400	10	44000	480	10.9
Vaccine efficacy			50%			50%			41%

* Over a period of 10 years.

7.2 Adjusting for confounding variables

A powerful way of removing the effect of a confounding variable is to restrict comparative analyses to individuals who share a common level of the confounding variable and then to combine the results across the different levels in such a way so as to avoid bias. Thus, in the example in Table 21.8, if the vaccine efficacy was first estimated separately for rural and urban dwellers, and then the two estimates were to be combined, the estimate of efficacy obtained (50%) would be free of the confounding bias of the place of residence. In general, to control for confounding, the study population is divided into a number of *strata*. Within each stratum, individuals share a common level of the confounding variable. Estimates of risk, rate or mean differences, or ratios are made within each stratum, and the resulting estimates are then *pooled* in some way across strata, in order to obtain an overall measure of the effect which is free of any confounding due to the variable on which the stratification was made. Such stratification may be carried out on several confounding variables simultaneously (for example, age and sex).

If it is known, when a study is planned, that it will be necessary to allow for confounding variables in the analysis, it is desirable to give consideration to this at the design stage, both in terms of the information which must be collected and because it will require an increase in the required sample sizes (to achieve the desired statistical power, see Chapter 5). Usually, the necessary increase in sample size to allow for confounding variables is not great (for example, less than 20%), and often the information needed for these sample size calculations is not available before the study starts anyway. Formal methods for calculating sample sizes, allowing for adjustment for confounding variables, are given in Breslow and Day (1987).

7.3 Adjusting risks

7.3.1 Overall test of significance

After stratifying on the basis of the confounding variable(s), the analysis is conducted one stratum at a time, and then the results are pooled. In the *i*th stratum, the data may be depicted, as shown in Table 21.9.

To test the hypothesis that the relative risk is 1 in all strata or equivalently that the risk difference is zero in each stratum, a generalization of the method given in Section 4.2 may be used. The statistical test is known as the Mantel–Haenszel test.

Table 21.9 Comparison of proportions developing disease in two intervention groups for individuals in the *i*th stratum

Intervention group	Developed disease	Did not develop disease	Total
1	a_i	b_i	$a_i + b_i = n_{1i}$
2	c_i	d_i	$c_i + d_i = n_{2i}$
Total	$a_i + c_i = m_{1i}$	$b_i + d_i = m_{2i}$	N_i

In the *i*th stratum:

$$\text{Expected value of } a_i = E(a_i) = m_{1i}n_{1i}/N_i \quad (21.11).$$

$$\text{Variance of } a_i = V(a_i) = n_{1i}n_{2i}m_{1i}m_{2i}/\left[N_i^2(N_i-1)\right] \quad (21.12).$$

An overall test of the null hypothesis that the relative risk is unity is given by calculating $\chi^2 = (|\Sigma a_i - \Sigma E(a_i)| - 0.5)^2 / \Sigma V(a_i)$, where the summation is over all strata, which may be tested for statistical significance using tables of the chi-squared distribution with one df.

The calculations are illustrated in Table 21.10, with data on disease incidence rates in vaccinated and unvaccinated individuals in three areas—urban, semi-urban, and rural.

$$\Sigma a_i = 530; \; \Sigma E(a_i) = 738; \; \Sigma V(a_i) = 284.21.$$

Thus:

$$\chi^2 = (|530 - 738| - 0.5)^2 / 284.21 = 151.49.$$

Thus, there is very strong evidence against the null hypothesis, as p < 0.000001 (from tables of the chi-squared distribution).

Table 21.10 Disease incidence rates in urban, semi-urban, and rural areas, according to vaccination status

Area (*i*)	Vaccinated			Unvaccinated			Grand total (N_i)	$E(a_i)$	$V(a_i)$
	Cases (a_i)	Non-cases (b_i)	Total (n_{1i})	Cases (c_i)	Non-cases (d_i)	Total (n_{2i})			
Urban (1)	160	15840	16000	80	3920	4000	20000	192	37.94
Semi-urban (2)	170	23830	24000	240	15760	16000	40000	246	97.39
Rural (3)	200	39800	40000	400	39600	40000	80000	300	148.88
Total	530	79470	80000	720	59280	60000	140000	738	284.21

7.3.2 Pooled estimate of risk difference

If it is considered that the risk *difference* (rather than the risk ratio) is likely to be constant across different strata, a pooled estimate of the common risk difference may be required. This is obtained by taking a weighted average of the risk differences in each stratum, weighting each by the inverse of its variance (as this may be shown to give the 'best' estimate of the common risk difference).

In the ith stratum, the risk difference is:

$$d_i = p_{1i} - p_{2i} = (a_i/n_{1i}) - (c_i/n_{2i})$$

and the variance of the risk difference is:

$$V(d_i) = \{p_i(1-p_i)[(1/n_{1i}) + (1/n_{2i})]\}$$

(as given also in Section 4.2), where:

$$p_i = [n_{1i}p_{1i} + n_{2i}p_{2i}]/(n_{1i} + n_{2i}) = (a_i + c_i)/(n_{1i} + n_{2i}).$$

Now, let $w_i = 1/V(d_i)$.

The pooled estimate of the common risk difference is given by $d = \Sigma w_i d_i / \Sigma w_i$. For the data in the example given in Table 21.10, the computations for the common risk difference are shown in Table 21.11.

Pooled estimate of the common risk difference $d = \Sigma w_i d_i / \Sigma w_i = -0.0083$.

7.3.3 Pooled estimate of risk ratio

A pooled estimate of the common risk ratio R across strata may be obtained, using the following formulae.

In the ith stratum, the risk ratio is given by:

$$R_i = (a_i/n_{1i})/(c_i/n_{2i}) = a_i n_{2i}/(c_i n_{1i}) \tag{21.13}.$$

A pooled estimate across all strata is given by:

$$R = \Sigma(a_i n_{2i}/N_i)/\Sigma(c_i n_{1i}/N_i).$$

Table 21.11 Computation of the common risk difference for the data in Table 21.10

Area	p_{1i}	p_{2i}	d_i	$V(d_i)$	w_i
Urban	0.0100	0.0200	−0.0100	3.705 × 10⁻⁶	270 × 10³
Semi-urban	0.0071	0.0150	−0.0079	1.057 × 10⁻⁶	946 × 10³
Rural	0.0050	0.0100	−0.0050	37.219 × 10⁻⁶	27 × 10³

Thus, for the example in Table 21.10:

$$R = \{[(160)(4000)/20\,000] + [(170)(16\,000)/40\,000]$$
$$+ [(200)(40\,000)/80\,000]\} / \{[(80)(16\,000)/20\,000] + [(240)(24\,000)/40\,000]$$
$$+ [(400)(40\,000)/80\,000]\} = 200/408 = 0.49.$$

7.3.4 Confidence intervals

The easiest way of obtaining CIs on the estimates of the common risk difference or the common risk ratio is to use the 'test-based' method (Miettinen, 1976).

The approximate 95% CI on the risk difference is given by:

$$d\left(1 \pm 1.96/\sqrt{\chi^2}\right) \qquad (21.15).$$

Thus, in the example in Tables 21.10 and 21.11, the confidence limits are:

$$-0.0083\left(1 \pm 1.96/\sqrt{151.49}\right) = -0.0096 \text{ to } -0.0070.$$

The 95% CI on the logarithm of the relative risk is given by:

$$\log_e R\left(1 \pm 1.96/\sqrt{\chi^2}\right) \qquad (21.16).$$

In the example, the confidence limits are:

$$\log_e (0.49)\left(1 \pm 1.96/\sqrt{151.49}\right) = -0.8269 \text{ to } -0.5998.$$

And thus the confidence limits on the relative risk are 0.44 to 0.55.

7.4 Adjusting rates

The computations for adjusting rates are very similar to those for adjusting risks and involve only some changes to the formulae given in Section 7.3.

Suppose the results observed in the *i*th stratum are as shown in Table 21.12.

7.4.1 Overall test of significance

In the *i*th stratum, e_{1i} is the number of individuals who developed disease in group 1.

Table 21.12 Disease rates in two intervention groups for individuals in the *i*th stratum

Intervention group	Developed disease	Person-years-at-risk
1	e_{1i}	y_{1i}
2	e_{2i}	y_{2i}
Total	e_i	y_i

Expected value of $e_{1i} = E(e_{1i}) = e_i y_{1i}/y_i$ (21.17).

Variance of $e_{1i} = V(e_{1i}) = e_i y_{1i} y_{2i}/y_i^2$ (21.18).

An overall test of significance (that the common rate ratio is unity or the common rate difference is zero) is given by:

$$x^2 = \left(\left|\Sigma e_{1i} - \Sigma E(e_{1i})\right| - 0.5\right)^2 / \Sigma V(e_{1i})$$ (21.19)

where the summation is over all strata.

The value calculated should be looked up in tables of the chi-squared distribution with one df.

7.4.2 Pooled estimate of rate difference

In the *i*th stratum, the rate difference is:

$$d_i = r_{1i} - r_{2i} = (e_{1i}/y_{1i}) - (e_{2i}/y_{2i}).$$

Its estimated variance is:

$$V(d_i) = (r_{1i}/y_{1i} + r_{2i}/y_{2i}).$$

Let $w_i = 1/V(d_i)$, then the estimate of the common rate difference across all strata is given by:

$$d = \sum w_i d_i / \sum w_i.$$

7.4.3 Pooled estimate of rate ratio

In the *i*th stratum, the rate ratio is:

$$R_i = r_{1i}/r_{2i} = (e_{1i}/y_{1i})/(e_{2i}/y_{2i}) = e_{1i} y_{2i}/(e_{2i} y_{1i}).$$

A pooled estimate of the common rate ratio is given by:

$$R = \Sigma(e_{1i} y_{2i}/y_i) / \Sigma(e_{2i} y_{1i}/y_i)$$ (21.20).

7.4.4 Confidence intervals

The 95% CI on the common rate difference is given by:

$$d(1 \pm 1.96/\sqrt{x^2})$$ (21.21).

The 95% CI on the logarithm of the common rate ratio is given by:

$$\log_e R(1 \pm 1.96/\sqrt{x^2})$$ (21.22).

Table 21.13 Disease incidence rates in urban, semi-urban, and rural areas, according to vaccination status

Area (i)	Vaccinated Cases (e_{1i})	Vaccinated Person-years (y_{1i})	Unvaccinated Cases (e_{2i})	Unvaccinated Person-years (y_{2i})	Both groups Cases (e_i)	Both groups Person-years (y_i)	$E(e_{1i})$	$V(e_{1i})$
Urban (1)	80	8000	40	2000	120	10000	96	19.2
Semi-urban (2)	85	12000	120	8000	205	20000	123	49.2
Rural (3)	80	20000	200	20000	280	40000	140	70.0
Total	245	40000	360	30000	605	70000	359	138.4

Example: In Table 21.13, the numerical computations are illustrated, as before, with data on the disease incidence in vaccinated and unvaccinated individuals in three areas: urban, semi-urban, and rural.
Overall test of significance:

$$\chi^2 = \left(\left|\Sigma e_{1i} - \Sigma E(e_{1i})\right| - 0.5\right)^2 / \Sigma V(e_{1i}) \qquad (21.23)$$

$$= (|245 - 359| - 0.5)^2 / 138.40 = 93.08 \, (p < 0.000001).$$

The estimation of the common rate difference is shown in Table 21.14.

$$d = \Sigma w_i d_i / \Sigma w_i = -0.0066.$$

The 95% CI on the common rate difference is:

$$d(1 \pm 1.96/\sqrt{\chi^2}) = -0.0066(1 \pm 1.96/\sqrt{93.08}) \qquad (21.24)$$

$$= -0.0079 \text{ to } -0.0053.$$

The estimate of the common rate ratio is:

$$R = \Sigma(e_{1i} y_{2i} / y_i) / \Sigma(e_{2i} y_{1i} / y_i)$$

$$= \{[(80)(2000)/10\,000] + [(85)(8000)/20\,000]$$
$$+ [(80)(20\,000)/40\,000]\} / \{[(40)(8000)/10\,000] + [(120)(12\,000)/20\,000]$$
$$+ [(200)(20\,000)/40\,000]\} = 90/204 = 0.44.$$

Table 21.14 Computation of the common rate difference for the data in Table 21.13

Area (i)	r_{1i}	r_{2i}	Difference d_i	$V(d_i)$	$w_i = 1/V(d_i)$
Urban (1)	0.0100	0.0200	−0.0100	11.250 × 10⁻⁶	89 × 10³
Semi-urban (2)	0.0071	0.0150	−0.0079	2.465 × 10⁻⁶	406 × 10³
Rural (3)	0.0040	0.0100	−0.0060	0.700 × 10⁻⁶	1429 × 10³

The 95% confidence limits on the logarithm of the common rate ratio is:

$$\log_e R(1 \pm 1.96/\sqrt{x^2}) = \log_e (0.44)(1 \pm 1.96/\sqrt{93.08}) = -0.988 \text{ to } -0.654.$$

Taking the anti-logarithm, the 95% confidence limits on the common rate ratio are 0.37 to 0.52.

7.5 Adjusting means

If the outcome variable is a quantitative measure, other than a risk or rate, adjustment for the effects of a confounding variable involves performing a stratified t-test.

A numerical example is given in Table 21.15 where the comparison is between subjects using mosquito nets (intervention group) and those not using them (control group), and the outcome measure (x) is the number of episodes of malaria over a period of 1 year. In this example, age is considered as the confounding variable, and the stratification has been made by dividing the study subjects into three age groups. The size of each subgroup has been made small to simplify the computations for illustrative purposes.

The data may be represented algebraically for those in the ith stratum, as shown in Table 21.16.

An estimate of the common difference in response between the intervention and control groups is obtained by calculating a weighted average of the differences within each stratum:

$$d = \Sigma w_i d_i / \Sigma w_i$$

where $w_i = [n_{1i} n_{2i} / (n_{1i} + n_{2i})]$.

$$\text{Difference } d_i = \bar{x}_{1i} - \bar{x}_{2i}.$$

Thus, in the example:

$$d = \{[(-0.75)32/12] + [(-0.45)132/23] + [(-0.20)50/15]\} / \{(32/12) + (132/23)$$
$$+ (50/15)\} = -5.25/11.74 = -0.45.$$

Table 21.15 Attacks of malaria in children of different ages in those using (intervention) and not using (control) mosquito-nets

(Stratum) Age group		Attacks of malaria/ child (x)	No. of children (n)	Mean ($\bar{x}$)	Standard deviation (s)
(1) <2y	I*	1,0,2,3,1,2,1,0	8	1.25	1.0351
	C*	2,3,1,2	4	2.00	0.8165
(2) 2–3y	I	0,1,1,2,1,1,0,2,2,1,1,0	12	1.00	0.7385
	C	2,2,1,1,1,2,1,1,2,2,1	11	1.45	0.5222
(3) 4–5y	I	1,0,1,1,1	5	0.80	0.4472
	C	1,1,2,0,1,1,0,2,1,1	10	1.00	0.6667

* I, intervention group; C, control group.

Table 21.16 Algebraic representation of data in Table 21.15 for those in the ith stratum

Intervention group	No. in group	Mean	Standard deviation
1 (I)	n_{1i}	$\bar{x}_{1i}$	s_{1i}
2 (C)	n_{2i}	$\bar{x}_{2i}$	s_{2i}

An overall test of significance is obtained by calculating a test statistic as:

$$\Sigma w_i d_i / \left[s\sqrt{\Sigma w_i} \right]$$

where $s = \sqrt{\{[\Sigma(n_{1i}-1)s_{1i}^2 + \Sigma(n_{2i}-1)s_{2i}^2]/\Sigma(n_{1i}+n_{2i}-2)\}}$, and the value of the test statistic can be compared with tables of the t-distribution with $\Sigma(n_{1i}+n_{2i}-2)$ df.

In the example:

$$s = \sqrt{(23.0265/44)} = 0.7234.$$

The test statistic (44 df) is:

$$-5.25 \left[0.7234 \times \sqrt{(11.74)} \right] = -2.12.$$

The absolute value is larger than 2.02, which is the tabulated 5% value for t with 44 df. Thus, there is statistically significant evidence regarding the efficacy of intervention; the reduction in the average number of episodes of malaria is estimated as 0.45 per child per year. The 95% confidence limits on the difference are given by:

$$(\Sigma w_i d_i / \Sigma w_i) \pm ts/\Sigma w_i \qquad (21.26)$$

where t is taken from tables of the t-distribution for 95% confidence limits with $\Sigma(n_{1i}+n_{2i}-2)$ df.

Thus, the 95% confidence limits are:

$$-0.45 \pm 2.02(0.7234)/\sqrt{(11.74)} = -0.88 \text{ to } -0.02 \text{ episodes/year/child}.$$

If it is thought that the intervention is likely to affect the response measured in a *relative*, rather than an *absolute*, fashion (i.e. a constant percentage reduction in the number of malaria attacks, rather than a constant absolute reduction in the number of malaria attacks), then it would be appropriate to *transform* the data initially by taking logarithms of the number of attacks (or, say, $\log_e$(number of attacks + 0.1) to avoid zero numbers) and to perform the calculation on the transformed values.

8 Analyses when communities have been randomized

In some intervention studies, communities, rather than individuals, are used as the unit of randomization. If this has been done, it is inappropriate to base analyses on responses of individuals, ignoring the fact that randomization was over larger units. An appropriate method of analysis would be to summarize the response in each sampling unit by a single value and analyse these summary values as though they were individual values.

8: ANALYSES WHEN COMMUNITIES HAVE BEEN RANDOMIZED | 389

The analysis of such trials, often called 'cluster randomized trials', is not straightforward, and only simple methods for performing statistical tests are given here. A comprehensive discussion of the design and analysis of such trials is given in Hayes and Moulton (2009).

8.1 Calculation of standardized responses

Often, trials in which communities have been randomized suffer from problems with confounding variables. If the number of units randomized is large, confounding variables are likely to balance out between groups, but, if the number of units is small (as may be the case when communities have been randomized, even though the number of individuals in each community is large), confounding may be a potentially serious problem, and some adjustment should be made in the analysis. One method of doing this is by *standardization*.

Within each community, the sampled population is divided into strata on the basis of the confounding variable(s) (for example, age and sex groups). The average value of the outcome measure is computed for those in each stratum (for example, a disease incidence rate). A weighted average of the rates in the different strata is then computed to give a single 'standardized' measure for the community, the weights being based on some 'standard' population. The same standard population is used for each community, and thus the standardized measures for each community are not biased by the differential composition of each community, with respect to the confounding variable that is being standardized for.

This method is called the 'direct' method of standardization. If the number of individuals in some strata is small, it may be better to use the 'indirect' method, and details of both are given (see Armitage and Berry (1987) for a more detailed discussion of these methods).

Consider a community in which disease risks p_i have been measured for individuals in k strata (for example, age groups). This may be represented in Table 21.17. Also shown are the corresponding data for a 'standard' population. For example, this might be chosen as the combined data for all communities in the study.

The *directly standardized* disease risk for the community (standardized to the standard population) is given by: $(\Sigma p_i N_i)/\Sigma N_i$.

Table 21.17 Disease risks in study community and in standard population in each of k strata

Stratum	Study community			Standard population		
	Total	Cases		Total	Cases	
		No.	Risk		No.	Risk
1	n_1	a_1	p_1	N_1	A_1	P_1
2	n_2	a_2	p_2	N_2	A_2	P_2
i	n_i	a_i	p_i	N_i	A_i	P_i
.	.	.	.	.	.	.
k	n_k	a_k	p_k	N_k	A_k	P_k
Total	n	a	p	N	A	P

The *indirectly standardized* disease risk for the community is given by: $[\Sigma a_i / (\Sigma n_i P_i)]/(A/N)$.

Having calculated standardized values for each community, the means of the standardized values for the intervention communities may be compared with those for the control communities, using a simple *t-test* (see Section 6.2).

It is usually safer, however, to perform a non-parametric test if the assumptions underlying the *t-test* are in any doubt (Armitage and Berry, 1987)), as it may be impossible to verify the assumptions if the study involves a small number of communities.

8.2 Non-parametric rank sum test

Suppose there are n_1 communities in one group and n_2 in the other $(n_1 \leq n_2)$ and a summary response has been derived for each community. To perform a non-parametric test, consider all the $(n_1 + n_2)$ observations together, and rank them, giving a rank of 1 to the smallest value and $(n_1 + n_2)$ to the highest. Tied ranks are allotted the mid rank of the group. Let $T_1 =$ sum of the ranks in group 1 with n_1 observations. Under the null hypothesis, the expectation of $T_1 = n_1(n_1 + n_2 + 1)/2$. Then calculate:

$T' = T_1$, if T_1 is less than or equal to the expected value

$T' = n_1(n_1 + n_2 + 1) - T_1$, if T_1 is more than its expected value.

T^1 may be compared with tabulated critical values (see Table A8 of Armitage and Berry, 1987) to determine the statistical significance.

Consider the example shown in Table 21.18 in which age-standardized leprosy prevalence rates are compared in 12 'intervention' villages and ten 'control' villages.

Table 21.18 Age-standardized leprosy prevalence rates and ranks in 12 'intervention', and ten 'control', villages

Intervention villages		Control villages	
Prevalence rate/1000	Rank	Prevalence rate/1000	Rank
3	1.5	10	18.5
9	15.5	13	22
8	12.5	6	7.5
6	7.5	11	21
5	5	10	18.5
5	5	7	9.5
7	9.5	8	12.5
3	1.5	8	12.5
10	18.5	5	5
8	12.5	9	15.5
10	18.5		
4	3		
Sum of ranks	$T_2 = 110.5$		$T_1 = 142.5$

The expected value of $T_1 = n_1(n_1+n_2+1)/2 = 10(10+12+1)/2 = 115$. As T_1 is greater than its expectation, T^1 is $10(10+12+1) - 142.5 = 87.5$. The critical value of T^1 at the 5% level of significance is 84 (from tables in Armitage and Berry, 1987). As T^1 is greater than the critical value, it is concluded that the intervention has not had a statistically significant effect (the average prevalence was 6.5 per thousand in intervention villages, and 8.7 per thousand in control villages).

8.3 Tests on paired data

In some study designs, communities may be 'paired' on the basis of similarity, with respect to confounding variables and baseline disease prevalence or incidence rates. Within each pair of communities, one receives the intervention and the other serves as the control. If this has been done, the analysis should take the pairing into account.

First, standardized response rates are computed for each community (as discussed in Section 8.1), and then the standardized response rates are compared using a paired t-test (Armitage and Berry, 1987) or a non-parametric test.

To perform a paired t-test for n pairs of communities, suppose d_i is the difference in outcome measured between the intervention and control unit for the ith pair. Calculate a test statistic $(\Sigma d_i/n)/(s/\sqrt{n})$ where s is the standard deviation of the n differences. This value of the test statistic may be compared to tabulated values of the t-distribution with $(n-1)$ df.

Consider the data shown in Table 21.19, which shows leprosy prevalence rates in ten pairs of communities.

The mean difference $d = -19/10 = -1.9$, and the standard deviation of the difference (s) is 2.23. Thus, the test statistic $= -1.9/(2.23/\sqrt{10}) = -2.69$ with 9 df. From tables of the t-distribution, p is <0.05, and it may be concluded that the prevalence of leprosy is significantly lower in the intervention villages.

Table 21.19 Leprosy prevalence rates in ten pairs of communities

Village pair no.	Prevalence of leprosy (per thousand)		Difference (d_i)	Rank (ignoring sign)
	Intervention	No Intervention		
1	6	10	−4	8
2	9	13	−4	8
3	3	6	−3	5
4	12	11	+1	1.5
5	10	10	0	
6	4	7	−3	5
7	7	8	−1	1.5
8	5	8	−3	5
9	7	5	+2	3
10	5	9	−4	8

Alternatively, a non-parametric test may be preferred. In this instance, the appropriate such test is Wilcoxon's signed rank test.

The differences between each pair of villages are arranged in ascending order of magnitude of the absolute value of the differences (i.e. ignoring the sign) and given ranks 1 to n; zero values are excluded from analysis. Any group of tied ranks is allotted the mid rank of the group. Let:

T+ = sum of ranks of positive differences

T− = sum of ranks of negative differences.

The smaller of the two (T+ and T−) is compared with the tabulated critical value (see Table A9 of Armitage and Berry, 1987). If it is lower than the tabulated value, it is concluded that there is a significant difference. For the data in the table, T+ = 4.5, and T− = 40.5; $n=9$ (excluding one zero difference). The tabulated critical 5% value is 5. Since T+ = 4.5 is less than 5, it is concluded that the difference is significant at the 5% level.

9 Prevented fraction of disease

The objective of most field trials is to measure the effect of an intervention in reducing disease rates. The results of such studies may be used to estimate the impact that an intervention might have on disease rates if it was introduced into a public health programme. In such circumstances, the overall effect is much influenced by the *coverage* achieved by the programme.

The *prevented fraction* among individuals exposed to an intervention measure is defined as the percentage of the disease incidence in such individuals that has been prevented due to having received the intervention. For example, if the efficacy of BCG vaccination against TB is 60%, among persons who receive BCG vaccination, 60% of the TB cases that would have developed otherwise have been prevented by the vaccination. For vaccine studies, the prevented fraction is directly equivalent to the *vaccine efficacy*, but the former term may be used for interventions other than vaccines.

The prevented fraction is computed by subtracting the disease risk in individuals with the intervention measure (for example, an anti-leprosy vaccine) from the disease risk in individuals without the intervention, and expressing the difference as a proportion of the latter. For example, if the annual incidence of leprosy is 2.8 per thousand in the vaccinated and 4.2 in the unvaccinated, the prevented fraction is equal to $[(4.2-2.8)/4.2] = 0.33$ (or 33%).

If the relative risk (R) (of disease in those who receive the intervention, compared to those who do not) is known, the prevented fraction may be obtained by calculating $(1-R)$. For example, if the relative risk of developing malaria in homes where mosquito-nets are used is a quarter of that in homes where they are not used, the prevented fraction is equal to $1 - 0.25$, i.e. 75%.

The *population prevented fraction* is defined as the proportion of cases of the disease in the *total population* that have been prevented by the intervention. If the relative risk (R) and the proportion of individuals in the population who receive the intervention measure (P) are known, the population prevented fraction is obtained by calculating

Table 21.20 Population prevented fraction, according to vaccination coverage and disease incidence rate

Vaccination coverage (%) ($P \times 100$)	Disease incidence in total population (per thousand) [$0.8P + 2.0(1 - P)$]	Population prevented fraction (%) [$P(1 - R) \times 100$]
0	2.00	0
20	1.76	12
40	1.52	24
60	1.28	36
80	1.04	48
100	0.80	60

$P(1-R)$. Thus, the extent of reduction possible in disease incidence in the total population, if all individuals were to receive the intervention measure ($P = 1$), is $(1-R)$.

Consider a situation in which the annual incidence of TB is 2.0 per thousand in those who do not receive BCG vaccination and 0.8 per thousand in those who do, i.e. the relative risk in those vaccinated is $0.8/2.0 = 0.4$. Table 21.20 shows the fraction of all cases prevented by the intervention, according to the disease incidence in the total population and the vaccination coverage.

References

Armitage, P. and Berry, G. 1987. *Statistical methods in medical research*. Oxford: Blackwell Scientific.

Breslow, N. E. and Day, N. E. 1980. *Statistical methods in cancer research. Volume 1. The analysis of case-control studies*. Lyon: International Agency for Research on Cancer.

Breslow, N. E. and Day, N. E. 1987. *Statistical methods in cancer research. Volume 2. The design and analysis of cohort studies*. Lyon: International Agency for Research on Cancer.

Hayes, R. J. and Moulton, L. H. 2009. *Cluster randomized trials*. Boca Raton, FL: Chapman & Hall/CRC.

Kirkwood, B. R. and Sterne, J. A. C. 2003. *Essential medical statistics*. Malden, MA: Blackwell Science.

Miettinen, O. 1976. Estimability and estimation in case-referent studies. *American Journal of Epidemiology*, **103**, 226–35.

Rothman, K. J., Greenland, S., and Lash, T. L. 2008. *Chapter 10: Precision and statistics in epidemiologic studies. Modern epidemiology*, 3rd ed. Philadelphia: Lippincott Williams & Wilkins.

Chapter 22

Phase IV studies

1 Introduction to Phase IV studies 394
  1.1 Efficacy and effectiveness 396
  1.2 Stakeholders 397
2 Types of Phase IV study 397
  2.1 Safety/pharmacovigilance 397
  2.2 Intervention effectiveness 398
3 The conduct of Phase IV studies 400
  3.1 Design issues 400
  3.2 Study sites 400
  3.3 Ethics and governance 401
  3.4 Stakeholder involvement 401
  3.5 Data collection, processing, and analysis 401
  3.6 Contextual and confounding factors 402
  3.7 Reporting and dissemination 402
  3.8 Funding 402
4 Examples of real-world effectiveness studies 403
  4.1 The INDEPTH Effectiveness and Safety Studies (INESS) platform 403
  4.2 Effectiveness of intermittent preventive treatment for malaria 404

1 Introduction to Phase IV studies

The main focus of this book is on randomized controlled field trials of health interventions in LMICs, many of which can be classified as Phase III trials (see Chapter 2, Section 3). This chapter gives a brief overview of Phase IV studies that are often carried out after an intervention has been shown to be efficacious in Phase III trials. We give a brief description of the rationale and some of the terminology used in such studies, outline the main types of Phase IV study, discuss some key issues in the design of such studies, and give a brief description of two specific Phase IV studies.

For new drugs or vaccines, the evidence from one or more Phase III trials, taken together with the results of the Phase I and II trials, will be presented to licensing authorities to register the product for clinical or public health use. However, the total number of participants included in Phase I to III trials of a new product will often be no more than a few thousand, and there are usually important public health issues that will have been incompletely addressed at the time a product is licensed. For example, individuals included in Phase III trials will often have been a carefully selected sample of the population and will not include all of those eligible for eventual administration of the product. Particular groups may have been excluded, such as children and adolescents, the very undernourished, or pregnant women, but these groups will often receive the product when it is in general use, and it is important to collect data on both the safety and the effectiveness of the product in these groups. Also, in most Phase III trials, great care will have been taken with product supply and storage, and, if the dosing regimen requires multiple doses, care will have been taken to ensure that the interval between doses was as recommended. Rigid adherence to such intervals is much less likely once the product is in general use. For these reasons, it will be important to measure whether the effect of the product, when it is administered in a routine health system or programme, is similar to the efficacy that was assessed in the Phase III trials conducted in a research setting. Phase IV studies are conducted to assess the *effectiveness* of an intervention when it is in public health use, as compared to the *efficacy* of the intervention as assessed in a carefully controlled Phase III trial (see Section 2.1).

Most Phase III trials will not have been large enough to detect reliably important, but relatively uncommon, side effects. For example, a serious adverse effect (SAE) of an intervention that occurs, on average, in one in every 2000 recipients may well be missed in a Phase III trial that involved only a few thousand participants. There may also be other unexpected effects when an intervention is implemented in a public health programme that were not apparent in the carefully controlled situation of a Phase III trial. For example, in a trial of a health education intervention in schools, teachers may be willing to promote condom use when they have been carefully trained, supported, and supervised, as part of the trial procedures. However, when the intervention is implemented on a widespread basis, in settings where condom use is unpopular and talking of such things with young people frowned upon, teachers might actually discourage use without the support that was included in the trial. It is important that studies are conducted to detect such adverse effects once an intervention is in routine use. Whenever possible, such Phase IV studies should be used as the basis for developing systems that persist after the study, so that routine health systems can continue to detect such events.

Historically, assessment of how interventions work in 'real-world' public health programmes has been relatively neglected. However, presently, such Phase IV research is receiving increasing attention. It encompasses post-marketing surveillance of the effect of interventions and implementation research which investigates better ways of ensuring the successful delivery of an intervention (such as how to increase the coverage of a vaccination programme). A common goal of Phase IV studies is to provide evidence that the health intervention can be successfully and safely integrated into public health or clinical practice where 'successful' means that it is not only feasible to do so, but also that the intervention remains effective and its implementation is not associated with any serious adverse effects.

This chapter focuses mainly on Phase IV studies related to the introduction of new drugs or vaccines, but similar studies can be used to evaluate other types of health intervention such as surgical procedures, health education, or peer supporters to encourage adherence to treatment regimens.

Phase IV research serves three major functions:

1. to support pharmacoviligance systems in monitoring the safety of new interventions used in large populations and in specific groups who were not studied adequately in the pre-marketing phases such as children, pregnant women, the elderly, or those with co-morbidities
2. to determine the effectiveness of an intervention in a routine health system, as opposed to within a carefully controlled trial
3. to assess new strategies of use of approved products or interventions, such as the evaluation of anti-malarials when used for intermittent presumptive treatment, rather than either for malaria prophylaxis or for treatment of a diagnosed malarial infection.

Furthermore, studies to seek ways of widening the coverage, ensuring a more equitable distribution or conducting an economic evaluation of an intervention (see Chapter 19) may also be encompassed by Phase IV studies. A key issue with respect to such studies is that they are conducted after a product has been licensed or is already in widespread use. Thus, placebo-controlled trials are generally ruled out for ethical reasons, and observational designs are often employed. A full description of all the potential observational study designs is beyond the scope of this chapter. However, because of the importance of Phase IV studies and the overlap with many of the field research issues covered in this book, after defining some of the key terms and concepts, Section 2 of this chapter gives a brief overview of some of the commonest Phase IV research approaches.

1.1 Efficacy and effectiveness

A distinction should be made between the effect of the intervention, as measured in a Phase III trial, called the *efficacy* of the intervention, and the effect of the intervention when it is delivered in a public health programme, called the *effectiveness* of the intervention. Generally, it is expected that the efficacy of an intervention will be greater than its effectiveness, for the reasons outlined in Section 1. However, this is not always the case. For example, when some vaccines are administered to large populations, there are at least two factors that may operate to reduce the incidence of disease. First, the vaccine may offer individual protection to recipients of the vaccine. Second, the reduction in the number of individuals who acquire the disease as a consequence of vaccination may reduce the overall level of infection in the community, and thus even those who are unvaccinated may be at lower risk of acquiring disease, simply because they are less likely to be exposed to someone with the infection. Such *herd effects* may be substantial for some person-to-person infections, for which humans are the main reservoir. If the vaccine coverage is high enough, the effectiveness of the vaccine may be higher than would have been predicted from Phase III efficacy trials, in which typically, at most, half of the eligible population is vaccinated. Fine et al. (2011) give an overview of herd effects.

The overall impact of an intervention against a disease in a population, sometimes known as the *community effectiveness* or *system effectiveness* of the intervention, will depend on the *effectiveness* of the intervention and its *effective coverage*, i.e. the proportion of the *target* population who receive it. The *target* population consists of all those who should receive (would benefit from receiving) the intervention. An example of how an evaluation of the effective coverage of a broad range of different health services was used to benchmark the performance of the health system in the various states of Mexico is given in Lozano et al. (2006).

1.2 Stakeholders

The primary audience for Phase IV studies is health policy decision makers, but other stakeholders may include regulatory agencies, industry, health care professionals, patients, community groups, media, and suppliers. Regulatory agencies and public health officials will seek to ensure the continuous evaluation of an intervention's risks and benefits. Industry engages in Phase IV research to determine the effects of long-term use, as requested or demanded by regulatory agencies, but also to inform key strategic and operational decisions related to the marketing of their products. Governments, decision makers, and policy makers need high-quality evidence on effectiveness and cost-effectiveness in the real world, as well as in Phase III trial settings, in order to design and implement public health programmes that optimize health gains and reduce health inequity. For clinicians, Phase IV study data can guide their prescribing and the advice they give to their patients.

2 Types of Phase IV study

2.1 Safety/pharmacovigilance

Pharmacovigilance is defined as 'the science and activities relating to the detection, assessment, understanding and prevention of adverse effects or any other possible drug-related problems' (World Health Organization, 2006). Pharmacovigilance studies are designed to detect and assess both long-term and short-term adverse effects of medicines (including drugs and vaccines). Regulatory agencies will often require that specific monitoring is conducted after a product is licensed (post-marketing safety monitoring or pharmacovigilance) that is designed to detect the occurrence of rare, but serious, adverse effects of the product. Similar issues apply to medical devices and prostheses.

Pharmacoviligance studies can include observational or intervention studies. Common designs include case-control studies, cohort studies (cohort event monitoring), and spontaneous (passive) reporting schemes. In some circumstances, RCTs might also be possible. The main method used in HICs is the collation of adverse drug reaction reports submitted by clinicians, which are compiled and analysed by national pharmacovigilance centres. The reports may also be submitted to the WHO Programme for International Drug Monitoring (<http://www.who-umc.org>). However, this reporting system is not yet functional in most LMICs, and, even in HICs, the system is acknowledged to be an imperfect way to detect all of the adverse events (AEs) that might be associated with a particular product. However, monitoring for product safety is particularly important in LMICs, often with their overburdened health care systems and frequent polypharmacy. Other potential safety issues in LMICs include the widespread manufacture and sale of counterfeit, substandard, or expired medicines, and potentially unsafe drug donation practices. An example of how pharmacovigilance can be built into a broader Phase IV study is given in Section 4.1.

2.2 Intervention effectiveness

As discussed in Section 1, the effectiveness of an intervention may well be different in the complex and dynamic situation of a routine health system, compared to the context of a carefully controlled Phase III trial. Effectiveness studies evaluate the impact of an intervention when delivered under real-world conditions in a routine health system. Such studies are especially important when a new intervention is first introduced into a public health programme. The decision to introduce the intervention will usually be based upon the results of one or more Phase III trials, including a cost-effectiveness analysis, often using data derived from the Phase III trials. However, it is important to evaluate both the effectiveness and cost of the intervention, as used in the public health programme, and this will generally require the setting up of specific studies. For example, a series of such studies were conducted when rotavirus vaccines were introduced into public health use (Patel et al., 2011).

Phase IV studies may also be appropriate for interventions which are relatively well established in a public health programme. These may be drugs or vaccines that have been in use for a number of years already, or other interventions which may have been implemented with or without preceding efficacy trials or for which the effectiveness of the intervention is unknown, even if the efficacy had been established in controlled intervention trials. For example, controlled trials were conducted to measure the impact of introducing insecticide-treated bed-nets (ITNs) as a measure to reduce deaths from malaria in malaria-endemic areas. These showed that this intervention had a substantial impact on child mortality. A Phase IV study to evaluate the impact of such bed-nets, when implemented in a public health programme, was conducted by Schellenberg et al. (2001). In this study, a programme was rolled out across two rural districts of southern Tanzania over a 2-year period, in which subsidized ITNs were made available at shops and kiosks. The proportion of young children who slept under an ITN was estimated through population-based surveys, and the impact on child mortality monitored through a case-control study, in which the prior use of an ITN was compared among children who had died from malaria and those who survived. All child deaths were identified within a demographic surveillance area. This Phase IV study confirmed that ITNs had a major impact on child mortality within a routine programme, and the study also elucidated ways in which that impact might be increased by modifications to the programme delivery system.

Phase IV studies of health system effectiveness are designed to understand reasons for the decay of the impact of an intervention that results from individual and system behaviour, including access to the intervention, diagnostic targeting, provider compliance, and patient adherence. Figure 22.1 summarizes the outcome of Phase IV studies conducted in Tanzania to determine why highly efficacious anti-malarial treatments had low community effectiveness. Controlled trials had shown that artimisinen combination treatments (ACTs) have very high efficacy for the treatment of uncomplicated malaria, with roughly 98% of patients who received treatment within carefully conducted efficacy trials cured. A community-based survey found that only 60% of those with malaria sought care from a clinic that had ACTs. Studies within the clinics showed that 95% of those who came to these clinics had an appropriate diagnostic test performed, and, in 95% of those diagnosed with malaria, the correct treatment was prescribed. Further studies in the patients who were given the correct prescription of ACT showed that only 70% of them adhered correctly to the treatment as prescribed. Taken together, this series of Phase IV studies showed that less than 40% of people with uncomplicated malaria in the community were effectively treated, despite ACTs, which had a 98% efficacy, being made available. Such Phase IV studies can not only document and measure the failings in the health system, but they can also be used to investigate the reasons behind these problems and the potential actions that can be taken to fix them (see Section 4.1).

Figure 22.1 represents what happened in the catchment population as a whole, but it is important, in such studies, to measure system effectiveness by socio-economic status, and among specific vulnerable groups, as this may reveal substantial heterogeneity in the findings, according to these factors.

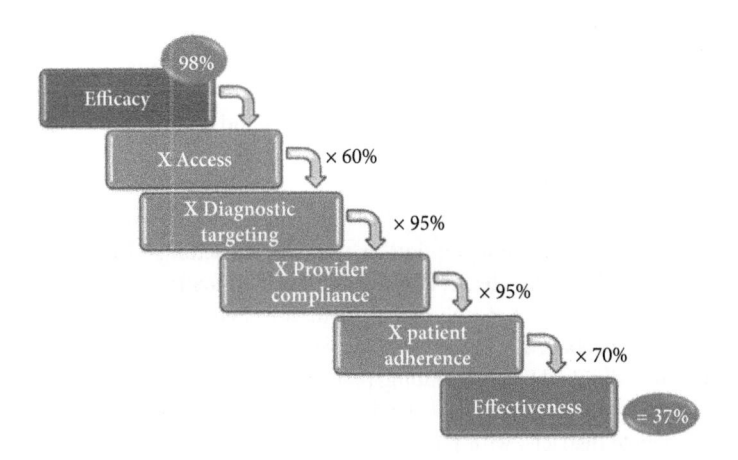

Figure 22.1 How the efficacy of highly efficacious malaria treatments translates into low community effectiveness for the treatment of malaria due to failings in the health system.

Reproduced courtesy of Don de Savigny (personal communication). This image is distributed under the terms of the Creative Commons Attribution Non Commercial 4.0 International licence (CC-BY-NC), a copy of which is available at http://creativecommons.org/licenses/by-nc/4.0/.

3 The conduct of Phase IV studies

Phase IV studies should follow the general guidelines, as described elsewhere in this book, with respect to the selection of the study population and study design, sample size calculations, ethics clearance and consideration of other governance issues, and the training and supervision of study staff.

3.1 Design issues

There are multiple observational designs and evaluation schemes that can be used in Phase IV studies to assess the effectiveness, cost-effectiveness, and safety of an intervention in real-world settings. Details of these approaches is beyond the scope of this book, but the use of non-randomized study designs to evaluate interventions is discussed in Victora et al. (2004) and Bonell et al. (2011).

3.2 Study sites

Whereas Phase I to III trials are often restricted to relatively small-scale research settings with good infrastructure, Phase IV studies are typically conducted over wider areas where health care and the intervention in question are delivered through routine health systems. A variety of service providers may be involved, including public, private-for-profit, private-not-for-profit, and community-based providers. A way of encompassing this complexity is to use the district as the unit of implementation and analysis within Phase IV studies. In many countries, districts are the core administrative unit for governmental health and other programmes, and the smallest unit that includes all the major features of the health system, from a hospital down to community health workers. They are usually the lowest unit that plans and allocates budgets, manages training, and aggregates health information. They are easily identifiable and often have some level of sociocultural and economic homogeneity. Wherever possible, Phase IV studies should support and strengthen existing health systems, rather than setting up special structures that may weaken the health system in the long term.

One of the challenges in conducting Phase IV studies in these situations is to balance the need to study the intervention in a real-world setting with the need to be able to collect reliable data. Health and demographic surveillance sites (HDSS) longitudinally monitor and register the total population living within a geographically defined area. They collect a broad array of important health-related parameters at the household and individual levels, including pregnancies, births, deaths, causes of death, socio-economic status, care-seeking behaviour, and immunization status. HDSS sometimes cover whole districts, with populations of 50 000 to more than 100 000 people, and therefore include the full range of health service providers. HDSS are increasingly being used for Phase IV studies of effectiveness and safety (see Section 4.1). Effectiveness studies involving HDSS can measure the effectiveness of the system in delivering the intervention to the whole community, as well as the effectiveness of the delivered intervention in affecting individual health status. The large numbers of exposures to the intervention that can be monitored longitudinally in HDSS make them useful for pharmacovigilance studies. The research infrastructure associated with HDSS also makes it possible to interpret results contextually and to estimate cost-effectiveness. The longitudinal history available on all residents in an HDSS provides data that makes HDSS highly valuable partners in effectiveness trials and Phase IV studies.

3.3 Ethics and governance

Planners of Phase IV studies are confronted with the need to maintain sufficient oversight of intervention delivery to ensure that the approach is as planned, while simultaneously allowing for realistic adaptation and tailoring by providers. Governance of such studies needs a balance between the requirements of routine health systems and international scientific standards. It is valuable to have a separate committee that involves donors, governments, regulators, industry, and key stakeholders who discuss the approaches used and to offer guidance as to their selection, interpretation, and use of results. Also see Chapters 6, 7, and 9.

Phase IV studies, in which any new data on people are collected, generally need ethical clearance from the relevant national and institutional bodies. Such studies pose some specific challenges, in terms of ethical considerations, as they may involve comparison of new vs old technology and expensive vs inexpensive drugs, and there may be concerns that some patients will not be receiving optimal care.

3.4 Stakeholder involvement

Mapping and involvement of stakeholders is even more important within Phase IV studies than in Phase III field trials, as described in Chapter 9. They should be part of the planning of large-scale activities that will affect policy and strategy, and they should have an active role in the selection of study sites. They should have the possibility to comment on study design, participate in the review and interpretation of preliminary results, and advise on the development of appropriate feedback mechanisms. Their active involvement will be essential for a successful translation of results into policy and programmes.

3.5 Data collection, processing, and analysis

Phase IV effectiveness studies can make judicious use of health service attendance and other data that are routinely collected by health programmes or other sources. Possibilities for linking population data with health facility data should be explored, although systems for doing this are difficult to set up in most LMIC contexts. Prospective studies provide greater opportunities than retrospective studies to gather essential additional data. Efforts should be made to simplify data collection and management and to improve data quality by introducing real-time data collection directly on to computers or mobile devices. When using routine data sources, one issue to resolve early on, among all partners, is the question of data ownership, and it is essential to have a clear agreement of where data will be managed, stored, cleaned, and analysed, and agreed publication and dissemination policies (also see Chapter 20). Additional study data collection is usually needed to fill data gaps and address specific questions. Potential methods include health facility and household surveys, longitudinal health status studies, and qualitative research.

3.6 Contextual and confounding factors

In order to be able to adjust for confounding factors, contextual factors need to be closely monitored in observational Phase IV studies—factors that are external to the programme or intervention under consideration. These usually include socio-economic, environmental, demographic, and health system factors, as well as other locally relevant factors. Health outcomes are affected by socio-economic progress, changes in both public and private health services, and other initiatives in health or other sectors in the same geographical area. Because these changes can happen concurrently with the assessment of the effectiveness of the study intervention, they require special attention and need to be integrated in the interpretation and analysis of the data. The aim should be to collect contextual data to allow the evaluation of whether or not it is plausible that factors, other than the intervention being studied, could explain any improvements seen (Victora et al., 2004). Again, HDSS can play a central role here, as they can provide information on contextual factors and health system dynamics.

3.7 Reporting and dissemination

As for Phase III trials, a well-thought out system for reporting and dissemination of results is crucial if the results of Phase IV studies are to feed into policy and programmatic action. Whereas reporting standards for Phases I to III trials have been widely agreed (see Chapter 2), those for observational research are more recent. However, the STROBE statement (STrengthening the Reporting of OBservational studies in Epidemiology) is widely accepted and has been endorsed by a growing number of biomedical journals (<http://www.strobe-statement.org>). Efforts are also being made to develop and strengthen scientific methods for conducting comparative effectiveness research to improve the consistency, applicability, reliability, and validity of comparative effectiveness research findings for informing the health care decisions of patients, providers, and policy makers. An example is the DEcIDE (Developing Evidence to Inform Decisions about Effectiveness) Network created in 2005 (<http://effectivehealthcare.ahrq.gov/index.cfm/who-is-involved-in-the-effective-health-care-program1/about-the-decide-network>).

3.8 Funding

Phase IV, and especially effectiveness, studies are often resource-intensive, due to large sample sizes and long follow-up periods. Also, a significant expansion of infrastructure and capacity is often required prior to the initiation of such studies, as many research groups are better placed to conduct efficacy trials than to conduct research within the health care delivery system. Raising funds for Phase IV research is challenging, but funders, including governments, have become increasingly interested in research to check that the interventions they fund provide the best possible value for money, so opportunities are improving.

4 Examples of real-world effectiveness studies

4.1 The INDEPTH Effectiveness and Safety Studies (INESS) platform

The development of new drugs and drug combinations for the treatment of malaria has created the need for countries to select and integrate new anti-malarial drugs into their health systems. INESS was designed as a platform for the conduct of Phase IV studies to provide objective data on the system effectiveness and safety of artemisinin combination therapies (ACTs) in real-world settings in Ghana, Burkina Faso, Tanzania, and Mozambique. The INESS research sites are based in districts with health and demographic surveillance systems and represent a diverse range of health system capacities and malaria endemicities. INESS looks at the overall performance (effectiveness) of deployment of the drug (ACT) in the system. It illuminates how the decay in the effectiveness of the ACTs occurs from efficacy to net or 'system' effectiveness, and at what levels the losses are the greatest (Figure 22.1). The research focuses on human behaviour, system behaviour, and drug behaviour in real-world contexts. Usually, there are lessons for all levels about how to optimize performance. By following a large number of patients with malaria who should benefit from the intervention through the system, this Phase IV study is in a powerful position to understand the net effectiveness of the intervention (see <http://www.indepth-network.org>).

Access and patient adherence seem to be the major bottlenecks creating the loss of effectiveness in the example shown in Figure 22.1. However, within each of the five compartments shown in the figure, the INESS study has identified and quantified the specific sub-determinants contributing to the loss in effectiveness. These include access failure (for example, due to distance, poverty, or lack of knowledge), diagnostics failure (for example, due to weaknesses in laboratory capacity or staff training), provider failure (for example, weaknesses in supply chain management, leading to drug or diagnostic test stock-outs, or poor prescribing), and patient adherence failure (for example, due to problems with taste, perceived side effects, stopping treatment when feeling better, or incorrect provider instructions).

INESS also conducts qualitative studies to understand community perceptions of the intervention under study, as well as the health system contexts, that help to explain the results from the quantitative system effectiveness studies. The INESS platform generates evidence that is sufficiently representative to inform local, national, and possibly global policy and practice. The results provide evidence on what human behaviour, health system, and drug issues need to be addressed and where the most urgent needs are. It also highlights issues for the industry to consider, in order to improve effectiveness. For the safety component, INESS strengthens the national spontaneous reporting system and also runs a separate event-monitoring cohort to detect and report AEs. Though initially developed to examine ACTs, the INESS platform has the potential to assess the effectiveness of other health interventions. Because the platform operates at the level of whole districts and follows a large number of exposures to the intervention, safety studies are easily incorporated.

4.2 Effectiveness of intermittent preventive treatment for malaria

The potential efficacy of intermittent preventive treatment for malaria in pregnancy (IPTp), infants (IPTi), and children (IPTc—now called seasonal malaria chemoprevention (SMC)) has been established in numerous safety and efficacy trials (Aponte et al., 2009). Yet, to move to public health action and promote it on a large scale, evidence is needed on the contextual determinants, costing, acceptability, and coverage rates. Taking IPTi using sulfadoxine–pyrimethamine (IPTi-SP) as an example, a cascade of activities has been undertaken by the IPTi consortium (<http://www.iptimalaria.org>) to establish the real-world effectiveness of this intervention if it were to be used on a large scale. First, a pooled analysis of the efficacy and safety of IPTi-SP was undertaken (Aponte et al., 2009), based on six studies conducted in different African countries. The effect of IPTi-SP on immune responses to Expanded Programme on Immunization (EPI) vaccines and on the development of naturally acquired immunity to malaria was also studied, as well as the effect of sulfadoxine–pyrimethamine (SP) drug resistance on the efficacy of IPTi-SP. An effectiveness study of IPTi was carried out in Tanzania and included cost-effectiveness (Manzi et al., 2008), acceptability (Gysels et al., 2009; Pool et al., 2008), and delivery through the existing health system, as IPTi is delivered through the EPI (Manzi et al., 2009). Then, a pilot study of the implementation of IPTi was carried out in six African countries, with careful evaluation of implementation bottlenecks and best practices, the evaluation of the impact of IPTi-SP on EPI coverage and other malaria interventions, its cost, acceptability, drug resistance, and pharmacoviligance safety profile. A separate study on the cost-effectiveness of IPTi followed and showed that IPTi-SP, when delivered alongside the EPI, is a highly cost-effective intervention. Overall, this series of Phase IV studies showed that IPTi-SP is a valuable addition to malaria control, but its benefits depend on the contextual factors of malaria endemicity and therapeutic efficacy of the drug. The decision on where to implement should take into account the local epidemiology of malaria. The IPTi consortium also conducted modelling of the impact of IPTi (Ross et al., 2008). One outcome of all these efforts is the IPTi decision support tool. It is a web-based tool, available at <http://ipti.lshtm.ac.uk>, and is intended to aid national and sub-national policy makers in assessing whether IPTi is a locally appropriate intervention. It includes drug resistance and cost-effectiveness components to assess the applicability of IPTi at a sub-national level.

References

Aponte, J. J., Schellenberg, D., Egan, A., *et al.* 2009. Efficacy and safety of intermittent preventive treatment with sulfadoxine-pyrimethamine for malaria in African infants: a pooled analysis of six randomised, placebo-controlled trials. *Lancet*, **374**, 1533–42.

Bonell, C. P., Hargreaves, J., Cousens, S., *et al.* 2011. Alternatives to randomisation in the evaluation of public health interventions: design challenges and solutions. *Journal of Epidemiology and Community Health*, **65**, 582–7.

Fine, P., Eames, K., and Heymann, D. L. 2011. 'Herd immunity': a rough guide. *Clinical Infectious Diseases*, **52**, 911–16.

Gysels, M., Pell, C., Mathanga, D. P., *et al.* 2009. Community response to intermittent preventive treatment of malaria in infants (IPTi) delivered through the expanded programme of immunization in five African settings. *Malaria Journal*, **8**, 191.

Lozano, R., Soliz, P., Gakidou, E., *et al.* 2006. Benchmarking of performance of Mexican states with effective coverage. *Lancet*, **368**, 1729–41.

Manzi, F., Hutton, G., Schellenberg, J., *et al.* 2008. From strategy development to routine implementation: the cost of Intermittent Preventive Treatment in Infants for malaria control. *BMC Health Services Research*, **8**, 165.

Manzi, F., Schellenberg, J., Hamis, Y., *et al.* 2009. Intermittent preventive treatment for malaria and anaemia control in Tanzanian infants; the development and implementation of a public health strategy. *Transactions of the Royal Society of Tropical Medicine and Hygiene*, **103**, 79–86.

Patel, M. M., Steele, D., Gentsch, J. R., Wecker, J., Glass, R. I., and Parashar, U. D. 2011. Real-world impact of rotavirus vaccination. *Pediatric Infectious Disease Journal*, **30**, S1–5.

Pool, R., Mushi, A., Schellenberg, J. A., *et al.* 2008. The acceptability of intermittent preventive treatment of malaria in infants (IPTi) delivered through the expanded programme of immunization in southern Tanzania. *Malaria Journal*, **7**, 213.

Ross, A., Penny, M., Maire, N., *et al.* 2008. Modelling the epidemiological impact of intermittent preventive treatment against malaria in infants. *PLoS One*, **3**, e2661.

Schellenberg, J. R., Abdulla, S., Nathan, R., *et al.* 2001. Effect of large-scale social marketing of insecticide-treated nets on child survival in rural Tanzania. *Lancet*, **357**, 1241–7.

Victora, C. G., Habicht, J. P., and Bryce, J. 2004. Evidence-based public health: moving beyond randomized trials. *American Journal of Public Health*, **94**, 400–5.

World Health Organization. 2006. *The safety of medicines in public health programmes: pharmacovigilance an essential tool* [Online]. Geneva: World Health Organization. Available at: <http://www.who.int/medicines/areas/quality_safety/safety_efficacy/Pharmacovigilance_B.pdf>.

Chapter 23

Reporting and using trial results

1 Planning communications 406
2 Communication before and during the trial 407
3 Reporting the final results 408
 3.1 Planning the sequence of communications 408
 3.2 Report to the sponsor 408
 3.3 Trial participants and the study communities 409
 3.4 Local and government officials 409
 3.5 Reporting in the scientific literature 409
 3.6 Media coverage 410
 3.7 The funding agency 411
4 From research findings to public health action 412
 4.1 Sharing and synthesizing findings 412
 4.2 Researchers and policy 412
 4.3 Introducing an intervention into public health programmes 415
Appendix 23.1 Guidance on how to write a scientific paper reporting the results of a trial 417
Appendix 23.2 Checklist of information to include when reporting a randomized trial 422
Appendix 23.3 A communication action plan for a trial 424

1 Planning communications

It is important to communicate the progress of a trial, from its initiation to its end, to all the people and institutions (the stakeholders) likely to have an interest in the trial and its results. Planning this communication should start before the proposal for the trial is submitted for clearance and funding, and the communication plan should be reviewed and updated periodically throughout the trial.

Many researchers do not give communication and dissemination sufficient attention. This can lead to resistance to its initiation, because community members or local or national officials feel annoyed that they have not been consulted or kept informed, and lack of communication may cause misunderstandings during the trial which may impede its progress. From an early stage in a trial, it is often useful to involve or to consult a person with past experience in communicating with policy makers and the general public about the conduct of a trial, ideally someone familiar with research in the context of the trial. At a minimum, in a large field trial, it is advisable to involve such an expert during the planning of the overall trial communication action plan and during the planning of the final dissemination of the findings of the trial.

A useful starting point is for the trial team to construct a list of all the potential stakeholders and to think through what information should be provided to each of them, in what format, and when. An example of extracts from the communication action plan for a trial of an adolescent sexual and reproductive health intervention in Tanzania is given in Appendix 23.3.

At a minimum, stakeholders must be told what the purpose of the trial is and what is going to happen from the start, be kept informed about the progress of the trial, and be given the results of the trial and a chance to comment on these.

There are many different communication formats and media, some, or all, of which can be used effectively at different stages in a trial. Depending on the circumstances, these may include public meetings, pamphlets, brochures, newsletters, films, press releases and briefings, web pages, academic journal articles, technical briefing documents, and policy briefing documents. While interested academics and researchers are likely to read journal articles reporting the design and results of a trial in detail, few other stakeholders will. Conversely, policy makers will want a brief and concise report that focuses on the main findings and their implications for policy. Managers of public health programmes will want suggestions as to how the results of the trial might cause them to consider making specific modifications to their programmes, and they are also likely to want an indication of what any changes are likely to cost. So it is essential to consider what communication formats are most useful for different audiences. Communication and dissemination of trial progress and results should not all be left to the end of the trial.

Comprehensive guidance on formulating a communication plan for a clinical trial is given in Robinson et al. (2010).

2 Communication before and during the trial

We have emphasized, in other chapters, the importance of adequate preparation before starting a trial. A very important aspect of these preparations includes meetings with community leaders, community advisory boards (CABs), and public meetings involving potential trial participants to explain fully the purposes of the trial and what it will involve. There should be ample time allocated at these meetings for questions, and indeed suggestions from those in the local community may lead to changes in the trial plan. It is also crucial to obtain permission from local and national officials for the conduct of the trial and to allocate sufficient time for discussions with those officials, who may also suggest modifications to the trial. Ideally, there will be representation from local and/or national officials on the trial steering committee, which is a good way of keeping them in touch and being able to call upon their advice at all stages of the trial.

Once the trial has started, to ensure the continuing collaboration from the trial participants, those in the community in which the trial is being conducted will need both information on the progress of the trial and the opportunity to comment throughout the trial. There will also be a need to keep the local health and government administration informed of activities. At a minimum, local and national officials should receive communication at least once a year; some may need this much more frequently (also see Chapters 7 and 9).

It is very important that any problems which are encountered during the conduct of the trial are rapidly identified by the trial investigators, and immediate steps are taken to make any necessary modifications to trial procedures and to explain to trial participants and community officials the reasons for any changes. Problems which are dealt with quickly are less likely to endanger the continued conduct of the trial than problems which are ignored for too long, with effective action either being delayed or not initiated. Regular meetings with the CAB should be a good conduit for early recognition of problems or issues being raised by trial participants or other members of the community.

3 Reporting the final results

In the absence of major problems during a trial, the most intensive phases of communication are before the initiation of the trial and when the final results are available. Dissemination of the reports of the trial findings is a substantial undertaking and must be considered an integral part of the conduct of the study and a major responsibility of the investigators. Research that is not appropriately disseminated is likely to fail to achieve its proper impact.

3.1 Planning the sequence of communications

The order of reporting of the results of a trial needs careful planning. In general, it is a good idea to follow a sequence whereby the results are first reported and discussed in confidence with all senior trial investigators, then, in confidence, with national and local health or other relevant government officials, representatives of the funding agency, and, when appropriate, with institutions who may be contacted by governments or the press to give their opinion on the results (such as UN agencies). All people involved in these steps should agree not to divulge the results to anyone else. These steps should occur, before the results are made public internationally. For example, it is bad practice for the results of a trial to be reported at an international conference or through a press release before the national and local government officials, trial participants, and representatives of the funding agency have been made aware of them. Also, some medical and scientific journals do not allow the results of a trial they are to publish to be presented at public conferences or released to the media before the journal article is published, so, where appropriate, it is worth trying to synchronize the publication of the trial results in a journal with the first international presentation of the results. Where this is not feasible (for example, the first suitable conference is not going to happen for several months after the results are ready, or the journal's review process will be too lengthy), it is important to discuss this with the journal in advance.

3.2 Report to the sponsor

Whatever the outcome of a trial, a number of different communications must be prepared. For all trials, it is recommended that a comprehensive report be prepared, detailing all the trial procedures and the full results. The preparation of this report should be a work in progress throughout the trial, with the final complete report serving as a permanent record for the study team and a reference for anyone who wants to know exactly what was done in the trial. It will also be invaluable for the conduct of any re-survey of the trial population and may provide legal documentation with respect to registration of a new product or if questions about the study arise, for any reason, in the future. If the results of a trial are to be used as part of the registration procedures for a new product, it is important to liaise with the regulatory authorities at an early stage in the planning of the trial, so that the appropriate records are kept and the proper recording procedures are used (see Chapter 20). Specific guidance has been prepared by the ICH on what should be included in a clinical study report that is going to be used to support registration of a new drug or vaccine (International Conference on Harmonisation, 1995).

3.3 Trial participants and the study communities

It is the responsibility of the investigators to report back the results to those whose participation made the trial possible, i.e. those in the study communities. As emphasized in Chapters 6, 7, and 9, the investigating team should be in regular communication with the participants and their communities throughout the trial, but there is a special responsibility to make the community aware of the findings at the end of the trial. This might be done through public meetings with community members, to answer any questions they may have regarding the study, and through meetings with community leaders and local officials. It might also be appropriate to prepare a short report on the findings, written in such a way as to be readily comprehensible to a lay audience and which can be distributed to community members.

3.4 Local and government officials

For most trials, it will have been necessary to have sought the permission for the conduct of the trial from the local administration, and often from the Ministry of Health (MOH). It is important that the results of a trial are carefully discussed with such officials, before they are made publicly available. When trial results are publicly released, it may be useful to have national meetings opened by the MOH or the Director of Medical Services, or their representatives, and to have regional, district, or local meetings opened by equivalent local officials. Sometimes, it is appropriate to also disseminate the findings of a trial through local, national, and international mass media (print, radio, TV, and/or webcast (a live broadcast via the Internet) or podcast (a digital audio or video file that can be downloaded from a website to a media player or computer)), or in the form of a film.

The findings should also be reported formally to the local and national research and health policy decision makers. As well as reporting the results in full, the implications that the findings have for the health system should be reviewed with all appropriate health authorities, both governmental and non-governmental. It is important that a clearly written summary of the main results and their implications is included, usually at the front of the report, as many of those for whom the results are relevant will not have the time or inclination to study all the fine details.

3.5 Reporting in the scientific literature

It is expected that the results of all intervention trials will be published in peer-reviewed journals. Investigators will generally wish their findings to reach a wide audience and may target international journals as an outlet for the results of a trial. If the findings in a trial are mainly of local interest, a national journal may be more appropriate. Journal papers will generally be much shorter than the comprehensive study report discussed in Section 3.2. A general guide on how to write a paper reporting the results of a trial is given in Appendix 23.1. Specific guidance on the form a paper should take is detailed by the particular journal selected. The choice of the journal to which to submit a manuscript will be influenced by a number of factors, including the target audience for the scientific results, their local or international significance, how quickly the paper will be published (journals vary substantially in the time they take to have a paper peer-reviewed and processed for publication), how exciting the results are (it is unfortunately true that journals are biased towards publishing papers that have new or unexpected findings), and whether the journal has a history of publishing intervention trials of the kind conducted. It is a good idea to select the journal before starting to draft the article, as each journal has different requirements regarding, for example, the permissible length of articles and the referencing style for papers cited in the text. It is also strongly recommended that the most recent CONSORT guidelines are read for the particular trial design that has been used (<http://www.consort-statement.org>). These provide guidance on what information should be included in any report of results of a trial, and they have been adopted by many journals. For example, it is now widely considered to be essential that a flow diagram is prepared that starts with the number of all individuals (and, where appropriate, clusters of individuals) who were invited to participate in the trial and ends with all those who provided data on the primary trial outcome(s), showing when and why any participants or potential participants 'dropped out'. An example of a CONSORT diagram is shown in Figure 23.1. A checklist of items that the CONSORT guidelines specify should be included in the report of a randomized trial is given in Appendix 23.2.

Since different journals have different target audiences, it may be important to publish different aspects of the study in different journals, in order to ensure dissemination of specific findings to the most relevant groups. As mentioned in Chapter 7, to report trials in most journals, it is now essential that the trial has been registered on an internationally recognized trial registration site, so this must be done before the first participant is enrolled into the trial.

Traditionally, publication of an article in a scientific journal was free to the author, but the reader (or their library) needed to pay for the journal issue or individual article. However, in the era of electronic publishing, there is a rapidly increasing number of 'open access' journals, in which the author pays for publication, but the article is then free to the reader. Also, it is increasingly possible for authors to pay so that an electronic version of their article is freely available to readers of traditional 'closed access' journals. Some funding agencies now insist on all research that they have paid for being open access. Such costs should be included in the trial budget, though some journals give discounts or waive the publication fees for articles submitted by research teams from LMICs. One major advantage of publishing in an open access journal is that readers who do not have access to well-resourced libraries, many of whom are in LMICs, but do have access to the Internet, can access the articles without payment.

3.6 Media coverage

A common practice is to prepare and disseminate a press release to selected media outlets a day or two in advance of the formal release of the trial results. This is to allow

3: REPORTING THE FINAL RESULTS | 411

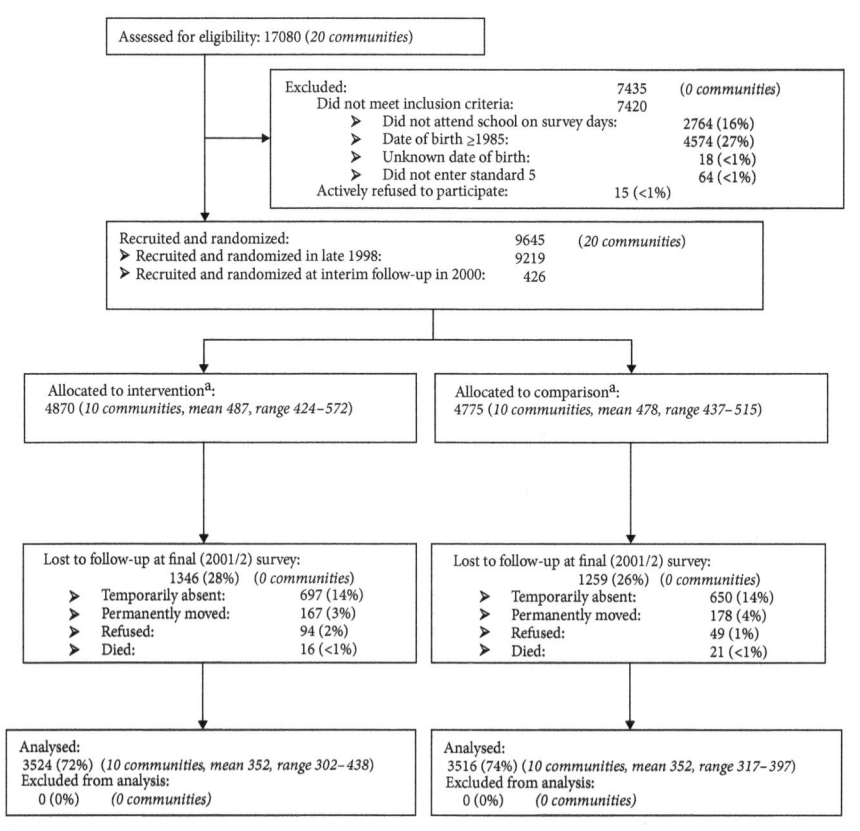

```
Assessed for eligibility: 17080 (20 communities)

Excluded:                                               7435    (0 communities)
  Did not meet inclusion criteria:                      7420
    ➤ Did not attend school on survey days:                     2764 (16%)
    ➤ Date of birth ≥1985:                                      4574 (27%)
    ➤ Unknown date of birth:                                    18 (<1%)
    ➤ Did not enter standard 5                                  64 (<1%)
  Actively refused to participate:                      15 (<1%)

Recruited and randomized:                               9645    (20 communities)
  ➤ Recruited and randomized in late 1998:              9219
  ➤ Recruited and randomized at interim follow-up in 2000:  426

Allocated to intervention^a:                    Allocated to comparison^a:
4870 (10 communities, mean 487, range 424–572)  4775 (10 communities, mean 478, range 437–515)

Lost to follow-up at final (2001/2) survey:     Lost to follow-up at final (2001/2) survey:
  1346 (28%)  (0 communities)                     1259 (26%)  (0 communities)
  ➤ Temporarily absent:   697 (14%)               ➤ Temporarily absent:   650 (14%)
  ➤ Permanently moved:    167 (3%)                ➤ Permanently moved:    178 (4%)
  ➤ Refused:              94 (2%)                 ➤ Refused:              49 (1%)
  ➤ Died:                 16 (<1%)                ➤ Died:                 21 (<1%)

Analysed:                                       Analysed:
3524 (72%) (10 communities, mean 352, range 302–438)  3516 (74%) (10 communities, mean 352, range 317–397)
Excluded from analysis:                         Excluded from analysis:
0 (0%)    (0 communities)                       0 (0%)    (0 communities)
```

Key:
[a]Although the interventions were available to all cohort members, there was no way of recording each individual's receipt of each of the components of the intervention

Figure 23.1 CONSORT diagram for a cluster randomized trial of an adolescent sexual and reproductive health intervention in Tanzania.

Reproduced from Ross, D. A., et al., Biological and behavioural impact of an adolescent sexual health intervention in Tanzania: a community-randomized trial, *AIDS,* Volume 21, Issue 7, pp. 1943–55, Copyright © 2007, with permission from Lippincott Williams & Wilkins, Inc. This image is not covered by the Creative Commons licence terms of this publication. For permission to reuse please contact the rights holder.

journalists to prepare their stories in advance. All such press releases should clearly state that the information they contain is 'embargoed' until a particular time and date. This means that the journalist is not permitted to publish the results until after that deadline.

3.7 The funding agency

The funding agency will also require a final report on the outcome of the study, as well as a financial report. Sometimes, it is sufficient to send drafts of papers that are to be published, but often the agencies will require a special report in a specific format.

Successful investigators need funding for their research, and many field trials cost very large amounts, so it is sensible to put considerable effort into ensuring that there is excellent communication and feedback provided to the funding agency—both to facilitate the current trial and future approaches for funding! Whenever possible, the investigators should seek an opportunity to report and discuss the findings of the trial with a person in the funding agency. As well as ensuring they know the outcomes that their funds have helped to generate, it also gives the investigators the opportunity to discuss how the funding agency might be able to help with implementation of the recommendations arising from the trial and to discuss further research ideas.

Most funding agencies are also keen to participate in the dissemination of research results and will, for example, put out a press release to coincide with the publication of a paper on a trial they have supported.

4 From research findings to public health action

4.1 Sharing and synthesizing findings

Major changes in public health policy are rarely based on the results of a single trial. It is important therefore for investigators to make themselves aware of any other trials that are being, or have been, conducted to answer similar questions to their own and to be open to the possibility of sharing their results, so they can be synthesized. If contact is made with those who are conducting other trials at an early stage, it may be possible to ensure that the data collected are comparable, which will greatly facilitate such synthesis and the formal meta-analysis of the results (see Chapter 3).

4.2 Researchers and policy

Final analyses and the dissemination of results are essential tasks that must be completed at the end of a trial, but an important further responsibility of researchers is to review the findings with the relevant government and non-governmental authorities and to explore implications for the overall health policy of the country and for the design of specific disease control strategies and programmes. From the beginning of the planning of a trial directed towards an important public health problem, the appropriate policy and planning (as well as implementation) arms of the MOH should be involved. Where the intervention involves other ministries, such as education, social services, agriculture, youth, women's affairs, this applies equally to them. Even when the Ministry does not have direct responsibility for the actual conduct of the trial, formulation of conclusions from the analysis of trial results requires their input and participation, as they are usually responsible for changes to health programmes that may be necessary because of the results of the trial.

Sometimes, trials are conducted to establish a principle (for example, a particular way of constructing a vaccine results in some protection against the target disease), and they may be an intermediate step in developing an intervention that might be of public health value. However, most field trials are of interventions that could be potentially used for specific public health actions. While the rigorous conduct of a trial is the primary responsibility of the researchers, the responsibility for ensuring that research findings are put to their proper use in public health programmes generally lies with policy makers, especially in the MOH. Unfortunately, in most countries, policy makers have a poor understanding, and sometimes appreciation, of health research, and frequently health researchers have a similarly poor understanding of the role and function of policy makers and of what they require from researchers to be able to do their job well. All too often in the past, researchers have considered that once they have conducted the trial and communicated the findings to the policy makers their job is done. As discussed in the next section of this chapter, it is not!

Furthermore, it is not sufficient for the research team to merely forward the main trial report or scientific article to the policy makers. Few will have the time to read such reports, and even fewer will have the inclination to do so. It is essential that the research team provides policy makers and programme managers with the results and their interpretation in a language and format that they will both understand and find easy to act upon. An example of how the abstract of a scientific article describing trial results was converted into a suitable summary for policy makers is given in Box 23.1.

Box 23.1 Example of how results in a technical journal article were rewritten for policy makers

Document A is the abstract from a paper that presented the main results from two parallel trials that compared vitamin A supplementation of young children vs placebo in northern Ghana. Document B is an excerpt from the Policy Brief prepared for dissemination of the results of the trials within Ghana and internationally.

A. The abstract from the scientific publication

Although most studies on the effect of vitamin A supplementation have reported reductions in child mortality, the effects on child morbidity are less clear. We have carried out two double-blind, randomized, placebo-controlled trials of vitamin A supplementation in adjacent populations in northern Ghana to assess the impact on childhood morbidity and mortality.

The Survival Study included 21 906 children aged 6–90 months in 185 geographical clusters, who were followed for up to 26 months. The Health Study included 1 455 children aged 6–59 months, who were monitored weekly for a year. Children were randomly assigned either 200 000 IU retinol equivalent (100 000 IU under 12 months) or placebo every 4 months; randomisation was by individual in the Health Study and by cluster in the Survival Study.

There were no significant differences in the Health Study between the vitamin A and placebo groups in the prevalence of diarrhoea or acute respiratory infections; of the symptoms and conditions specifically asked about, only vomiting and anorexia were significantly less frequent in the supplemented children. Vitamin A supplemented children had significantly fewer attendances at clinics (rate ratio 0.88 (95% CI 0.81–0.95), p = 0.001), hospital admissions (0.62 (0.42–0.93), p = 0.02), and deaths (0.81 (0.68–0.98), p = 0.03) than children who received placebo.

> **Box 23.1 Example of how results in a technical journal article were rewritten for policy makers (continued)**
>
> The extent of the effect on morbidity and mortality did not vary significantly with age or sex. However, the mortality rate due to acute gastroenteritis was lower in vitamin A supplemented than in placebo clusters (0.66 (0.47–0.92), p = 0.02); mortality rates for all other causes except acute lower respiratory infections and malaria were also lower in vitamin A clusters, but not significantly so.
>
> Improving the vitamin A intake of young children in populations where xerophthalmia exists, even at relatively low prevalence, should be a high priority for health and agricultural services in Africa and elsewhere.
>
> ## B. The policy brief (excerpt)
>
> Two randomised controlled trials were carried out in northern Ghana to evaluate the effect of 4-monthly vitamin supplements on child mortality and morbidity. They were conducted in neighbouring populations, where xerophthalmia, the eye disease caused by severe vitamin A deficiency, occurred but was not very common.
>
> The mortality trial showed that vitamin A supplementation reduced child mortality by 19%, and this result was very unlikely to have occurred by chance. This result confirms the results of earlier trials in Asia, but is the first in Africa to show such an effect.
>
> The morbidity trial results were intriguing in that they showed that vitamin A supplementation reduced indicators of severe illness—hospital admissions and clinic attendances—but did not reduce the overall frequency of illnesses. In other words, it appears that vitamin A supplementation may not reduce the number of illnesses that children will suffer from, but will reduce the number of those infections that go on to cause severe and life-threatening illness or death.
>
> Taken together, these two trials' results may help to explain puzzling findings reported by previous morbidity trials which did not find any impact of vitamin A supplementation on the frequency of child morbidity, but only measured the overall frequency of illnesses rather than their severity.
>
> The two trials show that improving the vitamin A status of young children should be given high priority by health and agricultural services in Africa and elsewhere in populations where xerophthalmia occurs, even when it is not very common.
>
> Adapted from the *Lancet*, Volume 342, Issue 8862, Ghana VAST Study Team, Vitamin A supplementation in northern Ghana: effects on clinic attendances, hospital admissions, and child mortality, pp.7–12, Copyright © 1993, with permission from Elsevier, http://www.sciencedirect.com/science/journal/01406736; and from Ghana VAST Study Team, *Results and policy implications of the Ghana Vitamin A Supplementation Trials*, Copyright © 1993. This box is not covered by the Creative Commons licence terms of this publication. For permission to reuse please contact the rights holders.

A variety of useful mechanisms that would assist in communication between decision makers and researchers are implemented in some countries. Health planning units may have responsibility for regularly reviewing, and even funding, health systems research. Other mechanisms include ad hoc, or regular, seminars at the Ministry level. A more comprehensive approach can be achieved through national health policy or epidemiology boards. These boards are composed of scientists, government policy makers, leaders in non-governmental organizations, and often lay people, and they have responsibility for reviewing and funding important public health research activities. Whether this mechanism or some other is used, it is of critical importance to have a way of effectively and speedily translating research results into public health action.

Many health systems in developing countries have partially devolved responsibility for health care to sub-national levels such as the district level. Thus, health intervention research should be mentioned in the district health plan, even if the research itself is not undertaken by the district health team but by a specialized research group. This will ensure regular review of the progress and implications of the research. Decentralization offers an excellent opportunity to link research with local public health practice.

4.3 Introducing an intervention into public health programmes

The main results from a trial will state what the effects of the intervention were on the primary and secondary trial outcomes. However, for a policy maker to be able to decide whether a successful intervention should be introduced, they need additional information. This includes knowing what the intervention will cost, how the intervention can best be integrated into existing health and social systems and what the likely positive or negative secondary effects of introducing such interventions will be on other interventions or outcomes, and whether the intervention is likely to be equally effective in all contexts or will only be effective in some, such as among specific age, sex, and socio-economic groups, or in certain geographical areas. While collecting such information may well require additional research, sometimes through Phase IV studies (see Chapter 22), trial investigators should carefully think through whether it would be possible to collect some useful information on these areas during the original trial. For example, it is usually possible to collect data on the costs of the trial intervention (see Chapter 19), to document any implications for other health and social interventions, and to conduct appropriate analyses to provide some indications as to whether the effects of the intervention differed by subgroup. Further useful information on the likely reproducibility of the findings of the trial in other populations can also come from the synthesis of findings from different trials (see Chapter 3).

The costs of introducing a new intervention must also be analysed, and some of the key issues involved in collecting information of intervention costs have been covered in Chapter 19. Ideally, these costs should be assessed in relation to other uses of the resources, and the benefits (years of healthy life gained or loss of DALYs averted) per unit expenditure required for adding the intervention to the health system would be compared with benefits that could be gained by the same expenditure on another health programme. Issues related to such cost-effectiveness analyses have been discussed in Chapter 19. Even if cost-effectiveness analyses are not carried out, it is essential that the trial investigators are able to report what it costs to deliver the intervention within the trial. Such costs should exclude the costs of the evaluation of that intervention (see Chapter 19).

Before a newly proven intervention can be put into operation, the Ministry must consider how the new intervention should best be integrated with other existing interventions. For example, malaria vaccines, when developed, will have to be integrated into the existing vaccination programme for other diseases and will have to be added to whatever the existing malaria control strategy is, which may include vector control (for example, through insecticide spraying), vector–human biting reduction (for example, through the provision of insecticide-treated nets), and case detection and treatment measures. An overall integrated strategy for control will have to be developed, and this might require trials of various combinations of interventions to determine the optimal mix. Such studies are discussed in Chapter 22.

Another important issue that the Ministry must consider is that the efficacy of an intervention measured in the circumstances of a trial can rarely be attained when the intervention is implemented under routine circumstances. System-level or community effectiveness (coverage and efficacy as actually achieved by the routine health service), rather than trial eficacy, is the measure of relevance for the Ministry (Tanner et al., 1993). Demonstration of high levels of efficacy under field trial conditions is important but, by itself, is not necessarily sufficient to justify the widespread introduction of the intervention, without further studies directly relevant to its implementation. Practical examples of this approach are given in Chapter 22.

The importance of understanding the setting and circumstances in which the intervention will be used in a public health programme must be understood both by policy makers and researchers. When the public health importance of an intervention is being assessed, managerial constraints must be considered that may make it impossible to achieve useful levels of efficacy. The principles and methods of continuous quality improvement management, with its emphasis on making sure that the right things get done, in the right way, and at the right time, are proving to be a useful approach to the management of health systems in developing countries. Such approaches may help ensure that the efficacy, as demonstrated under trial conditions, can be approached under routine conditions. An example of the use of these methods applied to improving the primary health care system in rural Nigeria is given in Zeitz et al. (1993).

References

Doyle, A. M., Ross, D. A., Maganja, K., *et al.* 2010. Long-term biological and behavioural impact of an adolescent sexual health intervention in Tanzania: follow-up survey of the community-based MEMA kwa Vijana Trial. *PLoS Med*, **7**, e1000287.

International Conference On Harmonisation. 1995. *Structure and content of clinical study reports (E3)* [Online]. Available at: <http://www.ich.org/fileadmin/Public_Web_Site/ICH_Products/Guidelines/Efficacy/E3/E3_Guideline.pdf>.

Obasi, A. I., Cleophas, B., Ross, D. A., *et al.* 2006. Rationale and design of the MEMA kwa Vijana adolescent sexual and reproductive health intervention in Mwanza Region, Tanzania. *AIDS Care*, **18**, 311–22.

Robinson, E. T., Baron, D., Heise, L. L., Moffett, J., and Harlan, S. V. 2010. *Communications handbook for clinical trials: strategies, tips, and tools to manage controversy, convey your* message, and disseminate results* [Online]. North Carolina: Family Health International. Available at: <http://www.fhi360.org/resource/communications-handbook-clinical-trials-strategies-tips-and-tools-manage-controversy-convey>.

Schulz, K. F., Altman, D. G., and Moher, D. 2010. CONSORT 2010 statement: updated guidelines for reporting parallel group randomised trials. *PLoS Med*, **7**, e1000251.

Tanner, M., Lengeler, C., and Lorenz, N. 1993. Case studies from the biomedical and health systems research activities of the Swiss Tropical Institute in Africa. *Transactions of the Royal Society of Tropical Medicine and Hygiene*, **87**, 518–23.

Zeitz, P. S., Salami, C. G., Burnham, G., Goings, S. A., Tijani, K., and Morrow, R. H. 1993. Quality assurance management methods applied to a local-level primary health care system in rural Nigeria. *International Journal of Health Planning and Management*, **8**, 235–44.

Appendix 23.1 **Guidance on how to write a scientific paper reporting the results of a trial**

Planning the publication strategy

It is important that the results of an intervention trial are published as soon as possible after the trial data have been analysed and the results are available. Generally, the sponsor will require a comprehensive report covering all aspects of the trial. Once such a report has been prepared, papers for publication in scientific journals can be prepared, based on the full report. It is good practice to try to include all of the important findings from the trial in one main paper and to avoid so-called 'confetti' publishing where the results are distributed among multiple different papers. While the trial is ongoing, it may be worth publishing a paper on the design and methods used in the trial (some journals specialize in publishing summaries of trial protocols, for example, *Trials* <http://www.trialsjournal.com>), as then reference can be made to this paper when the main results are published, without having to repeat details of the methodology.

The choice of which journal to submit a paper to will depend on the topic under study, and unfortunately on the results. Some journals are more likely to publish papers with 'positive' findings than those showing no effect of an intervention. Most authors will seek to publish their results in a journal with high 'impact' (i.e. likely to be read by many people), but it is important to think about who the target audience for the paper is and which journals that audience is most likely to read. It is a good idea to scan past issues of the journal to see the sorts of paper they publish to judge whether there is likely to be interest in publication of the results of a specific trial.

Once the decision has been made of which journal to submit a paper to, it is important to read the instructions to authors, as these vary from journal to journal. Links to websites, which provide instructions to authors for over 6000 journals in the health and life sciences, are given at <http://mulford.utoledo.edu/instr/>.

Drafting a paper

Shown in Box A23.1 is the general structure that most scientific papers have if they are presenting original study results. Approaches to writing papers vary from author to

Box A23.1 Structure of paper and suggested order in which to write the sections

1, 13	Title
2	Authors
10	Abstract/summary
9	Introduction/background
8	Materials and methods
6	Results
7	Discussion
12	Acknowledgements
11	References
3	Tables
5	Legends to figures
4	Figures

author, but one that we have found useful is outlined here. Also shown in the box is the order in which we suggest different sections of the paper might be drafted.

What parts of a paper are read and by whom?

The vast majority of readers of a journal will scan the title of a paper, and they may look at the list of authors. It is important therefore to highlight, in so far as is possible, the subject of the research and the 'headline' finding in the title, in order to provoke interest in reading further. A much smaller proportion of readers will read the abstract/summary than the title, but it is important to try to get all of the messages you want to convey into the summary, as a very small proportion of readers will go beyond that point and read the main body of a paper. A small number of readers will scan the tables and figures, so these should be made as comprehensible as possible, without having to read the paper. Unfortunately, in most instances, a miniscule proportion of those who access the journal will read the whole paper, but these may be the people who really matter!

A good place to start the writing of a paper is to decide on the title! It is suggested that this is revisited, once the drafting of the paper is finished, to consider whether any revision is appropriate. Thus, it is listed as both 1 and 13 in Box A23.1.

Authorship

An issue which is frequently contentious is who should be included as an author in a paper and in which order the authors should appear. Journals give guidelines as to what contributions are sufficient to merit authorship. Also many journals require that an account is given of the contribution that each author made to the research reported. There is no simple answer as to who should, and who should not, be included as an author, but it is good practice to plan the publications that are likely to come out of a specific trial well in advance of the final analysis of the results and to agree who will be included as an author in different publications. It should also be decided who will be the 'lead' authors with the primary responsibility of producing the first draft of specific papers. However, all authors share responsibility for the contents of the paper. It is important to remember this, even if you are only one of many authors in the middle of the publication list. Errors in a publication are usually permanent, and, even if corrections are made in a subsequent communication, these are often missed by readers.

Tables

The most critical component in constructing a paper is deciding on, and designing, the tables (or figures) that are needed to describe the study and to summarize the results. Once the tables and figures have been constructed, writing the paper around them should be relatively straightforward. There are four aspects of a trial to which the tables will generally relate:

1. description of the characteristics of the study population
2. main results
3. secondary findings
4. your findings in the context of other studies (though a table on these is not always needed).

Ensure that the title of each table is adequate to inform the reader of its content. Try to work out a complete description of the trial results through tables (and figures), even if later the content of smaller tables might be incorporated into the text. Avoid duplication of data in tables *and* figures. Plan the tables and figures, such that the paper can be largely 'read', based on these alone. Keep tables as simple as possible, and avoid unnecessary data, especially data that are not referred to in the text. Two simple tables are better than one complicated table. Label the rows and columns of each table very clearly, and, to the extent possible, avoid abbreviations. Avoid too many significant figures after the decimal point in numbers. For example, an OR of 4.7 is probably sufficient, rather than 4.735. In general, relate the number of decimal places included to the width of the CIs. For example, OR = 1.2 (95% CI: 0.1, 9.7) is more appropriate than OR = 1.23 (95% CI: 0.13, 9.68), whereas OR = 1.48 (95% CI: 1.41, 1.55) is more appropriate than OR = 1.5 (95% CI: 1.4, 1.6). When the tables (and figures) have been drafted, it is a good idea to give them to a colleague who is unfamiliar with the trial for them to tell you how they interpret them.

Figures

Figures may be a very powerful way of illustrating findings in a trial. They should be kept as simple as possible, but, if they are too simple, question whether they are really necessary. Consider whether a specific point is better made with a figure or table, and use one or the other, but not both. Label all axes of a graph very clearly, and give the units of measurement either in the figure or in the legend to the figure. For maps and similar diagrams, give a key to all of the symbols used, and show the scale diagrammatically (not 1 cm = 1 km, as the journal may shrink the figure). Have an arrow pointing north on all maps. Avoid using multiple colours, unless really necessary, as many journals are either only printed in black and white or charge extra for colour figures; and, anyway, many readers will print or photocopy a colour figure in black and white.

Results

The section of a paper describing the results of the trial should follow directly from the tables. Summarize what is shown in the tables, with appropriate reference to them. Start with the simplest analysis, for example, simple description of differences, without adjustment for confounding factors, etc. Then develop and describe more sophisticated analyses, as appropriate. Comment on all data shown in each table. If data are not commented upon, question the need to include them in tables. When estimates of effect are given (for example, vaccine efficacy), also include the CIs (usually 95%) and the 'p-value', but only if this contributes information beyond the CI.

Discussion

In the initial part of the discussion, focus on the key result(s) of the trial being presented, and summarize the overall findings. Discuss the strengths and limitations of the trial, for example, possible biases that could have influenced the results, and discuss the additional analyses that have been performed to control for potential biases, as appropriate. Then, put the findings of the trial in the context of other such studies, summarizing those studies as necessary, possibly in tabular or figure form. Then, draw overall conclusions derivable from the present study and other similar studies. Finally, make any recommendations for public health action or further research.

Materials and methods

Much of the materials and methods section may have been included in a previous paper, and it may be sufficient merely to summarize them and make reference back to that paper. However, this section of the paper must provide sufficient information for the reader to understand what was done, without having to go back to any previously published paper. The kinds of information that a reader will hope to glean from this section (or the earlier paper) are summarized in Box A23.2.

Introduction/background

The introductory section of the paper should be kept as brief as possible, giving the minimum necessary background information to explain any current controversies and why the trial was conducted. Make reference to any recent review papers, as appropriate. Specify the hypotheses that the study was designed to evaluate in quantitative terms.

Summary/abstract

Most journals will give specific instructions of how the summary should be formatted and the maximum number of words allowed. The reasons for doing the trial and why

> **Box A23.2 Information that should be included in the Materials and Methods section of a paper**
>
> Descriptions of:
> - study area (relevant features)
> - study design adopted (for example, cluster randomized trial)
> - study population
> - sample size determination
> - methods of selection/exclusion of participants
> - randomization methods and blinding
> - informed consent procedures
> - measurement methods
> - laboratory assays
> - follow-up methods
> - computing and statistical packages used
> - statistical methods employed
> - ethical approval (and data and safety monitoring arrangements).

it is important should be summarized in one or two sentences. There should then be a concise summary of results, using the maximum number of words allowed by the journal. Include as many of the key findings as possible, including summary estimates of the effect, with CIs and p-values. Finally, in a sentence or two, summarize the implications of the results and their public health relevance.

Acknowledgements

Funding agencies for a trial will often require their contribution to be referred to in a specific way (for example, including the grant reference). There should also be acknowledgement of the contributions of all those who facilitated the conduct of the trial who are not included as authors. These will usually include local health authorities, study participants, fieldworkers, laboratory workers, other study staff, including key administrative staff, local medical staff, and any advisors or consultants. If in doubt as to whether someone should be acknowledged or not, it is generally diplomatic to include them!

References

Authors should avoid trying to impress with how widely read they are and should only include references to papers which are key to the content of the current paper. Use recent review articles, and select from more accessible journals (for example, open access), wherever possible. Make sure that all of the references are complete (for example, check using PubMed at <http://www.ncbi.nlm.nih.gov/pubmed>), and it is bad practice to include references to articles you have not read! Pay strict attention to the instructions that the journal gives for the formatting of references. For this purpose, it is useful to have invested in a good reference manager system (for example, Reference Manager, Endnote, or Mendeley (<http://www.mendeley.com>)—which is free).

Appendix 23.2 Checklist of information to include when reporting a randomized trial

The Consolidated Standards of Reporting Trials (CONSORT) Group have produced several very useful documents (see <http://www.consort-statement.org/>) about how to report trials. These include a very useful checklist (Schulz et al., 2010) which is reproduced with permission in Table A23.1 (abstracted from <http://www.consort-statement.org>).

Table A23.1 Consort 2010—checklist of information to include when reporting a randomized trial

Section/topic	Item no.	Checklist item
Title and abstract		
	1a	Identification as a randomized trial in the title
	1b	Structured summary of trial design, methods, results, and conclusions (for specific guidance, see CONSORT for abstracts)
Introduction		
Background and objectives	2a	Scientific background and explanation of rationale
	2b	Specific objectives or hypotheses
Methods		
Trial design	3a	Description of trial design (such as parallel, factorial), including allocation ratio
	3b	Important changes to methods after trial commencement (such as eligibility criteria), with reasons
Participants	4a	Eligibility criteria for participants
	4b	Settings and locations where the data were collected
Interventions	5	The interventions for each group with sufficient details to allow replication, including how and when they were actually administered
Outcomes	6a	Completely defined pre-specified primary and secondary outcome measures, including how and when they were assessed
	6b	Any changes to trial outcomes after the trial commenced, with reasons

Table A23.1 (continued) Consort 2010—checklist of information to include when reporting a randomized trial

Section/topic	Item no.	Checklist item
Sample size	7a	How sample size was determined
	7b	When applicable, explanation of any interim analyses and stopping guidelines
Randomization		
Sequence generation	8a	Method used to generate the random allocation sequence
	8b	Type of randomization; details of any restriction (such as blocking and block size)
Allocation concealment mechanism	9	Mechanism used to implement the random allocation sequence (such as sequentially numbered containers), describing any steps taken to conceal the sequence until interventions were assigned
Implementation	10	Who generated the random allocation sequence, who enrolled participants, and who assigned participants to interventions
Blinding	11a	If done, who was blinded after assignment to interventions (for example, participants, care providers, those assessing outcomes) and how
	11b	If relevant, description of the similarity of interventions
Statistical methods	12a	Statistical methods used to compare groups for primary and secondary outcomes
	12b	Methods for additional analyses such as subgroup analyses and adjusted analyses
Results		
Participant flow (a diagram is strongly recommended)	13a	For each group, the numbers of participants who were randomly assigned, received intended treatment, and were analysed for the primary outcome
	13b	For each group, losses and exclusions after randomization, together with reasons
Recruitment	14a	Dates defining the periods of recruitment and follow-up
	14b	Why the trial ended or was stopped
Baseline data	15	A table showing baseline demographic and clinical characteristics for each group
Numbers analysed	16	For each group, number of participants (denominator) included in each analysis and whether the analysis was by original assigned groups
Outcomes and estimation	17a	For each primary and secondary outcome, results for each group, and the estimated effect size and its precision (such as 95% CI)

continued

Table A23.1 (continued) Consort 2010—checklist of information to include when reporting a randomized trial

Section/topic	Item no.	Checklist item
	17b	For binary outcomes, presentation of both absolute and relative effect sizes is recommended
Ancillary analyses	18	Results of any other analyses performed, including subgroup analyses and adjusted analyses, distinguishing pre-specified from exploratory
Harms	19	All important harms or unintended effects in each group (for specific guidance, see CONSORT for harms)
Discussion		
Limitations	20	Trial limitations, addressing sources of potential bias, imprecision, and, if relevant, multiplicity of analyses
Generalizability	21	Generalizability (external validity, applicability) of the trial findings
Interpretation	22	Interpretation consistent with results, balancing benefits, and harms, and considering other relevant evidence
Other information		
Registration	23	Registration number and name of trial registry
Protocol	24	Where the full trial protocol can be accessed, if available
Funding	25	Sources of funding and other support (such as supply of drugs), role of funders

Adapted from Schulz, K. F. et al., CONSORT 2010 statement: updated guidelines for reporting parallel group randomised trials, *PLoS Medicine*, Volume 7, Issue 3, Copyright © Shulz et al. 2010. Reproduced under the Creative Commons Attribution (CC BY) licence. This table is adapted from an open-access article distributed under the terms of the Creative Commons Attribution License, which permits unrestricted use, distribution, and reproduction in any medium, provided the original author and source are credited.

Appendix 23.3 A communication action plan for a trial (Annabelle South, Aoife Doyle, David Ross, personal communication)

These extracts are from the aims and objectives and then two key tables (Tables A23.2 and A23.3) and a box (Box A23.3) within the initial communication action plan for the MEMA kwa Vijana (MkV) Trial's Long-term Evaluation (Doyle et al., 2010). This was

Table A23.2 Example of extracts from a communication action plan for a trial: target audiences

Level	Audience	Importance	Influence	Objectives addressed
1. International	1.1 All-party UK parliamentary group on SRH and HIV	Moderate. Potential facilitator	Well placed to help to increase awareness of MkV and stimulate debate about ASRH policy and programming	(1) (2)
	1.2 USAID	Moderate. Potential facilitator		(1) (2)
	1.3 CIDA	Moderate. Potential facilitator		(1) (2)
	1.4 DFID, UK	High. Potential facilitator	DFID African Policy Department and Irish Aid are co-funding the trial and are well placed to help to increase awareness of MkV and stimulate debate about ASRH policy and programming	(1) (2)
	1.5 Irish Aid	High. Potential facilitator		(1) (2)
	1.6 Scientific community	High. Potential facilitators and blockers	Can help to disseminate our results and materials at scientific conferences and in publications. Could try to block our findings if do not accept them	(2)
2. African regional	2.1 African Union Commission	Moderate. Potential facilitator or blocker	Could disseminate findings and materials to high-level policy makers in Africa	(1) (2)
	2.2 Southern African Development Community	Moderate. Potential facilitator or blocker	Their recent expert Think Tank meeting recommended further studies to strengthen the evidence base in this area as an urgent priority	(1) (2)
	2.3 New Partnership for Africa's Development	Low. Potential facilitator	Not clear yet how influential this group will be. Keep under review	(1) (2)
	2.4 Pan-African Parliament's Committee on Health, Labour, and Social Affairs	Low. Potential facilitator or blocker	Not clear yet how influential this group will be. Keep under review	(1) (2)
	2.5 Health Ministers' and Education Ministers' Forum	High. Potential facilitator or blocker	Well placed to help to increase awareness of MkV and stimulate debate about ASRH policy and programming	(1) (2)

continued

Table A23.2 (continued) Example of extracts from a communication action plan for a trial: target audiences

Level	Audience	Importance	Influence	Objectives addressed
3. National	3.1 Ministry of Labour, Employment, and Youth Development, Department of Youth Development (DYD)	Medium. Implementer. Potential facilitator or blocker	DYD oversees National Youth Policy and deals with out-of-school youth. Potential implementer of Youth Condom Promoter and Distributor Component of MkV Intervention	(1) (2)
	3.2 Ministry of Education and Vocational Training (MOEVT), AIDS Coordinating Unit (ACU)	High. Potential facilitator or blocker	ACU coordinates all HIV and AIDS activities within MOEVT and handles NGO involvement	(1) (2)
	3.3 MOEVT, Department of Primary Education (DPE)	Very high. Implementer of in-school component of MkV intervention. Potential facilitator or blocker	DPE oversees activities in primary school	(1) (2)
	3.4 Ministry of Health and Social Welfare, Reproductive and Child Health Services Section (RCHS) and Adolescent Reproductive Health Working Group (ARHWG)	Very high. Implementer of youth-friendly health services component of MkV intervention. Potential facilitator or blocker	The RCHS has taken the lead in developing and promoting multi-sectoral ASRH materials. ARHWG has direct policy influencing capacity	(1) (2)
	3.5 Tanzania Commission on AIDS (TACAIDS)	High. Potential facilitator or blocker	Is within the Prime Minister's office and has the mandate for the coordination of all activities concerning the national response to HIV/AIDS	(1) (2)
	3.6 Family Health International (FHI), Usadi, Juhudi, Ari, Nguzo za Afya (UJANA) Project and Co-ordinating Committee of Youth Programming (CCYP)	High. Potential facilitators or blockers	UJANA is likely to be the largest youth HIV programme in Tanzania for the next 4 years. CCYP is supported by FHI and is a useful forum for national coalition building	(1) (2) (3)

Table A23.2 (continued) Example of extracts from a communication action plan for a trial: target audiences

Level	Audience	Importance	Influence	Objectives addressed
4. Regional	4.1 Regional Commissioner's Office	High. Potential facilitator or blocker	Overall responsibility for all activities within the Mwanza region. The Regional Administrative Secretary has been fully informed and involved in MkV from the outset and appears supportive but may be transferred	(1) (2)
	4.2 Regional Education Office and Forums	High. Potential facilitator or blocker	The Regional Education Office provides the policy link between MOEVT national and district levels. The forums provide an important venue for influencing regional, and hence district, policy, and for information being conveyed to national level	(1) (2)
	4.3 Regional Health Management Team (RHMT)	High. Potential facilitator or blocker	RHMT is the policy link between Ministry of Health and Social Welfare (MOHSW) headquarters, the regional administration, and the districts	(1) (2)
	4.4 Mwanza Policy Initiative (MPI)	Low. Potential facilitator or blocker	The initiative builds capacity to strengthen civil society engagement in policy processes. Potential venue for publicizing MkV and its findings	(1) (2) (3)
5. District, ward, and village	5.1 Full Council	High. Enabler	Main decision-making body in the district. ASRH is already within district plans	(1) (2)
	5.2 Council's Multi-sectoral AIDS Committee	High. Potential facilitator or blocker	Brings together all sectors to address HIV and AIDS	(1) (2) (3)
	5.3 Young people	High. Enablers and primary target group	Aim should be to actively engage young people in all aspects of the intervention	(1) (2)
	5.4 Farming associations	Low. Potential facilitators or blockers	MkV unlikely to be seen as important to their mandate	(1) (2) (3)
	5.5 Religious leaders	Moderate. Potential facilitators or (especially) blockers	Could order young people not to participate in MkV activities but could also support our messages and contribute choirs, etc. to events	(1) (2) (3)

Source: data courtesy of Annabelle South, Aoife Doyle, and David Ross (personal communication).

Table A23.3 Example of extracts from a communication action plan for a trial: list of activities

Activities	Target	Time	Lead person	Expected results	Indicator
1. MkV Advisory Committee	Gatekeepers in key government ministries from national and regional levels; trial funders; researchers; Key NGOs working in ASRH	Annual meetings: Jun 2007, 2008, 2009	PI	Forum to update key stakeholders on MkV-related research and to receive feedback	Attendance lists and minutes from advisory committee meetings
2. Set up mailing, e-mail, and phone lists	National policy makers Regional/district officials NGOs/CSOs Media Scientific community	May 2007 and then kept up to date	Communications officer	Mechanism for communicating with key stakeholders	Complete up-to-date lists
3. Develop and disseminate MkV introductory information packs	National policy makers Regional/district officials NGOs/CSOs Media Scientific community Young people	Development April 2007–July 2007. (a) Must be ready for national stakeholders' meeting	Communications officer	MkV advocacy materials in a consistent, innovative, and professional format (MkV brand) that are suitable for different stakeholders. Greater local and national interest in MkV interventions and trial results when they become available	(a)–(f) Availability of information packs Also: (d) Number of newspaper articles, radio/television pieces mentioning MkV (e) Articles, reports, presentations that mention MkV

Table A23.3 (continued) Example of extracts from a communication action plan for a trial: list of activities

Activities	Target	Time	Lead person	Expected results	Indicator
4. Development of MkV website (online publications, intervention materials, photos of activities, and provides links to other ASRH projects and organizations)	National policy makers Regional/district officials NGOs/CSOs Media Scientific community Young people	July 2007, then updated frequently with new material	Communications officer	Greater local, national, and global interest in MkV interventions, and trial results when they become available	Website metrics (hits, time, etc.)
5. Video shows with MkV video	Ward and village level authorities and community members	September 2007	Communications officer	Greater local understanding and acceptance of MkV interventions	Number attending, informal feedback from organizers and attendees

Source: data courtesy of Annabelle South, Aoife Doyle, and David Ross (personal communication).

Box A23.3 Example messages for different audiences (drafted after the trial results were known)

Messages about the MkV interventions

- MkV aims to help young people to protect themselves from STIs and unwanted pregnancies.
- MkV is an innovative adolescent health programme, including teacher-led, peer-assisted sessions in school classrooms. It uses carefully designed and tested education materials and provides youth-friendly health services.

General information on SRH education in schools

- Half of all students in primary schools in rural Mwanza Region have had sex by the time they are 15 years old.
- ASRH education in schools has previously been shown not to increase students' sexual activity in many studies around the world.
- ASRH interventions in schools and health units need to be supported by sustained interventions in the wider community.

> **Box A23.3 Example messages for different audiences (drafted after the trial results were known) (continued)**
>
> ## Messages for international technical agencies (WHO, UNAIDS, UNESCO, UNFPA, etc.)
>
> ♦ The MkV trial in Tanzania rigorously evaluated the impact of an innovative, multi-component package of interventions delivered by government departments.
> ♦ It demonstrated that the package of MkV interventions substantially improved participants' sexual health-related knowledge, reported attitudes, and some reported sexual risk behaviours, but there was no evidence that it reduced HIV, other STIs, or pregnancies.
>
> ## Message for government department of primary education
>
> ♦ After a pilot project in 60 schools, the MkV sexual health education programme has been successfully scaled up to over 600 schools through existing government systems and has been shown to improve students' knowledge.
>
> Source: data courtesy of Annabelle South, Aoife Doyle, and David Ross (personal communication).

a cluster randomized trial of an adolescent sexual and reproductive health (ASRH) intervention in rural Tanzania. The intervention had four main components (Obasi et al., 2006):

1 *in-school sexual and reproductive health education* through teacher-led, peer-assisted participatory lessons that included the use of drama, stories, and games
2 *youth-friendly reproductive health services*, education of health workers about the needs, and methods of providing sexual and reproductive health (SRH) services to youth
3 *community-based condom promotion and distribution*, for and by youth
4 *community activities* to create a supportive environment for the adolescent sexual health interventions.

MEMA kwa Vijana (MkV) Communication Strategy (excerpts)

Aims

1 Inform ASRH policy and programme design in Tanzania and internationally.
2 Increase national and international awareness and uptake of relevant MkV findings, materials, and activities.

Objectives

1 Increase stakeholder awareness of, and commitment to, the importance of evidence-based ASRH policy making.
2 Improve awareness of availability and policy relevance, and increase uptake of MkV findings, materials, and activities.
3 Strengthen ASRH programming and implementation within non-governmental organizations and other civil society organizations through their involvement and partnership in networks and capacity-building activities.

Index

A
Abbey, M. 70
Abdulla, S. 158, 182, 266, 405
abstracts
  reviewing 25–6
  writing 33, 420–1, 422
Access software 342, 355
accounting 275–6, 300–1, 307–10, 311–13, 316
  see also budgeting
accuracy of test results 296
acknowledgements 421
add-on studies 210
addresses, recording 173, 181
Adjuik, M. 197
adverse events (AEs)
  monitoring 56, 63, 107, 124–5
  as outcomes 207–8
  Phase IV trials 118, 395, 397–8
age, estimation 174–9
  children 174–5
  heaping 179
  men 176–9
  shifting 179
  women 175, 179
Ahmed, Y. 267
aims and objectives
  of literature reviews 21–2
  of trials 14, 40–3, 138
Ajayi, I. O. 255, 265
Akter, T. 69
Aldy, J. E. 327, 337
aliquoting samples 292
allocation 67
  concealment 67, 184
  groups 48–52, 189–92, 256
  individuals 47–8, 183–8
  non-random 52–3, 184
Alonso, P. L. 182
Altman, D. G. 36, 70, 119, 417
Amenga-Etego, S. 182
Amuron, B. 18, 336
analysis of data *see* data analysis
analysis of variance (ANOVA) 379–80
Anantharaman, D. S. 70
Angwenyi, V. 149, 155, 157, 158
Aponte, J. J. 404
archives 360, 361
Arifeen, S. E. 47, 69
Armitage, P. 366, 369, 370, 379, 389, 390, 391, 392, 393
attrition bias 29, 61, 94

audit
  of accounts 307–8, 312–13
  of data 345, 353
Australian Safety and Compensation Council 327, 336
authorship of papers 418–19
autonomy *see* consent
Awasthi, S. 45, 69
Ayles, H. M. 45, 70

B
backups of data 345–6, 359–60
Bakhai, A. 87, 97
Bamgboye, E. A. 265
Baqui, A. H. 119
bar codes 196, 290
Baron, D. 416
Barros, F. C. 181
baseline studies 60, 190, 217
Bassett, M. T. 266
before vs after studies 52, 53
Beg, S. 337
behavioural change interventions 8–9, 13–15, 47, 206, 209
behavioural research 249–65
Bejon, P. 157
beneficence/nonmaleficence 100, 110, 111–12
Bennett, S. 92, 97
Bernard, H. W. 264, 265
Berry, G. 366, 369, 370, 379, 389, 390, 391, 392, 393
Beyers, N. 70
bias
  assessment of risk of 29–30
  attrition 29, 61, 94
  avoidance *see* randomization
  outcome measures 206, 213–14
  publication 20, 22, 95, 129
  selection 29, 204
binary variables 76–7, 80–2, 371–3
Binka, F. N. 186, 197
biohazards 289, 298–9
Blackwelder, W. C. 89, 97
blinding 11, 48, 193–4, 213–14
  double 48, 185, 193
  role of DSMB 63, 123, 124
blood samples
  collection and storage 141, 288–9, 291–2
  feedback of results 156–7
  payment for 156
  safe handling 289, 298–9

Bonell, C. P. 53, 70, 400, 404
Boniface, G. 265
Bossuyt, P. M. 18
Boutron, I. 109, 119
Braunholtz, D. A. 119
Breslow, N. E. 374, 381, 393
Brown, C. A. 13, 18, 51, 70
Brown, J. A. 193, 197
Bryce, J. 70, 405
Bryman, A. 261, 265
Buchanan, D. 158
budgeting 39, 140, 275–6, 300–13, 410
  prevention of fraud 278, 313–17
buildings 276–7, 304
Burgess, B. 158
Burnham, G. 417
Byass, P. 182

C

CAGs/CABs (Community Advisory Groups/ Boards) 147, 149–51, 408
capital costs 304–5
case definitions
  clinical 201–4
  death 54, 204–5
  non-clinical 205–6
case finding 11, 12
case-control studies 29
Cataldo, F. 266
categorical variables 363
censuses 159–62, 166–81, 276
  mapping 160, 162–5
cerebrospinal fluid (CSF) 289
Chambers, L. W. 225, 240
Chambers, R. 148, 157
Chan, A. W. 65, 69, 70
Chandler, C. I. 251, 259, 261, 263, 265, 266
Changalucha, J. 70, 197, 215
Chantler, T. 158
chaperones 202
Chasela, C. 267
Cheah, P. Y. 149, 157
check digits/characters 169, 170, 195–6
Cheesbrough, M. 286, 299
chi-squared (χ^2) statistic 372, 373, 377, 378
children
  age 174–5
  census data 168, 172, 173, 174–5
  consent 103
  death 205
  gathering data concerning 168, 238–9
Chinbuah, M. A. 51, 70
Chirowodza, A. 165, 181
Chow, S.-C. 72, 97
chronic diseases 12
CI *see* confidence interval
CIOMS (Council for International Organizations of Medical Sciences) 101, 109, 119
Clark, S. 20, 36

Clemens, J. D. 263, 266
Cleophas, B. 222, 416
clinical trial phases 2, 16–17
  see also Phase IV trials
cluster randomized trials 48–50
  analysis 388–92
  blinding 214
  consent 111, 117
  randomization 50, 189–92, 256
  size 90–2, 96
Coates, T. 181
Cochrane Collaboration 22, 32
coding
  breaking 124, 125, 194
  check digits/characters 169, 170, 195–6
  cost codes 310, 311
  family relationships 171–3
  individuals 169–70, 179
  interventions 194–6
  location data 164
  questionnaire data 233–4, 240–2, 358–9
  re-coding 359, 362–3
  samples 297–8
coefficient of variation (k) 90
coercion of subjects 102, 105
communication
  communication action plans 406–7, 424–9
  with the community 59, 117, 155, 157, 255, 409
  trial progress 407–8
  trial results 408–12
  see also reporting of results
Community Advisory Groups/Boards (CAGs/CABs) 147, 149–51, 408
community engagement 59, 139, 145–57, 407
  censuses 161, 168
  community leaders 111, 148–9, 152–3
  and compliance 58
  influencing trial design 147, 256–7
  obtaining consent 103, 110–11, 117, 257
  participatory research 148, 265
  Phase IV trials 401
  in randomization 186
  reporting trial results 59, 117, 156–7, 409
compensation
  trial participants 102, 112, 156
  for harm 156
competence (for consent) 103
complex interventions 13–15, 47, 249–65
compliance 58–9
computers 277, 340–2, 351, 354
  see also software
confidence interval (CI) 367–8
  for means 378–9
  for proportions 371–3
  for rates 375–6, 385–7
  for risk 384
  and trial size 72–3, 94–5
confidentiality 105, 117, 350

confirmatory ('me-too') trials 41
confounding variables 188–90, 366, 380–8, 389–90, 402
consent 102–5, 106
  censuses 168
  communal 110–11, 117
  formative research improves 257
  Phase IV trials 118
consistency checks 180, 237, 283, 357
CONSORT statement (2010) 109, 410, 422–4
consultants 305
consumables 277, 293, 305
contamination (non-compliance) 58–9
contextualization 261
control groups 45, 46, 58–9, 113–14
Convit, J. 195, 197
cost–benefit analysis (CBA) 326–7
cost-effectiveness analysis (CEA) 325, 327–36
cost-utility analysis (CUA) 325–6
costs
  of implementing interventions 323–36, 415–16
  of publication 410
  of running the trial 39, 140, 275–6, 300–21
  to recipients 252, 329–31
Council for International Organizations of Medical Sciences (CIOMS) 101, 109, 119
Cousens, S. 70, 404
Cowan, F. M. 240, 266
Coyle, J. 267
Craig, P. 8, 18
Creese, A. 328, 336
Cutts, F. T. 196, 197, 199, 215

D

DALY (disability-adjusted life-year) 326, 333
DAMOCLES Study Group (UK) 128, 130
D'Arcy Hart, P. 115, 119
data analysis 138, 366–93
  in community randomization 388–92
  confounding variables 366, 380–8, 389–90, 402
  interim 62–3, 93, 125–6
  means 378–80, 387–8
  prevented fraction of disease 392–3
  proportions 371–3
  published 420
  rates 374–8, 384–7
  risks 374, 381–4
  spatial 165
  statistical analysis plan 62, 369–71
data management 67–8, 339–63
  backup 345–6, 359–60
  coding 233–4, 358–9
  re-coding 359, 362–3
  collection 60, 351–4
    censuses 168–9, 180
    questionnaires 237–8, 246–8, 351
    test results 248, 298, 351–2
  confidentiality 350
  data flow 346–50
  entry into database 180, 348, 354–5, 356
  error detection/prevention 282–4, 348–9, 353, 354–8
  hardware 237–8, 340–2, 351
  locking the database 359
  longitudinal studies 297, 352–3, 356
  metadata 360, 362
  paper forms 237, 340, 343, 344, 351, 361
  Phase IV trials 401–2
  preparation for analysis 362–3
  presentation in a paper 419–20
  qualitative data 257, 258, 262–5, 359
  quality control 281–4, 344–6, 349–50, 353
  sharing of data 360–1, 412
  software 342, 349, 351, 355, 356, 370
  staff 343–4, 350
  storage 341, 360, 361
Data and Safety Monitoring Boards/Committees (DSMBs/DSMCs) 63–4, 122–8
date of birth 174–9
Day, N. E. 374, 381, 393
de Craen, A. J. 193, 197
de facto/de jure populations 167–8
death
  censuses 181
  reporting to the DSMB 124
  as trial outcome 54, 55, 204–5
debtors 315
DEcIDE network 402
Deeks, J. J. 36
delivery strategies, trials of 18
demographic surveillance 180–1, 205
design effect 92
design of a trial 37–69, 138
  formative research 152, 250–7
  pilot studies 220–1
  preliminary studies 218–20
desirability bias 206
diagnosis 12, 201–3
  sensitivity and specificity 211–13, 214–15
  see also laboratory methods
diaries, trial 273
Dieppe, P. 18
digital maps 163–5
Diliberto, D. 265
direct observation 261–3
disability-adjusted life-year (DALY) 326, 333
discussion sections in documents 35–6, 420, 424
documentation
  consent forms 102–3
  field manuals 236–7, 273, 277
  financial 307–13, 316
  laboratory methods 292–4
  SOPs 293–4, 349
dosage 2, 16
double-blinding 48, 185, 193
double-entry of data 348, 354–5

Doyle, A. M. 36, 416, 424
drivers 278, 314–15
drug interventions 10–11
Drummond. M. F. 333, 336
DSMBs/DSMCs (Data and Safety Monitoring Boards/Committees) 63–4, 122–8
Dupont, W. D. 95, 97
duration of a trial 44, 55–6, 114–16
dwelling units 167
Dye, C. 337

E

Eames, K. 404
early termination of a trial 63–4, 93, 124, 125–6
economic analysis of implementation costs 323–36, 415–16
educational interventions 8–9, 209
Edwards, S. J. 117, 119
effectiveness 41, 395, 396–7, 398–9, 416
 see also Phase IV trials
efficacy 16, 396, 416
 vaccination 41, 115, 211–13, 377, 392
Egan, A. 404
Egger, M. 21, 36
Eichler, H. G. 333, 336
electricity supply 277, 341
electronic data capture 63, 180, 237–8, 246–8, 275, 351, 353–4
endpoints see outcome measures
enumeration of a population (census) 159–62, 166–81, 276
environmental alterations 9
Enwere, G. 197, 215
Epi-Info software 342, 355, 370
equipment 277–9, 291, 340–2
 budgets and accounts 304–5, 309
 maintenance 293
equivalence trials 41, 88–9
errors
 in data 282–4, 348–9, 353, 354–8
  check digits/characters 169, 170, 195–6
 in lab tests 294
ethics 39–40, 99–118
 adverse events 107, 116–17, 118
 beneficence/nonmaleficence 101, 110, 111–12
 cluster randomized trials 111, 117
 coercion/voluntariness 102, 105
 committees 99, 106–8, 116
 confidentiality 105, 117, 350
 consent 102–5, 106, 110–11, 117, 118, 168
 control intervention 20, 46–7, 51, 113–14
 Declaration of Helsinki 100–1, 108–9, 119
 duration and size of a trial 114–16
 at the end of a trial 117–18
 endpoints 74, 114
 equity 40, 99, 101–2
 guidance documents 68–9, 108–9, 117
 medical care of subjects 102, 112–13, 118
 payments to subjects 102, 112, 156
 Phase IV trials 118, 401

ethnography 259–60, 262–3
Ettling, M. B. 331, 336
Evans, C. 260, 266
Evans, M. H. 266
exclusion criteria 57, 204
explanatory trials 17–18, 57, 74
explorative flexibility 260–1
external validity 56, 334
Ezzati, M. 337

F

facilities 276–7, 286, 291, 298–9, 304
factorial trials 45, 88
faecal samples 289–90
Falade, C. O. 265
family relationships, coding 171–3
feasibility studies 59, 216–20, 254
 see also pilot studies
feedback
 to funding agencies 144, 411–12
 to individuals/communities 59, 117, 156–7, 409
fellowships 134
fevers, questions about 229, 230
field manuals 236–7, 273, 277
field organization 60, 268–79
fieldworkers 59, 273–6
 accommodation 277
 administering questionnaires 62, 234–7
 in the community 153–5
 delivering interventions 255
 measuring outcomes 203
 supervision 62, 214, 275, 282–4
 training 154, 162, 203, 221, 235, 274
figures in a paper 419–20
finance
 budgeting and accounting 39, 140, 275–6, 300–17, 410
 glossary of terms 317–21
 insurance 108, 121, 306
 payments to subjects 102, 112, 156, 306
 see also grant applications
financial interventions 12–13
Fine, P. 396, 404
Fisher's exact test 372
focus groups 264–5
follow-up losses 61, 94, 161
Fonn, S. 265, 266
forest plots 30–1
formative research 152, 250–7
forms, handling 237, 340, 343, 344, 351, 361
Foster, S. 18, 336, 337
fraud 278, 313–17
funding agencies 133–4, 135–6, 141, 143–4
 data sharing policies 361
 feedback to 144, 411–12
 Phase IV trials 402
 as sponsors 121
 see also grant applications

G

Gakidou, E. 405
Gambia Hepatitis Study Group (1987) 51, 70, 179, 182, 268, 284
Gantt charts 139
GCLP (Good Clinical Laboratory Practice) 286
GCP (Good Clinical Practice) 279–81, 344–6, 349–50, 359
Geissler, P. W. 157, 158
Geller, N. L. 93, 97
Gentsch, J. R. 405
geographical information systems (GIS) 165, 247
Gerth, W. C. 336
Ghana, event calendars 176–8
Ghana Health Assessment Project Team 326, 336
Ghana VAST Study Team 193, 197, 413–14
Gikonyo, C. 149, 157
Gilbert, C. E. 197
Gitlin, L. N. 144
Glass, R. I. 405
Glasziou, P. 21, 36
global positioning system (GPS) 163
Godfrey-Faussett, P. 70, 337
Goings, S. A. 417
Good Clinical Laboratory Practice (GCLP) 286
Good Clinical Practice (GCP) 279–81, 344–6, 349–50, 359
Gotzsche, P. C. 70
governance 40, 120–30
 DSMBs/DSMCs 63–4, 122–8
 Phase IV trials 401
 sponsors 121–2, 126–7
 steering committees 122, 124, 140
government
 census data 161
 and planning trials 38, 151–2, 397, 401
 reporting results to 407, 409, 412–16, 430
GPS (global positioning system) devices 163
GRADE system 32
Gramiccia, G. 118, 119
grant applications 55–6, 132–44
 budgeting 39, 140, 303–7
 funding agencies 133–4, 135–6, 141, 143–4, 402
 preliminary studies 218–19
graphs 419–20
Green, S. P. 21, 24, 29, 36
Greenland, S. 393
'grey' literature 22
Grigorenko, E. L. 181
group allocation/randomization 48–52, 189–92, 256
 size of a trial 89–93, 96
 statistical analysis 388–92
Group, C. 119
Group, P. 36
Groves, A. K. 103, 119
Gui, Q. F. 36
Gupte, M. D. 44, 46, 70, 160, 181

Guyatt, G. H. 32, 36, 53, 70
Gysels, M. 404, 405

H

Haaland, A. 255, 266
Habicht, J. P. 70, 405
Hargreaves, J. 70, 404
Harlan, S. V. 416
Hawthorne effect 214
Hayes, R. J. 70, 92, 95, 97, 189, 190, 191, 192, 197, 389, 393
health belief model 252
health care for trial participants 102, 112–13, 118, 306
health and demographic surveillance sites (HDSS) 400–1
health education 8, 209
health and safety (of staff) 278, 289, 298–9
health systems interventions 13
Heise, L. L. 416
hepatitis B vaccination 51–2, 328
Hernandez, M. J. 339, 364
Heymann, D. L. 404
hierarchy of evidence 53
Higgins, J. P. 21, 24, 29, 31, 36
historical event calendars 175, 177–8
historical recall 229
HIV
 post-exposure prophylaxis 298–9
 trials 23–4, 45, 192, 200, 335–6
home visits 162, 214, 276
Hoque, D. M. 69
Horton, R. 20, 36
households 167, 170–1
Hu, Q. Q. 36
Hurt, L. 182
Hutchinson, E. 266
Hutton, G. 405
Hyder, A. A. 325, 336
hypothesis-generating research 259–60
hypothesis-testing research 259

I

I^2 statistic 31–2
ICD (International Classification of Diseases) 201, 215
ICH see International Conference on Harmonisation
identification of individuals 60, 169–70, 290, 352
Iliff, P. J. 255, 266
illustrations 419–20
immunization see vaccination
impact models 43
implementation of interventions 13, 323–36, 415–16
incentives to participants 112
incidence rates 77–8, 83–5, 86, 96
inclusion criteria
 literature review 23–4
 subjects 57, 204

incremental cost-effectiveness ratio (ICER) 332-3, 334
INDEPTH network 54, 160
indirect costs 140, 306-7
INESS platform 403
informed consent *see* consent
injury prevention in the field 278
injury prevention interventions 11
insect vector control 9-10, 49, 206-7
insurance 108, 121, 306
interaction testing 88
interim analysis 62-3, 93, 125-6
International Classification of Diseases (ICD) 201, 215
International Committee of Medical Journal Editors (ICMJE) 129
International Conference On Harmonisation (ICH) 107, 108, 119, 120, 121, 122, 130-1, 280-1, 284, 409, 416
internet access 277, 342
interventions
 allocation 47-53, 189-92, 256
 costing 323-36, 415-16
 kinds of 6-15
 quality control 61
 selection 43-7
interviewers 234-7
interviews
 in-depth 263-4
 questionnaires 62, 238-40
 see also censuses
introduction sections in documents 33, 66, 420, 422
iteration 261

J

Jaffar, S. 13, 18, 330, 336
James, S. 158
Jenkins, M. 22, 36
job descriptions 273-4
Jones, C. 265
Jönsson, B. 336
Joseph, P. 181
Joshi, P. 266
journals
 publishing in 129, 408, 409-10, 417-24
 searching 22-6
Jukes, M. C. 160, 181
Juma, K. 265
Juma, O. 158

K

Kager, P. A. 70
Kahigwa, E. 215
Kale, O. 265
Kamali, A. 221
Kamau, E. M. 119
Kamuya, D. M. 150, 154, 157, 158

Kasindi, S. 158, 222, 266, 267
key informants 152, 253, 260-4
Khan, K. S. 21, 36
Kielmann, K. 261, 266
Kirkwood, B. R. 164, 182, 366, 369, 370, 372, 379, 393
Kleijnen, J. 197
Kombe, F. K. 157
Kong, S. X. 336
Krachaiklin, S. 336
Kubaje, A. 197

L

labelling of samples 290-1, 297-8, 352
laboratory methods 285-99
 data management 298, 351-2
 documentation 292-4
 links with other labs 296, 297
 quality control 62, 286, 295-6
 safety 289, 298-9
 sample collection and storage 141, 286-92
Lambert, H. 260, 266
Langhaug, L. F. 224, 240, 266
Lash, T. L. 393
Lavery, J. V. 147, 157
Law, J. 301, 322
Leach, A. 217, 221
legal interventions 12
legal liability 108, 121
Lellouch, J. 18
Lema, V. M. 103, 119
Lengeler, C. 417
length of a trial 44, 55-6, 114-16
Leonard De Vries, A. 197
leprosy vaccines 46, 212, 392
letters of intent 135
Lewis, T. 301, 302, 307, 313, 317, 321, 322
Liberati, A. 21, 36
Lievens, M. 221
Lilford, R. J. 13, 18, 51, 70, 119
linkage of laboratory specimens 297-8
literacy 102, 224
literature reviews 19-36, 101, 138, 252-4
Little, P. 70
logic models 254
Lopez, A. D. 205, 215, 337
Lorenz, N. 417
losses to follow-up 61, 94, 161
Lozano, R. 215, 337, 397, 405
Lukwago, E. 182
Lwin, K. M. 157
Lyons, K. J. 144

M

Mabey, D. M. 197
McCormack, S. 218, 221
McFadden, E. 339, 364
Machin, D 72, 97
Macintyre, S. 18

Madiega, P. A. 158
Maganja, K. 416
Maire, N. 405
Makhanya, N. 119
malaria
　ethics of vaccine trials 46, 115–16
　mosquito control 9–10
　Phase IV trials 398–9, 403–4
Maman, S. 119
Mantel–Haenszel test 381–2
manual
　field operations 273
　interviewers 236–7
Manzi, F. 404, 405
mapping 160, 162–5, 420
marriage, and age 175
Marsh, D. R. 266
Marsh, V. M. 149, 157, 158
Masiye, F. 158
matched-pairs randomization 189, 391–2
Material Transfer Agreements (MTAs) 297
maternal health 7–8
Mathanga, D. P. 405
Mathers, C. D. 328, 337
Maude, G. H. 197
Mavros, P. 336
Mbaabu, L. 158
Mbondo, M. 119
mean ($\bar{x}$) 378–80, 387–8
　and trial size 78–9, 85, 86
Medical Research Council (UK) 252, 266
men, age 176–9
Mendy, M. 284
Menendez, C. 215
meta-analysis 30–2
metadata 360, 362
methods sections in documents 33–4, 66–8, 417, 420, 422–3
Michie, S. 18
Miettinen, O. 384, 393
migration rates 56, 161, 181
Mills, A. 337
Mlamba, A. M. 158
mobile phones 275, 341
　data capture using 238, 246–8, 351
modification of a trial 126, 147
Moffett, J. 416
Moher, D. 27, 32, 36, 119, 417
Molineaux, L. 118, 119
Molyneux, S. 152, 156, 157, 158
monitoring groups
　DSMBs 63–4, 122–8
　ethics committees 107, 116–17
Montgomery, A. A. 45, 70
monthly calendars 174–5, 176–7
Moodley, D. 119
Morgan, D. 197
Morrow, R. H. v–vii 336, 417
Moscicki, A. B. 266

Moulton, L. H. 50, 70, 92, 95, 97, 189, 190, 197, 389, 393
Msomi, S. 119
Mtonga, A. S. 266
Mulupi, S. 158
Munalula, E. 158
Murray, C. J. 215, 326, 337
Murrell, P. 339, 364
Mushi, A. 405
Mwachiro, D. 157

N

Naidoo, N. 158
names 173
Nanda, K. 222
Napierala Mavedzenge, S. M. 21, 26, 28, 30, 36
Nathan, R. 182, 266, 405
National Institute for Health and Clinical Excellence (NICE) (UK) 254, 266
National Research Council (USA) 361, 364
Nayiga, S. 265
Nazareth, I. 18
Ndebele, P. M. 155, 158
Needham, D. M. 331, 337
neonates 8, 173
Nichter, M. 257, 266
Njuguna, P. 157
Nkoloma, H. C. 266
non-compliance 58–9
non-inferiority trials 41, 88–9
nonmaleficence/beneficence 100, 110, 111–12
non-parametric tests 92, 293, 390–1
non-respondents 239–40, 276
normal distribution 367–8
Nuffield Council on Bioethics (UK) 109, 113, 119
null hypothesis 73, 368–9
numbers, used to identify individuals 169–70, 179, 352–3
nutritional interventions 7
Nyamurera, T. 266

O

Obasi, A. I. 70, 215, 217, 222, 416, 430
objectives *see* aims and objectives
observation, in qualitative research 260–3
obstetric care 7–8
Oladepo, O. 265
onchocerciasis 42, 46, 193, 207
open access journals 410
open questions 230, 244, 257
open source software 342, 351
Opoku, B. K. 222
outcome measures 199–215
　adverse events 207–8
　behavioural changes 206
　case definitions 201–4

outcome measures (*continued*)
  choosing 54–6, 208–10
  death 54, 55, 204–5
  frequency of occurrence 44, 55
  intermediate/surrogate 43, 55, 115, 116, 209
  multiple 74–5
  primary 42, 55, 74, 114, 200–1
  quality control 62, 203–4, 210–15
  secondary/tertiary 42–3, 74, 114, 201
  and statistical analysis method 27, 367
  transmission reduction 206–7
  and trial size/duration 55–6, 74–5
overhead costs 140, 306–7
Oxman, A. D. 36, 70

P

p-value 79, 93, 368–9
paired data 189, 391–2
paired t-test 391
Palmer, J. 266
paper forms, handling 237, 340, 343, 344, 351, 361
Parashar, U. D. 405
Parker, D. 328, 336
Parker, M. J. 158
Participants in the Community Engagement Consent Workshop (2013) 145, 146, 155, 158
participants in trials *see* subjects
participatory research 148, 265
Patel, M. M. 398, 405
pathways of change evaluation 259–60
Peeling, R. W. 12, 18
peer review 135, 141–2
Pell, C. 405
Penny, M. 405
person-years-at-risk 374
personal digital assistants (PDAs) 63, 168, 237–8, 246–8, 341, 351
personnel *see* staff
Peters, T. J. 70
Peterson, L. 217, 222
Peto, R. 69
Petticrew, M. 18
petty cash 308, 309, 310
Phaiphun, L. 157
pharmacovigilance 118, 396, 397–8
Phase IV trials 17, 64–5, 394–404
  effectiveness 395, 396–7, 398–9, 416
  ethics 118, 401
  outcome measures 203
phased introduction (stepped wedge) trials 51–2, 92–3
Phillips, M. R. 329, 337
photographs 179, 248
physical examinations 202, 276
pilot studies 59, 220–1, 254–5, 344, 350
  see also preliminary studies
Pinder, M. 181

Piwoz, E. G. 266
placebos 46, 47, 193–4
planning
  budgets 39, 140, 303–7
  censuses 160–2
  communication of results 406–7, 408, 424–9
  data analysis 62, 369–71
  data management 340–50
  need for 38–9
  organizational 60, 139, 268–79
Plummer, W. D., Jr. 95, 97
Pocock, S. J. 93, 97
policy makers 38, 151–2, 397, 412–16
Pool, R. 404, 405
population
  enumeration (censuses) 159–62, 166–81, 276
  mapping 160, 162–5
  see also subjects
post-marketing trials *see* Phase IV trials
Powell, G. 339, 364
Power, R. 254, 266
power supply 277, 341
power of a trial 73–4, 79–86
  power curves 75–6, 80, 83
'pragmatic' trials 18
precision
  of test results 295–6
  and trial size 72–3, 76–9, 86
pregnancy 7–8, 57, 181
preliminary studies 59, 190, 216–20
  see also formative research; pilot studies
press releases 410–11
prevented fraction of disease 392–3
primary outcome (endpoint) 42, 55, 74, 114, 200–1
principal investigator (PI) 121, 122, 134, 305
PRISMA guidelines 32, 33–6
privacy 239, 276
process evaluation 257–9
programme grants 134
project ethnography 259–60
project grants 134
Prokscha, S. 339, 364
proof of principle trials 17–18, 57, 74
prophylactic interventions 6–7, 10–11
proportions 371–3
  and size of a trial 76–7, 80–2, 86, 96
protocols for clinical trials 65–9
Pryor, G. 339, 364
pseudo-randomization 184
public health actions 412–16
public meetings 153, 156, 407, 409
publication bias 20, 22, 95, 129
publication of results 129, 335–6, 408, 409–10, 417–24
purchasing 278, 314–15
purpose (goal) of a trial 41–2
Puvanashandra, P. 336

INDEX | **441**

Q
qualitative research *see* social research
quality control (QC) 60–2
  censuses 180
  data management 281–4, 344–6, 349–50, 353
  GCP 279–81, 344–6, 349–50, 359
  in the laboratory 62, 286, 295–6
  outcome measures 62, 203–4, 210–15
  and public health programmes 416
  questionnaires 62, 230–1, 235–6, 283
quality-adjusted life-year (QALY) 326, 333
questionnaires 224–48
  censuses 162, 170–1
  coding 233–4, 240–2, 358–9, 362–3
  data collection 237–8, 246–8, 351, 357
  interviewers 234–7
  interviews 62, 238–40
  layout 233, 242–3
  length 226, 231–2
  non-respondents 239–40, 276
  pre-testing 162, 220
  quality control 62, 230–1, 235–6, 283
  questions 225–9, 357
    open/closed 230, 244, 257
    order 232
  self-administered 224, 245, 356
  translation 231
  verbal autopsies 54, 205

R
Ramjee, G. 221
randomization 47–8, 183–92
  of groups 50, 189, 256
    matched-pairs 189, 391–2
    restricted 190–2
    statistical analysis 388–92
    stratification 50, 189–90
  of individuals
    restricted (blocked) 184, 186–8
    stratified 188
    unrestricted 185–6
rank sum test 92, 390–1
rate ratio (relative rate) 77, 84, 212, 377, 385–7
rates 374–8, 384–7
  and trial size 77–8, 83–5, 86
Ratliff, T. A. 295, 299
Ravaud, P. 119
Read, S. 69
recruitment of staff 162, 234–5, 274, 278
Reddy, P. 149, 158
references 421–2
reflexivity 261
registration
  of death 181, 205
  of interventions 17, 120, 409
  of a trial 129–30
regulatory requirements 120, 280–1, 397, 409
relative rate (rate ratio) 77, 84, 212, 377, 385–7
relative risk (risk ratio) 76–7, 82, 372–3, 383–4

religious groups 151
reporting of results 64, 140–1, 406–12
  CONSORT checklist 109, 422–4
  cost-effectiveness studies 332–3
  maps 165
  Phase IV trials 402
  publication 335–6, 408, 409–11, 417–22
  systematic reviews 32–6
  to the funding agency 144, 411–12
  to the individual/community 117, 156–7, 409
  to policy makers 409, 412–16
reproducibility
  outcome measures 210–11
  questionnaires 231, 235–6
  test results 295–6
research question 21–2, 101, 136
residency 167–8
results *see* reporting of results
Revill, W. D. 182
Reyburn, H. 265
Reynolds, J. L. 266
Richter, L. 181
Rid, A. 113, 119
risk 374
risk management plans 139
risk ratio (relative risk) 76–7, 82, 372–3, 383–4
Robinson, E. T. 407, 416
Roos, P. J. 197
Ross, A. 404, 405
Ross, D. A. 36, 45, 70, 197, 200, 215, 222, 411, 416
Rothman, K. J. 366, 393
Ryan, G. W. 264, 265
Rykushin, Y. P. 182

S
safety
  of staff 278, 289, 298–9
  of subjects *see* adverse events
Salami, C. G. 417
Salomon, J. A. 337
samples
  collection 286–90
  feedback of results 156–7
  labelling 290–1, 297–8, 352
  payment for 156
  safe handling 289, 298–9
  storage 141, 291–2
sampling error 72–3, 367
Sampson, C. 197
SAS software 95
Saunders, R. P. 258, 266
Saunderson, P. R. 331, 337
Saxena, A. 119
Schellenberg, D. 200, 215, 404
Schellenberg, J. R. 162, 182, 255, 266, 398, 405
Schulz, K. F. 109, 119, 184, 197, 417, 422–4
Schwartz, D. 18
Scott, T. W. 157
secondary outcome (endpoint) 42–3, 74, 114, 201

Seeley, J. 266
selection
  of interventions 43–7
  of subjects 56–7, 101–2, 204
selection bias 29, 204
self-administered questionnaires 224, 245, 356
self-reported outcomes 205, 206
sensitivity 211–13, 214–15, 230
sensitivity analysis 29, 334
serious adverse events (SAE) 107, 124–5, 207, 208
sexual health interventions in adolescents 28, 55, 192, 200, 219, 424–31
Shagi, C. 147, 158, 222, 257, 266, 267
Shao, J. 97
Sharifu, R. 158
Shepard, D. 326, 337
Shepard, D. S. 336
Sherr, L. 240
Shibuya, K. 215
Shiffman, S. 266
Shubis, K. 149, 158
Sifunda, S. 158
significance testing 73, 79, 368–9
Sikotoyi, S. 181
Sismanidis, C. 50, 70
site of a trial 256, 276–7, 400–1
size of a trial 57–8, 71–97
  for comparing
    incidence rates 77–8, 83–5, 86, 96
    means 78–9, 85–6
    multiple groups 44, 87–8
    proportions 76–7, 80–2, 86, 96
    unequally sized groups 86–7
  equivalence trials 88–9
  ethics 114–16
  factorial trials 88
  group allocation 89–93, 96
  interim analysis 93
  losses to follow-up 61, 94, 161
  with multiple outcomes 74–5
  power 73–4, 79–86
    power curves 75–6, 80, 83
  practical constraints 75–6
  precision 72–3, 76–9, 86
  preliminary and pilot studies 217, 221
  software 95–7
  too small 94–5
Smith, G. D. 36
Smith, P. G. 18, 53, 70, 172, 182
Snow, R. W. 182
social research 13–15, 47, 249–65
  evaluation 257–60
  formative 152, 250–7
  methods 148, 260–5
software
  data management 342, 349, 351, 355, 356, 370
  mapping 163, 165
  random number generation 185

systematic reviews 32
trial size calculations 95–7
Soliz, P. 405
SOPs (standard operating procedures) 293–4, 349
spatial analysis 165
specificity 211–13, 214–15, 230
specimens *see* samples
SPIRIT 2013 checklist 65–9
sponsors 121–2, 126–7, 408–9
sputum samples 290
staff 59, 273–6
  accommodation 277, 306, 315
  costs (salary, allowances, advances) 275–6, 305, 306, 315, 329
  data management staff 343–4, 350
  front-line staff *see* fieldworkers
  management 62, 139, 214, 274, 275, 282–4, 343, 353
  recruitment 162, 234–5, 274, 278
  safety 278, 289, 298–9
  training *see* training
standard deviation (σ) 378, 379
  in calculation of trial size 78–9, 85
standard error (SE) 367, 371, 378, 379
standard operating procedures (SOPs) 293–4, 349
standardization
  in data analysis 389–90
  of interviews 235–6
  of outcome measures 203–4
Stanton, B. F. 263, 266
STATA software 95, 370
statistical analysis plan 62, 369–71
  see also data analysis
Steele, D. 405
steering committees 122, 124, 140
Stephens, J. 181, 182
stepped wedge trials 51–2, 92–3
Sterne, J. A. C. 366, 369, 370, 372, 379, 393
Sternin, J. 266
Sternin, M. 252, 266
Stevens, A. J. 119
Stevens, W. 286, 299
Stone, M. M. 193, 197
stool samples 289–90
stopping a trial early 63–4, 93, 124, 125–6
storage
  of data 341, 360, 361
  of samples 141, 291–2
stratification
  groups 50, 189–90
  individuals 188, 381
STROBE statement 402
subjects
  census data 169–79
  ethics 101–5, 112–13, 118
  feedback to 117, 156–7, 409
  health care 102, 112–13, 118, 306
  ID numbers 169–70, 179, 352–3

payments to 102, 112, 156, 306
safety *see* adverse events
selection 56–7, 101–2, 204
vulnerable 103, 107
superiority trials 41
supervision of staff 62, 214, 275, 282–4
supplies 277, 293, 305
surgery 11
surveillance
  demographic 180–1, 205
  pharmacovigilance 118, 396, 397–8
Sutherland, I. 119
systematic reviews 19–36, 101, 138

T
t-value 378
tables
  of data 419
  dummy 62, 356
Tanner, M. 416, 417
Tavengwa, N. V. 266
taxes/taxpayers 12, 161, 309
Taylor, D. W. 197
Taylor, J. 267
Tetzlaff, J. M. 36, 70
theft 278, 279
Thimasarn, K. 336
Thomas, J. 119
Thompson, P. J. 266
Thompson, S. G. 36
Tijani, K. 417
timescales in economic analysis 328
timetables for field activities 161–2, 218, 221, 279
Tinadana, P. O. 157
titles of proposals/papers 138, 418, 422
training
  data management 343, 350, 353
  front-line staff 154, 162, 203, 221, 235, 274
  GCP 280
translation 231
transmission control 9–10, 49, 206–7
transport
  of samples 287
  vehicles 277–9, 305, 314–15
travel costs 305, 306
trend tests 373, 377–8
Treweek, S. 267
triangulation 261
Tuberculosis Prevention Trial Madras (1979) 179, 182, 194, 197
tuberculosis (TB) 115, 213, 331, 380
two-sided tests 369

U
urine samples 289

V
vaccination 6–7
  efficacy 41, 115, 211–13, 377, 392
  ethics 46, 115–16
  herd effect 396
validation
  data management 345, 350
  questionnaires 230–1
Vallely, A. 158, 218, 222, 257, 266, 267
Vallishayee, R. S. 70
van der Horst, C. 256, 267
van der Sande, M. 268, 284
Van Rooyen, H. 181
Vander Hoorn, S. 337
Vaughan, J. P. 181
vector control 9–10, 49, 206–7
vehicles 277–9, 305
  fuel fraud 278, 314–15
Vekemans, J. 221
verbal autopsies 54, 205
Victora, C. G. 53, 70, 181, 400, 402, 405
Viscusi, W. K. 327, 337
Vist, G. E. 36, 70
vitamin supplements 7, 44
  A 47, 193, 413–14
Vos, T. 337

W
Waight, P. 284
Walther, L. 301, 302, 322
Wang, D. 87, 97
Wang, H. 97
Wassenaar, D. 158
Wecker, J. 405
Wells, M. 261, 267
Werner, A. 13, 18
Whitty, C. J. 265
Whitworth, J. A. G. 196, 197
WHO *see* World Health Organization
Wilcoxon's signed rank test 392
Williams, B. 267
Williams, T. N. 158
Wilson, D. 266
women, age 175, 179
Woodward, C. A. 225, 240
World Bank 326, 337
World Health Organization (WHO)
  on costs 331, 337
  on drug safety 397, 405
  on DSMBs 123, 131
  on ethics 106, 108
  ICD 201, 215
  on lab techniques 286, 288, 289, 290, 291, 293, 299
  on verbal autopsies 205, 215
World Medical Association (Declaration of Helsinki) 100–1, 108–9, 119
writing
  grant applications 136–41, 142
  research papers 417–22
  systematic reviews 32–6

X
X-rays 202
Xu, Z. R. 36

Y
Yang, Y. M. 36

Z
Zaman, S. M. 197, 215
Zeckhauser, R. 326, 337
Zeitz, P. S. 416, 417
Zhang, L. N. 21, 25, 26, 31, 36
Zuniga, M. 197